MY STORY

A Memoir – A Trilogy

DR THEODORE K. AGBLE

Editing, design, typesetting and publishing by UK Book Publishing

www.ukbookpublishing.com

ISBN: 978-1-915338-10-5

DEDICATION

This book is dedicated to my late parents – my father, Erastus Lambert Kwame Agble and my mother, Kate Ama Agble, nee Apo, whose love, care and good example of Christian living have stood me in good stead and taken me safely on my life's journey. And to our sons Brian Kofi, Neil Yaw, Dugald Komla and Ronald Kwadzo, plus their progeny Noah Kofi, Danielle, Joshua Selorm, and Sarai Dzifa, so that they, too, may benefit from their Ghanaian roots.

CONTENTS

FOREWORD

Is it by coincidence that this book is being published in year 2021? Or, is it yet another example of predestination and the amazing symmetry which bedecks "My Story: A Memoir – A Trilogy" of Dr. Theodore K. Agble? The story began around World War II which ended in 1945. The story is being published in year 2021 when the world is gripped in the jaws of Covid-19, a pandemic, another world war, except that the enemy is invisible. The enemy is a virus. Everything has changed.

It is a privilege to contribute the foreword for a book written by a man of many parts. In an era of social distancing, this contributor respectfully invites parents, teachers and mentors to be creative and secure ways and means for their offspring, wards and mentees to access this book, and, read it. The content is informative and priceless. Its impact on character-building matches that of saints'.

Readers' attention will be drawn here to a selection of striking themes in the book. They include in the beginning up to the diaspora, multilingual education, the British Council connection, facts and an eye for detail. Some of Dr. Agble's virtues and insights are outlined in subsections entitled (in alphabetic order) Compassion, Empathy, Hope, Humility, Passing on the baton, Philosophy: Life is a Sea Journey, Racism, Transparency and Truth and Unafraid to accept challenge. Finally, this contributor shares with the author and his readers alike a poem which, in his humble opinion, may be considered the sum of the matter. It is entitled **The Final Liberation.**

The Compassion of Dr. Theodore K. Agble

Compassion, empathy and kindness are in the DNA of Dr. Agble (Ted, to this contributor). I well recall a few decades ago that I paid an urgent important visit to Accra to see a Director of an organisation, he bore the same surname as Dr Agble. The Agbles are a small clan, I assumed he was a relative of Ted's and so I prevailed upon him to accompany me to the gentleman's home. Although he had not been there before, he offered to drive, took me there and although not a relative, we were warmly received and the mission was successfully accomplished. It was only on our way back that I learnt from Ted that he and his wife were flying to New York early next morning! A reliable friend indeed, and such is how close he and this contributor are.

In The Beginning

Our origins and education run a striking symmetry. He comes from the Volta Region. So do I. He attended Achimota Secondary School, first in Accra and Mfanspim Cape Coast second. I was in PRESEC, Krobo Odumase first and St. Augustin's Cape Coast second. He received undergraduate medical education in Aberdeen, Scotland, and residency training in Glasgow. I attended Glasgow University as an undergraduate followed by my residency training.

Dr. Agble's father "was educated to the highest level attainable at that time. He understood the value of education". I lost my father when I was seven. My mother looked after me. She was illiterate. But, this is what was written about her:

"Eté: A Woman Of Africa"

Education was her next battle ground.	And were better off married ASAP.
It was the year of the Kaisers and the wars.	It was then that this woman decreed
In our villages schools did not abound.	*All the children must be schooled* And by letters, must be ruled.
Sons were assets like machetes and oars.	
And, conventional wisdom had it that	
Daughters must stay at home with pots, pans and peas	

Concerning elementary school, Dr. Agble wrote: "Our dressing was the wrap of cloth with the ends tied behind our neck." So was mine. He wrote: "I was eight years old then". I was four. "We walked bare-footed". So did I.

Dr. Agble wrote: "The teachers each had the Standard Seven School Leaving Certificate, but had not been to a Training College." Let us put this in context. Read part of this poem.

1	2	3
We clutched you with pride and framed you with light.	The gentle nobility of priesthood	Stan'seven School Leaving Certificate!
We stepped	Beckoned from the cold climes of	No ordinary decorated cardboard!
out, lion-like, to replicate	Akropong	A sufficient and
Gladsome scenes	Or the mystique hills of Amedzofe.	worthy prize, a crown
of heroes returning	(Amedzofe, our Eden, the origins of Man.)	Fought for, and hard won at this Olympiad:
home		
To heroes' welcome. Mere lads and lasses	Priests were priests, not raiders	Solid, good old fashioned education.
Between fourteen and twentysomething.	of flocks, their own.	

Multilingual Education

Dr. Agble wrote: "My teacher in Standard 1 was Mr Atiega. Teaching was conducted in Ewe; *English was taught as a second language.* Mr Atiega invited us to submit to him the Ewe words for which we wanted their English equivalent. This way, we quickly acquired a wide range of vocabulary in the English language. *It constituted a major bridge* into the English language. I suddenly experienced a quantum jump in my class performances. I acquitted myself very well in all the class subjects."

What a profound truth! During the Danquah Memorial Lectures February 2020, the speaker addressed Multilingual Education.

"How would multilingual education benefit monolingual English-speaking students? Research shows that bilingualism benefits cognitive and social-linguistic skills, throughout the individual's lifespan. Infants who are raised in a bilingual environment are more flexible (psychologically) than infants raised in monolingual environments. Their perceptual flexibility lasts into adulthood and makes learning a third language easier. They have a better understanding of the communicative functions and grammatical conventions of language. Furthermore, three rate-limiting cognitive skills are enhanced. These skills are attention, inhibition, and switching. Multilingual education can benefit all students not only academically during childhood, but also cognitively, socially, and linguistically across their lifespan.

Is it any wonder, therefore, that Dr. Agble bore this witness? "I suddenly experienced a quantum jump in my class performances and acquitted myself very well in all the class subjects."

The British Council Connection

This is another example of the uncanny symmetry in Dr. Agble's life. He wrote: "When Yolande and I arrived in Kumasi, the BC Director was Mr Bruce Smith. Bruce, a true Scot, was friendly and affable. My Aberdeen and Glasgow background quickly catalysed our relationship with his Scottish wife, Anne, and three young daughters. Our two families glued together into a firm family friendship.

The Diaspora

Dr. Agble spent a few years in The Middle East. This contributor spent decades there. Here are a few lines which tell the tale.

This zone diminishes the soul.	But the eyes had it
Though deeds of bravery are not rare	And now all bemused as if laughing with angels.
They are signed with their doers' hair.	I dive therein and grasp heaven's gift:
And many a hero remains unsung.	My own, my very own private shades
This is the battle front	*for this most crowded of Empty Quarters.*
And flack is our daily bread.	

Truth & Transparency

Dr. Agble is disarmingly truthful and transparent. He is bold, upright and unafraid to say it as it is. Here are three examples.

- "My allocation was Aberdeen in the far north of Scotland. *My initial reaction was to reject it straightaway.*"

- "His response was 'Young man, I am not God, I cannot tell you that on such a date you will go back to Britain. It was *the worst encounter with a senior official which I had ever experienced and it remains buried in my memory to the present.*"

- "My obstetric skills and knowledge were greatly enhanced in Glasgow. There was not a commensurate amount of gynaecological experience in Glasgow. I found Leeds more scenically attractive and appealing than Glasgow."

Facts and An Eye for Detail

The informative component of Dr. Agble's Story includes subjects such as Architecture, Classical Music, Football, History, Landscaping, Politics (Non-partisan), Tennis and Training Programmes. Dr. Agble has an eye for detail. Its impact is informative and entertaining.

Examples are:

- "The famous Achimota golf course was located on the Western Campus. *A Botanical g*arden was sited there.

- The Administration Block with its tall and huge clock tower, the well-tended grounds and lawns, the avenues of tall palm trees and the dormitory houses in Gothic architectural style all combined to leave an everlasting impression.

- "He (an instructor) was affable and friendly, sighted only in one eye."

- "The consultant oncologist was stocky and square-faced, with a thin lip-wide moustache; he wore a half-moon pair of spectacles."

- "Dr Sutherland was the departmental head. A Presbyter, heavy in build, he was a teetotaller, a non–smoker who was very strict and ran the department as a school headmaster. Dr Mair, a Welshman, was the exact opposite. Of middle build, debonair, a worldly figure, he enjoyed his whisky and cigarettes.

- "Whereas in England gynaecologists are addressed as Mr, in Scotland they are addressed as Doctor.

- "Mr. Redman and I quickly gelled together and he became my mentor. Respect for each other was mutual. Trivial though it was, we shared the same first name of Theodore. We both shared an interest in and love for opera.

- "The 1954-55 team included Dennis Law later joined Manchester United where he attained a legendary status. Alex Ferguson was snatched by Manchester United. He took with him the midfielder, Gordon Strachan; the rest is history."

- He provided a list of the hierarchy in Korle Bu Teaching Hospital in the mid-60s. Examples are Dr Obuabasa Bannerman, Dr Charles Easmon, Dr Emmanuel Baidoo, Dr, Kwashie Quartey and "David (ENT), an Englishman".

- When he came to the requirements for the MRCOG examination, Dr. Agble was in his professional element. He went full tilt. He used no fewer than 287 words.

Philosophy: Life is a Sea Journey

As a man of many parts, Dr. Agble also demonstrates considerable philosophical traits. There was much more in life other than being an expert in one's chosen field of professional pursuit. *"No one professional has monopoly of insight into his/her own profession"*.

- "From the top of the ladder as a final year medical student, I was going to start a new phase in the medical profession from the very bottom of the ladder. Such is life, a sea journey from port to port.

- "Glasgow, the largest and most populous city in Scotland is the industrial centre. Glasgow University is an acclaimed centre of learning and scholarship. It is the home to Glasgow Rangers and Celtic, the two famous football teams. During my Aberdeen student days, I visited the city twice. My first was to watch the football match between Scotland and the 'auld enemy', England. My second was to represent Aberdeen University in a tennis tournament against Glasgow University. I had now come in pursuit of the MRCOG." Indeed, *"life is a voyage from port to port."*

Racism

He bore witness on racism. Refusing to make sweeping statements, he was insightful enough to dismiss the subject with one word: *ignorance*. He wrote: "There was colour prejudice" but it was *in a section of the population*. NOT throughout all of Aberdeen. And, its cause? Colour prejudice was *based on ignorance*.

Humility

Dr. Agble admitted: "The very limited jobs in Medicine were normally given to the top three, *and, that ruled me out*." He reminds this contributor of Dr. J.B. Danquah about whom he had written: "How many teachers or professors have dared to admit their failures, saying: "Once upon a time I also failed an exam?" But, Dr. J.B. Danquah, role model extraordinaire, did just that. In his Poem entitled "Half-A-Century", he wrote: "I tried Matric # and failed it; # I tried **twice more#** And passed it."

Passing on the Baton

Dr Agble wrote: "They (parents) were proud of me, their youngest child who had successfully completed his studies abroad and returned home as a qualified doctor." When he also became a father, he passed on the baton. He is a loving husband and a caring father.

God Knows Best

Here is another example of symmetry. "Dr. Bannerman, because of my background in Sir Dugald's unit, took a special interest in my clinical activities." That was yet another fruit from the Aberdeen connection. It is the same Aberdeen of which Dr Agble had written: "My allocation was Aberdeen... *My initial reaction was to reject it* straightaway. Evidently, God knows best."

Unafraid to Accept Challenge

"Although I was the most junior Medical Officer in the department, Dr Bannerman told me that he was assigning to me the more challenging ward and to handle the more serious cases. I was pleased to note the confidence he had in me and the challenge he offered me."

The Sum of the Matter

In conclusion of the Foreword to "My Story: A Memoir – A Trilogy" by Dr. Theodore K. Agble, this contributor would like to share with the author and his readers alike part of a poem which, in his humble opinion, may be considered the sum of the matter. The poem is entitled **The Final Liberation.**

1.	2.	3.
I shoot the rapids of life	Betting my soul on this knowledge:	No longer scared of terminal darkness
Glide off the cliffs at dawn	Every gain is loss; every loss gain	I see it father of final light. To be in love with everyone But
And surf the thermals at dusk.	I dance to inner tunes of glory	expect naught from anyone Godsufficient by the sunset: That is
If you would ride roller coaster	Barefoot on the embers of fortune.	the final liberation.
Stick around. If not, bail out now.		

PROF LADÉ WOSORNU, FGA.

14th May, 2020

PREFACE

In 2007, after completing an enquiry on a maternal death at Korle Bu Maternity Department by a committee which I chaired, the seed of a memoir was sown. After relating some anecdotes on Korle Bu to the secretary of the committee, she strongly suggested that I should write my memoirs. I thought over the idea and finally decided to write my story. Thus, the seed germinated.

My story begins with my birth in 1931 in Hohoe and ends with my final departure from Tabuk in Saudi Arabia at the end of my years in the Diaspora in the year 2000.

The first part which covers my childhood and education is in three phases: the first phase covers my primary school education; the second covers my secondary school education; and the third covers my years at the infant University College of the Gold Coast (UCGC). This is followed by my years in Aberdeen University studying medicine. After returning home as a doctor, I worked as a Medical Officer in Winneba, Korle Bu Hospital and Kumasi for two years and returned to Britain to specialize in Obstetrics and Gynaecology.

Now married, I worked as a Specialist Gynaecologist and commenced a family life.

Some chapters tell the story of my family life, while some centre on my professional and social activities both in the government and private sectors.

My professional life was most fulfilling. I followed the dictum of my revered mentor, Sir Dugald Baird, that in the practice of medicine, one should take into account the environmental milieu in which one is practising: namely socio-economic factors, to which I would add religion and cultural factors. It is in this connection that I advocated the following: symphysiotomy, craniotomy, vaginal breech delivery when the indications are present; caesarean hysterectomy should be total. In my advocacy of symphysiotomy, I know that I belong to an endangered species of obstetricians preaching to a large number of sceptics.

In my days at Korle Bu and Komfo Anokye Hospital, Kumasi, I was a ringside spectator at the birth of Korle Bu and Komfo Anokye Teaching Hospitals. The products of these two medical schools may appreciate reading this memoir about them.

I have written the memoir from memory; any mistakes and shortcomings are my responsibility.

I am indebted to Professor Francis Agbodeka and Mr. Martin Meredith for using information from their books. Prof Agbodeka's book on the History of Achimota provided material on Achimota College in the national setting. I culled essential material and facts from the well-researched publication by Mr. Martin Meredith in providing the authoritative political and economic landscape of Ghana in the 60s, 70s and 80s. The New York Times proved valuable as a resource on World Affairs.

In writing this memoir, I received encouragement and support from my wife and four sons. Although I denied her the role of an amanuensis, because of her gift as an appealing writer, she kindly agreed to write the closing addendum.

I wish to extend my thanks to the following: Mr. Stanley Tormeti of Accra and Valentine Garraway of New York. They both assisted me in writing up my story on the computer.

I wish to express my special thanks and gratitude to Professor Lade Wosornu for the honour in accepting my invitation to write the foreword after only short notice. Lade is an eminent renowned surgeon, teacher, author and scholar.

Chapter 1
CHILDHOOD IN HOHOE

I was born on Tuesday, 21st July, 1931 at Gbi Hohoe in the Volta Region known then as the British Mandated Togoland (BMT). Togoland had been a German colony before the First World War (1914-18). After the war, Togoland was divided into two: one half became French Mandated Togoland with its capital at Lome; the other half was BMT, which was administered from Accra in the Gold Coast. Hohoe was under the Kpando administrative district. Although I cannot precisely date my earliest childhood memories now, some pictures have emerged in my conscious memory.

Hohoe was a vibrant town. It was the largest of the seven divisions of the Gbi state. Hohoe was also the commercial centre in the BMT. All the major trading companies in the Gold Coast had principal bases there. These companies were the United Africa Company (UAC) of the Unilever Brothers conglomerate, G.B. Ollivant (G.B.O.), the Union Trading Company (U.T.C.), the Commonwealth Trading Company Limited (C.T.L.) and the John Holt Company. UAC, John Holt and G.B. Ollivant were by far the largest trading companies. There were other smaller traders with shops owned by Syrians, Portuguese and Kwahus. UAC and John Holt companies each maintained at least two or three European expatriate managers. The expatriates lived in special bungalows at the Ridge area in Gbi Bla. They had tennis courts located on the UAC premises in Hohoe. Senior Africans such as storekeepers were allowed to play tennis on these courts; there was no element of apartheid at the tennis club. Other sporting activities, such as football, were encouraged and promoted on a grand scale. The trading companies had a formidable football team, known as the Spirocids X1. They played competitive, eagerly watched matches against other teams in the territory; their local rivals were the Gbi Bla X1.

As children we were thrilled by the entertainment provided by visiting magicians; they attracted large crowds to their performances. Hohoe town itself boasted of having a local magician, a person held in awe and fear; he was a Sierra Leonean called Mr Priddy. Other entertainers came from Accra and Koforidua.

Religion and religious activities played a significant role in my childhood years. The major Christian denominations in the Gbi state were Roman Catholicism and Presbyterianism. Hohoe was very predominantly Presbyterian whilst Roman Catholics dominated Bla and the Kpeme environs entirely. My parents were Presbyterians; I was therefore baptized and christened as a Presbyterian. Both denominations had their own separate infant, junior and senior elementary schools. The Presbyterian senior school in Hohoe was famous, and had a catchment district which included Gbi Kledzoe, Wegbe, Kpoeta, Likpe and Golokwati. There were similar, well known Presbyterian senior schools, known as Key-schools, located at Kpando and Ho in BMT and Peki and Keta in the Gold Coast Colony. The Hohoe Ewe Presbyterian (EP) Church was located near the EP infant and junior schools and the teachers' residential quarters. The foundation stone of the present church was laid in the early 1940s when I was in the junior school; it took a few decades to complete the building of the present church. The church library was named Agble Library after my late father.

The Roman Catholic schools and their Cathedral were sited at Gbi Bla; they also had a convent for girls. Their institutions were run by resident white nuns and priests; they could be spotted easily from afar as they rode on their bicycles to Hohoe.

Central Hohoe was centred on the big market which was sited at the place now occupied by the Bank of Ghana. It was a large triangular area bordered by the Accra-Kadjebi road, the Hohoe-Bla road and the road leading from the Bla road to the Presbyterian Church and schools. These roads constituted the High Street, and the various commercial houses were located along them. The Post Office site has not changed, and has remained on the Hohoe Fodome road. The Magistrates Law Courts were further up on the Fodome road.

The commercial houses had stores where various kinds of merchandise were sold. Some of the commercial companies, notably UAC, G. B. Ollivant, and John Holt, had local produce purchasing divisions; the produce division purchased cocoa and coffee beans for exporting to Britain. Cocoa and coffee were grown in farms in the Buem districts of Kadjebi, Ahamansu, Likpe and Lolobi.

My school years in Hohoe were in the period of the Second World War (1939-45). The impact of the war was severe and was felt everywhere. Although the purchase of cocoa beans continued during the war years, because of German forces' torpedo activities in the Gulf of Guinea, sinking ships with goods to and from Britain, for periods of time the cocoa beans could not be exported. The cocoa beans were, as a result, piled up into mountainous heaps and then incinerated. Likewise, the importation of essential items of merchandise was severely limited as the availability of many basic essential items depended on their arrival from Britain by boat. One of the most important items was kerosene, which was used for lighting lamps; Hohoe had no electricity at the time. Kerosene was stored and transported in four-gallon tins and 44-gallon drums. The arrival of kerosene from Akuse was always eagerly awaited and greeted with great relief and jubilation. The sale and distribution of kerosene by the major commercial houses was always a highly-disciplined exercise on a basis of rationing. Papa, as a major storekeeper, had a team of about four assistant-storekeepers and a labourer to conduct the kerosene sale. There was an element of prioritisation: schools, the church and teachers carried some clout. We, in our household, were of course in a privileged position; we always had some kerosene. Kerosene lamps were supplemented with small lamps which used palm kernel oil as fuel. Candles, also imported, were also regularly in short supply. Tinned evaporated and condensed milk, tinned butter and corned beef were highly prized items for the elite to obtain.

We had as a neighbour, who lived opposite our house, just across the road, Torgbe (Honourable) Gomli. He was a farmer and a hunter. More importantly, he was not only a `jujuman', but the chief `jujuman' to the paramount chief of Gbi Hohoe, Torgbe Gabusu. I recall him as a genial man in his late fifties; he had a chronic sore on one of his legs which never appeared to heal. His `juju' hut with its thatched roof was clearly visible from our house. He had constant visits from clients coming from near and far. Our family did not believe in juju, but I was fascinated by his activities and his clientele. If there was going to be a big football match involving any of the Hohoe teams, there would be a steady stream of players and supporters calling on him to influence the match in their favour. If the team lost, in juju fashion, a blame-worthy excuse or scapegoat could always be found.

My brother Willie returned home in 1955 from the USA with M.Sc. and Ph.D. degrees in Agricultural Science, with specialization in Plant Genetics; he was the first from the Gold Coast to qualify as an Agricultural Scientist. On his first visit home to Hohoe to see our parents, he paid a courtesy visit to Torgbe Gomli. Torgbe Gomli reportedly received him very warmly and felt proud of his achievement. He told him that although many people would laudably hail his achievement, a few may cast envious eyes on him and indeed plan evil deeds. The attempt might be a resort to juju. He went on to say that spiritual 'juju' could achieve nothing in itself; evil could only be rendered by ingesting a poisoned item such as a drink or food item. My brother was therefore advised on what sort of care he should take of himself. This advice and opinion was from the top Gbi 'jujuman'!

What was the populace of Hohoe like? Hohoe was by all accounts very cosmopolitan. The populace of the six other Gbi divisions was mainly composed of Gbi indigenes. The Hohoe populace had Ewes from the coastal region of Keta, Anyako, Anloga (all generally known as Anlos) and Ewes from Northern Eweland such as Peki, Kpando and Have; there were residents from the Buem districts of Likpe, Lolobi and Akpafu; there were Kwahus and Gas. The Northerners, known as Hausas, resided in a skirt area known as Zongo. There was a fairly large number of Nigerians, known as Lagosians; they indulged in the petty trade business. Quite apart from the white European managers who resided in bungalows at the Ridge in Bla, there were some Portuguese, Syrian and Lebanese traders who resided in Hohoe. Hohoe was indeed indisputably a very cosmopolitan town.

There was a small colonial-type hospital located on the road from the town centre to the Zongo area; the present one was built in the early 1950s. The old hospital consisted of a doctor's consulting room, a wound-dressing room, a dispensary, an operating theatre and two wards for inpatients; I do not think that they had more than 20 beds. In my early childhood, the Medical Officer was Dr Huppenbaure, a German, who sported a long and grey goatee beard. I was always frightened whenever I was told that I would be taken down to be seen by Dr Huppenbaure. Why? A consultation invariably ended with a painful injection. Dr Huppenbaure was followed in turn by Dr Bannerman, Dr Amorin and then Dr Eustace Akwei.

The hospital's wound-dressing unit was the busiest unit. In this pre-antibiotics era, wounds were septic and healed by granulation; dressing was an integral part of management. Mr Sekyi and Mr Dabri were dispensers who dressed the septic wounds on my legs. The next most senior member of staff to the doctor was the pharmacist. I did not know up to what level of cases the doctors handled and managed, but I knew that people often travelled from Hohoe to Kpalime in French Togoland for treatment and surgical operations. My sister Felicia was taken there with a dental complaint; a dental extraction was performed on her, which was followed by a frightening haemorrhage.

Hohoe did not have electric power at that time; my first experience with electricity was in 1943 when I visited my brother Emmanuel at Koforidua, where he was employed as a G.B. Ollivant storekeeper. Hohoe also did not have a pipe-borne water supply. Water was fetched from the Dayi River for drinking and cooking. During the rainy season water was collected from the roofing structure which had gutters, and stored in tanks and drums. We had a well in our compound which provided water for washing dishes and clothes. I did some swimming in River Dayi when I was in the EP Senior School, 1944-45. I nearly got drowned in the river during one rainy season when the water level had risen significantly and the base had been rendered very muddy, soft and unsafe. After this rather frightening experience, I never tried to swim again in the River Dayi.

Our house was located in the Trevi area of Hohoe, very near to the Hohoe-Bla road. Our neighbours were family-friendly. They included the Senoos (Reverend Father Hilary's father's family), the Kudjoes, the Akus, the Demanyas, Mr. Pomary and Madam Asamoah family. The elites in Hohoe, comprising the highly educated, mainly the most senior employees of the major trading firms, formed a society, called The Scholars' Union. My father, Papa, was the President/Chairman of the society for as long as I can remember. They held regular meetings and entertainment functions in our house. The food items for the parties were always catered for by a caterer; favourites served were roasted goat meat, barbecued pork and other tasty items.

Members of the Scholars' Union comprised Hohoe indigenes and others from various areas of Ewe land, known collectively as Strangers. Because Papa, my father, hailed from Peki in the Gold Coast, he was a Stranger, and was known as the Chief Stranger. This appellation and recognition carried with it some element of unofficial responsibility. If any traveller arrived in transit in the evening by lorry, and had nowhere to stay for the night, he was directed to our house. Papa always obliged by providing accommodation. They were often people from Peki who had their farms in Kadjebi, Ahamansu or Likpe in the Buem district and therefore travelled to or from Peki.

During the 1940s, Mfantsipim Secondary School, like all the other few secondary schools at the time (Adisadel, St Augustine in Cape Coast) conducted its own entrance examination at various principal towns. Hohoe was their centre in the BMT. The examiners always came to lodge with us. My father was reputed to place a high premium on education. Since Hohoe was a commercial and a postal centre, some parents not resident in Hohoe, but located in the hinterland, and having wards in secondary schools in Accra or Cape Coast, deposited funds with Papa for periodic transfer to their wards' schools. It was a service my father was pleased to render freely.

I was the youngest of my parents' children. I grew up throughout my childhood days with my parents in Hohoe until I left the elementary school for Achimota School. My father had a son and a daughter with two separate women before he married my mother, who bore him three children. Our eldest sibling was called Emmanuel, followed by Comfort Akua. My mother, Kate Ama, hailed from Saisi in Krobo Agormanya. My mother's children were William Kwasi, Felicia Ama and me, Theodore Komla.

During his early days in elementary school, Willie stayed for a brief period with Mr Kwame in Hohoe. Mr Kwame, then a school teacher, a renowned musician, later a Reverend Pastor, ended up as the Synod Clerk of the EP Church. Willie next went to Ada to stay with Mr Apo, a school teacher. Mr Apo was an Akropong trained teacher, who was an uncle from our maternal Krobo side. When Mr Apo was transferred to Christiansborg in Accra, Willie went along with him. After his senior school days in Salem, Christiansborg, Willie proceeded to Accra Academy Secondary School as a Day student. After a year at

Accra Academy, Willie was transferred to Mfantsipim School in Cape Coast. It was a treasured tradition in those days of yore to send your young son to stay with a school teacher, preferably a relative or a close family friend in order to acquire knowledge and discipline. Felicia, my sister, being a female, stayed with us in Hohoe and attended the Roman Catholic Girl's Convent School at Bla as a Day student until she completed the junior school. After the Convent school at Bla, Felicia was transferred to the Krobo Girls' School. This was a famous and prestigious Presbyterian boarding institution at that time in the country.

An exception was made for me, perhaps because I was the youngest. Living with my parents at Hohoe in my early years was a privilege which I loved. I was not pampered. Because of the tedium of travelling long journeys on the lorries, Willie joined us only at Christmas time during the school holidays. I very eagerly awaited Willie's arrival for the yearly family reunion. He always thrilled me with stories about Accra, the big city which I had never before visited. Our eldest brother, Emmanuel, was a student at Achimota Secondary School and joined us regularly in Hohoe for the Christmas. He would arrive wearing the Achimota blazer with its college black and white keyboard emblem crest and sporting a pork-pie hat; it was an impressive and enviable attire. Papa wanted Emmanuel to have the best education then available and spared no effort in this direction. He was outfitted with three-piece woollen suits ordered from Bradford in England, he owned a camera, an item not commonly seen then; Papa also bought him a number of musical instruments; including a cornet and other woodwind classical instruments. My half-sister Comfort Akua stayed with us in Hohoe and attended the Presbyterian elementary school up to standard three after which she joined her mother in Ayoma.

My mother was a trader, baker and a farmer, all rolled into one; her entrepreneurship and hard work were unsurpassed. Because of the extent of her activities, she had several maids in the house who assisted her. These maids came mostly from Krobo, her hometown; some were sent by their parents from Hohoe and the nearby towns of Likpe, Lolobi and Santrokofi to be taught the art of marketing, trading, house-keeping and baking. One of the maids I grew up with in the house was the daughter of Togbe Gabusu, the Paramount Chief of

Hohoe. The training given to maids by my mother was much sought after.

My mother had a store in the central market; the merchandise was mainly textiles and Krobo beads. On specific market days in the other towns in the Hohoe district, mainly Ayoma and Likpe, my mother would dispatch a senior maid with her merchandise to sell. Mammy was probably the most prominent and successful trader at that time in the Hohoe market. She also embarked on baking bread and cakes for sale for some time; a large oven was specially built in the house for this activity.

Each year, a large acre of virgin land at the Fodome road area was cleared by a group of hired labourers for the planting of yam, water-yam and cassava. The harvest time for the yam and water yam was usually in December, during the cold, dry and dusty Harmattan season. I always looked forward to the harvest trips to the farm on Saturdays; we only took home produce enough to last for about a fortnight. The remainder of the harvested produce was stored in specially built storage barns on the farm; the stored yam was never stolen, such was the level of honesty at the time.

The EP Church and its schools played a major role in my childhood in Hohoe. The schools comprised infant, junior and senior elementary schools. Each had classroom blocks, assembly grounds, playing fields and toilet blocks. Because the senior school was a boarding school, there were dormitory blocks as well as a dining block, and bathroom blocks. The infant school was headed by a headteacher; the junior and senior schools were each headed by a headmaster. All three schools came under the overall management of the Hohoe district Reverend Pastor.

My parents were religious and played leading roles in the church as Presbyters. Our family was generally regarded as affluent at that time. Each morning, it was my duty to sweep my father's bedroom, the dining room and the large living room, set up his table for breakfast, polish his shoes, as well as the living room furniture, which consisted of chairs, side tables and a large ornate harmonium. The harmonium was a tall, dark brown and elegant one which my father had bought by order from Canada; it was the largest in the Hohoe region. Papa and my brother Emmanuel played the harmonium regularly. Papa started me on lessons on how to play this instrument, and I made satisfactory progress reading and playing the notes until we got to flats and sharps. I regrettably gave up when I encountered difficulties with these notes. It remains one of my greatest regrets that I cannot read nor play musical notes. Perhaps, Papa should have used the stick on me; it was the accepted practice at the time. On this note, it is germane to state that my parents NEVER smacked me. After my failure with the sharps and flats, I took the easy way of playing popular tunes by ear, to the admiration of passers-by and visitors.

Each morning on weekdays, Papa, after breakfast would take a minute's walk from the house to the store, dressed in white trousers and white shirt, sporting a white or khaki-coloured pith helmet. Lunch was prepared by my mother and carried on a tray by a maid to my father in the store. His afternoon tea was regularly, without fail, sent at 4pm prompt daily; the pot of tea, cup with saucer, sugar and milk were carried in a deep round blue coloured tray. The store always closed at 5pm, after which Papa would walk back home; he would then change into casual attire, sit comfortably in his chair and read the daily newspapers. The newspapers at the time were *The African Morning Post* and *The Spectator Daily*. Both papers were published and printed in Accra, and delivered to Hohoe twice a week, on Tuesdays and Fridays. Another paper, published and printed by the colonial government during the years of the Second World War, was *The Empire at War;* this was freely available. At about 6pm Papa would go to the Post Office to meet his friend and colleague, Mr Gbedema. At the Post Office they received the latest news about the war from the postmaster, who got the news by wireless, the quickest way of communication at the time. Radio broadcast was not yet available in Hohoe then. I think that my interest in current affairs and habit of reading papers and journals dated from this period; in like manner, I attribute my habit of tea drinking to this lifestyle of my father's.

The War effort was carried on various fronts. The Government Broadcasting Department had a mobile cinema unit which toured the country, showing newsreels on the war and the depraved activities by the Nazi regime under Adolf Hitler. The film shows always ended with light-hearted comedies featuring Charlie Chaplin; these were very popular, and our only exposure to the cinema. The Government also organized activities to raise funds with the aim of paying for the cost of a Spitfire fighter plane to be used in fighting the Germans. Strong persuasive efforts were made to recruit young men to join the army.

At this juncture, it is germane to relate a chronicle. In 1942, the late Brigadier Michel was then an Akropong-trained school teacher, teaching at an EP school in Kpando. Michel's uncle was Mr Ansre from Peki; Mr Ansre, my father's cousin, was then a school headmaster in Worawora. One morning I was told that Michel had been recruited to join the army and was in fact in transit at the government recruiting centre on the Fodome Road My father gave me a message to give to him at the recruiting centre, and I delivered it. In those days, the general opinion was that only dropouts and the unemployed would join the army, and certainly not a person of middle class background like Michel. Why he joined the army was a big question. When I went to see him, he did not look a happy person to me, but I could be wrong since I was only 11 years old at the time. Michel went on to perform brilliantly and later rose in rank to become a Brigadier. In 1961, he was appointed to command the United Nations forces in the Congo by Mr Dag Hammarskjöld, the UN Secretary General. He was the first African military officer to attain that level of international distinction. Kwame Nkrumah was delighted and proud of this honour conferred on a Ghanaian. Shortly before leaving for the Congo assignment, he was on a flight from Accra to the Ashanti Region in a military aircraft to inspect a centre for training guerrilla soldiers. The plane crashed in the Ashanti jungle with serious consequences. Michel sustained very extensive third degree burn injuries, involving about 70% of his body; he was also a diabetic. He and the other passengers on the aircraft were conveyed to the Kumasi Central Hospital (now Komfo Anokye Teaching Hospital). I was at that time a Medical Officer in the surgical department of the hospital. Michel was admitted to the surgical ward where I saw him, and he recognized me. He was placed under the direct care of the most senior surgeons and physicians; the prognosis was obviously poor. He was transferred the following day to the 37 Military Hospital in Accra where he died not long after; a sad end to a brilliant career. The Michel Camp in Tema was fittingly named after him. Dag Hammarskjöld died in a similar plane crash while on a peace mission to the Belgian Congo in the same year.

The Congo had been a Belgian colony; the world's largest deposit of uranium, the vital element in the nuclear era, was found there in large quantities. The United States of America (USA) and the Soviet Union, the two major powers, did not want the Congo to fall under the influence of either adversary (the USA and Soviet Union). The Cold War was at its coldest stage. It was under this shadow that the two crashes chronicled with fatalities above occurred. I hold my tongue.

ELEMENTARY SCHOOL – 1945

My father had been educated to the highest level then attainable at his time in Peki and Keta. He understood the importance and value of education. It was his aim that his children should attain the highest level of education which was then available; he spared no effort towards this goal. He heaped praises on anyone he knew in BMT who was brilliant in school. A notable example was Master Dornyo who was excelling at Achimota College. He was awarded a government scholarship to go to Britain to study Medicine, a rare achievement in the 1940s.

My earliest formal education commenced when I was enrolled into the EP Kindergarten class. The classes were held at the Church premises. We were ten in number. Our form of dressing was the wrap of cloth with the ends tied behind our neck. I was eight years old then; we walked bare-footed. I was soon moved into the Infant school. The school had three graded classes: one, two and three; and there were three teachers, one for each class. The teachers each had the Standard 7 School Leaving Certificate, but had not been to a Training College. The school had an assembly ground and a playing field; there were toilet huts. We were taught to write the alphabet and numbers on the black, individual, portable wooden slates, using chalk; we also used chalk of various colours for drawing. The class teacher was good. We had an examination at the end of the year; I was placed in the ninth position above a big girl. We all gained promotion to class two the following year. I spent the following two years in classes two and three. More serious and progressively advanced lessons were taught. The full alphabet in Ewe and the times tables from one to 12 were mastered. The La Coombs exercise books, specially prepared and designed by the Education Department, were then in use in all schools. We were taught to read and write with pencils in exercise books. Marks were given on the quality of writing and one's ability in art and craft work. My classwork improved from year to year and gained me a promotion from class three to Standard 1 in the junior school in 1941.

The junior school was a moderately large institution. It consisted of a large block with three classrooms, each holding 30 to 40 pupils. There were three teachers, and it was headed by the Headmaster, Mr Mensah, a trained teacher. There was a large playing field, an assembly ground and toilet block. The playing field grass was kept in pristine condition by the pupils. Garden flowers were planted in the school compound and well tended. The EP school system and ethos laid great emphasis on manual work, with special attention to horticulture and agriculture.

My teacher in Standard 1 was Mr Atiega, who was excellent at his vocation. Teaching was conducted in Ewe; English was taught as a second language. Mr Atiega invited us to submit to him all the Ewe words for which we wanted their English equivalent. This way, we quickly acquired the knowledge of a wide range of vocabulary, especially verbs and nouns in the English language. This provided a major bridge into the language. I suddenly experienced a quantum jump in my class performances. I acquitted myself very well in all the class subjects, except arts and crafts.

There was a boy in my class who excelled in all the subjects, but was above all very talented in the field of arts and crafts. There was no limit to his handicraft in modelling clay, weaving, sculpturing, woodwork, painting and drawing. His name was Glikpo and he came from a humble and rather poor family. He always came first in our class examinations. Given the opportunity, he could have attained any height in his chosen field of pursuit. As an artist, he could have become a Picasso or Le Corbusier. On completing the senior school and obtaining the Standard 7 School Leaving Certificate, my father took him on as a store-assistant; he was provided with accommodation in our house. I do not know what happened to him later. In Standard 3, we were taught by the Headmaster, Mr Mensah, who also hailed from Peki, like my father; he was an excellent teacher. In our Standard 3 class we were joined by two brothers, named Godstime and Godsway Tay. The younger Tay, Godstime, later changed his name to Goza Tay. He graduated in Physics, obtained a PhD, and lectured at the Kwame Nkrumah University of Science and Technology (KNUST) in Kumasi; he was one of the pioneer scientists at the Ghana Atomic Research Institute.

The next stage of my educational ladder was at the EP Senior School in Hohoe. It was a boarding school for the Hohoe district; one of the 'Key' schools in the BMT. The catchment area included the Gbi state EP divisions, Likpe, Golokwati and Leklebi. Because of the limited number of intakes, an entrance examination had to be taken to gain admission to Standard 4 in the senior school. I passed the entrance examination and gained admission to Standard 4 in 1944.

The senior school occupied a larger acreage than its sister junior school; the classrooms were larger and more commodious. There were four classrooms for the four classes from Standard 4 to Standard 7 and it consisted of a large assembly ground, a major football playing field and two minor grassed playing fields. There were separate dormitory and dining blocks, as well as separate bathroom and toilet blocks. The grounds were beautifully landscaped with hedges, flowering plants and foliage; some tall trees provided an attractive arboreal ambience to the whole school. There were five trained teachers at the school, of whom the most senior was the Headmaster, Mr Anku. He had a special interest in arts and crafts, especially pottery. In addition to teaching pottery in a dedicated way, he was given much credit for building a Domestic Science block for the school. He had supervised the pupils in making the blocks and the roofing tiles, and their colouring to produce a durable and attractive burnt brick edifice. He hailed from Gbadzeme in the Amedzofe area.

There was also a resident housemaster at the school, one Mr Dumoga, an Achimota-trained teacher. In addition to teaching, he was responsible for the accommodation of pupils and other extracurricular activities.

The school also had a band with a wide range of woodwind musical instruments. The band and the school's choral activity came under Mr Geku, the music master. He was a brilliant Akropong-trained teacher and musician, he taught the top Standard 7 class. He owned a harmonium, a priceless acquisition. All the teachers assisted in running sports and recreational activities. Emphasis was laid on maintaining a clean and hygienic environment. The dormitories were regularly inspected by the housemaster. Our wooden beds had to be dismantled and thoroughly checked for bedbugs before each inspection. We used cutlasses to cut the grass on the playing fields to maintain an appealing environment. The EP educational system placed a great emphasis on manual labour, as mentioned before. All the teachers had little farms for cultivating food crops. The pupils assisted in tending these farms after class hours.

Hitherto, I had lived with my parents at home, the sole sibling doing so. There were many maids in our house, most of them being trained. Willie was in Accra, while Felicia was at Krobo Girls in Odumasi. I had now moved to join other young boys in the famous EP Senior School as a boarder. I looked forward to this new challenging experience. I was 13 years old. The World War was still raging.

We were allocated to our various dormitories, each of which was a mixture of junior and senior pupils. The day began with an early wakeup call, after which we had our bath from our personal individual buckets of water. Khaki school uniforms were standard from the infant to the senior schools. We purchased our breakfast from vendors who set up their food stalls near the dining hall. Lunch took a similar form of purchasing food from vendors. The morning school session started with the entire school assembled on the assembly ground. The pupils all stood class by class, facing the teachers. Following the announcements by the Headmaster or other teachers, and the singing of hymns, the assembly was then dismissed, the pupils marched class by class to their respective classrooms. The morning class session ended at 12 noon. The school was co-educational and comprised boys and girls, although the girls were day pupils only. There was also a handful of boys who did not board, but stayed with teachers or the pastor.

Mr Vulor, our teacher, hailed from Gbi Kpoeta; he was a good teacher. In our first week, we bought our books from the bookstore which was stocked with all those which were required. The textbooks were the Longmans, published in English. We had now graduated from writing with pencil to writing with pen and ink. The medium of teaching was a mix of English and Ewe, which was quite effective. The subjects were Arithmetic, English, Nature Study, Hygiene, Civics and General Knowledge. The English lessons consisted of grammar, spelling, syntax, sentence structure and reading simple stories. I enjoyed my curricular lessons under Mr Vulor.

The class teachers for Standards 5 and 6 were Mr Adjanku and Mr Dumoga respectively; they were both Achimota-trained teachers. As already stated, the Standard 7 teacher was Mr Geku, the music master.

The afternoon classes ended at 4pm, and this period was followed by sports, agricultural and horticultural activities. My ability and skill at football were undeniable. The school at that time had a crop of older and very gifted footballers; the town of Likpe in particular seemed to produce excellent footballers. The school team played matches occasionally against other schools in the region, except the Roman Catholic schools. The team also played against Hohoe Spirocids team occasionally.

A very sad event occurred in 1944 which needs to be chronicled. One of my classmates was Dorothea Kpetoe. She was fair in complexion, and probably the most beautiful girl in the whole school. Her desk was directly in front of mine. Very early one morning her body was found just outside our football pitch on a footpath; there was no sign of external injury. The story which gained currency was that she became pregnant and the person responsible for the pregnancy gave her something to ingest to cause an abortion. The alleged abortifacient turned out to be something very toxic, which resulted in Dorothea's death. The suspected gentleman was a well known married school teacher. He lived in a house in the teachers' quarters, not far from the place where the body had been found. Dorothea was buried in the late afternoon the same day, after viewing in their house. It was my first time of seeing a dead person, and it left an unforgettable imprint on my mind. A Criminal Investigations Department (CID) operative was sent from Accra to conduct an investigation into Dorothea's death, but I do not think that any evidence of guilt on the suspected teacher was found. He left Hohoe EP School for another school in a faraway region in the Gold Coast with his entire family. This teacher, by a most strange irony of fate, suffered a sad end to his life.

He had been keen on the Boy Scouts movement in his role as a teacher in the schools he taught in. In his new school, there was a fire outbreak in the town; and as a dedicated Boy Scout he went to assist in putting it out. Very sadly, he was consumed by the fire and died tragically. It sounds like the enactment of the last scene of Mozart's Don Giovani. Several decades later, a medical colleague of some disrepute suffered a similar fate.

At the end of 1944, we were all promoted to Standard 5 for the following year. I had enjoyed my first year in the boarding school; the fun on the football field, swimming in the river Dayi till my scare of nearly drowning, the school mischiefs on April Fools' Day, and a lot more.

My brother Willie and sister Felicia came from Accra and Krobo respectively to Hohoe for Christmas holidays. Papa always held a party in the house for the inmates and our neighbours on Christmas Eve after the Nativity church service. The decorations were modest, with the use of palm branches and a few imported decorative items as the dictates of the wartime permitted. On Christmas Day, a goat was always slaughtered, along with some fowls for the luncheon meal; imported biscuits, and home-made cakes provided extra treats.

The school year in 1945 opened with me in Standard 5. Our teacher was Mr Adjanku, Achimota-trained. He was short, modest and rather self-effacing. He hailed from Peki. There had been some staff changes: Mr Paul Kpeto, Achimota-trained, hailing from Hohoe joined the staff to take charge of Standard 6, whilst Mr Dormelo from Likpe, also trained at Achimota, took over Standard 4 from Mr Vulor, who was transferred to another school. Mr Dumoga was moved from Standard 6 to take over the Standard 7 school leaving class. Mr Kpeto came from a well known Hohoe family. He was a famous footballer who had played for the Achimota College team, a creditable achievement for a person from Hohoe in those days. Mr Anku remained as the Headmaster and added on the role of music master.

We were joined in our Standard 5 class by two brothers, namely Cephas and Simon Kpedekpo. They had been promoted from Standard 3 and jumped by two classes to Standard 5. Why? They were mature students who had attended and completed the French Togoland primary senior school three years earlier. Their knowledge of Arithmetic and other subjects was far more advanced than those they came to join from Standard 4; they were also naturally bright students. It is germane to add here that they displaced me from my position as the top of the class; it was indeed a good challenge for me. I was embroiled in all school activities. I was no longer a junior; I was a step up the seniority ladder. The language of communication on the campus was Ewe; the medium of teaching was a mix of English and Ewe. A new school rule was promulgated, much to the consternation of most of the students. The new rule was that on Wednesdays for the 24-hour period, no one should speak in the Ewe Language. A breach of this rule entailed a punishment to be administered by a teacher. Wednesdays as a result became silent days. Many of the known school bullies were visibly quiet and inconspicuous on Wednesdays, while confident, smarter students moved around, chattering with a bit of a swagger.

EP School ethic was discipline and scholastic achievement. It was an era when the rod was not spared in applying discipline. A serious offence was addressed with corporal punishment at the general school morning assembly. Some teachers earned the reputation for severe application of the cane. The cane was never used for poor scholastic performance though.

The afternoon sporting activities were followed by dinner, the meal of the day. Each student was provided with a meal from their home or a caterer's. My food was prepared at home by my mother and brought to me in a bowl by a maid. My mother, an excellent cook, provided me with delicious and sumptuous dishes and my meals were viewed with envy by fellow students. It was the practice to share one's meal with one or two other colleagues. The classmates with whom I shared my meals were considered lucky to be my pals. Dinner was followed by a period of private study lasting an hour in our respective classrooms. After the private study we retired to our dormitories. On Wednesday evenings we marched up to the EP church to attend evening service. In like manner, we dressed up in white shorts and shirts and marched to the EP church to attend Sunday morning service with the congregation.

In the annals of world history, 1945 will forever remain a great and significant landmark. Nazi Germany began to crumble in World War 2 under the combined onslaught of the Allied forces under the command of General Eisenhower, the American, and his British deputy,

General Montgomery. In April 1945, President FD Roosevelt of the USA died suddenly; the news of his sudden death was conveyed to his Vice President, Mr Harry Truman, as he was having his late afternoon tea. Mr Truman, hitherto a little-known person, became the new US President. Mussolini, the Italian Fascist Prime Minister and dictator, who was an ally of Hitler, was overthrown; he was executed and his corpse was hung in the city square for public viewing. To avoid a similar fate in Germany, Hitler retreated to his bunker where he made his will, and then shot himself fatally in the temple; his body was burned in accordance with his instructions. His newly wedded wife, Eva Braun, took her own life with cyanide. Germany surrendered in July 1945, and signed the unconditional treaty accepting defeat. Victory in Europe was celebrated worldwide, including in Hohoe in the BMT. A month later, the nuclear bomb millennium was opened by the dropping of the atom bomb on the Japanese cities of Hiroshima and Nagasaki. Japan's unconditional surrender to General MacArthur, the American, brought to an end the Second World War. This event also received worldwide celebration and was greeted with long pent-up relief.

A personal memoir is not meant to be a history book, but important events are worth chronicling. On the home front, two events in this period received much press coverage.

The first was the Kibi murder case. A prominent chief of Kibi was ritually murdered in Kibi. Investigations led to the prosecution of six people; they were all found guilty and sentenced to death. Appeal after appeal ended at the Privy Council in England. Some prominent Kibi citizens figured in this saga. Ghanaians of a certain vintage would know how this ended…

The second, which also received considerable press coverage was the Kojo Thompson case. Mr Kojo Thompson was a famous lawyer and national politician in Accra. In a case with national political overtones, he was accused of perjury, a criminal offence. He was found guilty and jailed for one minute! The British legal system with all its foibles was on clear view! It ended his legal and political career. Not much has since been written about this case.

In 1945, my father asked me to prepare myself to take the entrance examination to Achimota Secondary School. At that time, there was no common entrance examination to the few secondary schools in the Gold Coast; there was certainly none in the BMT. The test would be in English, Arithmetic and General Intelligence. The examination was open to students in Standard 5, 6, and 7. My father intended this to be a trial run for me with a more serious attempt in the following year when I would be in Standard 6, a higher grade. Hohoe was an examination centre for Achimota and Mfantsipim. The entrance examination to Mfantsipim could only be taken by those in Standard 7. Admission to the Akropong Training College was based on the Standard 7 School Leaving Examination results. Students who obtained three distinctions were offered admission with a full scholarship.

I prepared myself well and sat for the Achimota entrance paper one morning and was interviewed in the afternoon. I was interviewed by Mr Riberio and Mr Whittaker, Ghanaian and an Englishman respectively. The latter's wife, Mrs Whittaker, was a young mixed-race Ghanaian; she came to Hohoe with her husband on this examination visit, when she renewed her acquaintance with Mrs Emma Dumelo, with whom she had attended the School of Midwifery at Korle Bu. Emma (nee Emma Asamoah, the elder sister of Obed Asamoah) was probably the first trained midwife from this part of the country. I do not know how I felt after the written paper and the interview; I was certainly relaxed since it was only meant to be a trial run for me.

A few weeks after the examination, my father received a telegram, the fastest mode of sending written information at the time, from Achimota School. The message to my father was that I had passed the competitive entrance examination and that I was being offered admission to the school. With a half scholarship, you paid half of the fees. Outstanding students obtained full scholarships, while the less outstanding were offered half scholarships. I believe the status and financial ability of parents were factors taken into consideration when an offer was made to a ward. However, be that as it may, here I was, a 14-year old boy in Standard 5 being offered a place in Form two, a place open normally only to students from Standard 7. It meant a two-year jump in class. Very creditably for the Hohoe EP School, three other students were offered admission to Achimota. Gilbert Osei from Standard 5, and Festus Asamoah from Standard 6 to Form one and Ebenezer Amengor from Standard 7 to Form two. This was a very high success rate for the school, probably the highest in its history. Achimota, unlike other secondary schools, did not like to take students above a certain age. For this reason, some applicants to Achimota School reduced their age on their application forms to render themselves suitable for admission; birth certificates were not demanded then. It became an accepted fact in later years that there was the real age and the school age. Many people lived the remainder of their lives with this age duplicity. I did not have to alter my date of birth when I applied to go to Achimota.

My father accepted the offer to me from Achimota to attend as a full fee-paying student at 33 pounds sterling a year; this was a great amount of money in those days. A civil servant with the London matriculation certificate was paid four pounds a month, and a newly engaged non-expatriate medical doctor was paid 12 pounds a month initially for six months. These examples in salary are to put incomes at the time into perspective. My father, however, felt very apprehensive about the double jump from Standard 5 to Form two. What would be the consequence if the jump proved to be too steep for me? I could possibly face expulsion on academic grounds. This would have to be a wait and see game. The Hohoe EP School had acquitted itself very well with the excellent Achimota entrance results in 1945. To put this in its proper perspective, a little anecdote here is germane. About three years later, a girl from Gbi Atabu passed the entrance examination to gain admission to the Roman Catholic Holy Child Training College in Cape Coast. This success was celebrated sensationally. There was a march past through the principal streets of Hohoe, with a brass band accompanying the successful student marching in front of the procession. This may sound extreme, but it was quite an achievement then, when all academic success was hailed and celebrated grandly!

The ethic of discipline, the cornerstone of the EP Church educational system, established by the founding Bremen Mission, was matched by its deep religious and church activities. Senior teachers played a significant role and assisted the pastors in conducting church services. The church programme each year ended with the celebration of the church anniversary (Nkekenyuie) of the district on a rotational basis in various towns. Parishioners from other towns all converged on the chosen town venue on the Sunday for the anniversary church service. The EP Senior School played an important role in the celebrations. It was held in Likpe in 1944 and in Golokwati in 1945. We, the students, undertook the journeys by walking from Hohoe to the destinations on the preceding Saturday afternoon. As we approached any little township on our way, we assembled at its border, then marched through the township to brass band music. This process was repeated all along the way until our arrival at our destination, when the final grand march through the main street of the town was enacted to the welcoming and cheering crowd of the town. Since we were young, the relatively long distances we walked exhausted us. Food was provided by the local parishioners, quite an effort for them. The Sunday anniversary programme consisted of sermons, messages, and hymns interspersed with choral and brass band music. The Kpandu EP School band, wearing their blue tunic uniforms, well drilled and marshalled by their famous music master, Mr Kwame (later, Rev. Kwame of the Kwame musical family). He was always in demand for these church anniversaries in the region. The return journeys home on Sunday afternoon were less arduous. I recall these anniversaries with nostalgia.

The 1945 anniversary brought to an end my educational and associated church activities in Hohoe. I had benefited in no small way from the institution. I was also blessed with the good fortune of having parents who loved and cared for me; some of my mates were not so lucky. No doubt that I was very likely influenced by this example when I later became a parent.

Chapter 2
ACHIMOTA SECONDARY SCHOOL

ACHIMOTA IN THE NATIONAL SETTING

Achimota College, initially known as The Prince of Wales College, was founded by Sir Gordon Guggisberg, the Governor of the Gold Coast in 1927. He was the great pioneer who built Takoradi Harbour and Korle Bu Hospital. He appointed Reverend A. G. Fraser, a Scotsman, as the first Principal. A. G. Fraser, then in Kandy in Ceylon (now Sri Lanka), accepted the post on condition that Kwegyir Aggrey, who had hailed from Anomabu, but then in the USA, was also appointed as his assistant. Guggisberg, Fraser and Aggrey thus became known as the Founders of Achimota.

The aim was to establish a unique educational experiment in West Africa. They aimed to produce students with a Western intellectual and scientific attitude without neglecting the African cultural and traditional background. The school was to have a character along Christian religious lines, producing leaders who would solve problems in the Gold Coast. The History of Achimota was well researched and chronicled by the late Professor Francis Agbodeka, my Achimota contemporary, in his publication, *Achimota in the National Setting*.

To achieve its aim, Achimota recruited staff of very high calibre. In 1939, when the college population was 750, Achimota had a staff of 60 graduates and 40 nongraduate teachers. Achimota was a crucible of excellence. It was better endowed than Eton, Harrow and Winchester in England. Great emphasis had been laid on the practical aspect of education including agriculture. The Second World War imposed severe restrictions on recruiting expatriate graduate staffing. Emphasis also shifted more to the academic aspect of education. The Rev. Stopford, the Principal at the time, was credited with this shift.

The Principal of the college had always been a Reverend Minister. When the college ceased training teachers, and was only run as a secondary school, Achimota came to be known as Achimota School and no longer as Achimota College. It was during this phase of shift in emphasis that I made my humble entry as a freshman (or Ninoboy) into the portals of Achimota.

Achimota had two campuses, the Eastern and the Western. The Eastern campus hosted the Administration block with its famous tower, the dining hall, several Houses for boys and girls, classroom and science blocks, the gymnasium, arts and crafts blocks, large playing fields, an arboretum and the school farm. The hospital, the Post Office, the swimming pool, and the Police Station were sited between the two campuses. The Anumle village constituted the quarters for the junior staff. The Western campus, as part of the College, had dormitory halls of residence, a dining hall, and staff residential buildings. During the Second World War the Western campus was taken over by the British Military forces and converted into the Headquarters of the British West African Regiment. It thus became a very important place during the war. It was headed by Lord Swinton, the resident British Minister who was a member of Prime Minister Sir Winston Churchill's cabinet.

After the war, the Western campus was taken over by the newly emerging University College of the Gold Coast (UCGC). Mr David Balme, the first Principal, took up residence in Lugard House before moving to Legon later.

In 1946, the first year after the war, I made all the necessary preparations to travel to Accra. I had never been to the capital city before, but had been regaled with many stories about it by my brother Willie. My trunk was fully packed with all the necessary personal listed items in the school prospectus. My chop-box was also bursting with provision, items like powdered milk, sugar, Ovaltine, Tono, tins of sardine, corned beef, Keta oil shito and most important of all, gari. Since my father was a storekeeper, the contents of my chopbox invited a justifiable envy from many. I travelled from Hohoe to Accra in a lorry, leaving in the morning. Before my departure, my father gave me a sum of 17 shillings and six pence, the minimum amount stated in the school prospectus as my pocket money for the first term; my father was very strict financially. My mother, on realising the small amount of money that my father had given me, topped it up very generously, a typical maternal response! Our driver, wearing the heavy round metal driving licence plate on his neck as required by law, drove the lorry with passengers on the laterite road from Hohoe to Senchi. At Senchi, the UAC firm operated a ferry which ferried lorries and passengers across the River Volta; it carried five vehicles at a time, working from morning till 6pm. Senchi was therefore an important stop for vehicles and passengers from BMT to Accra. The fufu 'chop bars' served tasty dishes of soup with smoked fish and goat meat; passengers looked forward to this treat on their journey to and from Accra. The second part of the journey was the drive from Senchi to Accra on a macadamized road through Kpong, Somanya and Dodowa. The journey lasted a whole day. I was naturally thrilled and excited when we finally arrived in Accra at the lorry park, which was located near the Makola market, close to Tudu. I spent the night in Mr Opare's house, which was near the main Post Office building. Mr Opare, a good friend of my father's, was expecting me, although I had not met him before. I had an anxious wait for the following day to make my way to Achimota. The following day, I boarded the Achimota bus at the present Opera Square with my trunk and chop-box and set off for Achimota.

No one from any part of the world, let alone a young boy of 15 from colonial BMT, could fail to be impressed by the physical layout of Achimota in 1946.

The Administration Block with its tall and huge clock tower, the well-tended grounds and lawns, the avenues of tall palm trees and the dormitory houses in Gothic architectural style, all combined to leave an everlasting impression. I was in the first batch of intakes after the Second World War; it was the largest intake hitherto. We came from all corners of the country. The admissions were for the secondary school only, as admission for the training college was discontinued. There was a novel batch of girls admitted for a pre-nursing course to last for one year. Although we came from different parts of the country, ethnicity was not a factor in the choice of friends and associates. Unlike the EP School, where the medium of communication was Ewe, in my new school, English was decidedly the lingua franca.

The admission process was conducted very orderly in the Administration Block. I was allocated to a junior dormitory – Livingstone

House. There were five boys' houses and two girls' houses. Two of the boys' houses, Livingstone and Lugard, were junior houses, while the remaining three, namely Aggrey, Gyamfi and Cadbury were senior houses. The girls' houses were Slessor and Kingsley. There were also some round single houses, called Yaba houses, which were occupied by intermediate degree students. The Eastern campus of Achimota then housed the secondary school and the training college sections. The training college was a four-year course, running from T1 to T4. As already stated, admission to the training college had been discontinued; the course was in the process of being phased out. When I arrived at the school in 1946, only the T3 and T4 students were there. The admission process involved house allocation, issuance of school uniforms, the highly prized Achimota sandal footwear, the unique Achimota College blazer with its emblazoned school badge stating the school motto of "Ut Omnes Unum Sint" extended over a couple of days. Bullying of new students (Ninos) by older students formed part of the ethos, especially in the early days of admission; I did not escape it as a victim, but it took a relatively innocuous form.

After our allocation and placement in various classes, we collected our textbooks and exercise books from the book store. Up until 1945, Achimota had a Primary School section, the students from the Primary School gained entry into the secondary school at S1. Students from other Primary schools in the country coming from Standard 6 were admitted to S1 while those from Standard 7 were admitted to S2. The secondary school course leading to the Cambridge School Leaving Certificate at 'O' level in Achimota lasted for four years, terminating in S5. All other secondary schools in the country ran a five-year course terminating in S6 for the Cambridge school leaving examination. In 1946, Achimota had six students in S6; they had sat for the school leaving examination in S5 and were being prepared to commence a two-year Intermediate degree course. They were known as the citizens; they were all brilliant students who had been carefully selected. They were Ampofo (Gynaecologist), K.K. Korsah (Gynaecologist), Yaw Asirifi (Pediatrician), SA Amegashie (Accountant), Patrick Anin (Jurist) and Frank Mensah Bonsu (Solicitor); five of them of blessed memory. These six students had all been classmates of Alex Kwapong in S2. Because the teachers found Alex Kwapong, hailing from the Akwapim

Presbyterian background, exceptionally bright, they put him through an accelerated school programme, and prepared him to sit for the Cambridge school leaving examination in S4 – that is in just three years. Alex did not disappoint them; he passed the examination with grade one and obtained 6As from the seven subjects which Achimota permitted to be offered.

In its earlier days as already noted, Achimota College did not place great emphasis on academic excellence; Rev. Stopford was responsible for this seismic change towards academic performance. If a student was not performing well academically, he or she was expelled from the school after one year; the exercise was known as 'Stopfordisation'. It was under this intimidating atmosphere that I entered Achimota, jumping from Standard 5 to S2. A fellow student from Hohoe EP School Standard 6 was admitted at the same time to S1. My father had advised me quite wisely that if I found the course difficult, I should go to see Mr Nyaho Chapman, and ask him to intervene and arrange for my transfer to S1. Mr Chapman, an Ewe, was an Oxford University Geography graduate then on the school staff; he was also the school librarian.

YEARS IN ACHIMOTA

At the time I entered Achimota, there was no substantive Principal or Headmaster. The Acting Headmaster was Mr H C Neil, a Cambridge University Classics scholar. We did not get a substantive Headmaster until 1949, and his tenure at the post was short-lived. The senior teaching staff were mostly British European graduate teachers. The graduate African staff included Mr Dowuona, Mr Chapman, Mr M. A. Ribeiro and Mr P. D. Quartey; they were joined later by Messrs Kwame (Music), Oddoi, Mills, B. A. Brown and B. A. Attafuah. The non-graduate African staff included Messrs Boateng, Gbeho, and the legendary Ephraim Amu (whom my father had taught at the Peki Blengo EP Middle School). The school supplemented the permanent teaching staff with younger short-term teachers. These were products of the school who had sat for the intermediate degree examinations in science or arts (inter B.Sc. or Inter BA) and were awaiting their results before proceeding to the United Kingdom for the completion of their full University degree courses; they were bright young men, who taught mainly in S2 and S3 classes. During my time, I was taught by the following—S.P.O. Kumi, Silas Dodu, A. Armar, F.T. Sai, E. A. Boateng, Carl Reindorf and last, but not least, Alex Kwapong, my iconic mentor in Latin when he became my teacher in S4. He inspired me to learn, memorize and recite by rote a long piece of Cicero, parts of which I remember and still recite to him occasionally when we meet. Among the senior staff there were some very distinguished, highly qualified and devoted teachers. The group included Mr C.P. Woodhouse, Mr MA Ribeiro, Dr Royter (with a PhD in Chemistry), Rev. Father Leesage, Messrs Kwame and Ephraim Amu.

I went through the traditional school initiation ceremony. I had not been privy to the fact that the Ninos' examination at the end of the first week was meant to be a big practical academic joke, and that failure in the examination did not mean you were on your way out of the school, back home from where you came. I could not answer most of the questions, and so I was naturally very upset and worried. Mr Colin Wise, a senior master, wearing an academic gown, master of ceremonies, spared no effort to frighten us. I thought I was on my way back to Hohoe, until the element of fun was revealed later on that Saturday entertainment evening.

I settled down quickly in Livingstone House. Those of us in this house were juniors in S1 and S2, except the House Prefect and Assistant Prefect, Papafio and Kwakwa respectively, both in S5. The house master was Mr Boateng. It was a delightful experience and a novelty to have electric lights and WC toilet facilities. I was introduced to the game of cricket. Cricket and cross-country running (three or five miles) were the sporting activities in the first term; football was played competitively in the second term while hockey and athletics were third term activities. Volleyball and swimming had no assigned term. We played non-competitive football on house grounds all the year round.

In 1946, for the first time, there were four streams in S2, classified as 2A, 2B, 2C and 2D; they were not by order of merit. The form above us, S3, had only two streams.

I was placed in form S2A. I faced a new range of subjects which included Algebra, Geometry, Latin, Biology, Physics, and Chemistry. I was already familiar with the norms in Geography, Scriptures, History and Arithmetic. The medium of instruction was entirely English. I joined the pottery class in arts and crafts; I had acquired some interest and skill in in my previous two years at Hohoe EP Senior School under the tutelage of Mr. V.O. Anku. We had two excellent teachers, namely Mr Angba and Mr Ziga, who taught pottery. Several years later, the legendary Mr Ziga established a pottery industry at Golokwati in the Volta Region. I also enrolled in the lettering class which I enjoyed tremendously as a hobby. It is a shame that the art of lettering has faded away. I tried my hand at painting, but did not succeed. I joined the woodwork class, but dropped out for lack of interest. My mate and friend Emmanuel Asare enjoyed the woodwork class to such an extent that he offered it as a subject for the Cambridge school leaving 'O' level examination. He passed with an A. I took part in the practical work on the school farm. My domestic and EP School background in Hohoe made farming activity appealing, unlike the attitude of my mates from Accra and Cape Coast who were not used to manual work.

Cultural activities played an important role in the educational programme in Achimota. This dimension of education was absent in other schools and colleges in the country. Ewe, Ga, and Twi were taught, and could be offered as subjects for the Cambridge school leaving examination. Ewe classes were taught by Messrs Gbeho and Potakey. Tribal drumming was an entertainment activity which was held on some Saturdays. Mr Gbeho was the charismatic enthusiast who was in charge of the Ewe group. The Ewe group often excelled and was always adjudged the best performers. Music was taught as an academic subject by Mr Amu and Mr Gbeho. If you were academically interested in Music, there was an opportunity to listen to and enjoy classical music. After Sunday evening church service, Mr Amu played pieces of classical music from the porch of the first floor of the Administration Block through a loud speaker; this was in the HMV Gramophone era. Interested students stood on the lawn in front of the Administration Block to listen. This was my first exposure to classical music as opposed to church choral and hymnal music. It is a memory I still remember and cherish. This exposure was later supplemented by Messrs Kwame and Holmes.

One of the great achievements of Rev. A. G. Fraser was the recruitment of Ephraim Amu to join the Achimota College teaching staff.

Mr Amu had been dismissed from the staff of the famous Akropong Presbyterian Teachers Training College because he wore the Ghanaian attire of a jumper and cloth instead of a suit with a tie, as a Catechist, to preach the sermon in the church; it was considered an act of sacrilege. His dismissal received the full support of the Presbyterian Synod, the supreme and ultimate ruling Council of the Church in the country. Rev. A.G. Fraser wasted no time in recruiting this famous African musicologist and a true and genuine Christian.

The African cultural tradition which Rev. A.G. Fraser, a Scot, embraced early was also evident in the collegial dressing code; the attire for Sunday evening service was the cloth, with or without the jumper for boys and the kaba for the girls. This was also the attire for other important occasions such as the Founders Day. At this point in time, all the Cape Coast colleges and schools, namely Adisadel, Mfantsipim and St Augustine, stuck to the all-white trousers, shirt, with the blazer and tie. The colonial mentality despised the African culture in toto. One of the aims of the Founders was to inculcate the merits of the African tradition and culture in its students. This they succeeded in doing admirably.

Sporting activities played a major and significant role in the school programme. Cricket and cross-country running at three miles for juniors and five miles for seniors were the first term events. Inter-house competitions were held in all these events among the senior houses. Achimota School Cricket team played competitive matches against the Accra European cricket team and also against Mfantsipim School. The cricket coaches at Achimota were Mr P. D. Quartey and Mr Joseph (Paa Joe). Mr Joseph, a Sri Lankan (then known as Ceylonese), was brought from Kandy by Rev. A.G. Fraser to be in charge of sports as the Sports master. He excelled at this post and produced many notable cricketers and athletes for Achimota and the whole country. In recognition of his contribution to sports, the sports ground at KNUST in Kumasi was named after him. In 1946, two outstanding cricketers from the school represented the country in the match against the Nigerian national cricket team, by no means a small feat.

The second term was the season for football and athletics. Apart from inter-house matches, the school team played against Akropong Teachers Training College and the Cape Coast schools and colleges. The great competitive caucus was the annual intercollege sports, which was held on a rotational basis in athletics events. In 1946, my first year, it was held at Wesley College in Kumasi. All the secondary schools and teacher training colleges participated in the caucus. I remember some of the results to this day even though I was not there. Achimota not only won the competition very decisively, but it was at this venue that my late senior and friend K. K. Korsah excelled. He won the 100 yards, 220 yards, long jump, hurdles and pole-vault events as well as the sprint relays. He personally won 22 points out of a total of just over 40 for the school; this was more than the total gained by Mfantsipim, our regular rivals in all endeavours. Korsah was also the goalkeeper for the school football team, as well as the school's senior prefect. In physical appearance, he was tall and handsome. When he went to Britain later to study medicine, he continued to excel in athletics. In 1952, he belonged to the same athletic club as McDonald Bailey; Korsah was the second fastest in Britain then; Bailey won the Olympic gold that year in Helsinki.

The College had its own hospital. The doctor in charge at the time I went to Achimota was Dr Wilson, M.D, MRCP; both post graduate medical degrees, namely Doctorate in Medicine and Member of the Royal College of Physicians. These qualifications were not common at that time and were minimal qualifications for senior posts in medical academia. Achimota was 'sui generis' without an equal in Africa. It was not subjected to the Government Education department like all other schools; its governance and financial control were directly from the colonial Governor through the special Achimota College Council. In scholastic terms, it was comparable to Eton, Harrow and Winchester in England. It was this ethos of Achimota into which I became immersed.

Because my parents were religious, religion and church attendances had an influence on me. The college had a Presbyterian priest, by name Rev. Fraser (no relation to Rev. A. G. Fraser, although a fellow Scot) He had a strong Scottish accent, looked holier than the Pope, and would not step on an ant, figuratively speaking. The college chaplain was Father Bardsley, an Englishman who was the Housemaster of Aggrey House. Father Bardsley regularly, without fail, came to have lunch on Wednesdays with the students in the college dining hall, the only expatriate master to do so. Why? Groundnut soup with boiled yam and fried ripe plantain was the dish of the day and it was his favourite. There were three other Anglican priests, namely Father Persico (from British Guiana), Father Perry and a Ghanaian whose name I cannot remember. Father Persico was the Assistant House master in Cadbury House; he had an aura of holiness about him. Rev. Father Bronck was the Roman Catholic priest; he later became the Bishop of Lome, in French Togoland. Father Fraser held confirmation classes for a few of us new Presbyterians at the school for a few months; we were confirmed a few weeks after the end of the classes. Mrs Doris Owusu-Addo (nee Adu) was in this group. Evening nondenominational Sunday services were held for Protestants. The Roman Catholics held separate services. There were no known Muslims in the school at the time. Visiting priests came occasionally to preach the sermon. Bishop Anglioby of Accra was the preacher on one occasion when I was there. He it was who established the first municipal library in Accra, named after him, the Anglioby Library, located in the Legislative (now Parliament) House.

How did I fare academically? Most of the subjects were as new to me as to my classmates in S2 who had come from Standard 7 or Achimota S1. I struggled a bit with English as a subject. The other subjects, new to all of us, did not pose any problem to me. At the end of the term, I was certainly not at the bottom of the class; the first term was decidedly not as daunting as I had feared; there was no need for me to go to see Mr Chapman to arrange a transfer to S1. I found the school library very useful and patronized it. I cultivated the habit of going to read books there and also borrowing books to take home to read. This was an extra-curricular activity I enjoyed. William Kwaku (a fellow Ewe student in S2, coming in from Standard 7) and I established a close friendship which was buttressed by our mutual love of books and reading; we were bibliophiles. I spent my first term vacation with my aunt Minah in Agormenya, Krobo. I was joined there by my sister Felicia, who had come from the Wesley Girls school in Cape Coast. I read a few books which I had borrowed from the school library; these included *The Brothers Komazarov by Dostvevsky*, the

Russian novelist. I enjoyed reading this tome. I returned to Achimota for the second term. As the term rolled on, I grew more and more in confidence which remained unimpeded in the third and final term of my first year. I received a good report, gained promotion to S3, and was not 'stopfordised'. I was assigned to S3A – Form three would have four streams as follows: S3A, SB, S3C and S3NL (Non-Latin). Since Latin was regarded as the epitome of scholarship, it was not flattering to be in S3NL (nicknamed Non-Thinking).

At the end of the first year in December, I travelled home to Hohoe for the Christmas vacation in a lorry on a Monday, arriving in the evening. The harmattan season was at its peak; it was cold and very dusty. On the preceding Saturday in Achimota, I had developed a bad cough with productive, brown sputum; I felt feverish, anorexic and very unwell. I reported at the school hospital. A nurse attended to me, instead of the doctor, who was presumably away. The fever worsened during the day. My parents were shocked to see me for the first time on my arrival home, they were alarmed to see me in such a seriously ill condition. I went straight to bed where I had a very restless night, with rapid and distressed breathing. I was taken without delay the following morning to the hospital to be seen by the medical officer, Dr Eustace Akwei. He examined me very thoroughly; he percussed and auscultated my chest with his stethoscope. My breathing was rapid at twenty-four plus breaths per minute; my body temperature was one hundred and one degrees Fahrenheit. Dr Akwei diagnosed me as a case of right lobar pneumonia. He told my parents that it was very serious. This was in the pre-antibiotics era. He prescribed for me M&B (May and Baker) tablets; these were sulphonamides which had just emerged as potent drugs for treating a wide range of common infections About 12 hours after my commencement of the sulphonamides, I started feeling better, my temperature began to fall and my general condition began to improve gradually. Dr Akwei told my parents that without the sulphonamides, I might not have survived the next 24 hours. My life had been saved; we attribute this to the ALMIGHTY as well as to the sulphonamides. As I was to learn later in medical school, lobar pneumonia ended in death or by a process of resolution called crisis when the patient's inbuilt resistance caused a sudden drop in temperature. With sulphonamide treatment, the temperature fell gradually, in a process called lysis, as in my case. Dr Akwei advised me to have a chest X-ray done on my return to Achimota; there was no X-ray facility in Hohoe at that time. My Hohoe EP School mates now in Standard 6 and other friends visited me at home when they heard of my serious illness. They showed great concern, and felt great relief at my recovery. They were also very proud of my initial success in Achimota. Although my chest X-ray was reported to be normal, I used it as a reason to be excused from running the cross-country sports event, which I never liked.

The school year ran from January to December. On my return to Achimota in January, I was moved from Livingstone House, a junior house, to Guggisberg House. Guggisberg House was a newly-created senior house and students in S1 to S5 were brought from other houses to constitute the pioneers of this new house. Lugard House remained the only junior house for a few S1 students. The House-master of Guggisberg House was Rev Father Wilde. He had served in the Second World War as a Major and had been demobilized ("demobbed" in the parlance of the time). He still liked sporting his old khaki military uniform on his hefty physical frame. His assistant housemasters were Messrs Fry, an Englishman and A. B. Attafuah. Mr Fry was a graduate Chemistry master. Mr Attafuah had just returned from Oxford where he graduated in History. I did not know the academic credentials of Father Wilde. I engaged myself in all the house activities. I succeeded in gaining exemption from running the cross country because of my recent history of lobar pneumonia. We had an outstanding long distance runner in our house called Tommy Thompson. He was apparently a famed horse-jockey who hailed from a famous Ga family in Accra.

I played football and even though I was a relative junior in the house, I represented it in inter-house football tournaments. The school staged its first junior under-seventeen football match that year, 1947. The match was against its Adisadel College counterpart and was played in Achimota. I was selected to play in the right fullback position in defence, Peter Mensah partnered me on the left. Kwabena Owusu, in S2, played in the key position of centre half; this was in the standard 2-3-5 formation at the time. The Adisadel team included Fredua Mensah (now, Nana), who played directly opposite me in their left wing position. We played an exciting and excellent match and won. Kwabena Owusu, the pivot of our team at centre half, was outstanding.

Although I was a. bibliophile, I indulged myself in extracurricular activities. I joined the Red Cross Organization; our group was led by Mr Fry. Our activities included going to Anumle village to dress wounds. One of the clubs to which I belonged was 'The Plato Club'; its motto was *the unexamined life is not worth living*. The club invited notable personalities to deliver lectures. A memorable one I recall was delivered by Mr R. P. Baffuor. Mr Baffuor was an Engineer who had graduated from the Achimota Engineering School with a B. Eng. Degree, then a rarity; this was decades before he became the Foundation Vice-Chancellor of KNUST. He spoke on the River Volta Dam, which was then just a dream, but in this lecture, the nationalist fired our imagination. To this day, it has been my view that R.P. Baffour would have been a great President of Ghana; Ghana, sadly, was denied this opportunity.

I was put into Form S3A. This class had most of, but by no means all, the brightest students in the form. All the S3 students studied the same subjects except those in S3NL who did not study Latin At the end of the year, each student had to choose the seven subjects he or she wanted to study in the following two years for the Cambridge school leaving examination. Four subjects were made compulsory by the school and therefore each student had to choose three other subjects. The four compulsory subjects were English, Mathematics, General Science, and Geography. The choice of the other subjects was from the following list: Additional Mathematics, General Science Two, English Literature, Latin, History, Vernacular Language, Arts and Crafts, and Religious Knowledge.

I enjoyed all the subjects which were taught and can recall a few of the masters. Mr B.A. Brown taught us Mathematics; although Algebra and Arithmetic came across to me easily, that was not the case with Geometry. Mr C. P. Woodhouse (nicknamed Caput, because of his somewhat triangularly shaped head) introduced us to Trigonometry; he had written a text-book on the subject which was easy to understand. He was the Housemaster of Cadbury House and was reputedly the most powerful and influential person in the college. The Latin master was Mr P. O. Sanful, a colourful Ghanaian, confident and a mature teacher. Mr Sanful had been recruited from Adisadel College. He proclaimed to us "Get on to my Latin wings and I will fly off with you to the mountain of success. Your unseen will become seen".

He was a good and an inspiring teacher. He was later replaced by Rev. Father Perry, an affable and dedicated Englishman. His wife was also a member of staff. Under Father Perry, we translated Ovid and Virgil. He also taught us a tuneful song in Latin which I still love and remember, and hum and sing sometimes. The simple and short lyrics in two Latin verses run as follows:

Ludi magister
Quantos labores
Nobis dedisti
Nepe innocens tu
Imberbis infants
Nunquam fuisti

I believe it is some of this nostalgia of my school days which endeared me to the film "The Browning Version".

The Geography lessons were taught by Mr Norfolk, an Englishman who had served in the army and had been demobilized. He was a serious and dedicated teacher who made an impact immediately. Mr A. B. Attafuah was assigned to our class soon after his arrival from Oxford University where he had graduated in History. He claimed to have fallen in love with Oxford and was anxious to infect us with the Oxford ethos. In his first History lesson he started by asking us to define History. Verbal answer after answer from different students received an emphatic "rubbish" or "nonsense" from him. This went on for almost the entire 40-minute period. I then got up on impulse and asked him for his definition of history. He welcomed my question and in a very polished Oxford English accent said, "By History, we mean rattling the bones of Caesar, and breathing in (with gesticulating hands) our sympathies." On this note, with a self-satisfying broad smile, he packed his books, about four thick ones, then walked out triumphantly with a swagger, in his khaki shorts! Our History class with him did not last long after that introductory one. He was replaced by Mr M. A. Ribeiro. Mr Ribeiro taught me History for the next three years from S3 to S5. He made me fall in love with it as a subject. Mr Ribeiro was undoubtedly one of the best, or probably the best teacher I had the privilege to have had. Physics was taught by Mr Mills, a Ghanaian graduate who had just arrived from Britain. Mr Oddoi, also, soon after arrival from Britain, taught us Biology. Mr Joslin, an Englishman taught us Chemistry, as did Mr Fry.

A notice appeared on the college notice board in 1947, stating that Mr Torto, an old boy of the college, had just been awarded a PhD degree in Chemistry by London University, the first Ghanaian to achieve this feat; an epoch-making achievement. He returned home to Ghana to lecture at the infant University College of the Gold Coast, and later University of Ghana at Legon.

In my first year at Achimota, there were only four Ghanaian graduates on the staff, namely, Chapman, Dowuona, Ribeiro and Quartey. This was followed by a trickle with Oddoi, Mills, Brown, Kwame and Attafuah. This trickle grew into a drizzle in the whole country; the drizzle increased in intensity in the early 1950s when the early graduates emerged from the UCGC; with the move to Legon, it turned into a steady downpour.

In 1947, my brother Willie was in his final year at Mfantsipim in Cape Coast while Felicia was in her penultimate year at Wesley Girls High school. It was decided that I should go to Cape Coast to join my siblings for the first term holidays. Felicia stayed with one of her teachers. Willie hired a room in Aboom Wells, which was temporarily vacated by a fellow student from Kumasi. E. D. Kom, Willie's classmate, hailing from Peki who was also preparing for the school certificate examination, acquired a rented room in the same area. We cooked our own meals. I indulged myself by walking to downtown Cape Coast to buy very tasty "tatale" and beans from a vendor near the Victoria Park. It was during this period that the country experienced at midday a total eclipse of the sun. It was impressive and an unforgettable phenomenon. I recall the chickens running into their coops at midday and coming out when it was all over and sunlight was restored.

At the end of the year, I thought I had acquitted myself very well, and gained promotion to S4. Unlike the previous year when a few did not make it to S3, everyone was promoted to S4. Felix Konotey-Ahulu had joined us in S3 in a transfer from Presbyterian Odumase Secondary School. I went home to Hohoe at the end of the year to spend Christmas with my parents and siblings.

I returned to Achimota in January 1948 as a S4 student, and as a senior, I could raise the collar of my shirt in Cantona fashion. During the course of the year, my brother Willie sailed by boat to the USA to pursue further studies. I travelled to Sekondi to see him off. It served as a sibling reunion as we stayed with Brother Emmanuel. Willie went to Sheybougan with the late Alex Ababio to study for a BSc course in the state of Wisconsin. He later went to Minnesota State University for a PhD degree in Agriculture, specializing in Plant Breeding and Genetics. Felicia returned to Wesley Girls High school for her final year. She passed the Cambridge school leaving examination at the end of 1948 creditably. She was one of the earliest girls, if not the first, resident in Hohoe to accomplish this. Brother Emmanuel was a Provisions storekeeper with GBO in Sekondi, a high profile job at the time.

Although my memoir is not intended to be a historical treatise or document, it is nevertheless germane to reflect on the political landscape at the time. Soldiers from the Gold Coast had served in the British Armed Forces and fought in battles in East Africa, India and Burma in defence of freedom. They had now returned home; some of them with great distinction. Major Seth Anthony from Anlo state in Eweland became the first African to attain the rank of Major in His Majesty the King's British Army; I believe the second one was the Reverend Ampofo from Peki who also attained the rank of Major. The idea of freedom generated in its wake political activism.

A movement of unification of all the different Ewe groups into one country was launched. Prominent Ewes, including Ephraim Amu and Daniel Chapman, played leading roles in the Movement. Mr Chapman's high appointment with the newly created United Nations Organization seemed to take the steam and driving force from the Movement in 1947. In the Gold Coast colony, Paa Grant convened a historic meeting in Saltpond in 1947. Paa Grant was a very successful timber merchant. He invited some of the leading lawyers and politicians in the colony to this meeting. They included J. B. Danquah, Ako Adjei, Akufo Addo and Obetsebi Lamptey. Thus was formed the United Gold Coast Convention (UGCC), the political movement which aimed to agitate and seek independence for the Gold Coast. Ako Adjei was appointed the first General Secretary. They founded a newspaper called the *Observer*, a paper of very high quality. Numbered among its contributory columnists was the learned and protean medical doctor, Dr R. E. G. Armattoe. Dr Kwame Nkrumah was invited to come from Britain to take up the position of General Secretary. The rest is history.

The year 1948 was a significant year in the history of the Gold Coast; it served and still serves as a milestone. The pervading spirit of freedom and justice impelled a group of ex-servicemen to undertake a march to Christiansborg Castle, the seat of government, and also the Governor's residence. They were unarmed, and carried along with them a petition to present to the Governor. They paid no heed to the command of the British police officer to stop. The police officer, one Mr Imray, ordered the police to open fire on the unarmed ex-servicemen. Sergeant Adjetey and others were killed at Osu crossroads; a monument to their memory forms part of the Black Star Square. After the fatal shooting on 24th February 1948, the Colonial Secretary in Britain set up a commission of enquiry headed by a legal luminary, Mr Watson. In his report, Mr Watson stated that the constitution governing the country was bogus and out-dated, and that there was a need for a new one. This led to the setting up of the Coussey Committee to draw up and prepare a new constitution for the whole country. The rest is history.

Great Britain at the height of its colonial power had almost a third of the globe under its sway. After World War One, the global depression of the early 1930s and the Second World War, Britain's world power began to decline. Britain was superseded by, and was dependent economically on, the USA. The decline and liquidation affected the governance of her previous dependent colonies. The Indian subcontinent was granted independence in 1947, resulting in the creation of the two nation states of India and Pakistan; they were one secular state but their creation or division into two was based on religious population factors.

In 1947, a news item attracted great interest and the attention of the intelligentsia in the country. It was a visit back home by Dr R.E Armattoe. Armattoe, born in the Keta district, attended schools in Keta and Mfantsipim in Cape Coast. He had studied medicine in Germany where he achieved great fame as a scientist, anthropologist, poet and as a writer. His interests were protean, and he moved in high academic and intellectual circles in Britain and Europe. He was also invited as a guest at a Nobel laureates' award ceremony. His achievements and his home visit created great interest and also inspired many of us of the younger generation. He died in Germany at the relatively young age of 40 years. I must confess, however, that I do not know the depth of his researches in the varied fields of science, medicine, anthropology and literature credited to him.

I remained in Guggisberg House in form four. The house prefect was Moses Baeta. He was a mature student; he had completed the teachers training course in T4 at Achimota and was now enrolled into the secondary school course at S4 to do a two-year course in preparation for sitting for the Cambridge school leaving certificate examination. Achimota had adopted this novel system for a handful of trained teachers. The beneficiaries of this scheme came from Akropong Training college. During my time in Achimota, these included Ampene, Bampoe (later Librarian at KNUST), Ampofo and Victor Kisseih (later a judge).

There were four streams in S4, namely S4A, S4B, S4C and S4D; I was placed in form 4D class. The classes were based on the choice of subjects being offered for the school leaving examination. The 4D class had students who were offering General Science II and Latin in addition to the four other compulsory subjects. I chose eight subjects initially, but later, on reflection, replaced Pottery and Ewe with History, totalling seven subjects. It fitted into the class timetable better. I therefore offered History for the Cambridge school certificate examination. Many of the brightest students in form four were in the 4D class.

We were assigned new teachers in several subjects. Mr Ribeiro took the history class. The syllabus for the examination was British and European history from 1688 to 1815. A popular one with some other schools was British Empire history. Mr W. E. Ward, a former History master in Achimota, had written a book, "*History of the Gold Coast*"; it was in general use in the schools in the country. Many students from 4B and 4C also offered history for the examination. Miss Anderson, a young newly-arrived Scottish lady, a graduate of course, joined the staff in 1948; she was assigned to teach us Geography in 4D. Tall, plump and vivacious, she enjoyed teaching us. The standard Geography textbooks in use were one by Dudley Stamp and another one by Stembridge. Mr B. A. Brown carried on with us in Mathematics, while

Mills and Oddoi handled Physics and Biology respectively. The science textbooks in use were General Science by Daniels, books one, two, three, and four, the latter being the most advanced. Mr Joslin, Mr Fry and Dr Royter taught Chemistry. The standard of teaching was very high. All the teachers except one were graduates. The Latin teacher, Alex Kwapong, had successfully passed the Inter BA examination in Classics. Effusing with knowledge, he was assigned to teach us Latin. The core in learning Latin was to master the grammar, declension of nouns, conjugating verbs, syntax, the ablative absolute and of course, as much of the vocabulary as one could muster. We had all the necessary textbooks. The test of your comprehension was in your translation of Latin into an attractive and polished English prose, not a literal word for word translation.

Alex guided us and inspired us to translate works by Cicero. He inspired me to learn and recite one particular piece of Cicero which I could still recite by rote many years later. I attempted to recite it to him when I met him at the function in launching a book by the late Henry Sekyi. The little piece of Cicero was the introductory paragraph when Cicero got up in court to defend voluntarily the accused in the dock.

The Latin piece, with my apologies for any omissions and misspellings, went like this:

"Credo ego vos iudices, cum homines nobilisimi sedeant, ego potisimu, qui neque aetate et ingenio suxerim... Audacisimus ego sum omnibus, et tantum officiosor quam ceteri? Minime".

Alex left the school in the same year, 1948, for Cambridge University where he gained a double first in the tripos in classics, an outstanding feat. He returned home to Ghana to lecture, where he ended his unique pacesetting and outstanding educational and national career as the first Ghanaian Vice-Chancellor at the University of Ghana, Legon.

We had a little problem with the English lady who taught us English in 4D. She was Mrs Varley, wife of Prof. Varley, the Foundation Professor of Geography in the University College of the Gold Coast (UCGC). She was a pretty and charming lady, with a keen interest in Photography. Although we did not have a class prefect, I unofficially was the spokesman. Anytime we had a new class teacher, I would raise my hand and ask about his or her university degree, not a common acquisition in those days of yore. On disclosure of the degree, the whole class would applaud. I enjoyed playing this role of information officer. Mrs Varley's conduct of our English class was different from what was going on in our sister 4A, 4B and 4C classes. Each time she entered the classroom, she would write a short quotation on the blackboard, often of a political or social nature, and invite the class to discuss it. This method of teaching English went on for a couple of weeks while our sister classes were being taught how to write, construct essays and coached on how to précis. These were standard school leaving examination format questions we would face the following year. Mrs Varley had never asked us to write any essay or compose a précis.

One morning, following her arrival in the class to commence English class, sitting at the back of the class at my usual desk, I raised my hand in a gesture to say something. I said that for several weeks now, we had not been asked to write any essays nor perform any exercises in the art of composing a précis, unlike what was going on in the other sister classes. I proceeded to ask her very politely when we would also embark on this other form of learning. She looked shocked and angry, and took umbrage at what I had said. She said that if I did not like her method of teaching, I should walk out of the class; of course, I did not walk out. She asked the whole class to do silent reading for the remaining period of 40 minutes. After the end of the period, some of the class members congratulated me. Mrs Varley was replaced by a new English Mistress for the next and all subsequent lessons. The new Mistress took us right up to the Cambridge school certificate examination in 1949, the following year. Mrs Varley apparently left her teaching assignment soon after her episode with me. I felt sorry that it ended that way. About two years after, she saw me and another classmate at the university college campus near her husband's department. She quickly recognized us, and greeted us very warmly with a smile. No hard feelings, all was forgotten and forgiven; a civilized lady she was.

I realized that the Anglioby library in Accra had some useful books which the Achimota school library did not possess. It was a well-patronized library. William Kwaku was my associate in the bibliophilic excursions to Accra to widen my knowledge. After receiving letters from my brother Willie in America, I started making plans to go to the USA for tertiary education. I wrote to Harvard and Yale Universities for their prospectuses with a view to studying Medicine. I was unashamedly ambitious. The late Amon Neequaye, a year my senior, was in Guggisberg House with me, as was Reginald Amonoo (now Prof. in French), whose bed was next to mine in the dormitory. Amon Neequaye shared a mutual ambition with me to pursue tertiary education in the USA. Whenever I received a letter from my brother Willie, I passed it on to Amon Neequaye to read. Amon was a quiet, brilliant, but modest student. After his school certificate examination, he went to Amherst College in the USA, and Harvard University later. On his return home to Ghana, he held the high profile meritocratic positions of Governorship of Bank of Ghana and Minister of Finance.

My academic work did not restrict my sporting activities. I was not a swimmer by any standard; I merely waded in the swimming pool. The accomplished and the best swimmer in the whole school was Teddy Christian, a member of Guggisburg House, and a year my junior. Years later, when he was a medical student in Cork, Ireland, he was in consideration to represent Ghana at the Olympic Games in the swimming event. I did no serious athletics, and abhorred the cross-country event. I continued to play football; I represented my house in inter-house matches, and the school in the second team.

I performed very well in all my school subjects and gained promotion to S5. I did not win any prizes, but I was pleased to have obtained good marks in all my subjects. I went home to spend the Christmas holidays with my parents and Felicia. Sister Felicia had sat for the Cambridge school leaving certificate examination in December, 1948. My parents later completed arrangements for her to go to England to study Domestic Science.

I returned to Achimota in January, 1949 as a form five student. My house remained the same, Guggisberg. Dormitory monitors and prefects were appointed from my year group, but I was not one of them. I was not at all disappointed at this; indeed I was delighted; I knew that I was not in the good books of both the house master and his assistant, for no particular omission or commission on my part.

Scholastic work continued on schedule. The school certificate examination in Latin entailed translation from Latin into English. This came in two forms: seens and unseens. The seens comprised pieces from selected writings chosen by the examination board. For our year the chosen pieces were parts of Virgil's Aeneid, which we were coached in translating. The unseens could come from anywhere.

In preparing us for the school leaving examination in History, Mr Ribeiro went above the syllabus for a select few of us. He adopted the Oxbridge system for us: he gave each of us a different topic on which to write an essay for which we had ample time for preparation. There were five in my group. On the appointed day we went to Mr Ribeiro's bungalow in the afternoon to read out our essays. The essays were then critically assessed by him. We all spent time and effort writing the essays which entailed going to the library, combing through the thick volumes of history books by my favourite authors, HAL Fisher, G.M Trevelyan and Ramsay Muir. I aimed at writing in their style with the result that I lifted sentences from the tomes without due accreditation. Richard Donkor (aka Saffo Adu), later Dr Adu, was easily the best, and the undoubted scholar in our year. His essays were excellent, making you wonder whether he was indeed a fellow classmate. His all-round academic brilliance continued to his tertiary years in education. Such was the level of dedicated teaching targeted at some of us by Mr Ribeiro that I fell in love with History as a subject.

In 1949, Achimota students would start a sixth form course to extend over a two-year period at the end of which the students would sit for the Cambridge A level examination. It was a completely new and novel programme in the country, with syllabuses for Arts and Science courses. Students who were successful in the A level examination would then proceed to the University College to complete their respective full degree courses in their chosen subjects. The pioneer students were selected from Achimota students who had just completed their O level in 1948. Representative students were also admitted from Mfantsipim, Adisadel College, and St Augustine College. These representatives included Laing (Botanist), De Heer (Medical Doctor), Debra (Diplomat) and Eshun (Physician). Our year group would provide students for the second intake of sixth formers in 1950. The University College began running courses for the Intermediate degrees of Inter BSc and Inter BA. Successful candidates from these courses proceeded to study for the full London degrees. One had to pass an entrance examination before being admitted to the University College to study for the initial Intermediate degree course. The secondary school year ran from

January to December, whereas the University year ran from September to June in step with their United Kingdom counterparts.

The description above was the educational ladder ahead of me in form five. I applied myself studiously in preparation for the O level Cambridge examination at the end of the year. I spent the first term vacation in Accra with Auntie Cecilia Apo, my mother's first cousin, and daughter of Rev. Apo. She lived in a splendid house in Christiansborg with her husband. She looked after me caringly and with affection. During this vacation, I spent much of the time on the translation of Virgil's Aeneid. My confidence leapt by bounds at the end of the vacation and on my return to Achimota.

I was not earmarked nor selected for the sixth form in Achimota in the following year. I was reluctant to apply for entry into the University College because I wanted my father to send me to a university abroad (UK or USA) and not to an infant, local one. When he learned about my intention, I received an urgent message from my father to come to see him at home. I responded and paid a quick visit to Hohoe, going one day and returning the next. My father placed all the cards on the table. He said that he did not have the necessary funds to finance my intention to study abroad. If I insisted on going abroad, I would end up financially stranded without any support from him. A word to the wise is enough, goes the old adage. It was therefore logical to take the entrance examination for entry into the University College Stowing away on a boat to the USA had been glamourized at this time, but this appealed to a certain class of people, certainly not me. I earnestly and quickly understood all that my father told me and returned to Achimota. In due course, I sat for the entrance examination to the University College, and also the Cambridge O level examination. London University also conducted their Matriculation examination; I sat for this latter examination as a security measure to gain admission to the University College; obtaining the London matriculation or gaining an exemption from it in the Cambridge O level was an essential prerequisite to pursue a London degree course. This was an important fine point.

The examinations ended my secondary school odyssey in Achimota Eastern campus. I had arrived there four years earlier with an air of diffidence from Standard 5 from Hohoe EP School. My life had now been enriched in this unique educational establishment. I did not know what the future held for me, but that I had gained much in confidence and knowledge was not at all in doubt.

The Cambridge school leaving results were received in early 1950. I passed the examination with 6As, flying colours. One student, Aidam, topped our form with 8As, including three A1s (he had added Ewe as a subject in addition to the mandatory seven). Aidam was a very modest and unassuming student. Next in merit of passes was Henry Richter who obtained 7As; he was followed by six of us who obtained 6As. About 60% of those who offered History passed with an A. A great credit to Mr. Ribeiro, who had taught all those who offered History; thus our year group was rated as the best year group hitherto in the history of the school. On a lesser note, I believed that I was the first student to enter the school from Standard 5 and successfully complete the secondary school course and pass the O level in four years. I had held this belief till 2009 when a trusted old Achimotan, and a contemporary informed me that Richard Donkor (aka Dr Sarfo Adu), my classmate, had also come from Standard 5 in Kumasi to start the Form two class with me in 1946. Richard Donkor was the one I had rated as my intellectual superior. Apparently, his elder brother had been admitted from Standard 7 to Form 1 in 1946. The conclusion is that Richard and I were the first to come from Standard 5 to do the course successfully in four years.

The procedure following the entrance examination to the University College results were not straightforward. There were three categories for entry. In the first category, it was a direct entry in September 1950; in the second category, candidates would undergo a two-term pre-university course in Cape Coast either at Mfantsipim or St Augustine College for Science and Arts before entry into the university in September 1950. In the third category, you had to do five terms of pre-university course at Mfantsipim or St Augustine College before proceeding to the university in September 1951.

I received a letter to go to Mfantsipim School for an interview for the pre-university course. Although I was not by nature a proud or arrogant person, I was furious. I thought I had merited a direct admission in September 1950, I thought it was unfair to be asked to go to Mfantsipim from Achimota for my kind of course. I travelled on the Adra bus, popular with the elites of the time, from Accra to Cape Coast.

I stayed with B. Ohene, a friend and classmate in Achimota. I went for my interview the following morning at Mfantsipim. I was interviewed by Mr Saunders, an Englishman and the Physics master. During the course of the interview, on detecting an air of arrogance and perhaps false air of superiority, he warned me that there was no certainty that I might even be offered a place for a five-term pre-university course. I therefore had to calm down, swallow my pride, and change my attitude into a sober interviewee. At the end of the interview, Mr Saunders announced to me that I was being offered a place for the 5-term pre-university course. I found it very difficult to accept this verdict, such as it was. So I decided to do something about this injustice.

I returned to Accra the same day and decided to go to Achimota the following day to have an audience with Mr Balme, the Principal of the University College. I had a strong feeling that there had been some foul play. As planned, the next morning I went to Achimota and made my way to the residence of Mr Balme, formerly Lugard House, and also the residence of Lord Swinton during the war. Mr Balme was not at home when I got there – the steward boy told me that he had gone to do his rounds of inspection on the on-going construction work at Achimota Western Campus. He offered me a chair to sit on the ground floor porch to wait for Mr Balme. On his return home, a little to my surprise, Mr Balme received me very well with a smile, and asked the steward boy to serve me with fruit juice. He then enquired about my mission. Here, in colonial Gold Coast sat a teenager in front of an academic colossus; it was a daunting occasion. I plucked up courage and made a brief presentation of my resume as follows: I entered Achimota School from Standard 5 in 1946 from the EP School in Hohoe. I was admitted to Form two and had just completed the four-year course. I believed that I was the first to achieve this. The Cambridge school certificate O level results had just recently been received and I had passed with 6As, an outstanding performance. I had just attended an interview at Mfantsipim and was told that I would be admitted to do a five-term pre-university course before reporting at the university in 1951. In my view, I said, this was unjust and unfair. I also stated that it was possible that an ethnic factor might be operating against me, and that he might wish to look into it. Mr Balme listened to my complaint with sympathy and great understanding. At the end he advised me to accept the offer and go on to do the five-term course. Because of the sympathy he showed, I willingly accepted his advice, with a modicum of satisfaction. I think, too, that this soul baring was cathartic.

Mr David Balme, of average build, was the Foundation Principal of the budding University College of the Gold Coast (UCGC). An ex-Cambridge Classics scholar with a graduating BA degree, he had not even bothered to upgrade it to an MA. He was held in very high esteem both as an academic and as an administrator. He was at the helm when the college was on the Achimota Western Campus and supervised the constructional work at Legon by the Wimpey Construction Company. He masterminded and steered it from its years as a branch of the University College of London to its transition into the full University of Legon as we know it today. The University Library is fittingly named after him in his memory. I saw him several times later when I was a student at the college.

Because the residential block at Mfantsipim was not ready early enough, only the two termers were admitted in January 1950. They were accommodated in Onitsha House in town at the foot of the hill on which the school was perched. We, the five termers, joined them in April at Picot Hall.

MFANTSIPIM SECONDARY SCHOOL

I was an old boy of Achimota now going to enter another famous educational institution in the Gold Coast. Mfantsipim was founded and established by the Methodist Mission. Over the following decades, it produced famous scholars and earned the status of the leading secondary school in the country, next to Achimota. My brother Willie had told me a lot about the school. The students of Mfantsipim, both old and new, wore the black school blazer with its encrusted school badge in a black and red design and bearing the school motto of "Dwen, Hwe Kan" (meaning, Look and Think Ahead) with great and obvious pride; this pride is still undiminished.

Despite this well deserved reputation of Mfantsipim, I felt that I had descended several notches when I arrived at the school in April at the beginning of the second term; I had spent the first term in Hohoe and in Sekondi with brother Emmanuel.

The residential house for the pre-university students, Picot House, a newly constructed building, had been completed in March. It was a single-storeyed building with a number of cubicles. Three students shared a cubicle, I shared mine with two two-term students, namely EP Sowah (years later a top official at the Bank of Ghana) and Mills (later an engineer). We numbered about 20 in all, about a third of which were two-termers. The students were almost all from Achimota and Mfantsipim. The other five-termers from Achimota were Felix Konotey-Ahulu, Nyame Kumi and Peter Mensah, while the sole two-termer from Achimota was Samuel Ofosu-Amaah. We shared the dining hall with the secondary school students and the resident teachers, but sat at a separate table. A few steps down from our block and further down from the bathroom, was a tennis court which was hardly patronized.

Mr F.L. Bartels, the renowned educationist, was then the school Headmaster. Small in stature, handsome and bespectacled, he carried with him an air of authority and great respect. His wife was from the Phillips family of Cape Coast. Mr Saunders, my previous interviewer, was assigned to teach us Physics, while Mr Oduro, a graduate teacher, took us in Biology; I cannot recall the Chemistry teacher's name. We had a visiting French master, a Frenchman who taught us French. Everything about him, mannerism, and attire, you name it, bore the French stamp. He was a good language teacher. The purpose of learning French was to prepare us as future scientists to be able to read French scientific journals. We all, two- and five-termers, attended the same lectures. A female student, Victoria Zwennes, a two-termer, attended the classes regularly. She was a student of Holy Child College in Cape Coast and continued to board there for her pre-university course; a vehicle conveyed her daily for the classes. Physics seemed to dominate the teaching syllabus in this first term. We all took the lessons seriously. There was a natural feeling of intellectual superiority on the part of some of the two-termers, perhaps unavoidably.

Mates and masters in Mfantsipim - 1950

The school had a football playing field which was made available to us to patronize. We did not, however, mix with the secondary school students, since we were held in high esteem. I got a tennis racquet and started playing tennis for the first time. Yofi Bartels, a five-termer and a younger brother of the Headmaster, and E.D. Osafo (later a Forestry Consultant), who were also novices, were my playing partners. My skill and ability increased rapidly. I also took up boxing as a sport as well as a recreational activity with GCB Anteson, a two-termer from Presbyterian Odumase Secondary School. I enjoyed outdoor extracurricular activities; I was not just a bookworm.

Football as a game was widely played in the country at all levels in every village, school and every other community. It generated a competitive spirit in all the secondary schools in the country. Odorgono Secondary School in Accra, not highly regarded academically, had the most formidable football team. A confrontational football match was staged in Cape Coast while I was there.

Odorgono Secondary School came to Cape Coast to play two matches on successive days against Mfantsipim and Adisadel College.

As a Boxer at Mfantsipim -1950

The Adisadel team was the most fearsome of the Cape Coast schools and the confrontation with Odorgono was the match everyone was anxious to watch. Some students of the Odorgono school team actually played for leading top teams in the country, such as Accra Hearts of Oak and Asante Kotoko. One of the most famous and skilled players in the country was James Adjei, an Ashanti student at Odorgono who normally played for Asante Kotoko. There was a story that on one occasion when Accra Hearts of Oak were due to play against Ashanti Kotoko, their arch rivals, the Ga Mantse (Paramount Chief of Accra) sent his linguist to plead with James Adjei, then an Odorgono student, to play for the Accra team rather than his home team of Kumasi Asante Kotoko. Such was the background to the Odorgono trip to Cape Coast, and they came to Cape Coast with a large squad for two matches. They fielded a reserve team against Mfantsipim on a Friday and the first team against Adisadel on the following day, Saturday. Mfantsipim lost its match on its home ground. Adisadel College fielded a strong team against Odorgono; some of their players also played for leading teams in their region such as Cape Coast Dwarfs, Vipers and Sekondi Hassacas and Eleven Wise. The referee was the charismatic Mr. Akyeampong, an art master at St Augustine College. It was a great and memorable match which lived up to its expectation in both excitement and the skills displayed by both teams. It was the first time that I witnessed James Adjei displaying his legendary skill with the ball, which seemed to be glued to his foot! He would get the ball, dribble past about five or more opponents in quick succession and then pass it on; unbelievable to behold. Odorgono, of course, won comfortably; it was a football treat for the spectating crowd.

A historic sporting event occurred in 1950 and I offer no apologies in chronicling it in my memoir. Prior to then, Accra did not have a sports stadium. The Owusu Memorial Park, a grassless pitch without seats or an enclosing fence, had served as the venue for all major matches. The Unilever Brothers Company, owners of UAC Trading Company, the major trading company in the Gold Coast, in its wisdom and generosity, built a stadium in Accra, named it Accra Sports Stadium and made a gift of it to the country. For its grand dedication and opening, a football match between the Gold Coast Colony and Ashanti, a historic encounter, was the major feature for the occasion (the Gold Coast at the time comprised the Colony, Ashanti Region and the Northern Territories; the BMT, although administered from Accra was an entirely different entity).

This match was unprecedented. The Colony boasted then of teams such as Accra Hearts of Oak, Olympics, Cape Coast Dwarfs, Vipers, and Sekondi Hassacas, Eleven Wise and Koforidua Argonaughts. Ashanti had Asante Kotoko and Evergreens. I went to witness the dedication ceremony and watch the football encounter. The Colony fielded famous players such as Tim Darbar, Chris Briandt, legendary C. K. Gyamfy, Anante Akrah, McCauley and the youngster Pobee (later a cardiologist); James Adjei and Aggrey featured prominently in the Ashanti team. They all played bare-footed in the 2-3-5 formation, then the one in vogue. About two years later when the Gold Coast sent a team to tour England, they played there bare-footed, but with legs bandaged from ankle to knee. The Colony beat Ashanti in the encounter.

How was I performing academically? I thought that I had a good grasp of all the subjects, including the French lessons which I enjoyed. About halfway through the term, Mr Saunders conducted a Physics examination for both two- and five-termers alike. The examination covered the field he had taught us. When he released the results, I realized that I had topped with the highest mark of 87%. Abbiw Jackson, a brilliant mathematician from Mfantsipim, a two-termer, came second, followed in the third place by Nyame Kumi, an Achimotan five-termer.

Not very long after this, the results of the London Matriculation results were received in Accra from London. An old school mate of mine in Hohoe, now attending Accra Academy secondary school, saw the results in the Education Department in Accra. Although we had lost touch with each other over a period of time, he quickly and with obvious pleasure sent me a telegram at Mfantsipim. The message was that I had not only passed the examination, but that I had been placed in the first division. The passes were graded into first and ordinary divisions. I was one of the 12 placed in the first division in the whole country. Two of the Mfantsipim two-termers had not matriculated and therefore were not eligible to enter the University College in September 1950. This provided me with an opportunity which I would not let go without protest! I wrote a personal letter to Mr David Balme, in which I stated that he might recall my visit to him earlier in the year when I expressed my disappointment at the offer to me to do five terms at Mfantsipim. I then went on to state that in a recent Physics examination, the only one we had had so far at Mfantsipim, I came first in merit in the class. I went on to point out that two of the two-termers scheduled to enter the university in September 1950 had not matriculated and were therefore ineligible to enter in this year. Perhaps, he might wish to review my case and admit me in 1950 instead of 1951? I did not disclose my letter to anyone. There was a prompt response from the University College. I received a letter advising me to report for admission to the college in September 1950. My friend and mate Nyame Kumi, the five-termer who came third in the examination, received a similar letter to mine. We decided to have a culinary celebration for this excellent news. We ordered a whole roast chicken, an item then savoured by the elite. Nyame Kumi and I thus ended up doing only one term; one term less than the two- and five-termers. In the process, we were in the unique position of ending up as old boys of Mfantsipim and Achimota. On deeper reflection on my educational odyssey, I count myself lucky for having been the beneficiary of two famous educational institutions. They had both enriched my life and education. I returned to Hohoe to prepare myself for the next phase of my studies.

In concluding the Mfantsipim and Hohoe saga, it is appropriate to pay tribute to an old boy of Mfantsipim from the Hohoe district. This figure who deserves a high place in the gallery of famous sons of Gbi is Mr Francis Morny from Gbi Kledjoe. After his elementary school education in Hohoe, he went to Mfantsipim and successfully passed the Cambridge school leaving examination in the early forties. He provided guidance to my brother Willie when he went to Mfantsipim in 1943. Francis was probably the first from the Gbi district to obtain the Cambridge school certificate. He worked as a civil servant in the Education Department in Accra and hosted a few of us in his small apartment in Tudu on some occasions. There was no secondary school in BMT at the time. Driven by a force to fill this gap, he set about founding and starting a secondary school. I was privileged in joining the group discussion on the choice of a name for the school. We finally settled on "Wenega" secondary school; it was a semi-Anglicized form of Ewenyigba, or Eweland. Francis next engaged the services of a few Ewe students who had just completed their Cambridge school certificate courses. These included the late Nyaho Tamakloe and Steven Gadegbeku. It was a brave and commendable foray into higher education in BMT, but it succumbed to an early closure because of lack of funds and support. Francis soon after went to Wales in Britain where he trained as an optician. He returned home to Ghana as one of the earliest trained opticians in the country. He launched a successful practice in Kumasi where he trained several other opticians. He pursued further education himself and assisted in a big way in the establishment of a Department of Optometry at KNUST in Kumasi. He remained a figure of stature in the development of the Gbi district until his death. I believe his funeral was akin to a state burial, and deservedly so. He was honoured posthumously with a doctorate degree.

Chapter 3
UNIVERSITY COLLEGE OF THE GOLD COAST

The period of the early fifties was a time of rapid evolutionary changes in the Gold Coast, not only in politics, but also in education. Several new secondary schools were built and the University College of the Gold Coast (UCGC) was founded. It was one of three such colleges established in the British colonies under the aegis of the University of London; the other two were at Ibadan (Nigeria) and Kingston (Jamaica). They were all external colleges of London University. Graduates from these colleges were automatically London University graduates. London University therefore played a crucial role in these infant budding centres of learning and research.

The UCGC was located on the Western Campus of Achimota in its early years as a temporary site. Legon had been chosen as the permanent site and the Wimpey Construction Company was given the contract to build the UCGC. A number of asbestos buildings were erected at the Achimota Western Campus to supplement the existing solid buildings in Gothic architectural design. The College buildings consisted of halls of residence for students, a large dining hall, residential houses for senior and junior staff, a library, two Church buildings (one for Roman Catholics, and another for Protestants), laboratories, lecture rooms, a Senior Common Room (SCR), a Junior Common Room (JCR), an administration block and several other structures. A football pitch, a golf course, a hockey pitch, and two clay tennis courts constituted the sports and games arena. The famous Achimota golf course was located on the Western Campus, as was the Botanical Gardens. The UCGC shared the hospital, the Post Office and the Police Station with the school.

In 1950 and 1951 the Western Campus complex was shared between the UCGC and the Teachers Training College, a new two-year post-secondary school institution, headed by Lord Hemmingford.

The Training College was transferred later to KNUST and eventually to Winneba on the tortuous journey to its final location.

Mr David Balme, Principal of UCGC, was the head of the College when it was founded. A Classical scholar, he had graduated with a double first at Cambridge in the Tripos, and taught and lectured at Cambridge. He joined the Royal Air Force (RAF) in the Second World War and served with distinction, bravery and valour as a squadron leader. Following his return to Cambridge as an academic, he was persuaded to accept the post of Principal of UCGC. Mr Balme headed the academic and administrative staff. The administrative staff were directly under the Registrar, Mr Smith; his assistant, his Deputy was Mr Dowuona.

At the time I entered the College, these were the following faculties that were active: Science, Arts, Sociology, Divinity, Agriculture and Archaeology. The Science Faculty comprised the following departments: Botany, Zoology, Chemistry, Physics and Mathematics. The Arts Faculty embraced the departments of English, History, Geography and Classics.

I was assigned to Guggisberg Hall as my residence in the first and second years. The other halls were McCarthy, Aggrey, Fraser, North and South halls. North and South halls were asbestos buildings, meant to be temporary structures; the others were solid, in Gothic style. We were all given individual rooms and each hall had a senior member of staff as warden, with another as assistant. Mr Hilton, Geography lecturer, was our warden, with Mr Ward, a Physics lecturer, as his assistant. A senior student served as the students' representative/ supervisor. The late VC Dadson played this role. There was an influential senior member of staff, with the title of Dean who handled all non-academic and non-administrative matters; he was an affable and friendly man, sighted only in one eye. He was Reverend Duckworth, a man with a sense of humour, who seemed to know everyone and was also very well informed about campus affairs. He had reportedly served in the Intelligence Service and spent some time in China before coming to the Gold Coast.

I was now a university undergraduate, and no longer a schoolboy. The university environment was different. I was not expected to wear a school uniform, but to appear publicly in decent attire. Gabardine trousers and tefatex shirts replaced the khaki shorts and tussore shirts of school years. The wearing of suits made by a bespoke tailor in Accra was the order of the day. I was introduced to Mr Dan Morton, the bespoke tailor in Adabraka, Accra. The debate centred on the style of the coat's lapel, single or double breasted (SB or DB).

At the UCGC - 21st Birthday

My brother Willie in the USA flooded me with colourful casual shirts which were not obtainable in the Gold Coast. Since no one else had such glamorous shirts, my mates nicknamed me 'senior Yankee'. We were required to wear our blue coloured gowns to lectures and for meals in the dining hall. They also had to be worn to church and for all university functions, and when one had audience with one's warden; this was the little Oxbridge in the Gold Coast.

At UCGC   *At UCGC - 1951*

I had to choose the science subjects I intended to study, and as I had now decided on a medical career, I chose Botany, Zoology, Physics and Chemistry. Prior to this time, students who were awarded scholarships to go overseas to study Medicine were selected after obtaining the Inter BSc. Mr David Balme, in his wisdom, reckoned that if students continued to be selected in this way, the nascent UCGC would be deprived of the best science students for the full degree courses in science. It was therefore stipulated that one had to complete the full degree course before being eligible for selection to go on to study Medicine. This new regulation affected me and those one to three years ahead of me; my class would constitute the fourth batch of graduates from the UCGC. My science class consisted of those who gained direct admission and those who had done the Pre-University course at Mfantsipim, like myself. Amable and Leone Buckle (later de Graft) were my classmates from Achimota who had gained direct admission for the science course.

The Botany Department was headed by Prof. Boughey; Mr Adams and Mrs Booth were the lecturers in the department. The course consisted of lectures, practicals in the laboratory and ecology field trips. The Zoology Department was headed by Prof. Edwards, a grey-haired Welshman. Prof. Edwards, with a D.Scs. (Lond.), was the only academic on the campus who held this highly venerated degree. There were three lecturers in the department, namely Mr Booth, Mr Bassingdale and Miss Tazelar. The Chemistry Department had the following members on the teaching staff: Prof. Graham (Head), Dr Torto, Mr Higman and Mr Fridiga. Mr Higman, who was an all-round scholar as well as an accomplished pianist, staged a few piano recitals. Dr Torto, an old Achimotan, was the only African in the Science Faculty. The Physics Department was headed by Prof Huntly, a South African. The lecturers were Mr Ward and Reverend Father Koster, a brilliant, slim and tall Jesuit priest of high intellectual calibre.

All the science courses consisted of lectures in the mornings and practicals in the afternoons, finishing at 4pm, after which tea and snacks followed. The lectures and practicals ran from Monday to Friday, and the period following afternoon tea was free for recreational activities – football, hockey, athletics or tennis. I played tennis at least four times a week; my tennis attire was white gabardine trousers and a white jersey. I enjoyed tennis greatly and improved in skill with time. Because of the limited availability and the number of tennis players, both experienced and novices, my game centred on doubles rather than singles. Evening dinner was formal, with the senior members of staff, all gowned and sitting at the high table; grace was said in Latin. Dinner was a three-course meal and the cuisine rated highly in standard.

The JCR elected a committee yearly which planned and arranged entertainment programmes for Saturday evenings. A formal dance was held once a term which entailed some planning, such as booking the dance band of choice, much sought after. Because ladies were in short supply, a bus had to be arranged to bring nurses from Korle Bu Hospital in Accra to the campus. Despite this, the men still outnumbered the ladies at an unfavourable ratio. Since many of us new undergraduates did not know how to dance, some older and more mature students (former teachers or civil servants) gave us lessons in ballroom dancing. It was socially necessary to be able to dance the waltz, foxtrot, slow foxtrot, quickstep, blues, cha-cha-cha, la conga and of course the highlife and calypso – a tall order. There were a few societies, including the Debating Society; I did not join any of them.

The Gold Coast political scene was dominated by the two political parties of the day – Kwame Nkrumah's Convention Peoples Party (CPP) and J.B. Danquah's United Gold Coast Convention (UGCC). Kwame Nkrumah's rabble-rousing Positive Action Now politics did not win many adherents from us at the UCGC. For some reason, Kwame Nkrumah carefully avoided and declined invitations to come to participate in debates at the College. The African members of the senior staff were not many at that time; they included the following: Prof. CG Baeta (Theology), Prof. Busia (Sociology), Mr E.A. Boateng (Geography), Dr Torto, Mr Ofosu-Appiah, (Classics), Mr Alex Kwapong (Classics), Mr Dowuona (Deputy Registrar), and Mr Campbell, a Cambridge alumnus who had won a tripos in Mathematics lectured in Mathematics. Mr Campbell, tall and handsome, was a fellow African descendant from Barbados.

Social and recreational life was stimulating and refreshing. The publishers of the British Daily Mirror Group revolutionized newspaper coverage of world and local news when they launched the Daily Graphic newspaper in 1950. It was an epoch-making event. It became the first newspaper with a colour front page. The first editor was Mr. Bankole Timothy of Sierra Leone. It quickly became the paper of choice in the Gold Coast with a high distribution figure. It covered sporting activities very fully with pictorial and narrative reporting.

One sporting event in 1950 merits chronicling. It was a boxing event. A boxer from the British colony of the Gold Coast, Roy Ankrah by name, went to Britain and was excelling in the art and skill of the sport. Roy Ankrah and others who followed him in this field hailed from the tiny area of James Town in Accra. Roy Ankrah's boxing feats in Britain received great coverage way back home in Ghana, not least in the Daily Graphic newspaper. Then came his challenge for the British Empire Featherweight belt then held by Clayton. No African had hitherto attained this level of excellence and prestige in boxing. The widely held prediction was that Roy Ankrah would not succeed against such a skilled and formidable boxer as Clayton. The event was broadcast live on BBC Radio. The whole campus of the College was tuned to the live commentary. All through the contest, round after round, the impression from the commentator was that Clayton was leading comfortably.

Roy Ankrah usually out-boxed his opponents by skilful boxing and clever footwork, thus piling up points as the fight progressed, but he appeared to lack the knockout punch. Nearing the end of the match suddenly came a bombshell: Clayton was floored by Roy Ankrah and failed to beat the count to ten. Roy Ankrah had won the British Empire title, thus becoming the first African to win such a title. The whole of the Western Achimota Campus resounded in cheers such as one may witness if the Black Stars football team were to win the FIFA World Cup. Such was the joy and the uplift felt throughout the country. An African can climb to the top in human endeavour! These achievements have to be viewed in a historical perspective, and not judged by present day standards; the performers were breaking new grounds and frontiers.

Students at the UCGC were drawn from the few secondary schools in the country at the time. These were Mfantsipim, Achimota, St Augustine College, Adisadel and Accra Academy. There were also students who had attended Teachers Training College, but then studied on their own and matriculated after taking the London University examination. Because of the limited catchment base of the incoming students, the Education Department of the Gold Coast Government embarked on a programme of building several new secondary schools, known as the Trust Schools, throughout the country. Pari passu with this programme, the Christian Churches, notably the Roman Catholic and Presbyterian Churches, also embarked on a similar project of building a number of secondary schools throughout the country. Notable schools in this group include Mawuli, Prempeh, Opoku Ware and St Peters.

Football featured as the main and most popular sporting activity. The first team consisted of UCGC students and students from the Teachers Training College. The first team was a strong, formidable one; it included E. A. Haizel, Kofi Ampofo and GCB Anteson (Gynaecologist). E. A. Haizel was the best complete all-round sportsman of his generation, he excelled in tennis, football, cricket, hockey, long jump and the sprint athletic events. He competed at international level in some of these, representing the Gold Coast. Kofi Ampofo, short and diminutive in build, was a skilled footballer as an attacking midfielder. Anteson was an uncanny centre-forward (striker) with pace and deadly well-placed shots at goal. A transition was emerging; some of the players started playing in canvas shoes rather than barefooted. The team played against the famous Accra teams of the day, namely Accra Hearts of Oak, All Blacks and Olympics. The tennis club was an active one. I was a club member, but as a relative novice, I did not feature in competitive matches against other clubs; the more experienced players included E.A. Haizel, T. R. Addae, Patrick Hulede and Ziga (famed in ceramics industry). I played tennis regularly with John Hodasi (Zoologist).

There were a few cultural activities for those interested in such forms of entertainment. Mr Lerner, a South African who was a lecturer in English, formed an amateur theatre group which staged plays. He greatly motivated his students, one of the first of whom was the late Mr Joe De Graft. De Graft later became a famous actor and producer of plays; he married Leone Buckle, my classmate at Achimota and UCGC. Mr Higman, chemistry lecturer, staged a number of classical music concerts with his chamber orchestral group which included Laing, a student (later Botany Prof). We also received invitations from the British Council in Accra to attend classical music concerts which they organized. I took full advantage of these opportunities to enrich my social life.

There was an extramural activity in which I participated and which merits chronicling on the grounds of its historic significance. The Extramural Studies Department of the UCGC had Mr David Kimble as its Director. He was an active and creative person with a strong driving force. He planned to build a Residential Extramural School at Tsito in the Volta Region, then BMT. He appealed to the Political Discussion Society, of which I was a member, for volunteers to go along with him to Tsito to start the building. The chief of Tsito at the time was Torgbe Kofi Agbo. He was an old Achimotan, a business entrepreneur, a charismatic man and a traditional leader with very progressive ideas. About ten of us volunteered and proceeded to Tsito for the assignment. We were all housed in the classrooms of the Presbyterian school there. We were entertained to some delicious dishes during our stay, which lasted about ten days. I recall E. A. Haizel, E. O. Dodu and Ulzen as some of the participants. We dug the foundations, mixed the mortar with water which was delivered to the site by the Tsito women folk, and laid the blocks for the foundations.

We provided the manual labour force under the guidance of a professional instructor in laying the foundations and the platform.

It was community work which drew admiration from many people. Thus began the Adult Extramural Educational Institute at Tsito. Because UCGC was in its infancy, the student body consisted of both young students who had just come straight from secondary schools and mature (older) students who had been either school teachers, including secondary schools, or civil servants.

Jake Amekor Blukoo Allotey -1951

One of our classmates was Mr Bucknor, a great and renowned artist who had been teaching science at St Augustine College. I made new friends at the College which included Nyame Kumi and Tom Sekyi; Tom had gained a direct entry from St Augustine College with me in 1950. Prominent among my new friends was Jake Amekor Bluko-

Allotey. Jake, a year my senior, had come from Accra Academy to study for the BSc science degree. The friendship commenced almost instantaneously at our first meeting in Guggisberg Hall where he was also a resident. We chatted for over an hour at this initial meeting. Our friendship subsequently grew in strength and flourished into a life-long one, attaining a sibling relationship; years later, it embraced both our families. My friendship with Godfied Agbemebiese, a two-termer from Mfanfsipim, also commenced at the UCGC. He later changed his name to Kwashivie Doe (Gynaecologist).

In our first year science, whether young or old, we were a bunch of undergraduates starting at the bottom of the academic ladder. The science class was a mixed and overlapping one; while we all studied Physics and Chemistry, the Biology group did Botany and Zoology, while the pure science group did Pure and Applied Mathematics instead of the Biology subjects.

How did I perform in my first year? I had a fulfilling first year at the UCGC. The first batch of six students graduated with the BSc (Lond.) degree. It was an epoch-making event and accomplishment. Almost all of the new graduates were awarded scholarships to go abroad to study Medicine.

Amable, the ace scholar, my Achimota classmate, who had gained direct entry, dominated in our class in Physics and Chemistry examinations in which he consistently obtained the highest marks. I followed him in second place in both subjects. In the Pure Science group of Pure and Applied Mathematics, Amable met his match in Abbiw Jackson from Mfantsipim who beat him soundly in both Maths examinations. Abbiw was a Maths genius who went on to become the first person to obtain a first class in the London University Honours examination at UCGC in 1955. The unique family tradition continued to be maintained by his younger siblings. I obtained the highest mark in the end-of-year Zoology examination, but did not extend this performance to the Botany examination. In all this, there was a quiet subterranean competition between the Achimotans and those from Mfantsipim. I thought that I had acquitted myself very well in the first year, putting to shame the cautionary warning from Mr Saunders at the interview that it was indeed doubtful whether I even merited an admission to do a five-term pre-university course before going to the UCGC.

The academic year ended in June and I went home to Hohoe for the long vacation. During this vacation, I honoured an invitation from Tom Sekyi to visit him in Kumasi; it was my first visit to that city. I stayed with him at their house in Asafo. He had told me a lot about Wilbern Hotel, a place not to miss on a visit to the Garden City. We had a great time. I went to Sekondi from Kumasi to spend some days with Brother Emmanuel before returning to Hohoe. I was the only university student at the time in Hohoe. The late Jaisey, an old Achimotan, was reading for a History degree at the UCGC; he hailed from Lolobi, but often spent short spells in Hohoe. It was the same with Mr Akoto Ampaw, who was keen on national politics and was then reading for an Arts degree at the UCGC.

I returned to the College for the Michaelmas term in 1951. My assigned hall of residence, Guggisberg, remained unchanged. My social, cultural and sporting life was pursued with more enthusiasm. Visiting Professors came from abroad to deliver open lectures. One of them, Prof. Herkowitz, an anthropologist of great renown, gave a series of impressive lectures.

The first batch of A-level students from Achimota joined the third year students in both the Arts and Science full degree courses. The science students included the late Dr Ohui Agbetor, a brilliant female old Achimotan. Others were C. Marbel, (Pathologist), Joseph Eshun (Physician Specialist), Ludwig Henkel (Surgeon), Deheer (Public Health Physician), Jasper Tamaklo (GP) and Laing (Botanist). The A level Arts students included Mr E. M. Debrah (Diplomat), and Nti. My own classmates from our first year included Bucknor, Kwesi Renner, E. D. Osafo (Forestry), Ado Ashong (Forestry) and Adu Ampomah.

I plunged myself fully into the academic programme with zest. I enjoyed the following subjects best: Physics, Chemistry and Zoology; I was not very keen on Botany, even though it was a biological subject. If I was pressed to do an honours degree in any of the above, it would certainly have been in Physics or Chemistry. There was an element of logic in them which appealed to me. We had two resourceful lecturers in Zoology. They were Miss Tazelar, a tall, shapely, somewhat domineering, very knowledgeable lady in her fifties, and Mr Bassingdale. Miss Tazelar made us pay great attention to the details of the subject and the importance of dissection in the study of Zoology.

Greyhaired Prof Edwards was the grand eminence in the Science Faculty. Mr Booth, another lecturer, was a tall authoritative figure whose interest was in Mamalia. (I believe he died after a short illness at a young age while conducting research in the forest area.) Chemistry lectures for our class were assigned to Dr Torto and Mr Hulme. Dr Torto covered Organic Chemistry while Mr Hulme undertook the lectures in Physical and Inorganic Chemistry. Prof. Boughey, Mr Adams and Mrs Booth gave us lectures in Botany as well as instructing us in the laboratory practicals and guiding us on field and ecology trips. Prof. Huntly, Mr Ward and Rev. Father Koster all handled our lectures and practicals in Physics.

Achimota was hit in the early harmatan season by a serious water shortage, brought on by severe drought. As a result, the full Michaelmas term was terminated early. No end of term examination in Zoology was therefore conducted. The Zoology Department, in its wisdom, gave us five questions to answer during the Christmas vacation. It was meant, we all assumed, to keep us educationally active. The questions took the familiar forms of 'describe, discuss, compare and contrast'. This was not, however, going to be done under the examination atmosphere of time and invigilation, nor the absence of textbooks and notes. This could not be a real examination, but an educative assignment, I thought. I enjoyed the Christmas vacation as did most of my mates. I paid no heed to answering the questions. On our return to the College, we were generously granted an extra week before submitting our answers. I rushed through and answered all the five questions. About two days before the day of submitting the answers, Mr X came to my room in the evening and enquired whether I had completed all my answers, to which I responded in the affirmative. Mr X was a bright student. He asked me if I would lend him my answers to read through. I did not hesitate in complying with his request and handed all of them to him. He returned them to me on the day of submitting them to our teachers, which we all did as requested.

About 19 days after, we had a lecture given by Prof Edwards. Before the lecture, he made a brief announcement that two students were to report to his office after the lecture, the last one before lunch. The two students were myself and Mr X. Most of the class stamped their feet on the floor and murmured the word 'honours'. The various science departments were desirous of recruiting promising students to do the honours degree courses in their field subjects instead of leaving them for the General BSc degree course. Our mates felt that Mr X and I fell within the honours category. At the end of the lecture, Mr X and I went to Prof. Edwards' office where he was sitting at his wide desk, grim faced, flanked on either side by two lecturers seated beside him We were left standing, facing the very stern featured Prof. Edwards. He began by stating that at the end of Michaelmas term, we were given examination questions to answer. Our answers, he went on to say, were so similar that the only conclusion they could arrive at was that we had copied from each other. This amounted to collaboration in an examination. He went on to say that the University was not going to tolerate this malpractice and was determined to stamp it out straightaway. (Very unfortunately for us, at the end of the previous academic year, our class Chemistry examination questions had leaked out. This was detected and the results were nullified. We then had to take a second Chemistry examination.) Prof. Edwards ended by telling me and Mr X that he was therefore going to report us to Mr Balme, the Principal. I tried my best to explain to Prof Edwards that I did not consciously collaborate in answering the questions, but to no avail; he was unmoved and adamant in reporting us to Mr Balme. On this note, he dismissed us from his office.

I left the office with a feeling of great foreboding. My colleague, Mr X, swore he had not copied my answers (but in Ghanaian parlance "Book no lie"). If we were reported to Mr. Balme, there was no doubt in my mind that we would both be expelled from the College. In the colonial setup at the time, your future was in very serious jeopardy; the consequences were unthinkable. When we joined our colleagues in the dining hall, the feverish question was how the honours course interview ended. We did not disclose the nature or subject matter of the interview. I had no appetite for lunch; I was thrown into such a great state of depression that I did not go to play tennis later that afternoon.

I went to see my warden and Hall tutor, Mr Hilton, and narrated to him the story of the Zoology examination and the problem facing me after the meeting with Prof Edwards. He responded that there was nothing he could do to assist me. Mr X also went to see his tutor, Mr Adams, to seek his assistance with Prof Edwards and the Zoology department. Our future hung in the balance. Day followed day without any news. After about a week, I was summoned by Mr Hilton, my tutor, to see him in his flat. He was pleased, he stated, to inform me that Prof. Edwards had changed his mind about reporting us to Mr Balme; a punishment was, however, imposed on me. I was to write an essay on the topic of "The Importance of Zoology in the Development of the Gold Coast" in a thousand words; secondly, I was gated for the rest of the term, meaning that I was not to go to Accra or anywhere else for the rest of the term. My sense of relief and joy was boundless; my prayers had been answered. A similar punishment was meted out to Mr X. I complied with the punishment by writing the very long essay and not leaving the campus for the rest of the term, a very tolerable punishment for my malfeasance. Mr X went on later to do the honours degree course in Zoology. He followed it up with a PhD degree and ended up as an eminent Professor of Zoology and attained high acclaim. It is my sole decision to refer to him in my chronicle as Mr X, but I needed to narrate it as I truly consider it a crucial turning point in my life, one of those 'what ifs' events!

Such is the irony of fate. I had a narrow escape from expulsion. In the course of human affairs, a little twist or incident can lead to an entirely unexpected and adverse outcome.

I completed my second year at the UCGC, and passed the Inter BSc degree examination in June 1952; this was a prerequisite for proceeding to the final degree course. Sadly, some of my mates failed the Inter BSc examination and therefore could not carry on with the full degree course.

A batch of students graduated with BSc General in 1952. The group included the late Harold Philips. The general degree course lasted two years, while the honours degree courses lasted three years after the Intermediates. The BSc General in the Biological Science was reckoned to be a difficult course as there was a tremendous amount of ground to cover in just two years. An ordinary pass in the final examination was regarded as a good achievement, a 2nd class an excellent result, while a 1st class was thought to be almost unattainable. With the honours courses, which lasted three years, a 2nd or a 1st class was regarded excellent, but attainable. The examinations consisted of theory and practicals. Since the degrees were London University degrees, the

University played a major and significant role in the examinations. The format was that a number of questions in each subject was set by the local UCGC staff and submitted to London University for vetting and approval. London University would then select, modify or reset the final questions for the examination. After the examination, the local UCGC marked the answers and then sent them to London University where they were marked again separately. The UCGC examiners then went to London for a joint assessment of the answers and issued the final mutually agreed result. The final result was released and sent to the Gold Coast; in Achimota this was usually in August. Although London University was keen on maintaining its acknowledged high academic standard, the prevailing opinion at the time was that the local UCGC staff were stricter on, and less generous to the candidates.

Harold Philips was the most brilliant in his year group, and expectations were high that he would pass with a 2nd class, hitherto unattained in the BSc General; he passed at the ordinary class.

As a memoir, it may be germane to recall some of the pioneer science students. Ewusie Wilson was the first to do the Botany honours degree course; he was followed shortly after by Laing and Kootin Sanwu. Amaah-Attoh was the first to do the Zoology honours whilst Badu was the first with Chemistry honours. Adjei Bekoe followed Badu in Chemistry. VC Dadson pioneered the honours course in Mathematics, followed by Abbiw Jackson. They were both Old boys of Mfantsipim, and they both hailed from Saltpond, a remarkable contribution from this Fante town. They came under the tutelage of Prof. Blakely, Mr Sawyer and Mr Campbell. My classmate Amable was the first to do the Physics honours with Bampoe. De Graft, Djokoto and Kwakwa were the first to do the honours degree in English, while Henry Sakyi and PO Sanful pioneered the honours course in Classics. Most of these pioneers are no longer with us, but they were stalwarts who were breaking into new academic grounds with no predecessors to follow. They set the pace for others to follow. We salute them all.

What was the political landscape like in the Gold Coast at the time? The Gold Coast was in a political ferment at this time. The first elections for governance and political power were held. Many of us from the UCGC monitored the elections at polling stations in various parts of the colony. The contest was between the two major political parties of the time, namely, the CPP and the UGCC. Kwame Nkrumah, founder of the CPP, with its foot soldiers of "veranda boys", was then serving a political jail sentence in Accra's Usher Fort. Mr K. Agbeli Gbedemah was credited with a masterful grassroots organization of the CPP, making the party a popular and appealing party for the ordinary Gold Coaster on the street. The UGCC, led by J. B. Danquah, the veteran politician, appealed more to the intelligentsia of the country, who detected some hollowness and an element of superficiality in the leadership of the CPP. The UGCC had some supporters and adherents at the UCGC; the CPP was despised and held in contempt.

I was in a group which was sent to Winneba to monitor the election. After an early breakfast, we boarded a coach and were driven there. The polling was orderly and there were no incidents of malpractice. When the countrywide results were declared, the CPP had won resoundingly. Although Nkrumah was in jail, he had stood as a candidate in Accra Central; he won the seat decisively. The colonial Governor, Sir Arden Clarke, in his great wisdom, released Nkrumah from jail and asked him to form a government. It was the repeat of the India independence story with Pandit Nehru becoming the first Prime Minister of India. Gold Coast had been granted internal self-government. What this meant was that Nkrumah was to appoint his cabinet ministers for the various ministries except the three important ones of Finance, Defence and Foreign Affairs; these three were retained for the colonial British civil servants who were directly under the Governor, Sir Arden Clarke. Kwame Nkrumah thus became the first Prime Minister. The Accra Evening News newspaper was the mouthpiece of the CPP. The colonial government built some attractive and colourfully painted bungalows along the then Dodowa road (now the Ridge) for the incoming ministers of state to occupy. The Evening News newspaper announced in its publication that the ministers of state were the representatives of their people and therefore would continue to live with their people. The bungalows were too tempting to leave unoccupied. A few days after their initial announcement, the same newspaper, the CPP mouthpiece, stated that if the 'people' so wish, the ministers would take occupation of the bungalows, and they did without any referendum. "Vox Populi" indeed. The Pig farm story all over again. Indeed!

I was admitted in the Michaelmas term of 1952 for my final BSc course. We were joined in this third year by our colleagues from Achimota who had passed their A levels in the Cambridge examination. Not all of those who had sat for the A level passed the examination to join us; in like manner, those of our mates who failed in the Inter BSc could not join us for the full degree course. There were about 20 of us in the third year opting for the degree course in the BSc general in the Biological class; this was the largest class hitherto. Included in this class were Safo Adu (aka Richard Donkor), Emmanuel Manukure now Asare, George Swaniker, Henry Richter, Ofosu Amaah and Thomas Sekyi. A few in our class opted for the full degree course in the pure science combinations of Physics, Chemistry and Mathematics (Pure and Applied). This group included the late Ato Wilson, (Diplomat, brother of Gynaecologist Dr Wilson). My friend Nyame Kumi, after passing the Inter BSc in the pure science category, was awarded a scholarship by the Asanteman Council to go to Britain to pursue a degree course in Engineering. The Asanteman Council was eager to award scholarships to its promising and aspiring Ashanti students; this was commendable. There was no such body in the Ga, Fante or BMT regions. Shell Oil Company was visionary in this respect and deserves credit for its efforts. The Company awarded three scholarships to three of my Achimota school mates who had passed their A levels in the Physical sciences to go to pursue degree courses in Engineering. The recipients were E. K. Aidam, William Parker and Wiliam Quansah. Amable from our year group opted to do the honours course in Physics, while Abbew Jackson chose to do the honours degree in Mathematics. Amon Nii Kotey, another gifted and brilliant mate from Achimota, came via the A level course to join us in the third year to do the honours course in English.

I cannot resist the temptation of stating that the 1949 Achimota O level students were an outstanding group of students. I have only mentioned a few, not all of them; it is not the purpose of my memoirs. The 1950 year group also had a cream of some outstanding and brilliant scholars. Their group includes the following: Reginald Amonoo (French scholar), Thomas Mensah (Jurist, Philosopher, and Diplomat), KB Asante (Economist, Jurist, now a chief), and Tuffour (Historian).

In historical perspective I would like to state that we had an opportunity not presented to an earlier group of potentially brilliant students of a previous generation.

In my third year I was allocated a room in South Hall, one the prefabricated asbestos buildings. Although the rooms were large and commodious, it was humid and hot inside, making them not very satisfactory for mental cogitation. The rooms on either side of mine were occupied by Blukoo-Allotey and Ashong Mettle. Ashong Mettle was a mature student, married and reading for a degree in Economics. Other students in the block included W.Z. Coker and Buahin, both old Achimotans, and a year my senior, and both reading for the honours degree in Zoology. Adoglah, reading for a degree in Economics, was also a resident in one of the rooms.

The first hall in Legon was completed and the first group of students was assigned there. Initially, it provided only lodging, the students had all their meals at Achimota. A bus service conveyed them to and from, between Achimota and Legon. At a later date they had all their meals at Legon. All the lectures continued to be held in Achimota. On entering Achimota in 1946, my first career choice was to become an agricultural officer. The reason for this choice was that an agricultural officer who had been trained overseas and was stationed at the Government Agricultural Station in Kpeve paid regular visits to Hohoe. On these visits, he brought some very nice, somewhat exotic to me, vegetables to give to my mother. In my mind, this officer had attained the pinnacle of higher education. Apart from teaching, there was no other comparable profession in our limited horizon of the time. Because my brother Willie had already embarked on a university degree in Agriculture in the USA, and being exposed to a widening horizon in Achimota, I changed my mind and aimed to become a Medical Officer instead. The opportunity for this had not previously registered on me.

My choice of subjects for the full BSc degree had to be relevant to pursuing a medical degree course later. I chose Zoology, Botany and Chemistry for my degree course in compliance with the recommended combination. Sadly, I had to drop Physics, one of my favourite science subjects. A few of my mates opted to do the honours degree courses as already mentioned. The late Kwesi Renner was the pioneer in Geology.

The Bookstore was very well stocked with all the necessary textbooks in all the relevant subjects. The Bookstore manager was an efficient Englishman called Mr Braimah. In Zoology, we covered Invertebrates and Vertebrates. The volume on Vertebrates by J.Z. Young was the standard textbook, the contents of which had to be assimilated; a great deal of ground had to be covered. Organic Chemistry by Finnar and Inorganic Chemistry by Partington were standard textbooks we used. There was also a thick volume in Physical Chemistry. Mr Higman delivered the lectures in Physical Chemistry. I never got round to understanding Eisenberg's Principle of Uncertainty, however much I tried. I was not the only one in this category. I found Inorganic Chemistry fairly straightforward and logical. We covered new grounds in Botany. The knowledge of Krebs cycle in plant physiology would prove useful later in the study of human physiology in Medicine. Since the flora in the Gold Coast differed in many ways from the temperate climate flora described in the Western authored standard textbooks of the day, we had to rely to a great extent on the lectures given by our lecturers. Unfortunately, they were placed in a somewhat similar position and could therefore not convey or impart much information or knowledge on some topics we needed to have. There was a Ghanaian nongraduate on the staff of the Botany Department who knew all the plants by their generic and species names whenever we went on ecology trips. He was a modest, self-effacing gentleman called Mr Akpabla. He had been a field assistant to the legendary and renowned Dr Irving who researched and authored the seminal work on West Africa Flora. Mr Akpabla was a regular visitor/consultant to London's Kew Gardens. He deserved the popular epithet of "Walking Encyclopaedia". In my view, he truly deserved an honorary University Science degree such as an MSc or even a Doctorate. I do not know whether he ever received any; if not, it is a sad and regrettable lack of recognition and appreciation for a giant who strode the field of West African flora.

The most popular Arts honours degree course was in History; the department was headed by Prof Fage. Busia, appointed a Professor in Sociology, attracted three students to pioneer the honours degree course. These students were Austin Tetteh, Ampene and De Graft Johnson. They graduated in 1954. The Economics Department also attracted a few students to undertake the honours degree course. These included J.H. Mensah and Addade (later a Jurist), followed later by Frimpong Ansah (later Governor of Bank of Ghana). JH Mensah later became an iconic economist and a leading politician. Omaboe gained admission to the UCGC from Accra Academy in 1952 to commence a course in Economics. After passing the Intermediate examination he went to the London School of Economics and Political Science to complete an honours course in Statistics; he excelled and obtained a first class degree, a great achievement. All these were blazing a trail as pioneers for others to follow.

Young E. Acheampong entered the UCGC in 1952 from Accra Academy to start the Inter BSc course. He went on years later to attain great heights as the iconic Prof of Surgery and Dean of Korle Bu Teaching Hospital. Some of my contemporaries who read for the honours courses gained either a first class or upper second, progressed into academia at Legon or KNUST. They constituted the distillate from the early products of the UCGC. The UCGC had been criticized in some circles for setting up too high a standard in its formative years; I do not subscribe to this view. The group of academicians includes the following: Adu Boahen (History), Agbodeka (History), Abbew Jackson (Mathematics) Adjei Bekoe (Chemistry), Hodasi (Zoology), Laing (Botany), Kootin Sanwu, Tawiah (Botany), Austin Tetteh (Planning), Peter Dziwornu, Goza Tay (Physics), the Dickson brothers in Geography and Theology, Gilbert Ansre (Theology) and Abrahams (Philosophy).

At the UCGC in my third year, we were all highly motivated and took our studies very seriously. We were all on scholarships and paid no fees. Success in the final examination opened avenues for a career in the civil service, educational service or a pursuit in medicine. Outstanding honours students with a first class degree were likely to proceed to Cambridge or Oxford Universities in England for a post-graduate course in preparation for their career in Legon academia. High educational attainment was profoundly esteemed and indeed envied. Monetary considerations were secondary and not at the fore in those days; idealism prevailed; failure in an examination was unpalatable. The salary structure was partly based on academic qualification; there was no intermediate scale between a London University matriculant and someone with a full degree.

During the course of my third year, a Commission of Enquiry from England came to assess the feasibility of setting up a medical school at the UCGC. A member of the team was Professor J.Z. Young, author of the textbook on Vertebrates in Zoology. A gangly figure, he was the Anatomy Professor at London University; his interest was the human brain.

Although I was studious in my third year, I also took my tennis seriously, playing often on the court which was just a stone's throw from my cubicle. I developed a powerful forearm drive and backhand. The backhand was single-handed, unlike its double-handed style as pertains now. During the vacation periods in Hohoe I was a regular player at the UAC tennis courts. Lambert Quarcoo, hailing from Lolobi, entered the UCGC from St Augustine in 1952 to start an Inter BSc course. Because his parents lived in Hohoe, he spent his vacations there as I did.

Albert Menka and I at the Tennis Court at UCGC

He was a good and keen tennis player and the two of us formed a tennis duo in Hohoe; we happened to be the only UCGC students in Hohoe at the time. I keenly followed the Wimbledon tennis broadcasts on BBC radio; you could follow the tournament broadcast, ball by ball on the radio. I got to know of Trabert, McGregor, Jaroslav Drobny, Ken Rosewall and Lew Hoad before seeing them on television years later.

Social and recreational activities complemented my studious academic work. My routine after the formal evening dinner was to retire to my cubicle, sit at the desk, and read and read.

The Ewe Students at Achimota Western Campus
- UCGC, Training College - 1950

The venue of the social activities was the JCR situated near the football pitch. Although one could attend nightclubs in Accra at the weekends, I did not have the inclination to do this. Some of the more mature students did indulge in such pastimes. The JCR Social Committee organized ballroom dancing at the end of each term. Since the famous dance bands of the time were in great demand (not only in the Gold Coast but also in Nigeria), it was important to book the band early and far in advance. The leading band of the time was the legendary ET Mensah's Tempos Band, followed later by the

Ramblers Band. These bands were famous for their Highlife and Blues tunes. Saturday night dances had a programme which was followed almost to the printed letter. This included waltz, slow foxtrot, quickstep, La Conga, Samba, and Rumba, in addition to the very popular Highlife, Blues and Calypso. There was the occasional Cha-cha-cha on request. It was a serious handicap if you did not know how to dance. In my third year, I was an accomplished dancer and could execute all the above numbers with ease. The ladies were usually outnumbered by the men, but I had no difficulty in booking dancing partners for the dance floor.

I followed and maintained interest in world affairs and local politics on the home front. Prof. Busia was becoming very seriously involved in politics and became an active member of the UGCC, the main Opposition Party, led by J. B. Danquah. Richard Donkor (aka Safu Adu), my friend and classmate who was also interested in politics, and I visited Prof. Busia twice in his bungalow to listen and discuss with him the prevailing political conundrum in the country. At the end of the academic year, I gained promotion to the fourth and final year in the UCGC.

At this juncture in the memoir a brief recall of world affairs may not be inappropriate, but rather refreshing and informative for my readers. McCarthyism in USA drew worldwide attention. McCarthy's fraudulent, extreme, rightwing anti-communism style in politics was finally exposed, condemned, discredited and ridiculed. King George the sixth died suddenly of lung cancer when his daughter, young Princess Elizabeth, and her husband Prince Philip were on tour in Kenya in 1952. The announcement in London was 'The King is dead, Long live the Queen'! Elizabeth thus became Queen of Britain, while Conrad Adenaur was Chancellor in Germany and Joseph Stalin was the omnipotent dictator in Soviet Russia. He fell into a coma as a result of a severe cerebral haemorrhage which proved fatal. He was succeeded very briefly by Malenkov. Malenkov fell victim to a palace coup which was masterminded by Mr Khrushchev. Mr Khrushchev became Secretary General of the Communist Party and the dictator. Mr Beria, head of the dreaded KGB, was assassinated. Eisenhower was the President of the USA and Mao Tse Tung ruled in China as a dictator. Pandit Nehru was the Prime Minister of India and leader of the Non-Aligned nations. The Cold War was at its coldest. On the local scene, Kwame Nkrumah and the CPP continued to rule in the Gold Coast.

At the end of my third year, some of my fellow students graduated in the Arts and Science subjects. Some of the new graduates obtained appointments as Assistant Government Agents (DCs), or went to teach in secondary schools which had begun to mushroom throughout the country. Science graduates from the 1953 group who wanted to do Medicine had been interviewed earlier in the year, selected, and awarded scholarships to travel to Britain for their medical course. Numbered in this group were C. Marbel, Ludwig Henkel, CR Neequaye, Ohui Agbetor, Osa Simmonds, and Joe Ashun Frank Lloyd, all now of blessed memory. Others in this group included Deheer, Jasper Tamaklo, GK Asamoah and Blukoo-Allotey. There was an open avenue in the country to successful students. My friend Jake (Blukoo-Allotey) travelled on one of the Elder Dempster Lines boats to Liverpool in the summer of 1953 to study at the Liverpool Medical School. I very eagerly awaited the first letter from him. I had not yet been interviewed for a place in a Medical School until the following year, but looked forward with much anticipation to the occasion.

I entered the final lap of my university BSc degree course in the Michaelmas term in 1953 and was allocated to New Hall. Like the South Hall of my previous year, it was an asbestos prefabricated building, and similar in character in every respect. I was determined to perform well in the final examination. No one had hitherto passed the General BSc with a second class degree – the pass mark was reputedly set at 33%. The London University examination questions in two of the subjects I was offering – Zoology and Botany – had a format which was often repeated. Since the fields covered in these subjects were not only wide, but also entailed a detailed knowledge from Protozoa to the various phyla in Vertebrate Zoology and a similar situation obtained in Botany, there was a place for examination technique. It was a wise step to obtain the examination questions of the previous five years; these were easily obtainable. This way, one could discern the type of questions to expect and prepare for them accordingly. In subjects such as Botany and Zoology there was a premium on factual knowledge rather than the application of principles in a subject such as Chemistry. In Zoology and Botany, the questions were usually framed as describe, or compare and contrast, or discuss. My forte had been a deductive approach from the knowledge of the principles rather than one with a photographic memory. Others might have a different approach that worked for them. One of my mates had a most daunting approach. He prepared the full answers to all the Zoology and Botany questions in the previous five years in readiness for our final BSc examination. It took a tremendous amount of effort, but that was his proclaimed style which he said had served him well in previous examinations. He did indeed carry out his plan and memorised the answers he had painstakingly prepared. My approach, though different and less taxing, had also served me well. There was no change in my lifestyle or in my social and sporting activities.

World affairs were dominated by the fighting in Vietnam between France, the colonial power, and the Vietnamese nationals. France was fighting with its back to the wall. It all ended with the capitulation of France in Dien Bien Phu. In Egypt, the playboy King Farouk was overthrown in a coup d'état. It was masterminded by Abdel Nasser, but he installed General Naguib as President. After a few months, Nasser took over the Presidency of Egypt.

During the course of the year, the Ministry of Health invited applications from aspirants who wanted to study Medicine in Britain. I naturally applied, and I was interviewed in Accra. The interview was fairly innocuous. I was delighted to have been selected. In all, ten of us were awarded scholarships to go to Britain to study Medicine that year, the highest number hitherto. Our opportunities and luck were in the ascendancy. Our names were forwarded to London for placements in medical schools in Britain. Nigeria had its own Medical School at Ibadan, the British West Indies in Kingston, Jamaica, whilst Makerere Medical School catered for East Africa.

We awaited our medical school placements with a feeling of great anticipation. I had gained a little notoriety among some of my friends for teasing. The popular and prestigious medical schools we knew were those in London, Edinburgh and Glasgow. Since very little was known about St Andrews and Aberdeen medical schools, I pronounced that it would be a shame and misfortune if anyone received a placing in either of these schools in Scotland. The placings arrived in a steady stream, with most of my mates being allocated to London schools. My allocation was the last to arrive. What was it? It was Aberdeen, in the far north of Scotland. I was shocked and dumbfounded. My initial reaction was to reject it straightaway. I kept it a secret from my friends who kept asking me about my placing. I accepted the offer philosophically and eventually broke the news to them. I learned later that my application had originally been sent to Emmanuel College, Cambridge, but had been unsuccessful; this accounted for the delay in receiving my placement in Accra.

We sat for the final BSc examination at the end of the year. I thought I had acquitted myself well enough to pass comfortably although I was not too happy with my Zoology practicals. Several candidates complained about the Chemistry paper, but I did not have any qualms about it.

The academic year ended with the annual end of year dance. E.T. Mensah's band had been booked long in advance to provide the music. The entertainment committee appointed me as the Master of Ceremonies (MC) for the night. My star had risen high socially, and I considered it a great honour to be assigned this role. The dance was open to both members of the JCR and SCR. A bus was hired to transport nurses and other ladies from Accra to Achimota for the occasion. The bar was fully stocked with drinks of all kind. The Dining Hall served as the dance floor, tables and chairs were arranged on the spacious forecourt. I followed the programme and made all the necessary announcements befitting the evening, including taking special music requests. I made sure that I booked my ladies for the various dances – as a rule one did not stick to one particular dancing partner; even with couples, there was free mixing. The dance was a memorable one with which to end the year; it went on until late in the night. It is appropriate here to chronicle a mini episode. I had booked a pretty UCGC student for the final Highlife medley. After announcing the number from the podium and approaching the table at which the lady was sitting, a young lecturer shoved me aside and took her to dance. I thus missed out on the long final Highlife medley, the climax of the evening. I was greatly delighted to learn that this dance was followed by a romance and courtship which ended in a lasting marriage; especially more so as the gentleman had been my iconic academic. In those days of yore, dance hall meetings often presaged lifelong partnerships.

The UCGC released the BSc examination results in July or August 1954 after they had been received from London. To my great joy and relief, I had passed the examination. I had, however, missed out on the 2nd class on which I had set my sights. I could now append the suffix BSc (Lond.) to my name. A London University degree was not a common commodity. Out of our class of about 20, a mere 50% passed the BSc examination. My mind went back to the interview in January 1950 at Mfantsipim, when I was warned that it was not even certain whether I would be offered a place for a five-term pre-university course. Mere mortals, we do not always have the last word!

In my educational odyssey I had spent four very important years at the UCGC. I had grown from boyhood into manhood as a young adult. I had attained some maturity, not only academically, but also socially, in sporting activity and in the acquisition of knowledge. I had made new friends and acquaintances with backgrounds different from my own. Some in this group belonged to the cream and distillate of the early products of the UCGC who would later join the emerging African academia of Legon and KNUST. I cherish my formative years on the Eastern and Western campuses of Achimota, ending up with the BSc (Lond.) degree. Was I the first from the Volta Region to obtain this degree from the UCGC?

The next big assignment was preparation for my travel overseas. We were all asked to go to Korle Bu Hospital for a medical examination, which we attended in groups. The examination was conducted by a Dr X (I refrain from stating his name for reasons of confidentiality, and also in consideration for his relatives of a younger generation.). I found him unprincipled and detestable. He asked us all to strip ourselves stark naked and jump up and down several times in the course of the medical examination! As incredulous as this may sound, it was nonetheless true. I believe he remained a perpetual bachelor. He requested me, the only one of the group, to have an X-ray done of my hips when there was no need for it. He claimed quite falsely that one of my legs was shorter than the other. My hip was duly X-rayed as requested by the radiologist, an Englishman, who told me that there was no abnormality. When I took the X-ray film to him later, he pronounced that 'this is unacceptable'! All this entailed time-wasting trips from Achimota to Korle Bu in Accra to see Dr X. When I realized that I was the only one subjected to this unnecessary going back and forth, I went to the Ministry to make enquiries on our medical reports. I found out that a satisfactory report on all the students had been submitted a long time ago. I stopped my trips to Korle Bu after that. I could not at the time fathom out what Dr X wanted from me, but he was certainly not one of the best doctors I have ever encountered in my experience, in fact quite the contrary. Several years later, when I became more worldly wise, I did entertain some guesses on his lifestyle.

The Government was not the only institution at the time to award scholarships to students to go abroad to study Medicine or other disciplines. The Cocoa Marketing Board (CMB), with its huge funds, started awarding a number of scholarships from 1951 onwards to post-secondary students to go to Germany for further study. The students on arrival there first had to learn the German language before enrolment in medical school. Most of the recipients at the time were Achimotans. The prevailing opinion then was that these Achimotans were not the cream of the crop in their year groups. It should, however, be stated here that on their return home to Ghana as doctors, they made equally great contributions in medical care as their colleagues who trained in Britain.

Travel to Britain in pursuit of higher education was an event of great uplift. Although it opened the door to a bright future, there had been some cases of notable failure. There was the case of Mr Dornya from the Volta Region in the early forties. Dornya had attended Achimota School and was reportedly very brilliant in the science subjects. After obtaining the Inter BSc, he was awarded one of the very few (probably two) scholarships by the Gold Coast Government to go to study Medicine in Britain My father never ceased praising him to all and sundry; his was a household name in the Volta Region at the time. During the early part of his course in Medicine, he had to be sent back home to the Gold Coast because of 'brain fag' or a serious case of depression. Bluntly put, he could not cope with the academic and the social environmental challenge which he encountered. This was not an uncommon occurrence. I personally knew another person who had suffered this trauma. In this new era there was a steady stream of students going abroad to study, which was great for morale and other support. I therefore did not have any feeling of fear or foreboding on going to study in Britain.

A new elitist class was emerging in the Gold Coast. It consisted of those who had returned home after a professional degree course abroad, usually Britain. They were known as 'been-to'. It was even popularized in a highlife tune, the lyrics of which stated that 'we the elite ladies are only interested in the been-tos, who own a car, a refrigerator (carful, fridgful been-tos, nome worle, in the Ga language)'. Such was the ethos and perception at the time.

The British Council organized and held seminars for those who were going to Britain for further education. This major British institute, which propagates and advances British culture in its widest sense, is neither political nor religious. The Goethe Institute and the Alliance Francaise are its German and French equivalents respectively. At the seminar it provided advice on British etiquette, life and culture. The "dos" and "don'ts" were mentioned, and advice was given on how to comport oneself. It served a useful purpose since culture varies from country to country.

ACCRA / ABERDEEN

Travel to Britain was mainly by sea; a few travelled by air. The Elder Dempster Lines operated three passenger ships, namely MV Apapa, MV Accra and MV Aureol, which sailed between the West African ports and Liverpool in England. They all called at Las Palmas, a popular stop-over port. I was booked to travel by air to London.

My flight from Accra to London was on a small Hunting Clan aeroplane. The plane flew at a low altitude, making stops in almost all the countries we flew over. We left the old, small Accra airport on a Friday morning and arrived in London at about 4pm on Sunday; the journey lasted three days. The other passengers on the plane with me included Samuel OfosuAmaah (my classmate from Achimota and the late Cromwell Quist (solicitor/lawyer). We touched down in Dakar, Senegal in the evening of the first day. We spent the night in a hotel which was booked for us. It was a top grade hotel and our first experience of hotel accommodation. I was fascinated to see and watch, with gastric juices churning, the cook frying steak in a sizzling pan at our table in the restaurant as we waited to be served. On the second day we flew across the Sahara, making only one stop-over at a French military outpost; the outpost reminded me of "Beau Geste", a book I had read in my secondary school days in Achimota. We arrived and touched down in Algiers on the north coast of Africa on Saturday evening. We spent the night in a modest and less elegant hotel. We took off after breakfast on Sunday morning, crossed the Mediterranean and touched down in Bordeaux, France in the afternoon. After lunch at the airport, we set off on our final leg for London and arrived at about 4pm on a grey Sunday.

We, the three students, were met and welcomed by a British Council official who took us to a hotel at Russell Square, near London University Senate House. This completed one chapter of my life and would mark the beginning of a new one. I had arrived in Britain as a green-horn and was now readying myself to commence my future career.

A British Council official came to the hotel on Monday morning to check on our state of comfort and wellbeing. The British Council, I would discover, was going to play a most supportive and significant role in my early days, nay months, in my new environment in Britain. With neither relatives nor close friends around, even though I was now an adult, it was reassuring. The British Council (BC) official took us to their office on a street off Regent Street in Central London. The spectacle of tall, majestic buildings, and red double decker buses was in marked contrast to the Accra buildings and layout, with the 'tro-tros' and 'mammy trucks'. The population was almost entirely Caucasian; some of them were engaged in manual labour. Prior to my coming to Britain, all the Caucasians I had met and seen in the Gold Coast were managers, senior civil servants or academicians. I must confess to a naivety in having a simplistic view in my observations. It was late summertime and the weather was not unlike the one I had just left in the Gold Coast.

Since Ofosu-Amaah and I were bound for Medical School in Scotland, we received our briefings together. We were scheduled to spend a week in London after which we would proceed to Edinburgh; we would then go our separate ways from Edinburgh to our respective destinations of Aberdeen and Glasgow. After the briefing in the BC office, we were taken to Bush House in Aldwych by a BC officer where the Gold Coast students Supervisor's office was located, and we were taken there to see him. To our great surprise and delight, the Supervisor was Mr Ribeiro, who had not only taught me History to obtain an A in my Cambridge O level examination, but had kindled in me a lifelong interest and love of the subject, encompassing it in its widest sense— e.g. history of medicine, of tennis, of opera etc. Mr Ribeiro was equally delighted to see us and to brief and advise us. He felt extremely proud of us and offered his warmest congratulations to both of us on having passed the formidable BSc examination only a few weeks earlier. He informed me that an attempt to place me at Emmanuel College in Cambridge had failed, hence my placing in Aberdeen. He assured us that Scotland had indeed established a reputation for the training of doctors better than elsewhere in Britain at that time. He went on to say that we were ambassadors of our country and should therefore comport ourselves in a way to bring credit to ourselves and to our country. He then cautiously addressed the delicate matter of having girlfriends. At that time, returning home with a Caucasian companion created a problem of a sort, in general. The prevailing wisdom was to avoid this discomfiture. Mr Ribeiro raised the matter in his advice to us. We were adults, he said, and were likely in a long course of medical education, to have female friends. He advised us on a dignified way of overcoming the problem, ending his advice with a hilarious quotation. It was a friendly and memorable meeting with my iconic teacher. I have always held Mr Ribeiro in the highest esteem. I met two of his sons more than 40 years later separately, in Accra and in London at social functions, and gave them my testimony on their late father. One of them, an eminent London surgeon, received a Knighthood when he became the President of the Royal College of Surgeons of England (PRCS). He was the first African, and probably the first non-Caucasian, to hold that venerable position. He was later elevated to the peerage and became Lord Ribeiro of Achimota. This speaks volumes of his father as well as the son who comported himself with a blend of confidence, modesty and supreme dignity, without any air of either arrogance or ostentation.

Sammy and I stayed in London for about a week, sightseeing, doing some modest shopping and familiarizing ourselves with the London environment. After the week in London, we boarded the "Flying Scotsman" train at King's Cross Station for Edinburgh. The six-hour journey began at 10am and terminated at the famous Waverley Station in Edinburgh. The train traversed beautiful countryside of varying foliage with a number of major stops on its way. It was a journey I would repeat several times over a few years. My addiction to the meals in the dining coach originated from this first journey. We were met again by a BC official and taken to a BC hostel for students. The hostel hosted students from the British Commonwealth; most of the students were from the West Indies and British West Africa. We settled in quickly. We then went to the BC office in Edinburgh where we met Mr Carmichael, the official who dealt with Gold Coast students. Mr Carmichael was a warm, friendly man who put you at ease when you met him. I believe that he was later on recruited by the Gold Coast Government for an important position in the country. He briefed me and Sammy on our respective Universities of Aberdeen and Glasgow, and the travel arrangements to our destinations after a week in Edinburgh. We did as much sightseeing as we could. The beauty of the castle with its famous landscaped valley was not lost on me. Sammy and I went to the cinema to see a film which had received titillating reviews; it was the "Glenn Miller Story". Like the first in everything, it got stored in my memory. It was an excellent film with Stewart as the star, featuring the Glenn Miller band with many tuneful, appealing jazz numbers. When I bought my record player in Aberdeen, the first long playing record I bought was the one on The Glenn Miller story.

After a week in Edinburgh, I embarked from Waverley Station on the train journey to Aberdeen, the final leg of my travels. It was a four-hour journey. There was no other person of colour on the train. We arrived in the evening after leaving in the afternoon. As usual, a BC official was at the station to meet and welcome me. I was driven in a car to my residence at 75 Bonnymuir Place. This was a two-storey tenement in an appealing part of the city. Two rooms on the first floor were allocated for rental as "digs". The landlady was Mrs Duthie, a widow in her 70s. She was a caring, motherly and friendly lady with grey well-coiffured hair.

Already in digs in one of the rooms on the first floor was Victor Adu, also a student from the Gold Coast. He had arrived a few days earlier to study for a soil science degree at the university. He was the older brother of Ammishadai Adu, my classmate at Achimota School and the UCGC. The BC was thoughtful, as I would learn later. The BC did not have an easy time in finding suitable digs for the students from overseas, which were necessary since the university did not have any halls of residence at that time; these came many years later. The local Aberdeen population had had very little exposure to people of colour then.

I arrived in Aberdeen in the autumn of 1954. I left Aberdeen in November 1960 after six years of career launching and very fulfilling years. I had loathed the thought of going to Aberdeen when I was at the UCGC, but grew to love the place. On leaving Aberdeen and for many years thereafter, I regarded the city as my second home.

Aberdeen, the capital of the Grampian, or the North East region of Scotland, is situated on the NE coast of Scotland. To its north lies Peterhead, and to its west Balmoral Castle, and further north-west is Inverness. There was a big fishing port which created a great fishing industry. After the discovery of offshore oil, Aberdeen was transformed and attained a status of great importance as a major oil industry centre.

The city of Aberdeen was bordered by the rivers Don and Dee at either end. A tramway car ran on a line from the Bridge of Don to the Bridge of Dee. The high street, known as Union Street, ran from East to West of the city. The city gained the epithet of the "Granite City". Why? All the buildings were built with granite stone and this lent a unique glitter to their exterior, especially when the sun shone. It has to be seen to be fully appreciated.

Chapter 4
UNIVERSITY OF ABERDEEN

A Aberdeen University (AU), Scotland's third and the UK's fifth oldest university, consisted of two colleges: King's College and Marischal College, located in Old Aberdeen and the city centre, respectively. There was also Robert Gordon College, another tertiary establishment. All the Arts faculties, Agriculture, Forestry, Physics and Chemistry departments and the main university library were located at King's College. The departments of Human Anatomy, Physiology, Biochemistry, and Zoology as well as the Faculty of Engineering were situated at Marischal College. The Students Union building and the university bookshop were situated just across the road from the main majestic entrance to Marischal College.

AU at that time had no halls of residence or hostels for its students. Students therefore had to seek for accommodation in "digs". The Students Union building therefore served as the centre of students' activity. There was a large restaurant, a spacious entertainment hall, a small reading room, a music room, a commodious basement bar, and several shower rooms. Lunch was served to allcomers, both students and the teaching staff, during the academic term. It was heavily patronized by students and staff from both university colleges. Ballroom dances were held regularly on Saturday nights in the entertainment hall. A resident band, Jim Moore and his orchestra, provided music.

The BC played a major role in the welfare of all Commonwealth students in Britain, and as such, Aberdeen was no exception. The BC, with its headquarters in London, had several branches in the country; mainly in the university cities. Major among its activities was assisting Commonwealth students in every way in the pursuit of their studies. It involved meeting them on arrival, seeking suitable accommodation for them, providing recreational extra-curricular activities, and exposing them to British culture in a non-patronizing way. The students were mainly from the West Indies and British West Africa. The Aberdeen BC was located in Provost Ross House, the previous residence of the Lord

Mayor, situated not far from the Students Union building. There were administrative offices, a large reading room, an entertainment hall for hosting dances and other sundry activities, a little canteen, and restrooms. The staff consisted of the director, two assistants, a secretary and a canteen lady. Mr Le Fanu was the director, Betty Imray the secretary, and Clara an assistant, in my early days. Aberdeen at the time had very few people of colour; this community consisted almost entirely of the overseas students at the university. There was therefore an inevitable colour prejudice in a section of the local population, based on ignorance. The BC faced a challenging task in procuring suitable accommodation for the students from overseas. They had a list of landladies who would take in students irrespective of hue. This way, Victor and I were accommodated at 75 Bonnymuir Place with Mrs Duthie. The overseas students at this time numbered about 30.

Scotland boasts a reputation of its golf courses and the Aberdeen golf course was no exception. Aberdeen Pittodrie Football Park with the Dons Football Club as its host team was equally famous. The Dons were in the first division of the Scottish Football League. The first division had always been dominated by the two Glasgow giants, or firms, known as Rangers and Celtic (you had to be a Roman Catholic to play for Celtic). The 1954-55 season was dominated by the Dons of Aberdeen. The team included players such as Paddy Bucklie, and Dennis Law. Dennis Law, hailing from Aberdeen, later joined Manchester United where he attained legendary status. The Dons won the Scottish league in 1955. This feat was never repeated until the early 80s when they added the European Cup to their trophy haul of silverware. They were guided in this foray by Alex Ferguson, then relatively unknown as a football coach; he was then snatched by Manchester United from Aberdeen. He took along with him from Aberdeen the very talented and skilled midfielder, Gordon Strachan; the rest is history.

City Hall in Aberdeen was where visiting orchestras such as the Scottish BBC Symphony Orchestra gave performances. I recall an opportunity and the privilege to watch Otto Klempere conduct there. The city also had a large theatre where visiting performing companies such as London's Sadler Wells staged their productions. On their visits, the Sadler Wells group would stage at least four or five operas during a session. The 'What's More Players', a talented group, and one of my favourite visiting theatre companies, would also stage about four or five plays during their season. Anyone who was interested in the theatre, classical music or opera did not in any way feel culturally deprived in Aberdeen.

The cinema halls provided a regular venue for evening entertainment. There were several of these, with the prominent ones sited on Union Street. Television had not arrived in Aberdeen in my early years. In the cold winter months, the cosy warmth of the cinemas was an added attraction. The dance halls provided an extra venue on Wednesdays and Saturdays for social intercourse. The Mecca group was a major company which had dance halls located in most cities of the country, with their own resident dance bands.

The university sports fields were located at King's College. Sporting activity depended on the season. Rugby was played during the autumn and winter season, whilst soccer took over in the spring and summer. Tennis was played on outdoor courts in the summer.

75 Bonnymuir Place, my new home, was in the nicer residential area of Aberdeen. Mrs Duthie, our landlady, was a widow; her deceased husband had been a dentist. Of the two children, one, the son, was also a dentist. The daughter was married to Mr Alexander Mutch (Sandy). They were a friendly and caring family. We realized later that the BC held her in high esteem as a landlady. She kept our bedrooms clean and comfortable, providing all the linen. She served us breakfast in the morning, and dinner – or high tea as it was known in Scotland – daily. She provided lunch on Sundays as well; the meals were good. We were entitled to one hot water-bath weekly; this, to my surprise, was the standard practice. It was of course, entirely new to me since at home in the Gold Coast two baths a day were the norm. In Aberdeen, with a different climate, perspiration was minimal. The skin was so dry that my vests and shirts showed very little sign of dirt for days. I found it desirable to supplement my weekly bath with a weekly hot shower with copious water at the Students Union building; this proved very refreshing.

This was the Aberdeen in the autumn of 1954 which I remember and recall as the temperature started to fall and it began to get cold.

The university year formally opened. There were overseas students from Nigeria, Gold Coast, Sierra Leone, Jamaica, Trinidad, British

Guiana and Cyprus. There were four of us from the Gold Coast; the other two were Joe Eshun and Emmanuel Asiedu, both medical students; Asiedu was in my year group. Joe had arrived in 1953, the previous year, after obtaining the BSc degree from the UCGC, and had started the medical course in the second year. He would turn out to be the first AU medical graduate from the Gold Coast. The first Gold Coaster to graduate from AU was Mr Arkust, who had graduated in Economics; well before my time, I never met him.

The university medical course lasted six years. Joe Eshun arrived in 1953 with the BSc (Lond.) general degree in Zoology, Botany and Chemistry, a formidable combination. Joe was a brilliant student. He was told to start the course from the first year. After commencing the course, he realized that he had already covered the first year science subjects in his BSc degree course. Being the fighter he was, Joe boldly approached the Dean of the Medical School, Sir David Campbell, and asked to be allowed to join the second year group of students. His request was granted on condition that he performed satisfactorily. He complied. Joe performed excellently and gained promotion to the third year. Because Joe, the pioneer, had prepared the ground, on my arrival in Aberdeen with a BSc degree, I was automatically placed in the second year. This year group class included Deji Femi-Pearse from Nigeria, Asiedu from the Gold Coast and Betsy Davies from Jamaica. We constituted the people of colour in our class. The first year class had the following students of colour: Francis Egbuonu, Bayo Oshinkalu, (Nigerians), Karl Smith, Jerry Batson, and Rudy Archer (Jamaicans), Hugh Spicer (Trinidad), Percy Nylander (Nigeria), Adams (British Guiana) and Sadik (India) were third year students; Bayo Akinkugbe (Nigeria) and Miss Evans (Jamaica) were fourth year students while Abu Imam (Nigeria) was in the fifth year. There were a few more from the Caribbean studying Medicine whose names I cannot recall at present; they were in the fifth and sixth years. Otto Ndukar was a Nigerian in his final year of History; Carl Brown was an elegant, handsome fellow from British Guiana in his final year of an Arts degree course. Mr Sowah from Accra came to extend his knowledge in fishing, not in the university, but at the fishing port; he was a down-to-earth, mature man who called a spade a spade, no pretentiousness. Two pretty ladies, both old Achimotans, Ethel Armateifio and Elise Henkel, came to pursue courses in Domestic Science. This was the mix of students in my first year at Aberdeen. We came from all corners of the Commonwealth, and there was great camaraderie and friendliness among us all.

As a student on Government scholarship, I received an allowance of twenty-eight pounds sterling a month. This was the standard amount for students in the provinces outside London; London students received thirty-one pounds a month. The allowance was adequate for all my needs; it was sent and received regularly and promptly. The university tuition and examination fees were paid for by the Gold Coast Government directly to the university. A separate allowance was given for the purchase of books. I paid my landlady from my student's allowance. I was rather particular about dressing properly. I purchased my suits from the bespoke tailors, Jackson the Tailor and Burton. I added a tweed jacket to my wardrobe to combat the cold in my new northern altitude.

Now enrolled as a second year Medical student, I bought all the necessary textbooks for the subjects to be covered in the following five terms of the preclinical course. The subjects were Human anatomy, Physiology and Biochemistry. There was a bar examination at the end of the fifth term, known as the 2nd MB examination. It was the pons asinorum; one had to pass before proceeding to the clinical course. The anatomy course had earned a reputation of being the most difficult to assimilate and requiring considerable effort. The course consisted of systematic lectures and dissection sessions of the cadaver in the drain (the dissection rooms) from head to tail. The department was headed by Prof. Lockhart, the eminence grande, in the preclinical course – grey-haired, and of medium height, with a square face.

Lockhart was always immaculately dressed with an impressive tie clip and cuff-links to match. He was held in awe by all, students and teachers alike. He remained a bachelor. There were two other lecturers, including one called Dr Fyffe, a very knowledgeable anatomist, who later left Aberdeen to take up a chair in Anatomy in Newfoundland. The lecturers were assisted in supervising students in the drain by young doctors who were preparing to sit for the first part of the FRCS examination. These assistants included Drs Charles Clark and Duguid. Dr Clark later qualified as a surgeon, and scaled the academic ladder to become Professor of Surgery at University College Hospital, London.

He was a Gastroenterologist. Dr Duguid later became an eminent Ophthalmologist at London's Moorfields Hospital.

Cunningham's Anatomy was the textbook of choice in all Scottish Medical schools, while Gray's Anatomy was the choice in England. Prof. Lockhart's special area of interest was Myology and action of muscles. The chapter on muscles in Cunningham's Anatomy was written by him. He also published a book on Surface Anatomy. Dr Fyffe held a special interest in the brain and nerves. We were 60 in number in our class and a cadaver was allotted to a group of five for dissection. I thoroughly enjoyed the dissection sessions; an examination, called the spotter, was held at about four weekly intervals to test our detailed knowledge of the dissections we had been doing. My forte had been the deductive application of principles in mastering knowledge. This method was not exactly applicable to the spotter examination; a detailed knowledge at your fingertips was necessary and demanding. I had to adjust myself to this requirement quickly. Betsy Davies from Jamaica always came in the top three in the examinations, with Alexander McKenzie (Sandy), and David McKay. Physiology and Biochemistry were subjects nearer my mettle (my BSc being an added advantage). I performed creditably well in the terminal examinations in these subjects. The Biochemistry Professor, even though blind in both eyes, delivered the lectures. The story was that he sustained the blindness while performing an experiment. One of the lecturers was Dr Kosterlitz, presumably Belgian, who spoke English with a strong German accent. Some decades later, a research centre at the University was named after him.

A typical day started with an early breakfast, after which I would board a bus at a stop very near Bonnymuir Place and take a ride to Marischal College for morning lectures and practicals until midday lunch. The Union building was at its busiest during lunch break. The lunch queue was always long. My favourite dishes were fish and chips, stovies, fried cod roes, and bread and butter pudding; I still miss the cod roes. After lunch I would go to the reading room to read the day's newspapers. The Aberdeen Press and Journal, the P and J, was the local morning paper. I also read the Manchester Guardian, now known simply as the Guardian, and then published in Manchester. Although this was one of the most serious papers, it was noticeable to me that only a few students read it. The lunch break period was also the time to meet other students and share in social discourse. The afternoon academic session was spent in the drain dissecting a cadaver. Sometimes, the afternoon was free, when I would go to the Music Room to play and listen to classical music. This was played on the gramophone using the old 78rpm 12inch fragile records. It took several discs to play through a Mozart symphony. The long playing (LP) records were just about to arrive. Aberdeen had half day working on Wednesdays, when all shops and commercial activities closed at 2pm. At the end of the college activities, I would go to the British Council, often to play table tennis, usually against Deji Femi Pearse, and always very competitively. After the recreational activities I would board a bus and go home. High tea was served at about 6pm. After high tea, I would retreat to my room to study and listen to my radio for the rest of the evening. Television had not then arrived in Aberdeen. The radio I bought became a prized possession. The BBC had three standard channels – the Light Service, the Home Service and the Third Programme. The Light Service provided popular music and entertainment; the Home Service broadcast the news and discussions on current affairs, both local and international. The Third Programme, broadcast only in the evenings, was highbrow and deeply intellectual in content. I was usually drawn to the Home Service and the Third Programme. I had the radio on all the time even while reading serious academic work. The cooler weather in Aberdeen made studying and mental cogitation easier compared with the hot and humid atmosphere in the prefabricated asbestos rooms at UCGC.

I kept myself well informed on local and international affairs. The Cold War was getting colder. Winston Churchill was Prime Minister in Britain; Eisenhower was the President in the USA; Mao Tse Tung was untouchable and unchallenged in China. Visits to China by other statesmen were a rarity. It was therefore historical and sensational when Field Marshal Montgomery, the famous British General of World War Two, was allowed to visit China where he met Mao Tse Tung. The press coverage was profuse. On his return, he was asked about his impression of the Chinese leader. He was reported to have replied in this paraphrase 'he is a person with whom I can confidently venture into a dark thick forest'! Events in Cyprus, then a British colony agitating for independence, involving Enokas, an independence movement led by Bishop Makarios, played centre stage in the daily news.

For an overseas student, the British Council (BC) played an important and useful role in my life in Aberdeen. There was always a social entertainment event on a Wednesday evening, often a dance night or a film show. One of the films I saw there and to which I have forever been endeared was "The Browning Version" with Judi Dench starring in it. Music for dancing was provided usually by playing gramophone records, or occasionally by a small dance band. At the Students Union, dances were held in the main entertainment hall, with music by Jim Moore and his orchestra. On Saturday nights, the bar on the basement floor was popular and a great attraction. Meandering your way through the crowd to the service counter to procure your mug of beer, and drinking with friends who shared your experience and interest, was rejuvenating in this spirit of camaraderie.

Since there was no TV at the time, the cinema halls were very well patronized. Before the film show there was a news bulletin, titled Scottish Movietone. The cinema houses showed two films each evening, and as they were all well heated in the winter this provided an extra attraction. Ballroom dancing was popular, especially with young men and women, as it provided another opportunity for social discourse, as well as for dance enthusiasts. The Mecca dance halls thus fulfilled this need amply. People of colour were not many in Aberdeen and requests for a dance with a local lassie could quite often be refused with a 'No', accompanied by a shaking of the head. This factor deterred some people of colour from attending such dance halls. I recall an Engineering student from a British West African country, good-looking and always immaculately dressed, who would ignore repeated 'No's from the ladies and carry on requesting several of them in turn, in plain sight of everyone, until he finally found a willing dance partner. He never took one 'No' as a deterrent in his forays as others did. He succeeded in following up to date several of these ladies. Such then was the manifestation of colour prejudice at the time. It was also not uncommon that while on a bus with many passengers, a child might stare at you, and with finger pointing would say "Mummy, see a Darkie", with utter indifference from the mother as the other passengers looked on, amused. To clear their doubt or inexplicable ignorance, some would entice a smile or laugh from you to see the colour of your teeth, black or white. Not all people of colour could cope with such experiences. If there was difficulty in the academic work, a brain fag was not far off.

Joe Eshun had a single room apartment in the desirable West End of the city. His flat served as a venue for visits and parties for the few of us from the Gold Coast. Joe was an excellent host, and we all felt at home from home in his place. As the winter wore on, the weather got colder and colder. I received a heavy winter coat, with a thick alpaca lining and fur collar from my brother Willy in the USA. It was striking when I wore it for the first time. Mrs Duthie, my landlady, was quite fascinated by this attire from the American Midwest. In December, I woke up one morning and what did I see? Snow had fallen heavily during the night, and it was feet high over land, rooftops and elsewhere. I saw snow for the first time in my life – not just flakes, but knee deep! Like the first in everything, it was endearing and memorable, a picture of beauty all its own, never mind the bitter cold!

A belated profile on Victor Adu and Emmauel Asiedu is appropriate here. Victor was an old boy of Odumase (Krobo) Presbyterian Secondary School (now Accra Presec). He joined the infant department of Soil Science after his Cambridge O level examination where he worked as an assistant to the Soil Scientist, Mr Charter. Obviously impressed by Victor, Mr Charter recommended him for a scholarship award to go to Britain to study for a Soil Science degree. This brought Victor to Aberdeen via Dundee, where he studied for a year to obtain the mandatory Scottish Preliminaries. Emmanuel Asiedu, on the other hand, had trained and worked as a nurse in the colonial hospitals in the Gold Coast. He came to Britain on his own as a private student. After passing the Scottish Prelims, he gained admission to study Medicine in AU. He was therefore a much older and more mature student than the rest of us. Of a medium physical build and slightly fair complexioned, with a patch of receding baldness in front of the head, somewhat befitting his age, we the Ghanaians referred to him as 'Opanyin', the revered term for an old man. He was married and had children, all resident at home in the Gold Coast. His wife joined him later in 1956. He was reserved by nature and a true gentleman by any definition or standard. I treasure his friendship. We all got along very well together.

I settled down quite well in Aberdeen during the first term in the new environment I have described above. I wrote letters home to my parents informing them of my new home and experiences. I also kept in touch with my friend Thomas Sekyi, who informed me of current events in the Gold Coast. Tom was one of the successful BSc graduates from our class. He was bonded to teach and was therefore sent to Opoku Ware Secondary School in Kumasi. I think he was the first African graduate science teacher in the school. Although he was very keen on going abroad to study medicine, despite all his efforts, he did not succeed in being released from his bond.

On completing my first academic term, I stayed on in Aberdeen for Xmas and the New Year. I realized that the Scots celebrate the New Year grandly, and regarded it as important as Xmas. The New Year eve, known as 'Hogmanay night', is a special occasion when the tradition is to have a person of dark skinned hue to be the first person to set foot in your house (first footing); it brings with it good fortune. The first-footer is warmly welcomed with a drink of Scotch whisky. We, the students of colour, were therefore in high demand to first foot. Victor and I first footed our neighbours to their great delight.

At the end of the Xmas holidays, Victor and I were informed that, on account of her health, Mrs Duthie could no longer cope with her responsibilities as a landlady for us. This news came to us as a shock and disappointment because she appeared to have been coping quite well, except that she constantly complained of painful and troublesome knees. Since the domestic atmosphere had been friendly, cordial and free of any incidents, we accepted the reason as genuine. The BC assisted us in getting new accommodation, a large house, rather like a small hostel. The landlady had five students, two of whom were from Singapore. The atmosphere was less homely. The move was somewhat unsettling. After a couple of weeks there, we found and moved into new digs. The new place, easily accessible, was located in the Font Hill area, a nice district; there were four rooms for four students, and it was run by two middle-aged dedicated sisters. The other two students were Mr Roy and a lady from Sweden. Mr Roy was on PhD course in Soil Science. The atmosphere was friendly and the culinary standard was high.

Aberdeen Class Reunion

I kept in touch with Jake who was studying in Liverpool. He invited me to come over to Liverpool for the Easter vacation. I obliged and travelled to Liverpool and joined him in his digs. Jake's landlady, Mrs Walker, grey-haired and in her sixties, was a widow who cared for Jake as her own son. I was allocated a room to myself and cared for as Jake's sibling. I spent all the three weeks' vacation in Liverpool. Each day, after a very late midday breakfast, we made our daily visit to the local BC where we met other students from the Gold Coast. These included the late Dr Arbenser, Dr Gabriel Kemavor and Harry AsafuAdjaye, all medical students at the time, also all old Achimotans, and my contemporaries. I returned to Aberdeen after a most enjoyable vacation to commence the third term in my first year. I completed the academic year in the early summer of 1955 and gained promotion to the third year starting in September 1955. Jake and I had planned to spend the summer holidays in London; it was indeed the standard practice for students in the provinces to gravitate to London for the summer holidays.

My first summer vacation in London was as memorable and fruitful as it was enjoyable. I travelled by the night sleeper train from Aberdeen to London (Ethel Amatefio was on the train as well). The train fare was a meagre four pounds sterling; unbelievable in 2015. My accommodation in London had been arranged by the Aberdeen BC. I was booked to stay at the BC hostel at 3 Hans Crescent of historic fame, just three doors from the famous Harrods. It was a very large hostel with several floors, and provided accommodation for a number of Commonwealth students.

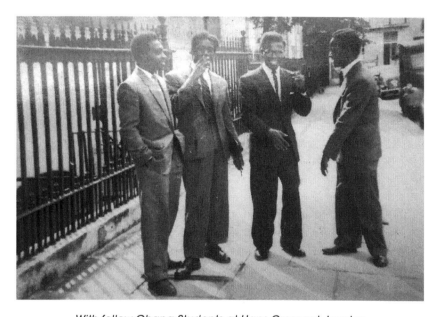

With fellow Ghana Students at Hans Crescent, London

It doubled as a club for other male Commonwealth students who resided elsewhere in London, such as WASU (West African Students Union) hostel. On the ground floor were the administrative offices, a large reading and sitting room, a large dining hall, kitchen and rest rooms. The hostel served English breakfast and dinner daily. The dining hall also served as the entertainment hall for dances, musical concerts and other functions. The central location of the hostel in a desirable part of London was a great advantage. Some of my mates during my stay included CR Neequaye, Ebenezer Aquaye, Kweku Hudson, Jasper Tamakloe, all of blessed memory, and of course Jake Blukoo Allotey. Other students in London who frequented the hostel were the late Bonito Olympio, the late Harold Phillips, Pomeyie Daniels and Sammy Brew Graves.

Jake and I decided to earn some income by doing a vacation job. We were lucky to obtain jobs in a fur coat factory in the Elephant and Castle district of London. I was assigned to a rather senior post in the laboratory. First of all, I was to familiarize myself with the various laboratory tests and then follow up with formulating new tests aimed at improving on and updating the current ones. Even though I was a London University BSc science graduate, my level of knowledge in organic chemistry was not, in my view, sufficiently high to devise new tests in organic chemistry within my limited short period there; very bluntly put, it was beyond my ken.

It was a particularly hot summer and the demand for ice cream was phenomenally high. Walls Ice Cream Company, the premier ice cream makers, was working 24 hours a day around the clock to meet the demand for ice cream and associated products. The company, which was located in Acton, West London, had vacancies on a day-by-day basis. The pay was good, very attractive. Each morning, a long queue would form outside the entrance gate of the factory with a crowd of people wanting a job. The hourly rate of pay on Saturdays was one and a half times the rate on a weekday, and twice the weekday rate if you worked on a Sunday and public holidays. This meant that if you completed all the weekday working hours and also worked on Saturday and Sunday, you almost doubled your total weekday earnings. It was therefore tempting and irresistible to work nonstop, seven nights a week, week after week. Jake and I did just that. I was placed in the chocolate bar section with another young fellow from Sierra Leone. Jake was sent to a different section. Harold Phillips was assigned to the cold storage room, a physically demanding area. Eshun and Daniels also worked at the factory. Jake and I worked continuously for six weeks there. The earnings, plus our regular student allowances, made us feel like millionaires after our six-week stint.

Near to our hostel in Knightsbridge was the famous Harrods store, the preserve of the affluent for shopping. Britain was then a highly class-divided society and Harrods catered for the needs of the upper classes (social classes one, two and three). The store had a reputation that it could obtain any item you wished to purchase, no matter how rare or esoteric; the royal appointment crest had been conferred upon it. Jake and I decided to do some shopping in Harrods with our newly acquired money. I bought an expensive long-sleeved pullover to wear in the cold winter months of Scotland. It remained in very good condition up to the eighties, when I passed it on to our youngest son.

A little anecdote here may amuse my readers in Ghana. It is the story told about the wife of a famous judge from the Gold Coast. She travelled with her husband to London on 'home leave'. (Since the Gold Coast judiciary was almost all white British expatriates, who spent their leave at home in Britain, their few handpicked counterparts who were natives of the Gold Coast were also granted the so-called 'home leave' to Britain.) The wife of the judge from the Gold Coast went to do some shopping at Harrods in keeping with her privileged class. She selected an item to buy, and as the story goes, asked for the cost. On being told what it was, she was alleged to have said "Ah, too much; reduce small, your last price". The salesman, exquisitely attired in a bespoke suit, was reportedly completely flabbergasted since he had never before been faced with a shopper in Harrods making such a request. It was an embarrassing faux pas by this high class lady from the Gold Coast. Since I was not there, I cannot attest to its veracity or otherwise.

Jake and I decided to go to Paris for a ten-day visit. It was at that time not common for students to go to continental Europe on holiday, partly because of the cost. Jake and I had enough money to undertake such a venture; we also wanted to broaden our outlook. We booked return flights to Paris.

On our arrival in Paris, because we were students in British universities, we sought accommodation at the Cite Universitaire, the Paris University housing complex. It was a vast campus with several houses, each bearing the name of different countries and colonies belonging to the vast French Republic. We were assigned to Monaco House. A large modern restaurant provided meals to all the residents in the houses. The food was excellent and of great variety. We were surprised to find fish fried almost exactly the same, kenam, as at home in the Gold Coast! And spinach cooked and prepared like 'kontomire' at home, too. The meals were not only delicious, but also plentiful. I was introduced to the long French bread, the baguette, to which I am still addicted. The culinary experience is to this day unforgettable. The African students (mainly from French West Africa) appeared to be more at home in France and comported themselves with more of an air of confidence, compared with those of us in Britain. We did extensive sightseeing and visited the entertainment night spots in Paris. It was a fulfilling, memorable and, above all, a confidence-boosting fortnight in Paris. We returned to London in a spirit of exhilaration and great 'bonhomie'.

We returned to London and spent the rest of the summer vacation in utter relaxation and in the company of other students from the Gold Coast.

The day started with a full English breakfast, followed by reading the day's papers in the reading room with other students. All the major papers were available: The Times, The Manchester Guardian, The Daily Telegraph, The Mail and The Express. News items of interest were discussed. The central figure in these discussions was a Nigerian law student, very knowledgeable and with the bearing of an academic don. Jake and I still recall a spirited and serious discussion when another law student, but from the Gold Coast, apparently well-informed, quoted a supposedly leading authority on the subject under discussion. Our Nigerian scholar was quick to authoritatively retort "forget about? ...", thus confidently dismissing the leading authority who had been quoted by this other contributor to our discussion. Setting himself above this leading authority, who had been quoted with such an air of confidence, was both telling and impressive. The discussions were renewed and carried on later in the evening after dinner in a pub near the Knightsbridge tube station. We regaled ourselves in a spirit of camaraderie with lager beer and a new drink I discovered – Rough Cider, quite potent indeed!

Being summertime with sunny skies and long daylight hours, I had time for outdoor sports activities. My interest in tennis had not waned. I went to the Battersea Park by bus several times to play tennis with Ebenezer Acquaye, who resided in the hostel, and I played table tennis and billiards there. My zeal for tennis was further enhanced by watching the Wimbledon tennis championship matches on television – transmission was then in black and white. I watched the leading players of the time in competitive matches; they included Yaroslav Drobny, an Egyptian of Yugoslavian origin, Ken Rosewall, Lew Hoad, Trabert, McGregor, Tony Roche, Davidson and several others. Drobny was impressive with his overhead smash and lobs to his opponent's left hand corner in the singles matches. Young Ken Rosewall was famous for his singlehanded backhand drives, while his fellow Australian Lew Hoad, also quite young, attained a legendary status for his fast service and decisive volley. It was the era of the Slazenger wooden tennis racket.

At the intellectual level, I extended my reading to History, my perpetual love. Arnold Toynbee, the renowned historian of the generation, had just published his ten volumes opus, titled "The Study of History". It had received very favourable critical reviews. The massive ten volumes were abridged into a single equally massive tome. I bought the abridged version and tried to read as much of it as I could, but I did not, however, succeed in reading the whole book. Arnold Toynbee's main theme was that over the past centuries, history kept repeating itself and went to great lengths to prove his argument. H.A.L. Fisher, another legendary historian, whose literary prose style I had always admired, held exactly the opposite view. The comparison and verdict as an exercise on these opposing views is, in my opinion, left to professional historians. I am a mere bystander, in awe at their level of scholarship, an admirer of their literary style.

During this summer vacation a significant encounter in my musical life occurred. I went to London's Covent Garden Opera House to see an opera for the first time in my life. My first taste of such musical form was watching the performance of a cantata in Hohoe in 1943 when I was in junior school. The opera on this unique occasion at Covent Garden was Mozart's Magic Flute (Die Zauberflote). I was completely overwhelmed and overawed by the production, staging, and orchestral play, and not least of all the singing, all this with the Covent Garden setting and ambience, combined at the end of the performance to convert me into a lifelong opera lover. Zarastro's two famous bass arias (Isis und Osiris, and In diesen halen hagen), Pamina and Tamino's arias and duets, and the coralatura soprano arias of the Queen of the Night, all sank into my indelible memory. I attended a couple more operas at Sadler's Wells in London's Islington. I bought a book on opera to learn more about this form of music, which opened to me a new chapter in music appreciation. The introduction to opera through Mozart was also critical; no other opera could have had a similar effect.

My brother Willie arrived in London from Trinidad during this summer on his return to the Gold Coast. After obtaining the MSc and PhD degrees in Agricultural Science in America, the British Colonial Office sent him to the Tropical Agricultural College in Trinidad for a year's course to prepare him in Tropical Agriculture before returning home. He completed the year and passed through London on his way home, thus providing the fortuitous opportunity for us to meet and have a reunion; we had not met since 1948 when he left to study abroad. After about a week in London, he left for the Gold Coast. In his odyssey, he had become the first Agricultural Scientist in the Gold Coast, a great achievement.

I continued to receive news about my friends and quondam mates at the UCGC. The UCGC London University examination results for 1955 had just been released. Amable, my classmate from Achimota who did Physics, obtained a 1st class honours and Abbiw Jackson, my mate from Mfantsipim preuniversity days, also gained 1st class honours in Mathematics. Amable and Abbiw Jackson were thus the first in their respective fields to perform these feats at the UCGC. I was delighted and felt justifiable pride in their achievements. I was informed that they had both been selected to proceed to Cambridge University to pursue further and more advanced courses in their respective fields. Very sadly, I learned later, that Amable suffered a mental breakdown and could not, therefore, proceed to Cambridge to study nuclear physics; Abbiw continued to Cambridge, with a successful outcome.

I had a wonderful, educative and most self-fulfilling summer vacation. I met my brother Willie for the first time in seven years. I had a toe dipping experience into French culture. My exposure to opera had begun in all seriousness. And I was ready to return to Aberdeen to continue my studies in the third year.

I went back to my digs in Font Hill. I was starting my second year in Aberdeen as a third year medical student with some confidence and perhaps a bit of a swagger, after my recent experiences in London and Paris; very few of my contemporaries could boast of a holiday in Paris then. Some new overseas students came to join the BC Community. These included the following from the Gold Coast: Chris Adomakoh, Asare, Amonoo Neizer. Chris, an old boy of St Augustine College, had come from the UCGC to study medicine. Asare and Neizer, both old boys of Achimota, had come to study Forestry and Engineering respectively. Chris was also fortunate in being listed to start from the second year medical class in the sense that he had come from his third year at the UCGC when he had not sat for the final BSc examination, normally taken at the end of the fourth year. This stands as a testimony of the high standard the UCGC had attained. Miss Ethel Amatefio did not return to Aberdeen because she had now enrolled at London University for a degree course in Nutritional Science.

My academic and social life in Aberdeen proceeded without any hitch. More and more I was becoming a native Aberdonian, but without their distinctive broad accent. Aberdonians had their own regional accent and colloquialisms. As an example "Fit yerdeing?" translates as "what are you doing?" And "I di ner ken" also translates as "I do not know".

My second Xmas was again spent in Aberdeen. The Principal of Aberdeen University, Sir Thomas Taylor, was also a Presbyter of the Presbyterian Church at King's College. My classmate Emmanuel Asiedu was a regular attendee at that church on Sundays, but although a fellow Presbyterian, I had not attended any church service in Britain since my arrival. Sir Thomas Taylor invited Emmanuel Asiedu for Christmas lunch and asked him to bring along any fellow student. Emmanuel extended this very kind invitation to me, which I gladly accepted; coming from such an eminent person was indeed an honour, and especially at such an occasion. Emmanuel suggested in his gentlemanly manner that it would be proper for me to attend the Christmas morning service at King's College Presbyterian Church before going to Sir Thomas Taylor's residence for lunch. I obliged very willingly and attended the service with him, my first time in Britain. After the service we went straightaway to Sir Thomas's residence in Old

Aberdeen, the official residence of the Aberdeen University Principal. It was a huge house, with a large living room, splendid with very cosy sofas and chairs. It was seasonally decorated with a Christmas tree and other Xmas paraphernalia. A burning coal fire kept the living room comfortably warm, adding to the receptive ambience of the home. I had looked forward with great anticipation to spending Christmas Day in the august company of the University Principal and his family. Emmanuel and I received a warm welcome from Sir Thomas and Lady Taylor. I recall that they had a teenage son and probably one or two other children.

The table was set for the traditional Xmas lunch. There was a huge brown roast turkey which set the gastric juices in motion, as well as several other dishes. I looked forward to a sizeable cut of the turkey, which was rather sliced into thin portions and served on our plates. A delightful Xmas dinner, hugely enjoyed and followed by a special rich Scottish Xmas pudding served with Drambuie cream was a fitting end to this sumptuous Xmas dinner.

We all retired from the table and settled ourselves on the sofas in the warm living room with the welcoming coal fire crackling in the background We then indulged in conversation, covering a wide field of topics. Although I cannot recall which subjects we discussed, there is no doubt that the Gold Coast, our home country, was prominent among them. What I distinctly remember is that the subject of History came up and my interest in it surfaced. Since I had read part of Arnold Toynbee's abridged version of 'The Study of History', I put on my History cap. I was able to articulate Toynbee's views on History and the opposite view of H.A.L. Fisher in my discourse with Sir Taylor, an Art, but not a Science man. Such a discussion in History with a medical student, hailing from colonial Gold Coast, must have been a little surprising to our hosts. Emmanuel and I felt grateful for having been given such hospitality by this eminent Scots family. We on our side did not let our country down; we were good ambassadors. There was, however, a caveat: we still had British passports.

At the beginning of the second term in January 1956, I moved from my digs in Font Hill to another one near the Bridge of Don. I do not recall the reason for the move, but Emmanuel was staying there and recommended it, adding that it would facilitate having joint revision in preparation for our forthcoming 2nd MB, ChB examination. It was further away from the University, but the landlady was a good cook, and the domestic atmosphere was friendly. We passed the 2nd MB, ChB examination at the end of the term, thus completing our pre-clinical course, and ready to embark on the clinical course. Once again I went to Liverpool to spend the Easter vacation with Jake.

On my return from Liverpool, I moved from my digs at the Bridge of Don to a new place in Forrester Hill to commence my clinical course; this was because the Medical School complex and the main Teaching Hospital (The Aberdeen Infirmary) were in Forrester Hill. The proximity of my new digs to the Medical School complex and the Teaching Hospital involved only a short ride on the bus instead of the long ride on a tramcar from the Bridge of Don followed by another ride on a bus from Union Street to Forrester Hill. My new digs, located in an attractive area of Aberdeen, was in a semi-detached single-storeyed house. I was the only tenant, and the landlady kept the house in a very clean condition. She provided me with breakfast and the Scottish High Tea daily, and also lunch on Sundays. The food measured up to only a fair standard, not up to that of my two previous digs. After each high tea meal, the landlady would say to me with a broad smile "that was a nice meal; wasn't it?". Although the adjective 'nice' could not always be applied to the meals, I always nevertheless diplomatically replied in the affirmative.

The Aberdeen Medical School complex and the Teaching Hospital were an imposing architectural complex befitting the Aberdeen Medical School, one of the oldest Medical Schools in Britain, and by logical extension or inference, in the English-speaking world. The building spread over a gently rising low hill; on entering from the main entrance and to the right was the main Medical School block. To the immediate far left was the obstetric department, much further up at the end of the complex was the School of Nursing with the Nurses' block adjacent to it. The slightly hilly topography, beautifully landscaped, lent to the vast complex an aesthetic beauty. The Aberdeen Medical School was rated at the time as one of the very best in Britain; the rating included the student products.

The Medical School block housed the departments of Pathology, Bacteriology, Public Health and the Department of Materia Medica and Therapeutics. A large lecture hall, where all the lectures were delivered, was located on the ground floor, as were the administrative offices. A big noticeboard in the foyer of the ground floor served as the bearer of news, both good and bad; all examination results were posted on it. The Infirmary building housed the surgical wards, the medical wards, the Gynaecological wards and several operating theatres. The housemen's cubicles and several offices were located in this storey building with long corridors and a multitude of rooms. The Obstetric hospital, a complex of its own, was linked physically to the Infirmary through a commonly shared restaurant. The obstetric block housed the antenatal, labour and postnatal wards, lecture hall, operating theatre and administrative offices, and doctors' offices. A wing of the building was double-storeyed, the upper floor of which housed rooms for resident housemen and the Medical Research Unit. The Medical Research Unit was a unique and famous institute, the only such unit in Obstetrics in the country. The medical records department, located in the basement, was a unit of worldwide repute, which attracted visitors from abroad who came to observe its working methodology. In this unit, patients' records could be retrieved within minutes in this pre-digital and non-electronic era. The research unit was created and headed by the legendary Sir Dugald Baird. Behind the Obstetric hospital, and further downhill on a slowly undulating landscape, was the Children's Hospital. A students' hostel was located between these two hospitals.

The Dean of the Medical School was Sir David Campbell. He was the Professor of Materia Medica and Therapeutics. He was a short, rotund, square-faced, genial person. Double-chinned, he wore half-moon spectacles and a bow-tie on his signature three piece suit. He was a striking and impressive looking gentleman. Sir David was also the President of the General Medical Council (GMC) of Great Britain, a most prestigious position He was an expert raconteur, with a gift for relating interesting anecdotes.

The hospitals in Forrester Hill were not the only ones in Aberdeen where teaching was conducted. The Woodend Hospital situated at the northern end of the city had medical wards with two consultant physicians where bedside teaching was conducted, the City Hospital for infectious diseases and tuberculosis in another part of Aberdeen was another where the hospital's consultants provided bedside teaching. Teaching sessions were also held at the Psychiatric Hospital near Forrester Hill and at the Accident Unit in the city centre. The Aberdeen Medical School, therefore, had a multitude of teaching centres with the catchment population of the Grampian region providing teaching material for its medical students.

Now as students in the clinical course, we had to make some adjustments; we would be dealing with patients rather than cadavers. Personal appearance and suitable attire were important. I made some improvement in my wardrobe by acquiring some new suits from Jackson the Tailor and Burton. A good suit could then be purchased for less than fifteen pounds sterling.

We had introductory lectures in Medicine and Surgery aimed at preparing us for hospital ward rounds. These were followed by systematic lectures in medicine, surgery, pathology and bacteriology. The department of medicine was headed by Professor Fullerton, tall and somewhat austere in appearance with a short lip length moustache. His lectures were precise, lucid and excellent. He lectured at such a speed and pace in so clear a tone that you could write down every word he uttered. You could rely entirely on his lecture notes without any resort to a textbook on the topics he covered. His main interest was in cardiology. He was assisted in the lecturing role by Dr Palmer and Dr McCleod. Dr Palmer, an Englishman, was the Senior Lecturer, with interest in respiratory diseases. Dr McCleod, a Scottish Nephrologist, delivered the lectures in nephrology. Dr Dawson, a lady, completed the teaching team in Medicine in the didactic lectures; they constituted the Professorial unit in the medical ward rounds. There were two other medical units, each headed by a senior consultant. These other consultants, assisted by their Registrars, shared in the bedside teaching of medical students. For the ward rounds, we were required to have our individual diagnostic sets and stethoscopes. Dr Palmer offered us advice and a caveat on the purchase of stethoscopes. The cost price of stethoscopes, he averred, varied; some were expensive while others were cheaper. He then pointed out that in the use of the various types of stethoscope, the most important aspect was not the link from the chest piece to the earpiece, but rather from the ear to the brain of the clinician, or the clinician-to-be! Astute advice and comment!

We were put into groups of five or six for the teaching sessions ward rounds. The standard textbook in Medicine was 'Principles of Medicine' by Davidson, with all the contributing authors drawn from Scotland. Scotland had earned a reputation over generations for the training of doctors and engineers, many of whom crossed the border southwards to take up eminent positions in their fields.

The Department of Surgery was headed by Professor Wilson. Dr Wilkinson was the Senior Lecturer, and Dr Dudley the lecturer. Dr Wilkinson left Aberdeen to take up the Foundation Chair in Paediatric Surgery at London's Great Ormond Street Hospital. Dr Dudley also left Aberdeen later for St Mary's Hospital in London as Professor of Surgery. Aberdeen's Teaching Hospitals in a way turned into a nursery for budding Professors in the clinical field for the rest of the country. The lecturers were assisted in the bedside teaching ward rounds by the Registrars. The textbook of choice was" Principles of Surgery" by Bailey and Love. The textbooks in Surgery and Medicine each had its complementary book of Physical Signs in Medicine and Surgery respectively. Lectures and demonstrations in Pathology and Bacteriology completed the first term timetable. After the lectures and ward round sessions, we had our lunch break. Most of us would then go to the Students Union building by bus for lunch and return later for the afternoon session of lectures and demonstrations in Pathology and Bacteriology.

After the sessions in Forrester Hill, my extracurricular activities at the Students Union and the BC determined the time of my return to my digs. I had acquired a portable record player and started collecting long playing (LP) records. The first LP records I bought were two 10-inch LPs namely, "The Glenn Miller Story" and Mozart's D Minor Piano Concerto (K466). There are only a few pieces of music, in my view, which can surpass the beauty of the second movement (the adagio) of the latter. Glenn Miller's "String of Pearls" is also a gem. The habit of collecting recorded music grew exponentially in subsequent years; it has not yet abated completely. I maintained my interest in current affairs by listening to the radio and reading the serious newspapers. The BBC Home Service and the Third Programme were still my choice in channels. I spent most of Sunday reading The Observer and Sunday Times. I occasionally took a look at the 'News of the World', which was considered non-upper class (non-U) to be seen reading, but it was irresistible – the contents were always so juicy to read. Such was the prevailing climate of hypocrisy and pretence. People who bought the highbrow quality papers concealed their copies of The News of the World within the pages of the serious papers.

It was during this period that The Observer broke with its tradition and devoted its entire Sunday publication on one occasion to the entire speech Khrushchev, the supremo in USSR, gave to the General Congress of the Communist Party behind closed doors. Stalin had been revered and his image had remained unsullied in Russia following his death in 1953. Khrushchev debunked this image ruthlessly and revealed for the first time the atrocities, mass murders and the mass movement of millions to Siberia, which Stalin had orchestrated. He condemned Stalin in no uncertain terms and rewrote the history of the USSR. This was during the era of the Iron Curtain when the USSR was impenetrable to the outside world. The revelations on Stalin therefore came as a shock and were most unexpected. The Cold War showed no signs of thawing. The Observer wasted no time in exposing this; it was a major media coup. Winston Churchill had succumbed to Alzheimer symptoms and Sir Anthony Eden had succeeded him as the Prime Minister of Britain.

At the end of the term, I started planning for the summer vacation. Some district hospitals in England offered clerkships to medical students in their clinical years and provided them with full board and lodgings for four to six weeks.

The students attended the outpatient clinics, ward rounds and operating sessions in the theatre of the consultants. They followed and observed the Registrars on their duty roles. Deji Femi-Pearse and I decided to take advantage of this and applied to Pontefract District Hospital in Yorkshire. We were lucky to be accepted for surgical clerkships for six weeks. It was all free; we did not have to pay for anything, not even for the three daily meals. The doctors appeared to like having us, medical students, around. The Casualty (ER) doctor was an Indian with an FRCS degree. The Registrar, also an Indian called Dr Dutta, had passed the part one of the FRCS and was preparing for the final part two. They were all a friendly lot, eager to teach us.

Unlike me, Deji was a private student. His father was apparently a successful medical doctor in general practice in Lagos, Nigeria. Deji, bespectacled, with bushy hair showing early silvery strands of grey, belying his youth, was a jovial, most likeable colleague. He was financially very comfortable; his younger sister, Funke was also studying in England. We visited some other towns in Yorkshire, such as Wakefield. After six educative and pleasurable weeks in Pontecraft, we completed our medical clerkships. Deji then set off to Italy on a sightseeing tour.

I followed with a train journey to London where I joined Jake and other Gold Coast students at #3 Hans Crescent, the BC hostel. I did not do any vacation work in London on this occasion, which was spent leisurely, socializing with fellow students, and attending a couple of dances at entertainment spots. I renewed my interest in opera by attending performances at Sadler's Wells opera house and Covent Garden. I had become an opera fan and went to see as many as I could. I played tennis at the Batttersea Park. The Wimbledon tennis championship TV broadcast remained a vital part of my sporting activities.

We were introduced to a new eating venue at India House Restaurant. Pandit Nehru was the Prime Minister of India and his sister served as Indian's High Commissioner to the Court of St. James. Nehru had forged a strong link between India and the Gold Coast. The India House restaurant, highly subsidized, served excellent rice and curry cheaply to Indian students. Because of the link with the Gold Coast, this culinary lunch privilege was extended to students from the Gold Coast. We could therefore go to India House and have a delicious rice and curry lunch at a very reasonable price. Occasionally I went to the Veeraswamy Restaurant, on Regent Street, reputedly the best Indian restaurant in London and which boasted a wide circle of patrons. It was founded by a former British colonial civil servant in India. The chefs were reputedly head-hunted after a rigorous and competitive search in the subcontinent. It was not cheap going there for a meal, but was well worth the price.

It was during this summer that the world was convulsed by the Suez Canal Crisis. The Suez Canal was constructed and opened to shipping in 1869. Before then, ships from Europe on their way to India and the Far East had to sail round the Cape of Good Hope in South Africa and then northwards over the Indian Ocean to reach their destination, a very long and circuitous journey. The canal was constructed across the straits in Egypt to bypass the long South African detour and shorten the journey significantly. It instantly became a very important sea route, serving a similar function to the Panama Canal. Some people incorrectly claimed that Verdi, the Italian opera composer, was asked to compose an opera (Aida) to celebrate the official opening of the Suez Canal. The correct version is that, a year before he composed the Aida opera, he was requested to compose an anthem to celebrate the opening of the Suez Canal, but he refused. He did, however, accept a commission to compose an opera to open the Cairo opera theatre. This he did by composing Aida, one of the most famous and popular in the opera repertory.

The Suez Canal was operated by the British Suez Company. Abdel Nasser was the President of Egypt in 1956. The Russians under Khrushchev had promised to build a dam across the River Nile to be known as the Aswan Dam. The Aswan Dam would not only provide an enormous amount of hydroelectric power but would also provide water for irrigation, thus transforming Egypt's industry and agriculture. The Egyptians naturally placed great hopes and expectations on the Aswan Dam project. The Russians for some reason decided not to proceed with the project. It is possible that they were deterred by the enormous cost entailed. President Nasser and his fellow countrymen were naturally struck with great disappointment, disbelief and anger. Nasser's response was dramatic. He decided to nationalise the Suez Canal and use the proceeds thereof to generate funds to propel the country's economy. His argument was that the canal traversed Egyptian land and was therefore Egyptian national property. This claim with its argument was bluntly rejected by the British government under Sir Anthony Eden. Britain also claimed that the Egyptians did not have the necessary expertise and personnel to operate this crucial and important international waterway. There was just a mere handful (fewer than five) of Egyptian pilots, out of about 30 pilots, who could safely navigate the ships through the 120.1 mile stretch of the canal.

The British government in collusion with its French counterpart decided to launch a military attack and seize control of the canal and its operation. Britain was going to send troops to take physical control of the canal. Nasser, Eden argued, was another Adolf Hitler in the making and had to be checked by military means. Eden's decision created great division and controversy in Britain. The Labour opposition party, headed by Hugh Gaitskell, opposed Anthony Eden on this front. The British press was equally divided, but with the majority displaying full nationalistic jingoism. The Daily Express at the height of the crisis had pictures of British troops on its front page with captions and headlines reading, "Nasser, HERE WE COME". Eisenhower was the USA President, with Foster Dulles as his Secretary of State. Foster Dulles dictated USA foreign policy. The USA at this time after the Second World War appeared to support independent movements in countries all around the world in challenge to the USSR. The USA in its wisdom decided not to support France and Britain in this dangerous Suez confrontation with Nasser. With the pound sterling in jeopardy without the support of the US dollar, and Britain no longer great as in the days of yore, the country had to capitulate quietly and accept the nationalization as a fait accompli, and the blockade of the canal was lifted. The Suez Crisis could have easily led to a major war. It signalled, if indeed a signal was necessary, the beginning of the visible fall of the British Empire. The USA had emerged as the Superpower in the Suez Crisis without firing a shot in anger.

The Suez Crisis and the saga of its conclusion, was a great humiliation for Sir Anthony Eden. Eden suffered from gall bladder problems at about this time and had to go to the USA for surgery to treat the condition. Russia's Khrushchev made an unsporting joke on the inflammation of Eden's canal. The governing Tory Party in Britain found it timely and also convenient to replace Eden as Prime Minister with the astute Harold Macmillan, of Scottish origin. With his bushy moustache Macmillan was a respected and accomplished Foreign Secretary; he had advised against the Suez adventure.

It was a politically eventful, if somewhat restless summer vacation in London. The events provided daily fodder for our discussions in the BC reading room in the mornings and the evening post-dinner discussions in the pub. I recall young Obed Asamoah, then a law student, as an interested participant. The Asamoah family from Likpe Bala had been known to my family in Hohoe for many years. An older sister, Ema, the first professional midwife in Hohoe, had been a close friend of my mother's. An older brother had also been my mate in EP Senior School and Achimota Secondary School. Decades later, Obed Asamoah was to play a prominent role in politics during the Rawlings regime and thereafter.

I returned to Aberdeen at the end of the summer holidays and prepared myself in readiness to start the fourth year in medicine. There were new arrivals from the Gold Coast. Janet Asiedu, Emmanuel's wife, came to join him, but not as a student. Asibey had come to study for a Forestry degree. David Acquaye, an old boy of Accra Academy, arrived from the USA to do a PhD course in Soil Science in AU.

On my return from London, I went back to my digs in Aberdeen. While still there and before the commencement of lectures, I was informed that there was a flat available at 14 Bedford Road for rental. The flat was in a three-storeyed tenement building. The building had two-roomed apartments on the second and third floors, and an attic was also available. There was a grocery store/corner shop on the ground floor, run by the landlord, Mr Jimmy Coutts. The toilet facilities were located outdoors, nothing indoors. Generally speaking, it was in a decent working class area, well-served with bus services to Forrester Hill. I took the most desirable flat on the second floor. One of the two bedsitters was much larger than the other. The flat consisted of the two bedsitters and a kitchen. What was the rental fee? It was two pounds sterling a week!

The phenomenon of inflation was decades ahead of us. I took the larger room and sublet the smaller one to another medical student for seventeen shillings and sixpence a week, so that I paid one pound, two shillings and sixpence a week for my room. We used an electric bar for heating in our rooms. The kitchen had a fireplace for coal fire heating, but we hardly used it. My subtenant was Percy Nylander, a Nigerian medical student, a year my senior in the fifth year. He had been a senior civil servant in the Finance Ministry in Lagos before coming to Britain to study medicine. He was therefore much older than I. He had been a cathedral organist in Lagos, as well as an accomplished pianist. To maintain and sustain his pianoforte skill, he purchased a second-hand piano for the lowly sum of four pounds and installed it in the kitchen. He practised and played this piano for his remaining two years in Aberdeen Medical School. He gave performances at the BC on some special occasions to the great admiration and adulation of all. He also played the pipe organ at one of the cathedrals in Aberdeen on some Sundays. Joe Eshun, his classmate from the Gold Coast, had also been a cathedral organist in his Roman Catholic Church in the Gold Coast. In my first term in digs at Bonnymuir place, Joe would visit me and Victor Adu on some Sundays, sit at Mrs Duthie's small organ to play hymns as we accompanied in singing them, to Mrs Duthie's great admiration. We certainly were not lacking in musical talent along the West African coast. Percy was a helpful and supportive flatmate. We did our cooking separately, but got on very well together. The first floor had similar rooms and were rented by Deji Femi-Pearse and Francis Egbuonu, also a Nigerian medical student in his third year. Francis was a very good tennis player. The attic was rented by David Acquaye. Such was my new abode and the neighbours I had, a little West African colony.

I never missed the annual BBC Reith Lectures delivered on the Third Programme. I recall the memorable one delivered by the American diplomat George Keenan on 'Russia, The Atom And The West'. The Nigerian playwright Amos Tutuola received a favourable critical review of his book, 'The Palm Wine Drunkard' on the BBC Third Programme. It was lauded because of the prose style in pidgin-English, a style despised by educated West Africans. I continued with my patronage of the Aberdeen Theatre when visiting opera and theatre companies came for their seasons. My collection of LP records increased in scope. My collections centred on Beethoven (all the symphonies and piano concertos), Mozart, and Haydn. Each time I saw a new opera, I bought the recordings of the highlights of the opera. This way I familiarized myself with most of the arias, duets, ensembles and choruses of all the operas I saw. I managed to save some money from my students' allowance to purchase a wooden record player with excellent acoustics; it was not cheap, but in the field of musical sound rendering and appreciation, it was great value for money.

I started indulging in the vice of smoking cigarettes from my days in the UCGC. It was then fashionable to smoke them held in a cigarette-holder; so was the possession and use of fanciful cigarette lighters. When I started my clinical course in Medicine, our attention was drawn to the link between lung cancer and cigarette smoking. This link was repeated and hammered on at lectures in Pathology and Surgery ad nauseam. The message began to sink in with me, as there was no such link with pipe smoking, except a possible very low risk with cancer of the lip, I therefore switched from smoking cigarettes to the pipe; I became an inveterate pipe smoker. What about the second vice of drinking alcohol? I have never been a teetotaller, my choice in alcoholic drinks, dating from my days at the UCGC, had been Lager beer with lime juice. It was a cocktail mix I enjoyed for many years before finally settling on plain lager. I later added to my choice in drinks, single malt whisky, taken neat, without soda, water nor ice, the purist's and connoisseur's way of enjoying the Scotch whisky. This explains my present day attraction to The Glenlivet, Glenfiddich and Antiquary. The vices in which I indulged, such as they were, were only done in moderation. I was not a chain smoker, nor did I ever drink to a level of inebriation.

We celebrated Xmas and the New Year with parties in our tenement flat and at the BC. I followed events which were unfolding in the Gold Coast: 6th March 1957 had been chosen as the date for the declaration of the country's independence with GHANA as its new name. Pre-colonial West Africa had had three famous empire states in its history, namely Ghana, Mali and Songhai. Ghana was chosen from this trio of former empire states. The Gold Coast was to be the first British colony after India and Pakistan to attain independence. The fame of the country was spreading far and wide. We, the Gold Coast students in Aberdeen, planned to celebrate the Independence Day, and although we were few in number, this factor was no deterrent. The following were the Gold Coasters, soon to be Ghanaians, in Aberdeen: Mr and Mrs Asiedu, Mr Joe Eshun, Victor Adu, Mr David Acquaye, Mr Asibey (all of blessed memory), Chris Adomakoh, Elise Henkel and myself. Joe Eshun was our chosen President and I was elected as the secretary of our small union. We kept in touch with the Gold Coast High Commission in London. We informed the BC of our planned programme of celebratory activities which they concurred to host. The programme centred on a formal reception at the BC on the evening of 6th March 1957.

The Ghanaian Students in Aberdeen on Independence Day - 6/03/1957

The Gold Coast High Commission sent us two large new Ghana flags in the now familiar red, gold and green with its black star insignia for the event. In addition to all the students under the wing of the BC, we also invited several VIPs from the city of Aberdeen and the University. As befitting such a historic occasion in the annals of not only the Gold Coast, but the British Empire, the cocktail reception was to be followed by entertainment and dancing. Joe Eshun as President presided over the evening's function while I played the role of Master of Ceremonies. I made a short speech to welcome our guests and left the main role of speechifying to Joe. It was undoubtedly a most successful and entertaining evening.

Now time for a little anecdote. Balmoral Castle, where the Queen normally spent part of her summer holidays, was located to the west of Aberdeen. On 7th March, a day after our independence day celebrations, two Scottish university students came to see me at the BC. They had been informed that I was the custodian of the new Ghana flags, which they asked to borrow. For what purpose, I enquired of them. They planned to go to Balmoral Castle, with the flag, climb the walls surrounding the castle in an unauthorized way and hoist the Ghana flag atop the tower. I, of course, politely declined to give them the flag. Next day, it was reported in the Aberdeen Press and Journal daily newspaper that two students had gone to hoist a flag atop the tower at Balmoral Castle. It was a prank, and there was the picture of a flag hoisted atop of the tower. The report went on to state that the students had at first attempted to obtain a Ghana flag from Mr Theodore Agble, a medical student from Ghana. Mr Agble, the report continued, the custodian of the flag, refused to part with his country's banner. It was in this patriotic role in which I was chronicled that I first received a mention in the media. As Ghanaians, we held our heads high; we were the cynosure of all eyes. I think that it was in that year or the following one that the Black Stars (the national football team) thrashed its Nigerian counterpart with a 7-0 score line, thus equalling the number of letters in the name N-I-G-E-R-I-A !!!

The independence celebration events in Ghana received worldwide attention and coverage. Vice-President Richard Nixon headed the official USA delegation representing his country, while Britain's Princess Alexandra represented Queen Elizabeth II. Vice-President Nixon was reported to have met Martin Luther King, an invited guest at the celebration in Accra.

Mr Richard Nixon, so goes the story, went on to congratulate Mr Martin Luther King, the African American civil rights activist, on having achieved independence. Mr King's reply to this 'faux pas' was 'I am Martin Luther King from the USA, and I am not yet independent in my own country'. President Kwame Nkrumah on his first visit to Britain later was hosted at Balmoral Castle. Kwame Nkrumah was being courted all over the globe, from the East to the West, from the USA to the USSR.

I completed my fourth year medicine and had to plan for my summer holidays which were shorter in duration for clinical year students than for those in the preclinical course. Deji and I again arranged to do medical clerkships in a district hospital. We were again successful in obtaining clerkships, in Barnsley District Hospital in Yorkshire. The medical clerkship this time would most appropriately be in internal medicine for four weeks. We would enjoy free board and lodging. We were assigned to a Senior Consultant Physician and his Registrar. The Physician, a middle-aged Jewish man, was very knowledgeable and had an air of confidence, bordering on flamboyance. The Registrar, a very pleasant Indian, had just passed the London MRCP (then for some reason regarded the most prestigious of the Physicians' qualifications) and was oozing with knowledge and charm. This duo of excellent Physicians took us under their wings and taught us all we needed to know, almost up to the MRCP level. There was no doubt that they wanted to impress on us that even though they were District Hospital Physicians, they ranked in every respect with their colleagues in Teaching Hospitals. Their confidence radiated on me at the end of the four weeks' clerkship. I learned a lot of clinical medicine in this short period.

During this summer, the Commonwealth Games were held in London with competing athletes coming from all the corners of the British Commonwealth. It received full TV coverage. For the first time, some Kenyan athletes running bare-footed, began to make an impact in the middle and long distance events. It was obvious that although they lacked the necessary experience at international level, they were knocking at the door of international fame and recognition. Another remarkable event occurred when Mirka Singh, a turbaned Indian, won the 440 (or 880) yard event in a full flowing style, comfortably. The commentator remarked that this was the first time an Indian had won an international running event in athletics. An almost epoch making event!

I maintained my interest in football. The big event was the annual encounter between Scotland and England (referred to as "The Auld Enemy"). Scotland had over the years produced great footballers, and their national team had always been worthy opponents against England, the acclaimed founders of the game. The Scotland team was selected mostly from Glasgow Rangers and Celtic, known as the "Old Firm". The Scotland #5 (centre half) was invariably the Rangers #5. I travelled to Glasgow from Aberdeen to watch this highly anticipated confrontation between these age-old rivals. The venue, Glasgow's Hampden Park, was full to capacity. It lived up to expectation; it was a close and memorable encounter. It was pure pleasure to watch England's Duncan Edwards, playing at the right wing half, and Bill Wright at centre half. Duncan Edwards was one of the most gifted players to wear the England jersey. Very sadly he was one of the players who died in the Manchester United Munich air disaster the following year, 1958. I had travelled to Glasgow earlier in the summer to represent Aberdeen University in a tennis match against Glasgow University.

After the medical clerkship in Barnsley, I went to London to spend the rest of the holidays at 3 Hans Crescent BC hostel where I enjoyed reunions with my friends from Ghana. The Ghana Students Union held a meeting at Belgrave Square where the new Ghana High Commission was located. I attended the meeting, presided over by the President, the late Mr Nelson, with Jake, Sammy Brew-Graves and Pomeyie. I attended a number of operas, as a matter of course. I returned to Aberdeen at the end of the summer vacation.

On my return to Aberdeen, I took occupation of my flat on Bedford Road. Mr Coutts normally rented out the apartment to tourists during the summer holiday season. Percy Nylander, my flatmate, had also returned from his summer holidays, part of which had been spent in Scandinavia. This was an excellent package which took him to Denmark, Sweden and Norway. It was a trip sponsored for medical students in Europe and heavily subsidized by a group of drug companies.

The students paid very little for the trip. Percy strongly recommended it to me for the following year. I was now in my fifth year, while Percy was in his final year. Two Ghanaian students, Arkurst and Ayivor, arrived to commence courses in Medicine.

I had two years more left to complete my course. There were a few more examinations in an increasing number of subjects. These required more concentration and application in my studies. There was, however, no significant change in my lifestyle.

We had lectures in General Medicine, Surgery, Orthopaedics, Paediatrics, Psychiatry, Anaesthesia, Ophthalmology and Public Health in the following two years. Clinical ward teaching was provided in the Forrester Hill Infirmary wards, as well as in the associated hospitals at Woodend and City Hospital. The three consultant Physicians at Woodend, namely Morgan, Nedham and Gauld, were assisted by their Registrars in the ward teaching sessions. Woodend Hospital was a much sought after hospital for housemanship jobs. City Hospital was the hospital for infectious diseases and tuberculosis. The Casualty Department (ER) was centrally located in the city centre so that it could serve its purpose of attending to emergency accident cases.

It also served as a teaching centre. The Obstetric Hospital, (known as the 'Matee') was headed by Sir Dugald Baird. Dr McGillivary was the Senior lecturer and Dr McNaughtan was the lecturer. They constituted the Professorial unit who gave all the didactic lectures in Obstetrics and Gynaecology. The other consultants with their registrars who provided clinical teaching were Drs Milne, Wyper and Bernard. As students, we had to spend two weeks in an adjacent students' hostel to enable us to be supervised in delivering five babies each. My interest in Obstetrics and Gynaecology was not kindled until I was in the first term of my final year.

In the first term of our fifth year, my clinical group of about eight students, including Deji, went to the City Hospital. We had to change and put on white gowns before entering a cubicle to be shown a case of chicken-pox. The differential diagnostic points from small-pox were demonstrated by the consultant to us. About 12 days later, Deji developed a full blown case of chicken pox. Two days later, I followed him with a similar ailment. We were the only students of colour in our group and we both resided on Bedford Road. We had to stay quarantined for the mandatory period of one week, thus avoid attending classes. There was no acknowledged therapy for the condition except perhaps some palliatives for skin discomfort. When I contracted measles in 1944 at the EP senior boarding school, the traditional treatment was spraying palm-wine over the whole body.

World events proceeded apace, some to convulse the world. The arms race between the USA and Russia was fierce. Following the detonation of the atom bomb on Hiroshima and Nagasaki in Japan in 1945, the Russians worked around the clock to attain nuclear power status. Allegedly, with help from spies, Russia succeeded in developing and producing the atom bomb. Rosenberg, an American scientist who had worked at America's Manhattan Project, had passed the secret on to the Russians. He was tried with his wife for treason, found guilty and both were executed. The American team, led by Oppenheimer, went on to produce the Hydrogen bomb, a thousand times more powerful than the Hiroshma and Nagasaki atom bombs. The nuclear race continued, and the Russians again caught up in this escalation of nuclear technology. Pari pasu, quietly and secretly, a race in space was going on. One day, the Russians suddenly and out of the blue announced that they had launched the Sputnik, a gigantic spaceship, into space, orbiting our planet earth. The Americans, now acclaimed leaders of the West, were shocked and alarmed. The British had a large telescope, the Jodrell Bank Telescope in Manchester, which monitored the Sputnik and issued reports regularly as it orbited our earth. The message was clear and unmistakable: the Russians had overtaken the Americans in space. The Americans increased their research efforts and succeeded in launching a device, although quite small in comparison, into space to orbit the earth. It took a few more years for them to catch up. Several years later, the Americans succeeded in landing a man on the moon. The race was fierce and relentless.

The Third World emerged in the Cold War era. It was formed initially by countries that had originally been colonies of European countries, notably Britain and France. Pandit Nehru, Prime Minister of India, was the towering figure who headed this group. Nehru had been a political prisoner with Mahatma Gandhi during India's fight for independence. When India and Pakistan attained independence, he became India's first Prime Minister. With his peaked prisoner's cap, his signature head adornment, he commenced the Nehru political dynasty in India. His sister was India's High Commissioner to the Court of St. James in London. His daughter, Indira Gandhi, was later to succeed the short-lived premiership of Shastri. Indira Gandhi was to be followed in turn by her son; the dynasty continued. Burma and Egypt (under Nasser) were leading Third World countries.

My interest in football remained unabated. Sweden hosted the quadrennial football World Cup Championship tournament in 1958. It was during this tournament that a little known 17 year-old player from Brazil, called Pele, created a sensation to emerge some years later as the world's best player in the history of the game.

Football team formation was then a strict 2-3-5 as follows: two fullbacks, three half backs and five forwards. The centre-half, wearing the #5 jersey, was the fulcrum of the team, while the centre forward (#9) was the acknowledged striker. The inside wings (#8 and 10) played the role of present-day midfielders. The Brazilians came to the tournament and completely revolutionized this almost sacred, decades-old formation. They introduced a 4-2-4 system, now familiar and well-known to anyone with the slightest iota of interest in football. Their players had the necessary skill to execute this new formation successfully. The two middle players joined the back to defend the goal, then navigated the midfield with the ball to join the four attackers in front to launch an attack to score the goal. It required an ambidextrous skill in both feet of ball control and pace. It also required a strong stamina to last the 90 minutes of the game. Brazil had two such players in Didi and the young 17 year-old Pele. Their solid defence included the outstanding Zito, while the front attackers included the legendary Vava and Garrincha. Brazil defeated a resolute and skilled French team which included the famous Fountain in a semi-final match. Brazil then played Sweden, the host team, in the finals. It was a memorable match in many respects. Pele scored one of his most famous goals in that match. With his back facing the goal, and surrounded by several Swedish players, he headed, chested, knocked the ball on to his thigh all in quick and rapid sequence before turning himself round to convert the ball into a goal. It was breath-taking and sensational, more so coming from a hitherto unknown teenager. (We were to learn later that not all who competed in FIFA under-17 tournaments from different countries were genuinely under 17 years of age.) Brazil deservedly won the cup and in launching the 4-2-4 formation rewrote the annals of history in the world's most popular game of football. Pele took off from this launching pad as an icon in the game.

The summer term brought to a close my fifth year in medicine. Joe Eshun and Percy Nylander passed their finals and qualified as doctors. They both left Aberdeen to do their housemanship jobs elsewhere. Victor Adu and Elise Henkel also completed their courses and departed Aberdeen for Ghana.

Percy had highly recommended to me the Scandinavian trip for the summer holidays. I was fortunate to be one of the limited number of 30 students who paid very little for the trip. Participating students came from Britain, Germany, Yugoslavia and the Scandinavian countries. Included in the group were GCB Anteson, an old colleague from UCGC, then studying in Leeds, and William Kwaku, a close friend in Achimota, now studying in Germany. I travelled by boat from Yarmouth in England to Aarhus in Denmark, from where I teamed up with the other participants. The programme began with lectures in the morning, followed by clinical ward rounds in their teaching hospitals; we were also taken to some of their medical research centres. Lunch was light, consisting of the open Danish sandwich, the 'smorgasbord'. After lunch we were taken around some industrial centres and breweries and on sightseeing trips. The evenings were free, and it was the time to attend nightclubs or parties. We spent five days in Aarhus from where we went to Copenhagen, the Danish capital. After a week in Copenhagen, we left for Gothenburg in Sweden to spend a week. We ended up with another week in Oslo, Norway. The pattern of the programme followed a similar one of lectures, visits to leading hospitals in the mornings and sightseeing in the afternoons. I fondly recall my visits to Tivoli Gardens in Copenhagen and the evenings at the Students' Union, with the jazz music sessions. While in Oslo, we were taken on a boat trip around some of the fjords, on a Saturday, when we were treated to some delicious large prawns and lobsters. On Saturday night, we were hosted to a grand dinner/dance by a millionaire. He was a relatively young man, in his forties, who was in the whaling business which he had inherited, and was reputedly one of the richest people in the area. He lived in a magnificent palatial house, oil paintings adorned the walls of the banqueting hall and wall at the top of the richly carpeted staircase. We were hosted to a sumptuous dinner in the banqueting hall, after which dancing followed. A number of young ladies, matching us males in number, had been specially invited for the dance. The ambience was magnificent, I had never been entertained by a millionaire before. After dinner, the tables were cleared for the dance session. After a few dances, the hostess, a very attractive lady, requested to dance with me. She claimed I was the best dancer and wished to dance with me for the rest of the evening. She herself was a very good dancer and I obliged by dancing with her for most of the evening. I confess to being rather flattered by the engaging attention of our very attractive hostess. We returned to Oslo on Sunday. The British ambassador hosted us to a cocktail reception and a buffet dinner in the evening. This brought to an end our educational and entertaining trip to Scandinavia. To me the vacation proved educative in more than one sense. I noticed no sign of racial prejudice nor discrimination; indeed in Gothenburg, Sweden, I experienced admiration for my skin hue. Since I had enjoyed Copenhagen best of all, I returned there for about ten days.

I stayed with a caring and friendly middle-class couple in their detached house, located some distance from the city centre. It served my tourist purpose well. I made a very useful purchase in Copenhagen – an LP record on cardiology had just come out on which were recorded normal heart sounds as well as all the pathological aberrations, taking in all the arrhythmias and the murmurs; this record was then not available in Britain. I mastered cardiology up to MRCP level by listening to and studying the record. I gained great confidence in auscultating patients. It was to play a significant role when I was examined in Obstetrics in 1965 for the MRCOG examination.

After my Copenhagen sojourn, I travelled by the night train to Brussels in Belgium, which was then staging an International World Trade Fair. I planned to attend this highly touted and anticipated exhibition. I succeeded in obtaining comfortable board and lodging accommodation which was in very high demand. Many countries erected their own pavilions on the wide expanse of land at the Trade Fair site. As its centrepiece was a huge globular structure called the Atominium, depicting an atom. It was a most impressive architectural masterpiece symbolising the atomic age. Prominent among the pavilions were the Russian, American and Czechoslovakian ones. At the front of the huge Russian pavilion was an exact replica of the Sputnik, the original of which had been launched into space to orbit the earth just about a year before the Fair. Architecturally and structurally, the American pavilion was also impressive. The Czechoslovakian pavilion stylishly portrayed the country's glass industry. There were numerous attractions of absorbing interest, day and night; it required several days to see all the exhibits on show.

A little experience at the Russian pavilion is worth narrating. Walking through one of the halls of the Russian pavilion, one was overcome by a stereophonic rendering of the slow movement from Beethoven's Fifth Piano Concerto. You could not trace the source of the piano and orchestral music; they seemed to emanate from all sides, as well as the roof of the hall. People walking through the exhibition halls stopped and stood still in dead silence on entering, almost all to a man, to listen to the enchanting and overpowering rendition of Beethoven's music. The soloist was either Gilels or Richter. After a week in Brussels, I travelled by the night train to Paris.

I had fallen in love with Paris from my first visit there in 1955 and looked forward to another joyful experience. I was again lucky to obtain a room at the Universitaire, my earlier haunt. I met Samuel Ofosu-Amah there; he was also on vacation. I did quite a bit of sightseeing and indulged in the night entertainments which I fancied. I tucked in and enjoyed as much of French cuisine as was possible in the brief period of one week. Sammy and I went to the Paris Opera to see Aida. The Paris Opera House, a great tourist attraction as a magnificent architectural edifice, was a beauty to behold. I entered its portals to see one of Verdi's greatest works. The winding staircase in marble, richly carpeted, lent it an air of elegant grandeur. It was my first time of seeing a performance of Aida. This was indeed an excellent one, featuring a live elephant on the stage; a great spectacle and also musically absorbing.

On a separate day I went to the nearby Opera Café, the most famous café in Europe and enjoyed a drink of coffee. Sitting and sipping coffee there, so goes the adage, you can see the rest of the world's who's who, pass by. This ended my long eventful sojourn in Europe. It was undoubtedly the best vacation I ever had; I had seen the best of Europe. My only regret was that I could not fit in West Germany. I travelled back from Paris to London where I spent a week, before returning to Aberdeen.

I arrived in Aberdeen to commence my final year in medicine. Aberdeen had become my second home. The flat at Bedford Road which I had rented from Mr Coutts had been my secure residence. On my return, much to my shock, Jimmy Coutts told me that the flat was no longer available to me. There was no plausible reason for this, and he had not served me with any prior notice. It was not going to be easy to get a suitable flat at such short notice. I reported the case to the University Students Union and also the British Council. Within days, the matter was resolved to my great relief and satisfaction. Mr Coutts had rented my apartment to someone else while I was away on vacation; however, he had a very similar apartment in the same vicinity which was vacant. He offered this one to me for the same rental fee.

Percy Nylander and Joe Eshun had both passed their finals and left Aberdeen for their House jobs before returning to their respective home countries. Chris Adomakoh joined me in the tenement apartment as my new sub-tenant. I cannot remember the new address now, but it very quickly became my second home. There was no significant change in my lifestyle, socially and recreationally, in my final year. I planned my studies to cover all the necessary grounds in preparation for the final MB, ChB examination scheduled for June 1959. I had passed the examinations in Pathology, Bacteriology, Forensic medicine, Therapeutics and Materia Medica. The final examinations were to consist of Medicine, Surgery and Obstetrics/Gynaecology. We were, however, warned that questions in General Medicine could include Paediatrics, Ophthalmology, Anaesthesia and Psychiatry in the final examination. This meant that a wide field needed to be covered in my reading in preparation for the finals.

We sat for our finals in June. The exam in each speciality consisted of a written paper and a viva voce. I was smartly dressed for the viva voce sessions. Having the name Agble starting with the letter 'A', I found out that I was often the second opening batsman in almost all the viva voces. I had no problem with the vivas in Medicine and Obstetrics/ Gynaecology; I encountered a problem in Surgery. It happened this way: you were assigned a patient; you took the medical history; you then examined the patient methodically and fully. As a result of the foregoing, you rendered a diagnosis. You were allotted a period of time to accomplish all the above before the examiners came to interrogate and examine you.

The importance of obtaining a good medical history had been emphasized and drilled into us during our period in training. A good history, we were advised, took you far in the viva voce examination. With this advice in mind, I took a good history and just when I started examining the patient, the two examiners came to the patient's bedside. I was caught in the conundrum of the opening batsman; the examiners had come earlier than my allotted time. Of the two examiners, one was Professor Wilson. He was partially deaf and as students, we had to shout out our answers to his questions, right or wrong. The second was the external examiner, not a familiar face. Rather kindly, and aware of their early entry, they asked me how far I had gone with the patient. I told them that I had taken a history and was just beginning the physical examination as they walked in. 'Let's have the history then' was their next request. The patient, I said, complained of a pain in a region (which in my knowledge, would be described as right renal region). According to the textbooks, the abdomen is divided into nine regions which are demarcated by drawing two horizontal and two vertical lines connecting certain distinct anatomical landmarks. The patient's pain originated from the right renal region going by the above classification. Professor Wilson stopped me in my tracks at this point and asked me to point with my hand at the site of the pain. I obliged. To me the area I pointed at fell within the area described in Cunningham's textbook of Anatomy and another standard textbook I was using. Professor Wilson then asked me, 'Where do you come from?' In reply, I said, 'I come from Ghana.' His response then was, 'Do you think that Ghana would like to have doctors who do not know where the renal region is?' I said, "No Sir." He went on, 'Now, my son, is the renal region at the back or at where you are pointing ?' The message was unmistakably clear. I responded that the renal region was at the back (I think the Professor, with due respect, was referring to the renal ANGLE as opposed to the renal REGION, according to the textbooks). After overcoming this hurdle, the rest of the viva was uneventful. A second examiner is a useful cushion and insurance. In due course, the results of the examinations were released and posted on the notice board. I passed the final MB, ChB examination and thus qualified as a doctor. I could now append to my name B.Sc.(Lon), MB, ChB(Aberd). Emmanuel Asiedu and Deji Femi-Pearse also passed. I cannot recall the form of my celebration.

A date was fixed for the graduation ceremony. My Scottish mates had their relatives in attendance to witness this important milestone of their graduation. Deji's father flew over from Lagos to witness with pride his son's graduation. Janet also witnessed with deserved pride the graduation of Emmanuel, her husband. I had no such relatives, but had the support of a friend of long-standing. She was a lady of high intellect and not lacking in charm, beauty and elegance (she had been crowned as the Aberdeen University Charities Beauty Queen in 1953). After the graduation ceremony, Deji's father entertained some of us to drinks of champagne; it was my first time of drinking champagne. The graduating class held a black-tie dinner dance at the Caledonian Hotel (the best hotel in the city); some of our teachers were invited to attend. The class produced a photograph album which had a passport-sized photograph picture of all members of the class. The organizing committee selected a short quotation, each one befitting the graduand, below his or her picture. Mine was "A man not old, but mellow, like good wine". There was one other very fitting quotation. It was the quotation for the most attractive lassie in our class by name Leonora Murray (now MacAndrew). The quote was "Even Beethoven made overtures to me". My graduation news was of course sent home to my parents and siblings.

Graduation Picture - 1959

With fellow Graduation and some Teaching
staff at Graduation Dinner - 1959

(L) On Graduation Day in Aberdeen
(R) At a party with Elma Mennie (1959) with Elma Mennie

HOUSEMANSHIP JOBS

I was a Medical doctor, a professional man, and no longer a medical student. I was ready to commence a new phase in my life. I got my temporary medical registration which entitled me to practise as a doctor for one year. After the two six-month mandatory recognized house jobs in General Medicine and Surgery, I would obtain the full medical registration which entitled you to a life-long practice as a doctor. From the top of the ladder as a final year medical student, I was going to start a new phase in the medical profession from the very bottom of the ladder. Such is life, a sea journey from port to port. The tradition was to do the house jobs in Britain before returning home to Ghana and I intended to do just that. I planned to do my first job in Medicine and the second one in Surgery. The very limited jobs in Medicine were normally given to the top three and that ruled me out.

I applied for one of the very limited jobs at Wood End hospital but was informed that there was no vacancy. I was offered a job at the infirmary in Forrester Hill which I did not find particularly attractive. It was a house job in a mixed ward for Dermatology, Dental and breast cancer cases, but recognized as a job in General Medicine. I reluctantly accepted the job because it was in a Teaching hospital; it meant I was going to be in Aberdeen for another six months.

Most of the patients in the ward (Ward 14) were breast cancer cases. Mr Philip was the consultant oncologist. Stocky in build and square-faced, with a thin lip-wide moustache, he wore a half-moon pair of spectacles. He was a very skilled surgeon. I found him parochial, perhaps bordering on crude, and not at all graced with sophistication. I worked under him for six months, but did not like his attitude and demeanour towards me. Although all the staff addressed me simply as Dr Agble, he persisted in addressing me as 'Joe' (not my name). I regarded it as a somewhat racist and condescending attitude. His Senior Registrar, a Greek, Tsapogas by name, was a sophisticated gentleman. He had trained and qualified as a surgeon in Greece and came to Britain to obtain the British qualification as a surgeon. Indeed, years later he delivered the 'Hunterian Lectures' in London. Dr Tsapogas realized that I had a problem with Mr Philip and always gave me full support. I held a holistic view of life in general. There was much more in life other than being an expert in one's chosen field of professional pursuit. I should, however, place on record that I learned a lot from Mr Philip, the surgeon. It was pleasant working under Drs Anderson and Lyall, the two consultant Dermatologists; they were both respectful and not patronizing.

The houseman's job was to clerk and examine all patients on admission. You were responsible for all routine investigations and writing up all progress notes. All venipunctures for the commencement of IV fluids and blood were done by the houseman. All the wards had side-rooms where the houseman performed all the urine tests for protein, sugar and pus cells. There were no lab sticks then. There was a microscope in the side-room for the houseman to do all the blood count for WBC (White Blood Cells) and platelets. It was taxing and very demanding to be a houseman in a Teaching Hospital, but equally educative. Blood transfusion was administered through a red rubber tubing from a glass bottle. If you encountered difficulty with the venipuncture, you could seek assistance from the Registrar. I also assisted at operations in the theatre. Mr Philip performed masterfully with skill in dissecting out invaded lymph glands in patients with breast cancer. I did ward rounds at night to prescribe medications.

Halfway through my job, I was assigned a daunting task. The Registrar for Dermatology asked me to clerk and examine a patient who had been admitted to a side-room in the medical ward, and to report to him after I was finished clerking the patient. Who was this patient, I asked. The patient was Sir David Campbell, Dean of the Medical School, Professor in Therapeutics and Materia medica, also President of the British General Medical Council. I pleaded with the Registrar to undertake the clerking of this very distinguished patient, but in vain. He refused bluntly and stated correctly that it was my duty to clerk my erstwhile teacher. I went meekly to the room where Sir David had been admitted under Dr Anderson. I took a full history. It was a case of a generalized eruptive dermatological condition. After a routine auscultation of the chest, I did not intend to do a full examination of the body surface, leaving that to the Registrar. Sir David asked why I had stopped short of a full general body examination. He then went on to strip himself completely, to put me at ease to examine him fully. I still held him in awe. When I finished examining him, he thanked and complimented me. I reported my findings to the Registrar who then prescribed the appropriate treatment. My intervention with Sir David was not yet over. I had to see him later during my evening ward round with the ward sister. During the ward round when I asked him which sedative, if any he required, his response was that he left the decision entirely to me. The esteemed Professor of Therapeutics and Materia Medica left me, a junior houseman in his medical infancy to take the decision on his medication. I prescribed for him a standard sedative in use at the time. He asked me to come back after finishing my ward round.

After my ward round I went to Sir David's room and sat down on a chair at his request; all he wanted was to have a chat with me. His genial, sociable and fatherly personality was revealed and fully on show. Partly because he was then President of the British General Medical Council, he had travelled very widely to many countries; he was very well-informed and broadminded (in marked contrast to Mr Philip). He related me with several anecdotes and relished me with jokes; a raconteur par excellence. I spent about an hour, most convivial and entertaining, with him. This was repeated each evening for the few days he stayed in the hospital.

My social life had meantime undergone some change. Since I was no longer a student, I restricted my visits to the Students' Union. Similarly, I avoided the nanny role of the British Council for which I was so grateful and highly appreciative in the preceding five years, but felt that the time had now arrived for me to steer my own canoe. I joined my fellow housemen in some social outings together.

Halfway through my first house job, I began planning for my next job in Surgery. A house job in a District hospital, preferably in England, was regarded as the best for a young doctor like me who would be returning home, as I was more likely to gain hands-on experience there than at a Teaching hospital. The image of Sir Dugald Baird's Unit began to build in my mind. It was a very prestigious unit and lucky were the few who got jobs there. I decided to do a six-month job there after completing my second job in Surgery. Was this possible? I went to see Dr Arnold Klopper. Tall and easily approachable, he was a Consultant Gynaecologist who conducted research in Gynaecological endocrinology at the MRC (Medical Research Council) unit. Originally hailing from South Africa, he was a pioneer in his field and was the leading authority on oestrogens. I expressed to him my interest in Obstetrics and Gynaecology. He took note of my interest, but pointed out that there was normally a two-year waiting list and that it would be difficult if not impossible to fit me in soon after my second house job. He promised to pass my request on to Sir Dugald, and advised me to keep in touch with him. I applied for several surgical jobs and received an offer from Warrington General Hospital, which I accepted. I completed my first job on 31st December 1959 and was scheduled to start the second one in Warrington, Lancashire on the 1st January 1960.

I travelled to Warrington and reported at the General hospital (there was a second hospital, the Infirmary, in Warrington). The General hospital consisted of single-storeyed buildings spread over a large green landscaped site. It catered for General Medicine, Surgery, ENT and Obstetrics/Gynaecology cases. The Surgical staff consisted of a Senior Consultant, a Junior Consultant, an ENT consultant, a Registrar and two housemen. The Obstetrics unit had a senior consultant, a Registrar and an SHO.

My duties consisted of clerking cases in General and ENT surgery, writing up progress notes and assisting at operations when called upon, and doing venipuncture.

The senior consultant in Surgery was Mr Philip. He was a tall, well-mannered, confident and experienced skilled surgeon of Scottish lineage. He was held in esteem by the junior consultant surgeon, who was both competent and likeable. I often assisted the junior surgeon and the ENT surgeon. The Registrar, a lady by the name of Melville, very plain, hardly ever with a lady's makeup, she did her utmost to ingratiate herself to Mr Philip and displayed uninhibited favouritism towards the second houseman, a young female Indian doctor, newly arrived from India, very diffident and trying to find her feet. Dr Melville had passed the part 1 of the FRCS and was preparing for the final part 2. Although I posed no threat to her, she displayed an attitude of resentment towards me and I did not find her a likeable person. The ENT surgeon, a pleasant young consultant whom I assisted during his operations, highly appreciated and commended me on my assistance to him.

The six-month period in Warrington passed rather quickly. Although I did not perform any surgical operations, I acquired a substantial amount of knowledge and experience. One of my friends who had trained in London told me that as a houseman in a London hospital, he had personally performed 39 appendectomies; I envied him, but I took on a more decision-making role than in my first job in Aberdeen.

A little episode here demands chronicling. I was called one evening to see a patient in the emergency room. The patient was a young lady in her early twenties, complaining of pain in the epigastric region of her abdomen. After obtaining the history and examining her, I arrived at a diagnosis and instituted a management schedule for her; she required no surgery. I reported the case to the consultant surgeon on call. The patient apparently was a famous well-known singer, married to an equally famous singer. On the following day, a report appeared in the Daily Telegraph newspaper that this lady had been admitted to the Warrington General Hospital as an emergency case. She was seen by Dr Theodore Agble, the report went on, and surgeons kept an all-night vigil on her. There was an element of exaggeration and sensationalism of the seriousness of her condition. Be that as it may, that was the second time I figured in a newspaper report.

In the course of my second job in Warrington, I received some good news from Aberdeen. A vacancy at the Maternity unit for a 10-week period after my second house job was offered to me; there was the possibility of its extension to six months. It was a great opportunity for me to enter the portals of the most prestigious Obstetrics department in the United Kingdom. I had to plan for this unfolding, very favourable development, including obtaining permission from the Ghana government to delay the time of my return home. Returning home soon after finishing the second house job and acquiring the full Medical Registration, had been obligatory.

My friend Sammy Brew Graves was in his clinical years at St Thomas Medical School in London. He wrote to me to arrange for a medical clerkship in my hospital at Warrington. I succeeded in obtaining a clerkship for him in Medicine. We had a memorable time together in Warrington. I discussed with him my prospective third job in Aberdeen and the need to delay my return journey home. He advised me to go to see Mr Ivor Cummings, the official responsible for all such affairs in the Ghana Office in London. I went to London and accompanied by Sammy went to Mr Cumming's apartment to present my case on a Saturday afternoon. Mr Cummings was a cultured and well spoken gentleman, probably an Oxbridge product. I explained to him that the Aberdeen Maternity unit was the most prestigious in the country and that I was extremely lucky in receiving an offer of a job there. It was my aim, I stated, to train and qualify as a Gynaecologist and that a six-month extension would further enable me to obtain the Diploma Certificate (DRCOG), in the first instance. It would be a great loss if this unique opportunity were left to waste. He was sufficiently impressed by my request and promised to do his best to obtain its approval. I returned to Warrington the same day in a hopeful mood. Not long after my return, I received news of approval from Mr Cummings. Permission was granted for me to do the initial 10 weeks with the possibility of an extension for six months. I was delighted and grateful to Sammy and Mr Cummings.

During this period in Warrington, I took driving lessons, but did not proceed to take a test to obtain a driving licence. I paid visits to Liverpool, Leeds and Manchester. I went to see an opera and a play at a theatre in Manchester. In Leeds I met Emmanuel Asare, now also a qualified doctor. He introduced me to his wife, Joan, pushing their first baby, Margaret, in a pram.

While in Warrington, I acquired knowledge of a new English word. The BBC TV showed a regular programme called "Brain of Britain". About three contestants appeared at a time to answer questions on myriad topics. A question was put to them as follows: "What is the meaning of going Fante?" Two of the contestants did not know the answer, but the third, a doctor, came out with the correct answer. He said that the Fantes were a tribe in the coastal region of Ghana, previously known as the Gold Coast, a former British Colony. Some British officials, he explained, tried to adopt some local native practices in Cape Coast, then the erstwhile capital of the Gold Coast. The practice of adopting a native mode was termed as "going Fante", thus the word "Fante", probably the only Ghanaian word, got into the Oxford English dictionary.

The European football season for 1959/60 ended while I was in Warrington. Entrechat had humbled Glasgow Rangers in one of the semi-finals. Eintracht Frankfurt was impressive and looked invincible. The European Cup final was played in Glasgow at Hampden Park between Eintracht Frankfurt and Spain's Real Madrid. The match was televised and broadcast worldwide in the black and white mode, then the medium. It was a match to remember; all those who watched this match rated it as the best they had ever seen. To this day, I belong to this group. The magic of the legendary Alfredo di Stefano and Puskas was unveiled for all to see. Real Madrid humiliated Eintracht in an excellent and most exciting football match. At the Wimbledon Tennis Championships, two fellow Australians, Anderson and Cooper, met in the Men's Singles final; Anderson defeated Cooper to take the trophy.

After completing my second job, I obtained my Full Medical Registration. I took a short break before going to Aberdeen for my third job. I went to London where I was provided with comfortable accommodation at a hostel for London University's Institute of Education. Mrs Stevenson, the warden, a genial and friendly lady in her fifties, was always caring and always provided me with the best accommodation she could muster on my visits to London. I was joined in London by a friend who had come from Scotland. We went to Paris, lodged at Cite Universite. We spent a week in Paris and returned to London. I always enjoyed my trips to Paris and this was no exception.

I returned to Aberdeen and reported at the Maternity hospital (the department was headed by Sir Dugald). Dr MacGillivary was the Senior Lecturer, and Callum MacNaughton was the Lecturer. Dr Arnold Kloppan was a Research Fellow and Consultant. The other consultants were Drs Wyper, Milne and Bernard. (Whereas in England Gynaecologists are addressed as Mr as are Surgeons; in Scotland, they are addressed as Dr; surgeons are, however, addressed as Mr if they are male). The Registrars were Dr Paintin, Ivor Fairweather, John Davies, Sandy Herriot, Aitken and Sinnathuray (from Ceylon/Sri Lanka). Not long after I joined the staff, Dr Selwyn Crawford was appointed as a Consultant Obstetric Anaesthetist, probably the first to be appointed to such a post in the country. He later pioneered epidural anaesthesia and rose in fame for his work in this procedure; he later moved from Aberdeen to Birmingham.

The 'Matey' was a creation of Sir Dugald Baird. As a relatively young man of 35, he was appointed to the Regius Chair in Obstetrics and

Gynaecology. He had been a protégé of the legendary Munroe Kerr in Glasgow and had drawn attention with the presentation of a paper on ureteric dilatation and urinary stasis in pregnancy. Obstetrics and Gynaecology reputedly, had been badly taught in Medical schools, hitherto. Young Dugald Baird decided to rectify this. Steadily, and step by step, he built a fine teaching department and a Research Unit which attracted universal attention. He wrote a textbook, "A Combined Textbook of Obstetrics and Gynaecology", with several contributors which became the standard textbook on the subject in all medical schools in Scotland and several in England. (The London medical schools stuck to "Ten Teachers in Obstetrics and Gynaecology, the first, in the country.) The MRC staff included Dr Klopper and Dr Thompson, a Sociologist. The department acquired a unique and enviable status as a nursery of future professors in the specialty, not only in Britain, but also in the British Commonwealth. In a memoir, such as mine, this fact needs to be stated and put on record. In 1960, the medical schools in Britain were relatively few, not as many as now, and there was never more than one professor in a department; deserving figures of professorial status were appointed to a Readership. At this time in Britain, two professors, including Professor Walker in Dundee, had passed through the Aberdeen nursery. Professor Stewart in Kingston, Jamaica had also passed through this nursery. He had co-authored with Professor JB Lawson of Ibadan, 'Obstetrics and Gynaecology in the Tropics', a most valuable book, and the first of its kind. When Sir Dugald retired, Professor Lawson was seriously considered as being worthy of taking on the baton in Aberdeen. When I met him in 1969 on my visit to Kingston, Jamaica, he told me that he had preferred to stay put in the warmer climate of Jamaica rather than going to the cold one of Aberdeen. He was, however, then contemplating in 1969 taking up a chair in Newfoundland in Zoology, a far removed field.

ARRIVAL IN ABERDEEN The Second Coming

On arrival in Aberdeen, I entered the portals of the 'Matee' where I was to spend 10 weeks. The foundation stone of my career in Obstetrics and Gynaecology was laid there; I became a protégée of the legendary Sir Dugald Baird.

The department had four wards – the antenatal, labour, postnatal and gynaecology. There was also a Delivery unit outside the hospital. We were five housemen, which included Anne Staddon and Dave McKay. We were rotated through the wards at two-weekly intervals. On our team there were also five Registrars and five Consultants.

I commenced my duties on the labour ward, where I worked directly with a team of midwives under the supervision of the Registrar on call. Progress in labour was monitored by vaginal examination and foetal heart auscultation, using the Pinard stethoscope. This method was soon to be upgraded by the cardiotocography (CTG) devised by Dr Alan Turnbull, a protégée of Sir Dugald's, then based at Cardiff University. I spent a busy two weeks in the labour ward where I learnt a lot about the management of and progress in labour. This was to stand me in good stead. I supplemented my knowledge by reading through Ian Donald's great book on Progress in Labour. It is pertinent here to chronicle one of the cases in my first week. The management of breech presentation at the time was to perform external cephalic version (ECV) at 36 weeks gestation; if successful the patient would go on to have a normal delivery, if not successful a breech delivery at term if the patient's pelvis was judged to be adequate. Performance of the ECV was usually done by a Registrar. On this particular occasion, after the ECV was done, the patient complained of feeling wet and on examination the sheet under her it was found to be bloody and soaked. Placenta praevia was diagnosed. This was an obstetric emergency of the highest grade. Sir Dugald was summoned and quickly appeared on the scene to perform an emergency C-section. In the changing room it was decided that I should be the junior to assist the Chief. A great honour and an opportunity to assist in surgery at its zenith! Fast and effortlessly, a live, but very asphyxiated baby was delivered, but died soon after. Undiagnosed placenta praevia was in the pre-ultrasound era. After this, ECV was only done after placenta praevia had been excluded. Assisting Sir Dugald at this emergency section was a great first experience.

Sir Dugald had been a protégé of Munroe Kerr, the legendary Glasgow Obstetrician, who decades earlier had advocated that lower segment Caesarean section was better than and superior to Classical Caesarean section. The battle between the two had raged for many years before the final capitulation in 1931 at the British Congress of Obstetricians.

This episode of severe bleeding following ECV left me with an unforgettable lesson. Even in the ultrasound age when placenta praevia can be confidently excluded before performing ECV, the entire vulval area should be left exposed.

Delay in the second stage of labour with a cephalic presentation was managed by a forceps delivery if this was feasible and possible. Ventouse delivery had just been pioneered and started in Sweden. The Aberdeen unit adopted the practice, but this resulted in a few cases of necrosis of the skin on the baby's scalp. Sir Dugald therefore sent Callum MacNaughton to Sweden to learn more about the procedure. The Aberdeen unit as a result of fine-tuning was establishing the right suction and the duration of the application to the foetal head. There were no cases of scalp necrosis at the time I was there.

My fortnight in the labour ward was intensive and fruitful. I learned a lot about the progress of labour and its management. John Dennis taught me the way to perform assisted breech delivery and also the manual removal of a retained placenta. Within this relatively short period I gained sufficient practical and theoretical experience to imbue me with confidence in the labour ward. But my judgement received a severe setback with a case in my second week.

I was called to the labour ward one night to see a patient, a grade 4 cardiac due to a rheumatic heart disease. She had spent a long time, several weeks, if not months, in the antenatal ward because of the severity of her condition. Indeed, earlier on in the pregnancy, termination on maternal grounds was offered, but rejected. She had been under the joint care of a consultant cardiologist and was on oral Digoxin to control her cardiac condition, but this had been discontinued on account of Digoxin poisoning a few days before she went into labour. Her medical folder was very thick with many sheets of progress notes. Because I did not cover the antenatal ward, I was neither familiar with her history, nor had ever seen her. I rapidly scanned through the notes to glean a gist of her history, treatments and condition. She was well propped up with pillows and appeared to be comfortable. I examined her and assessed her progress thus far in labour. I allowed her to continue in labour and went back to my room. I then read over and over again Ian Donald's 'Practical Obstetric Problems' chapter on the management of cardiac patients in labour. I wanted to make sure that I was doing the right thing in the management. I was called repeatedly, about four times, during the night to come to see the patient. I never slept, but kept on reading in between the intermittent calls from the midwives on the labour ward. In the early hours of the morning, I was called to the ward because the patient was in the second stage of labour. On my arrival I found the patient in a satisfactory condition. Fortunately, the second stage was short and she had a spontaneous vaginal delivery. The live baby was however asphyxiated and was immediately taken to another room for resuscitation by the midwives. Meanwhile I stayed on in the delivery room to oversee the completion of the third stage, a critical stage in cardiac patients. Shortly after the expulsion of the placenta, the patient developed severe dyspnoea. I felt that she needed to be digitalised because of her cardiac condition. I asked a midwife to inject her with Digoxin. She declined and I therefore injected the Digoxin myself. Her condition improved appreciably on this medication and the continuous administration of Oxygen. I was then summoned to the room where the baby was, to be informed that the baby had not responded successfully to the resuscitation efforts. I felt devastated by the perinatal death. I should of course have informed the registrar on call with me at the very beginning when the patient was transferred to the labour ward. I had been taking relatively important decisions in my second house job in Warrington, and felt that I should not disturb the registrar.

When I went for breakfast in the restaurant, I sat at the table and directly sitting opposite me was the registrar on call with me that night, Dr David Paintin. I narrated to him the events of the night and he listened very attentively without any interruption. At the stage of my narration when I stated that the baby did not respond to resuscitation,

David was holding a fork with a piece of bacon and sausage halfway up to his mouth. In utter shock he dropped the knife and fork, got up without saying a word, and departed the canteen straight for the labour ward. I finished my breakfast and went to the labour ward. Any perinatal death was unwelcome in the department, but this particular one was singularly most unwelcome because of the patient's history and a long stay in the antenatal ward. Indeed, it was regarded as a disaster. Dr Aitken, the registrar now on-call, was assigned the task of investigating and writing a report on the case. He summoned me and interviewed me. He asked me to narrate the events of the night and confirm the statements from the midwives. It was a humiliating encounter with him. He asserted that the severity of the patient's condition made it mandatory for a consultant, not even a registrar, to manage. He, however, at no point said that the case had been badly managed medically – for sure he would have made a song and dance about it; nevertheless, I felt very depressed after my meeting with Dr Aitken. The midwifery sister on duty with me should have suggested to me to inform the registrar during the night. A report was duly submitted to Sir Dugald. How could I face him after this disaster?

Strange things do happen. A few days later, Sir Dugald saw me walking along a corridor and accosted me. With a smile on his face he said he was aware of the events of recent days. He went on to say that I should not be too upset by the incident; such things, he said, happen from time to time. In spite of this or even perhaps, because of this, I became his protégé. It is a case I never forgot. My management of the case was probably faultless; in retrospect, an assisted forceps lift out in the second stage would have been obligatory. The department normally held a perinatal mortality and morbidity meeting jointly with the Paediatric department each month. My case was not included in the list of those for review that month. Was this a deliberate omission? I only know that it was one of my worst experiences, thankfully never again repeated.

I continued my rotation in the antenatal and postnatal wards. Birth control by tubal ligation on the third postnatal day was practised in Aberdeen by the prevailing opinion and standard at the time. Sir Dugald had a liberal approach to birth control: he would recommend or perform the termination of pregnancy on exceptional social grounds.

Puerperal tubal ligation was known as the "Aberdeen operation"; it was avant-garde. He inculcated in us his philosophy that in the practice of Medicine, socioeconomic factors should be taken into account. The decision to perform a Caesarean section, for instance, may be influenced by socio-economic factors. My final rotation was at a Peripheral District Delivery home; there were three such homes which all came under the "Martee". Low-risk cases were booked for delivery in these homes which were staffed with midwives under the direct management of rotating housemen. The housemen could perform simple forceps deliveries and also repair episiotomies. Any problematic case was referred to the "Martee". My training in the labour ward and frequent perusal of Ian Donald's book gave me sufficient confidence to manage cases in the Homes.

Towards the end of my 10-week period, Dr Klopper hinted to me that Sir Dugald was considering the extension of my locum period to six months which I had originally requested. Things were moving up favourably for me in the department. I informed Mr Ivor Cummings about it and requested permission for an extension of my stay. To my great disappointment, he informed me that I had to return home on completing my 10 weeks locum. He was in no position to recommend an extension; indeed, it would place his job on the line. Why? The political crisis in the Congo in 1960 had arisen and Kwame Nkrumah, the Prime Minister, had decided to play a major role. He dispatched a number of Ghanaian doctors to the Congo to assist them in their serious medical need. Ghana itself had only a few doctors in the country and was in no position to provide doctors to the vast country of Congo. The Ghana government, therefore, instructed the London office to dispatch home all Ghanaian doctors without delay to fill up the vacancies. It was obvious that Mr Ivor Cummings was in no position to do anything about my case. I had to accept the fact that I had to return home. I informed Drs Klopper and MacGillivray; they sympathized with my decision to leave, and went on to promise me a job if and when I was granted permission to return to Britain – very reassuring and confidence-boosting. I prayed and hoped for an early return.

It is germane here to recall a visit to the Aberdeen unit by Professor J.B. Lawson of Ibadan Medical School, Nigeria. He had been newly appointed to the chair following the resignation of the Foundation Professor. It was a learning visit for him: he was particularly interested in the record keeping and storage model for which the Aberdeen unit was famous. He no doubt picked up some bits and pieces on the management of an academic unit. He delivered a lecture on the Ibadan experience of Ruptured Uterus in Labour. The subject was part of the blood and thunder of Obstetrics in Developing countries. It was a common problem in Ibadan, but a rarity in Britain. It was an excellent lecture. The accepted management at the time was by a Caesarean hysterectomy. Ibadan, according to his lecture, advocated for repair of the uterus instead of its total excision. Judging from the case management and statistics, tropical obstetrics was a challenging field.

Events in world affairs were exciting and moving fast. The American Presidential election campaign was in full swing. Nixon, the incumbent Vice-President to Eisenhower, was the Republican candidate against the tall, handsome, rich and appealing JF Kennedy. For the first time in history, a Roman Catholic, JF Kennedy, was running for the Presidency of the USA. Also for the first time, a debate was staged between the two candidates and broadcast worldwide on television. I also recall a most telling advertisement caption against Nixon. Below a large unflattering photograph of Nixon, unshaved, was this caption: 'Would you buy a 2nd hand car from this person?' It was telling and delivered a knockout blow message. The rest is history. Kennedy did win, but with a slim margin.

In boxing, Floyd Patterson, the African American, reigned supreme as the World Heavyweight Champion: he was regarded as invincible. He was challenged by the Swede Ingemar Johansson in a title fight and against all odds, was floored a couple of times before finally being knocked out. It was a most sensational result. Johansson repeated the feat later in the return encounter, soon after Patterson retired from boxing.

George Bernard Shaw's play, 'Pygmalion', was made into a musical, 'My Fair Lady'. It opened in New York's Broadway to very high critical acclaim. Several special return flights from London to New York with enthusiasts were made to see the musical.

As my final days in Aberdeen were drawing to an end I was overcome with a feeling of great emotion. As I pen these memoirs, this section is particularly done with thankful memories. I remember my seniors and colleagues with a feeling of great nostalgia. One of the housemen, Dave McKay, with blue eyes, was the best student in our year. He was brilliant. He suffered from an incurable inherited CNS disease. He died only a few years after completing his house jobs. I moved from the hospital into a hotel in the West End for a few days before departing for London. I stayed in London for a fortnight. Mrs Stevenson provided me with accommodation at Russell Square. I had a final reunion with my friends in London. Jake came down from Liverpool to wish me a safe journey home. He and Sammy hosted me for dinner. I attended an opera in Covent Garden. I went to Drury Lane to see "My Fair Lady" with a friend who had travelled from Scotland to bid me farewell. My Fair Lady is the best of its genre. The cast, lyrics, music and the entire production bore comparison in music to the best of the operas of Mozart, Verdi, Puccini and Wagner.

Chapter 5
MY RETURN HOME TO GHANA

After very emotional and memorable farewells, I was seen off at the London Airport by Sammy Brew-Graves and Fred Engmann on a Friday evening. I flew off on a BOAC plane and arrived on Saturday morning at Accra airport. My brother Willie and an official from the Ministry of Health were there to welcome me. The official handed over a letter to me which stated that I had one week disembarkation leave, after which I would go on a posting to Winneba Hospital as a Medical Officer. I would report to the MOH office on Monday morning.

I had a very warm welcome from my brother who at that time was the Crops Research Director and based in Accra. He took me to his bungalow at the Ridge, and later for a drive around Accra. The changes were impressive – UTC and KINGSWAY were both new and moving away from their colonial past, they now obtained goods and merchandise from Europe and the USA. We had lunch with my sister Felicia at her house in Osu, and in the evening my brother took me to the best night spot in Accra at the time –The Seaview Hotel – where I met a couple of my old friends.

The plan was to go to Hohoe to visit my parents after my scheduled visit to the MOH on Monday. I set off early to meet the Acting Director of Medical Services, Dr Phillips, at his office on the top floor of the Ministry Building. I knocked on the door and was asked to enter. On doing so Dr Phillips said 'yes', but continued with his perusal of the document he had in front of him. It was rather strange not to be offered a seat, and to remain standing, while he carried on a conversation with a senior official who appeared to pay no attention to me. When he did decide to address me, it was to remind me that after my one week disembarkation leave I was to report to Winneba Hospital as a medical officer. I then ventured to say that I thought the usual practice was a posting at Korle Bu Hospital for new arrivals to orientate them, before they were sent to district hospitals. In my case, I had arrived on Saturday by air, without any of my medical books and no tropical medicine experience. His response, said rather rudely, was that he could not send everyone to Korle Bu. At any rate I would not be alone as there was another M.O. at Winneba! Despite the very unwelcoming atmosphere, I plucked up the courage to broach a subject which was very important to me: my specialization in Obstetrics and Gynaecology and a need to return to Britain in order to accomplish this. This comment appeared to stoke a fire in him. His apparent annoyance with me, for no good reason, reached its limits. His exact response was: 'Young man, I am not God, I cannot tell you that on such a date, in such a year that you will go back to Britain." It was the worst encounter with a senior official that I had ever experienced and it remains buried in my memory to the present. This was an administrative malfeasance which should not be tolerated by anyone, and especially not a very senior colleague. I met Dr Phillips later in much more pleasant circumstances, when I was best man to his cousin, Dr Harold Philips, at his wedding.

After this sobering encounter, I proceeded to Hohoe to visit my parents. My brother had kindly provided a car and chauffeur to facilitate this trip. My parents were overjoyed to see me, and their welcome was more than warm. They were proud of me – their youngest child who had successfully completed his studies abroad and returned home as a qualified doctor. After an absence of seven years the feeling of happiness at seeing them again was mutual. I spent two very happy days there, during which many friends and relatives dropped by to greet and welcome me back home. As custom demanded, I returned their visits. It was a very enjoyable time. On my journey back to Accra in preparation for my Winneba posting (it is pertinent to mention here that my very good friend Fred Engmann had returned on the Monday after I did and was posted to Korle Bu), I passed through Agormanya to visit relatives on my mother's side –the Venerable Presbyterian pastor Rev Apo, her cousin, and his daughter Aunty Cissy, who remains a great favourite of mine. My mother joined me in Winneba and did a marvellous job of settling me in my new home. My brother was very instrumental in getting me a very good cook and house boy, Philip, who remained with me for a number of years.

My accommodation at Winneba was a G45 type bungalow, very nice, quite roomy and facing the sea. We unpacked the few items I had with me. My neighbours were the District Engineer and an old classmate of mine from UGCC, who was the District Education Officer, Mr Otinkorang. The engineer, an old Achimotan, was married to a Swedish lady called Britt; we all got along very well as neighbours. The MO whom I joined was an experienced English fellow, called Dr Mann. My predecessor was a Dr Oduro who had just left for Britain to specialize in Anaesthesia. Dr Mann was very pleasant and friendly, and invited me to join him and his wife for dinner at their place on that very first night when we met. It was a very pleasant evening and Dr Mann took the opportunity to brief me about the hospital. I realized how inadequate my knowledge was and that I would have to rely on him quite a bit. My mother returned to Hohoe after seeing me settled in. I got a car from the hospital and went to the nearest big town –Swedru –to do some shopping; and so began my new life in my country as a medical officer.

The Winneba District Hospital was like any other of its kind at the time. It consisted of two single-storeyed blocks – female ward with a labour ward, one male ward, an outpatients block, a dispensary, and a theatre block. There were two consulting rooms in the OPD and I started work there two days after my arrival, seeing and examining patients, prescribing drugs. Dr Mann was very good about guiding me. The work was very different from that in Aberdeen and Warrington in the UK where I had worked recently. One incident during my first week warrants mentioning. Dr Mann went to Accra to do some shopping and I was left on my own. He did check the labour ward before he left, ensuring that there would be no incipient problems. Shortly after he left, I was called to see a patient who had been admitted – a multiparous woman in the second stage of labour, who clearly needed assistance. After examining her I told the midwife that we should give her more time in the second stage, knowing that eventually she would need a C-Section. After the time period had expired, I went to see the patient. I was in no doubt that her uterus would rupture if action was not taken soon. I asked the midwife to inform the theatre to prepare for a C-section. Apparently, the theatre was already prepared! No more delaying tactics here. I had never done a C-section before, I had only assisted in Aberdeen. It was a daunting task. I went to the OPD consulting room before going to the theatre. As I walked to the theatre a car drove in: it was Dr Mann! I was never happier to see someone! We went straight to the theatre together and he performed a lifesaving C-Section. Shortly after, a case of ruptured ectopic pregnancy came in and I assisted him with that, too. This was before the days of the mobile phone. I was eternally grateful to whichever power got Dr Mann to the hospital in time to save me from a huge catastrophe!

It was clear that I needed a car. When I arrived in Accra I had decided to get an Opel Rekord after visiting some showrooms. One day, a salesman with SCOA from Accra, one Mr Odonkor (son of Reverend Odonkor), came to see me in Winneba; he had heard that I had recently returned from abroad and would need a car. He had a promotional offer of a brand-new Peugeot 404 with a full tank, to try out for a week. If I liked the performance I could pay for it and keep it. If I did not, he would take it back. As I had already decided on the Opel Rekord, I had to decline this very tempting offer. Such was the level of salesmanship at that time.

Three weeks after my arrival in Winneba, I had a call from the hospital on a Sunday morning to meet Dr Bannerman who had come from Accra. By the time I arrived at the hospital in the ambulance which came to collect me, he had left. Dr Bannerman was the Acting Director of Medical Services (DMS). He was gone without leaving any message for me, and I had no idea of the purpose of his visit. A few days later, I received a letter from him, asking me to move to Korle Bu and report for duties at the Department of Obstetrics and Gynaecology. This was very welcome news, like Mozartean music to my ears; it had been utterly unexpected. I had not sunk any roots in Winneba, and I forthwith made preparations to leave. My mother had returned to Hohoe after seeing me well settled after a week. The District Commissioner (DC) and the Police Commissioner had heard about my transfer to Accra. They were unhappy about it. If I granted them my consent, they would write a letter of protest against my transfer, and collect a number of signatures. This way, my transfer to Accra would be aborted. I told them that it was indeed my desire to be posted to the Korle Bu Maternity Unit, and the matter ended there. And so it came to pass that after exactly a month in Winneba, I found myself in Korle Bu.

Not very long after my transfer episode, Dr Bannerman retired from the Ministry of Health (MOH) as Acting DMS and was appointed a

Senior Medical Officer (MO) at the KNUST Hospital in Kumasi. Several years later when I was the senior Gynaecologist at Komfo Anokye Hospital (KAH), we met at the Kumasi airport and engaged in a conversation. With unconcealed pleasure at meeting me, he asked how I was getting on professionally. Following my response, with a great sense of satisfaction, he revealed to me that at the time of my arrival home in 1960 as a young MO, he was the Acting DMS, and had been on a pre-retirement terminal leave. The only thing he did before his retirement, he went on to say, was to nullify an administrative malfeasance which had been perpetrated on me. The injustice was of course my posting to Winneba by Dr Phillips. Dr Bannerman's action, to me, was a magnificent stroke of fair and professional administrative conduct. It is germane to record here that we had both very principled and unprincipled senior medical administrators in the service in the persons of Dr Bannerman and Dr Phillips respectively.

On my arrival at Korle-Bu, I was given a temporary accommodation on the first floor of the two-storey building which housed the Post Office on the ground floor. I was moved to a bungalow on Slater Avenue about two weeks later. This was a commodious G45 type, with boys' quarters for Philip, my cook/steward. There was a modest garden and it was very conveniently near the hospital and the tennis court. Philip was responsible for cleaning the house, cooking all my meals, my laundry and maintaining the garden in a satisfactory and attractive condition.

I was an Old Achimotan. Achimota was built by Sir Gordon Guggisberg. I had now entered the portals of the second of his three creations. His third historic creation was the Takoradi Harbour.

Korle Bu was the flagship Health Care Centre in Ghana. It was lauded and many High Life music lyrics praised its name.

The hospital consisted of the double storeyed Administrative block in an impressive Gothic architecture at the front, two storeyed wards, Dispensary and theatre blocks at the back. A considerable amount of extension blocks have been added to the original edifice.

There were four major clinical departments, namely: Medicine, Surgery, Obstetrics and Gynaecology (OB/GY), and Paediatrics. There were ancillary departments of Pathology, Bacteriology, Pharmacy, Radiology and Public Health. The complex also hosted the Schools of Nursing and Midwifery. There were also schools for the training of pharmacists, radiographers, and laboratory technicians. The hospital served as the major training centre for newly-arrived doctors before posting to District hospitals. The programme was supposed to be six months in Medicine, six months in Surgery, six months in OB/GY and about a month in Administration. After the completion of the course, the doctor was considered 'ripe' for a District hospital.

MEDICAL OFFICER AT KORLE-BU

I reported to Dr Obuabasa Bannerman, Specialist Gynaecologist, and Head of OB/GY Department. Dr Bannerman had obtained the MRCOG, the specialist qualification, in 1956, the first African from Sub-Sahara Africa to obtain this qualification. The next most senior in the department was Dr A. A. Armar, who had obtained the MRCOG in 1960, the second Ghanaian to do so. He held a position as a Special Grade MO in the department. Promotion to the Specialist grade followed a period of acquisition of experience and knowledge. The following MOs completed the medical staff of the department: Drs CR Neequaye, Hammond Quaye, Hugh Lassey, Marbel, and Chinnery.

The Surgery Department was headed by Dr Charles Easmon. The other surgeons were Drs Baidoo, Quartey and David (ENT), an Englishman. The Department of Medicine was headed by Dr Silas Dodu. The other Physician Specialists were Drs F.T. Sai and Hawe. Dr Hawe, an Englishman, was the doyen of the Physicians, he had served for decades in the colonial medical service. (My mother told me that he had treated me when I was an ailing toddler, at Akuse District Hospital.) Dr Laing was the Specialist Pathologist. Drs Easmon and Sai were soon handed extra duties. Dr Easmon was appointed DMS and Sai his deputy at the MOH, both demanding responsibilities in addition to their clinical workload. A new crop of young doctors, mostly my colleagues from the UCGC days, had begun returning home. Many were posted to Korle Bu while a few were posted to Kumasi or Sekondi.

I commenced work in the OB/GY Department; this consisted of attending to the outpatients in OB/GY, treating them or referring them to Dr Bannerman. Dr Bannerman, I believe, because of my background in Sir Dugald's unit, quite early took a special interest in my clinical activities and my clinical assessment of cases. The labour ward consisted of two units: one for booked patients who had been attending the Korle Bu antenatal clinic and had been booked for delivery in the hospital, and a second unit for patients who were referred from outside by midwives, or other medical centres, or just came in with no medical record. The latter were admitted to the NIB (Not In the Book) ward. The NIB cases were the more serious and challenging. Although I was the most junior MO in the department, Dr Bannerman called me to his office to inform me that he was assigning to me the more challenging ward to handle the more serious cases. I should not hesitate, he stated, in calling him to solve any problem I would face. He hoped, he concluded, that he was not pushing me too far. I was pleased to note the confidence he had in me and the challenge which it offered. My stint in the labour ward in Aberdeen and the knowledge acquired from Ian Donald's treatise in "Practical Obstetric Problems" stood me in good stead and provided me with the necessary confidence. At the start, I assisted at Caesarean-section (C-section) and laparotomies for ectopic pregnancy. In my early days, the operations were done by Drs Bannerman, Armar or Hamond Quaye. These were the bread and butter operations in the department.

Dr Bannerman, small in stature, being the only Specialist Gynaecologist in Accra, was kept very busy. His duties extended to the Ridge Hospital, which catered for the elites in Accra at the time. His gynaecology outpatients clinics commenced in the morning and extended into the late afternoon. Referrals came from near and far, from the entire country. The clinics were often interrupted by surgical emergency operations, such as Caesarean hysterectomy for cases of ruptured uterus. He developed an interest in Fallopian tube blockage as a factor in the management of infertility, and also the repair of vesico-vaginal fistulae. He realized that these were problems which faced Gynaecologists practising in Ghana, not necessarily facing their counterparts in Britain. In my view, this remains the yardstick by which to judge and assess fellow practitioners in this part of the world. He addressed these problems as best he could. He was a dedicated and hard worker, as well as an academic.

There was a daily surgical session in the operating theatre for cases of incomplete abortion of which there was no dearth, and surgical evacuation of the uterus was done by the MO on duty for the day.

Soon after Christmas, Dr Bannerman had to travel to Russia on an invitation. Dr Armar was also on a short leave. I was on duty with Dr C. R. Neequaye on 31st December 1960. Dr Charles Easmon, Head of Dept. of Surgery and also the DMS, was on call for any surgical emergency for the OB/GY Dept. Around midnight, we had a case of obstructed labour, requiring an urgent C-section. Dr Easmon was to be called from the Coconut Grove, a famous nightclub when required for any emergency cases. We phoned him and he promised to come soon. We waited and waited, by which time we were getting worried about the patient's condition. We phoned again and set ourselves a time limit after which we would go ahead and perform the operation ourselves. The time limit passed with Dr Easmon not yet on the scene. Dr Neequaye and I changed into operating attire and proceeded to scrub up. Although I was the more junior doctor and was going to assist Dr Nequaye, I had positioned myself and started scrubbing at the tap normally used by the operating surgeon, while Dr Neequaye scrubbed at another tap. Soon after we started scrubbing, Dr Easmon arrived and entered the theatre. We felt embarrassed, especially I, since it would appear that I was playing the key role in going ahead with the operation. I apologized to Dr Easmon. His response was that there was no need to apologize and that I should continue scrubbing up and go ahead and perform the operation. Neither Neequaye nor I had ever done a C-section before. Dr Easmon did not scrub up, but stood by to watch me as I operated. As I made the incisions and delivered the baby, encouraging words came from Dr Easmon. During the repair stage of the uterine incision, I encountered severe ceaseless bleeding. Dr Easmon verbally guided me to control the bleeding without any success by me. He was finally obliged to scrub up and take over. With a few ligation sutures he stopped the bleeding. He then asked me to complete the operation, which I did. He congratulated me on my first C-section. There was no post-operative complication and the patient was discharged home in a satisfactory condition. This was my initiation into laparotomy surgery, welcoming the year 1961 and the new decade. After this historic event, the rest is history.

I was thereafter permitted to perform C-sections on my own without assistance from another doctor; assistance was provided by theatre nurses or midwives. I was initiated into performing laparotomies on cases of ruptured ectopic pregnancies. These constituted the major emergency surgical operations. By the end of June 1961, I had performed about 40 C-sections. I was pleased and satisfied with my surgical skill. I had endlessly practised the skill of tying surgical knots fast and safely.

I immersed myself into the vibrant social life in Accra. I had decided to buy a two-toned Opel Rekord car from UTC Motors. Although I was entitled to obtain a loan from the government to buy a car, my mother offered and insisted on buying it for me herself. Mammy, my mother, thus paid for the car which cost six hundred and fifty pounds sterling. She was a loving and generous lady, 'sui generis' (in those days, it cost less to buy a car in Ghana than in Britain). Now as a young doctor, and a bachelor – with a car! – I was the cynosure of the eyes of a few ladies, and was indeed targeted.

I renewed my friendships with some former colleagues and mates from the UCGC. J.S Addo, a former mate from Achimota, was prominently placed as the Secretary of the infant Bank of Ghana.

On a visit to the Barclays Bank on the High Street, I met Alex Kuma there, in the hall. He was delighted to see me after several years; he had been three years my senior at the E.P Senior school in Hohoe in the 1940s. He was a brilliant student who went to Akropong and trained to become a teacher. He taught for a while and then went to Dublin in Ireland to study and qualify as a lawyer. Back in Ghana, he practised as a prominent lawyer, and became a very high ranking member of the ruling CPP political party. He was very close to Kwame Nkrumah. He was indeed very pleased to see me after all those years and felt proud of my achievement and new status. He offered to assist me in any way I might need him. He told me that he was a board member of Barclays Bank, and then took me straightaway to the manager's office and introduced me to him. My account with the bank was opened without delay. Alex was also the head of one of the six very special law chambers which handled lucrative government cases. He had also been appointed to a special chair, Osagyefo Professor of Law and Jurisprudence at Legon University of Ghana. This indicated the full extent of his power and influence in the realm. He had a direct telephone line to Kwame Nkrumah, the President. His wife was an Indian whom he had met in Dublin. She was an MO in the Department of Paediatrics in Korle Bu Hospital. They lived in a bungalow at Achimota West End. They honoured me by hosting a special buffet dinner in their residence on a Saturday evening with about 15-20 other invited guests. It was a memorable and touching gesture from my Hohoe EP Senior School alumnus, pleased with the achievements of his junior classmate.

I also renewed my friendship with Reginald Amonoo. Reggie, a year my junior in Achimota, and my dormitory neighbour in Guggisberg House, was the first to graduate in French at UCGC, with honours. He was also an excellent and accomplished pianist. He entertained me to a reunion dinner at Legon; sadly, it was a short-lived reunion as I was soon after transferred to Kumasi. Many years later in my semi-retirement years in Accra, we renewed our friendship once more.

Cromwell Quist had also returned to Accra from Britain as a qualified Solicitor. One morning he accompanied his wife, Dawn, an English lady, to the maternity unit, when she was in an advanced stage of labour. I was on duty, but was not covering her ward. I, however, broke the joyful news of the birth of his first child to him.

DS Quarcopome, my colleague from UCGC, held the sensitive and high position of the officer in charge of Internal State Security. G. A. Bonsu (nicknamed Guy Chu from our Achimota School days) was an Assistant Principal Secretary in one of the high profile ministries. In short, many of my mates from Achimota and the UCGC were in highly placed positions in the Civil or Educational Service. I got to know Mr Eric Adjorlolo, the head of the Broadcasting Corporation, an extremely sensitive post at the time. A very pleasant man, Eric was married to an African American lady and his residence was adjacent to Flagstaff House, the seat of government. They entertained me with meals on several occasions. This was a time for nation building and each of us felt duty-bound to contribute positively in the process.

The general political climate appeared to be stable. Agbeli Gbedemah, the respected Minister of Finance, Kojo Botsio, Kofi Baako and Krobo Edusei were the prominent and influential ministers. JF Kennedy had just acceded to the Presidency of the USA. His inauguration speech was a landmark in world affairs. 'Ask not what your country can do for you, but what you can do for your country' became iconic quotes on nationhood and national dedication. In my view, JF Kennedy transformed the method of choosing members of a ruling cabinet and senior advisers. He had a team of talent hunters who combed the length and breadth of the country, selecting suitable people, irrespective of their political or religious lineage. In Arthur Schlesinger, he had an excellent and unsurpassed speech writer. He established the Peace Corps programme which was to contribute greatly to the development of Third World countries. Khrushchev was the ruler in the USSR, the Cold War was at its bleakest stage, Dag Hammarskjöld, a devout Christian, was the Secretary General of the United Nations Organization (UNO). He steered a neutral course as much as he could, and sought the interests of Third World countries, now known as Developing Countries. In the pursuit of this, he flew to the Congo Republic which had declared her independence from Belgium, its colonial master. Patrice Lumumba, its Prime Minister, was struggling to administer the vast mineral-rich country. It was the world's main source of Uranium, the main ingredient for nuclear power. The West was anxious not to allow the Congo to fall under Soviet hegemony. Kwame Nkrumah immersed himself and the infant Ghana nation into this struggle of giants by providing personnel from Ghana to assist Lumumba. The stakes were high. The plane flying Dag Hammarskjöld to the Congo had a crash in the Congo, killing Dag Hammarskjold. The crash was described as mysterious. I was greatly saddened by his death; not the way to terminate the life of a great Christian and a dedicated UNO Secretary General. Was any country or individual responsible for this accident?

President Kennedy soon after his inauguration took a momentous decision on Ghana. He decided that the USA should assist Ghana in the Volta River Project. He had apparently taken this decision personally against the official advice he had been given. Ghana had placed great store and expectation on the Volta River Project. The approval raised Kwame Nkrumah's image nationally and internationally. He was being courted by the East and the West. On the following Sunday after the announcement of the American approval, an international football match was played at the Accra Stadium. Nkrumah was driven in a car at the stadium all-round the playing pitch as he waved a white handkerchief to a cheering crowd. This was my first time of seeing Kwame Nkrumah. The Black Stars, the national football team under the legendary Ohene Djan, were twinkling like little stars. They dominated the football scene in Africa and also excelled outside Africa. At their peak they played a drawn game in Accra against Spain's Real Madrid, also then at its peak, with a 3-3 score line. Real Madrid's team included Alfredo di Stefano, Puskas and Gento, whilst the Black Stars side included Ado Odametey, Kwame Adarkwa and Acquah.

I revived my interest in playing tennis. There were some eager and good tennis players around in Korle Bu at the time. The group included Drs Silas Dodu, Sam Afuakwa and Emmanuel Asare. Young Edmond Anan also joined our group. He was one of a group of young boys whom an Englishman outfitted, equipped and coached with his own income. He guided them to become national stars who played in international matches to represent Ghana. The group included Narh Tetteh, Lartey and Odartey Anan. Our last set on the tennis court was followed by cold beer at Silas Dodu's bungalow. We played several days in a week. It was for me a glowing sporting and social life which combined well with a satisfying and fulfilling professional experience.

The MOs who were my contemporaries in Korle Bu at the time included the following doctors: Jake Blukoo-Allotey, Samuel Ofosu-Amah, Felix Konotey-Ahulu, Kweku Hudson, Ludwig Henkel, Fred Engman, EO Arbenser, Solo Odamten, and Harold Philips.

Kwasivi Agbemebiese (aka Doe) had also returned from Britain and been posted to Cape Coast Hospital. Early in 1961, he decided to marry his sweetheart of several years, Afi Quist. Afi was Cromwell Quist's sister, I had known the Quist family well for several years. Godfried Agbemebiese asked me to be his best-man at the wedding. I accepted the request graciously. The wedding was held at the Ewe Presbyterian Church in Keta. It was for me a memorable event which I treasure. It was my first, but not the last, in this role.

Fred Engman also decided to get married about this time. Like Godfried, he had been my colleague at pre-university Mfantsipim and at UCGC, before going to Britain to train to become a doctor. He met a German lady in London and was engaged to her. About a fortnight before the arrival of his fiancée in Accra, Fred sought my advice on where to spend their honeymoon. I thought Winneba, with some nice chalets by the sea, would be ideal. We drove down to Winneba to inspect the facilities. They had a civil registry wedding ceremony a fortnight later, which I could not attend because of my clinical commitment in the hospital, but promised to visit them at a later date. Fred and I had other plans in mind. What were these plans? Easter was approaching and the Ghana Medical Association (GMA) was holding its annual congress in Kumasi during the Easter holiday period. Fred and I planned to travel together in his car to Kumasi. It was going to be a great social event and we looked forward with much anticipation to the entire event. I had been to Kumasi only once before as a guest of Thomas Sekyi's several years previously. The social programme for the congress was particularly attractive.

I was scheduled to be on duty on Good Friday night till 8am the following day. We therefore planned to leave Accra for Kumasi soon after 8am. I was to accompany Fred and his wife in their car. It would be my first opportunity to meet Mrs Engman. On Thursday, I was informed by my seniors that the duty roster had to be reviewed, entailing my finishing at 12pm instead of 8am. The alteration meant a departure time for Kumasi after 12pm. I protested against the change in the roster, but in vain. I did not know the reason assigned for the change. I informed Fred about the change, and the implication of a delayed departure time soon after 12pm. Fred found a late arrival time in Kumasi unsuitable. A dinner/dance on Saturday night was an event to which we were all looking forward. The conclusion was that Fred and his wife would leave Accra in the morning as planned, and take a rest on arrival before attending the evening social function. If I still wanted to go to Kumasi, I had to make my own travel arrangements. I decided not to go to Kumasi after all for the congress.

I performed my on-call duties and finished at 12pm as scheduled. I went home, had lunch, rested and later went to play tennis with Mrs Genievive Easmon, a good tennis player (all the male tennis players had gone to Kumasi). After my evening dinner, I went to bed. At about 4am, my telephone rang. I picked up the phone, annoyed at the interruption of my deep slumber. Assuming that it was a hospital call, without listening, I just said 'I am not on call' and banged down the receiver. About five minutes later, the phone rang again. I picked it up and listened this time. The call came from my girlfriend at the time, who had gone to Kumasi on Thursday, and was expecting me to arrive with Fred. The message was 'we were expecting you here in Kumasi with the Engmans. Fred's car was involved in a serious accident 23 miles away from Kumasi. His wife died on the spot. Fred himself sustained a fracture of the femur, and is in a state of surgical shock. He is under observation, and a rupture of the spleen has not yet been ruled out. Can you please pass the message on to Fred's relatives in Accra?'. This was the message I received in the early hours of Easter Sunday! I was numb with disbelief, but it was not a nightmare; it was true. I was scheduled to be in that car, but I was prevented from doing so by the sudden revision of the duty roster on Thursday. It was not yet my time. With my Presbyterian faith, I do believe in the doctrine of predestination.

I then phoned George Swaniker, also from Osu, to give him the sad news and asked him to accompany me to Osu to pass on the news to Fred's relatives. George was the hospital Biochemist. A brilliant student, he had been my classmate in Achimota up to UCGC where he also obtained the coveted B.Sc. (Lond.) degree. George drove to pick me up from my bungalow. We first went to Fred's brother's house at Osu to convey the sad news to him, then we went to Fred's sister's house with the message. This great tragedy had befallen the Engmann family on Easter Sunday, the most joyous day in the Christian calendar. Later that afternoon, the body of Mrs Engmann was flown from Kumasi to Accra. The German embassy arranged for her burial the same day in the Osu cemetery. Thus ended the life of Mrs Engman, a lady I never met, who lived in Ghana for approximately three weeks. She had an appointment with death in Ghana. Fate had decreed it, and fate had excluded me from the tragedy.

Fortunately, Fred did not sustain a rupture of the spleen. He was transferred from Kumasi to the 37 Military Hospital in Accra where he remained for several weeks before he was discharged home. I visited him a few times in the hospital. Fred returned to Britain later to specialize in Radiology and while pursuing the course he met another German lady whom he married. On their return to Ghana, at a later date they visited Kumasi, my wife, Yolande, and I hosted them to dinner. Not very long after the visit, Fred and his wife migrated to Canada via Britain.

We have lost touch with each other, although he visited me in Accra in 2004 when he paid a brief visit to Ghana.

Some of my medical colleagues were romantically linked and felt the need to settle down to married life. One such colleague was Harold Ebo Philips. A few years my senior, Harold was a friend. He was an old boy of Mfantsipim and we first met at the UCGC, where he was a brilliant student; he graduated with the London BSc degree in 1952. He proceeded to London on scholarship to study Medicine. After his second MB, he was selected to do the special course in Physiology for an Honours degree. He completed this course and continued with the clinical course and then qualified as a doctor with the MB, BS medical degree. On his return to Ghana, he was posted to Korle Bu, where he was assigned to the Medical ward under Drs Silas Dodu and Hawe as MO. Harold was a knowledgeable and confident doctor who was popular with patients and colleagues alike.

Harold was in love with Gladys Tamakloe, a pretty and vivacious young lady. Gladys was at the time staying with her elder sister, Virginia, an equally pretty and attractive lady, then the Nursing Sister in charge of the Medical Ward in Korle Bu. She resided in a bungalow on Slater Avenue, not far from mine. Harold decided to take Gladys to the altar and asked me to be his best man. A grand wedding was held at Legon, officiated by Rev Professor Baeta. The toast to the couple was proposed by His Honour Justice Van Lare. Several of my UCGC contemporaries were among the invited guests and old friendships were renewed. It was an honour to play this role for Ebo Philips since he had other close friends of longer standing; so passed my second role as a best man.

I had by now obtained a driving licence and I drove to Hohoe to visit my parents. Although still a bachelor, no pressure was exerted on me to get married soon; I was left to my own devices! Peki Tsame Presbyterian Church celebrated its centenary (Peki Blengo and Keta had celebrated theirs in 1947 and 1953 respectively). I drove to Peki to attend the celebration, at which one of the keynote speakers was a young Scottish missionary priest, whose name I have forgotten. He was a theology student in Aberdeen during my student days there and I often met him in the Students Union building. His sermon was in faultless, admirable and impressive Ewe. Phrases, abstract words and sentences were delivered in the correct tones. It was a memorable performance. I have always admired linguists like him and Westerman, the German linguist and author of the first Ewe-English dictionary.

Dr Bannerman invited me and some other junior doctors to his wife's birthday party one Saturday evening. My impression had been that he was not on close terms with his senior doctors' peers. We were about 20 in number, and halfway through the party, a VIP in the person of Krobo Edusei arrived with a retinue of about six people. Krobo Edusei was one of the most famous political figures in the CPP, Nkrumah's governing political party. Rather short in height, and an Ashanti with limited educational background, he was one of the most influential ministers in the regime. Sometimes derided as a buffoon, he was shrewd and had an appealing charisma; no need to explain why the lyrics of a popular Highlife tune extolled his virtues. He was very close to Kwame Nkrumah. It was alleged that he had quietly alerted his fellow Akan, Dr Busia, about his impending arrest and incarceration as a political prisoner under PDA (Preventive Detection Act), thus enabling him to slip out of the country to Britain, where he remained until the overthrow of Nkrumah. This was my first time of meeting Krobo Edusei. Soon after his colourful entrance, he announced that the party would soon move to the Lido nightclub. This nightclub, owned and run by a Lebanese, was one of the leading ones in the city at the time. Most of us then drove up to the nightclub, which was located opposite the Alms Hotel, and currently near the Nkrumah Circle. On our arrival, the club was already full, but this posed no problem for Krobo Edusei. On waving his hand, the Lebanese manager appeared on the scene. In a few minutes a large table was cleared for Krobo Edusei and his guests, numbering about 20. After we were all seated, waiters came along and placed a bottle of champagne in front of each guest. I had never before been presented with such copious and limitless amount of champagne. It was certainly a night to remember. I attended quite a number of parties in Accra.

On the medical front, a confrontation was building up at a senior level. In order to present the correct perspective of the confrontation, it is germane at this juncture to give a picture of the senior medical personalities at the time. There were not many Ghanaian doctors then with postgraduate qualifications, and most of them were in

Korle Bu. Drs Silas Dodu and FT Sai were the only two with MRCP; in Surgery, Charles Easmon, E. Baidoo and Quartey had the FRCS; in OB/GY, Bannerman and Armar had the MRCOG, while Dr Laing had the Specialist qualification in Pathology. Dr De Graft Johnson, FRCS was the surgeon in Tamale and Dr Teddy Christian was the specialist Pathologist in Kumasi. This was the list of the Ghanaians with specialist qualifications.

Drs Dodu, Baidoo and Armar were alumni of Sheffield University Medical School and so were identified by some as the 'Sheffield group'. Kwame Nkrumah had as a Special Medical Adviser, Professor Gilman, a South African Jew who wielded great power and influence in medical affairs in the country at the time.

Dr Bannerman held the rank of a Specialist Gynaecologist, while Dr Armar held the lower rank of Special Grade Medical Officer. I had known Dr Armar since my school days in Achimota when he taught me Physics in Form two, before he left for Britain to study medicine. He felt very strongly that he should be upgraded to the rank of a Specialist Gynaecologist. Dr Bannerman held a contrary opinion. His view was that Dr Armar needed to have more experience before being upgraded to the Specialist position. This resulted in an overt conflict between them in the department of which all the staff in the unit were aware. I was personally placed in a difficult and invidious position. Because of my friendship with Dr Armar he would narrate to me his side of the conflict. On the other hand, as a result of the keen interest taken in my clinical work and professional progress, Dr Bannerman also told me his side. I was the most junior doctor in the department and felt myself somewhat squeezed in between the two warring seniors. I never disclosed to either of them what the other had told me. I nevertheless offered such advice as I could muster to these senior colleagues. This way, I believe, my relationship with them was kept on an even keel. The conflict level reached such a peak that on one occasion it escalated in the theatre changing room, and almost resulted in a physical altercation. This scene was witnessed by myself and Dr Hugh Lassey, another MO. The conflict had allegedly spread to involve their respective families and some political heavyweights. This unseemly and highly unethical situation did not work in the interest of patients or staff. The MOH quite rightly decided to intervene at this stage. A committee of enquiry was set up by the MOH to which Dr Lassey and I were summoned and asked some questions pertaining to the quarrel. I answered the questions as objectively as I could, without proffering my opinion.

The outcome was quite radical. Dr Armar was to be elevated to the Specialist grade forthwith and to be transferred to Kumasi Central Hospital immediately and assume the position of departmental head in OB/GY. Dr Bannerman was to go on an immediate transfer to Sekondi/Takoradi Hospital as head of OB/GY Department. (This was in fact a demotion from the premier post in Accra) Dr Bentsi-Enchil in Kumasi was to move to Accra in the musical chair exercise and take charge of the most senior and premier post in the country. All the changes were to take immediate effect. This was in April 1961. The transfers did not end at the senior level; junior MOs were also transferred. Dr CR Neequaye was transferred to Koforidua District Hospital, Dr Hugh Lassey to Kibi District Hospital, both one man stations. Dr C. Marbel was transferred to Kumasi to work under Teddy Christian in the Pathology Department, in preparation for a specialist course. Dr Chinery was moved to the Department of Medicine in preparation for a post-graduate course in Britain. I was the only one left behind in the department. I think that my stint in Winneba spared me. These were undoubtedly radical changes. The transfer of Dr Bannerman was controversial. As the first West African with the MRCOG, an innovative and hardworking Gynaecologist who set the pace in his field, he should have been kept in Korle Bu. The country would have reaped more benefit from his experience and expertise while at post in Accra rather than Sekondi. I believe the decision was dictated by the politics of the time.

Although Dr Bannerman was the Gynaecologist in Accra, the task, nay privilege, of acting as the Gynaecologist to the First Lady, Madam Fathia, wife of Kwame Nkrumah, was not offered to him. This was entrusted to an Indian expatriate, Dr S.C. Bose, who was stationed in faraway Kumasi. He had to travel to Accra periodically for Madam Fathia's antenatal care visits and stay there for four weeks to await her labour and delivery. This may sound incredible, but it is nevertheless true.

Dr Bannerman obeyed the MOH's orders and left Accra for Sekondi. Before leaving, he invited me to his office to say goodbye and wish me well in my career. He then presented me with a book, inscribed with the following: from RHB to TKA. It was the newly published English translation of the New Testament Bible. In parting, he said that despite all my efforts at reconciliation, the eventual result was not what had been expected. I was very deeply touched by this fitting goodbye. On reflection, perhaps, it was his wish and blessing on me for a future in Obstetrics and Gynaecology; only fate and the future could unfold this. I never met him again.

After a few months in Sekondi, Dr Bannerman was appointed a Senior Lecturer in Obstetrics and Gynaecology in Ibadan, Nigeria under Prof. Lawson. Ghana's loss was Nigeria's gain. He later went to work for the World Health Organization (WHO) in Geneva before finally retiring and returning home to Ghana. He died in Accra in the year 2000. I attended the funeral service. Despite the brevity of our association, I admired him and cherish his memory.

Dr Kwesi Bentsi-Enchil came to replace Dr Bannerman in Accra around April 1961. There was a prevailing rumour at the time that after an unspecified period, Dr Armar would be transferred back to Accra to head the department. Dr Bentsi-Enchil's alleged response was that he had not come to Accra to warm the seat for anyone to return to occupy. The department was ushered into a new phase. Recruitment of expatriate specialist doctors in all the major specialities had begun in full swing. They were mostly Indians, Bengalis from Calcutta with the British Specialist qualifications of FRCS, MRCP and MRCOG. Dr Tara Ghosh joined the OB/GY Department after a stint at Adeoye Hospital in Ibadan, Nigeria. Dr Medine, a Canadian, also came to join the OB/GY Department. Kwame Nkrumah had been in a political relationship with President Tito of Yugoslavia, an upshot of this, Dr Jokic, a Yugoslavian Gynaecologist, made his entry on to the Ghanaian scene. Heavy in build and an extrovert, he joined the department as a specialist. The Israelis under Golda-Meir, their female Prime Minister, were also making a strong impact in Ghana. An Israeli team which included an outstanding Paediatrician and a very skilled Surgeon joined the Korle Bu staff. The Ghana Black Star Shipping Line benefited greatly from its Israeli association. The Israelis assisted in the establishment of a viable poultry farming industry in the country.

With the new staffing, the OB/GY Department was transformed in a way. Dr Kofi Newman came from Ho as an MO to join the department in preparation for his return to Britain to specialize. Candidates for post-graduate courses on scholarship were vetted and the scholarship award went to the more senior candidates. Sir Dugald Baird had reserved a Supernumerary Registrar post for me commencing in 1961.

Prof. Bentsi-Enchill. Foundation Prof. of OB/GY, Korle-Bu Teaching Hospital

I applied for a scholarship to avail myself for the Aberdeen post but failed to obtain one. I felt greatly disappointed at this outcome, but bore it stoically and left matters to Destiny.

I was assigned to Dr Ghosh as his MO. He granted me full responsibility and I functioned as a Registrar in the British system. Dr Ghosh taught me a lot and this boosted my confidence greatly. My unaccompanied luggage, including my books, had arrived on the Elder Dempster lines. The books included Ian Donald's Practical Obstetrics Problems and Dugald Baird's Combined Textbook of Obstetrics and Gynaecology. I mastered the contents of these books, especially the former. The workload was mainly Obstetrics; the Gynaecological cases were relatively few. The operative work was almost entirely Caesarean section and laparotomy for ectopic pregnancy.

Until then, all the Ghanaian doctors had been trained in Britain; Ibadan Medical School was the only one of its kind in British West Africa. The Ibadan School and a similar one in Kingston, Jamaica were under the tutelage of London University. Ghana quite rightly felt that it was now time to have its own medical school. Events began to move at a fast pace and with interesting drama; the alumni of Korle Bu Medical School perhaps may be interested in its unfolding. Ghana decided to have a medical school patterned on the Ibadan and Kingston model under the tutelage of London University. Professor Morgan of Khartoum Medical School in Sudan was appointed the Dean of the envisaged school. Even though a dean had been appointed, quiet negotiations were going on between the USA and Kwame Nkrumah's government. President J. F. Kennedy had only a couple of months earlier given approval for the Volta River Project. The USA was aware of the fact that a medical school was needed in Accra and that Britain (London University) was involved in its establishment. The USA decided to outbid the British influence in this sector. The USA therefore offered to build a health-care complex to include a medical school, school of nursing and a school of pharmacy for the people of Ghana. The offer was irresistible and the Ghana government therefore accepted it. A site for the complex was chosen on the Accra-Legon road and would be associated with the University of Philadelphia in the USA. Professor Morgan, unaware of these developments, flew to Accra to inspect and acquaint himself with the Korle Bu setup. On arrival, he learnt with shock that there was no longer a job awaiting him in Accra. He flew back the same day on the same plane to Sudan. The story was that, luckily for him, he had not submitted a letter of resignation from his chair in Khartoum before his brief visit to Ghana. This way, he returned to his post. Following the acceptance of the American offer, a number of Ghanaian doctors were selected to go to Philadelphia University to pursue post-graduate studies with the view to returning to teach in the Medical School. Dr Blukoo-Allotey was selected for Pharmacology, Harold Philips for Physiology and Teddy Christian for Pathology.

The level of USA commitment to Ghana was high, and a little episode merits recalling for my readers. A carrier of the USA Navy made a friendly call at a Ghana port. There was a helicopter on the carrier; hitherto, no helicopter had flown and landed in Ghana. In demonstrating a spirit of friendship, the helicopter was to be landed at Korle Bu on a football playing pitch. (The football pitch is now the site of the Maternity Block.) Several Accra dignitaries, including the Ga Mantse (the traditional chief of the Ga people), were invited and were part of the large crowd that gathered to await the arrival and landing of the helicopter. The helicopter flew in to land but in the process created a sandy storm of such magnitude that the crowd, including the Ga Mantse had to flee the ground. Visibility was reduced to almost zero. It took quite some time for the dust to settle. It was an embarrassing episode for the Americans on a goodwill mission. The helicopter take-off was no less stormy, but only a few of the original crowd stayed on to have another dose of a sandy dust bath.

All was now set for an American model medical school, but not quite yet. Professor Gilman, the South African, who was a special adviser to Kwame Nkrumah on medical affairs, went to see Nkrumah to offer some advice. He told him that he had a warning for him. What was the warning? The Americans' offer to build the health-care complex was aimed at gaining a strong foothold in Ghana. The next step would be to see the overthrow of his regime. Nkrumah was reported to have said 'Is that so? Thank you very much for your warning and advice'. Nkrumah then summoned the American representatives and told them that he was rejecting the offer to build the healthcare complex. He no longer wanted the Americans around. Next, he summoned Dr Charles Easmon, (DMS and Head of Surgery Dept.) to his office at the Flagstaff House. He told Dr Easmon that he had rejected the American offer to build the healthcare complex. He went on to tell him that we, the Ghanaians, would build the medical school by ourselves. "I therefore appoint you to be the Dean. You go ahead and start the medical school in Korle Bu." Dr Easmon was reported to have replied that he had never taught in a medical school before and that he was basically a clinical surgeon and with the added administrative duties as DMS. Nkrumah reportedly countered that since he had himself been taught by clinicians in medical school, he should also be able to teach medical students. This was a formidable and incisive retort. Dr Easmon had trained at Edinburgh University in Scotland. He very wisely went to Scotland to seek advice from his quondam colleagues and mates. Thus began the genesis of the medical school. I was an MO in Korle Bu at the time and therefore I had a ringside view of the events. The rest is history. The story of the medical school would undoubtedly have been different, but for the intervention by Prof. Gilman.

Following his influence on the medical school history, Prof. Gilman tried to extend it in other ways. It was his view that there was no need to send Ghanaian doctors to pursue specialist post-graduate training abroad, and that they should do this locally in Ghana. He was mistaken in this view and thankfully no heed was paid to his advice in this direction; wiser opinions prevailed. By June, Kofi Newman had left Ghana for Scotland for his MRCOG course, soon to be followed by Ampofo for the same course. I received my marching orders in June 1961 to go to Kumasi Central Hospital on transfer.

I was in a resigned mood for leaving Accra. Not long before my departure from Accra, I received a telephone call from Dr Jasper Tamakloe in Sunyani. He had been a year my senior and was MO in charge of Sunyani hospital. He had been informed by Dr Djoleto, Regional MO for Ashanti and Brong Ahafo Regions, but based in Kumasi, that I was coming from Accra to join him in Sunyani. Dr Tamakloe was anxious and desperate for an MO to join him and wanted to know how soon I was leaving Accra for Sunyani? I was surprised and shocked to receive this news. The plan by Dr Djoleto was that on my arrival in Kumasi from Accra, I would be asked to proceed straight on to Sunyani, without disembarking in Kumasi. The decision to transfer me to Kumasi had been taken by Dr F. T. Sai, the Deputy DMS. I therefore went straight to see him about the news of my planned transfer to Sunyani. He was not privy to Dr Djoleto's plan to send me to Sunyani, and was genuinely furious about it. This was to be my second transfer in eight months, and I naturally protested at being a victim of "transferitis". Some of my colleagues in Korle Bu had had no transfers at all. Dr Sai assured me that my transfer decision to Kumasi would stand unaltered; on no account should I be sent to Sunyani. Dr Djoleto was informed about this. Accommodation in Kumasi should be arranged for me and the keys were to be handed to me on my arrival from Accra. I was pleased and grateful to Dr Sai, especially the firm manner in which he handled my case. He went on to say that if he had known that I was going to be a victim of "transferitis", he would not have initiated my transfer from Accra at all. My luck was serendipity of the telephone call from Jasper. It was all part of Destiny with Fate.

MEDICAL OFFICER IN KUMASI

I arrived in Kumasi, the Garden City by fame in June 1961. The tree-lined streets and the hills of the city provided a marked contrast to Accra. I was handed the keys to my apartment in the maisonette flats. The building was relatively new, and the rooms were in good condition. Philip again, and for the third time in eight months, unpacked my few bachelor possessions from the truck that had been provided for my transportation; he again set up my new home. The apartment consisted of a large ground floor living room with an adjoining dining room section and kitchen; a commodious bedroom with an ensuite bathroom and the toilet was on the first floor. There was a boy's quarters for Philip.

I instantly found Kumasi an attractive and welcoming location. Kumasi Central Hospital, the Ashanti Regional Hospital, a five hundred-bed hospital, built not long ago, architecturally attractive, was the most modern in West Africa. The drive-in was beautifully designed and attractively landscaped with the greenery for which Kumasi was famous. The hospital building comprised the following: an extensive ground-floor area with the OPD (Outpatient Department) with several Consulting rooms, Casualty unit (ER) and Pharmacy. The Administrative offices, Dental and Ophthalmology units, X-Ray Department, Pathology department, Doctors' lounge, the operating theatre complex unit were all sited on the first floor. Four towering multi-storey blocks constituted the wards. A number of single storey blocks behind the main building provided the location for the mortuary and the hospital workshop. Adjoining the hospital building was the School of Nursing and Midwifery with the nurses' accommodation units.

I reported for duties and to the Hospital Medical Superintendent, Dr Rail. Dr Rail was a Physician Specialist, a Caucasian, from Southern

Rhodesia (now Zimbabwe). An affable and easily approachable man, he was a seasoned coaster and a keen golfer. He was assisted in the administrative duties by the Hospital Secretary, Mr Tackey. The Hospital Matron was Miss Ward-Brew. The medical staff was cosmopolitan in composition. There was a Russian team of three doctors as follows: Dr Yasnov (Surgeon), Dr Parafinik (Physician Specialist), and a female, Dr Zotikova (Gynaecologist). An Israeli team of two doctors comprised a surgeon (Dr Peer) and a Paediatrician, whose name I cannot now recall. An Italian Surgeon, Dr Rovis and Dr Yogaratnam (a Sri Lankan), an Orthopaedic surgeon were in the Surgical unit, which was headed by Dr Evans-Anfom, the Ghanaian. Reference has already been made to Dr S.C. Bose, the Indian Gynaecologist who attended to the First Lady. An eminent and very knowledgeable Canadian Physician Specialist, Dr French, headed the Department of Medicine. He had apparently joined the staff in preparation for taking up the foundation chair in Medicine at Korle Bu when the Medical School was envisaged to come under the tutelage of London University. When this original plan was axed, Dr French left Ghana soon after. He had previously turned down a very attractive post in one of the oil-rich Middle-East countries. There were two Bengali Physicians with MRCP, who held the Special Grade Medical Officer posts in the Medical Department. They were Dr Das Gupta and Dr Thakurta. The MOs at the time included the following doctors: Selby, Emmanuel Asare, Owusu Ansah, Joy Nicholas, Blankson Heyman, Asafo Adjei, Gabriel Kemavor and C. Marbel (all Ghanaians); Photiades (Greek), De Vries (Dutch lady) Summasundram (Sri Lankan) and an African-American. The latter was a strange loner, who resented social intercourse of any kind with any non–African colleagues, particularly Caucasians. Indeed, he once attempted to chastise me for engaging a Caucasian colleague in a convivial conversation in the doctors' lounge. This of course was not my style, nor part of my background in racial terms, having had such an international mixture of races in teachers and colleagues from my secondary school days. People were just people to me, some you got on with, some you did not, but not because of race or colour.

The Department of Surgery was headed by Dr Evans-Anfom. The following headed other units: Dr Peer, Dr Rovis, Dr Yasnov and Dr Yogaratnam. Dr French headed the Department of Medicine and one of the two units; the second unit was headed by Dr Parafinik, a Russian. Dr Armar, recently transferred from Accra, headed the Department of OB/GY; he headed a unit; the two other units were each headed by Dr SC Bose and Dr Zotikova (the Russian lady), all Specialists. An Israeli Paediatrician Specialist was the only doctor in that department. Dr Teddy Christian was the Specialist Pathologist. Dr Marbel worked as an MO in the Pathology Department in preparation for returning to Britain to specialize in that field. There was also a Specialist Ophthalmologist, an Indian, whose name I cannot recall.

In my view, the hospital was adequately staffed. Some of the Specialists were excellent; very sadly though, some were not. We all mixed freely in the lounge during the morning coffee break, held discussions on various topics in a friendly and collegial atmosphere. The Russian doctors did not mix at all and abstained from all discussions; this was not because of any linguistic limitation. They were apparently following instruction from their embassy not to socialize with anyone and not to accept any invitations for dinners, parties, etc.; an imposition of a monastic lifestyle.

Dr Rail, the Medical Superintendent, assigned me to the school children out-patients' department (OPD). It was my responsibility to see all the school children who complained of illness. I was assisted by a nurse who served a dual role as an interpreter since I could not speak the local language, Twi. The complaints were of a general medical nature and I had to make a quick diagnosis and prescribe the necessary treatment/ medication. It was a large and busy clinic and so I had to work fast. I devised my modus operandi. I consulted my books on Tropical Medicine, drew up a list of ailments and their treatments. This proved extremely useful. A few months later, I was transferred to the Department of Surgery and replaced by Dr Kormey. He had just arrived from Britain as a novice MO, with no experience nor exposure to children's complaints in the tropical setting. I made a copy of my protocol and presented it to him. He was extremely grateful and felt a great sense of relief. No matter how brilliant or well-trained, the situation was the same for all those arriving from Europe and being plunged into an outpatient setting. I gained some experience during my stint at the OPD. I also did turns at the ER (Casualty Dept.) on a rotational basis during the weekends. It entailed some minor surgery of suturing fresh cuts, admitting emergency surgical, medical, paediatric and gynaecological cases. Pregnant women in labour were sent straight to the labour ward. I also attended the grand medical ward round when Dr French was doing his turn. He was a very knowledgeable and impressive physician. His ward rounds were the best I had ever attended; I learnt a lot from him. Dr Parafinik, in marked contrast, had a poor knowledge of Medicine; almost any complaint was diagnosed as being caused by tuberculosis, which was not at all rampant. MOs were reluctant to be assigned to his unit because there was nothing to learn from him. After my transfer to the Surgical Department, I could no longer attend Dr French's grand ward round because of its clash with surgical duties, a sad and regrettable miss.

On the social front, I was experiencing a pleasant and entertaining lifestyle. Several of my colleagues from the UCGC were on the staff of Kwame Nkrumah University of Science and Technology (KNUST). The campus was beautifully landscaped, with well maintained green lawns; it compared favourably with any campus I had seen abroad. The Vice-Chancellor, Mr R. P. Baffour, deservedly earned a reputation as a great leader and an administrator, sui generis. The Registrar was Mr Ulzen, a former colleague from UCGC. Austin Tetteh was on the staff as a planner in the Faculty of Architecture; so was John Owusu Addo (architect); they were to remain life-long friends. Thomas Sekyi, my fellow BSc graduate from UCGC, was teaching at Opoku Ware Secondary School, the first Ghanaian science graduate teacher in that famous school. Steven Gadegbeku and Mr Adoglah of Survey Department and British Petroleum (BP) respectively, both UCGC colleagues, were based in Kumasi. Teddy Christian, Pathologist and an old Achimotan and a friend was in a serious courtship with Miss Dorothy Hutton-Mills, a nursing sister. We socialized together a lot. Teddy and Dorothy very much enjoyed the culinary offerings of akpledze, okro and garden egg stew with banku, in which Philip, my cook/ steward excelled.

Later in the year, Dr Christian Adomakoh returned home from Aberdeen. He was posted to Kumasi, a most welcome posting for us – we renewed our association and friendship. Chris had travelled home on an Elder Dempster liner. On board the ship and also returning home after studies in Britain was Miss Victoria Bright-Davies, an attractive lady.

A courtship which commenced on board continued after landing. I met Vic for the first time when she paid a brief visit to Kumasi. I instantly knew that Chris had met his life partner; and so it proved to be.

Harold Philips had introduced me to Mr J. A. Addison, who was a very successful businessman in Kumasi. What started as a casual acquaintanceship grew, flourished and blossomed into a close friendship. Years my senior, he treated me as a younger sibling.

My social and sporting life was fulsome. I joined the Maxwell Tennis Club and played tennis regularly. The leading players at the time were Messrs Dedeji, Awuah and Kofi Pobee. Kofi Pobee, a lawyer, had been my contemporary at UCGC with his brother, the physician.

On the football front, Asante Kotoko was in a raging rivalry with Accra Hearts of Oak. I never missed their encounters at the Kumasi Sports Stadium. The Ghana Black Stars continued to twinkle and forge a reputation for Ghana under Ohene Djan. It was about this time that they played host to Spain's Real Madrid in Accra. Although I did not watch the match, I listened to the radio commentary. The formidable and famous Real Madrid fielded Alfredo di Stefano, Puskas and Gento in their team with other outstanding and legendary names. It was a combative encounter, and the Black Stars stood up toe–to-toe with the visitors. A Real player received a yellow card. The Black Stars led 1-0, 2-1, 3 -2 and finally drew at 3-3.

On the political front, there was great uneasiness. The Preventive Detention Act (PDA) was not only divisive but made life and free communication unsafe. Any personal score could be settled by reporting someone as anti-CPP without any questions being asked.

The fear of PDA greatly influenced the assessment of the Russian doctors who were sent to Kumasi. Dr Parafinik could not, in my view, pass as a low grade MO because of his poor knowledge of Medicine. Dr Yasnov, the surgeon, was reportedly heading for a chair in Surgery before his posting to Ghana. Dr Rail assigned me to Dr Yasnov's unit despite my protest. Dr Rail argued that an MO had to be assigned to Dr Yasnov, and the axe fell on me.

Although I did not work in the Maternity Department, reports emanating from there about Dr Zotikova were very disturbing. She struggled, it was alleged, to perform a Lower Segment Caesarean Section (LSCS). It could take her two and a half hours (as an MO in

Korle Bu, I could perform it in half an hour). She often preferred to perform a classical C-section which was indicated in only rare cases; which took her an equally long time to perform. She struggled to operate on cases of ectopic pregnancy. These cases constituted the bread and butter of surgery in OB/GY. Her performance could be attributed to incompetence and lack of experience. Unfortunately, and very sadly, some of her performances were of a serious and criminal nature. It was reported that when she was confronted with a case of obstructed labour with the cervix fully dilated and a live foetus, instead of performing a LSCS, she would perform a craniotomy by perforating the live baby's head and extracting the baby. Dr De Vries, her Dutch female MO, would leave the theatre, go outside and cry rather than witness the criminal procedure. Because she was a Russian, and regarded untouchable and with the fear of PDA, there was a reluctance to blow the whistle. I was not working in the OB/GY Department and therefore did not personally witness any of the reported cases mentioned above., but I had no reason to doubt their authenticity. Someone eventually blew the whistle. Suddenly, over one weekend, the three Russian Specialists, such was their designation, were quietly sent back home to Russia. Whoever was the whistle-blower, it brought to an end the grotesque medical malfeasance committed in Kumasi Central Hospital in 1961/62. God listened and responded to our prayers.

Following my move to the surgery department I was assigned to Dr Yasnov as already stated. Dr Owusu Ansah was assigned to Evans-Anfom, Selby to Rovis, and Asare to Peer. Yogaratman (orthopaedics) had no MO. Dr Photiades acted in a senior registrar role to Dr Evans Anfom. I soon realized that I was not learning much from Dr Yasnov. While on call with him, on a few occasions, I would admit patients with acute retention of usually the result of benign enlargement of the prostate. Dr Yasnov's management was to deflate the bladder by suprapubic aspiration, then send the patient home without any follow-up for a definitive treatment of the enlarged prostate. They would return with the problem at a later date and luckily face a different team who would render definitive treatment. Dr Yasnov never performed a prostatectomy. I envied Dr Asare a lot because Dr Peer taught him to perform a wide range of surgical operations. Dr Asare was also skilled with his hands, and it was my view that he had the potential to become a great surgeon in the future.

When the Russians were sent back home, I had another hiccup. An MO was needed in Wenchi in Brong Ahafo Region. Dr Rail summoned me to his office and gave me my marching orders to go to Wenchi. I pointed out to him that Kumasi was my third posting in less than a year since my return from Britain. There were some other MOs, without mentioning names, with a similar return duration who had had never been transferred. Enough was enough. My bachelorhood status was no reason for exploitation for "transferitis" (my own word, or worse transferoma, the malignant form). Res ipsa loquitor. There the matter rested. Dr Selby was dispatched to Wenchi, the home town of Dr Busia, the politician. It is possible, although I cannot vouch for this, that this early meeting laid the foundation stone of the close association some years later between the two gentlemen.

Now and again in the course of human affairs, fortune and fate play a significant role. After the dispatch of Dr Yasnov back home to Russia, Dr Asare was moved and paired with Dr Yogaratman, and I was in turn moved to join Dr Peer. Dr Peer was one of the very experienced Specialists sent from Israel by Golda Meir, their Prime Minister. Middle-aged, short in stature, he was always attired in white shorts and shirt. He and his wife quickly took great interest, almost parental, in my welfare. If I had a flu or felt unwell, Dr Peer would offer to take all my calls himself if our team was on duty. He would send me home to bed and ask his wife to prepare a light meal or some soup for me. Not long after joining his unit, an Indian doctor on contract and preparing for his FRCS examination requested to be assigned to him. Dr Peer refused bluntly, stating that he had come to Ghana to train Ghanaians, and not Indian doctors.

In the sensitive politico-medical atmosphere prevailing at the time, it was dangerous to express any view against the ruling CPP government. He advised me on how to comport myself without endangering my future. I was no admirer of the ruling party, but I kept my views to myself. I sought no martyrdom, but equally despised those who sang the praises of the CPP.

General anaesthesia for surgical operations was administered by specially trained Nurse-anaesthetists. The most senior and experienced of these was Mr Kusi; grey-haired, cool and very skilled, he compared very favourably with the doctor anaesthetists I had previously encountered.

Dr Peer taught me basic operative surgery from A to Z: holding the scalpel for a stab incision, peritoneal drainage and toileting, resection and anastomosis of small intestines, distortion of volvulus, retropubic prostatectomy, bur-holing of the skull and drainage of epidural blood and several other procedures. These were added to my modest and meagre repertoire of obstetric operations.

One of my day-case lists was the passing of bougies for the dilatation of male urethral strictures resulting as a late complication of gonococcal infection; urethral stricture was common at the time. The procedure was performed under a short general anaesthesia, using Pentothal. It required an exercise of great caution to avoid the creation of false iatrogenic passages.

Dr Photiades developed an interest in electro-anaesthesia, a form of anaesthesia hitherto unknown in Ghana in 1962. The technique consisted of connecting an electrical device to both parietal parts of the scalp of the patient. When the electrical device was switched on at the appropriate voltage and amperage, the patient passed through a brief period of jerky convulsion into a state of unconsciousness. Surgical procedures could then be carried out as under a general anaesthesia. It was decided to carry out a trial programme with this novel form of anaesthesia in Kumasi Central Hospital, starting with the dilatation of urethral strictures. It was performed by me on about 20 patients successfully. The patients all woke up soon after the device was switched off. There were neither complications nor sequela. Dr Anfom and other surgeons carried out other procedures under eletro-anaesthesia without any complications in 1962.

Drs Anfom and Photiades went to Korle Bu to present the series of cases done under electro-anaesthesia in Kumasi without any complications or sequelae. It received front page press coverage and Kumasi Central Hospital was lauded.

Since no complications followed any of the cases, it was decided to move on to more serious cases. A female patient with typhoid intestinal perforations was admitted under Dr Peer. Her condition, with severe peritonitis, was rather poor. Dr Peer assisted me in performing the laparotomy in the standard way. I had performed several such cases before under conventional general anaesthesia. This patient was operated on under electro-anaesthesia. On the completion of the operation, the electro-anaesthesia was switched off but the patient did not resume consciousness as expected. She died about an hour after the completion of the operation. We attributed the cause of her death to the fact that her condition was rather poor before the commencement of surgery and not to the electro-anaesthesia. Dr Peer assigned to me a case of enlarged prostate in a healthy man for my first attempt, with his assistance, at the retro pubic prostatectomy. It was the more difficult, but in his view better than the transvesical approach. Dr Peer guided me step by step through the operation from the beginning to a successful end. I felt elated and was filled with a sense of achievement nearing the end of the operation. The operation was being carried out under electro-anaesthesia. Dr Peer left me alone as I started closing the incision. As I was tying knots on bleeding small vessels, I noticed that the bleeding had suddenly stopped spontaneously. I alerted Drs Peer and Photiades immediately. The patient had developed cardiac arrest, and attempts at resuscitation by external cardiac massage and the administration of oxygen failed to revive him; he was declared dead on the operating table. It was a devastating outcome following a technically successful prostatectomy. The only attributable cause was the electro-anaesthesia. With two mortalities in this novel electro-anaesthesia, it was decided to discontinue this form of anaesthesia. Sadly though, I had to bear the burden of being the surgeon in the two deaths.

I spent about nine months in the department of surgery of which seven were under the tutelage of Dr Peer. He instilled in me confidence in surgical operation for which I am forever grateful. Not many doctors are granted a surgical mentor with the unique character, experience and devotion of Dr Peer.

In June 1962, I was transferred to the Department of Medicine. My work entailed the clerking and management of inpatients. I carried out procedures such as lumber puncture, setting up difficult IV lines which the nurses could not handle, bone marrow aspiration for laboratory investigations, paracentesis abdominis and thoracis for the drainage of fluid. I was exposed to a wide range of clinical medical cases. I relished the exposure and experience I gained from them. As a medical student, Medicine had been my first love and favourite subject. I was, however, still hoping to be awarded a scholarship to return to Aberdeen to pursue my career in OB/GY.

The political climate in Ghana was undergoing a change at this time. Mr Agbeli Gbedemah, second in command to Kwame Nkrumah for a long time, a shrewd and highly respected minister of finance, found it necessary to leave Kwame Nkrumah and the CPP. It was a momentous and unprecedented event. The opposition party was driven underground; sycophancy within the party was rife to an unpleasant degree. To illustrate this point, I recall a well-known politician in the higher realm of the CPP in a sycophantic pronouncement saying that he would like Kwame Nkrumah to spit into his mouth so that he could also mimic his oratorical power. I decline from naming this Ga politician in deference to his family. Such was the depth of sycophancy and infighting in the CPP. In Korle-Bu Hospital, one of the most feared and powerful persons was the man who operated the simple lift; he was a prominent member of the Trades Union Congress (TUC). He had more clout and influence than the specialist doctors and as such was much feared. It reminds me of an observation that in the capital city of one of the great Western countries, the chauffeur in the Russian embassy was in fact the most powerful, not the ambassador, member of staff.

Queen Elizabeth and Prince Philip were scheduled to pay a state visit to Ghana in 1962. A few weeks before the visit, a bomb planted near Parliament House in Accra exploded. Although it caused no serious damage, such an event was unprecedented in Ghana. It threw serious doubt on the safety of the Queen's visit. There was political tension also in the country. Mr Duncan Sandys, the Commonwealth Secretary in Harold Macmillan's British cabinet, decided to visit Ghana to assess for himself the safety and wisdom of the Queen's visit. He came to Accra and was driven in a car along the route the Queen would be driven on her visit. Following this reconnaissance visit, the British government approved of the Queen's visit; apparently, the Queen herself insisted on it and her wish prevailed. The Queen and Prince Philip duly arrived in Accra for the State visit. The Royals paid two separate one-day visits to Kumasi and Sekondi/ Takoradi. The visits received wide national and international media coverage, most prominently by the BBC.

I had a ringside view of her visits to Kumasi and Sekondi. The Queen and the Duke were driven through the principal streets of Kumasi to the Central Hospital amidst cheering and welcoming crowds.

An incident occurred in the hospital which demands chronicling. The hospital programme commenced with a visit to the wards by the Queen, Prince Philip and Kwame Nkrumah with the accompanying retinue. The paediatric ward was one of the wards to be visited. Anthony Appiah, then about eight years old, was an inpatient in the paediatric ward. Anthony was the son of the legendary politician, Joe Appiah, and Peggy Appiah. Joe, an Ashanti royal, was then a political prisoner under Nkrumah's PDA. Peggy was the daughter of Sir Stafford Cripps, the Chancellor of the Exchequer in Clement Attlee's British cabinet. Two days before the Queen's visit Anthony was admitted to the ward for some investigations for a non-acute condition. Mounted on Anthony's bedside table was a photograph of his father. During the inspection tour of the ward, the Queen and Kwame Nkrumah walked down the aisle on the right side while Prince Philip walked on the left side. Anthony's bed was on the left side just by the aisle. When Prince Philip reached Anthony's bed, he stopped and exchanged some pleasantries with him. The Prince saw the framed photograph of Joe, and enquired of him from his son, he then asked Anthony to extend his regards to him. The international group of cameramen covering the royal visit did not miss the opportunity to take several pictures at this juncture. I was in the ward and witnessed the whole incident. The news hit the front pages of the British papers the following day. It created a great political thunderstorm and embarrassment for Kwame Nkrumah worldwide. It highlighted Nkrumah's PDA and the internal political tension. The economy was in a sharp decline. Two days after the visit, when I went to see Dr Rail in his office, he showed me some copies of the British press with their reports on Anthony, the Prince and Joe Appiah. It was reported to have been a setup to embarrass Kwame Nkrumah with his PDA regime; to me this sounded credible. Dr Rail, in an agitated mood strongly denied that he was involved in any setup and indeed threatened a lawsuit against the press. It was obvious and predictable that Nkrumah would dismiss him from the service. Dr Rail was initially transferred to Sekondi and not long after dismissed from the government service.

My second ring-side view of the royal visit was in Sekondi/ Takoradi. Mr Eric Adjorlolo, a good friend of mine who was then the news editor of Ghana Broadcasting Services (GBS), extended an invitation to me to join his press crew in covering the royal visit to Sekondi/Takoradi. It was an appealing and irresistible offer. I travelled from Kumasi to Accra to join the crew. We left Accra for Sekondi very early in the morning of the day so that we would be at the airport long before the arrival of the Queen's flight from Accra. At the Takoradi airport, Eric indicated to me to join a small group of about five people at the reception counter. Not long after, Kwame Nkrumah with a small retinue, including Kojo Botsio, arrived in the reception room. Nkrumah stood about six feet away from me and then moved to the front of the building to await the arrival of the Queen's flight. That was the closest I ever got to him. As I stood leaning on the reception counter, two gentlemen, one in a cloth, and the other wearing a suit, came and stood on either side of me. They obviously did not know who I was and were puzzled. Next, the one in cloth said to me in English: "Short men do not die." Looking puzzled, I responded saying; "I beg your pardon." The two gentlemen exchanged a puzzled look on their faces and then left me alone. The men were obviously security personnel who thought that I was one of their numbers who would be privy to their password for that occasion. They may well have concluded that I was a security man from Britain involved with the royals. The Queen's plane arrived and the royals were met and welcomed by Kwame Nkrumah on the tarmac. They were driven through the principal streets of Sekondi and Takoradi with cheering crowds to Gyandu Park for a durbar. The durbar, grand in style with chiefs from the Western and Central Regions, was held under a scorching sun. I was positioned near the BBC correspondent who was recording a live broadcast. To my great surprise, I saw and met a Scottish lady, Gwen, in the crowd, not far from me. She had attended the social functions at the British Council frequently during my student days in Aberdeen. She was a friend of a Ghanaian Engineering student. She had come to Ghana and was then teaching in a secondary school in Sekondi. Thus, I ended my involvement with the Queen's state visit to Ghana in 1962 with an unsolicited ring-side view.

The royal visit made no difference to the Nkrumah regime. The economy continued to plummet; the cedi was weak and inflation was high. Kwame Nkrumah sought economic advice from Mr Kaldor, the famous Hungarian economist at the London School of Economics and Political Science (LSE). Other developing countries had sought advice from this guru, but the story was that in applying his recommendations, their economy in fact deteriorated further! Bribery and corruption were rife. Kwame Nkrumah (aka Osagyefo) was feared and held in awe. Because he was President-for-life, societies and associations which by their constitution would have their most senior officers addressed as president avoided this term, using the rather inappropriate term of Chairman. This of course bred resentment.

The Kulungugu bomb incident occurred about this time. Nkrumah travelled by road to visit Northern Ghana. In the course of the journey, a massive bomb which had been planted at the roadside exploded. The car in which Nkrumah was travelling was reportedly blown off the road, but there did not appear to have been any serious injuries to anyone. The news was conveyed early to the Medical Superintendent of Kumasi Central Hospital as an alert. Dr Vanderpuje, a tall bespectacled figure and a chain smoker, played the party game of CPP shamelessly. He was instructed to alert the medical staff in readiness for any casualties. He told me to alert Dr Christian, the Pathologist, to have enough blood in the blood bank in readiness. Dr Christian and I had a most hilarious discussion on the blood group, the nature of which I am not narrating. In the event, we did not receive any casualties in Kumasi. The general public reaction to the incident was muted and concealed as revealed in the often-quoted comment by an Accra market-woman on hearing of the bombing attempt on Nkrumah. An English rendering of her comment in the Ga language goes as follows: 'Is he dead or?' This portrayed the prevailing political atmosphere.

Most institutions and departments were obliged to set up 'study groups' to study and discuss Kwame Nkrumah's political philosophy; political activists played prominent roles in the study groups. I did not join the hospital study group. Soon after my return from Britain, my father obtained a CPP registration card in Hohoe in my name without my knowledge or consent and gave it to me. Although my father was not politically active, he did this to protect and 'immunize' me; I never had to use it for any purpose.

The entire hospital staff was summoned one afternoon to attend a meeting in the large Nurses' hall. The Regional Minister was scheduled to address the meeting, and this was to be followed by a political discussion. I decided not to attend the meeting, faking an excuse of being on duty in surgery. On knowing of my intention, Dr Peer, my Israeli mentor and boss, summoned me to his office. He counselled me in a fatherly manner and advised me to attend the meeting. My failure to attend could adversely affect my future, more so since I was planning to return to Britain for a postgraduate course in OB/GY. I obliged and went to the meeting venue; the hall was fully packed. As the minister with his retinue entered the hall, everyone stood up until the minister and Dr Vanderpuje, chairman for the meeting, were seated on the dais. We were then asked to stand up and recite an oath, with our hands held up. This was all strange and bizarre to me. A couple of my fellow MOs were familiar with this and participated in reciting the oath. After the address by the minister and following his departure, Dr Vanderpuje took over the centre stage as Chairman of the study group discussion. He said that all those on duty should return to their various stations. No one was obliged to stay on for the discussions, but, he added darkly, "we will find out about anyone who falsely claims to be on duty". I reflected on what Dr Peer had told and counselled me about. I was not seeking martyrdom. I stayed on, listened to the discussions, and watched Dr Vanderpuje as he presided, smoking one cigarette after another on a long cigarette holder, then fashionable, endlessly.

Professor Gilman remained a dominant figure in health affairs in the country. He planned and organized a training course in Accra for MOs in Public Health. The course would run for three months. The following doctors were selected to participate in the course: Chris Adomako, Jacob Blukoo Allotey, De Heer, and Hutton-Mills. During this course, which included the Easter month of March in 1962, another unfortunate incident occurred. Chris decided to take advantage of the long Easter holidays to visit his mother in the Ashanti Region. I was expecting him in Kumasi as his first port of call. On Good Friday, I received a distressed telephone call from Miss Victoria Bright-Davies, his girlfriend in Accra. She reported to me that Chris had been involved in a serious car accident near the town of Suhum on his way to Kumasi. The Mercedes car he was driving had overturned and was a write-off. Chris sustained severe cuts on his hand and had been admitted to the Suhum District Hospital. This was distressing news for me, coming exactly a year after the Engman episode. I prayed for him and awaited news of a reassuring nature. To my great relief there was no report of any other serious injury. Chris was soon transferred to 37 Military hospital for definitive and appropriate surgery on his hand. He recovered fully without any sequelae. Such were the events of both Easters on my return home to Ghana.

It was now time for some good news. First, I received a letter from the Ministry of Health offering me a three-year scholarship to return to Britain to study and obtain the MRCOG qualification. It was the joyous news for which I had been praying and waiting quite a long time. I wrote to Dr Arnold Klopper in Aberdeen to inform him about my returning to the UK for the MRCOG course.

The second piece of good news was that the wedding bells for Chris and Vic began to ring, and again, I was given the honour of playing the role of best man; for the third time in 18 months. The wedding was held in Accra at the Anglican Holy Trinity Cathedral.

The bachelor fraternity was shrinking in size. Jake Blukoo-Allotey, my 'paddyman', a very eligible gentleman on the Accra scene, was in a serious courtship with Miss Cynthia Chinery, a very pretty young lady. I remained to be the lonely, single, unattached bachelor. Still there was no pressure on me from my relatives and well-wishers.

Chris had expressed an interest in Psychiatry; as a result, he was transferred to the Accra Psychiatry Hospital after the Gilman course in Public Health. He was soon after offered a scholarship to return to study and obtain the appropriate specialist qualification in Psychiatry. Similarly, Jake Blukoo-Allotey was awarded a scholarship to go to Philadelphia in the USA to study Pharmacology and return to teach it in the infant medical school. Dr Harold Philips was a recipient of a similar scholarship in Physiology.

Bestman at the wedding of Chris & Vic (1962)

Drs Hugh Lassey and C R Neequaye were also offered scholarships to go to Britain for the MRCOG course, just like I was. Placement in recognized jobs in Britain, mandatory before sitting for the examination, was a hurdle both Lassey and Chris had to overcome. Fortunately for me, I had Sir Dugald Baird and Dr Arnold Klopper as my mentors to look after that. In due course I received a letter from Dr Klopper in Aberdeen. I was informed that the single supernumerary position which was passed on to Dr Akinkugbe in the previous year had continued to be filled by him, a Nigerian alumnus, two years my senior in Aberdeen. Since there was no longer a vacancy in Aberdeen, Sir Dugald arranged for me to go to Dr Tennent's unit in Bellshill, Scotland. (Dr Tennent, brother of Lady Baird, hailed from the famous brewery family.) I was to take up a position as a supernumerary Registrar. I was satisfied with the arrangements which were made for me, although somewhat disappointed by my missing out on Aberdeen, my quondam second home. Recognized posts were not easy to obtain; the jobs were not only limited in number, but attracted applicants from Commonwealth countries in addition to the local British doctors. The competition was fierce. A couple of weeks later, I received another letter from Dr Klopper. In this letter, Dr Klopper stated that since it would take some time for the RCOG to grant recognition for the post I would be occupying in Bellshill, the situation would not favour my interest. In view of this, Sir Dugald made an alternative arrangement for me. Sir Dugald arranged for me to take up a substantive paid job in the NHS as a Senior House Officer (SHO) at Southern General Hospital in Dr Arthur Sutherland's Unit in Glasgow. I was free to go there any time starting from August 1962. It would run for 12 months (1st January to 31st December, 1963); anything I would do before then would count as a locum job. This was an excellent arrangement for me. I had been confirmed as a protégé of Sir Dugald. Dr Emmanuel Asare was earmarked to go to Australia or Britain to train in Surgery. Some other MOs received awards to go abroad for post-graduate courses. It was our time; opportunities and avenues were being opened for us to exploit.

I decided to leave for Britain as soon as possible because I did not want to risk taking any chances with a political upheaval. I went to Hohoe to bid my parents farewell. On my return journey, I passed through Agormanya to bid my uncle, Rev Apo, farewell as well. I was booked to travel by boat on an Elder Dempster liner, MV Accra, embarking from Takoradi. I decided to take along with me my car, the Opel Rekord. I bade farewell to my friends and colleagues. Dr Peer was delighted and felt very proud of me; he expressed great confidence in my future and offered an invitation to me to visit him anytime in the future. I obtained a testimonial from Dr Anfom in which he stated my nine months' surgical rotation in the surgical department; this would prove crucially important in the future.

On reflection and in retrospect, it was fortuitous that I had not been granted the scholarship in 1961, the previous year, for the supernumerary Registrar post in Aberdeen. The extra year which I spent in Kumasi inducted me into Tropical Medicine and General Surgery. It enabled me to gain a great amount of surgical skill and knowledge and boosted my confidence. The brief period in the medical ward was also priceless and an extra bonus; it buttressed my knowledge and experience in tropical internal medicine.

I drove my car to Takoradi accompanied by Philip, my cook/steward. I stayed overnight in the government guest house before my departure the following day. Chris Adomakoh and Jake Blukoo Allotey drove up from Accra to see me off. This trio friendship would remain life-long. Chris was booked to fly to Britain a few days later; this resulted in his arrival in Britain before me. Jake was also due to leave soon for the USA.

This was my first sea journey to Britain and it was a relaxed, pleasant and an enjoyable journey. The cuisine was excellent. On board were Dr Prempeh, Mrs Yaw Asirifie, and Mrs Fredua Mensah with a toddler and a baby. Dr Prempeh was going to study Public Health, and Mrs Asirifie was going to join her husband, then studying for the MRCP and DCH. The ship had a stopover at Las Palmas. After the experience of a stormy sail through the Bay of Biscay, we enjoyed a calm sail to the port of Liverpool. The train journey to London's Euston station completed my return journey to Britain. Chris was at the station to meet me; he took me to our hotel where we had a little reunion.

I still had about two to three weeks before commencing my SHO locum job in Glasgow. I met Dr Gabriel Kemavor and Abbew Jackson; the latter gave me a room in his flat in Fulham to stay in for the period I chose to stay in London. The Wimbledon tennis championships were over, and the football season had not yet started, but the Commonwealth Games were being held in Australia. The Ghanaian long jumper, Mike Ahey, in winning the gold medal, came fractionally close to breaking the very longstanding world record set by Jesse Owens. Starved as I had been of opera for two years, I quenched my thirst with attendances at Covent Garden and Sadler's Wells opera houses. After three weeks of disembarkation leave in London, I travelled by train to Glasgow to start my post-graduate course in OB/GY. A new chapter in my life was about to begin.

Chapter 6
POST-GRADUATE
RESIDENCE IN GLASGOW

Glasgow, the largest and most populous city in Scotland, is its industrial centre. Glasgow University is an acclaimed centre of learning and scholarship; legendary obstetricians had practised in its medical institutions. It is home to Glasgow Rangers and Celtic, the two famous football teams. During my Aberdeen student days, I had visited the city twice. My first visit was to go to watch the annual football match between Scotland and the 'auld enemy', England, while my second visit was to represent Aberdeen University in a tennis tournament against Glasgow University. I had now come in pursuit of the MRCOG.

Southern General Hospital (SGH) was the largest hospital in Scotland, and the second largest in Britain. It was located in the Govan district, the ship-building industrial area of the city. The obstetric wards were located at SGH campus and the gynaecological wards at David Elder Infirmary (DEI), about half a mile away from SGH. SGH, a sprawling complex, housed several other departments apart from the obstetric department. DEI housed the administrative offices of the OB/GY department, outpatients unit, operating theatre and wards for gynaecological cases; a small nurses' hostel and rooms for two resident doctors.

The medical staff consisted of three consultants, one senior registrar, two registrars, one SHO and one houseman. The consultants were Drs Arthur Sutherland, Theodore Mair and Donald Bruce. Dr Sutherland was the departmental head. A Presbyter in his church, heavy in build, he was a teetotaller and non–smoker who was very strict and ran the department as a school headmaster. Dr Mair, a Welshman, was the exact opposite, of middle build, debonair, a worldly figure, he enjoyed his whisky and cigarettes. Dr Bruce of a diminutive build was the junior consultant. He was in perpetual awe of Dr Sutherland; to whom he reportedly had been a senior registrar for a long time before being made a consultant. I saw him on more than one occasion concealing a cigarette he had been smoking behind his back when Dr Sutherland entered his office. Dr Sandy Herriot, as Senior Registrar, completed the list of the senior doctors. Sandy, red-headed, slim and a heavy smoker, had been a junior registrar in Sir Dugald Baird's unit in Aberdeen when I was there as a houseman. The two registrars were Jimmy Johnson and Peter Hirsch. Dr Johnson was in possession of the MRCOG, and had been on the staff for a number of years. Short in height and always restlessly active, he wore strong-lensed spectacles. He was a skilled and dexterous obstetrician, but bore a marred image as a gossiper. Woe unto you if you told him something in confidence. He was very loyal to Dr Sutherland and followed him around like a puppy. The unspoken opinion at the time was that able and very competent though he was, he was unlikely to be offered a consultant post in Scotland. He eventually got a consultant post in Ireland. Peter Hirsch, a Dundee graduate, was, like myself, preparing for the MRCOG examination. This constituted the medical staff on my arrival. We were soon joined by a houseman, Dr Maat, a Syrian, somewhat senior in years, who had come to seek the MRCOG. A couple of months later a second houseman was appointed to join the staff.

There were certain requirements to be fulfilled before gaining eligibility to sit for the MRCOG examination. After obtaining the full medical registration, you must complete two years of a combined job in obstetrics and gynaecology or a full year at a prestigious hospital in obstetrics and gynaecology at certain recognized posts in approved hospitals. The hospitals and posts were under the jurisdiction of the Hospital Inspection Committee of the RCOG. One must also have done a six-month post registration job in Surgery at a post recognized for the part one examination of any of the RCS (Royal College of Surgeons). Almost all the house officer posts in teaching hospitals were recognized as training posts for the MRCOG. Some District Hospital Registrar posts were not recognized as training posts. (District hospitals could and yet not qualify to sit for the MRCOG examination.) Some registrar posts in some district hospitals were, however, remarkably not recognized as training posts for the MRCOG. A house officer in a prestigious teaching hospital was most unlikely to perform an operation such as a Caesarean section or hysterectomy on his own. A registrar in an unrecognised district hospital was not qualified to sit for the examination, whereas a houseman in a prestigious hospital could sit and pass the MRCOG with very limited operative experience. Obtaining recognized jobs was competitive and not easy in those days. There were only a few postgraduate books for acquiring the desired knowledge for the examination. In teaching hospitals, it was acknowledged that a trainee was exposed to current knowledge and practice, thereby increasing his chance of passing the examination, unlike his counterpart trainee in a somewhat remote district hospital. Some fine-tuning and luck were needed in obtaining the right job.

I had gained some experience in obstetrics at Korle Bu Hospital, but had not done any obstetrics and gynaecology for more than a year. The locum SHO job from August to December was an appropriate one to start with. Dr Maat clerked all the patients on admission and reported to me.

I was provided with accommodation at DEI (David Elder Infirmary) in relative luxury. My apartment consisted of a roomy bedroom and a commodious well-furnished living room. All my meals were provided free in the DEI restaurant which was shared with the few nurses in the hospital. Since the post was an NHS one, I received a salary. As an MO, I received my full salary from the Ghana government; I was financially comfortable.

I plunged myself into clinical activity. I adjusted myself to the pace and method of work at the hospital. I had full guidance and support from Drs Herriot and Mair. With encouragement, Dr Herriot assisted me in performing a number of Caesarean sections. In my view, Dr Sutherland was far too strict in delegation of surgery; Dr Mair was reasonably liberal, with a balanced approach.

A major requirement of the RCOG was the submission by the candidate of a book of 20 cases each in obstetrics and gynaecology; each case was to be essentially handled by the candidate and followed with a brief commentary. Another requirement was a long commentary on any chosen topic, one in obstetrics and a second one in gynaecology. The cases had to be authenticated and signed by the consultant in charge of the case. The acceptance and approval of the book was mandatory for a candidate's eligibility to sit for the examination. With the prerequisites in mind, I planned my programme. I ordered the following books from Ferrier, the medical booksellers in Edinburgh: Gynaecology by Jeffcoat, Victor Bonney's Operative Gynaecology, Gynaecological Pathology by Haines and Taylor, Operative Obstetrics by Munro Kerr, Antenatal Postnatal Care by McClure Browne. These books and a regular attention to the British Journal of Obstetrics and Gynaecology (BJOG) would serve as my bibliographical resource for the MRCOG examination. I later acquired Shaw's Operative Gynaecology.

About a week after my arrival in Glasgow, my Opel Rekord car was delivered to me. I had travelled on the boat with it. I was in possession of an International Driver's Licence. The Opel model was a rarity in Glasgow. It was useful to have the car in Glasgow since I had to commute daily between DEI and SGH.

Dr Samuel Ofosu Amaah, my classmate from Achimota and UCGC, and an alumnus of Glasgow Medical School, had arrived in Glasgow from Korle Bu long before I did to commence a postgraduate course in Paediatrics for the MRCP and DCH. He was on attachment to SGH. He introduced me to a number of Ghanaian medical students and Dr Portuphy Lamptey who had also come to pursue a postgraduate course. The medical students, all in their final year, were Kluffio, Lade Wosornu and Miss Doris Hayfron-Benjamin. Lade and his wife at a later date entertained me in a homely way to a dinner of Ghanaian cuisine. I was delighted at a later date to meet Mr Jones Adzimah, a medical student, hailing from Hohoe. We had grown up together as children and neighbours in Hohoe; I had not seen nor met him again for many years.

Since Glasgow was a big city, it was possible for me to quench my thirst for opera. I went to see an opera whenever a touring company, notably the Scottish National Opera Company under Alexander Gibson, featured. I arranged once and swapped my call duty with Dr Peter Hirsch without inconveniencing anyone. Somehow to my surprise, this did not go down well with Jimmy Johnson, who although senior to both of us, was in no way involved in the swap. I felt somewhat awkward because of the mumbling and rumbling inferring an air of elitism on my part. I never again requested to swap.

It is now germane to chronicle an episode involving the opera. The Glasgow opera house was for some inexplicable reason located in the Gorbals district. The district had a notorious reputation as a centre of crime. Indeed, the cop who had worked to clean it and sanitize it to a degree was reported to have earned a knighthood for his achievement. I was notified to collect a parcel of books I had ordered from Edinburgh. I drove up to collect the parcel of books and then went to the opera house. I parked my car, locked, on a side street next to the theatre. When the performance was over, as I walked over towards my car, I was accosted by two uniformed policemen. They enquired from me whether I was the owner of the car to which I replied in the affirmative. I wondered whether I had committed a crime. I had not. The police informed me that soon after leaving my car, two men were seen to have broken into the car; they opened the package, but realizing that the contents were just books on OB/ GY, they left the car without taking away any items. Someone in an adjacent building saw them when the exercise was going on and informed the police by telephone, who soon appeared on the scene and awaited my arrival. They asked me to check whether I had any items missing. I checked and found that I had nothing missing; there was no damage to the car either. The criminals were not only clever, but arguably intelligent and considerate as well. This was my initiation experience into Glasgow. The Doctors' Common room was located in the SGH; there was a TV set, which had its pictures in black and white (in the non-colour era). There were only a few channels. One programme on Saturday nights which attracted millions of viewers. was 'That Was The Week That Was (TWTWTW)' Sammy and I never missed it. It was a political satirical programme with an exhibition of humour and great talent.

In November 1963, after a busy day, I drove up from DEI to SGH early in the evening. Soon on my arrival, Sammy gave me the shocking news of the assassination of President JF Kennedy. He was the political icon, idol and statesman of millions if not billions of us worldwide. It was a tragedy. Almost everyone of that generation knew where he was or what she was doing at the time of hearing the news. Johnson succeeded him as President. I followed the succeeding events closely. The burial was attended by all the world's who's who in Washington. It was a very moving event. The hooves on the feet of the horses drawing the carriage were reversed backwards.

In Britain, a big scandal was unfolding. It was a sexual scandal involving Mr. John Profumo, a high-ranking Minister in Harold Macmillan's cabinet. Mr Profumo, educated at Eton and Oxford, and married to Valerie Hobson, the film star, was the Secretary of State for War. He saw Christine Keeler as she emerged from the swimming pool in the nude at Lord Astor's Cliveden estate. After meeting her, Mr Profumo commenced and carried on a love affair with her. When rumours of the affair were increasing in crescendo, Mr Profumo in a statement to parliament categorically and in a challenging tone denied any impropriety whatsoever in his relationship with Miss Keeler, only to confess later and resign in disgrace. The scandal was compounded by the revelation that Miss Keeler was at the same time having a relationship with Mr Yevgeny (Eugene) Ivanov, a Soviet Naval attaché in London. This, at the height of the Cold War with Russia, had ominous implications. Miss Keeler and her fellow showgirl Miss Mandy Rice-Davies, a prettier and more alluring girl, became household names. Miss Rice-Davies' quip in a giggle to Mr Profumo's original denial that "he would say that, wouldn't he," became a famous quote. Dr Stephen Ward, a West End osteopath, who was friendly with both girls and was very well connected with several famous clients, got involved in the scandal. At its height, he committed suicide with a drug overdose.

As Harold Macmillan's government was tottering on account of the scandal, Mr Macmillan set up a commission of enquiry to look into it, headed by the distinguished Law Lord, Denning. He completed the enquiry and wrote a report, the gist of the conclusion which I cannot recall now. What I remember is the high standard and quality of the prose. The prose style of short, precise and concise sentences, 'sui generis' for which he was famous, was appealing and unforgettable. The Daily Telegraph newspaper not only published the full report in a special supplement, but wrote an editorial extolling the quality of the English prose Lord Denning had rendered. (Lord Denning had obtained a Tripos in Mathematics at Cambridge before switching on to Law.) Such was the background of the genius on the bench. I became his admirer and bought copies of all the books he wrote. One of the last was his "Family History". A copy of this was bought for me in London by my future wife, who had it autographed by his Lordship at its launch in London. I was fortunate to have the opportunity to meet him in Kumasi when he visited Ghana in the seventies.

The Profumo affair contributed to the decline of the premiership of Mr Harold Macmillan, for whom I had great admiration and respect. I was appalled to read in a book some revelations about Lady Macmillan, his wife. Apparently, Lady Macmillan was reputed to have had a long affair with Lord Boothby, the Scottish politician. The depth of the affair was revealed in a statement made by her saying that she was being faithful to Lord Boothby by denying conjugal rights to Harold Macmillan, her husband. An incredible statement. Despite this, Sir Harold Macmillan elevated Mr Boothby, then a parliamentarian, to a knighthood; he was later elevated to a peerage. I must confess that I am sometimes puzzled by the behaviour of members of the British aristocracy. When Mountbatten (an uncle of Prince Philip) was the Viceroy of India at the transitional period of gaining her independence, the saintly Pandit Nehru was reported to have been having a passionate affair with the Viceroy's wife in India.

When Sir Harold Macmillan resigned as Prime Minister, to the surprise of all the political pundits of the time, he handed the premiership over to Sir Alec Douglas Home, rather than Butler. According to well informed opinion of the time, Alec Douglas Home was not the smartest of people. Indeed, on the (TWTWTW) satire programme, he could only count by using match sticks.

I went to Edinburgh a few times at the weekends on Saturday visits to Chris Adomakoh and his family. He had come to Edinburgh in pursuit of the Diploma in Psychiatry. He was joined there by Vic and their firstborn child, Nana. They always entertained me in style on these visits. I also met Adjei Duah, then a medical student, and Frank Vardon, studying accountancy.

I interacted with the medical students in Glasgow. In this respect, it is worthy to commend Lade Wosornu on his high academic achievements at Glasgow Medical School. The school had the largest class intake in Britain at about 200, compared with smaller numbers elsewhere. Lade's achievement lay in the fact that he topped his class in almost all the subjects, no small feat.

Lade visited me in my DEI apartment one day and sought my advice on which speciality he should pursue on qualifying as a doctor. It was not an easy question to answer, particularly from a person with such a marvellous brain. With his indisputable brain, he could, I opined, choose any speciality. I was quite frank with him. In my view, Pathology and research therein was the foundation stone and basis of medicine on which patient care is based. It should therefore attract the best brains. It was, however, the least financially rewarding, more so in Ghana. Among the clinicians in Ghana, I was told that the Gynaecologists fared best, but pointed out that it was the least mentally challenging. Internal medicine was lucrative and mentally challenging while I ranked General Surgery between Gynaecology and Internal Medicine. The choice, I opined, was entirely his own inclination. After he had passed the MB, ChB, with acclaimed honours, I believe, almost all the professors tried to persuade him to follow their respective speciality. He won the most prestigious prize in the final year examination; it was reported in the Observer newspaper as the first African to have won this award; a great honour to Ghana. Normally, Ghanaian doctors had to return home after their house jobs before returning to specialize. Dr F.T. Sai in his wisdom granted Lade permission to specialize in General Surgery before returning home. Lade pursued the FRCS course and obtained the diploma in the minimum time. He then undertook a research course at the prestigious Hammersmith Hospital in London before returning home to join the staff of the medical school.

The obstetric workload consisted of antenatal care and the management of patients in labour. The catchment population in the Govan district was mainly working class of the ship building industry. It was in an era when the sequelae of rheumatic fever in the form of valvular cardiac disease were not uncommon. The unit was renowned for the management of pregnancy with cardiac disease; the antenatal ward always had a significant number of such patients with varying grades of severity in the ward. The short stature of the working class patients had some degree of contracted pelvis. Although most of the patients had spontaneous normal vaginal delivery, some of them with dystocia required assisted vaginal instrumental delivery. A mid-cavity arrest was managed by manual rotation, followed by forceps application and delivery, or by Kjellands forceps application, rotation and delivery. The flat pelvis made the application of Kjellands forceps for rotation risky and unwise; the use of Kjellands forceps was therefore not permitted in the department. On the other hand, manual rotation of the arrested head in mid-cavity, a procedure requiring a fine manual skill and dexterity, was the preferred method. I was taught this procedure by Sandy Herriot and Jimmy Johnson, who were both adept at it. It was not an easy manoeuvre to acquire, and therefore required supervision in order to gain the experience and confidence. I gained the necessary skill to list it in my operation repertoire. In those days, the aim was to achieve a safe vaginal delivery, when there was a thin line between the concept of "Trial Forceps" and "Failed Forceps". Indeed, this fine line came under severe scrutiny in the following decade in a medico-legal test case which went to the highest court in Britain. The defendant was then a Senior Registrar. Both the prosecuting and defending teams had very eminent obstetricians as expert witnesses. Although the defendant was found guilty, it did not adversely affect his career. He rose in rank to become consultant, an eminent consultant Oncologist.

In gynaecology, Dr Arthur Sutherland had established a worldwide reputation as an authority on pelvic tuberculosis. The literature on the subject was littered with his name. Almost all the cases in Scotland were referred to him for management. He established and formulated strict protocols for the investigation and treatment of pelvic tuberculosis. The diagnosis entailed a D and C (Dilatation and Curettage) and a laboratory workup. The treatment consisted of the administering of a triad of anti-tuberculosis drugs for at least 18 months. Most patients responded favourably to drug therapy; in the few cases where the response was poor, a total hysterectomy was performed by Dr Arthur Sutherland. The other routine major gynaecological operations, such as abdominal hysterectomy and pelvic floor repair for prolapse, were performed by Drs Mair and Herriot. Family Planning and Oral contraceptives had not yet arrived on the scene. Gynaecological endocrinology was limited to the estimation of oestriol and pregnanediol levels.

In preparation for the MRCOG, I started collecting a series of cases in obstetrics and gynaecology under the guidance of Sandy

Herriot. I wrote them all up. I chose "Accidental Haemorrhage" for my long obstetric commentary and "Cyst of Gartners' Duct" for my long gynaecological commentary. They received authentication signatures from Dr Arthur Sutherland.

SGH held Grand Round presentations monthly in departmental rotation. It came to my turn in the department to make a presentation. I researched the subject as well as I could and made my presentation. This constituted part of the postgraduate activity. I think my presentation was well received.

We experienced a case of mortality in the gynaecological department at DEI in 1963. Very occasionally, when a case of pelvic tuberculosis proved refractory to the drug therapy, hysterectomy was performed as a final resort by Dr Sutherland. One such case arose in 1963 when I was in DEI. Sandy and Jimmy advised me to go to the theatre to watch the operation to serve as a learning experience for me. The case was the only one booked for that afternoon, when I was free, and not scheduled for any duty. I went to the theatre and watched the operation from beginning to the end, lasting about two hours. There appeared to have been a fair amount of oozing of blood, but haemostasis seemed to have been controlled on the completion of the operation. The patient after recovery from the general anaesthesia was transferred to a single bed cubicle. A couple of hours after the operation, the patient went into a state of shock. There was no clinical sign of bleeding. A consultant physician was summoned for an opinion. There was no intensive care unit in those days. The patient was given a blood transfusion to combat the shock. Despite all the attempts at resuscitation, the patient's condition deteriorated and she died later on the same day. We were all very saddened by the event. Although I was not on duty, I was there all the time and witnessed everything. I do not recall whether a post-mortem examination was done, and if so, what the findings were. Years later, I wondered whether this was a case of septic shock, which carries a high mortality rate.

Many years later, when I was a senior consultant gynaecologist in Kumasi, Ghana and in my regimen of reading journals voraciously to keep abreast of current practice, I read an article in a gynaecological journal published by Dr Arthur Sutherland. In this article, with his decades-long experience and probably the largest number of pelvic tuberculosis cases under his belt, he presented a report on the management. He provided figures for all the cases which responded favourably to drug therapy and all those that ended up with a hysterectomy. He claimed a zero mortality in his series on a total hysterectomy. The period on which he reported he reported on included 1963. He indicated that his series on hysterectomy had no mortality. This, of course, was not true. I was shocked with his claim of zero mortality. I refrained from writing a rejoinder to the article because of my loyalty to an institute which had played a commendable role in my training to become a highly acclaimed gynaecologist. I agree that this is an arguable excuse and that I could be faulted on that.

In the year 2000, I was working at the Northwest Military Hospital in Tabuk, Saudi Arabia, as a senior consultant gynaecologist. Again I read an article in a reputable gynaecological journal written by Dr Arthur Sutherland. It was the reproduction of a lecture he had given in Switzerland on his decades-long experience in the management of pelvic tuberculosis. Once again, he quoted zero mortality for the cases which required hysterectomy. This time, I could not resist writing to him a personal rejoinder, but not to the journal. In the letter, I told him who I was and acknowledged my training period under him in 1962/63. I listed all the doctors in the department at the time, including Dr Bruce Donald, the third consultant. I stated that I witnessed one case of postoperative mortality after watching him perform the hysterectomy. I stated that this may have escaped his memory. A few weeks later, I received a short, blunt and rather unfriendly reply from him. He acknowledged the receipt of my letter and stated bluntly that I was wrong. To authenticate my wrongness, he stated that there was no Dr 'Bruce Donald' in the department. I had, I fully admit, mistakenly stated Dr 'Bruce Donald' instead of Dr Donald Bruce. This was the way he chose to deny the falsification of records. I gain nothing in relating an incident with a sad ending, and not writing a rejoinder to the journal to expose an untruth and rather writing directly to the major character to correct an error. A fellow gynaecologist who was once associated with SGH told me some time ago when we met at a congress that a dispute involving case notes emerged when Dr Sutherland retired. He had apparently claimed personal ownership of the case notes of some patients. I cannot attest to the veracity of this. Be it as it may, this fortified my belief in not accepting all statistical reports as faithful.

As 1963 was drawing to its end, I realized that I had to find and secure another job starting in January 1964 for another year. Sixteen months at SGH was enough; it was desirable to move to another hospital in order to gain varied experience. When Dr Mair entertained me to a Sunday lunch with his family, he suggested to me that I should approach Professor Ian Donald, at Glasgow's Queen Mother's Hospital and of ultrasound fame, for a job in his unit. He followed it up by making an appointment for me to see him at an interview. I went and had an interview with the Professor, but did not receive an offer of a job. Dr Mair tried another channel for me; in him I found another mentor. He indicated that he could get a job offer for me in London's prestigious Hammersmith Postgraduate Hospital and arranged an interview for me with Professor McClure Browne; he was obviously well-connected and influential. I was interviewed but again failed to get an offer of a job; the jobs there were high profile jobs and very competitively sought after. Although they merited highly in the acquisition of the latest knowledge and advances in the speciality, they fell short on hands-on experience in operative work, an important factor for someone like me who would return home soon after obtaining the MRCOG.

I applied for suitable jobs which were advertised in the British Medical Journal (BMJ). The jobs in England attracted my attention most. A job in St. James Hospital in Leeds and a district hospital job attracted me. They were both recognized jobs, of course. I was invited to attend interviews for both jobs on two successive days, the district hospital one being the first. Dr Mair, sharing Theodore with me as a first name, had taken a fatherly interest in both my training and future. He advised me to go for the job in Leeds in preference to the district hospital one for the reason that with Leeds being a big city, it was more likely that I would meet my life's partner there! I travelled from Glasgow and was interviewed as were other interviewees. At the end of my interview, I was asked "When can you start work if we offer you the job?" I gambled by answering that I would like to think it over in the next 24 hours. A hospital official told me later that I was not offered the job because it was discerned that I was not really interested in it. I proceeded straight on to Leeds uu77777777F Redman, a consultant gynaecologist. I was offered the post of SHO under Mr Redman. I was delighted. I collected my travel fares for each interview journey from Glasgow; not a bad trip from the financial point of view. I returned to Glasgow and prepared to leave for Leeds. SGH (and perhaps Scotland as a whole) was an excellent training centre in obstetrics. My obstetric skill and knowledge were greatly enhanced in Glasgow. The flip side was the absence of a commensurate amount of gynaecological experience in Glasgow. I did not see nor assist at a single case of vaginal hysterectomy or Wertheim radical hysterectomy.

RESIDENCE IN LEEDS

I found Leeds more scenically attractive and appealing than Glasgow. It was one of the three major cities in the county of Yorkshire, the other two being Sheffield and York. Like its sister city of Sheffield, it was a famous university city. St James Hospital (SJH) and Leeds General Infirmary (LGI) were the two major hospitals in the city. LGI was the main University Teaching Hospital. SJH was regarded as the largest hospital in Europe. The consultants held teaching posts in LGI, and had beds there. Entering SJH from Elland Road, you were ushered into an appealing frontage landscape, the administrative block and the chapel. The rest of the hospital was a sprawling complex, very similar in style to the red brick complex of SGH. The SJH blocks were almost all double-storeyed buildings housing the various departmental wards. The antenatal, labour, postnatal wards and the obstetric offices occupied one block; the gynaecology wards, two in number, occupied one floor in a separate block located further away from the obstetric block.

The senior staff consisted of four consultants and two Senior Registrars. The junior staff consisted of one junior registrar, one SHO and one House Officer. Three consultants, namely Mr Agar, Mr Farquar and Mr Redman, had obstetrics and gynaecology beds in the hospital whereas Mr Currie, the fourth, had only gynaecology beds in the hospital (my readers will note that whereas in England male gynaecologists are addressed as Mr, in Scotland they are addressed as Dr). The Senior Registrars were Mr Cyndie and Mr Begg.

The registrar was Dr Attit; he was replaced later on a rotation basis by Dr Gooneshila, both Indians. The House Officer was Dr Tom Kargbo, a Sierra Leonean. Mr Cyndie was responsible for Mr Currie's patients, Dr Attit for Mr Farquar's patients and Mr Begg for Mr Agar's patients. I was responsible for Mr Redman's patients. My predecessor was an Australian who left after obtaining the MRCOG.

I worked as an SHO under Mr Redman for the next 22 months. Mr Redman, stout in stature and handsome, was a very confident consultant; he strode the department with his signature short bowtie. He was an excellent teacher in every respect. Mr. Redman and I quickly gelled together and he became my mentor. Respect for each other was mutual. Trivial though it was, we shared the same first name of Theodore, like Dr Mair in SGH. We discovered later that we both shared an interest in and love for opera.

Dr Attit, from Bombay, was also attempting to obtain the MRCOG. He had worked as a houseman in obstetrics at Warrington in 1960 when I was a houseman there in general surgery. We renewed our collegial association which later developed into a friendship. He told me that the SHO post under Mr Redman was the most coveted and envied training post in the Leeds region. At the end of my tenure, it was an opinion I would not dispute.

The antenatal clinics were held in a single storeyed block at the right forefront of the hospital three times a week. The patients were booked under the consultants who held their sessions there, namely Mr Agar, Mr Farquar and Mr Redman. The junior medical staff assisted in attending to the patients; the sessions were held in the morning. Mr Redman held his weekly morning gynaecology outpatients' clinics in the city centre in Leeds. Each consultant had one operating session on an afternoon once a week. Saturday morning operating session was allotted to Mr Redman's SHO, which was me. One of the two gynaecology wards was allotted entirely to Mr Redman's patients, while the remaining three consultants shared the second ward. Mr Redman thus had half of all the gynaecology patients at SJH. As the "de facto" registrar, the onus of the resident management and care fell on my shoulder.

The profiles of the other three consultants were as follows:

the most senior consultant was Mr David Currie. Mr Currie had earned a reputation in the management of cervical carcinoma by his skill in performing the radical Wertheim's hysterectomy, the Everest in gynaecological surgery. The five-year survival rate of his cases was the best in Britain, and the second best worldwide. Most of his gynaecological cases were managed in another hospital and not in SJH. He did his ward rounds in SJH on Sunday mornings. Dapperly dressed in a bespoke suit with a rose in his breast pocket, he conducted his ward rounds accompanied by Mr Cyndie, his senior registrar. It was said that if you worked under him as a houseman, you were guaranteed a pass at the MRCOG examination on your first attempt.

The next most senior consultant was Mr Agar. Slim and tall, his appearance in suit did not lend the elegant image of a consultant gynaecologist. The following is an anecdote about him: he went to the house of an aristocrat in Leeds on a domiciliary consultation visit. When he pressed the front doorbell, a butler emerged from the door. On seeing Mr Agar, without a word, the butler indicated to him to pass through the tradesman's entrance at the back. After disclosing his identity, the butler opened the front door to let him in. As a surgeon, he possessed an unmatched remarkable skill and speed at operation. His operation field was almost bloodless. He had apparently trained and practised as a surgeon before branching into gynaecology.

The third consultant was Mr Farquar. Physically well built, he was always immaculately dressed with excellent taste in ties, shirts and cuff links. He drove a Rolls-Royce which was kept immaculately clean and shiny. He had a great sense of humour. Dr Attit was his registrar. He was later replaced by Dr Gooneshila on rotational basis. Such was the composition of the medical staff in 1964.

The resident staff of housemen, SHOs, and registrars were accommodated in the Residents' Quarters. This was a two storeyed block with single-bed sitters on the upper floor, and ground floor housing a large common-room, restaurant and TV room.

Soon after my arrival in Leeds SJH, I plunged myself into my new environment. I attended to patients at the antenatal clinics; these were held on fixed days for each consultant in the mornings. The hospital had a large population catchment area, with patients of lower middle and lower classes, which included some from the Caribbean countries. There was no standard protocol for patient management in those days; each consultant had his own approach to antenatal patient care and for those in labour. We as residents complied with each consultant's management. Nevertheless, there was a great deal of uniformity. We saw patients with a pathetic history of repeated stillbirths on account of Rhesus isoimmunisation. Lilley in New Zealand had devised the practice of intrauterine blood transfusion on affected foetuses. Just about this time, research by Clarke in Liverpool and by others in the USA resulted in the prevention of this serious problem by the administration of the Rhesus D gamma globulin. This major breakthrough, in my view, merited a Nobel Prize in Medicine. The Neonatal Intensive Care Unit (NICU) in Paediatrics had not yet arrived on the scene.

Dr Attit and I took turns in the management of patients in labour. Assisted vaginal delivery, breech vaginal delivery and Caesarean section operations rested on us. I had to perform forceps deliveries in SJH, mid-cavity arrest in the second stage of labour was managed by the application of Kjelands forceps plus rotation followed by delivery; the type of pelvis dictated the option. The use of the Kjelands forceps was in vogue and its skilled application and use partly constituted the yardstick of assessing an obstetrician's ability. Dr Attit and Dr Begg guided me in the careful use of the Kjelands forceps. With the exception of Mr Begg, there was not much familiarity with the skill in manual rotation. I ended up acquiring the skill in manual rotation and the skilled use of the Kjelands forceps; therein lies the advantage in working in different hospitals like SGH and SJH.

If a patient in labour, in my opinion, needed a Caesarean section (CS), I would ring the consultant under whom she was booked for his approval. Two of the consultants would invariably request me to go ahead and perform the CS; the third one would invariably argue that the operation could be deferred before finally approving. I soon adopted an approach of just giving him all the details of the case and leaving him to conclude and decide that a CS should be done.

There was no controversy about the management of breech presentation. External cephalic version at 36 weeks gestation was the practice. A failed version was followed by X-ray pelvimetry to assess the pelvic adequacy. If there was doubt about the adequacy, an elective CS would be carried out. If the pelvis was adequate, an assisted breech delivery with the application of forceps to the after-coming head would be done. An Anaesthetist always had to be present.

Mr Redman held his gynaecology outpatients' clinic once a week in the city centre. The patients were all those referred by General Practitioners (GPs). He was assisted in this by Mr Begg and me. My role was to take and write the history of all the patients; the examination and diagnosis were handled by Mr Redman and Mr Begg. After all the patients had been seen, I joined Mr Redman as he dictated his letters to the GPs. The letters embodied the summary of the clinical findings and the management plan, be it surgery or otherwise. Mr Redman would discuss with me interesting and instructive cases and their management plan. The list of cases billed for surgery was given to me to take to SJH to add to the waiting list cases in the book. It was my duty to select the cases for operation. I had to exercise some element of prioritisation, taking into account the clinical factors and the history. This was a priceless experience for me. After gaining confidence in my clinical judgment and case management, Mr Redman paid me the ultimate compliment.

He was due to take his annual leave, but decided not to cancel his outpatients' clinic, nor entrust it to the Senior Registrar as he apparently normally did. He asked me to run the clinic all by myself in his absence, without the Senior Registrar. This entailed clerking and examining all the referred patients, planning their management and writing back to the GPs to inform them of the diagnosis and the envisaged management plan; I had been inculcated with Mr Redman's management scheme. This was a high score in his trust and confidence in me; I was just an SHO and had not obtained the coveted MRCOG yet.

Mr Redman had one operating session a week in SJH. I selected and listed his cases for surgery from the waiting list book. The list was always a mix of minor and major cases. The majors included laparotomies, abdominal and vaginal hysterectomy, pelvic floor repair, Manchester repair and Wertheim's hysterectomy for earlier stage cervical carcinoma. Mr Begg and I assisted him at the major operations. I had not seen nor assisted at a vaginal hysterectomy and Wertheim's operations before I went to Leeds. The minor list included D and C, TOP and Shirodkar cerclage. He used a metal coil twisting it; it predated the use of the nylon tape.

The allotment of an operation session to me was based on the fact that half the total number of gynaecology beds were under Mr Redman. I exercised great care in selecting my cases, avoiding those which may require assistance from him while at the same time building up and consolidating my surgical repertoire. Mr Redman's management of cases of postmenopausal and climacteric bleeding was to perform a D and C; if the curetting macroscopically suggested that it was a carcinoma of the uterus, he would proceed on and perform an abdominal total hysterectomy and bilateral salpingo-oophorectomy (BSO). The curetting in such cases looked cheesy, and you could confidently diagnose it as a case of uterine carcinoma. In preparing my list of cases, I selected a couple of such suspicious cases with the hope that I would get some cases which might require a hysterectomy. This way, I got the chance to perform a hysterectomy, occasionally two on my Saturday session. I slowly gained skill and confidence in performing hysterectomies. This created some envy by the registrar to Mr. Farquar who had no such privilege. Indeed, Dr Gooneshila, Mr Farquar's registrar, approached Mr Redman and requested a Saturday operation session from him. Mr Redman, in his wisdom, told her to address her request to me (she was then in possession of the MRCOG and FRCS). My answer to her request was a polite, but emphatic 'No'. That was the end of that conundrum. Years later, after returning home to Bangalore, she attained fame; she pioneered Assisted Reproductive Technology (ART) and her unit was a pace-setter in Southern India.

In the passage of time, I grew in confidence in the management of acute and non-acute gynaecological cases. I could not have attained that level if I had remained in SGH. Indeed, in my second week at SJH, faced with an emergency while on duty, I performed a laparotomy on my own. It turned out to be a case of a twisted ovarian cyst. When I wrote to my erstwhile colleagues in SGH, they received the news almost with disbelief. I was of course authorized to perform the laparotomy. Managing cases of ectopic pregnancy, pelvic infection and abortions was bread and butter stuff for me in Leeds.

My daily programme after breakfast was first of all to go and do a ward round in the gynaecology ward, alone or join Mr Redman if he was present. If I was on call duty for obstetrics, I would then do a review of patients in labour. I would then join the team of houseman, registrar and the consultant for that day at the antenatal clinic. One of the housemen, whose tenure lasted six months, was Dr Tom Kargbo, a Sierra Leonean, the only other African doctor at SJH at the time. Several years later, in 1978, I met him in Freetown at the West African College of Surgeons' Congress. He had trained and qualified as a gynaecologist and was practising in Bole.

Dr Attit, the registrar, a heavy smoker, became a friend and we socialized together, including holidaying. There were three Senior Registrars when I was in SJH, namely, Mr Begg, Mr Cyndie and Mr Melville. Mr Begg, a true Scott, tall and handsome, was a Glasgow graduate and a heavy smoker; we both shared a taste and love for malt whisky; he was friendly and supportive and I learnt a lot from him. Mr Melville, from Barbados, West Indies, was a graduate of Birmingham and of Caucasian stock. He was a knowledgeable and skilled surgeon. Mr Begg and Mr Melville rotated as Senior Registrars under both Mr Agar and Mr Redman. Mr Melville was gratuitous with advice to me. Mr Cyndie, under Mr Currie, dealt only with gynaecology cases. Quiet and rather self-effacing, he told me that Dr Armar had been his mate in Sheffield Medical School. There were resident doctors from other clinical departments in the Residents' Block. A spirit of camaraderie prevailed; we all shared in the amenities provided. We did not have to pay for the meals, snacks and drinks; these were all gratis, unlike the case now.

After a rather brief period at SJH, Mr Melville left for a London Teaching Hospital, after which he was appointed Consultant at a Brighton hospital. We all felt pleased at his progress and in 1978, the year of my elevation to the Fellowship, he arranged a locum consultant job for me there. (I was then based in Kumasi, Ghana.) He hosted and entertained me a couple of times on my visits to England. Mr Begg was later also appointed to a consultant post in Dewsbury in Yorkshire where he and his wife Jean also hosted me on a few occasions. Sadly though, he died when still relatively young and at the peak of his career as a consultant gynaecologist. I still treasure my visits with them.

Dr Fred Amroliwala, a Parsee Indian from Bombay, joined SJH in 1965 as a registrar in the Department of Medicine. He had been a colleague and a friend of Dr Attit's for years. He lived with his family in a house outside the hospital. Tall and with a confident air, Fred was a worldly and sophisticated gentleman. He later joined the RAF where he rose spectacularly in rank to attain one of the highest, if not the highest, in the RAF Medical corps. We met a couple of decades later in London and Swindon, our respective homes at the time. His children have all had distinguished careers. One of them is the BBC TV anchorman, Matthew Amroliwala. The last time I met Fred was in Cyprus in the year 2000 when Yolande and I were holidaying there.

My duties included dictating all the discharge summary letters on patients for the secretary to type; after which I signed them to be forwarded to the various GPs. Mr Redman appreciated a good prose style – concise and precise. I was off-duty on Wednesdays. My lifestyle rubbed off on Dr Attit, who confessed to me that he had acquired and learnt a lot by our association. I also frequented the library in LGI to browse through the medical journals (the BMJ and BJOG), in order to keep abreast of current information and practice in the speciality.

During one of my visits to LGI, I paid a courtesy call on Dr Charles Clarke in the department of surgery. He was then the senior registrar to Professor Goliger, the legendary gastro-enterologist. Dr Clarke had taught me Anatomy and Surgery in Aberdeen. As a fellow Aberdonian, I was really pleased with his current status. He was later appointed to the chair in Surgery at London's UCH. Professor E. Q. Acheampong of Korle Bu told me that he did his Ch. M (Master in Surgery) degree under his tutelage at UCH. Dr Clarke was a heavy smoker. Sad to relate, he died rather relatively young when he was in his prime as a Professor.

Mr Agar did his operation lists on Wednesday afternoons, my off-duty days. He was assisted by Mr Begg. Because of Mr Agar's operative skill, Mr Begg would alert me if there was an interesting case to watch; I never missed an opportunity to do so.

There was a case of a third degree uterine prolapse in an elderly lady, for which she needed to have a vaginal hysterectomy with pelvic floor repair. This operation is usually done with the patient positioned in the lithotomy position. Unfortunately, she could not be positioned that way on account of arthrodesis at her knee joints. Indeed, because of this, she had earlier consulted a leading gynaecologist in his office. He offered and fitted her with a pessary; the device reportedly dropped out as she walked to board the car waiting to take her home. As a result of this unfortunate experience, she was advised to seek a second opinion. Mr Agar saw her and had her admitted for surgery. But how? Mr Begg and I wondered how Mr Agar would proceed in the non-lithotomy position. After the rendering of the general anaesthesia, the patient was laid flat in prone position; the legs were partially parted. The uterus was drawn down with tenacula applied to the cervix; the presenting anatomy was in the complete reverse to the lithotomy position. Mr Agar, seated and with two assistants, then carried out a vaginal hysterectomy with pelvic floor repair in his signature bloodless operating field with skill in 30 minutes. It was an experience a few of us were honoured and privileged to witness. When he finished the operation, he mumbled in sotto voce, "I believe this operation had been deemed impossible to perform". I am eternally grateful to Jim Begg for sharing this fantastic experience with me. I have related this experience on countless occasions to some of my gynaecological colleagues.

My SHO tenure at SJH was for one year; this would pass in the fulfilment of the prerequisite training before taking the MRCOG examination. I wrote up more cases in obstetrics and gynaecology to reflect a wider field. Another prerequisite was a six-month post-registration surgery approved by any one of the RCS for their Part 1 examination. My wide range of surgical experience would count for nought if not recognized by any of the RCS of London, Edinburgh, Glasgow and Ireland. I wrote in turn to all of them, seeking approval of my nine-month spell in Surgery in Kumasi, enclosing in each letter a copy of Dr Anfom's testimonial. I was distressed when letter after letter from three of the Colleges declined to recognize my job in Kumasi.

It was a great relief when I finally received a letter from the RCSE approving of my Kumasi surgical job for their Part 1 examination. I did not have to do a six-month job in surgery before the examination, what joy, what relief!

I completed my book of 20 cases each in obstetrics and gynaecology and the long commentaries in both fields. I had now completed all the prerequisites. I submitted my book with the letter of recognition and approval from the RCSE. My book was approved and returned to me in February 1965. It was two months late for eligibility for the next examination in June; six months was the minimum. I might have to wait for a long time to the end of the year for the next opportunity. This waiting period was too long for me since I had come from Ghana on scholarship, restricting me to three years. I decided to write to the secretary of the examination board to plead for an exemption to permit me to sit for the MRCOG in June. To my great surprise and joy, I was granted special permission to sit for the examination in June. Although there was no guarantee that I would pass on my first attempt, I had an inner sense of confidence that if I prepared adequately, I would be successful; it was a feeling of confidence rather than arrogance. The pass rate was reckoned to be 30-40% at the time, and not many passed on their first attempt. I was aware of the fact that I had a lot of ground to cover in assimilating factual knowledge. My colleague, Dr Attit, had been unsuccessful in at least two previous attempts; the last one in 1964, when I was already in Leeds, sent him into a state of deep depression for several days.

I met and socialized with a number of Ghanaians who were in Leeds at the time. One of them, Peter Mensah, an Old Achimotan, had been my classmate. He had trained in Edinburgh as a Dentist, practised in Kumasi in the army before returning to Britain to pursue a postgraduate course in Dentistry. Dr GAC Anteson, an associate from my Mfantsipim days, had trained and qualified in Leeds and was working in the Leeds area. An old schoolmate from my Hohoe days, Mr Clemence Atuwo and his wife resided in Leeds as he was studying accountancy. Dr Effiong, a Nigerian, was doing a postgraduate course in Paediatrics. This group attended parties and we all socialized together.

Social life was far from dull for me in Leeds. Leeds boasted of a very good theatre where plays and operas were performed by visiting companies. The newly formed ENO (English National Opera), and the Welsh Opera Company came seasonally to perform. I travelled once to York to see Mozart's Cosi fan Tutte by ENO. My TV viewing was mainly sports and current affairs. I never missed the performances of the comedian Harry Worth, whom I rate unsurpassed until now.

It was at this time that Mohammed Ali (aka Cassius Clay) broke into celebrity prominence. Young and handsome, he had won the Olympic Gold medal in the heavyweight division of boxing and turned professional. The world heavyweight champion was one fearsome Sonny Liston; he had remained undefeated, and looked like a murderer on the wanted list. Cassius Clay challenged him for the title. Everyone thought it was extremely reckless on Clay's part to challenge Liston and, in fact, asking for an execution. Some of us seriously prayed that there should be no fatal outcome. We all watched the encounter with a feeling of trepidation and anxiety as round followed round. The result is now history. Clay knocked out Liston in an early round to everyone's disbelief. We thought it was a fluke but Clay repeated the feat in a return fight to great admiration and applause.

In tennis, a great Brazilian, Miss Maria Bueno, returned to the scene after a long period recuperating from hepatitis. The demure tennis star with her signature poise met the athletic Australian champion Miss Margaret Court in the Wimbledon Ladies' Singles final; it was the mouth-watering encounter of the tournament. Miss Bueno defeated Margaret Court in three sets. It was in this match that I saw Maria play a backhand shot over her shoulder with her back facing the net to win a point at a critical stage in the match; I had never seen such a stroke before. She was cool and elegant on court. On her return home after winning the championship title, the day was declared a public holiday in Brazil.

It is the recall of sporting episodes such as those chronicled above which, in my view, constitute the essence of a memoir.

I was entitled to a fortnight leave in my first year. I chose a time which coincided with the London opera season. I also planned to visit Paris. Dr Attit had never been to Paris, and without much persuasion decided to join me on my trip. I made my usual preparations before going to Paris. This entailed revising my French, centring on the vocabulary and simple sentence structure, such as: "donnez moi …, s'il vous plait". Dr Attit and I travelled to Paris by air and had a wonderful and memorable time. On our return through London, I took Dr Attit to the newly built Hilton Hotel on Park Lane where we enjoyed the pleasures on offer. Dr Attit at the end of it all expressed to me his gratitude for introducing and exposing him to some of the finer things in life. In an entirely contradictory manner, in an attempt at upmanship when we were both invited to the Redmans for dinner, his insecurity was embarrassingly exposed.

In 1964, the Prostaglandins had not yet made an entry into clinical pharmacological practice. The following narrative of reminiscences will set it in its historical perspective. The North of England Obstetrical and Gynaecological Society held periodical meetings in Sheffield. Mr Farquar attended one such meeting and informed some of us at our coffee break during his antenatal clinic session the following morning that, someone had made a presentation on Prostaglandins. Mr. Farquar went on to say with a little chuckle, 'not even Jack Dewhurst asked any questions' (Mr Dewhurst, then a Senior Lecturer, had earned a reputation for being most informed and who would regularly ask questions or make a commentary at these meetings). His silence on Prostaglandins spoke volumes on the subject. This was my first time of hearing about Mr Dewhurst. He was later appointed to the prestigious chair of Obstetrics and Gynaecology at London's Postgraduate hospitals Hammersmith and Queen Charlotte. He later served as President of the RCOG. He authored a famous, almost biblical, textbook on Postgraduate Obstetrics and Gynaecology. A must-read for those preparing for the MRCOG examination. He deservedly earned a knighthood.

The Prostaglandins burst into clinical practice later. The pioneering research and clinical assessment work had been carried out in Makerere Medical School in Kampala, Uganda by Dr Kassim in termination of pregnancy. The literature in journals was dominated by Kassim's publications. All this was before Idi Amin came to power. With Idi Amin's governance of alleged brutality, many professionals, including Kassim and Trussel, left Uganda. When I met Kassim, he told me about the number of tantalizing offers of jobs he had received. I think he eventually went to Singapore. Trussel accepted the chair in OB/ GY in London's St George Hospital. The high image of Makerere Medical School declined thereafter.

The above discourse on Prostaglandins is to put into historical perspective the emergence of this powerful drug which is now widely used in obstetrics and gynaecology. I hope I have succeeded and that it is not a triviality.

My first year as SHO was due to end on 31st December 1964. To continue my tenure, I had to renew my contract. The registrar post in obstetrics at St Mary's Hospital, a sister hospital, would also be vacant about the same time. It was a less busy post offering plenty of free time for reading and studying for examination. I had in mind another ambition. If I succeeded in passing the MRCOG on my first attempt, I could proceed to read up on internal Medicine and sit for the Edinburgh MRCP (MRCPE) offering obstetrics and gynaecology as a speciality. My friend Percy Nylander had done just that. I was then being affected by the disease of multiple diplomatosis. Chris Adomakoh had obtained his Diploma in Psychiatry and was doing a medical job in Scotland to prepare to sit for the MRCPE examination. With this aim in mind, I applied for the registrar post at St Mary's Hospital. Mr Redman had some beds in this hospital. One of the other applicants, Dr Fernando, a Sri Lankan, with the MRCOG, had worked in the SJH group before. At my request, Mr Redman wrote a reference on me in support of my application. Mr Redman's secretary called me to her office one day and in "soto voce" asked me to read over the reference letter Mr Redman had written about me, and to share it with her in confidence. I felt flattered after reading the reference letter. It was not a long letter, but the word "excellent" appeared three times!!! I attended an interview conducted by two doctors I had not met before. It was a friendly interview, with no penetrative questions. The job was offered to Dr Fernando. Mr Redman's reference letter on me was enough satisfaction for me. At my request, Mr Redman arranged for the extension of my contract for a further six months.

After fulfilling all the prerequisites before sitting the examination, I had to plan and set a programme for myself. I had acquired great skill and experience in the speciality. The aim now was to complement this with the assimilation of factual knowledge. Jeffcoate's Textbook of Gynaecology was the primary book to be mastered from cover to cover. I had to be familiar with the contents of "Gynaecological Pathology" by Haines and Taylor, Shaw's "Operative Gynaecology", and Munroe Kerr's "Operative Obstetrics". I was already familiar with the contents of "Combined Textbook of Obstetrics and Gynaecology" by Dugald Baird, a book aimed at undergraduate students.

At the initial stage of preparation, Dr Attit and I decided to hold joint discussions on topics of interest. I soon realized that I had to acquire a lot of factual knowledge. I therefore suggested that we discontinue the discussion sessions until I had done sufficient reading; he agreed to this. I applied for a short leave, which was granted. I sat down, read and read, and assimilated a vast spectrum of factual knowledge. The deductive way of learning had been my métier for years and this approach enabled me to acquire comprehensive knowledge. Feeling satisfied that I had done enough reading, I invited Dr Attit to resume our discussion sessions. We acquired some past MRCOG examination questions, and used them as a guide on discussion topics. After only one discussion session when I was effusing with knowledge, Dr Attit felt diffident and insecure; he suggested that we should discontinue with any further discussion sessions; we stopped the joint revision programme.

In furtherance to my preparation for the examination, I applied to attend a special course at London's Postgraduate Hospital at Hammersmith, then the Mecca of all the medical specialities, and Queen Charlotte. Hammersmith earned a worldwide reputation as a great medical learning centre: the Great Ormond Street Hospital was its sister hospital in Paediatrics. The Obstetrics/ Gynaecology Institute ran a course lasting a fortnight twice a year. The attendees, limited to 25, came from Britain, South Africa, Australia and Canada. Although I was not entitled to attend the course, Mr Redman, in full support pushed my application through for me to be granted special permission to attend it. I was thrilled by my acceptance. The course consisted of lectures delivered by faculty members and invited guest lecturers. This was in an era before sub-specialization in the speciality. A gynaecologist covered everything in obstetrics and gynaecology, although some had an interest in certain areas, and were then acknowledged as authorities in those areas.

I travelled from Leeds to London and stayed at a hotel in Bayswater. Attendees to the course came from Britain, Australia, South Africa and the West Indies. Peter Hirsch from SGH and Dr Sonnendecker from South Africa were among the attendees. The course consisted of didactic lectures given by carefully selected lecturers who prepared their lectures thoroughly, covering and involving the latest information on the topic in the literature. The following were some of the lecturers: Professor McClure Browne, Dr (later Professor) Dixon, Dr (later Professor) SG Clayton, and later President of the RCOG. A wide range of topics was covered. Dr Clayton was outstanding and gave the highest number of lectures. There were no discussion sessions. There was a lecture on PCOS (Polycystic Ovarian Syndrome). At the end of which, the speaker intimated that a new drug would soon come out in the management of PCOS, and that it would be a major breakthrough in the management of the condition. The new drug was called Clomiphene citrate. Dr Clayton gave an impressive lecture on urinary tract fistulae, a problem I would face on my return home to Ghana. An open lecture was scheduled in the second week at the Postgraduate Institute hall. The speaker was to be Sir Dugald Baird.

Sir Dugald had retired as Professor in Aberdeen, and was now Emeritus. His retirement was celebrated with a special dinner held in his honour in Aberdeen. Dr Arnold Klopper sent me a special invitation with an enclosed menu. Unfortunately, I was unable to attend the historic function. A portrait painting of him by a famous artist was presented to him at the dinner. Although I did not attend the dinner, I felt a great sense of pride and honour in receiving the invitation; I had been admitted into an exclusive group.

Sir Dugald travelled from his home in Aberdeen (Fare me well) to London to give a lecture on "Perinatal Mortality: The Aberdeen Experience". The hall was fully packed as he was escorted to the dais by Dr Dixon and Professor McClure Browne. I sat on the right side in the middle of a row. Sir Dugald gave a scintillating lecture on a topic close to his heart. He illustrated the methodology involved in reducing the perinatal mortality over the decades in his unit in Aberdeen. He finished the lecture to a standing ovation. Sir Dugald then walked down the aisle towards the exit at the back of the hall escorted by the organisers. When he reached the row where I was sitting, almost near the wall, he spotted me. He then stopped and directed a broad smile towards me. I was obliged to meander my way towards him in the aisle to acknowledge his presence. Everything came to a standstill. I was amazed that he could spot and recognize me in the large audience, particularly so when he had not seen me for about five years. He enquired about how I was faring and went on to say that he had information that I was doing well. With a paternal smile of obvious delight, he continued on to the exit. I of course became the cynosure of all eyes in the hall; who was this fellow whom Sir Dugald had singled out for such attention? I felt highly honoured. I completed the course and returned to Leeds. It was a fortnight well spent; a memorable one.

I kept on reading in preparation for the forthcoming examination; I felt that I had prepared myself in every respect. Since I had not failed any examination before, I was confident and positive about the forthcoming one. I was nevertheless mindful of some quirks in examinations. The examination consisted of a written paper, clinical cases, and a viva voce. The written paper for candidates in the north of England was scheduled to be held in Sheffield whilst the clinical and viva voce for all the candidates were to be held in London.

Dr Attit and I went to Sheffield for the written paper. I felt comfortable with the questions. One of the questions was on urinary tract fistulae. I had read almost all the literature on this condition and had seen cases of vesico-vaginal fistula whilst I was working under Dr Bannerman in Accra. No matter how much knowledge you have on a question, it was unwise to spend an unnecessarily long time in answering that one question; you could not score more than 75% in close marking. I was fully aware of this fact. At the end, I thought I had acquitted myself in the written paper. One of the candidates, a lady from the Indian subcontinent, asked for permission to use the rest-room. She was caught reading her notes. She was dismissed from the examination. After the examination, Dr Attit and I returned to Leeds. This was my first visit to Sheffield.

About a week later, Dr Attit and I travelled to London for the clinicals and viva voce parts of the examination. Travelling with us on the train to London was Dr Currie (Junior), son of the gynaecologist, and registrar in internal medicine at SJH; he was on his way to London for the MRCP examination. Dr Attit and I lodged at a hotel in Bayswater. The venue for my clinical was the Wittington Hospital. I made a preliminary reconnaissance visit to the hospital on my arrival in London, a day before my examination. The clinical was held in the morning, followed by the viva voce in the afternoon at the RCOG located at Sussex Gardens, near Regent's Park.

My first case was an obstetrics one. I was presented with a young primigravida in her mid-twenties, who was about seven-eight months pregnant. She was not an inpatient. She was well and had no complaints, I took her case history and before I could start examining her, the two examiners strode in. My "A" opening batsman factor again at work. I told the examiners that I had not yet examined the patient. They beckoned me on to examine her in their presence. During the course of the examination, as I was auscultating the heart in the mitral area, I heard a faint diastolic murmur; as I was not too sure, I spent a little more time on this. As I listened, I caught the eye of one examiner blinking with some fascination towards the second examiner. I felt that I had hit on something interesting; a grade one cardiac with mitral stenosis. I followed on with the rest of the obstetric examination. Not many obstetricians would normally diagnose a case of low grade mitral stenosis. I was asked to present the case. I stated that I thought I had heard a faint diastolic murmur in the mitral area, but would defer to a Physician to confirm my finding. This was well received by the examiners. If my diagnosis was confirmed, the examiners asked me how I would manage and deliver the patient. In my answer, I stated that since she was asymptomatic, I would allow her to undergo a normal labour, but in her second stage, I stated that a forceps application and delivery would be "obligatory". There was nodding approval from both examiners. I must confess to a feeling of pride and satisfaction at my choice of the word "obligatory". I was next asked about the third stage of labour. At that time, there was a controversy on the use of the oxytocic. Ergometrine was available, but Syntocinon had not yet arrived on the scene. While some obstetricians administered Ergometrine, another school refrained from using it routinely in cardiac patients. I responded that Ergometrine was not used routinely at SGH, well known for the management of cardiac cases in pregnancy. I had not seen any harm from refraining from its use; I therefore would not use it on this patient in her third stage of labour. I stated that I was aware of the controversy surrounding its use. This assertion brought my case to its conclusion.

The next one was a gynaecological case, a lady in her fifties who presented with utero-vaginal prolapse. It was a straightforward case with no controversy about its management. This completed my clinical examination at Whittington Hospital that morning. I felt satisfied with my performance so far.

I went to the RCOG in the afternoon for the final part, the viva voce, of the examination. One had to pass in all the three parts to be successful at the MRCOG; excelling in two parts and failing in a third amounted to a total failure. I went to the RCOG well attired in a bespoke suit befitting a consultant gynaecologist. In the foyer, I met Dr Adotey Moffat, a fellow Ghanaian. Although he was also on Ghana government scholarship for the MRCOG, he had moved to Canada to prepare for this British examination. The nuances of examination make your location also important (Moffat had not abandoned his flamboyance which was on display when I met him in Achimota in 1946).

When I was called for my viva voce, I faced two examiners. One of them was Dr Halsted, an eminent gynaecologist practising in London. Like the legendary Sir John Stalworthy and Sir Zachary Cope, he hailed from Australia. Dr Halsted asked the questions while the second examiner looked on. The question which occupied most of the time was how I would handle a transverse lie during a Caesarean section operation. I answered that I would extract the baby by the legs and do a breech extraction. Dr Halsted tried his best to make me change my mind and do something different like pulling out the presenting shoulder. I stood my ground firmly, but politely. Although my answer was correct, his approach as an examiner was to make sure that it was safe to let the candidate loose as a new member of the RCOG. The viva voce lasted about 20 minutes. I cannot recall the question in gynaecology. On my dismissal, I felt I had acquitted myself satisfactorily. With the examination over, I returned to Leeds.

My period of waiting for the results was shrouded in anxiety and foreboding, as well as impatience. Dr Attit had told me that we would receive the results by mail in one to two weeks' time. The pass rate was reputedly 30-40%; whether this was a true reflection of the candidates' performance, or the application of a bar to limit the number of new members, I did not know. If it was the latter, then it was competitive.

I met Dr Attit at breakfast on a Monday morning. He informed me that we would receive our results that day. I had to leave him to join Mr Redman for his ward round. Dr Attit made a strange request from me as I left. The request was that on receiving the result, we should not disclose it to anyone till evening time. Although I found this peculiar and odd, I agreed to oblige, and proceeded to Ward 14 to join Mr Redman on his round, with a retinue of the ward sister and junior nurses. The ward was large and open with two single side rooms. While we were in the middle of the round, Dr Attit strode into the ward in a triumphant mood and declared loudly to Mr Redman and all around "I have passed my MRCOG". He then handed me somewhat challengingly, my mailed envelope with my result. I quietly put the envelope into my pocket without opening it. Everything had come to a standstill. Mr Redman asked me to open my envelope with a wink and an air of prescience. I obliged, opened the envelope, read the result that I had passed the MRCOG and quietly, pokerfaced, put the envelope back into my pocket without any comment. With the group and indeed all the patients holding their breath and on the prompting stare from Mr Redman, without any emotion, but with a little smile, I said "I have passed the MRCOG examination". Mr Redman jumped up with uncontrollable and celebratory joy. The spontaneous joy was shared by our team and on-looking patients alike. Why did Dr Attit break the pledge and behave the way he did? Suppose I had not passed the examination? It is best left to conjecture. The news of our success quickly went viral in the whole hospital, and congratulations were rendered by many, including the chaplain who told me that the examination was regarded as a difficult one to pass. Dr Currie (Jr), son of the Gynaecologist, a medical registrar, in congratulating me went on further to disclose to me a piece of information. He told me that his father was the examiner who marked all the written answer papers on the question about urinary tract fistulae; he disclosed that I had topped with the highest mark. He had been privy to this information for a long time, but deliberately refrained from telling me for a good reason: one could still fail the examination despite scoring the highest in one question. It was gratifying to know, nonetheless, that I had performed so well in that paper. I had never before then repaired a urinary fistula; it was a problem I would face on my return home to Ghana.

It was mandatory for me and Dr Attit to celebrate our examination success. Dr Freedom Amroliwala invited us to his house for a special dinner in the evening. Dr Attit and I bought and took along with us some bottles of champagne. Dr Amroliwala received us warmly and introduced us to his family. He had two young sons and a daughter. It was a memorable evening of jollity. I sent the news of my success home to my parents. I wrote to Sandy Herriot and Dr Mair in Glasgow; they were delighted and responded with congratulatory messages. I wrote to Dr Arnold Klopper in Aberdeen. In his warm congratulatory letter he went on further to offer me a research fellowship post in gynaecological endocrinology in the Aberdeen Medical Research Council unit. He was the leading gynaecological endocrinologist in Britain and the leading authority on Estrogenes in the world. I had to think hard about this super attractive offer.

I had acquired the MRCOG and would now append it to my name in addition to others. I had been addressed as Dr Agble, but with my new acquisition, my assignation reverted to Mr Agble, as is the designation of gynaecologists in England. With my new assignation, I attained a new level of confidence in every respect. Although I was still only an SHO, I performed duties normally assigned to registrars and sometimes senior registrars.

The RCOG wrote to inform me about the date of the convocation, when I would be formally admitted to the membership of the RCOG. I was allocated two tickets for my accompanying guests. I had established contact with Dr Tsapogas, my quondam registrar in Aberdeen in 1959. He moved to London and became a leading Peripheral Vascular Surgeon in leading London hospitals. He delivered the Hunterian lectures at the RCS in London in 1963. I invited him and his wife to the convocation ceremony at the RCOG as my supporters. He accepted the invitation graciously. Dr Attit and I travelled together to London for the occasion.

Elegantly gowned, I was admitted as a member of the RCOG, witnessed by my supporters. Some members were elevated to the Fellowship at the same function. After the ceremony, Dr and Mrs

Tsapogas entertained me to dinner in a very nice restaurant. Dr Attit and I returned to Leeds the following day.

The tenure of my SHO post had been extended for six months to enable me to sit for the examination, but could not be extended any longer. The Ghana High Commission was of course informed about my new status as an MRCOG. The government policy was to return home soon after acquiring a postgraduate degree without any delay. Without prolonging my stay, I certainly could not prepare and sit for the MRCPE examination, nor accept the research fellowship offer from Aberdeen. Other developments in another sphere were also in progress.

I had been blessed and fortunate in myriad ways. My surgical experience nurtured under Dr Peer and my exposure to Tropical Medicine in Kumasi were priceless assets. My first SHO job in SGH in Glasgow provided me with the opportunity to train and become a competent and a first class obstetrician. SJH in Leeds provided me with the venue and chance to acquire the training and expertise in gynaecology. I exploited the opportunity to its fullest extent. I was now a fully rounded and confident obstetrician/gynaecologist. With great modesty, I felt that not many of my peers had been as blessed and lucky as I was at the time. I had achieved the feat of obtaining the MRCOG on my first attempt when the pass rate was reputedly 30-40%. I was professionally ready to return home to Ghana.

I attended a meeting of the North of England OB/GY Society in Sheffield. The main speaker was Dr Una Lister. Una and her twin sister both practised as eminent gynaecologists in Nigeria. Una presented a paper on the repair of vesico-vaginal fistula, "The Ibadan Experience", a vast experience indeed. It was an impressive presentation. The acknowledged authority on the subject in Britain was Professor Chassar Moir at Oxford University; he had written the definitive monogram on the subject. Dr Lister, on this current visit to Britain, went to Oxford and observed Professor Moir perform a fistula repair. She went on to say that at the end of the operation, she asked him how he would describe the fistula. His stated response was 'a moderately difficult one'. Dr Una then continued in some sort of sotto voce, 'that is the sort of fistula we pass on to our registrars in Ibadan to repair'!

Ghana had started its first medical school at Korle Bu. Dr RH Bannerman, then a Senior Lecturer at Ibadan, was appointed as the foundation chair in OB/GY. In an answer to a question I asked her about Dr Bannerman, she confirmed that he had accepted the appointment and stated that he had some ambitious plans for his new department. I began to look forward to joining his team in Accra. I think that at that time I was the 10th or 11th Ghanaian to obtain the MRCOG. I was quite sure that if on his return to Korle Bu, I made a request to join his unit, he would very gladly agree to offer me a post there. I believed that I had a laudable CV (Curriculum Vitae). Visions of life in academia in clinical obstetrics and gynaecology began to unfold. With my established linkage with the department and research MRC unit in Aberdeen, I looked forward to the future with confidence and enthusiasm.

On my return to Britain, I was a mature young man who enjoyed the best things life could offer. I was socially engaging and enjoyed the company of friends of either gender.

The landscape of my life began to change towards the end of my first year in Leeds. It started in a most inconspicuous way. A Staff Nurse, Yolande Garraway by name, a Trinidadian, was assigned to the gynaecology ward (Ward 14) for a brief period of two weeks to solve some logistical staffing problems, much against her wishes. She was an SRN (State Registered Nurse) and had just qualified as a Midwife. Attractive, intelligent and of a rather quiet disposition, she took turns in rotation with the Ward Sister, Miss Kneeshaw. They had a disagreement one day on the duty roster. Unknown to them, I was within ear-shot and listened to the altercation. Miss Garraway wanted to attend a concert by Ray Charles, but Miss Kneeshaw had not taken this into consideration, despite being informed, when preparing the duty roster. The issue was apparently resolved and she was able to attend the concert. A few days later, she telephoned me about a newly admitted patient, I asked her whether she had enjoyed the Ray Charles concert. She was quite surprised to learn that I had been aware of her initial problem with Sister Kneeshaw. A lively and friendly chat was followed by a dinner out; thus began a friendship. Like all friendships, I did not envisage how it would continue or end. As I got to know of her background, interests and vice versa, the friendship escalated into a love affair. Introductions to a few Ghanaian friends received favourable comments of approval. Dr Kemavor, a senior colleague who was doing a post-graduate course in ENT (Ear, Nose and Throat) Surgery lived in Harrogate with his English wife, Anne. I drove up to Harrogate with Yolande to visit the Kemavor family (they had some young children then). We were very warmly entertained. Gabriel was due to return home to Ghana shortly. They said they looked forward to seeing us in Ghana as a couple.

During my post-graduate course in London, Yolande came to visit me over a weekend. I must have mentioned marriage during that weekend, although I have no recollection of a proposal as such, but I presented her with an engagement ring which she accepted, returning to Leeds as my fiancée. While in London, I took her to the Covent Garden Opera to see Bellini's NORMA with Joan Sutherland in the title role (Joan Sutherland emerged as a diva after this performance). Yolande had left SJH and commenced a six-month course in Health Visiting; this earned her a diploma in Public Health. Yolande resided in an apartment in the Headingley district of Leeds. I kept my parents informed of all the developments; they were pleased to learn that my days of bachelorhood would end soon. It is perhaps germane here to recall the advice Dr Mair in Glasgow had given me in 1963 that I should go to Leeds in preference to a district hospital because of a more likely chance of meeting a life partner. This came out of the blue, not prompted by any discussion on marriage. How prescient!

After obtaining the MRCOG, events moved fast. Yolande and I were invited to London by Comfort Blukoo Allotey, now Mrs Boakye (Mr Boakye was the CEO of the Ghana Black Star Shipping Line). Comfort, Jake's fond sister, and I had developed a closeness that approached surrogate siblinghood. She hosted a special party in our honour. Becoming engaged to Yolande, a Trinidadian, in Britain, spared me the traditional Ghana custom of 'door knocking' fee, dowry drinks and the lot. After we were married and relocated home to Ghana, Yolande was made aware of this custom – she claimed that she felt she had missed out, but I was never asked to compensate for it!

Back in Leeds, we fixed a date for our wedding. I was a Presbyterian although not currently a church attendant. Yolande was an Anglican, the dominant church in England, so a date was chosen for an

Anglican Church wedding. I had played the role of best man on three occasions in Ghana and had given away a bride, a Trinidadian friend of Yolande's, to a Sierra Leonean groom, earlier on in Leeds. Now the major male role as a groom was descending on me in a place far from home and my relatives.

The wedding was held on 2nd October 1965. Yolande's mother travelled from Trinidad with the traditional wedding cake, made by one of her aunts, to witness the occasion. It was her first visit to Britain. Peter Mensah, who had hosted a bachelors' night party the previous evening, was my best man. My cousin Gilbert Ansre (now Professor Reverend Dr Gilbert Ansre) travelled from London to witness and grace the occasion as the representative of my family. The guests who attended included Mr and Mrs Redman, Mr and Mrs Begg, Mr and Mrs Melville, Mr and Mrs Tom Skelton, Drs Attit, Anteson, Adjei-Sowah, Mr and Mrs Atuwo and a number of resident doctors from SJH, as well as a number of Yolande's friends. We numbered just over 50 The toasts and replies were humorous. The ceremony was historic, but not as grand as it would have been if it had been held in Ghana. My parents held a nuptial service simultaneously in Hohoe.

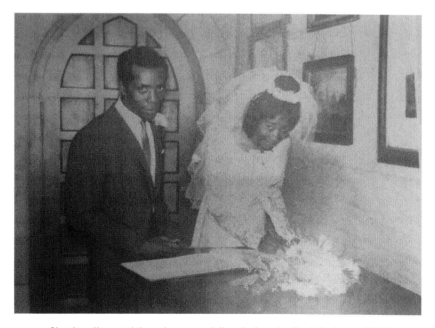

Signing the register at our wedding in Leeds, 2nd October 1965

We planned to go to Dublin for our honeymoon. Neither of us had been there before, but it appeared to be an ideal location, highly recommended by a very good Irish friend of Yolande's, Peggy Skelton, whose husband, Tom, had given Yolande away, in the absence of her father. About an hour after the reception, we were driven to the Leeds airport where we boarded a plane for Dublin.

Honeymoon is basically a holiday in an idyllic location for a newly married couple to get to know each other. Dublin was a city of historic beauty and eminence. The home of George Bernard Shaw and several Irish writers, Dublin was also a great seat of learning. The Rotunda Hospital was famous for its pioneering work in Obstetrics. We booked and lodged in a highly rated hotel, the Powers Royal, centrally sited; we were not disappointed in our choice. I was suddenly ushered into a new expenditure commitment; hitherto, on most occasions, payment of bills was for a single person; from now on the payment would be for two people, a new awakening demanding the appropriate budgeting. As tourists, we visited several places of interest in the urban and rural districts. It was a couple's start in life, lasting just over a week.

Although I cannot recall any anecdotal incidents, we made an acquaintance which initiated a friendship that lasted a long time. At our first breakfast, we met a dignified looking English man, Mr Wright, at the table. After the initial exchange of pleasantries, and introductions, we found a common ground and bonded. He was an architect and was taking over a new job in Dublin with an international company. He was taking over from Mr Bob Barclay. Bob Barclay had just been appointed to the chair in Building Technology in KNUST in Kumasi, Ghana. Bob was due to leave for Ghana in early 1966, the following year. We were due to leave for Ghana before the end of the year. The Barclays lived in Kent and Mr Wright thought that Mr Barclay would be pleased to meet us. He therefore arranged for a mutually suitable time for us to visit the Barclays in Kent. It was a fortuitous first day in Dublin.

On our return to Leeds, I moved into Yolande's flat, a single bedroom one. Yolande's mother soon after returned to Trinidad. We now fully engaged ourselves in preparation to travel to Ghana. Because of her connection with the Black Star Line and Elder Dempster Line, Comfort Blukoo Allotey undertook to arrange for our booking for our journey home. To add to the excitement of returning home, Jake was also due to arrive in England from the USA with Cynthia and baby John on his return journey home to Ghana. What could be more appropriate than both Jake and I travelling back home together on the boat journey with our families? Jake and I had not met for over three years when he and Chris came to see me off in Takoradi. Comfort set herself up and did just that; she arranged and secured a booking for us in November on M.V. Aureol, the most luxurious ship of the Elder Dempster line (the other two were M.V. Apapa and M.V. Accra). The port of departure was Liverpool. Yolande and I had to do some serious planning and packing. According to all reports, the Ghana economy was in a poor shape and the political climate was deteriorating. Dr Kemavor had returned home and wrote to advise me to bring along every possible item I would need; he listed some items which one would not normally think were necessary. A saloon car, a refrigerator, cooker, deep freezer were all "musts"; washing machine not necessary. We had several items of wedding gifts, some of which had to be supplemented with everyday crockery, pots and pans.

The choice of a saloon car exercised my thoughts to some extent. A Mercedes Benz car was sturdy, elegant and prestigious, but I associated it with corrupt politicians with ill-gotten money. I therefore chose the latest model of Opel Rekord. I instructed Comfort to purchase the car for me in Germany. She obliged and I paid for it. The car was shipped to London. Peter Mensah, then resident in London, at my request, arranged with M. O. Adjei (Old Achimotan classmate) to drive the car to Liverpool and deliver it to Elder Dempster to be placed on the Aureol to accompany me to Ghana. I saw the car for the first time on my arrival at Tema on 1st December.

Pari passu with all the developments noted above, Yolande and I had a busy programme before our departure. We honoured a few invitations to dinner. Yolande continued to work as a newly qualified Public Health nurse. We went to the cinema to see the film version of Bernard Shaw's "My Fair Lady"; a musical I still rate as the best produced musical.

Aberdeen had been my second home and had not ceased to be so. It was also my Obstetric place of birth under the wings of Sir Dugald Baird and Dr Arnold Klopper. I decided to squeeze a little time to pay a brief sentimental visit to the Granite City; this would be the most appropriate, fitting and timely occasion. My good old friend Victor Adu had just returned from Ghana to Aberdeen to commence a PhD course in soil science. I travelled by train from Leeds to Edinburgh where I changed trains into an Aberdeen–bound train with a restaurant coach. The culinary offerings back the nostalgia of the days of yore. I had booked and stayed in a hotel; the sights remained familiar and unchanged. The students from overseas whom I knew had completed their various courses and returned home; there were no familiar faces around.

I paid my pilgrimage visit to the Maternity Unit at Forester Hill. Dr Klopper was delighted and very pleased to see me. I thanked him for all his contributions towards my training and success. I renewed my bond with him. He understood and appreciated the reason for my return home to Ghana and not accepting his offer of a Fellowship in their Research Unit. Sir Dugald had retired and Dr MacGillivray was now the occupant of the Regius Chair; he had moved back from London's St Mary's Hospital, where, I learned, he had not been quite happy. Dr David Paintin, an Englishman, who had accompanied him from Aberdeen to St Mary's, however, stayed on. David attained fame later as the Editor of the BJOG and one of the leading personalities to have the law on abortion completely revised. Stepping into the shoes of iconic Sir Dugald could not have been the easiest of tasks for Ian MacGillivray. He had of course distinguished himself as one of the world authorities on pre-eclamptic toxaemia in pregnancy. Perhaps it takes more than that to create and achieved. I had achieved the main object of my mission. I did not, however, go as far as visiting Sir Dugald in his home at "Fare-me-well" on the outskirts of the city. This was attributable more to a feeling of awe, than anything else.

Victor Adu and I arranged and met at the Students Union building the following evening in the basement bar. It brought back sweet memories; we reminisced. He introduced me to a Malawian student. The student was delighted and excited to learn that I was a gynaecologist. He said that there was only one gynaecologist, a German expatriate, practising in the whole country. He tried his best to persuade me to go to work in Malawi; he seemed to be very well connected. We downed several rounds of beer before retiring from the Students Union building. I traced and located the new abode of

Mrs Duthie, my first landlady. She was her sweet self, with well coiffured hair, but now frail. She was delighted to see me. Her daughter, Mrs Mutch, was there to entertain me to an afternoon tea. We continued to keep in touch with an annual exchange of Christmas cards until she passed away.

I returned to Leeds after fulfilling the Aberdeen mission. I continued with the purchasing and preparations for eventual departure. We had received an invitation from the Barclays to visit them in Kent which we intended to honour. Yolande and I travelled by train to London on a Saturday and boarded another train for Kent. We were met at the Kent station by Mr Wright who then introduced us to the Barclays. It was a bright and sunny day. The Barclays, a cheerful and vivacious couple, were looking forward very much to meeting us in Ghana. We returned to Leeds in the evening.

The chapter of my life as a postgraduate had now come to a close. I had arrived in August 1962, a little over three years to the day. I had trained and qualified as a gynaecologist in just three years. I was an accomplished clinician and surgeon. There was still a lot to learn by way of experience which only comes with the passage of time. In Yolande, I had acquired a life partner. Yolande, a Trinidadian, had never before been outside her home country except England. She was now plunging herself into a new life in a place unknown to her. She showed no sign of fear, anxiety or insecurity. We completed all our packing and arranged with a removal company to collect our packages, numbering about 30 in all and delivered them to the port in Liverpool. I had sold my old Opel Rekord car for peanuts.

Yolande continued to work as a home visiting nurse till our final days in Leeds. Nearing our departure date, she felt lethargic and generally unwell. We bade our final farewells and travelled to Liverpool by train. We checked into a hotel close to the port, which we had booked. The departure date was scheduled for the following day. Jake and Cynthia arrived from London and came to visit us in our hotel, accompanied by Dr Joe Blankson. Dr Blankson, a fellow Ghanaian and a Liverpool Medical School alumnus, had come to see off the Blukoo-Alloteys. The meeting with Jake and Cynthia was the first for Yolande; it was the start of a family friendship, approaching surrogate siblinghood status at all levels. Yolande and I checked in on the MV Aureol the following day. The real nature of Yolande's malady had unfolded the previous evening when she suddenly felt lesions on her scalp! Characteristic spots appeared on her skin; she had chicken pox. Her earlier feelings of being unwell were the prodromal symptoms of chickenpox. A fortnight before our departure date, she was asked to do a home visit on a patient, a nun, with shingles and the fact that she was aware that shingles and chickenpox shared the same virus. Although she expressed her concern because of her forthcoming travel, her supervisor , lacking the in depth knowledge of infectious diseases, arrogantly dismissed her fears, and she obliged by conducting the visit. Yolande's concern now turned into a reality.

On checking in we were assigned a nice cabin. We next called on the ship's doctor to disclose to him Yolande's illness. He made no fuss over the disclosure, but after taking a history, imposed a five-day quarantine on her – there were a number of young children on board. Since I had a history of chickenpox I was thought to be immune to it. The MV Aureol was the flagship of the Elder Dempster Lines. It was a pleasure for me to travel on it for a second time. Other passengers on board included Dr Takyi (Surgeon), Dr David Acquaye (Soil Scientist) and a Duke who was a cousin of the Queen who was going to take up a diplomatic post in Lagos.

The sea journey lasted 14 days, with stops at Las Palmas and Freetown. The passage through the Bay of Biscay lived up to its notoriety, stormy with the fifteen thousand ton liner rolling from side to side and front to back, sending plates and objects to the floor told the story. Most of the voyage was smooth over a quiet Atlantic Ocean. During her days under quarantine, Yolande's meals were delivered to her in the cabin. She joined the rest of us at our selected and reserved table. Breakfast and lunch were casual, but formal dressing was mandatory for dinner. It was an opportunity for the ladies to dress up; Yolande and Cynthia did not disappoint us in this respect. We, the men, took turns in buying the alcoholic drinks. The cuisine was delicious, the company of fellow professionals and friends convivial, and entertaining. Yolande began her familiarization process with Ghanaians and Ghana. Her impression on the whole was a favourable one. We approached Ghana in a quiet sea and docked at Tema, the country's new industrial port.

*Yolande & I on the M.V. Aureol on Yolande's first
visit to Ghana in November 1965.*

At this juncture, it is timely to provide the political landscape and the state of the economy in Ghana in a historical perspective. What was the prevailing political climate like? What were the achievements of Kwame Nkrumah? These thoughts assailed my mind. Most of the facts and the bibliography were culled from the well-researched and scholarly chapter from Martin Meredith's book "The State of Africa (A History of Fifty Years of Independence)".

Kwame Nkrumah was sworn in as President in 1960 when Ghana became a Republic. His CPP party became supreme. A personality cult had built around him. His titles included His High Dedication, Man of Destiny, Star of Africa, and most famous of all, Osagyefo. Apparently, this façade concealed a loneliness and an isolated personality. Ms Genoviva Marais, a South African, and reputedly attractive confidante of Kwame Nkrumah, wrote in her memoirs "the more successful he was politically, the less he seemed capable of trusting his most intimate friends, no matter how loyal they had proved themselves to be. He gained the support of party activists, who only told him what they thought he wanted to know". He had arranged with Nasser of Egypt for a bride. Fathia's wedding to Nkrumah occurred on 30th December, 1957, the day of her arrival in Ghana. Fathia spoke only Arabic with a smattering of French. Nkrumah spoke neither Arabic nor French. The marriage produced three children. In a letter to Ms Erica Powell, his long-standing private secretary, Nkrumah confessed that marriage did nothing to lighten the sense of isolation he felt. Nkrumah built a citadel of power around himself. The 1960 Republican Constitution enabled him to rule by decree, to reject Parliamentary decisions, to dismiss any public servant or member of the Armed Forces or judiciary. He maintained total control over all the media. Using the Preventive Detention Act (PDA), and other security measures, the negligible opposition was buried and silenced. With the party supreme, a vast establishment was set up to control institutions such as the civil service, the TUC, farmers' organisations and youth groups to become subordinate to it. Tussles for power and influence arose in the party. With this came a tide of corruption. Adamafio in his memoirs wrote of corruption as "a howling monster threatening to wreck the whole nation". Government funds were squandered in every direction. To his credit, Nkrumah denounced this ugly development in 1961. Despite the setting up of an investigative committee to probe this, the corrupt activities of the party elite continued unchallenged and unabated.

With his plan to turn Ghana into a modern industrial society, Nkrumah initially made considerable progress. Schools, hospitals and roads were built at an unprecedented rate; a major hydroelectric scheme on the Volta River was completed, providing a lasting source of electricity and cheap energy. Impatient for results on a spectacular scale, Nkrumah pressed on with one project after another, with factories, steelworks, mining ventures and shipyards, almost any idea which caught his imagination. Some schemes were started simply for reasons of prestige. Nkrumah wanted, for example, to build the largest dry dock in Africa, regardless of its viability. Other schemes were impractical. An enterprising Romanian-born businessman convinced him of the need to build a huge set of concrete silos to store cocoa so that the price of cocoa could be controlled more effectively. Once built, the silos were condemned as unusable. One of Nkrumah's expatriate advisers, Robert Jackson, walked into Nkrumah's office on one occasion to find a European salesman peddling some far-fetched scheme. Nkrumah had his pen in his hand ready to sign a contract for more than a million pounds sterling. "Shall I just look it over?" suggested Mr Jackson. He carefully took the document away, and that day saved the exchequer a million pounds sterling. The more ambitious the project that was put forward, the more likely it was to gain approval. A footwear factory was set up with luxurious bungalows and lavish administrative block at a cost eight times higher than the price recommended at the time of independence by an expatriate adviser.

At the same time that the ideas, schemes and instructions were pouring forth from Nkrumah's office, Ghana was heading into economic difficulties. The external debt soared. Officially, it reached 184 million pounds sterling in 1963; a year later, it stood at 349 million pounds sterling. But no one could ascertain exactly to what extent the government was in debt because complete records of the contracts were not kept in government files. Nkrumah often awarded contracts personally without reference to the cabinet, the appropriate minister, or cabinet's contract committee. He resorted to using suppliers' credit, in effect, mortgaging Ghana's revenues for years ahead. But again, no one was sure in the absence of proper records, by how much. In later years, odd items, a five million pound sterling warship for the navy, a 7,500ton luxury boat built for Nkrumah himself, kept turning up. In some cases, the delivery of goods for which Ghana signed was never made.

The agricultural policies were equally disastrous. He favoured mechanized state farms and diverted government resources for their benefit, neglecting the need of peasant farmers. Disgruntled by the low prices offered by the state monopoly of state buying, farmers reacted by selling cocoa illegally across the borders and by refusing to plant more trees. The state farms, meanwhile, staffed by CPP supporters, their families and friends, made huge losses, producing yields that were less than a fifth of peasant agriculture. Most became graveyards of rusting machinery.

The overall result of Nkrumah's handling of the economy was disastrous. From being one of the most prosperous countries in the tropical world at the time of independence in 1957, Ghana by 1965 had become virtually bankrupt. At a cabinet meeting on 11th February 1963 when the Finance Minister announced that Ghana's reserves stood at less than five hundred thousand pounds sterling, Nkrumah was so shocked that he sat in silence for 15 minutes, then broke down and wept.

In foreign affairs, he spent huge amounts of time, energy and resources in campaigning for a United States of Africa, which he aimed to head himself. Other African leaders did not share his enthusiasm. He quarrelled with Julius Nyerere of Tanzania over his plans for an East African Federation since it conflicted with Nkrumah's own concept of African Unity. He also denounced the policies of "African Socialism", which other African leaders favoured over that of "Scientific Socialism" which Nkrumah regarded as the right road. He accused the Francophone states of West Africa of acting as puppets of French neo-colonialism. More seriously, he fell into disputes with neighbouring countries — Togo, Cote d'Ivoire, Nigeria, Upper Volta and Niger. In addition to setting up guerrilla training camps for African exiles from Southern Africa, Nkrumah readily supported the activities of subversive groups from neighbouring countries in the hope of helping them to power. After Ghanaian agents were implicated in an assassination attempt on Togo's President, Sylvanius Olympio, seven African heads of state threatened to break off diplomatic relations with Ghana. His Bureau of African Affairs ran subversive agents in nine African countries, and organised a host of training camps for anti-government dissidents with the help of East German and Chinese experts.

In the wider field of foreign affairs, he strove to act as a world statesman offering his services as a mediator. In support of these ambitions, he built up an extensive diplomatic network which included 57 embassies. The embassy network enriched party members who staffed them. Huge sums were spent on diplomatic properties, allowances and expenses of every kind.

The crowning folly of Nkrumah's regime was "Job 600", the construction of a grand complex of buildings for a single conference of OAU Heads of State in 1965, costing ten million pounds sterling, launched at a time when factories were short of raw materials. Food queues in town were common; hospitals were short of drugs; and state corporations were bankrupt. Nkrumah's dream was that it would also serve as the future capital of a Union Government of Africa. Nkrumah boasted proudly of Job 600; the 60 self-contained suites that would have satisfied the demands of millionaires, the banqueting hall capable of seating two thousand guests, the fountain operated by 72 jets with a multi-coloured interplay of lights rising to a height of 60 feet.

Yet the conference turned out to be an abject failure. Because Nkrumah's foreign policy had alienated so many governments, a large number of African leaders were reluctant to attend. A group of 14 leaders led by Felix Houphouet-Boigny agreed to boycott it in retaliation for Nkrumah's support of subversive activities against their governments. In the end 28 out of 36 members of OAU attended the meeting, but only 13 were represented by heads of state. No one supported his call for Union Government of Africa. Indeed, the conference rejected his plea for a subcommittee to consider the issue.

This was the tapestry of the political and economic landscape of my home country on which I would shortly disembark.

Chapter 7
ARRIVING AND
SETTLING IN GHANA

We docked at Tema port and stepped out on shore on 1st December 1965. It marked the end of our journey and the start of a new life. Our arrival had been keenly awaited by my nuclear family and friends. Among the welcoming party was my mother, clad in a white celebratory kaba. My sister Felicia, brother Willie, auntie Cecilia and some family friends constituted the welcoming group. Our pieces of luggage and the Opel Rekord car were unloaded. Two pieces of my luggage had gone missing and were never recovered. I saw my car for the first time; it was a beautiful car, probably the first of that model to arrive in the country. It was registered later and bore the registration of GF 4460. After all the disembarkation formalities, we were driven to Accra. Brother Willie was the Director of Crops Research unit of the CSIR. He had booked accommodation for me and Yolande at the CSIR Guest House at Ridge. The Ridge area was an appealing and attractive part of Accra with greenery and roads canopied with trees. Willie assigned to me his Mercedes-Benz car with a chauffeur, Mr Ben Ocloo, a young, pleasant, charismatic fellow, who knew his way around almost everything; he was an excellent driver. As a Man Friday, he was peerless. On the day we arrived, Felicia served us our first meal, fufu with ground-nut soup. Yolande was welcomed into the Agble family.

I had complied with the demand of the MOH (Ministry of Health) by returning home promptly after obtaining the MRCOG. Where was I going to be posted? I went to report at the MOH and was directed to see the DMS (Director of Medical Services) in his office. He welcomed me back home and told me that I was being posted to Ho Hospital in the Volta Region. I had hitherto worked in large busy hospitals and although I hailed from the region, I had my own reason for not welcoming the posting to Ho. My hope of working in Accra was dashed. After leaving the Director's office, as I walked along the corridor, I met Dr E. A. Baidoo, the eminent surgeon. He warmed up to me and greeted me cheerfully saying, "What? You are back already?" I had not been aware that he had known me that well. Next, he asked me about my posting. When I told him that I had just been told of my posting to Ho, his immediate advice was "Ho? Do not go there. You will be lucky to perform one hysterectomy in a month. What about Accra or Kumasi?"

This instantly instilled in me a resolve to fight for a posting to Accra. Since I thought the Ho posting was a fait accompli, I had not considered challenging it. But a fight against the DMS, the Supremo? I was advised to see the Principal Secretary of the MOH. On the following day, I went to the MOH to see the PS, Mr Winful. I told him that I had just arrived and was being posted to Ho when I had assumed that I would be posted to Accra. Mr Winful, speaking with an Oxbridge accent, impressed me as a thoughtful and broadminded officer; he was forthright and said that as a newly qualified specialist, I should work with other more senior specialists before being posted to a place to be on my own. He said that he had learned that acquiring the FRCS or the MRCOG did not mean that the doctor could necessarily operate well without understudying senior ones on arrival. Although I did not think that I fell within this category regarding operation skill, it was sweet Mozartean music to my ears. He promised to help me, but there were a number of "ifs".

There was the serious problem of lack of accommodation for doctors at Korle Bu Hospital. Dr Evans-Anfom, the Superintendent of Korle Bu, was responsible for providing accommodation for the doctors. Dr Kwesi Bentsi-Enchill was the head of the OB/GY department. If Dr Bentsi-Enchill was willing to accept me in his department and Dr Anfom could provide accommodation for me, Mr Winful assured me, he would post me to Accra; these were two big "ifs". Since I had worked under Dr Anfom in Kumasi as a junior MO, I did not think that he would fail to help me, if possible. Likewise, I had worked for a brief period in Accra when Dr Bentsi Enchil came to Korle Bu to replace Dr Bannerman, although I had only worked directly under Dr Ghosh in 1961. I had not been close to Dr Bentsi-Enchill. I was informed that Dr Bannerman, Professor-designate for OB/GY in Korle Bu, but still on the Ibadan staff, was in the country. He was reported to be resident in his house in Aburi. I decided to go there to see him with a view to discussing my desire to join him at Korle Bu. Ben Ocloo drove me and Yolande to Aburi when darkness had already set in. The driveway from the main road to the house perched on a hill, was gravelly and bushy. The surroundings were overgrown with grass and the house was in darkness and looked uninhabited. Dr Bannerman was obviously not around. I felt greatly disappointed and we returned to Accra.

In Accra, I went with Yolande to see Dr Anfom at his bungalow in Korle Bu. He and his wife Leonora received us warmly. I told him the reason for my visit. His response was positive and reassuring. Difficult though the accommodation situation was, Dr Anfom promised to fix me up if Bentsi-Enchill would accept me in his department. With this comforting assurance in the bag, I went with Yolande to see Dr Bentsi-Enchill in his bungalow. The initial reception in marked contrast was cold. I summoned up courage in my spirit of foreboding and made a request to join his department. In a cold way, he said the department was already full and that there was no room for me. The other Gynaecologists in the department at the time were Drs K. K. Korsah, Kofi Newman and Ghosh. He sounded my death knell and aborted my ambitions for a Korle Bu posting. I realized that heads of department played powerful roles in deciding the fates of other doctors; several years later a similar role would fall on my shoulders.

I went to the MOH to see Mr Winful and briefed him on my meetings with Drs Anfom and Bentsi-Enchill. He told me that he would attempt to place me in Kumasi. The departmental head there was Dr A. Armar, a friend and a senior colleague of long-standing. I had indeed written to him from Leeds before my return and was puzzled that he had apparently influenced the decision to post me to Ho. A few days later Mr Winful informed me that my posting to Ho was cancelled and I was supposed to go to Kumasi. After the Korle Bu fiasco, this news was very welcome. Kumasi had been my old hunting ground; I still had several friends there; my brother Willie was stationed there and his wife (Doma) was the matron of the hospital, now named Komfo Anokye Hospital, from the original Kumasi Central Hospital.

While awaiting Mr Winful's attempt on my posting to Kumasi, I decided to complete my return journey home by going to Hohoe, my place of birth, to see my father; my mother had returned to Hohoe after welcoming us at Tema. We received a warm and joyous welcome from my parents. Papa met Yolande for the first time; there was a great feeling of pride in us from my parents. An additional wing consisting of two bedrooms with an enclosed porch had been added to the main house as was a new structure with a bathroom and toilet. A high wall with a gate completed the quadrangular structure of the house. Features of the main, original house remained the same, unaltered. My father, now 75 years old, looked well and healthy. He had retired from GB Ollivant, but kept himself active and busy; he was self-sufficient financially and needed no support from his children. He put up a single-storeyed building on a piece of land just across the road opposite our house. It housed a shop which he operated with a young male assistant. Ghana State Transport Corporation had not extended its service from Accra to Hohoe, but Papa negotiated with the Managing Director, Mr Dompey, and had the service extended to Hohoe with my father as the terminal station officer. The front of the shop served as the bus terminal and as the location for parking the bus overnight for its return journey to Accra the following day. Papa sold the boarding tickets.

Ghana lottery, drawn weekly on Saturdays, was popular with some of the populace in Hohoe and the surrounding district. My father was involved in the lottery business; he not only sold out tickets to vendors, but paid out money to winners soon after the announcement of the draw. His desk location was the centre of thriving activities on Saturday afternoons and evenings. Despite this element of involvement, he never, on a point of principle, bought a lottery ticket for himself. He kept money locked in a safe in the house. The payments earned him a commission. These three commercial activities were efficiently run by the 'old man', as he was popularly and reverently called and addressed.

Although he was 75 years old, he functioned as someone in his sixties; he belied his age. He played an active role in the church and was a Presbyter. He and Yolande struck a mutual affinity instantly; it was the same with my mother except that there was the limiting factor of communication (my mother could only mutter a few words in English). Although her formal education ended at class three, her brain was razor-sharp; as an enterprising entrepreneur, she would score an A+++. The old Hohoe market had given way to the Bank of Ghana building, Hohoe's centre point. Mammy was allotted a shop on the Bla road, very near the old market site. She continued to ply her trading activities, concentrating on textile goods. Now at 65, she scaled down and stopped her previous activities in farming and commercial baking. She was active in the church and was also a Presbyter.

The Hohoe visit lasted only a few days. We visited family friends who in return visits brought along gifts. The Hohoe visit brought back memories and nostalgia of my younger days. My mother remembered my favourite simple Ghanaian dishes which she used to prepare for me lovingly (garden egg and okro stew with banku, hot kenkey "kela kela" with ground fresh pepper and corned beef or sardines); she did not disappoint me in this respect. Even though one needed to acquire a taste for these, Yolande quite quickly took a liking for them. I positioned myself in front of the harmonium and played some old highlife tunes and hymns I used to play in the natural key. To this day, one of my greatest regrets is that I did not persevere enough to learn to read and play music by notes (I read somewhere that Pavarotti, the legendary operatic tenor could not read musical notes either).

On our return journey from Hohoe to Accra, I decided to make a detour and pass through Ho (the Hohoe-Accra route was then over the Kpeve hills and via Tsito) to enable me to have a look at the Ho Hospital even though I was no longer going to be posted there. I did not include Peki in my itinerary. I made a brief visit at the Ho Hospital. From Ho, we drove on, crossing the Volta River at Adome over the new bridge to Saisi at Agormenya to pay a mandatory visit to Reverend Apo, a maternal uncle. He had retired as a Presbyterian minister, but still performed pastoral work in Saisi. Rev. Apo, his wife and daughter, Auntie Cecilia, welcomed me and Yolande very warmly and with unmitigated pride; auntie Mina, my mother's sister, who lived in my mother's adjacent house, joined the welcoming group. Rev Apo was his revered and affable self. After fulfilling these family obligations in Krobo, we continued on our journey to Accra, arriving rather late. It had been a crowded, but happy trip in its totality.

On our arrival in Accra, we found, to our utter shock and dismay, that the CSIR apartment we had been occupying was occupied by a

CSIR official; we could only re-occupy it the following day. Ben Ocloo, our driver, opined that Mr Cromwell Quist, a solicitor, and an old friend, might not mind hosting us for a night under the present circumstances. He drove us to his house at McCarthy Hill, an area then new to me. Cromwell and Dawn, his English wife, willingly, without prior notice, hosted us for the night. It served as a good opportunity for Yolande to meet and be entertained by some of my friends. We moved into our CSIR apartment the following morning and then went to see Mr Winful at the MOH. Mr Winful confirmed my posting to Kumasi, a great relief.

We completed our preparations before commencing our journey to Kumasi. Sister Felicia hosted us to several meals. Yolande and I were entertained to meals by Jake and Cynthia at Kokomlemle (Jake's mother's house) and Chris and Vic Adomako at their residence in the Ridge area. My Achimota and Guggisberg House classmates, GA Bonsu, RO Djan, both now Principal Secretaries, organized a luncheon party in my honour on a Saturday afternoon. Rather sadly, with my crowded programme, I got to their residence at Ridge late when some of the invited mates had left. There was a genuine feeling of pride in my achievement. I felt very embarrassed by my lateness, but my hosts were quite understanding of the circumstances and reason for it and were forgiving.

On the appointed date of my departure for Kumasi, I was provided with a government truck which would convey our belongings to Kumasi. The truck was duly loaded and despatched with all our shipped boxes, 28 instead of 30, as well as our personal luggage to Kumasi. I had taken delivery of my own car, Opel Rekord, with registration number GF 4460, and returned Bill's Mercedes-Benz. Bill still assigned Ben Ocloo to drive us until we got well settled in Kumasi; this was filial support par excellence. I was familiar with the Accra-Kumasi road because I had driven on it several times during my days as an MO in Kumasi. The route was through Aburi and Koforidua before the current one through Nsawam and Kibi was constructed by the Kassardjan Company. Yolande, coming from a small island country, found the 168 miles journey in four hours rather long; the road, although macadamized, she found somewhat dusty. The journey first carried you from savannah scrub vegetation that gradually merged into forest, which progressively thickened into dense forest , with the tree branches and foliage providing a picturesque canopy along parts of the road. It was and still is a scenic drive. We arrived in Kumasi late in the afternoon. Kumasi deservedly earned the sobriquet of the 'Garden City'. The road from Kojokrom to Asafo Roundabout was lined with trees, and canopied in parts with tree foliage. There was much greenery over the parks and undulating hills in parts of the city. I was informed on my arrival about my bungalow allocation and handed the keys. It was No.11 Danyame, sited in one of the most desirable areas at the time. Since we arrived in Kumasi rather late, we booked in at the government guest house for that day and arranged to unpack the following day in our bungalow at Danyame.

Number 11 Danyame, a G45 type government bungalow, was to be our home for several years. It consisted of a master bedroom, an adjoining smaller bedroom, a living room with two opposing entrance doors, a dining room with a door leading to a kitchen, and a large storeroom. A corridor, panelling the two bedrooms, led at one end into the bathroom and toilet and from the other end in to the living room. A large rectangular roofed front porch opening into the living room served as the main entrance to the house. A similar, but smaller porch at the back served the same purpose. A car garage adjoined the storeroom at the back of the building. The building was single-storeyed, but rose on a four step elevation. Surrounding the front and back of the bedrooms were designed gardens of flower plants, lending them to the whims and fancies of the occupants. The entire structure was architecturally appealing. A short driveway from the road led into the front yard. The front yard had a short mango tree, whose wide branches provided welcome shade. There was an outhouse (boy's quarters), fully contained with kitchen, bathroom and toilet at the rear of the bungalow. The bungalow was separated from similar bungalows on both sides by a thick hedge.

The previous occupants, an elderly East European couple, had kept the bungalow very well maintained, with particular attention to the garden. The PWD (Public Works Department) was responsible for maintaining all the bungalows, and no. 11 had been thoroughly cleaned before our arrival. The allocation of bungalows was done in the regional office. I believe that the hospital matron, my sister-in-law, played a significant role in its allocation to me. It was ideal because it was relatively not too far from the hospital, about a two miles distance, it was suitable for a gynaecologist to attend to urgent calls while on duty.

We arrived in Kumasi in the 2nd – 3rd week of December 1965, just before Xmas. I was not expected to commence work until January 2nd, 1966. We went to the PWD to select furniture items of our choice to set up our first real home. The officers were eager and willing to comply with our wishes. On the domestic front, we were inundated by a good number of cooks/stewards, all bringing along with them testimonials and references wanting to work for us; we wasted no time in making a choice.

My first official call at the hospital was not delayed for long, however. Now named Komfo Anokye Hospital (KAH) and no longer Kumasi Central Hospital, there was no physical change. It stood out as a magnificent building, reputedly and unarguably the most modern hospital building in West Africa then. I called on the Hospital Superintendent, Dr Armar, and the Matron, Ms Ward-Brew. Dr Armar, my former senior colleague, who doubled also as the OB\GY departmental head, was delighted to see me back; the delight was mutual. He acknowledged receiving a letter I had sent him from Leeds, requesting him to monitor my posting on my return to Ghana. According to him, long before my arrival, when he contacted the MOH on my posting, he was told that I had personally made a request to be posted to Ho. This was, of course, not true; I never made such a request personally, nor through an intermediary.

KAH had the standard four major clinical departments, namely Internal Medicine, General Surgery, Paediatrics and OB/GY; other supplementary departments were Pathology, Laboratory, Radiology, Ophthalmology, Dentistry, Anaesthesia and Physiotherapy. The ambulance unit functioned as a transport division for transporting doctors or nurses, rather than responding to emergency cases to convey patients to the hospital. The maintenance department was the workshop for the hospital. A School of Nursing and Midwifery was part of the hospital complex. KAH was a regional hospital with a wide catchment area and population. It was a referral centre for a number of district hospitals in the region. The district hospitals included

Bekwai Government Hospital, Offinso Catholic Hospital, Mampong Government Hospital and Mampong Mission Maternity Hospital.

The OB/GY department had three units, each headed by a Specialist; the specialists were assisted by a varying number of MOs. The specialists at the time of my arrival were Drs Armar, SC Bose (gynaecologist to the First Lady in Accra) and Victor Kumodji. Dr SC Bose, with a vast experience in tropical obstetrics, was the most senior, but attracted some controversy. The lucrative private practice in which he indulged did not endear him to his other colleagues. Victor Kumodji, two years my senior in Achimota and UCGC was a competent and knowledgeable gynaecologist, but harboured some questionable character traits. In his view, Dr Bose had overstayed in Ghana and did not merit an extension of his contract (with an eye on Bose's private patients, no doubt). To some extent, Dr Armar, too, thought it was time for Bose to leave the service.

There were three general surgeons, one ENT surgeon, an orthopaedic surgeon, one maximo facial surgeon. The surgery department was headed by Dr Akiwumi, a year my senior in Achimota. The medical department with three units was headed by Dr Bondzi-Simpson. The specialists were a mix of Ghanaians and Indians. The government policy stipulated that the departments be headed by a Ghanaian if he had the specialist qualification. Although I agree with the policy, I think that the head should know his clinical limitations and consult and seek advice when the need arose. Dr C Marbel headed the Pathology Department and Dr Adu Aryee headed the Dental Unit.

It is appropriate at this stage to list the other Ghanaian gynaecologists: Dr Kwarko, after a short stint in Kumasi was the only gynaecologist in Tamale; similarly, after a grooming stint in Kumasi, Dr Barte-Plange was the only gynaecologist in Sekondi/Takoradi. Dr Ampofo was stationed in his hometown, Mampong. Drs Bentsi-Enchil, K. K. Korsah and Newman were stationed in Accra. Dr Obeng, then the senior registrar to Sir John Peel, gynaecologist to Queen Elizabeth, was based in London.

As a young couple, Yolande and I embarked on setting up an ideal home with its salubrious surroundings. Our neighbours included the Kemavor family, whom we had visited in Harrogate, and Dr Akiwumi. Dr Akiwumi, a year my senior in Achimota, was married to an African-American, Carmita; they had a young son. An across the street neighbour was Mr Boret, an official in the Lands Department. His Nigerian wife was friendly and helpful towards Yolande. Other specialists lived in an entirely different neighbourhood.

I had to attend to some important affairs; which included banking. I had banked with Barclays Bank for several years, both in Ghana and Britain. I went to the main branch and got my account reactivated. The manager at the time was Mr Colin Basford, a Caucasian Trinidadian with an Oxbridge background. Because of the political climate, I avoided opening an account with the Ghana Commercial Bank, the national bank. Kingsway store was the main supermarket for almost all grocery items as well as domestic and clothing items. The store operated a credit account system for doctors and other professionals. After the customary introductions and recommendations, I opened an account with the Kingsway store. The credit had a limit which we never exceeded. It was desirable to join the Kumasi Club for social and recreational activities. It was centrally located, adjacent to the historic Kumasi Fort. It consisted of a large hall, a bar, an adjoining billiards room with three tables, and a cinema hall. There were also a cemented tennis court as well as a practice wall. The club dated back in history to the colonial era when it was known as the European Club and segregation was fully enforced, with membership limited to 'whites' only. Africans, however distinguished, were not permitted to join. Because of this, the Lebanese and Indians formed their own clubs. The situation was similar in Accra with the Accra European Club. The Roger Club in Accra catered for high-ranking and professional Africans. The equivalent club in Kumasi was the Maxwell Club. It was not until the early sixties that the racial segregation in the Kumasi Club ended. Mr Frank Mensah Bonsu was the first African to be admitted as a member. He had been the City Clerk of the Council; later as a Solicitor he handled the lease agreement for the Kumasi Club. He was made a member after this. A trickle of Lebanese and Indians followed. At the time of my arrival in Kumasi, there was a significant number of Africans as members.

I hardly played any tennis in Britain while on my postgraduate course. With my interest in the game now rekindled, I re-joined the Maxwell Tennis Club, which had two splendid clay courts, well and firmly maintained surfaces on which rollers were regularly used. Mr Acquah, then president of the club, lived close to the club house, and with this advantage kept a vigilant eye on the court and its property.

The KNUST campus was another centre of our social activities. Under the Vice-Chancellorship of Mr R. P. Baffour, physical appearance of the campus was impressive. Several members of the KNUST staff had been friends or colleagues from the UCGC; these included Mr Ulzen, the Registrar, Austin Tetteh and his family, John and Doris Owusu Addo. John and Austin were both lecturers in the Faculty of Architecture and in the fullness of time became Deans in the Faculty. They continued to be lifelong friends. Other campus associates were Abbiw-Jackson (Mathematician), Kutin-Sanwu (Botanist), T.K. Tawiah (Botanist), Amon Nii Kotey (English), and Thomas Sekyi (administration). This circle of friends would expand in later years to include Goza Tay, Peter Dziworno (both Physicists), Frank Kwame and David Tay (Engineers).

Yolande was introduced very early to Dr Emmanuel Asare and his English wife, Joan. When I left Kumasi for Britain in 1962, Dr Asare was scheduled to go to Australia to specialize in Surgery. Unfortunately, the course was never pursued. Emmanuel was posted to Wa Hospital as the MO. He contracted a severe and near fatal acute hepatitis from which he thankfully recovered. He returned to Kumasi and joined Dr Kofi Tagboto in General Practice at Adum. Dr Tagboto, also an Old Achimotan and a Leeds Medical School graduate, was a brilliant doctor. Hailing from Kpando, he was the first person from inland Eweland to train and qualify as a doctor. Dr Djoleto, although regarded by many as an Ewe, never claimed Ewe ethnicity. With heavy press censorship under the Nkrumah regime, the Daily Graphic and Ghanaian Times could not be described as quality newspapers. The British Council had its regional office in Kumasi centrally well located, not far from my bank. I enrolled to become a member of the British Council. This started a long association with the institute and its directors.

Such was the environment and the social milieu and the composition of my circle of friends when Yolande and I arrived to settle down in Kumasi in December 1965. I was not expected to commence work until January 2nd 1966; the December duty roster did not justifiably include me. An anecdote here is timely and germane.

Emmanuel and Joan invited us to join them for their Xmas luncheon. Since Yolande was keen on preparing our first Xmas lunch we graciously declined and postponed their invitation to another date; they were quite understanding. Very early on Xmas Day morning I received a telephone call from Dr Kumodji with a message. What was the message? He was scheduled to be on call for OB/GY department on Xmas Day. He called to say that he was unwell and feverish and would not be able to attend to calls. He was therefore asking me to be on call for the day; I had no choice, but to oblige. Not long after this call I received a call from the hospital labour ward requesting me to come and attend to some emergency cases. I left home immediately for the hospital. On my arrival in the Labour Ward, I found myself confronted with a number of cases requiring urgent surgery. The first case was a late case of ruptured uterus with peritonitis referred from the district. I promptly performed a Caesarean hysterectomy with peritoneal lavage and toileting. Despite heavy antibiotic therapy, the patient died postoperatively, most probably from the overwhelming infection. I ended up performing five laparotomies that day before returning home for my Xmas lunch, such as it was. Poor Yolande had fallen asleep after waiting several hours for me to come home and the local turkey dried up in the oven! After a brief rest following the lunch, I drove to Dr Kumodji's house to pass on the Yuletide greetings to him and wish him a quick recovery from his debilitating fever. When I got to his house, he was absent; but the steward boy was there. On enquiring about Dr Kumodji, the steward boy stated that he had left the house early in the day to attend a party from which he still had not returned. Strangely, I bore him no grudge. I had my baptism of fire into tropical obstetrics and was also initiated into the foibles of human behaviour and perhaps a hint of things to come, work wise!

I commenced full time clinical duties in January 1966. There were three units headed respectively by Drs Armar, S. C. Bose and Kumodji. Dr Armar assigned me to his unit and delegated all the clinical work to me while he concentrated on hospital administrative duties. Although office space was scarce, I was lucky in being assigned an office. I held my weekly outpatient clinics on Friday afternoons. I was given complete independence and could have my own protocol on my patient care. The MOs were few in number; the Korle Bu products had not yet started coming out. The MOs were Drs Forster (Cairo-trained), Djan (Canadian trained), Wontumi (Jamaica trained) and Joe Riverson (Belfast trained).

The hospital had a modest library; the OB\GY books were few and consisted of books of historical interest. The doctors' coffee room was a congregation point mainly between 10-11am, when most of the doctors came for refreshments. There was a good mix of doctors, junior and senior, Ghanaians and expatriates.

My working day in the hospital started with a ward round with my MO and ward nurses. The wards comprised the antenatal, postnatal and gynaecological wards. There was one VIP (Very Important People) ward. On my on call days, I started my rounds in the labour ward where patients in labour were reviewed and their management planned. Cases requiring surgical intervention were prepared and sent to the operating theatre. There were two operating theatres; one was used for major and abdominal cases, and the other one was used for minor and vaginal cases. Elective surgical cases were done by the specialist on the fixed on-call day. In this way, each specialist would have full control over both theatres and plan his operating list of emergency and elective accordingly. General anaesthesia for the cases was administered by specially trained male Nurse/Anaesthetists. Some of them were outstanding; the most experienced and senior was Mr Kissi. Dark in colour with grey hair. Mr Kissi was worth his weight in gold and compared favourably with consultant anaesthetists I had worked with in Britain. It was wise to seek him out for tricky and difficult cases. Messrs Seshie and Amoah reached his level of excellence in later years. The Anaesthesia Department later came under the headship of Dr Sen Gupta, a senior Bengali anaesthetist. He taught me how to administer epidural anaesthesia for operative surgery.

The dismal political and economic climate on our arrival has been already painted; it influenced the ethos of our life to some extent.

The tranquil early morning of 24th February 1966 was broken by a radio announcement starting as follows: "My dear fellow Ghanaians..." The Ghana Armed Forces had successfully staged a military coup d'état and overthrown the government of Kwame Nkrumah. The CPP as a political party was banned and its membership declared illegal and an offence. Nkrumah was on a self-appointed mission to Beijing and Hanoi to mediate in the Vietnam War. The Armed Forces were led by General Kotoka and Brigadier Kwasi Afrifa. There was an integral cooperation with the Ghana Police Force led by Mr Harley, IGP. The regular Ghana Army had been infiltrated by CPP spies, thus rendering the planning and execution of any military coup a very hazardous exercise. In creating the President's Own Guard Regiment, an elite private army, generously remunerated and treated, Nkrumah split the army and incurred the anger of the regular army. The troops of the coup executants travelled all the way from the north of Ghana by night and engaged the special Guard led by Brigadier Bawa at the Flagstaff in a fierce armed combat leading to the successful overthrow of Kwame Nkrumah.

The announcement was greeted with joyous disbelief through the length and breadth of the country. Nkrumah's statute in front of Parliament house was brought down and posters with Nkrumah's picture in all buildings were destroyed. The celebration was prolonged and lasted for a few days. Although the national hero was General Kotoka, a retired army General, Ankrah, was sworn in as the new Head of State. A trio of Kotoka, Afrifa and Harley constituted the new hierarchy. Prominent technocrats and some other revered figures were appointed to head various ministries and departments as a new government was installed in power. All political prisoners were released from jail; these included Mr Joe Appiah. Dr Danquah had died in jail some years earlier.

The coup was necessary and timely. Kwame Nkrumah had established a one-party state and declared himself President for life. He had brought down the economy from a peak of excellence to a bottomless abyss. Two earlier attempts at assassination had failed. In my later years, on reflection, I began to concede that in some respects, as a statesman of some stature, he was ahead of his time. Our notion of politics and world affairs was greatly influenced by a pseudo colonial mentality and an excessively proWest view in the Cold War geopolitics of the period. We failed to be sufficiently neutral. There was a dominant and pervasive Western aura at UCGC during my time of which we were hardly conscious, so insidious was it. The graduates were going to replace the British expatriate in high decision making positions. It was in Britain's interest to have the attitude and mentality suitably

257

moulded/cloned. This is in no way an attempt to denigrate the British standard and attitude. Indeed, the underlying legacy Mr David Balme left at Legon was that he insisted on establishing an unquestionably high academic standard. He aimed at establishing an Oxbridge at Legon, and I acknowledge this as a credit to his legacy. Several years later, I learned that while Mr Balme was Principal at UCGC, he also doubled as 'Head of British Intelligence in the Gold Coast. Although I have no direct evidence, a former close British expatriate friend of mine probably fell within this category. The naivety of the Ghanaian body politic comes for comment here. The USA embassy building in Accra, with no doubt all the news gathering technology at its disposal, was centrally sited at the ministry buildings. Sensitive intelligence of any kind on Ghana could easily be obtained.

Several years after the overthrow of Kwame Nkrumah, it was revealed that the coup had been planned and orchestrated by an American CIA agent in Accra who collaborated with members of the Ghana Armed Forces. After the coup, Nkrumah initially sought refuge in Yugoslavia. Some members of his retinue returned home to Ghana in disgrace. One of the returnees, an object of much hatred, was put in a specially constructed cage, and driven through the principal streets of Accra, like a caged animal from the zoo, to much ridicule and jeering from the crowds. The President of Guinea, Mr Sekou Toure, granted asylum to Nkrumah and also magnanimously declared him co-president of Guinea. Nkrumah lived in Guinea with a small group of close associates. He still believed that he would return to Ghana as president. He developed a liver malignancy and died in Guinea. The Ghana government sent a special delegation, headed by Mr Joe Appiah, who brought home Nkrumah's remains. Nkrumah's body was buried in his village, Nkroful. One of Nkrumah's close associates in Ghana and Guinea was Mr Stokely Carmichael. Originally from Trinidad, as an African-American, he espoused neocommunist ideology and was politically active. He married the famous South African singer Miriam Makeba. On his death bed, I learned Mr Stokely Carmichael confessed to having been a CIA agent in Nkrumah's camp during all the years he had spent with him!. The political stakes were high and some individuals were willing to make a sacrifice. Was Nkrumah's liver malignancy induced? We may never know.

The NLC (National Liberation Council) government ushered Ghana into a new era. Freedom had been attained at every level of human endeavour; the media were free to publish anything without fear or favour; expectations were high. In operatic analogy, it was like the final scene in Beethoven's Fidelio, his only opera, when the prisoners were all freed. Several commissions of enquiry were set up to find out what had gone wrong; why and how; and to many heads of government of emerging nations to learn lessons from them. Nkrumah was a victim of hero worship. To his great credit, although he was surrounded by corrupt people, he was not corrupt himself; he could not control this rotten aspect of governance. Many heads of government of emergent nations found themselves facing similar challenges.

Politicians who had fled the country under Nkrumah returned home after the coup. Prominent among the returnees was Professor Abrefa Busia, who hailed from Wenchi in the Brong Ahafo Region. A man of small and rather diminutive build, he was a brilliant scholar; he was one of the earliest Ghanaian Oxford graduates. He read Sociology and went on to obtain a PhD, then a rare achievement. He was one of the first Africans recruited by Mr David Balme to join the staff of the UCGC where he headed the department of Sociology. He drifted into politics, became an MP and led the opposition party to Nkrumah's ruling CPP. I admired and adored him at that time, but later events undermined my image of him; my idol had feet of clay! He was on the verge of political incarceration under the PDA, but was luckily tipped off by Krobo Adusei, a fellow Akan, thus enabling him to flee into exile in Britain. Being diabetic, he certainly would not have survived in prison. On his return to Ghana from exile, the NLC appointed him to lead a civil programme to educate the Ghanaian populace on democratic governance and the rule of law, through public lectures.

A year after the overthrow of Kwame Nkrumah, the country was plunged into grief by an abortive military coup d'état that claimed the life of General Kotoka. A regiment from Ho barracks arrived in Accra and in cold blood senselessly killed the popular hero of Nkrumah's overthrow. Kotoka's body was discovered a day after the abortive Guitar Boys coup. Return to an elected civilian government was decreed and the formation of political parties declared. General Ankrah's political manoeuvrings forced him to resign from being Head of State. Colonel Afrifa, young though he was, rather than Mr Harley was sworn in as the new Head of State. Two major political parties were formed, led respectively by Dr Busia and Mr Gbedemah. The election which was held was declared fair and free. I voted for Busia's Progress Party, much against the advice of Yolande, who on seeing him at Kumasi airport for the very first time, told me that she did not think he would be a good leader! I laughed it off, of course. After all, she had never met the fellow, whereas I knew him. Or so I thought. The Progress Party won the election comfortably. Victor Owusu was appointed Minister for Foreign Affairs, an influential position. His sister Christina, now Mrs Armar, seemed to wield great power and influence in the party. I witnessed a constant stream of lobbyists who came to seek appointments to juicy positions or as ambassadors.

My Old Achimotan classmate Richard Donkor (aka Safo Adu) won a Parliamentary seat in Kumasi and was appointed the Minister for Agriculture. Richard was the brilliant all-round classmate I had rated my intellectual superior from our days in Achimota and at UCGC. He went to King's College, London to study Medicine. He distinguished himself in the preclinical years and was ushered into Pharmacology wherein he obtained an honours degree. On his qualifying and obtaining the medical degree, the Ghana government awarded him a scholarship to pursue a postgraduate course in Pharmacology at Cambridge University. He left Cambridge and went to Ibadan Medical School, Nigeria, where he was appointed a lecturer in Pharmacology. Dr Easmon recruited him from Ibadan to join the staff of the infant Korle Bu Medical School in the Department of Pharmacology. Richard spent only a brief period in Korle Bu and left for Kumasi to commence work as a General Practitioner. A scholarly character with a debonair and cultured bearing, he was a talent.

Busia formed a government from which much was expected. He soon after revealed the true nature of his character which had hitherto been unknown to some of us. He dismissed a large number of state employees at all ranks, junior and senior, apparently on groundless reasons with a thick under-current element of tribalism. Tribalism had hitherto been unknown in Ghanaian body politic even in the woeful days of the Nkrumah regime. A deadly cancer, it was an issue that Ghana's first and foremost sociologist should not have entertained, let alone introduce into Ghana's politics. One of the dismissed officials, Mr Sallah, challenged his unlawful dismissal and went to court for legal redress. The court decided in his favour by declaring that his dismissal was unlawful. Busia went on radio to condemn the court decision stating in an angry and arrogant voice: "NO COURT, NO COURT" could challenge a personal decision he had made. He revealed an aggressive and arrogant character unknown to most Ghanaians. I was almost speechless with shock! To her credit, Yolande's 'I told you so' was rather muted.

As if on a rampage, Busia issued the Aliens Compliance Order. In brief, no non-Ghanaian citizen could own any property nor indulge in retail trading. Lebanese, Indians and especially Nigerians, most of whom had lived in Ghana for several decades, were forced by a stroke of the pen to leave. Most ethnic Nigerians had lived in Ghana for decades and generations, many of them, mainly Yorubas, did not even know which town or village their forebears had come from and assumed, quite rightly that they were Ghanaians. Almost every village in Ghana had a Mami Alata with a stall or corner shop where basic essential items such as candles, matches and soap were sold. I travelled to Accra during the expulsion exercise and stayed in a hotel sited at the present site of the Golden Tulip hotel. There I witnessed a pathetic scene. Several truckloads of commercial vehicles packed to overflowing with hundreds of Nigerians; they included children of all ages and also pregnant women. They were being deported to destinations in Nigeria unknown to most of them. How could anyone, let alone a sociologist and a highly regarded Methodist church preacher, enact and enforce such a draconian measure without a prick of conscience? He apparently carried out the exercise as the Prime Minister, without full cabinet approval. He surely must have seen the scenes I described above. Most Ghanaians were appalled at this.

The media had flourished under the NLC regime. The Legon Observer, a weekly journal, was launched. As a quality paper it could match any British weekly of similar pedigree. The level of scholarship and the high literary standard of its opinion column was one to admire. Yolande's rejoinder letters were always published. Yolande revealed a literary talent of which I had previously been unaware.

Cromwell Quist's television interview and talk shows on *Kaleidoscope* attracted large viewing audiences. He was articulate, fearless, forthright and entertaining; he was the Ghana Jeremy Paxman at the time. Yolande and I were delighted to host him when he paid a brief visit to honour an invitation to speak at a prestigious function in Kumasi. Busia, quite early, adopted an extravagant and publicity-attracting style which generated unfavourable comments. The chauffeur-driven car which drove him from his house to his office had a motorcade of outriders; neither General Ankrah nor Mr Akuffo-Addo, previous and current Presidents had paraded that style or image. Cromwell Quist brought up the matter in his television *Kaleidoscope* programme. Views were expressed and public opinion condemned the motorcade style. To Busia, Cromwell had crossed the red line; his programme was terminated and replaced with another programme. Mr Cameron Duodu, a journalist from Asiakwa, had been appointed Editor of the Ghanaian Times. He was an independent journalist, but I think a Busia supporter. The South African apartheid regime was at its most diabolical and despised stage; it was an international pariah state. Ghana in concert with all other African countries shared a policy of non-engagement of any kind with South Africa. Busia decided on his own to have some kind of relationship with this outcast regime in South Africa. Cameron Duodu opined in the Ghanaian Times that this adventure should be avoided by Ghana; if Busia, however, insisted on this mission, he should only do this personally on his own, the equivalent of 'banging his head against a stone wall'. What was the consequence? Cameron Duodu was dismissed as Editor of the Ghanaian Times. Is this the same Busia I had admired as a Liberal and for whom I had enthusiastically voted? Here was a tribalist and a dictator, now revealing its feet of clay and diabolical claws.

Mr Joe Appiah had been a prominent member of the opposition party to Nkrumah and his government; he was incarcerated in jail and released only after the overthrow of Nkrumah. During the Busia regime, he seemed to have been side-lined. Some years later, when Joe and his wife Peggy became close friends, she recounted to me the reason for this. During the time that Joe was in prison under the PDA, Peggy stayed on in Ghana, but raised considerable funds in Britain under the aegis of the World Council of Churches; the money was meant for the dependants of those incarcerated under Nkrumah's regime. Since Busia was then in safe exile in Oxford, Britain, he was made the custodian of the funds which Peggy had organized and raised. Busia was to hold the money in trust as the custodian. On Busia's return home from exile after Nkrumah's overthrow, the Appiahs asked him to render to them an account of the money placed under his trust. To their shock and dismay, he refused to do so. This led to a parting of the ways. In Oxford, Busia was a Fellow at St Anthony's College. Income generation in British academia is known to be meagre. Despite this, Busia was able to put up a magnificent, palatial building in Wenchi. How did he finance this? After the military coup by Colonel Acheampong which overthrew the Busia government, Joe Appiah was appointed a Special Advisor and Minister Plenipotentiary with an office in Christiansborg Castle, the seat of government. Acheampong discovered a letter and passed it on to Joe Appiah. It was a letter with the South African confidential seal from their Prime Minister to Busia; it was a friendly letter which Joe subsequently kept. I narrate this chronicle reluctantly, but only to illuminate part of the Busia legacy. Two more annotations would complete the story of the Busia legacy. Hohoe was and remained the commercial capital of the Volta Region. The Accra-Hohoe old road was a major road in the area. Originally a laterite road, it was in the process of being widened and macadamized. The modernisation of the road was halted 15 miles from Hohoe when the people in the Hohoe area voted in a referendum, conducted by the UNO, not to join the Gold Coast when the latter was attaining independence under Kwame Nkrumah. In halting the road work to Hohoe, Nkrumah meant to punish the people in the Hohoe area. After the overthrow of Nkrumah, the NLC government quite rightly decided to rectify this petty and petulant act of government. The modernization of the road was resumed and the road work had reached a point nine miles from Hohoe when the NLC handed over power to the Busia government. Almost immediately, the road work was stopped, all the machinery and workers were moved from the Volta Region to Brong Ahafo Region to construct and modernise roads in Busia's region. The remaining Hohoe road project was eventually only completed after the overthrow of the Busia regime by Acheampong.

The second chronicle centred on a couple of school teachers. A lady who attended my Friday gynaecology clinic requested for tubal ligation, as she did not want to have any more children. As was my habit, I took a brief social history from her. She and her husband were Ewes, teaching in an elementary school in the Brong Ahafo Region. I found this intriguing and probed further. She told me that she and her husband had attended and trained as teachers at St Francis Teachers Training College at Bla (Hohoe), a college held in high esteem. The graduates were normally sent to teach in the Volta Region. After graduation during the Busia regime, my patient continued to tell me, almost all of the newly graduated teachers were sent to teach in schools in the Brong Ahafo Region; she and her husband had remained in the region ever since. The Busia regime deprived the Volta Region of its teachers; this was quite revealing, I thought. Especially in light of his anti-Ewe stance.

From my earlier years in Achimota and UCGC I had held Busia in high esteem, influenced perhaps by my adoration of high education and scholarship; I had shared his political views in opposition to Kwame Nkrumah and voted for him during the election. A different personality, shorn of his scholarly attainments and professed Christian values, had now emerged. I could excuse him for vaingloriousness, but what I cannot forgive him for in his legacy was that he sowed the seeds of overt tribalism into Ghana body politic. It is a seed, which once sown, germinates and grows into a thicket; the resulting consequences are difficult or perhaps impossible to eradicate. Victor Owusu and Safu Adu, prominent ministers in his government, I believe, did not share this tragic flaw. Sadly, it has never quite gone away and lies dormant like a virus, ready to erupt at any time.

My full flow of clinical activity commenced in January 1966. There were three units and I functioned as the de facto head of one unit. In addition to the work at KAH, Dr Kumodji and I took turns one day each week to go to the Mampong Anglican Maternity Hospital. We attended to referred patients at the antenatal clinic in a morning session and performed elective Caesarean sections in an afternoon session. It was an outreach clinical activity in which I was pleased to participate. The nuns served me with lunch. This activity lasted for several months.

Dr S.C. Bose left in 1967, following the non-renewal of his contract. It is my view that he had contributed to obstetric practice in Kumasi in no small way over the years. He was replaced by Dr Jokic, a Yugoslav. Heavy set and burly in build, he played the political game well. As a gynaecologist, he was not in the same league as Dr Bose. Following his transfer to the Accra Military Hospital, when Afrifa was Head of State, Jokic was gynaecologist to the First Lady. Jokic was replaced in Kumasi by another Yugoslav, Dr Radovic; short and dapper, he was friendly and a good colleague to work with. Victor Kumodji was a competent and knowledgeable gynaecologist. After the departure of Dr Bose, he established a flourishing private practice with a core of clientele based on Lebanese and Indians (Bose's clientele). I also saw some patients privately in my office, but since the government ruling did not allow it, I charged no fees for my services; it was left entirely to the patient to show her gratitude in any manner. I received gifts in various forms including unsolicited cash. In this manner I earned the description of 'the Doctor who does not like money'.

An anecdote here is perhaps germane. I was a football enthusiast and relished watching the encounter between Asante Kotoko and Accra Hearts of Oak. The rivalry between the two teams was legendary. The teams were scheduled to meet on a Sunday and I succeeded in obtaining a ticket for a good seat. I was scheduled to be on call that day, and all I needed was to ask my colleague Dr Kumodjie to provide cover for me for a period of three hours to enable me to go and watch the match. After providing him with cover for the whole of Xmas Day without demur, I thought my request was a modest one. My request was very bluntly refused with an implied air of impropriety. I was stunned and dumbfounded and never again made a request of him. Medical practice in a large hospital requires teamwork and solidarity, especially so in obstetrics.

The department started experiencing serious problems in 1968. With a delivery rate of eight thousand a year, the workload fell on me and Dr Radovic as specialists with assistance from a few MOs. Dr Kumodji had been transferred to Akwapim Mampong to be on his own because he could not work in a team and for other reasons it would be inappropriate to delve into. Dr Martey arrived from Britain and was posted to Kumasi. An old boy of Mfantsipim, he had trained at Manchester Medical School. Several years later, we found out that we were related: his paternal grandmother and my maternal grandfather were siblings from Prampram. Dr Martey replaced Dr Kumodji. Dr Valnicek, a Czechoslovakian, came to replace Dr Radovic. Stan Valnicek, tall, athletic, blue-eyed with blond hair was a skilled and knowledgeable gynaecologist who showed great enthusiasm for work. He was a keen tennis player; we both shared much in common and worked well together as colleagues in a satisfying relationship. As a medical colleague and as a sportsman on the tennis court I was sorry he felt obliged to leave Ghana for Canada after the Russians invaded his home country of Czechoslovakia. Following his departure, a female Indian gynaecologist, Dr Chodagam, replaced him. After an 18-month tour of duty, she was replaced by Dr Djan. All the three units were from then on headed by Ghanaians.

With Dr Charles Easmon as Dean, and Mr Gbeho as the Registrar, the Korle-Bu Medical school had a humble, but courageous and dedicated beginning. Almost all the teaching staff had been British trained doctors, although none of them had ever taught in a medical school. Dr Quartey, the Urologist, led a team that taught Anatomy, while Dr Silas Dodu undertook the task of teaching Physiology, before Dr Harold Philips returned to take over. The students were the crop of the best science students who had emerged from the secondary schools. The clinical course, in line with the British system, would follow the pre-clinical course.

Dr Charles Easmon was appointed Professor in Surgery. An Old Achimotan, he had trained and qualified as a doctor at Edinburgh University. After postgraduate studies he became the first Ghanaian to obtain the FRCS. He worked in several hospitals throughout the country and acquired a tremendous amount of experience and knowledge; he was a skilled surgeon. He was the doyen of Ghanaian surgeons. He was assisted in teaching surgery by Drs EA Baidoo, Evans Anfom and Quartey, all Old Achimotans. Dr Silas Amu Dodu assumed the foundation chair in Medicine and Therapeutics. Silas Dodu, also an Old Achimotan, was tall, gangling, and light-complexioned with aquiline features that gave him the look of a Fulani. He had a distinguished academic background. Trained at Sheffield University, he was the gold medallist in his final year. He obtained the MRCP (London) on his first attempt, a commendable achievement in those days. On his return home to Ghana, he acquired great experience and kept himself abreast of current medical literature through the journals. His field of interest was cardiology. His weekly grand ward rounds were acclaimed to be comparable with any such rounds in Britain's teaching hospitals. He was assisted in his teaching unit by Drs Foley and Felix Konotey Ahulu. Some years later, the former acquired fame as a hepatologist, while the latter was recognized as one of the leading authorities on sickle cell disease.

The headship of the Paediatric Department was not easily decided. Dr Yaw Asirifi obtained the MRCP and DCH in Britain and returned home to practise as a Paediatric Specialist. Dr Susan Ofori-Atta, hailing from the Kibi royal family was the first Ghanaian female doctor. She had the DCH diploma, but not the prestigious MRCP. She was senior in years to Dr Asirifi and was the head of Princess Louise Children's Hospital in Accra. Although Susan was considered to have had more clinical Paediatric experience on the Ghanaian terrain, she did not possess the MRCP. There was yet a third candidate for the Paediatric Chair. He was Dr Carl Reindorf. Carl, like Yaw, an Old Achimotan, had trained at Newcastle in England and obtained the MRCP and DCH. He then went to Canada where he published some medical articles which counted as high sterling in appointments in medical academia. Carl, however, crucially lacked any experience in tropical Paediatric practice. After all the factors had been weighed, Yaw Asirifi received the nod to head the school's Paediatric Department.

The OB/GY Department posed a different, but more complex problem. Dr Obuabasa Bannerman, alluded to earlier, had been appointed to the chair in 1965 when he was in Ibadan. His return home to Ghana was eagerly awaited with high expectations. After a long period of anxious waiting, it became clear that he did not wish to return to Ghana for the chair. The unconfirmed reason for this, I was told, was that following the overthrow of Kwame Nkrumah, he did not find it secure for him to return to take the chair; I knew certainly that he was not an Nkrumaist. He felt that the personalities responsible for his transfer from Kole-Bu to Sekondi in 1961 were in prominent positions in the medical school hierarchy. Drs Ampofo and Kofi Newman had been appointed lecturers, and also doubled as specialists in the OB/

GY Department. Dr Bentsi-Enchill was the head of the department with the Ministry of Health, and Dr K. K. Korsah was a Specialist in the department under the MOH. Dr Bentsi-Enchill had deliberately not applied to join the medical school staff so as not to come under Dr Bannerman. With the passage of time and the realization that Dr Bannerman was no longer coming, it became urgent to appoint a head of OB/GY for the medical school. The obvious choice was Dr Bentsi-Enchill, a Fante from a well-known and affluent Cape Coast family. He had trained in Belfast as an undergraduate. On his return to Britain for his post graduate course, he was in MacCafees's unit in Belfast where he obtained the MRCOG, the third Ghanaian to do so. In Dr Obeng, Dr Bentsi-Enchill had a serious competitor for the chair in OB/ GY. Dr Obeng, an Old Achimotan hailing from the Buem area of the Volta Region, had trained at London's King's College and obtained the MRCOG. He was the Senior Registrar at King's College Hospital to Sir John Peel, the Gynaecologist to Queen Elizabeth and the royal household. He attracted an enviable clientele of prominent people of colour in or visiting London. Mr J.G. Amamoo, then the Editor of the Ghanaian Times, and a friend of Dr Obeng, wrote an editorial in which he extolled the outstanding achievements of Dr Obeng and pleaded for his appointment to the chair in OB/GY. Mr Amamoo was not a doctor and was not in a position to adjudicate on the appointment to the chair. Dr Obeng had not been exposed to obstetrics and gynaecology in the Ghanaian setting, an essential requirement, in my view. Dr Bentsi-Enchill was offered the headship of the medical school department of OB/GY with the status of a Senior Lecturer. Kwesi bluntly turned down the offer; he would only accept the offer if it was as Professor. He pointed out that neither Dr Easmon nor Dr Dodu had taught in a medical school before their appointments to their chairs, an argument which carried too much impregnable weight to refute. The board had no choice but to accede to Kwesi's demand. Thus was Bentsi-Enchill appointed to the foundation chair in OB/GY in Korle Bu. Dr Obeng had much earlier been appointed a lecturer, but never came to take the offer. He planned to return and engage in private practice. On one of his visits home, he brought a set of musical instruments to donate to a band in his hometown. The Sunday on which they came to collect the gift, very sadly, Dr Obeng suffered a fatal heart attack. Ghana was deprived of his contributions in gynaecology.

Dr Blukoo-Allotey and Dr Safu Adu were appointed as lecturer and senior lecturer respectively in Pharmacology. Safu Adu's tenure was short-lived. Drs Teddy Christian and Laing taught Pathology, Dr Adomako lectured in Psychiatry; Dr F. T. Sai taught Public Health.

Dr K.K Korsah & Dr Ampofo

By all accounts the students received excellent tuition along the British traditional lines in all the fields; the lecturers imparted to the students all they knew. The day of reckoning would come when the final examinations in Medicine, Surgery, Paediatrics and OB/GY were held. Almost all the external examiners came from Britain; this way, the examination results would be indisputable. The external examiners in OB/GY were Professor Trussel from Makerere, Uganda, and Professor Charles Douglas (London Royal Free Hospital), the Honorary Secretary of the RCOG. The results were awaited with great interest. When the results were released, they hit the front pages of the papers. The graduands received high accolades and praise from the team of distinguished and eminent external examiners. The general standard was acclaimed to be very high; due praise was showered on the tutors and teachers who had facilitated this achievement. A day after the release of the results, I received a call from Dr Bentsi-Enchill inviting me and Dr Martey to a cocktail reception to be held the following evening in honour of the two external examiners in OB\GY; he was keen on our presence. Dr Martey and I obliged and flew to Accra for the reception. Prof. Bentsi-Enchill at the time was an MRCOG; the whispering among my colleagues at the party was that it was an exercise towards his elevation to the Fellowship, FRCOG. In those days, elevation to the Fellowship did not come easily, especially if you were not based in Britain. Be it as it may, Kwesi fully merited an elevation at that time. Not long after this he was elevated to be FRCOG.

Korle Bu produced its first batch of MOs. From then onwards followed the quantum release of doctors, many of whom were posted to Kumasi to complete or commence their house jobs. Our department was a recipient of some of these doctors. Their general high standard was indisputable. My personal view was that their standard far surpassed those who had been trained in continental Europe.

I got another linkage with Korle Bu in the late 60s. The Midwifery Board appointed me the examiner for their board examinations in Accra. I performed this annual assignment for a couple of years. It was an exercise I thoroughly enjoyed. I had to prepare myself each time by reading through Margarate Myle's textbook of Midwifery to familiarize myself with what the midwives were expected to know; unwittingly, I learned some facts myself. An anecdote here on a strange dream I had merits narration.

On the night preceding my drive from Kumasi to Accra the following morning to conduct the examination, I had a dream. In the course of my journey, I reached a village. Some boys at the village waved their hands and directed me to a route different from the one I usually took. I ignored their advice and continued to drive on. The road suddenly turned steep and my car began to roll backwards, eliciting such fear that I woke up from my nightmare. It was just a dream and it constituted no reason to abort my journey to Accra. I embarked on my journey to Accra the following morning and on arriving at a village in the Kwahu area, some villagers stopped my car and advised me to turn into an alternative route. I ignored their advice (in retrospect, remembering my dream, was this wise or prudent?) and without asking for an explanation, continued to drive on. After driving for about two miles, I came to a halt; a large tree had fallen across the road; it was in the rainy season. I turned round, drove back to the village and humbly followed the advice and instructions of the villagers on an alternative route to Accra. This was a dream which foretold a future event. It was my first of such a dream, remarkable serendipity.

Although I had settled down very well in Kumasi in every respect, my interest in academia was awakened by an advertisement. The OB/GY Department in Korle-Bu advertised for a post of a lecturer. I responded by sending in my application for the post. I am still awaiting the letter of acknowledgement, nay appointment, in the second decade of the 21st century.

The initial batch of the Korle Bu graduates to my department included Drs Ankrah, Amponsah and Cudjoe. It was stimulating to take them on my ward rounds. In response to my question on the age of menarche (the first menstruation), I was given the standard one in the prevailing textbooks of the time. I pointed out that our teaching establishments should by then start research on such subjects, so that we in Ghana have our own original indices on various topics. I pointed out that Korle-Bu was failing us in some respects. On reflection, I quickly retracted my statement. There was no reason those of us outside the Korle Bu should not undertake such research projects, they did not have to be done in a Medical School establishment. I decided to embark on the task of finding out the age of the menarche in Ghana.

Although an accomplished clinician, I had had no background in research. It was an era without the internet and the source of medical information was through journals, in my case the BJOG.

I designed a questionnaire in two parts. The first part related to the social and environmental background of the subjects, while the second part centred on the age and nature of the menarche. I required a fairly large number of cohorts. Since I knew the Headmistresses of Aburi Girls' School and Achimota School, I approached them and obtained their consent. The Headmistress of St Louis Training College in Kumasi could not grant me this without the approval of the regional education boss. He was an Old Achimotan, Mr Boateng, a year my senior in Achimota. His response was quick and staggering. He not only gave an enthusiastic approval, but went on to suggest that the research should be conducted country-wide. I wrote to thank him, but being single-handed with limited resources, I decided to limit the participants to the three institutions only. The questions I asked were few, but pertinent enough for the exercise. On the whole, the response was satisfactory. The responses had to be fully analysed. On perusal of the first part, an interesting fact emerged. It was the vast difference in the social and environmental background of students in Achimota and Kumasi St Louis Training College. I took a week out of my annual leave to go through the responses. It was a tedious, but stimulating exercise. Since I had no knowledge of statistics, I sought for a statistician's services. I was lucky to find one. My brother Bill, Director of CRI, had a highly qualified statistician, Mr Ebbyn, on his staff. Mr Ebbyn, a Legon graduate in statistics, had done a postgraduate course in the subject in Britain. As he was willing to assist in my research project I handed over to him all the papers including the classifications I had done up till then. I gave him enough time to analyse and make his statistical input. We agreed to meet at a convenient date to discuss the results before publication. Mr Ebbyn postponed our meeting several times to my increasing distress. A few months later, I learned that he had left the CRI for an appointment elsewhere. I made several efforts through a number of intermediaries, including Dr Buahin, a senior Entomologist on the CRI staff, and an Old Achimotan, all to no avail to regain the papers I had given to him. He was appointed to the post of Regional Commissioner of Central Region. I believe he moved from there to take up a post with the Ghana Cocoa Board in London. The research papers he failed to return to me were priceless; they were never returned. So ended my first attempt at publishing an original research work entailing considerable input in man hours, despite a busy clinical commitment. The ensuing bitterness and sadness took a long time to go away. The exercise on the menarche was repeated about two decades later by Dr Adadevoh in collaboration with me and duly published in a journal.

When I arrived in Kumasi in 1965, my position was as a Special Grade Medical Officer. I was promoted to a Specialist grade in 1968.

In 1970, Dr Armar was transferred from Kumasi to Accra to head the Family Planning Unit. Dr Bondzi-Simpson, the Physician Specialist, was appointed the Medical Superintendent in KAH. He appointed me to head the OB/GY department in 1970. We had three units in the department with two headed by Valnicek and Martey. Initially, the MOs in the department had all been trained abroad as the Korle Bu products had not started coming out then. Among the MOs were Harry Poku, Wontumi, Forson, Djan and Riverson. Harry Poku, Bristol trained, was good looking, athletic and a very good tennis player; he was a dedicated, hardworking and brilliant doctor. We became close friends till his untimely death at a young age. Dr Wontumi had trained in Jamaica; he later went to Britain on scholarship to train and qualify as a gynaecologist. Dr Djan had trained in Canada; he returned there later to become a family doctor in Saskatchewan. Dr Turkson, two years my junior in Achimota, had trained in Germany; he returned there later to obtain his qualification as a gynaecologist. Dr Forson, an affable colleague, had trained in Cairo, Egypt; he later went to practise as a family doctor in Dunkwa. Dr Riverson, another dedicated colleague, had trained in Belfast.

On assuming the headship of the department, my aim was to promote as high a standard of patient care as was possible at the time. To this end I introduced the monthly maternal mortality and morbidity case review meetings. Dr RH Bannerman had initiated me into this practice in Accra. All maternal deaths were critically reviewed to learn and discover whether they could possibly be avoided. I made the attendance of the meetings compulsory for all the doctors and midwives; the meetings were educational and instructive in many respects. I always, in a preamble at the meeting, stated that it was not a court of law for finger pointing and this always went down well. The doctors always looked forward to attending these meetings. I chaired most of them, but occasionally rotated it with the two other Specialists. In Aberdeen, the equivalent was the monthly perinatal mortality meeting; maternal death being a rarity. Each year, I compiled the statistics for the department, showing the total number of deliveries, Caesarean sections (with rates), assisted vaginal deliveries, breech deliveries etc. Since I was the departmental head, the buck stopped with me. Sir Dugald Baird had inculcated in those of us who came under his tutelage the concept that the practice of Medicine is influenced in its milieu which is dictated by social, economic and prevailing environmental factors. Knowledge and access to current medical literature were equally important. I had in my personal library all the books I used while preparing for the MRCOG examination. I had subscribed to the monthly BJOG journal, the arrival of which I eagerly awaited. A priceless book in Tropical Obstetrics and Gynaecology authored by Professors J. B. Lawson of Ibadan and Stewart of Kingston appeared on the scene.

The Medical schools at Ibadan and Kingston were founded after World War II under the aegis of London University. These two schools established their own pedigree, several British gynaecological academics had gone to spend variable periods of time as Registrars or lecturers on their way to ascending to professorial chairs in Britain. These included Professors Dixon of Bristol and Charles Douglas of Oxford. This new book on Tropical Obstetrics and Gynaecology was the repository and definitive textbook on tropical OB/GY; it embodied facts and the experience of practitioners one could not find in other standard books at the time. The *Yearbook of Obstetrics and Gynaecology*, and Studd's *Progress in Obstetrics and Gynaecology* became regular acquisitions. I could therefore claim that I was extremely well informed, indeed as most in the gynaecology academia.

SPECIALIST GYNAECOLOGIST IN KUMASI

What clinical grounds did I cover? The catchment population was more than a million and the delivery rate was nine thousand to ten thousand a year. In Obstetrics, obstructed labour in primigravidae and multipara was common, as were their sequelae. Ruptured uterus resulting from obstructed labour in multipara with serious and sometimes fatal outcome was common; prolonged obstructed labour in primigravidae also resulted not infrequently in vesico-vaginal and/or recto-vaginal fistulae; these were unpleasant sequelae for the patients. The onus of repairing the fistulae lay with me by my own commitment; they were social outcasts, and only a few specialists were interested in repairing fistulae at that time. Dr Ghosh in Accra was outstanding in this regard and I referred cases which I found difficult to him. Blockage of the Fallopian tubes resulting from pelvic infection was a leading cause of infertility; this constituted a major gynaecological problem. I devoted myself to the management of cases of infertility and cervical cancer, more often than not at an advanced stage when presented to me. I managed them as best I could. The management of fibroids was fairly straightforward, based on the definitive approach by Victor Bonney; the fibroids varied in size from the small and numerous to the massive.

In obstetrics, I acquired the skill of performing the operation of symphysiotomy in cases of obstructed labour. To this day, I still advocate its application in selected cases depending on the environment in which the obstetrician is practising. I realize that in this advocacy, I belong to an endangered species preaching to the sceptics, the vast majority of our present day practitioners.

The repair of vesico-vaginal fistulae engaged my attention. I had been initiated into this malady by Dr Bannerman my mentor at Korle-Bu. The patients as aforementioned, were social outcasts and needed treatment. It was meaningless to me to score the highest mark in the MRCOG examination question on the topic and not tackle the issue practically. At this juncture, one should pay tribute to the Hamlin couple, both Gynaecologists from Australia, who went to Ethiopia and set up a hospital devoted entirely to repairing vesico-vaginal fistulae. It became the Mecca for treating the condition. Dr Ghosh, the outstanding Gynaecologist, who was the only one repairing vesico-vaginal fistulae in Accra, very commendably made his pilgrimage to the hospital in Ethiopia to learn from the Hamlins.

My second area of interest in Gynaecology was also traceable to Dr Bannerman. Patients complaining of infertility would travel any distance for treatment. My approach of diagnosis and treating the cause, by no means original, was at par with the management in the Western world; it was satisfying and fulfilling. Over time, I earned a reputation for addressing the problem, and indeed, some patients came from afar to consult me.

Cases of cervical cancer were more daunting. The management of early cases (stage 1 and 2a) was by Wertheim hysterectomy and Radiotherapy. There was no Radiotherapy facility in Ghana at the time. Although I could perform all the standard gynaecological operations when I returned to Ghana, I had never before performed a Wertheim's hysterectomy nor the alternative of Schautas radical vaginal hysterectomy. The latter was not done in Britain, but by a few in continental Europe. Mr Begg and I had assisted Mr Redman in performing the Wertheim's hysterectomy, a bloody, long and tedious operation. I had also watched the skilled and gifted Mr Agar do the same. It was regarded as the most difficult and daunting gynaecological operation, and not many gynaecologists attempted it. Dr Valnicek had assisted at many such operations in Czechoslovakia before he came to Kumasi. We therefore teamed up to operate jointly on early cases; both growing in confidence and skill, performing the Wertheim operation. I was sorry to see him leave Ghana for Canada. I continued performing the Wertheim on my own with assistance from my MOs. The MOs always looked forward to the cold bottle of beer after the two and a half hour marathon; anything beyond a stage 2a was abandoned. Although I was neither an Agar nor a David Currie of Leeds fame, I think that I acquitted myself reasonably well at the Wertheim; it entered my surgical repertoire.

Routine bread and butter surgery involved performing emergency and elective Caesarean sections, Caesarean hysterectomy for ruptured uterus, and laparotomy for twisted or ruptured ovarian cyst, ruptured or aborted ectopic pregnancy and pelvic peritonitis resulting from acute pelvic infection constituted the regular cases. One's diagnostic acumen was put to the test a few times by successfully diagnosing and performing laparotomies on cases of advanced abdominal pregnancy. I was familiar with the literature on a series of 12 cases in Kingston, Jamaica, published by Dixon in the BMJ in the early 60s. Craniotomy, followed by the extraction of a dead foetus, external cephalic version and assisted vaginal breech delivery were not uncommon undertakings in my practice at the time. It was also my duty and commitment to teach a succession of MOs in my unit to perform Caesarean sections and laparotomies on cases of ectopic pregnancy. They were methodically taught step by step and not rushed through; they also mastered the technique of evacuating the uterus in cases of incomplete abortion. Some of these MOs were Drs Atubra, Kplomedo and Turkson.

The field of clinical gynaecological endocrinology was still very limited. Up to the early sixties, for historical purposes, I venture to add the following footnote: pregnancy tests were still done biologically (using the toad or frog); it took three days; it now takes only seconds. The oral contraceptive was a few years away; the earliest IUD (intrauterine device) in the form of the Lippes loop was emerging in clinical practice. In 1969 the Ford Foundation in the USA sponsored a group of nine Gynaecologists from Nigeria and Ghana (five from Ghana, four from Nigeria), including myself, to tour a number of countries to observe how their Family Planning Programme worked We visited the following places: Washington, New York, Mexico City, Kingston in Jamaica and Caracas in Venezuela. It lasted four weeks. I personally had a bonus; since the tour ended in Caracas, my return journey home to Ghana was conveniently routed via Trinidad (Yolande's home country). On my return home, I was appointed the Programme Director of the Kumasi branch of the International Planned Parenthood Association of Ghana (IPPAG). The Kumasi branch, with offices on Harper Road, had a clinic which I ran weekly on Wednesdays. There, I inserted IUDs, dispensed oral contraceptives, administered long-acting progesterone. Family planning involved tubal ligation. In the era predating the laparoscope, I performed the operation through a minilap abdominal incision. The operations were all done at the KAH OB/GY department. After reading the medical journal, I performed tubal ligation operation through an incision in the posterior fornix, a posterior colpotomy incision vaginally. I later made a presentation of my series of cases to the Ghana group of Gynaecologists in Korle-Bu.

Yolande and I arrived in Kumasi and took residence as a family of two in 11 Danyame. On 16th December 1966, after a not very easy 1st and 2nd trimesters and a fairly protracted labour, the family size increased to three with the birth of our first son. As a Friday-born, he automatically acquired the name Kofi; and my father, as Ewe tradition dictates, added the name Dodzidenu (Trust in Him). The family size increased to four in January 1968, with the arrival of a second son, Yaw (a Thursday-born). Our first son was named Brian at his baptismal ceremony, which was held in our bungalow and conducted by a Presbyterian pastor; Dr Asare and Mr Austin Tetteh were Godfathers., and Joy Djan and Naakarley Tetteh were his godmothers. When Brian was three months old, we travelled to Peki with him for the Easter festivities. It also served the dual purpose of introducing Yolande to the Peki family. My father came to Peki for the Easter; my mother did not accompany him, but came to Kumasi at a later date to visit us. In the latter stage of her second pregnancy, Yolande travelled to Trinidad. Our second son was born and baptized in Trinidad as Yaw (Thursday-born) Neil Theodore Etriakor (He is Powerful) Agble.

Parenthood commenced with the arrival of the young Agbles. Our fairly recently acquired friends, Bob and Betty Barclay, had very kindly offered to purchase any nursery items required, however bulky, as they had a shipping consignment of goods in a container which they were sending from the UK. They were generous with their time, doing very careful shopping at the famed Army and Navy Stores in London. Nothing was left out – from baby cot to carry cot, bath and stand, pushchair and a very posh pram which lasted for all four boys.. John and Akua as our domestic staff laid the basis of our domestic life, devoid of stress. Yolande complemented her motherhood skills by reading Spock's standard book on the subject. The children had a nursery of their own, right next to our bedroom. This all worked together for a continued stress-free life as new parents.

Before our arrival in Kumasi, Yolande possessed no culinary skills to boast of; in fact, her mother was quite frank with me about this! We found ourselves plunged into a social and somewhat elitist milieu in Kumasi, Yolande quickly applied herself to acquiring the necessary culinary skills with the use of books and advice from friends and indeed her mother all the way in Trinidad! The Doctors' wives club, in a way a gourmet group, served as a place where ideas were exchanged. Titi Hudson sometimes accompanied Yolande to the market to shop; she also instructed Yolande on the cooking of all the popular Ghanaian dishes. Yolande in turn of course introduced several of them to Caribbean dishes. An American neighbour and new friend, Dorothy Mellor, wife of a Diplomat, introduced Yolande to cordon bleu dishes. Yolande thus attained an enviable level in the art of cooking varied tasty dishes. An invitation to attend a dinner party at the Agbles was one to which our many friends looked forward.

Miss Abbensett, the Domestic Bursar of the KNUST, acknowledged as an excellent cook in every respect, adopted my family and showered

278

us with very tasty ethnic dishes from time to time. Miss Abbensett, born of British Guyanese parentage, grew up in Sekondi. Our close family relationship followed the birth of her first and only child, a son, who very sadly passed away in his twenties.

My non-clinical activities were of a sporting, social and literary nature. The major companies, including Guinness Brewery and Star Brewery, Standard Chartered Bank and Barclays Bank, all had expatriates in senior positions; with the staff of the KNUST, Kumasi was quite a cosmopolitan city. Our friends with whom we socialized embraced this group and Ghanaians. City Hotel was in its prime, the Saturday curry lunch there was popular and heavily patronized.

Kumasi Club Tennis Group

I played tennis every day except on Sundays. In the early years, I played at the Kumasi Club on weekdays and at the Maxwell Club on Saturdays; in later years, I played on weekdays at the KNUST tennis courts. While Dr Lahiri's drop shots and drop volleys were generally admired, my powerful forearm and single-handed backhand drives were a force to reckon with. The doubles partnership of Drs Lahiri and Harry Poku and the singles performance of Mr Kofi Pobee were formidable. We played with the wooden Slazenger rackets, the best at that time. On a visit to the USA in 1969, I bought a steel racket which had just come on the market. I took it along to the tennis clubs, passed it around for all my tennis buddies to get the feel of a steel racket. I listened to the BBC radio broadcast of the Wimbledon Tennis Championships Men's Singles finals in July every year. As a football fan, I followed the encounters between Asante Kotoko (the soul of Ashanti) and Accra Hearts of Oak.

Yolande and I (like Papa, my father) were bibliophiles. My choice of books was on History; never a fast reader, I did not fancy reading novels. Yolande's interest centred on books on World War Two and British authors like Monica Dickens and Margaret Drabble, as well as P.G. Wodehouse, among others. Our modest library reflected our interests. I started collecting gramophone records, the long-playing records (LPs) of 12 inches and 10 inches width had replaced the fragile 78rpm of old. I had a collection of the smaller sized 45rpm. The record collection reflected my catholic taste in music. It included Ghanaian Highlife music, Calypso, Jazz and Western classical music. Because of my interest in opera, I had collections of highlights of several operas by Mozart, Verdi and Wagner. All the Beethoven symphonies and piano concertos, several Mozart symphonies and concerto records and selections from Chopin, Schubert, Tchaikovsky, Rachmaninov and Bach constituted my music library. My love of Calypso music dated back to the 1950s when Lord Kitchener was indeed the lord of Calypso. The titivating and naughty, tuneful lyrics (Nora, Dr Kitch, Tomato Calypso, Cricket Lovely Cricket, A Woman's Figure) figured in my collection. I also adored Sparrow, a fairly newcomer on the calypso scene, and collected a number of his calypsos. E. T. Mensah and his Tempos Band, Ramblers Band and the Uhuru Band were great exponents of Ghanaian Blues and Highlife music. My jazz interest extended from the traditional, through Louis Armstrong, Duke Ellington, Ella Fitzgerald, Charlie Parker, Benny Goodman and Glenn Miller to the Modern Jazz Quartet and virtuoso soloists as Dave Brubeck, Stan Getz and Oscar Peterson. The joy of listening to purveyors of this art, like Oscar Peterson or George Shearing, can match the rendition of Litstz's piano transcriptions of Beethoven's symphonies or Schubert's impromptus. This wide and almost complete musical range was always shared with our dinner guests, to their great delight. Of particular delightful listening pleasure were the many LPs which we purchased in boxed sets of 12 from The Readers Digest; we still derive enormous satisfaction from listening to them.

Some of my leisure hours were spent listening to my collection of music. The transition from records to the audio tape had not yet occurred. Ghana TV was in its infancy with the pictures in black and white, and for those of us in Kumasi an inconsistent and unreliable service.

I have mentioned earlier in the memoirs my visit to a couple of places when the Ford Foundation in the USA sponsored nine Gynaecologists from Ghana and Nigeria on a Family Planning mission. Starting with a week in Washington, we then went to Mexico City for a week.

The Ghana Embassy in Mexico City hosted a splendid dinner in our honour. This Embassy also then doubled as the representative of several other African countries (a legacy from Kwame Nkrumah's era). From Mexico we went to Kingston, Jamaica. We were hosted to an evening reception by the department of OB/GY in UWI (University of West Indies); it was a most convivial evening. I was delighted to meet Professor Stewart for the first time; he had co-authored (with Professor A. B. Lawson in Ibadan, Nigeria) the excellent book "Text Book of Tropical Obstetrics and Gynaecology". Prof. Stewart, although far more distinguished, like me, was a protégé of Sir Dugald Baird in Aberdeen. Indeed, when the chair in Aberdeen was due to be vacant on the retirement of Sir Dugald Baird, he was considered as the front-runner for the post; he apparently declined the proposal. In a friendly one-on-one conversation, and reminiscing about Aberdeen, he indeed confirmed this to me. He preferred the warm weather in Jamaica to the cold Aberdeen weather. He said that he would be taking a chair in Nova Scotia, in guess what, in ZOOLOGY. Both Professor Dixon of Bristol and Charles Douglas of Royal Free and later of Cambridge University had been lecturers under Prof Stewart in Kingston before ascending to prestigious chairs in Britain. Dr Ojo, a Nigerian in our touring group, did not desist from his machinations in academic appointments. He was an MRCOG, and in hierarchy, the most senior indigene in the Ibadan OB/GY Department. On meeting Dr Hugh Wynter, his Jamaican, but unassuming counterpart in UWI, he pressed him to agitate to have Prof Stewart removed for Wynter to head the department. I had a ringside view of Dr Ojo's machinations; I thought it was improper for him to be pushing Hugh that far. In the course of time, Dr Ojo got his way when Prof Lawson returned to Britain to continue with his very distinguished career in OB/GY with the RCOG and University of Newcastle. Dr Hugh Wynter also in due course succeeded Prof Stewart at Kingston.

We ended our Family Planning tours in Caracas, Venezuela; this is the nearest city to Trinidad. Since I had never before then been to Trinidad, I seized the opportunity to go there to visit my in-laws. I flew from Caracas to Port of Spain, Trinidad. I stayed for a night at Queens Park Hotel. I contacted Dr Hugh Spicer; he was an Aberdeen contemporary, now in general practice; he came over to the hotel for a mini-reunion.

The following day, Gloria, Yolande's sister, came from San Fernando, their hometown and took me to their home on Cipero Street. There I met Yolande's other siblings, Rica, Roland and Ronald. Yolande's second sister, Glenda, had come to see me at my hotel in New York when I was passing through from Washington to Mexico City. Gloria took me to Port of Spain to see Dr Maxwell Awon, the Minister of Health for some discussions. There was a very remote possibility of my going to work in Trinidad. Dr Awon was a fellow Gynaecologist with MRCOG, MRCPE and FRCSE (a veritable case of multiple diplomatosis), qualifications required to be a specialist Gynaecologist, Physician, and Surgeon respectively; he was obviously a brilliant doctor. Some doctors give up attempts at obtaining one of these diplomas after failing the examination a couple of times. The detour through Trinidad ended my Family Planning course. I returned to Ghana via London where I did some useful shopping. Following my appointment as the Regional Director of the IPPFG in Kumasi, it was my pleasure to attend two regional meetings in Ibadan and sub-Saharan meetings in Nairobi, the headquarters of IPPA.

My family planning activities were not confined to clinics and attendances at conferences in Accra, Ibadan and Nairobi; it was carried on at a personal level. Our third son was born in 1970 on a Tuesday and so, like his father, is Komla; my father gave him a family name of Agyabana (name of my great grandfather). He was christened with the Christian name of Dugald by the Presbyterian minister from Prempeh College. The name Dugald was chosen in recognition and as a tribute to my mentor Sir Dugald Baird of Aberdeen.

An important episode here needs narrating. When Yolande was eight months pregnant with Dugald, she was involved in a serious car accident. Driving her small Austin mini minor car to visit a friend at Nhyiaeso one morning, her car was hit at a crossroad at right angles by a big Mercedes car being driven at top speed by a rich Lebanese timber merchant, thus overturning Yolande's car. Neither of the two intersecting roads had been marked as the major road, and it was obvious that the Lebanese fellow was at fault by driving so fast in a residential area. Yolande was extricated from her car and taken to the ER (Emergency Room) at KAH. I was doing a ward round at the time of her admission, and I was alerted. Luckily, she did not sustain any injuries and the pregnancy remained intact. After a short period of observation, I drove her home. An intriguing legal episode followed.

The Lebanese driver got the appropriate authorities to mark the previously unmarked road he was driving on as the major of the two intersecting roads and the police to take the measurements of the scene and brake marks. This way, he would be adjudged as driving on the major road and not requiring to slow down at the junction. I went to see the Kumasi City Town Clerk, Mr Achampong, a lawyer by profession, and complained about this malfeasance; it came under his purview. His opinion was that this was most irregular; Yolande had already been pronounced guilty, so we appealed against the judgment. The appeal case was apparently called twice with the appellants, Yolande and I, absent. When I went to enquire from the magistrate's court as to why our case was never called, the clerk was quite puzzled. The bailiff with the necessary summons never delivered it to us; it appeared that there was some form of collusion between himself and the policeman to prevent the appeal from being heard. Apparently after the 'third no show' by the appellants, the matter would be finally dismissed. What was behind this was anybody's guess; the businessman was very influential in Kumasi. Suffice it to say that the case was reviewed in an open court, the magistrate ruled in our favour and all parties on the opposing side were properly reprimanded, especially the policeman.

This was not the end of the case for the policeman. His role in the affair was referred to the Chairman of the Kumasi Police Board, Mr Joe Appiah. He was punished for a severe misdemeanour and lowered in rank from being a sergeant to the rank of a corporal; he was also seriously reprimanded. That was the first time I saw Joe Appiah.

It is now timely to write briefly about the Appiah family. Mr Joe Appiah was a famous lawyer, politician and an Ashanti royal. He became famous during his student days in London as a soap box orator in London's Hyde Park Corner. His wife Peggy was the daughter of Sir Stafford Cripps, Chancellor of the Exchequer in Clement Attlee's government just after the Second World War. He was also the British Ambassador to the Kremlin during said war. Their wedding in the early 1950s (a famous African to a white aristocrat) hit the front pages of the media worldwide. He became a political prisoner when he was incarcerated by Kwame Nkrumah and was released only after the 1966 coup d'état which toppled Nkrumah.

The second time I met Joe was at a Robert Burns night; he was invited by mutual Scottish friends in Kumasi who were celebrating a colourful and entertaining Burns night. Short in height, with a thin lip wide moustache, he was clad in his signature Ghanaian cloth and had a heavy gold chain around his neck. He captivated the audience and we all marvelled at his oratory. At a later date, Yolande and I invited him and Peggy to dinner at our Danyame bungalow. We hosted about ten people in all to a most convivial and pleasant dinner, probably the best Yolande and I had ever staged.so far. Thereafter, Peggy took a special liking to our family; invitations to their house at Mbrom became regular; sometimes we were persuaded to stay overnight to watch video films on a player sent to them by Anthony from America, then a novelty. The family friendship extended to the children and flourished. We were out of the country when Joe passed away. Peggy virtually adopted Yolande as a surrogate younger sister. Almost every time we visited her in Kumasi, from Accra where we were later resident, she would give Yolande precious beads from her collection. She gave us copies of her book of Ananse Stories which she co-authored with Anthony; she also gave us three copies of her big tome on Akan Proverbs "Bu Me Abe". She adopted Kumasi, and Ghana completely as her home. The KNUST awarded her the honorary degree of D. Lit

(Doctorate in Literature.). After her death, the children named Yolande as one of the chief mourners and requested her to write a tribute. Yolande was honoured by this and wrote a fitting tribute to Peggy. Their only son, Anthony Kwame Appiah, is a renowned academic in Philosophy; he has been a don at Legon, Cambridge, Yale, Princeton and New York Universities. In 2016, he delivered the BBC's famous and prestigious Reith Lectures. His three sisters are Akua, Abena and Adjoa.

At this juncture, it is worth chronicling some significant world events. In June 1968, Reverend Martin Luther King (Jnr) was assassinated by a white gunman. ML King aged only 39, had achieved worldwide fame for advocating and preaching non-violence and universal racial brotherhood. He was a Nobel Peace Prize Laureate. The news was received with profound shock and with worldwide condemnation.

Barely two months after M. L. King's assassination, the USA and the outside world was again shocked and grief-stricken; Robert Kennedy, the younger brother of the assassinated President J. F. Kennedy, was also assassinated. He was a civil rights advocate and the frontrunner in the forthcoming Presidential election. After the assassination of his brother JFK, he assumed the headship of the Kennedy family and their political mission. The assassin, Sirhan Bishara Sirhan, was a Palestinian with Jordanian citizenship. The Kennedy mantle then descended on Edward Kennedy. The Vietnam War was raging and in claiming the lives of many American soldiers, gave the President, Lyndon Johnson, a low poll rating. In Czechoslovakia, an attempt to democratize the Communist regime western style, led President Brezhnev to send in the Red Army to restore the Communist regime.

In the Middle East, there was another conflagration. Following an unexpected attack by Syria and Egypt on the Israeli forces, with military help from her guardian and greatest ally, the USA, the Israelis responded very swiftly and decisively. In less than a week, known in history as the Six-Day War, the Israelis destroyed the Egyptian Air Force and drove Syrian troops from the Golan Heights.

In 1969, two American astronauts, Neil Armstrong and Edwin Aldrin, in Apollo 11 made history by landing on the moon. They stepped from their fragile four-legged lunar module and stepped onto rocky, arid ground. To the millions of awed TV viewers on planet earth, Armstrong proclaimed as he stepped on the terrain and planted an American flag, "That's one small step for man, one giant leap for mankind". Americans had taken the lead in the fierce competition in the space race. They returned to earth in triumph, adoration and adulation with a piece of rock from the moon. J. F. Kennedy's aim had been achieved.

Dr Christian Barnard in South Africa removed the heart of a very young woman who had died in a car accident and placed it in the chest of a 65-year old man, Mr Washkansky, whose heart was seriously diseased and failing. The announcement was hailed worldwide, but doctors said the crucial question was whether the body would accept the alien heart. Mr Washkansky died 18 days after the operation of pneumonia. As a surgical procedure, it was a success. Dr Barnard had trained in the USA as a cardiac surgeon. Many years later, much of the surgical success was attributed to a black South African. The apartheid regime then in power forbade any mention of his critical contribution. He was named and honoured after the fall of the apartheid regime.

Transplant surgery advanced and heart transplant without immunological rejection prolonged life for many. In less than 20 years, history was made by a Ghanaian, Dr Kwabena Frimpong Boateng, who led a team to perform a heart transplant in West Germany. It was a historic event which hit the front pages of the media in Ghana. Kwabena, a graduate from Korle Bu, had been an MO in my department in KAH before he went to Germany and trained under his German mentor. He fulfilled his personal mission and ambition of returning to Ghana to establish a Cardio-thoracic Unit in Korle-Bu, his Alma Mater. I recommend his book, "Deep Down My Heart" as a compulsory read to readers of these memoirs. For establishing this Unit, the first in sub-Saharan Africa, and unselfishly training many doctors from the continent in this craft, against all the prevailing odds, we should salute him.

Ghana attained the status of a democratic country and in its wake attracted visits from several distinguished and prominent people. One such visitor was Mr Roy Jenkins. Initially a leading Labour politician, he was one of the gang of four who broke away to form the Social Democratic Party; he ended his distinguished career as the Chancellor of Oxford University.

A delegation of parliamentarians including the Prime Minister of Barbados visited Ghana. On their brief visit to Kumasi, Yolande and I had the pleasure of entertaining them to a dinner at our bungalow.

During our final months in Leeds, Yolande had, as one of her patients, the elderly wife of Mr Roger Gallant; this lady required regular visits which she provided. Over a period of time she became very friendly with Mr Gallant, who treated her in a rather fatherly way. He kept in touch even after his wife passed away and professional visits were no longer required; in fact, he was a guest at our wedding. He continued to keep in touch with us and when we told him that we were leaving for Ghana he expressed the wish to visit us there. He was a man in his late seventies, although quite fit, so we wondered if he was serious about this desire. We kept in touch by mail, in those days 50 plus years ago there was a fairly reliable postal service between Ghana and most of the rest of the world! He was quite serious about visiting us, arrangements were made and we went to Accra to meet him at the airport. He stayed with us for almost two months! Uncle Roger, as he asked us to call him, as did most of our close friends, fitted in from the word go. No complaints about mosquitoes, heat, food or anything, he enjoyed everything; he was particularly fond of palm nut soup. He quickly established a routine: after breakfast donned in his white shorts and shirt, he would go for a walk around the Danyame area where we lived, chatting with anyone whom he met along the way, especially if they spoke English, then sit in the garden on his return, have his lunch inside or sometimes in the garden. He socialised with us and our friends in the evenings; they always included him in their invitations to us. During his visit, he celebrated his 80th birthday by personally hosting a grand dinner party at the City Hotel. All our friends were invited, including Drs Tagboto and Asare, both Leeds University graduates; he got along very well with everyone, especially Joan, Emmanuel's wife, who was from Accrington, near Leeds. Uncle Roger thoroughly enjoyed his visit, he was an excellent guest, gave no trouble at all, and we were as sad to see him go as he was to leave us. A truly remarkable gentleman.

Friendships and associations are forged in various ways. Our circle of friends in our initial years in Danyame gradually widened and included now were Miss Christina Owusu, Dick and Pat Kassardjian,

Gulpu and Betty Lahiri, Mr J. A. Addison, Bruce and Anne Smith and Nana Amanianpong, the Mamponghene, to mention just a few. I will write briefly on them in no particular order.

Dick Kassardjian, the son of the very well known road construction entrepreneur, was a Lebanese of Armenian stock. Dick's Ghanaian mother hailed from Yilo Krobo. He had met Pat in London where they got married. Pat was a pretty lady from Trinidad. They had a son of the same age as our son Brian and were expecting another child when they arrived in Kumasi. Pat had been referred to me by Professor Oduro, an Anaesthetist in Korle-Bu (also married to a Caribbean); Yolande was the only other Trinidadian in Kumasi and a very close friendship developed between our two families, including our children as they grew up as playmates, attending the same schools. Initially, the Kassardjians lived in a foundry bungalow sited on the Mampong road, 12 miles from Kumasi. They later moved into their own house in Nhyiaeso. Their house was directly opposite B. M. Kuffuor's mansion, which boasted a tennis court, a large swimming pool, a gazebo and a fish pond. Kuffuor was reputedly the richest man in Ashanti, if not the whole country (he had 12 cars, including a Rolls-Royce parked in his massive garage). It was my pleasure to deliver the two Kassardjian daughters. Our friendship blossomed, but relocations of our two families later made our meetings together rather infrequent. It was with a feeling of great sadness that Yolande and I received news of Dick's sudden death at a relatively young age. I renewed my acquaintance with his brothers Armen (owner of Accra's Shangri-la Hotel) and Maxwell.

I had known Dr Armar and his family for a number of years. Dr Armar was now married to Miss Christina Owusu, an Old Achimotan and the younger sister of Mr Victor Owusu, the legendary lawyer/politician. Miss Christina Owusu, popularly known as Auntie Christie, was then the Regional Education Officer. She was politically powerful and carried much clout, although her brother was the second in the political pecking order as the Minister for Foreign Affairs, the general belief was that she was more influential in the Busia regime than her brother. I witnessed a stream of people trooping into her house seeking ambassadorial or other prestigious or potentially lucrative political appointments. Plump, vivacious and very friendly, she lived in a bungalow not far from ours in Danyame. Auntie Christy quickly took a liking to Yolande and me and helped us in many ways. Yolande and I were greatly saddened when her only child with Dr Armar, a boy, died at a young age. We remained family friends until she passed away.

I got to know Nana Amanianpong, the Mamponghene, the occupant of the Ashanti Silver stool, when his wife was my patient. He visited me in my Danyame bungalow several times. Initially he would call in with a small retinue of traditional attendants, but with the passage of time when the friendship grew, he would come with only his chauffeur. We responded to his invitations to visit him in Mampon and we were very well received. We shared a lasting friendship until he passed away.

Nana Amanianpong was succeeded on the Silver stool by Mr Gyimah Kesse (aka Saint). Mr Gyimah Kesse, an only child, and a Legon graduate, trained and qualified as a lawyer. He joined the administrative department of KNUST and rose in rank to become the Registrar. Tall and athletic, he was a very good tennis player with whom I played regularly at the Maxwell and KNUST tennis clubs. His wife, also an only child and a Legon graduate, worked at the Bank of Ghana, and rose in rank to be its regional manager in Kumasi. She was professionally known to me, and I delivered their only daughter, now a medical doctor. I recall with pleasure my tennis playing days with Saint. I was abroad in Saudi Arabia when he ascended to the Silver stool, but I sent him a congratulatory letter.

After his degree courses in Aberdeen (ending with a PhD), Victor Adu, with his wife Victoria, was stationed at the Kwadaso Soil Research Institute in Kumasi Our two families naturally developed a close friendship, seeds of which had been sown in Aberdeen. They moved to their Nhyiaso residence later. I was pleased to be able to obtain two plots of prime land for them from the Samanhene in Nhyiaso. They built their house there, beautifully landscaped with an orchard of fruit trees. Victoria, a genuine Christian, caringly looked after Victor when his health was failing. Yolande and I were in Cape Town, South Africa, attending a FIGO Congress in 2009, when we received news that Victor had passed away.

Our friendships with some important members of staff in the Faculty of Architecture of KNUST conferred on us almost honorary membership of that Faculty.

First, Austin Tetteh and his family were in Kumasi when we arrived there. Austin and his wife Narkaley were one of the first old friends of mine to whom I introduced Yolande. The relationship between Austin and me, dating back to our UCGC days, had attained one of a surrogate siblinghood. Austin, rotund in build, round-faced and light complexioned was married to Narkaley, daughter of Mr K. G. Konuah, founder of Accra Academy Secondary School. On my return to Kumasi in 1965, Austin had risen in rank to be the head of the Planning Department in the Faculty; he later rose to the chair and the Deanship of the Faculty. Austin was an excellent cook; he enjoyed his time in the kitchen cooking delicious dishes. Austin enjoyed life as it should be enjoyed. Our two families with our growing children enjoyed happy times together. Yolande and I, once again, were abroad when Austin passed away. We still miss Austin dearly; it was a friendship we cherished and still do.

Mr John Owusu Addo became the first Ghanaian Professor and later Dean of the Faculty. He always had a friendly countenance and an infectious smile. I got to know him through his wife Doris from Amanokrom. Doris and I both entered Achimota school in 1946; she was a year my junior. We both attended the Presbyterian confirmation classes there run by Reverend Fraser. and were confirmed the same day. After two years post-secondary course at the UCGC, she went to study law at Hull University in Britain. On her return home as a lawyer, she scaled up the ladder of the bench. I recall giving her a lift in my car in 1961 from Accra to Kumasi; Doris was then far into her first pregnancy, carrying triplets. When I returned to Kumasi in 1965 with Yolande, Doris and John quite naturally constituted our group of family friends; it remains a life-long one.

When we decided to build our own house in Nhyiaeso, we approached John. He very willingly agreed to design a house to our taste and specification. Taking into account the sloping topography of the land, he designed a most attractive and beautiful house, winning him my accolade/nickname of 'Le Corbusier' (the famous and legendary architect). Because we intended to build the house through direct labour, with limited resources, John got for us a trusted and knowledgeable foreman, Ocloo by name, whose workmanship he held in high regard. The building of the house lasted one and a half years. John supervised the whole project. When it was completed, it was regarded by many as probably the most attractive in Kumasi at that time. John had done all that without demanding or taking a penny! Professionally and diligently, the nature of his character.

When two fellow colleagues and I agreed to build Bomso Clinic, John did the design and entire drawings and assisted in our attempt to raise funds from the bank. He also supervised the building of the clinic which was being done by direct labour. Again, because of me, it was all pro bono! It is rare to experience such acts of generosity these days. A keen golfer and a Freemason, try as he did, he did not succeed in enrolling me into Freemasonry. I never took to golf either. He is Godfather to our youngest son, Ronald. I lay great store on our friendship.

The third Faculty member was Professor Bob Barclay, an Englishman, mentioned earlier in these memoirs. A year after joining the staff as Professor of Building Technology, he became Dean of the Faculty. With his wife Betty, he not infrequently hosted cocktail parties in his bungalow at KNUST to which Yolande and I were regularly invited. Our association began in Kent, England, when they hosted us just about a month before Yolande and I sailed home in 1965. Our association grew and developed into a close friendship in Kumasi.

In 1977, Prince Charles of Britain visited Ghana for the celebration of Achimota's golden jubilee (Achimota College was initially named Prince of Wales College until the abdication of the uncrowned Prince of Wales). Bob was honoured with the OBE (Order of the British Empire) in Kumasi by Prince Charles. The ceremony was held in the Regional Office. In addition to Betty, his wife, Bob could invite three other couples as supporters to witness the exclusive royal event. Bob invited me and Yolande, the Vice-Chancellor of KNUST, Professor Banfo-Kwakye and his wife, and the Director of the British Council and his wife, Nigel and Janet Ross, completed his list of special guests. Prince Charles, dressed in a white naval uniform, struck Bob's shoulder gently with a sword as Bob knelt on a cushion to receive the honour. It was my second opportunity of seeing the Prince. Yolande and I felt highly honoured.

My first sight of Prince Charles had been at the Accra airport on his arrival from London the week before. We, the Old Achimotans, in our specially designed jubilee cloth, went to the airport to welcome our special guest, the Prince of Wales. He alighted from the plane and walked alongside the security barrier fencing, waving to the cheering crowd of Old Achimotans there to welcome him. As he passed in front of me, a pressman took a picture, unknown to me at the time. A couple of weeks later, Mr Denis Beasley, CEO of the Kumasi Star Brewery, and a friend, drew my attention to the weekly news magazine, West Africa, then a famous publication. On the front cover was a picture of Prince Charles as he passed just in front of me, KG and Leena Korsah waving in the crowd of Achimotans; a memorable copy of the magazine to acquire. I got three copies of that publication. The random list of my friends continues.

Mr Denis Beasley, an Englishman, was the CEO of the famous Star Beer Brewery in Kumasi in the 1960s and 1970s. With a flamboyant air of authority and bonhomie, he bore a close physical resemblance and also in diction to James Robertson Justice, the famous actor in 'Doctor in the House' series. He loved Ghana and had gone very Fante. He cultivated a friendship with me and Yolande quite early after our arrival in Kumasi. His parties were unforgettable and ones to cherish; good company, free flowing drinks and delicious food (the best palm nut soup I ever had in Kumasi was in his house, prepared by his cook). He had palm nut soup almost daily at 11am in his office – apart from liking it, he believed in its nutritional value. The Star Brewery was then the largest in Ghana, with Star beer being its flagship brew. The company launched Gulder, a stronger brew later; this was not popular initially, but I liked it and preferred it to the Star brand. Because of this, Denis Beasley sent me free cartons of Gulder beer on promotional exercises from time to time.

Denis also doubled as the British Consul in Kumasi. An unconfirmed story was that his visa was withdrawn in the 1970s, resulting in his departure from Ghana. The overseas company then posted him to Sierra Leone, a location he reportedly did not like. The Ghana military government took over the Tata Brewery, which had been founded and owned by Mr Siaw, a Kwahu entrepreneur, who fell foul of the then government. Tata Brewery became a state industry. The same government which had withdrawn Mr Beasley's visa then recruited him to return to Ghana to run the Tata Brewery as its CEO. I believe he was later enstooled as a traditional chief in Cape Coast. Despite failing health, he chose to stay in Ghana rather than return to England in his final days. My last meeting with Denis was in May 1987 at his office at Tata Brewery. He died in Ghana when I was out of the country. It was reported that he was accorded a Ghanaian traditional funeral befitting a Fante chief. I treasure his memory and friendship.

There was a second brewery in Kumasi, the Guinness Brewery, established by the parent Irish Dublin Company. It was a modern establishment run by a succession of British expatriates. Some of them had children who attended the same school, the Ridge International School, as our boys did. The friendships among the boys extended to the parents – Yolande and I received invitations to attend parties organized by the Guinness managers. The son of one of them, Mark, a great buddy of our son Neil, joined our family when we went to celebrate Easter in Peki one year. Mark's parents, Pat and Mary Kennedy, later relocated to Takoradi and hosted our family when we visited there.

Dr Emmanuel Asare and his English wife Joan, were among our closest family friends in Kumasi. My association with Emmanuel dated back to 1946 when he and his twin brother Enoch came from Mamfe to enrol at Achimota. After his sixth form, he joined our degree class at UCGC. He was one of the few who successfully obtained the London BSc degree in 1954. He went to Leeds Medical School and graduated at the same time that I graduated in Aberdeen. He married Joan from Accrington, Yorkshire. We both served as MOs in Korle-Bu and KAH. As an MO in Kumasi, he acquired a surgical dexterity which if pursued would have made him one of Ghana's greatest surgeons. This did not happen.

Emmanuel and Joan were our instant friends when we arrived in Kumasi in 1965. They had three daughters – Margaret, Tricia and Elizabeth – and a son, David. Joan, a trained teacher, taught at the Ridge International School; eventually becoming its Headmistress, a position she held for several years. She retired but was recalled for another long spell as Headmistress.

Our family friendship blossomed. Emmanuel was Godfather to our first son, Brian. Emmanuel, a keen tennis player, was my doubles partner for several years. Their only son, David, their youngest child, but two years older than Brian, was his playmate; he would often come to play with him and Neil after school. David suffered from asthma. I collected David, Brian and Neil from school one day and drove them to our house to play. Brian and David had their faces painted like Red Indians. After playing with the boys, I drove David home later in the afternoon. Very late that night, I received a telephone call from Joan to tell me that David was having a severe attack of asthma and that Emmanuel was giving him the kiss of life. Without any delay, I quickly dressed up to drive to their house near the stadium. Yolande, then expecting in mid-pregnancy and very unwell with pregnancy sickness, insisted on accompanying me. On arrival, we found to our profound shock and great sadness that David had passed away and was resting peacefully on Joan's lap; it was one of the saddest moments of my life. I aborted a trip to Accra which I had arranged for the following day so that I could give support with all the myriad things needing to be done in such tragic circumstances, as did Yolande, despite her condition. Not long after this, Yolande's pregnancy ended in miscarriage of a female conceptus, the only time we had conceived a girl! Our family friendship was maintained over the years in both adversity and joy, including our 16 years sojourn abroad.

In 1992, we came from England with our son Ronald to spend Christmas in Kumasi. Joan and Emmanuel invited us to a special, unforgettable Christmas lunch. The other guests were Jim and Joan Ofori. Mrs Ofori, an Australian, was the current Headmistress of the Ridge International School. Ronald, our son, was in his 2nd year at Emmanuel College, Cambridge University, as a medical student. Both Joan and Mrs Ofori had taught him at the Ridge School years earlier; he was now almost 6ft tall and towered above his petite headmistresses!

On our return to Ghana after 16 years in the diaspora, we relocated to Accra and lived in our newly-built house at Agbaamo Lane, Airport Residential Area. Yolande and I celebrated our fortieth wedding anniversary there in the year 2005. The highlights were a church service at the Accra Ridge church in the morning followed by a buffet dinner at our residence in the evening. Our four boys, from England,

and Yolande's mother, sister and niece came from the USA for the celebration. Joan and Emmanuel honoured our invitation and came from Kumasi to attend. Joan was dressed in a resplendent Ghana Kente kaba.

It was with great sadness that Yolande and I received the news in 2008 that Joan had passed away. Joan and Emmanuel had enriched our lives with their friendship. We received another blow in 2013. Margaret, the oldest of the three daughters, had passed away, succumbing to a relentless illness in London. Yolande and I were able to visit her at home in south London about two months before her demise; Margaret had died at a relatively young age.

Dr Gulpu Lahiri, a Bengali Indian General Surgeon from Calcutta with his English wife, Betty, were in Kumasi in the late 1960s and early 1970s. Gulpu was short and slight in build; Betty, quite petite, had a polished upper class English accent. They had a daughter, Kim, and two younger sons, Robin and Arun. Gulpu was a highly respected surgeon with tremendous experience and surgical skill. We both shared great interest in tennis; he was a member of the Kumasi Tennis Club. His doubles partnership with Dr Harry Poku rivalled that of Pobee and Sackey, the reigning Ashanti Region champions. The Lahiris remained family friends until their final departure for London where Gulpu was appointed a consultant surgeon at Kingston-upon-Thames. Our meetings with them are now infrequent.

Our Kumasi circle of friends in the late 1960s and early 1970s included Dan and Reggie Annan. Dan, tall, broad-faced and always with a smile, was a High Court Judge in Kumasi. He had a great interest in boxing and served a term as Chairman of the Ghana Boxing Board. I first met the Annans when Reggie was my patient at KAH. Reggie, an attractive lady, was a keen poultry farmer. A close family friendship developed between us. After the Rawlings military coup d'état, Dan stepped on to the political stage as a highly respected jurist. He ended up as the Speaker of Parliament when democratic government was restored. Both Reggie and Dan have moved on. Dan was deservedly accorded a State burial.

I cannot fail to include Mr J Addison in my list of friends. I introduced Yolande to Mr Addison quite early on my return to Kumasi in 1965. I had first met him at Harold Philips' wedding in Accra in 1961. He was then a middle-aged successful businessman and a bachelor. He lived in his unusually designed, but attractive house in the stadium area known as the "Sikafoyi amantem" (The Richmen's Village). He took a liking to Yolande instantly. A long lasting friendship developed until he left Kumasi for Takoradi to establish the first cement factory in the country. A self-made industrialist, he received an honorary doctorate degree from an Italian University. He was keen and active in national politics. I cannot forget the frequent invitations to his home for Sunday lunch of palm nut soup, expertly prepared with fufu and rice, by his cook of many years. We have sadly lost touch with one another.

Chapter 8
MY FIRST FORAY INTO PRIVATE PRACTICE – A FAILED AFFAIR

N ow and again in the course of one's life, an event may occur which affects one's fate and fortune for significant good or ill. Such was the above-mentioned affair. In early 1970, Yolande and I attended a cocktail reception on the well-manicured lawn at the bungalow of Mr David Howell, the Director of the British Council. During the course of the reception, a senior expatriate colleague and fellow guest, pulled me aside and made a proposal. This fellow had over the years established a very highly regarded private medical clinic, quite close to where the party was being held (one of the nicer areas in Kumasi), which he ran single-handedly. He told me that with his advancing age, he needed an assistant to join him as a junior partner and who would take over the clinic eventually. A senior Ghanaian surgeon based in Korle-Bu, who had been an assistant surgeon to him before, had been approached, but declined because he did not want to leave Accra. He said my name had been suggested to him as a possible partner. He asked me to think it over and let him know of my decision at a later date. I was initially flattered by the proposal and left it at that, there was no urgency, I would take time to mull it over.

My expatriate colleague was a British surgeon, one of twins, who came to the Gold Coast as a young surgeon in the colonial service. As one of the earliest surgeons, he acquired great experience and knowledge in tropical medicine and surgery. He trained many other surgeons and doctors in the country and attained an iconic status. He published a large volume on Tropical Surgery which merited compulsory reading by any surgeon practising in tropical countries. He left government service to establish his private clinic in a two-storey building located in an exclusive verdant residential area in Kumasi, with a nicely landscaped front garden. His patients included the elite (expatriates and Ghanaians alike) and the ordinary working class. He told me that it was reputedly ranked as the best in West Africa. His wife was an attractive Ghanaian lady from Mampong who had worked with him as a nurse. They lived in a beautiful two storeyed house with a large front lawn. They had no children of their own, but had adopted two young girls.

I thought over the proposal carefully and discussed it with Yolande. Private practice would yield more income than the government service; on the other hand, as a Gynaecologist, I would be deprived of seeing the rare and uncommon cases (my little side pleasure). The event of my finally taking over the practice made the proposal very appealing indeed. I had reached the pinnacle of my practice as a Gynaecologist and Dr XY seemed very keen on my joining him. I decided to accept the proposal of a partnership, after which he invited me to the clinic to take a critical look at the whole place. He took me round the ward (10 beds), the operating theatre, his consulting room, the room to be assigned to the Gynaecologist/Obstetrician, I could come to the clinic any time to see what was going on. Yolande's mother arrived in Kumasi to visit us for the first time, and on learning of her presence with us, he invited her for afternoon tea with him and his wife at their home; my mother-in-law was thus recruited in his courtship of me. There appeared to be no doubt of his desire to having me join him as a partner. There was, however, no urgency on my part as I still had to wait for at least nine months to complete my five-year bond in government service after obtaining the MRCOG. (Years later, many of my fellow Ghanaian doctors on government scholarships abroad never returned home to serve the country after obtaining their post-graduate qualification, there were greener pastures overseas especially financially.) My prospective partner on his part, said that he would be travelling home to Britain on leave during the summer and that while there, he would seek professional advice from solicitors who specialize in drawing up medical partnership contracts. On his return, he would apprise me of the details; it sounded sensible and professional.

With this prospect in view, I had to look for accommodation since I would have to vacate my government bungalow. In order to keep a low profile and not to alert anyone about my plan at this stage, I assigned the responsibility of looking for suitable accommodation to Yolande. Busia had promulgated the Aliens Compliance Order and as a result, many aliens, especially Lebanese, had to leave the country, thus rendering several bungalows vacant and available for renting. On viewing and inspection, we found none suitable despite being in really nice residential areas. Many were unkempt and rundown, needing extensive renovations to be brought up to our standard. The Estate Agent we engaged, realising our dilemma after very many of these inspections, made a suggestion to us, which seemed quite logical. Since I was going into private practice in Kumasi, I would be spending a long time, perhaps the rest of my professional life here. Would we not consider getting a plot of land and putting up our own house? It had not occurred to us before, but on thinking and talking it over, it seemed a good idea. Thus a decision was reached to build our own house.

Dr XY duly returned to Kumasi from his leave in the UK. He did not, however, bring along with him the draft of an agreement from specialist or any other solicitor in the UK as he had promised earlier. He would now prepare his own and submit it to me in due course. After a series of procrastinations, he submitted a draft for my consideration which had some disturbing, unpleasant and totally unacceptable clauses as follows:

I was to serve as an assistant to him for an initial period of two years after which a partnership offer would be made; the assistantship could be terminated at any time by either side with a three-month period of notice. (After leaving the government service, I would have no leg to stand on; the termination would likely originate from him.)

My monthly remuneration in the initial two-year period would be significantly less than what I was already earning in the government service. I was to acquire and pay for my accommodation (unlike the free government bungalow). I was also to pay the salaries of three out of about ten nurses. (If there were a guaranteed certainty that I would become a partner, it was arguable that one could make an initial financial sacrifice; the eventual acquisition of the practice may justify the initial financial input.)

I was not to perform any surgical termination of pregnancy. Although termination of pregnancy was a lucrative source of income for many doctors, it was well known that I never indulged in the practice. As a Gynaecologist, I terminated pregnancy only on medical indication and the patients were appropriately counselled. This was the rule I enforced as the departmental head in KAH. I considered the inclusion of this clause as an intrusion into my professional area of expertise.

I had to seek permission from the theatre sister before performing any operation. Doctors and theatre staff normally work as a team; no surgeon would just walk into a theatre and operate. The decision to operate rests with the surgeon, and not the theatre sister.

At this stage, I sought advice from Dr Kofi Tagboto, the most senior and experienced Ghanaian doctor in Private General Practice at the time, and also a personal friend. Dr XY tinkered with some irrelevant minor details, but left the main disturbing and indeed offensive clauses intact. It was at this point that I approached Mr Frank Mensah Bonsu for legal advice.

Mr Bonsu was a prominent solicitor/lawyer who had taken over a large and most lucrative legal practice in Kumasi from an expatriate Englishman. Their clientele included the Ashanti Gold Mines, Barclays and Standard Chartered Banks. He was also an old Achimotan, four years my senior. He was one of the first Ghanaians to train as a solicitor, and on his return home, he was appointed the Kumasi City Clerk, a prestigious post in those days. He held this position for a few years before taking on the current practice. I gave Frank a copy of my prospective partner's proposed agreement, after which he gave me an appointment to see him later. Soon after reading it through, he summoned me to his office. He first of all gave me a polite rebuke and scolding for not approaching him earlier. On this matter he condemned the whole document. He pointed out that although Dr XY was an eminent doctor, I was a Specialist, held in high regard not only in Kumasi, but in the country. With the evidence of his proposal I was being treated like a 'small boy' which was quite wrong and totally unacceptable The proposal, he pronounced, was insulting and should properly be rejected in its entirety; there was nothing to salvage from it. His consultation was completely pro bono, he was only too happy to be able to help. I then drafted a polite letter of rejection of the offer and sent it to Dr XY. I also withdrew my letter of resignation from the government service which I had earlier submitted to Dr Bondzi-Simpson, the Medical Superintendent. He returned it to me with a big sigh of relief. Thus ended my first foray into private practice. Dr XY did not get an assistant until several years later. At some stage, he appointed the Foundation Professor of OB/GY at the KNUST Medical School as a part-time consultant in his clinic. The appointment had to be quickly terminated after it was realized that the gentleman could not perform a straightforward Caesarean section. At some stage Dr XY was joined by another German trained doctor, a generalist, which was also short-lived. He and Dr Joe Hiadji taught Anatomy by giving didactic lectures to the initial batch of the KNUST medical students. Age and Alzheimer's took a toll on him. I was in Kumasi at the time on leave, during my years in the diaspora, when he passed away. I attended the burial service at the Ridge Church and the funeral rites in his house.

Despite our parting of the ways, thankfully before any great harm had been done, I acknowledge the immense contribution to the practice of surgery in Ghana and the Tropics at large made by my expatriate colleague and prospective partner. He deserves a place in Ghana's Hall of Fame.

KPLOMDEDIE

When we failed in getting a suitable bungalow during my negotiations to become a partner in private practice, logic demanded that we should build a house to our own taste and design. This entailed satisfying some prerequisites: we had to get a plot of land in a suitable location, without any legal ownership encumbrances and available funds to execute the project. The estate manager assured us that he could indeed get a suitable plot of land in a good area from the newly installed Saamahene. The chief, a charming, burly young man, had, by tradition, gained undisputed sole custodian/ownership of a large acreage of land in the Ahodwo village area, now known as Nhyiaeso. The plots of land could be easily accessed then by driving on a laterite road from the Nhyiaeso roundabout through the Ahodwo village or through the old Nhyiaeso residential bungalows area. The Samanhene, without any hesitation and after an initial search, allocated me two large plots of land when I needed only one. The plots of land bordered a tarred road, with, most crucially, a well-laid out infrastructure of water and electricity supply. There were only three existing buildings on the road; the rest of the land was virgin forest with trees and thick bushes The Samanhene, wishing to dispose of the land as quicky as possible so that it could be developed, insisted on selling me two adjacent plots. I obliged and paid for them from my personal savings; it was a mere six hundred cedis. The chief was so pleased that he asked me to persuade any of my friends who may be interested to get in touch with him. Thus I succeeded in getting a large plot each for Messrs Owusu Addo and Victor Adu.

Next was the financial wherewithal to build the house. In those days, you built a house from your own resources; mortgage facilities were not available. If you knew the CEO of the SIC (State Insurance Corporation) personally, you could get a loan to build a house on a plot in the airport residential area in Accra and rent it to any of the big companies for a handsome income., and many professionals in Accra took advantage of this perk. I was lucky to have succeeded in getting a plot of land at the airport residential area at that time through the good offices of Jake Blukoo Allotey. I, however, failed woefully to get a loan from the SIC (I did not have the right contacts). Barclays Bank, my bank for years, and Standard Chartered Bank operated a policy of not giving loans; certainly not to Ghanaian individuals. The manager of these banks, British expatriates, were my social colleagues, but still could not assist me in obtaining a loan. This paints a dark financial climate at the time. However, in the course of human events, certain situations unfold in accordance with the Lutheran doctrine of Predestination, to which I subscribe. The manager of Ghana Commercial Bank (GCB) in Kumasi was Mr Kofi Agyemang. His wife, an Old Achimotan, had been introduced to me by Miss Jackson, KAH Senior physiotherapist, when she was pregnant. I looked after her and delivered their baby. Mr Agyemang was very pleased with the care I had rendered to his wife, for which he thanked me with the usual gifts of provisions and a sheep as well as a traditional Ashanti stool. On leaving, he went on to say that if at any time in the future I should need assistance from him, I must not hesitate to ask.

I needed financial assistance from a bank to carry out my building project. Although I had no savings account with GCB, I went to see Mr Kofi Agyemang in his office to seek his advice. We discussed the options of building the Kumasi house. If you had adequate financial resources, you could ask a reputable building company, notably A Lang Company at the time, to build it. This was reputedly expensive, but freed you from other headaches. The second option was building by direct labour: you purchased the building materials, employed artisans to carry on with the building under your supervision; it was tedious and demanding, but was a less expensive option, particularly so for someone with limited financial resources, Mr Agyemang and I, after a detailed discussion, opted for the latter – building by direct labour. He offered to provide me with the necessary funds from the bank to execute the project as soon as we were ready to start. Although there was no pressure or request that I should switch accounts from Barclays to GCB, I did so willingly and speedily, out of a feeling of loyalty to this bank which was so ready to help me. He had to seek approval from his immediate boss in Accra, Mr Kweku Anin, Deputy MD of the GCB, which he obtained. I had met Mr Anin only once before then. We had no idea how much it would cost to build the house!

The architect of our choice was obvious; we asked Mr John Owusu Addo to design the building for us. John graciously and willingly agreed to do it; he sat me and Yolande down and asked us what form and style of house we wanted. John followed our request and prepared the drawings, taking into account the sloping topography of the landscape; it was an excellent design. John, without any solicitation, offered to assist in supervising the erection of the building. To execute and follow the erection in accordance with the drawings, we needed an experienced foreman; John knew just the right person, Mr Ocloo, and brought him along from Koforidua.

The GCB advanced me the first instalment of money with which to commence work. As a start, we purchased tools such as wheelbarrows, pans, pickaxes, spades etc. from Mr Wuaku's hardware store. The building site was cleared; several trees were felled, a few were left to preserve an arboreal and forested ambience, very important to Yolande with her love of trees.

The construction of a house runs in stages: the first, an important one, is the laying of the foundation and the ground floor; this is followed by erecting the block, but this is not all. Ceiling work, electrical wiring, plumbing flooring and other finishing works can be time-consuming and expensive. Plastering and painting comprise a major part of the final finish, which includes doors and window installation as well as locks. We learnt a lot from this experience which stood us in good stead decades later.

On the appointed day, we went to the building site. After a short prayer, work began in earnest. The foundation was dug. We had purchased earlier loads of sand, stone and cement; water was plentifully available at the site. Work proceeded according to plan. Yolande and I visited the site each morning and late afternoon each day as work proceeded. John also visited the site often to inspect on-going work and give instructions at various stages. Block by block, and stage by stage, the structure was erected. Long roofing sheets to span the building dimensions had been ordered from Tema. The very major exercise of conveying the roofing sheets to the site, chronicled later, was completed. The roofing stage was completed. Mr Agyemang visited the site a couple of times and was amazed at the amount of work which had been carried out with the relatively small sum of money advanced so far; the bank's funds had been spent very wisely and judiciously, and a request for further funds was promptly granted. At this stage a new manager came to replace Mr Agyemang; who had moved to Accra on promotion to the position of Deputy MD, while Mr Kweku Enin, also newly promoted, became the Managing Director.

The A Lang Building Company, a Swiss company, was the most famous, accomplished and prestigious in the country. Its headquarters were located in Kumasi; its workforce of experienced artisans was based in Kumasi. We could engage their artisans to work on our building at the weekends and provide the A Lang finish. Mr Kofi was a joiner/ carpenter foreman with the company, who very conveniently lived in the nearby Ahodwo village. The T and G wooden ceiling, wooden wall panelling and wooden parquet flooring works were assigned to Mr Kofi and his team on contract basis. We purchased all the wood materials from the Naja David timber factory. All the terrazzo flooring was similarly contracted to an A Lang group of three artisans. The plumbing work was assigned to Mr Sarkodee of Adum, on the high recommendation of Mr Wuaku. The electrical wiring and associated works were contracted to Mr Bolfrey. Thus, step by step, the building was nearing completion. The kitchen unit needed someone with expertise in this field. The AG Monta Company, a reputable Italian company, fitted the role and they installed a state-of-the-art kitchen unit. A family friendship with the Montas commenced from this initial contact. Some years later we did a joint school run with them, taking their son Carlo and our three sons, Brian, Neil and Dugald, to Prempeh College where they were all day students.

Amazing now to look back and review how this was accomplished with very little rancour with workmen, who were largely keen to work. In those days it was possible to get honest Ghanaian artisans who took pride in their work and before 'rip off' became an endemic and entrenched Ghanaian disease.

With the building completed and exquisitely finished, it was necessary to acquire furniture elegant and becoming enough for our very attractive house. Mr Osei Bonsu was a Ghanaian entrepreneur who owned a furniture company with a workshop headed by a creative and artistic Czechoslovakian, who was innovative in designing furniture. He had designed some living room sofas and chairs in prime wood, which had attracted much attention at the recently held International Trade Fair in Accra. For the dining room, he designed a round table in thick, solid afromosia wood for seating eight people on equally solid attractive chairs with leatherette cushions. A tall cocktail cabinet and a large wide sideboard, all in Afromosia wood, completed the dining room set. A wooden room divider with a nice set of shelves for objects d'art was built and installed in my study. A large section of the wall in the study was fitted with shelves designed in wood and iron to accommodate our large number of books. The very large family room was suitably furnished with soft leatherette seats. All the wooden beds were commissioned and made in the Osei Bonsu workshop. An appealing balustrade in brown Sapele wood leading from the staircase to the wall separated the dining area above from the living room three steps below.

The main house was built in the middle of one of the two plots, leaving large areas at the front, back and the sides. The second adjoining plot was initially left undeveloped; a large boys' quarters building was later erected at the back of the plot. It was my intention to construct a tennis court on the front part of the land, but this plan never materialized. It was imperative to build a fence wall, enclosing the entire plots, not only for security reasons, but also to prevent the incursion of all types of animals, not least, dangerous snakes, from the surrounding forested bush. A five-foot cement wall was built around the back and both sides of the entire land. The front wall, three feet in height, was constructed with red bricks. Hedges of thorny plants were planted all round the inside of the four enclosing walls as extra deterrent to any intruders. A driveway was constructed leading from a wide front gate at the entrance leading to the garage to the basement area at the side. Most of the natural vegetation on the estate was cleared and replaced with lawn grass, with particular attention to the area in front of the forecourt; there was a large playground for the boys with swings, seesaws, tepees and other garden toys, and the location of the gazebo and bar under one of the massive original trees which had been preserved, lent a great ambience for outdoor parties. It was in every way a splendid family home which we thoroughly enjoyed for the years in which we lived there. I named our house 'Kplomdedie', the Ewe translation for the Scottish 'Faer thee weil'. The building was both wide and long, and following the gradient slope was designed in the popular American 'split level 'style. The nearly flat, very wide roof had gutters at the front and back concealed by attractively designed frontals, characteristic of John's architectural designs. The left side of the entrance ushered you on the ground floor onto a large terrazzo floored front porch, to the left of which was a medium sized indoor garden. A large elegant sliding glass door on the right provided entry into a large open plan living room.

The three bedrooms are on the left on entry – a large master bedroom ensuite, and two bedrooms with a complete bathroom set between them which the boys shared A corridor alongside the boys' bedrooms led up five steps to the family room, study, dining room, kitchen and back porch leading down several steps to the maid's room, laundry room and large store room, very useful in later years when we were travelling. Another set of stairs from the family room and study led to the guest suite and garage. One of the very best things about working with John on this house was how involved he allowed us to be, especially Yolande, who had very definite ideas of rooms, sizes and location, so we ended up with a perfect house, thanks to John's indulgence. Both the interior and exterior were painted.

In conclusion, some people opined that it was probably the most beautiful house in Kumasi at the time. The highest credit for this achievement undoubtedly goes to Messrs John Owusu Ado, Kofi Agyemang and Kweku Anin. We give much credit, too, to the artisans whose skill and hard work helped to bring our dream to reality.

As a specialist in the government service, I was still entitled to live in the government bungalow. Good financial sense dictated that we rent out this beautiful house to acquire the funds to pay off the bank for the loan, but Yolande and I were as one in deciding that we wanted to live in this house and enjoy it with our children, only three in number at the time, and this we did. We have never regretted this decision. We believe that it greatly influenced their upbringing and self confidence, which served them well when they went abroad later for further studies and work. After a short thanksgiving ceremony, we moved in to Kplomdedie and settled there in 1971.

Kofi Agyemang, a gentleman in every sense of the word and Selena, his wife, a demure charming lady, became close family friends in Kumasi, and this continued when they transferred to Accra. Kofi was later posted to London as Manager of GCB there and rose in rank to be the CEO of GCB in Accra during my years in the diaspora. We lost touch with each other, but renewed our association on our return home to Accra.

Kweku Enin, son of a famous chief in Bechem, Brong Ahafo, was a brilliant scholar. After his secondary school education at Accra Academy and Achimota, he went to Cambridge (Selwyn College) where he graduated in Law and later qualified as a Solicitor. He joined GCB and became their Solicitor before being promoted as the CEO. I was introduced to him by Chris Adomako and we got along instantly. Kweku left Ghana for England in 1979 after Rawling's military coup d'état when there was great uneasiness in the country. During his period in London, I always met him on the few occasions I was there. On our relocation to Accra, our close association was renewed. Yolande and I spent many intellectually stimulating and enjoyable evenings with him at his Cantonment residence. He had written a couple of books, autographed copies of which he presented to us on several important aspects of Ghana's economy. In one of the books, he outlined in common sense and an easily understood way the solution to Ghana's economic problems, emphasizing that we should forgo our over-reliance on foreign aid. This, in my view, must be a compulsory read for any leader in Ghana. It is, however, sad to relate that even though he was closely related to a previous president by marriage, his ideas and services which were on offer were never utilized. He was financially comfortable and did not seek to enrich himself.

It was quite a few years before I found out how closely a path our lives had run since birth. I was born in Hohoe, Volta region on a Tuesday, 21st July, 1931, hence my middle name of Komla. Kweku Enin was born in Bechem, Brong Ahafo Region the following day, 22nd July, 1931, Wednesday, hence his name Kweku. While I was baptized in a Presbyterian Church at Hohoe as Theodore (Gift of God), Kweku was baptized at a Presbyterian Church in Bechem as Theophilus (Lover of God), a very interesting coincidence. Following the Theodore trend of my mentors in Theodore Mair of Glasgow and Theodore Redman of Leeds, Theophilus Enin joined this exclusive group of Theos who played a significant role in my life.

In 2006, on my way from our Agbaamo Lane residence with Yolande and Dugald, our son (on an Easter break from his London base), to Peki on Good Friday we passed Kweku's Cantonment residence. Unsolicited, Kweku had promised to donate a handsome sum of money to the Peki Tsame Presbyterian Church Easter Sunday offertory. He handed me the money after which we drove to Peki, returning to Accra after Easter. Not long after, Yolande and I travelled to London on a brief holiday. Very soon after our return, we learnt to our great shock that Kweku had died in a tragic car accident on his way from Brong Ahafo between Nsawam and Accra. It was a great loss from which it took me a very long time to recover. It created a vacuum for me to fill. He was a scholar and an intellectual, "sui generis", a most loyal friend, whose memory will always remain with me. A massive crowd attended his funeral service which was held in the Accra Roman Catholic Cathedral; Kweku had turned to Rome during his long sojourn in London. Living abroad has taught us to value every moment we spend with close friends and relatives; we never know if it would be our last.

Mr Isaac Ogbarmey-Tetteh was the senior solicitor of GCB from the early sixties till his retirement. Tall, charming and friendly, he bore himself with great dignity. I had known him (aka Ike) since our years in UCGC in the early 1950s when he came in the group from Accra Academy. After UCGC he went to Britain, trained and qualified as a solicitor, joining GCB on his return. We became close friends. During the time in which I made several frequent day trips between Kumasi and Accra, negotiating loans for Bomso clinic, his office served as my first port of call. I was invited to have lunch in the VIP section of their restaurant, reserved for the senior staff; it was always most delicious. I enjoyed those trips, on which I look back with nostalgia. He introduced me to Mr Ben Selormey, then the Deputy CEO to Kweku Anin (he was the husband of Aurora Lokko, my Achimota classmate, and the first Ghanaian female to qualify as a chartered accountant). Ike hosted me on several occasions in his residence on my extended visits to Accra. We kept in touch during my years in the diaspora. It was a delight to welcome him and his wife to our Christmas party at Kate Amaville in Accra in 2006; he appeared to be in good health. Alas, that was the last time I saw Ike; he passed away suddenly not long after. I responded to his wife's request to write a tribute, our association had been a long and very fond one.

A great historical event occurred when we were resident in our Danyame bungalow. It was the death of the Asantehene Osei Tutu Agyemang Prempeh II. We had met him once before at a private cocktail party in the residence of Mr Francis Eshun, then the Regional Manager of BP Oil Company. Osei Agyeman Prempeh Tutu II was a genial person, dignified, small in stature; we admired his wit and personal deportment. His funeral was a very grand traditional event. Yolande and I accompanied Mrs Christine Armar to view the body as he was laid in state at the Manhyia Palace at midnight, when all the streets in Kumasi were completely deserted. The scene was one of great traditional splendour. In accordance with Ashanti tradition, he was buried at a secret location at midnight. A fitting traditional funeral was held at a later date under his successor, Nana Opoku Ware II. Nana Opoku Ware had been a lawyer before ascending the Golden Stool. His senior wife was a sister of Mr Joe Appiah, the lawyer and politician.

Very early in my position as a Specialist Gynaecologist, I realized that international conference attendances were important. Such conferences increased your knowledge, and provided the opportunity to meet famous colleagues and also do some sight-seeing. The limiting factor was the availability of funds to travel and attend. The MOH funded conferences held in the West African region, but not elsewhere. I attended two such conferences in the 1970s in Ibadan, Nigeria. One in Obstetrics centred on the management of eclampsia with Diazepam; eclampsia in pregnancy carried a high mortality. Predating the ICU, patients with eclampsia were nursed in a dark room and sedated with rectally administered Bromethal. In attendance from Aberdeen was Professor Ian MacGillivray, a leading authority on the subject. I renewed my friendship with Percy Nylander, then a Senior Lecturer in Ibadan. The other Nigerian colleagues I met included Drs Ojo, Ladipo, Harrison and Bayo Akinkugbe. I attended a WACS conference which was held in Accra; there, I presented a paper on "Carcinoma of the Cervix, the Kumasi experience". In 1978, I attended a WACS conference in Freetown, Sierra Leone. Yolande and I, as already chronicled, were royally hosted by David and Nancy Howell. I met Dr Tom Kargbo at the conference; he had been my houseman in Leeds; now a specialist Gynaecologist in Sierra Leone. Professor JB Lawson, now based in Newcastle, England attended the conference. I held a long, stimulating discussion with him. I discussed with him his co-authored book on Tropical Obstetrics and Gynaecology; it was time for a new edition, I stated, and went on to offer a contribution in preparing some chapters. He was non-committal to my proposal and there the matter rested.

The RCOG held its triennial congresses in UK cities on a rotational basis. Prior to 1974, I had never attended any; K. K. Korsah was the only one who had. In 1974, it was scheduled to be held in London, and I decided to attend. The summer sports events were a great attraction. The FIFA Football World Cup was due to be held in West Germany. I was fortunate to find sponsorship for funding my trip to the UK. The Organon Pharmaceutical Company specialising in Hormonal drugs, had Mr Cross as their representative for the West African region. I had met him at the Kumasi tennis club; he was very knowledgeable and knew the ins and outs of the politics of the region and the rampant nature of corruption; he did not spare mentioning specific names. We got along really well, and when I mentioned that I was interested in attending this congress, he made a recommendation to his company to fund me. Thus Organon Company paid for my return trip to London and also the congress registration fee. This was superb generosity on the company's part. Mr Bruce Smith of the BC offered me accommodation in London. I was overwhelmed with generosity on every side. I found the congress educative and memorable; it whetted my appetite to attend future ones. Dr K. K. Korsah was the only other Ghanaian delegate. I met some old friends and made new acquaintances.

Dr Maat, a Syrian, the only Syrian with MRCOG, who had been my colleague in SGH in Glasgow, was also a delegate. He apparently had a flourishing practice in Damascus, Syria; he came with his wife. A few years earlier, he wrote to me in Kumasi expressing a serious desire to come and work under me in Kumasi. It was an expression of a high compliment as he had been my houseman in Glasgow. Very sadly, not long after his return to Syria, his death was reported in our BJOG.

The afternoon sessions of the congress witnessed a stiff competition in TV broadcast of two sporting events: the Wimbledon Tennis competition and the finals of the World Cup (Football) being held in West Germany. Many delegates disappeared to go and watch the TV broadcasts from West Germany and London SW19. The final match in the football was between West Germany, captained by Franz Beckenbauer (the Emperor) and Holland, the favourites, led by the charismatic and legendary Cruyff. The title in a famous and memorable match went to Germany. The match was a nail-biting one. Holland scored the first goal from a penalty kick in the first minute when no German had touched nor kicked the ball; the referee was an Englishman of high repute. The other RCOG Congresses which I attended while I was at KAH were held in Sheffield (1977) and Edinburgh (1980), which are chronicled later.

In 1976, the OB/GY department in KAH received two very distinguished visitors, whose visits merit narrating. Professor Charles Douglas (of Royal Free Hospital, London) came to conduct examinations at Korle Bu. After the examination, he expressed a desire to Prof. Bentsi-Enchill to visit Kumasi. Kwesi phoned to ask me if I could host Prof. Douglas's one-day visit. I agreed to do so if he would come on the forthcoming Thursday as I had planned to attend the funeral of Mr Bucknor (a famous artist, scientist and educationist who had been my classmate at UCGC) in Cape Coast the following Saturday. I met Prof. Charles Douglas at the Kumasi airport and drove him to KAH. I conducted him around all the wards and gave him a copy of our departmental report with the statistics of our performances of the previous year. Then I took him home, to Kplomdedie, for lunch and an informal discussion. He wore a dark suit., very distinguished looking and wore monocles instead of spectacles, which our two older sons found fascinating, not having seen this type of eyewear before. They tried very hard not to stare, but kept making occasional glances when they thought no one was looking! The chair in Cambridge had fallen vacant; although it was offered to David Baird of Edinburgh, it appeared that he was unlikely to move from Edinburgh to Cambridge. Prof Douglas at this time was awaiting the definitive offer from Cambridge. Our conversation covered a wide range of topics, personalities and some gossipy items. I knew a few of the people he knew and vice versa, it was as if we had known each other for a long time. When he told me that he was going to stand for election to the RCOG Council, I offered to vote for him, but he countered by stating that I could not because he was standing as a Fellow representative (only Fellows could vote for Fellows; and the same applied to Members voting). After the lunch break, and a well fulfilled day, I drove him to the airport. Prof Douglas was obviously satisfied with his day trip to the Garden City; and so was I as the host.

I went to Cape Coast the following day for the funeral as planned. On Saturday, after the burial service as the cortege advanced, Prof Bentsi-Enchill spotted me walking in the crowd from his car. He waved at me frantically, beckoning me towards his slowly moving car. When I got close he announced to me with much delight and excitement that Prof Douglas on his return to Accra told him how greatly he had enjoyed his Kumasi visit. Prof Douglas, he went on to say, was so impressed with me in every respect that he told Kwesi to recommend my elevation to the Fellowship of the RCOG immediately. Canvassing for elevation was strictly forbidden and I had not at any point in our long and most convivial conversation raised the matter. Up until then, I had had almost no contact with Prof Bentsi-Enchil. About a month after the above episode, I received an invitation from him to be an external examiner in Obstetrics and Gynaecology for the re-sit candidates.

Hitherto, the external examiners had always come from England, and always Caucasians. Kwesi thus appointed me the first Ghanaian, nay African, to be an External Examiner at Korle-Bu. Did this come about because of the accolades showered on me by Prof Charles Douglas? We can only speculate!

The second visitor to KAH was Professor John Dewhurst of the Postgraduate Institute in Hammersmith and Queen Charlotte's Hospital. He was the President of the RCOG (PRCOG). He was the author of the standard Postgraduate textbook of Obstetrics and Gynaecology, a must read for anyone attempting to obtain the MRCOG; he held a special interest in Paediatric gynaecology. His image as an academician loomed high worldwide. He had come to Accra as the PRCOG for the sole purpose of elevating Dr Ampofo, MRCOG, to the Fellowship: the first time this was being done outside the UK. I went to Accra to witness the ceremony, which was held at the Korle-Bu auditorium. I complied with the Chairman's request to make a brief speech and the vote of thanks.

Sir John Dewhurst spent about five days in Accra. Dr Armar, who had known Sir John in his student days in Sheffield, arranged for him to pay a visit to KAH in Kumasi. As the most senior gynaecologist in KAH, it fell on me to prepare a programme for Sir Jack and Lady Dewhurst. Dr Armar and I met the couple at the Kumasi airport in the morning. On our way to City Hotel, then in its prime, we passed the Manhyia Palace to pay a courtesy visit to the Asantehene, Nana Opoku Ware II; the visit had been arranged in advance by Dr Armar. The 20 minute visit to the traditional ruler in Ashanti went down very well.

We then drove the couple to City Hotel, where they would rest and have lunch. I briefed him on the programme I had prepared for him for the day. I would first conduct him on a tour of the OB/GY department, visiting the wards; next would be a meeting at the auditorium of the Nurses Training College. At the meeting, I would make a case presentation; the presentation would be followed by a lecture to be delivered by him on any subject of his choice. I gave him an idea of the composition of the audience (a few gynaecologists, general surgeons, physicians, MOs, nurses and midwives) to assist him in the choice of his topic and the level of pitching it.

In the tour round the wards, including the labour ward, he saw the range of cases we handled. I also presented him with a copy of our annual departmental report, which included the statistics of our activities. The afternoon programme would end with a tea and snacks reception, which would provide an opportunity for him to chat with a good cross-section of the hospital staff. I planned to host a buffet dinner in his honour at my residence, Kplomdedie, in the evening, inviting about 20 guests.

The afternoon programme was an undoubted success. For my case presentation, I chose a case of vesico vaginal fistula. It was a patient with a fistula so large that there was no palpable bladder wall anteriorly to mobilize and repair. The solution at that time was to mobilize the ureters and implant them into the sigmoid colon through a laparotomy incision; this way urinary continence was achieved with the anal sphincter musculature. I had done a couple before, but the case I presented was a recent one. I sent for the patient to report to the ward. She obliged and Sir John was able to examine her vagina in the ward before my presentation. He was the most distinguished medical personality to visit the KAH during that decade.

Yolande and I hosted a splendid, varied buffet dinner in the evening in honour of our distinguished guests. Apart from some senior hospital colleagues, the invited guests included the Director of the British Council and the Vice Chancellor of KNUST. We sat on the front porch in groups of four, but I moved the Dewhursts around from table to table at appropriate intervals for all the guests to engage them in sociable conversations. Yolande excelled as usual as an excellent cook and hostess.

It was a delightful evening. In a vote of thanks at the end of the dinner he said that although they travel around the world and are hosted quite often, there is something very special when you are invited to someone's home, which they always enjoyed and appreciated. The Dewhursts returned to Accra the following morning. On their return home to London, Sir Jack wrote to thank me and Yolande for the hospitality we provided them in Kumasi. It was a very genuine letter of appreciation. Unknown to me at the time, even though he had spent five days in Accra, there was nothing such as a clinical meeting and/ or presentation to engage his interest as the academician he was. Our solitary medical school at the time in my view should have arranged for a case presentation or something similar to stimulate his clinical interest. It was indeed a lapse, for which I hoped that we in Kumasi made up, with our modest effort.

The narration of the Kumasi visits should not end without a follow-up anecdote. In 1977, when I attended the RCOG Congress in Sheffield during the triennial Presidency of Sir Jack, I was fortunate in obtaining sponsorship funds from Mr Naja David, a very successful and generous Lebanese timber industrialist and also owner of a pharmaceutical company. A small number of Ghanaians and Nigerians attended. The delegates, mostly from the British Commonwealth countries, numbered almost a thousand. An evening cocktail reception on the first day opened the Congress. Sir Jack stood at the foot of the staircase which led upstairs to the very large reception hall, shaking hands and welcoming delegates to the function as they proceeded upstairs. When it got to my turn, he shook my hand warmly and said, "Ted, I am glad you have come. Is Yolande here with you?" I replied that I had come alone,. With a disappointed countenance on his face on Yolande's absence, he asked whether I had received an invitation in my registration bag to attend his party after the official cocktail that evening. I confirmed that I had received it, and he reminded me not to miss it. The queue of delegates to be welcomed was in the meantime held up by the President's extra conversation with me. My fellow West Africans were probably curious as to why the special attention from him! When the reception was drawing to a close, an announcement was made asking those attending the President's private party to go and board a coach waiting to convey them to the venue. I left my other colleagues and went to board the coach. We were just a few in number and were driven to a hotel sited about five miles away.

There were not more than 30 delegates at the party; I was the only non-Caucasian. Sir Jack introduced me to them as a senior colleague from Kumasi, Ghana. The other guests were all very eminent gynaecologists (Professors, RCOG Council Chairmen in various countries). The only familiar person was Mr Redman, my former boss in Leeds, who was playing a leading role in staging the congress in Sheffield. Initially, I felt somewhat diffident in this august company, but I quickly restored my self-confidence. The President had travelled widely to many countries and met many other prominent gynaecologists. To accord me this singular honour as a guest in this prestigious company at his private party was unforgettable. About a year earlier, Prof Charles Douglas (of Royal Free Hospital, and Cambridge, later) unveiled and revealed me to Prof Bentsi-Enchill of Korle-Bu. Early in 1978, I received a letter from the RCOG to me that I was being elevated to the Fellowship. I was naturally quite delighted, even if it were the visits of our two prestigious visitors in the past year which prompted it. In those days elevation to the Fellowship was less automatic than it is now, more particularly so in countries such as Ghana.

I travelled to London in the summer of 1978 with my eldest son Brian, then 11 years old and having just been successful in the common entrance exam, to be elevated ceremonially at the RCOG. The photograph of Brian, Sir Jack and me (gowned) is highly cherished.

Sir Jack, aware of my interest in furthering my knowledge in current practice, extended an invitation to me to attend and sit alongside him as he conducted his outpatient clinics at Queen Charlotte's Hospital. The invitation extended to his operation sessions in Chelsea Women's Hospital, the Mecca of operative gynaecology in the British Commonwealth. Most of the famous gynaecological surgeons of the millennium had sessions at the Chelsea. I went there to observe various gynaecologists operate. I also met a couple of visiting gynaecologists on a similar mission. (One of those was Prof Cohen from Israel, author of the book "Abdominal and Vaginal Hysterectomy". I had a stimulating conversation with him.) Shortly after my arrival in London, I would phone Sir Jack, who would quickly recognise my voice and would not hesitate to invite me to attend his clinic session. I cherish his memory and my association with him. His book on Postgraduate Obstetrics and Gynaecology is a worthy legacy.

During this visit to London, Brian and I stayed with Cynthia and Peter Grant, old Caribbean friends of Yolande's. They provided us with most comfortable accommodation at their home in Cheam, a suburb of London. Peter and Brian accompanied me to the RCOG in Sussex Gardens for the elevation ceremony.

The London trip was lucrative. Mr Melville, former Senior Registrar in Leeds, but now a consultant in Brighton, Sussex, arranged a locum consultant job in his hospital for me. It lasted a couple of weeks and proved financially rewarding. Brian accompanied me to the locum job and we both enjoyed watching the FIFA Football World Cup matches taking place in Argentina on TV. Once again, Holland, the favourites, were denied the title although they played brilliantly. Argentina lifted the cup; it was a joy to watch.

On my return to London, there was a treat for me. I had arranged for the purchase of surgical instruments from Down Brothers in Leeds through Pasico, their Ghana representative company. The surgical instruments were for Bomso clinic. I had been to Leeds and made a thoughtful and careful selection of surgical instruments earlier from an exhaustive list. On realizing my great interest in tennis and the on-going Wimbledon Championships, although late, they promised to try their best to obtain a ticket for me. They asked my preference in a match to watch. I said that I would be pleased with any of the men's semi-finals, if possible. A day later I received a telephone call from them; they had succeeded against all odds in obtaining a vantage ticket for the men's final for me. I was over the moon with sheer delight. The legendary Bjorn Borg was due to defend his title against Jimmy Connors. A chauffeur-driven car was sent to convey me from Cheam to SW19, Wimbledon. The driver was to wait and convey me back home after the match. After we arrived there, I dismissed the driver and said I would find my way home, which was easy and straightforward. I had an excellent seat, near the front row; the ticket must have cost a handsome sum of money. It was an exciting, nail-biting match which lived up to all the expectation. Borg retained the title of men's number one. A couple of people claimed to have spotted me on the TV broadcast; I was the only one of colour near the front row of seats. I was indeed grateful to the company for getting me the ticket. They told me that they discovered rather late that I was an opera fan; if they had known earlier, they would have tried to get me tickets to Covent Garden or the ENO (English National Opera). I was, however, quite satisfied with the Wimbledon outing.

On the day of our departure from London, the company sent a car to Cheam to convey me and Brian to the airport. This was unrivalled salesmanship which I appreciated highly. Brian travelled on his own by train to visit the Boal family in Edinburgh where he spent a week. Mr George Boal had taught Engineering at KNUST and he and his wife

Sylvia have been friends through their boys Lawrence and Norman being buddies of Brian and Neil. We have always kept in touch and it is a friendship still ongoing, even though George passed away a couple years ago. No trip to Edinburgh is made without meeting up with Sylvia.

The year 1978 was my "Annus mirabilis". I attended a regional IPPF meeting in Nairobi, Kenya, as a Ghanaian representative, then the WACS congress in Freetown, Sierra Leone (already chronicled); then the trip to Britain for my elevation to FRCOG in summer. Finally came my trip to Baltimore, USA.

I had cultivated an interest in the management of infertility. It was probably in recognition of this that I was selected to attend a two-week course at John Hopkins Hospital in Baltimore, USA. Another gynaecologist, Dr Issa Egala from the Accra Police Hospital, was selected from Ghana. The others came from other countries; we were about ten in all. The course was conducted by Dr John Rock who had just succeeded the legendary Dr Jones as head of the Infertility and Gynaecological Endocrinology Unit. A tall figure with a toothbrush moustache, Dr Rock was a friendly, affable and accommodating person. He had acquired some experience in microsurgery in the management of infertility. Some years later, when he had left Baltimore to take a chair elsewhere, he became the editor of the famous book by Te Linde "Operative Gynaecology". This tome is recognized widely as arguably the leading textbook in operative Gynaecology. It has run into several editions since its first publication.

The course consisted of didactic lectures on the latest developments in the management of infertility, case discussions, and watching Dr Rock and his team conduct an operation on a patient in the theatre. We witnessed his skill in using the operating microscope and also the magnifying glasses. It was a course from which I learned a lot. At the end of the course, I acquired a loop of magnifying glasses for operations in tubal surgery; I still use it when the need arises.

Earlier in the year 1978, baby Brown, the first test tube baby, had been born in England. This epoch-making event received worldwide publication in the media. Drs Edwards and Steptoe, had not at this time published details of their historic feat in any medical journal. In the course of our clinical case discussion, I raised the topic of baby Brown, the test tube baby. It was, in my view, relevant to our discussions on infertility. Dr Rock said that an in vitro fertilization was impossible and therefore any ensuing pregnancy was a hoax. He gave a multitude of reasons in support of his view. I had just been elevated to the Fellowship of the RCOG and therefore felt obliged to defend my august Fellow (Steptoe) and Dr Edwards DSc of Cambridge University. I stated that in my view, it was not a fraudulent claim and that in the fullness of time details of the medical breakthrough would be published in the medical journals. My defence of Drs Steptoe and Edwards was firm, but polite. Steptoe and Edwards published their work later in the medical journals and the rest is history. Not very long after this, Dr Jones, who had retired from John Hopkins Hospital, became the first person to set up an IVF Unit in the USA. I relate this episode not in any way to discredit nor denigrate Dr John Rock, but to paint a picture of the prevailing background at the time. Although one of the doctors who achieved the feat was honoured by the award of Order of Merit, in my view, they should both have been made peers of the realm. The Baltimore course helped me in refining my surgical management of infertility, tubal blockage in particular. In 1980, after the Edinburgh RCOG Congress, I went to the Hammersmith Hospital to observe Professor Liston perform some tubal surgery (he was renowned in this field). Prof Liston received a Knighthood and later a peer of the realm. Drs Steptoe and Edwards later established an IVF Unit at Bourne Hall. After the RCOG Congress in Edinburgh in 1980, permission was granted to me to visit Bourne Hall Unit. I travelled from London to Bourne Hall and spent a full day there. Initially, I sat with a doctor as he conducted the outpatients clinic. This was followed by a ward round. The wards consisted of several port cabins. I went to observe proceedings in the ultrasound room. Finally, I joined the medical staff at a meeting where cases were thoroughly reviewed. It was a stimulating and mind-enriching meeting. The beneficiary of my undying interest and knowledge in infertility were my patients. Surgery in establishing tubal patency did not necessarily guarantee success in producing a pregnancy. The functional aspect of the patent tube is often ignored. Therein lies the major breakthrough in IVF.

In 1980, the BC sponsored me to attend the RCOG Congress in Edinburgh. The RCOG Congress attendance was fruitful and nostalgic in many ways. The BC, one of my two sponsors, had made a provision for me to visit my two alma mater hospitals in Aberdeen and Leeds. Dr Ampofo had succeeded Bentsi-Enchill as the Professor of Ob/Gy at Korle Bu. Since he had never attended an RCOG Congress before, I thought it would be very useful for him to attend the Edinburgh Congress in 1980. I persuaded him to seek sponsorship to enable him to do so. He took my advice and succeeded in getting a sponsor; he and I were the two attendees from Ghana. At this congress, Sir Dugald Baird was awarded the quinquennial Gold Medal by the RCOG (the previous recipient in 1975 was Prof Ian Donald of ultrasound fame). I met Sir Dugald Baird during one of the interval periods. He was delighted to see me and we enjoyed a long period of interesting conversation and reminiscences. He projected a paternal image. During this congress, the Australian and New Zealand branches of the college were ceremonially granted their autonomy, thereby severing their link from London; this meant that their doctors no longer had to come to sit for the RCOG examinations in London. I also met Dr Dennis (now the Foundation Professor in Southampton Medical School). He had been my registrar in Aberdeen in 1961; we were pleased to see each other.

After the congress, I went to Leeds on my first pilgrimage visit. I was met at the train station by Mr Redman, then retired from SJH. SJH was now a medical school and the extended building dwarfed the old familiar building. He took me to the OB/GY Department where he introduced me warmly to Professor Lilford, a young and very bright fellow. Mr Redman then drove me to his home where we had a lovely luncheon, enhanced by favourite background opera music which we both enjoyed. It was a Saturday and the Wimbledon Men's singles final was being shown on TV. They obliged my request to watch the historic thrilling contest between Bjorn Borg and John McEnroe, reputedly the longest match then. Borg retained the title. Miss Goolagong, an Australian aborigine, won the Ladies' singles match, the first mother to do so. After this memorable day with Theo and Jay Redman, I was driven to my hotel. Dr Jim Begg, now a senior consultant in Dewsbury, was not going to be left out. He drove me to their beautiful house on a hill in Dewsbury and entertained me to a splendid dinner. This was topped off as the evening wore on with a selection of single malt whisky, of which Jim was a connoisseur. Jim smoked his cigarettes while I smoked my pipe; these were occasions to savour.

The next destination of my BC sponsored trip was Aberdeen. I enjoyed my train journey from Leeds to Aberdeen with nostalgia, marvelling at the changing scenery along the tracks. I booked in on arrival at the Caledonian Hotel on Union Street. My programme for the following day was a morning visit to the Aberdeen BC followed by a midday visit to the Forrester Hill Maternity Unit. On arrival in Aberdeen, I phoned Mr Sandy Mutch, the son-in-law of Mrs Duthie, my first landlady in Aberdeen. Sandy was a burly figure sporting a thick bushy lip-wide moustache and having a broad Scottish accent. From rather humble beginnings, without higher education, he rose to attain a very high status in Scotland. He started by selling second-hand cars and later TV sets when TV services reached Aberdeen, thus becoming a successful businessman. The quantum jump in his career came with the discovery of offshore oil in the Grampian region of Scotland (it involved travelling often to meet oil magnates in Texas, USA). Sandy was made Chairman of the cartel running the offshore oil business. On the political front, he rose from being a city councillor to the peak of being the Chairman of the Scottish Conservative Party. In this role he accompanied Prime Minister Ted Heath on his visits to Scotland. Sandy had become a prominent figure, not only in Aberdeen, but in Britain as a whole. His wife, meanwhile, had been made a City Councillor.

I phoned Sandy after my arrival in Aberdeen from my hotel room. After informing him about my programme for the following day, he invited me to come over to his house that evening for a reunion drink. I was happy to oblige and had some choice whisky and a pleasant reunion with his family. He offered to pick me up from my hotel the following day to show me his office establishment. This would be after my visit to the BC and before the visit to Forrester Hill. Sandy drove me back to my hotel after this very warm and friendly visit with him and his family. It was my first visit since October 1965. The following day, I paid a visit to the BC; it had not changed at all physically. The meeting with the current officials, all new faces, was not a prolonged affair. I returned to my hotel to await Sandy. At the appointed time of 10am, Sandy arrived at the hotel in his official car, a Rolls-Royce with a personal standard driven by an elegantly attired chauffeur. I was courteously ushered into a back seat of the noiselessly purring car, like a head of state on an official visit. We were driven to a most impressive skyscraper building in which the oil cartel offices were located. Sandy took me by the elevator to his office which was on the topmost floor of the skyscraper. It provided a most magnificent aerial view of Aberdeen. Sandy and I chatted endlessly and reminisced about Aberdeen in the fifties. As Sandy went on signing documents and papers delivered by different officials, a lady waitress served me with tea and a great assortment of Scottish cookies. When I genuinely apologized to Sandy for taking his time off work, he replied that the entire morning was mine alone. I should feel at home and we should both enjoy it as such; this was a great relief to me. Then he brought the Visitors' Book for me to sign.

There were two books: one of blue leather, and the other red, also leather covered. The only signatures in the red book were those of Queen Elizabeth II and Prince Philip, The Duke of Edinburgh. The blue book was the one for other distinguished visitors. The previous visitor before me was the Chinese Prime Minister who had signed in the blue book. Sandy then asked me to sign in the blue book, a great honour I thought. He went further by asking me to put my signature over a complete page, and not sequentially below the preceding signature, which was that of the Chinese Prime Minister. I was overawed. He and I shared a mutual admiration for the obvious progress we had made, he wanted to show this by the full page signature request. Although he insisted, I persuaded him that I was very honoured by his asking me to sign the book at all. I appended my signature under that of the Chinese Prime Minister. I had spent more than two hours there with Sandy and it was now time to leave and go to Forrester Hill Maternity Unit. Sandy took me round several offices on different floors on our way out. As we entered each office, the occupants got up from their seats after which he introduced me briefly; it was touching. This was repeated room by room until we reached the ground floor. I was escorted from the elevator to the Rolls-Royce, with the engine purring, and driven to Forrester Hill for my last engagement. My feeling was one of great achievement and recognition at a place I regarded as a second home.

I met Professor Arnold Klopper in his office. I had not seen him for a couple of decades and he had aged noticeably. He had been honoured with a personal chair. He welcomed me warmly and we renewed our association. I detected an element of disappointment that I had not been able to join his Research Unit when I obtained the MRCOG. I owed much to Arnold Klopper; he made an immense contribution towards my training in OB/GY. He was the mastermind behind the involvement of Sir Dugald Baird in my future speciality.

In 1978, my "annus mirabilis", my first travel outside Ghana was to Nairobi to represent Ghana at an IPPF regional meeting. I had attended a couple earlier. The meeting lasted for about a week. I went on some Safari tours in the game reserve, a most enjoyable visual experience. I also went to the Rift Valley area to visit Mr Merz, a Swiss national. He was a partner in the famous A Lang Building Construction Company in Ghana. I knew two of his sons very well and had indeed delivered one of his grandchildren. Mr and Mrs Merz hosted me to an excellent lunch in their very attractive house, which was located in a remote woodland area. I also visited the Nairobi Teaching Hospital, where Dr Ayim was the Chief of the Anaesthesia Department. I was very impressed with the ICU (Intensive Care Unit); this was my first time of seeing an ICU. Dr Ayim was a fellow Ghanaian from the Volta Region, and also an old Achimotan (a year my junior). He had trained as a doctor and later as an anaesthetist in Germany and Switzerland respectively; he was held in very high esteem in the hospital. Although he never returned home to practise in Ghana, he excelled as an ambassador of his country of birth.

On my return home, I received the letter from the RCOG which informed me of my elevation to the Fellowship.

My second travel outside Ghana was the trip to Freetown, Sierra Leone to attend the WACS meeting which has already been narrated in these memoirs. On our return journey home, Yolande and I passed through Abidjan where we spent about five days as guests of Mr Kwame Donkor Fordjour. Mr Fordjuor was then the Managing Director of the African Development Bank (ADB) with its head office in Abidjan. His residence was located in an exclusive leafy and attractive area of the city. We were wonderfully hosted (I had delivered their last baby). The highlight of our visit was the evening. Kwame took us out for dinner in a small, but obviously most exclusive restaurant; the only other guest was the Minister of Finance. The dinner was excellent and ranked as the best I had ever had; Yolande and I threw caution to the winds and tasted frogs legs a la Francais for the very first time: not bad. It was indeed an unforgettable evening.

The history of the Korle Bu Medical School has been already narrated in these memoirs; so have the accolades showered on the graduate products. To my pleasant surprise and satisfaction, Bentsi Enchil invited me the following year for the full examination, as one of three external examiners. The other two examiners were Dr (later Professor) Graham Harley from Belfast and the Professor from Makerere Medical School in Uganda (a Maltese whose name I cannot recall). We were lodged at the Ambassador Hotel, then in its prime. We spent a most friendly and stimulating time together. I took them along to pay a courtesy visit to the Dean of the Medical School, Prof Harold Philips (aka Ebo, my pal) in his office. We spent about half an hour with him, and he exuded his usual charm and witticism; a great conversationalist and raconteur. When we finally left his office, Dr Harley, having been so impressed with him, remarked to me that he was the most impressive Dean he had ever met. As Ebo's friend I basked in his glory and praise.

The examination ended on a Friday and I planned to return to Kumasi the following day, Saturday. Professor Bentsi-Enchill invited me to stay with him at his bungalow for the rest of the weekend, Saturday and Sunday. I agreed to avail myself of this singular honour and mark of genuine friendship. I spent a delightful weekend with him; we got to know each other better. He drove me to Aburi where we spent the afternoon in his stylishly constructed wooden chalet. It was built by the Forestry Department and exhibited at the Trade Fair. On our return journey, we had a stopover at Legon where his daughter was then studying law. He introduced me to her, an obviously very proud father. I believe she later married a very wealthy Nigerian.

I continued with my role as an external examiner for three years, had a break of one year as demanded by the college regulations, and then continued until 1982. Whether true or not, Kwesi told me that in his opinion, I was the best external examiner they have ever had in Obstetrics and Gynaecology and went on to say that I would remain an external examiner for as long as he occupied the chair. I was gratified by the comments which implied that I was indeed making a useful contribution to the professional education of my younger compatriots in our field. I was the first Ghanaian, indeed African, to play this role in the department in Korle-Bu. I did not indulge in the habit of passing every candidate – only those who merited it and would be safe to practise got through. I was conscientious about my own current knowledge – before each examination session, I would brush up on the facts in the textbooks. In examining each candidate, I had to be satisfied with the following: (a) does the candidate have the minimal amount of knowledge? (b) Is it wise and safe to unleash the candidate into the field to practise medicine as a generalist, but not as a specialist? I think I succeeded in acquitting myself creditably as an external examiner.

Professor Bentsi-Enchill passed away rather suddenly (after a short period of ill-health) at a relatively young age. I was greatly saddened by the event. I travelled from Kumasi to Accra to mourn and attend the funeral. Our friendship was a short-lived one. Although he was based in Accra and I in Kumasi, we were close enough for him to have placed trust and confidence in me. Our friendship would have been deeper, but for his early demise.

Dr Ata Ampofo succeeded Kwesi as Professor and Head of Department. He, without any hesitation, renewed the invitation to me to be an external examiner. Hitherto, I had been the only African external examiner in OB/GY. Although Ibadan Medical School was the premiere medical school in the former British West Africa, no Nigerian had ever been invited to examine in Korle Bu in OB/GY. Neither had any Ghanaian done so at Ibadan or Lagos. I pointed out this anomalous situation to Ata and he agreed with me that it should be rectified.

Ata usually listened carefully to my views and opinions, acting on those which he thought relevant or wise. He told me that since he did not know any of the Nigerian Gynaecologists at Ibadan, he would leave the selection of the Nigerian Gynaecologist to me. I did not hesitate in nominating Professor Percy Nylander. I had known Percy since our student days in Aberdeen. He had trained under Sir Dugald Baird, obtained the MRCOG and MRCPE in the shortest period of time before joining the staff at Ibadan under Professor J.B. Lawson. He climbed the academic ladder to become a Professor.

Prof Atta Ampofo

He was elevated and became FRCOG and FRCPE. He had done much research and published extensively on multiple pregnancies, known to have a high incidence among the Yorubas in Nigeria. Percy fitted the role perfectly and I left it to Ata to personally formalize an invitation to him to be an examiner. The Nylander family had originated from Sierra Leone, but some decades earlier, some of them migrated eastwards resulting in some of them settling in the Gold Coast (now Ghana) and others in Nigeria, hence Percy's Nigerian links. Percy would therefore have some relatives and kinsmen in Accra whom he had never met as this was his first visit to Ghana. The prospect of coming to Accra must have been irresistible and exciting. Percy was invited in 1980 as an external examiner at Korle-Bu, and he was overjoyed at the invitation. Percy and I were the only two external examiners. We were both accommodated at the medical school guest house. We had a memorable reunion as we had not met for a number of years. He seized the opportunity to meet some of the Nylanders in Accra whom he had never met before. It was an emotional visit for him. I introduced him to my friends in Accra. He expressed great admiration

326

for the beauty and cleanliness of the city. It was while we were in the guest house that we heard the news that Sgt Doe had staged a coup d'état to seize the government in Liberia. This completed my role as an external examiner at Korle Bu Teaching Hospital.

My next role at Korle Bu was Inspector in OB/GY on behalf of the Ghana Medical and Dental Council (GMADC). The President, Prof Christian Adomakoh, appointed me to this position. My role was that of an observer, to ascertain during the course of the examination that they complied fully with the expected standard. It was a relaxed role which I found very satisfying. I enjoyed my visits to Korle Bu and looked forward to them. My colleagues took turns in hosting me to meals and entertaining discourse. I truly felt part of a team, everyone doing their bit to ensure that our country continued to have doctors of a high calibre.

The subject of OB/GY was well-taught. The school produced doctors with a high level of knowledge in medicine on the whole, and could hold their own against products from any Western country. Our department received many of these doctors as housemen or as fully registered Medical Officers. A few of them later on went to attain fame.

Our circle of friends in Kumasi widened as the years rolled on. The circle included the Poku family, Mr Paul Sagoe, Mr Gyamfi and Dr Joe Hiadzi. It is germane to write about them, but in no particular order.

I got to know Dr Harry Poku in the late 1960s when he was a MO in my OB/GY department. Tall, athletic and handsome, he had trained in Bristol, England, and worked under Dr Tara Ghosh in Korle-Bu before his transfer to Kumasi. He taught me how to perform my first case of Symphysiotomy. This endeared him to me; a mutual friendship was born. He introduced me to some other members of the famous Poku family, notably Nelson, Francis and Fritz. Although I tried my best for him to be sponsored by the MOH to return to Britain to train and obtain the MRCOG to fulfil his desire, I did not succeed. Harry went into General Private Practice where he achieved great success. He erected a beautiful home, and was later enstooled as a traditional chief. Harry's health took a bad turn rapidly and he departed from us rather prematurely. I do miss him.

Nelson Poku was Harry's cousin; I had known him as a Beer Distributor before he branched into heavy haulage transport business.

His uncle Francis Poku was a tycoon in the very lucrative timber business. When I was building my house in Nhyiasu, on one particular day, I urgently needed a long truck to convey a large quantity of very long roofing sheets from a location 15 miles from Kumasi to the site. On enquiry, I was told that Nelson Poku was the appropriate person to approach. At that time he was a mere acquaintance and I was not sure whether he would assist me by releasing a truck for a four-hour period to fulfil the mission. The only truck which could handle the conveyance had already been fully loaded with timber in readiness to leave for the port city of Takoradi. Nelson ordered his workers to unload the truck immediately and release the truck and driver to comply with my task. The driver drove to the location, got the truck loaded and conveyed the roofing sheets to the building site. It took more than the estimated four hours. The truck, of course, could not undertake its original task of the day of conveying timber to Takoradi. This was done the following day. It was done free of charge. I never forgot this great act of generosity and kindness. It extended into a lasting family friendship. In later years whenever I had to travel outside the country, my car received safe storage facility in his transport depot. I became a surrogate member of the Poku family. Harry and Nelson were regular guests at our annual Christmas parties. Yolande and I were regular attendants at the exclusive New Year party hosted by Francis Poku.

Friendships originate in varied ways. Among my friends in Kumasi from the 1970s onwards was Paul Sagoe. Well-built, dark complexioned and affable, Paul was a young successful self-made timber businessman whose wife had been a patient. Paul and I became very good friends, he was helpful and supportive in very many ways, too numerous to mention. The most significant had to do with my Opel Rekord car, GF4460, the first and only car which I had owned since 1965. The bad roads in the city and country contributed in no small way to the numerous problems I incurred with it. I needed a new one, but could not afford it. It often had to be taken to the workshop for repair work. Not happy about the condition of my car, Paul drove one of his cars, an Opel model WR 1999, to my house one day and told me that I was now the rightful owner of the car, handing over the keys to me. The car was not new, but it was in a good condition. This eased my transportation tremendously.

In December 1982, my father passed away in Accra. I had to travel to Accra and Hohoe to fulfil some functions. Paul assigned to me his Mercedes-Benz car and driver to take me around for three days to complete all my errands He attended my father's funeral at Peki. Paul rose in prominence in Kumasi and a busy street in a central part of Adum was named after him, while still alive (Paul Sagoe Lane). We have also enjoyed free hospitality at his hotel on this street. He was enstooled a traditional chief in his town in the Central Region. Unfortunately, because of our relocations, we have not met for a long time. I still highly treasure our friendship.

Very high on my list of loyal and generous friends is Mr Yaw Gyamfi. I got to know Mr Yaw Gyamfi after delivering his second wife of a son which followed a long period of marriage. The delivery in January 1982, was the first one I conducted at Bomso Clinic. Mr Gyamfi, slightly built in stature, but mighty in character and modest to a fault, was a hardworking, principled and successful businessman. At that time, he was a cigarette distributor in the Ashanti Region. He owned a fuel depot to serve his vehicles (this was an era in Ghana when scarcity of fuel was regular and common, resulting in very long queues of vehicles at filling stations). Mr Gyamfi was charged the standard stipulated fee for the delivery at Bomso Clinic, he came to introduce himself to me in my consulting room. He thanked me profusely for what I had done for them as a couple and added that I should not hesitate in any way if I needed assistance from him in the future. Not too long after, there was an acute fuel shortage and I sought his help. He provided me with the much needed fuel from his depot without accepting payment. He further instructed his entire staff who were all summoned to his office, that if at any time I needed fuel and there was none available at the depot, fuel should be siphoned from any of their fleet of vehicles into my car tank. Because of me he extended this same rare and generous privilege to my other two partners at Bomso Clinic. Sad to relate, but reportedly true, that one of my partners did not show any sign of gratitude for this rare act of generosity of which he had been a beneficiary some years earlier, by refusing to see the grand-nephew of Mr Gyamfi's, a young child brought to the clinic ill! Mr Gyamfi on some occasions provided me with a driver when I had to undertake a long journey.

When my father died, transportation was very difficult countrywide because of fuel scarcity. Preparations for the funeral involving purchase of drinks and food items and their conveyance plus chairs from Kumasi to Peki posed a logistic problem. In full anticipation of my needs and without any solicitation from me, he came and offered a large vehicle to transport all the items from Kumasi to Peki in the Volta Region and return them to Kumasi after the funeral. I was greatly overwhelmed; it was a relief from the foreboding task of arranging for the transportation. I did not have to pay for it.

In 1983, Yolande went to London with Ronald, then eight years old, to do some moonlighting. I had to travel in the summer of 1983 to England to attend the RCOG Congress in Birmingham. I was driven in my car, GF 4460 (now 17 years old) from Kumasi to Accra to board my flight to London. While on the plane, my car on its return journey from Accra to Kumasi had a breakdown and had to be towed to Kumasi over a distance of 70 miles. A repair was carried out involving the purchase of some expensive spare parts. Mr Gyamfi paid the full bill for restoring the car to full service. On my return home, my son Neil related to me the incident with the car to which I had not been privy. Mr Gyamfi had told my children not to let me know anything about the breakdown, the towing and the repairs carried out. I naturally went to thank him for this act of generosity and friendship, but he initially faked ignorance and when pressed refused to accept any reimbursement.

While still retaining his office in Kumasi, he opened a Forex Bureau and Travel Agency in Accra on the Aviation R oad at the Airport residential area. This happened when I was out of the country during my years in the diaspora. We bought a good second-hand Mercedes–Benz car in London and shipped it to Accra: it was meant for our use on our final return home. At my request, Mr Gyamfi got the car cleared from the customs, took delivery of it and kept it under safe storage until we returned home to Ghana. Mr Gyamfi looked after my personal affairs in many ways which I cannot list; he had assumed the status of a surrogate elder sibling to me.

In the year 2000, Yolande and I decided to build a house on my plot at 12 Agbamo Lane at the airport residential area. The contract was given to the architect/contractor to execute on a stage-by-stage basis. Because we were still resident in London at the time, we entrusted the supervisory and payment roles to Mr Gyamfi in our absence. Mr Gyamfi and his nephew Issac Asamoah, in charge of the Kumasi office, performed innumerable tasks and assignments for me.

Yaw hailed from Sefwi and played a leading role in developing this very rural part of the Central Region. He got an Australian mining company to establish a gold mining industry in the area. His sudden and unexpected death following a short illness came as a devastating blow and shock to me and my family. Listed as one of the chief mourners, it was an honour for me to pay tribute to a great man.

Isaac continued to run the business his uncle had founded. It was a great pleasure to see him at my 80th birthday party with his wife in splendid attire in 2011. About two years later I met Mr Gyamfi's son, Kwadjo, the one I had delivered, in a shop. He had grown into a good looking young man and I was delighted to see him. I enquired about Isaac and received the shock of my life. He told me that Isaac had died about two years earlier, dating it barely a few months after my birthday party when he looked so well. I was profoundly shocked and greatly saddened. His fresh and friendly countenance has not faded from my memory. He had been supportive of my friendship with his uncle Yaw.

Dr Josiah Hiadzi stood out eminently as one of the outstanding founding members of the Kumasi Medical School. Selfless dedication to clinical surgery, scholarship and teaching were his hallmarks. It is, however, as a friend that merits this column in my memoirs. Joe, a year my junior in Achimota School, trained and qualified as a doctor and surgeon in West Germany. Tall, good-looking and with an elegant and imposing stature, he always had a friendly smile on his face. He joined the department of surgery when I was then head of OB/GY Department. He succeeded Dr Akiwumi when the latter left KAH. Joe was a skilled surgeon. The Kumasi Teaching Medical School started under humble and unplanned circumstances with hardly any experienced teaching staff. The onus of teaching Anatomy in the preclinical years fell on the shoulders of Joe, already burdened with a heavy clinical surgical workload, and Dr Charles Bowesman. In like manner the teaching of Surgery to clinical students descended on his shoulders and his team of surgeons. It certainly was wearisome and taxing though stimulating for him. Joe was widely read and a scholar in the History of the Ewe language; I believe his German language was flawless and erudite. He was twice married; first to a German, Rosemary, and secondly to Elizabeth, a fellow Ewe. Joe and I maintained a close social relationship. It was with sadness that Yolande and I watched his failing health when we relocated to Accra until he departed from us in Kumasi. When the history of the Kumasi Medical School is written, his name should appear in gold and figure prominently in its hall of fame.

THE FAMILY

Our nuclear family life started at No11 Danyame in Kumasi. Our number increased stepwise to five in 1970 when Dugald, our third son was born. After our move to Nhyiaeso, the number of children increased to four in 1975 with the birth of Ronald. At various times we were assisted by domestic staff comprising a steward boy and/or maid servant. We had two lovely dogs, Coocoo and Sambo.

My brother Bill also lived in Kumasi with his wife Dorma and family at Kwadaso Agricultural Research Centre. The children were Jemima, Patricia (the twins), Marilyn, Lambert and Kafui. We all met from time to time. Felicia, my sister, lived in Accra with her husband Wayo Crabbe and their children: Adawa, Sackitey, Paa Azu, Nii, Nicholas and Mama. We visited them on our visits to Accra. Adawa, their eldest child, came for a week's visit to us at Danyame.

When Brian, our first son was born, my mother travelled from Hohoe to Kumasi to visit us. She stayed for about two weeks. My father came to Kumasi several years later when we had moved to Kplomdedie at Nhyiaeso. We held a grand cocktail party in his honour on our front lawn. Beaming with smiles, well attired and enjoying a cigar, he was introduced to all our invited guests. He enjoyed the party tremendously.   He bonded well with his grandchildren. Papa was keen on the children acquiring the knowledge and ability to speak and write the Ewe language. To my everlasting regret and sorrow, I failed to enforce this paternal wish and advice.

Brother Bill and Family in Kwadaso, Kumasi

I drove the family each year, usually at Easter time, to visit my parents at Hohoe. The outward journey usually took us through Accra where we stayed with the Blukoo-Alloteys. Our children and their children thus bonded as cousins. Our return journey from Hohoe to Kumasi was usually a direct one through Adukrom and Koforidua. Although a long drive for me, the children enjoyed it.

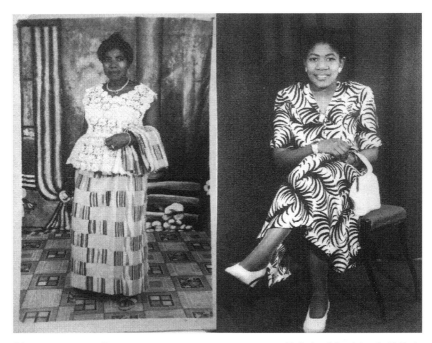

Mammy, my mother   *Felicia, My sister in Britain*

The year 1976 turned out to be our "annus horribilis". In that year, Mammy, my mother died; I contracted severe hepatitis B and my brother-in-law, Wayo Crabbe, also died. Rev Apo, my maternal uncle, had predeceased my mother at Agomenya.

Mammy had suffered from Diabetes and hypertension. Despite careful and painstaking management, her condition began to deteriorate in 1975. At this stage, she moved from Hohoe to Accra to stay with Felicia and received the necessary treatment from Dr Felix Konotey-Ahulu, a family friend and Physician Specialist. Yolande travelled with baby Ronald from Kumasi to Accra on the State Transport bus to pay a special visit to Mammy. It was during the heavy rainy season. Yolande and my mother shared a mutual affection for each other.

The Agble family planned to spend Easter at Peki. Papa had completed a new residential building at Peki Afeviefe for his three children. The dedication and house-warming celebration was planned for the joyous and joyful Easter weekend of 1976. The two-storey building consisted of two apartments, one each for Bill and me and a single storey bungalow for Felicia with car garages. They were attractive and spacious with ample surrounding grounds.

Papa and Mammy   *Papa - 31st March, 1974*

About a week before Easter, Mammy's health took a turn for the worse and she was admitted to the Ridge Hospital in Accra. I drove from Kumasi to Accra with my family on Good Friday and visited Mammy on Saturday morning. Before our departure for Peki, accompanied by Yolande, I drove to the Ridge hospital to pay my mother a farewell visit. I planted a gentle kiss on her forehead as a final act, turned round and straightaway departed for Peki. Bill and his family travelled to Peki and Papa went to Peki from Hohoe. Felicia stayed behind in Accra to attend to Mammy. Easter was observed in Peki and the new Agble home was blessed and dedicated, but under a heavy cloud of foreboding. After a cheerless Easter at Peki, I drove to Hohoe with my family on Easter Monday morning in order to spend a few days with Papa. On Easter Monday afternoon, a maid arrived from Accra with a letter from Felicia: Mammy had passed away peacefully on Easter Sunday. She had waited just long enough to dedicate the house before leaving us for eternity. Papa was of course devastated by the news, but bore it well.

We returned to Kumasi the following day. Although my mother was a Krobo from Saisi in Agomenya, it had been her wish to be buried at Peki. A fitting funeral was planned for her. Yolande and I were driven in my car to Accra by Mr Sampson, a very good, friendly hospital driver, who was specially released to me at my request by the KAH Superintendent, Dr Prempeh. We stayed in Accra with Mr Ogbarmey-Tetteh, my friend. The following day, Friday, Yolande was driven in my car by Mr Sampson to Peki. Bill and I took Mammy's body from the morgue at the Ridge Hospital. We drove in cortege from Accra first to Saisi, Agomenya for a brief family rite and then straight to Peki Afeviefe. Wake was held on Friday night, burial and thanksgiving service were held on Saturday. Mammy was buried at the Tsame cemetery. Friends and relatives from Hohoe, Krobo, Accra and Kumasi attended the funeral and mourned with us.

Hitherto, I had maintained and kept a smooth hairless face. Partly in her memory, I commenced sporting a little goatee beard.

Yolande and I returned to Kumasi via Accra where we spent a night at Ike Ogbarmey-Tetteh's house. I began feeling unwell and feverish on our arrival in Kumasi. The following day, the nature of the illness was clear and unmistakable. I had a full blown case of severe acute hepatitis with debilitating anorexia. I was confined to bed rest for the following four weeks and some dietary restrictions. A few days after our return to Kumasi, we received news from Accra that Mr Wayo Crabbe, my brother-in-law had passed away rather suddenly. Yolande went to Accra to represent me at his funeral. Thus, the year 1976 became the "annus horribilis". Because of the hepatitis B, some dietary and physical restrictions were imposed on me by my attending Physician colleague for at least six weeks. I was excluded from all forms of clinical activity. I was nursed by Yolande, observing strict quarantine guidelines, so no one else in our household developed the malady. There was an episode worth narrating.

My wife (Yolande) and I

While I was convalescing and preparing to resume work, one of my infertility patients on whom I had performed a bilateral tubal-uterine implantation was in the 35th week of her very precious first pregnancy. As my regular practice, in such cases, I had also performed a prophylactic Shirodkar cerclage on the cervix. Despite this precautionary cerclage, the patient went into preterm labour. Dr Martey, then deputising for me, phoned me late in the night about the case. I advised that an emergency Caesarean section should be done. I drove up to the hospital to observe the operation as it was carried out. I was very pleased and happy with the outcome of my initial surgery. The couple were forever grateful. The husband was a wealthy businessman, and the couple had been known to me for a long time. She had been a nurse at KAH. I delivered her of another baby two years later, after which she decided not to have any more children.

Papa continued to stay at Hohoe after the death of Mammy, and maintained an active life in his business, the church and community pursuits. He had a young assistant who handled all State Transport activities. A housekeeper was responsible for catering for his meals and house maintenance. Although we invited him to come to Kumasi to spend the Christmas with us, he declined it. The mountain would not go to Mohammed; we therefore decided to go to Hohoe and spend the Christmas with him. Bill's children also went to Hohoe to spend Christmas with Papa. It was a joyful Yuletide for the three generations of the Agble family. On Boxing Day, I took my family along on the Fodome Road to the Wli waterfalls; it was my first visit to this scenic, picturesque and wonderful site, reported to be the second largest in Africa (after the famous one in Zambesi). It entailed a long walk, with me piggy-backing the 18-month-old Ronald. This visit to Hohoe bonded the family more decisively. We continued to spend the Easter annually at Peki, sometimes extending the trip to Hohoe.

Papa later developed symptoms of prostatism. I drove from Kumasi to Hohoe, and took him to Accra. He was admitted to the Police Hospital under the care of Dr Andani Andan, my friend and colleague. An elective operation was planned for him. I returned to Kumasi and arranged to return to Accra for Papa's surgery. I returned to Accra with Yolande so that we would be around for the major surgery which was being done at an advanced age. We stayed with Roger and Sheila Korsah, with whom we became friends when Roger was in Kumasi as a High Court judge. The operation went successfully. Yolande, the true and affectionate nurse she was, and to my pride and admiration, spent a couple of nights in Papa's single room after the surgery. Papa recovered fully from the operation, spent some weeks recuperating with Felicia in Accra and returned to Hohoe. The mantle of the family matron had descended on Felicia and it was a role she has played with care and patience. The Korsahs provided us with excellent hospitality during the week we stayed with them.

About two years later, Papa now in his 90s, showed signs of failing health, which began to take a downward turn. He travelled to Accra to stay with Felicia; the two had always shared a great patri-filial relationship and love. We came from Kumasi to visit him a number of times. He remained cheerful and was always in good spirit even though he knew that his illness could not be cured. Felicia continued to be very caring to him. Early in December 1982, Yolande and I had to travel to Lagos to attend a wedding. Adjoa Appiah, daughter of Joe and Peggy Appiah, had had a wedding in Kumasi with her Nigerian spouse two weeks earlier and a repeat ceremony was planned to be held in Lagos. Yolande and I were invited to attend as special guests and we were pleased to oblige. Although it proved difficult to get flights to Lagos, we eventually succeeded. We visited Papa before our trip to Lagos and again on the morning of our return to Kumasi. About a week before Christmas, while consulting at Bomso Clinic, I received a telephone call from Felicia in Accra. The big and mighty tree had fallen. Papa had passed away peacefully at 92 years of age.

Funeral arrangements were quickly put into motion, with my brother Bill as the chief organizer. Papa had a status of a dual citizen of Gbi Peki and Gbi Hohoe. As an iconic figure in commerce, education, the Ewe Presbyterian Church, local politics and several other areas in Peki and Hohoe, the funeral would attract a large number of people. The Ghana economy was in dire straits at the time. Transportation was a problem because of continual fuel shortages in the whole country; the logistics of transportation were challenging. The funeral arrangements were therefore simplified as much as possible: wake on Saturday night, burial and thanksgiving service on Sunday morning, followed by burial at the Tsame EP Church compound constituted the plan. Burial would be followed by a reception at our Afeviefe grounds. This programme was followed and Papa was the first to be buried in the Tsame EP church grounds. Mourners came from far and wide to mourn with us. The Gbi Hohoe traditional area was represented by Togbe Gabusu and his Asafo Company. The Hohoe EP Church cancelled its Sunday service to enable the pastor, the choristers and the church members to be at Peki for the funeral. Friends from Kumasi and Accra made the long journeys to attend and pay their respects. It brought to an end an era. The EP Church in Hohoe dedicated a library in the church to his memory. In Peki Tsame, we, his children, later played a significant role in the construction of the new EP church.

An often quoted adage is that behind every successful man lies a good woman. If indeed I have achieved success, then the cap fits Yolande's head. Yolande had trained and qualified as a State Registered Nurse (SRN) in Trinidad. She then went to England where she trained and qualified as a Midwife as well as a Public Health Nurse.

Although I was the breadwinner, it would be useful in more than one sense if Yolande could practise her nursing profession. I excluded

KAH from her location of practice. An opportunity arose when the family size reached four. Opoku Ware Secondary School needed a school nurse and the required qualification for the post suited Yolande. A little diversion here may not be irrelevant.

When I went to Achimota school in 1946, there were very few boys' secondary schools in the country; these were Mfantsipim, Adisadel, St Augustine, Accra Academy, Odorgono and the Presbyterian Odumase Secondary School. There were only two girls' secondary schools, namely Wesley Girls and Holy Child in Cape Coast. The missions, notably the Roman Catholic, embarked on a laudable programme of building and establishing a number of secondary schools in the country in the 1940s and 1950s. This saw the birth of Opoku Ware and Prempeh College in Kumasi, Mawuli and Bishop Herman in the Volta Region, to name a few. The government also started to build the Trust schools in the 1950s and 1960s. All these schools benefited in staffing from the emerging new graduates from UCGC. My friend and mate Mr Thomas Sekyi, after graduating with a BSc in 1954, joined the staff of Opoku Ware as the first Ghanaian science graduate teacher there. Opoku Ware was a progressive school with an excellent track record. In appointing Yolande, it became the first school to appoint a school nurse. Achimota, of course, had a small hospital Headmaster – Mr Oduro was the first Ghanaian to hold the post. I bought a small second-hand Austin Mini car for Yolande from Prof. Barclay to use so that she could be independent of me for her transportation requirements. An assistant was assigned to Yolande for her work at the school dispensary. He was John Awurik, a Northerner of limited formal education, but very high intelligence. The small building comprised a consulting room, a dressing room and a small ward with four beds. Yolande established a successful unit which she ran for about a decade and half. John Awurik was a valued assistant; he was helpful in many ways and became a family friend and our "Man Friday". When Yolande left for England in 1984, John had gained enough experience to be appointed the Acting School Nurse although he had no nursing qualifications, apart from the training which she gave him!

He indeed was apparently addressed as doctor because of his confidence and performance. The fact that Yolande had a couple long white coats made for him as a uniform, no doubt helped to perpetuate this image! It was with great sadness that Yolande and I belatedly heard while we were in England that John had passed away. Yolande and I made determined efforts when we relocated to Accra to assist in the education of his children, but our efforts did not yield any positive response from them.

Yolande performed as a school nurse She regarded her role as being holistic, not only looking after their health needs, but social behaviour as well – she was a stickler for good manners and abhorred cruel bullying by older boys of younger ones; it was actually outlawed through her intervention. Mr Oduro and the senior teaching staff were very supportive of her efforts to instil discipline and good behaviour to the students. She was very caring and would go to any lengths to ensure that they had the best care. I will narrate an incident to illustrate the point. A student was struck in his head by a javelin which was thrown during a sporting event on the playing field. Although he did not lose consciousness, even when she removed the javelin, she thought it was necessary for him to be medically assessed by a Neurosurgeon. At that time, there was only one Neurosurgeon in the country, namely Dr Mustafa, based in Accra, Korle Bu (I knew Dr Mustafa very well, and indeed, I had once arranged for him to travel from Accra to deliver a lecture at KAH as my guest which he graciously did). I phoned Dr Mustafa about the incident and he agreed to see the student in Accra. The school speedily organised a return flight to Accra for the student, accompanied by Yolande. Although badly shaken up by the incident, Dr Mustafa found no serious sequelae to the javelin injury. He was kept on observation overnight, after which they both returned safely to Kumasi. Yolande had an arrangement with some of my medical colleagues to refer students with serious ailments directly to them with a note from her. She really cared about the students in her care.

Yolande saw through several generations of students at the school. Occasionally, she meets an old student, bearing a smile of recognition, whom she had treated at the school dispensary. Some of these encounters were on the underground train in London during our years in the diaspora, and even in New York.

The literary side of Yolande, hitherto unknown to me, and her political convictions unfolded after the 24th February 1966 coup d'état which toppled the Nkrumah regime. In its wake, Legon University launched the Legon Observer journal. This was a weekly publication which in quality matched any similar publication in Britain. In one of the early issues, Yolande responded in a rejoinder of high literary quality and content. She instantly became a regular contributor in writing rejoinders. She had an appealing prose style and the editors always welcomed her contributions, which were usually published. She became known among a certain group in her own right and I by association, as her husband.

The young members of the family needed to commence schooling, first in a Nursery for infants. There were a couple of them run by the wives of English expatriates. Brian and Neil attended one of these highly recommended nursery schools before moving to the Ridge International School (RIS). Dugald and Ronald attended a different Nursery school when we moved to Kplomdedie in Nhyiaeso, which was run by Mrs Adisi. Mrs Adisi, a Scottish lady, was married to Mr Joseph Adisi, a Ghanaian manager at the Star Brewery Company. They lived in a bungalow not far from our residence and were family friends as well. The boys moved on to the RIS later.

With my family

It is germane here to give a brief background of the RIS (these modest memoirs may interest some readers with an interest in social and educational history). The Kumasi RIS was built and established solely for the children of the European Caucasian stock, as was its equivalent in Accra. Children of mixed parentage did not qualify for admission to the international schools, irrespective of parental pedigree. So it was that Anthony Appiah was not eligible for admission at the Kumasi RIS and had to attend the KNUST Primary school. This was in the 1950s. Anthony was the son of Joe and Peggy Appiah, who have already been mentioned in these memoirs. This was pseudo-apartheid in Ghana only a few years before Ghana's independence in 1957. Change occurred before the end of the decade and Ghanaian children started attending the RIS. My nieces Patricia and Jemima and the children of Emmanuel and Joan Asare were some of the earliest pupils to attend school there. The pupils ranged from Africans to Caucasians of mixed and international ethnicity and nationality. The parents were middle class professionals. The teachers at the school were Ghanaian and British expatriates.

Yolande played a leading role in the affairs of the school. Having been a Brownie in school, she asked for and established a Brownie group at the RIS. They held their activities on Saturday mornings. It attained great popularity and prestige and in order to have a Brownie troop which was more diverse she accepted little Ghanaian girls who were not pupils at RIS. She took the group on several camping trips. With the assistance of Mrs Valerie Sackey, an English geology graduate who taught at Opoku Ware School, she staged plays with the Brownie group regularly at Xmas. Partly because of these activities, she was selected to lead a group of Brownies from Ghana to attend an international camp in Austria. The Ghanaians were grateful to her for instilling in them a spirit of confidence during their years as Brownies, as did the expatriate ones who even recently reached out to her from various countries abroad on FACEBOOK to see how she was.

The RIS each year organized an international bazaar day on a Saturday, a fundraising event for the school. Vendors put on sale various items, including food stands of different nationalities (Ghanaian, Caribbean, Indian, Lebanese, English, German etc.).

Yolande's stand of Trinidadian roti and curry and hot pepper sauce was very popular and always a sell-out success.

The quality of an educational institute should be judged less on the magnificence of the physical structure than its ability to instil a sense of worth and confidence in its pupils, as well as the quality of teaching. The teachers at the time were almost all females and included trained Ghanaian and expatriate teachers. Mrs Joan Asare was for many years the Headmistress of the school. She was succeeded by Mrs Joan Ofori, an Australian. After the untimely sad death of Mrs Joan Ofori, Joan Asare was summoned to the helm and served for several years until her final retirement.

The RIS had an active Parents/Teachers Association (PTA). Regular meetings were held where several matters about the school, including teaching and staff welfare, were discussed. Yolande was active and prominent in the discussion at these meetings. In due course, Yolande was elected President of the PTA, a post she held and at which she acquitted herself creditably.

The RIS took in pupils from the age of five; the classes ranged from one to six. Pupils wishing to continue their education in Ghana sat for the common entrance examination. Success at this examination enabled the successful ones to move on to their secondary school of choice. Entry into the leading secondary schools was very competitive. Our boys made their transition to secondary school when we moved to Kplomdedie at Nhyiaeso. The pupils at the RIS were a mix of nationalities—Ghanaians, Indians, Lebanese, and British. Because of this mix at a formative age, an air of confidence and self-esteem was instilled and inculcated in the children. An equally progressive home background played a positive role; this would manifest itself in the future.

There has been a revolution in educational institutions since my father's generation. After his primary education at Peki Blengo, he had to travel on a footpath from Peki to Keta, a hundred miles journey accompanied by an older sister and two other pupils. He stayed at the Keta Presbyterian Boarding Senior School for four years and another year at the teachers' training college, after which he returned home to Peki by foot. With progress, the boarding school in my case was different as already chronicled. My boys were driven to school as day students. Since I was an Old Achimotan, and I had benefited greatly from the boarding school ethos, I wanted Brian, our eldest son, to go to Achimota as well. Yolande had not attended a boarding school and saw it only from the perspective of a school nurse. She could list a number of negatives in the current system. Above all, she wanted the boys to be near us so that we could follow their progress and also make an input in their education. With our middle class environment and an appropriate domestic input, her argument prevailed. So we chose a school in Kumasi. Prempeh College was highly rated. We chose it in preference to Opoku Ware simply because Yolande worked there, so they would be more independent at Prempeh.

Prempeh College was founded and established by joint Methodist and Presbyterian churches in the late 1940s in the same way that the Roman Catholics founded Opoku Ware. The first Headmaster was Reverend Pearson. The school was well staffed and attracted bright students, and a high academic reputation was quickly established. The first Ghanaian Headmaster was Mr Osae. He had been my senior as a mature student at UCGC in the early 1950s. I was sure that our boys would receive the best academic education at Prempeh College.

Brian, Neil and Dugald passed their common entrance examinations in their respective years and gained admission to Prempeh College as day students. As such, our boys were required to report at the school by 8am for the morning school assembly every weekday. School lessons followed the assembly and ended between 1 to 2pm, after which the day students could return home. The day students were thus excused from the school's afternoon activities of sports and other pursuits. Their assigned homework had to be done at home. The day students were thus denied the boarding school ethos and camaraderie on which I placed great store.

Each morning, the boys were driven and dropped in turn first at the RIS, then at Prempeh College before 8am, a three mile journey, and collected from school later in reverse manner. Although it posed a daily logistic problem, it was solved and executed without much effort. Mr and Mrs Monta of the famous Italian building construction company lived in a house not far from our house. Their son Carlo was also a day student at Prempeh College. We arranged and took turns in driving the boys to school and bringing them back home. We normally did the outward journeys in the mornings. It worked out well to our mutual advantage.

Our residential house was a big one and was surrounded by a high wall with a wide gate. For several years, we had no immediate neighbours; we therefore had to engage the services of a night watchman for security reasons. The first watchman we engaged was Mr Ayitey, short and small in stature; he was afflicted with an advanced cataract in one eye. He hailed from Togoland and lived in the nearby Ahodwo village. A couple of years earlier, I had operated on his wife who had the most massive fibroids I had ever seen – about the size of 38 week gestation, one for the textbooks indeed! The second watchman who took over from Ayitey was Ewusie, also from Togoland and living in Ahodwo. Awusie, in his late 50s, was a competent artisan painter. We took him on in the middle 1970s and he remained in our service till our years in the diaspora. Awusie was very dedicated and loyal to our family. Very sadly, he passed away after a short illness when we were in London. John Awurik, Yolande's former school nurse assistant, in my absence from the country, played a highly commendable role. He arranged for the urgent admission of Awusie to KAH where he died shortly after. Because Awusie did not have any close relatives around, John arranged a fitting funeral and burial for him on my behalf. He wrote to me in London, providing me with details of the sad event.

During my next visit to Ghana, I made a brief trip to Kumasi.and accompanied by John Awurik, I went to the Kumasi cemetery to pay my respects at Awusie's grave. I arranged and held traditional funeral rites ceremony at our Kplomdedie house. The mourners were from a small group of Awusie's friends and the Ewe community at Ahodwo. Awusie's devotion and loyalty to the Agble family remained unsurpassed. I salute him for this. May his soul rest in perfect peace. John was a source of strength to me on this brief visit to Kumasi.

Because of the size of our family, my profession, and Yolande's work at Opoku Ware, it was necessary to engage the services of domestic staff: a maid, steward boy or both. It was not always easy to get the right people; it was a case of trial and error. We eventually got a suitably good maid when we were at Kplomdedie, called Akosua, from Brong Ahafo Region. She was pleasant, hardworking and caring towards the boys. Akosua worked for us for a longer period than any of her predecessors. On Christmas Day, Yolande gave her a beautiful wrist watch she had specially purchased in London for her. On Boxing Day, Akosua, beautifully dressed and sporting the new watch, accompanied our family when we went to my brother Bill's house at Kwadaso for our traditional luncheon. On our return home, I remarked that she was now part of the Agble family. She responded by saying "and I like it". We all went to bed in the evening after a tiring, but enjoyable day. On the following morning she did not come to the kitchen as was her routine to start the day's work. We called out to her, but there was no response. We went to her room and found it completely vacated with nothing of her belongings left behind. She had slipped away quietly without the notice even of the watchman, Awusie. It was a great shock and it took us some time to get over it. We learned at a much later date that she had left in order to get married to a Police officer from her region.

In our early years in Danyame, we acquired a cat and a dog. The cat had a variegated hue of brown, white and black of a striking beauty, and was a stray that had been picked up on the side of the road by Yolande, between school and our home. For some strange reason, we never named her. The dog was of mixed breed, given to us as a puppy by close friends, Bruce and Anne Smith; we called her Coocoo. The two pets got on well together. We woke up one morning to find that the cat had delivered some kittens, about four or five in number. They all lay in a corner of our front porch. I made an attempt to provide a bed for them all. Later in the day, we discovered to our shock and sorrow that the mother cat had suddenly turned cannibalistic and eaten up all her kittens. Guilt-driven, she climbed up to the roof of our bungalow and remained there. I summoned the veterinary department. It was a case of puerperal psychosis and they advised that she should be euthanised, which they did. (At this juncture, I recall a case of puerperal psychosis in Kumasi a few years later. An English lady, married to a Ghanaian, in a fit of puerperal psychosis, drowned her baby in a bath-tub.) Coocoo was an adorable dog in many ways, dark brown in colour with darker eyes. In time, she bore a son, Sambo, of jet black coat; we loved them and so did the boys. Nice playful pets and alert and protective watchdogs.

When we moved to Nhysiaso, Coocoo and Sambo were taken along with us and they seemed to have settled in well. A couple of weeks later we woke up to find that they were both missing! We looked everywhere, including several times at our 11 Danyame bungalow. No luck. This caused much sadness in our household, our boys were very upset, as indeed we were. The only conclusion was that they had been killed by criminal miscreants, a terrible loss. Several weeks later, I received a visit on a Sunday morning from a couple whose baby I had recently delivered. The man, who hailed from Hohoe, was a teacher at Opoku Ware Secondary School. They had dropped in to thank me for my services. When they were ready to leave, they asked if I would be kind enough to take them to their home as they did not have a car and transportation from our area was not easily available, especially on a Sunday. Not being particularly amused at having my one free day of relaxation disturbed, I nevertheless graciously agreed and drove them home, a distance of about two and a half miles. On my way back, in a non-built-up section of the road, a brown coloured dog, which looked very much like Coocoo, emerged from the adjacent bush. I stopped my car, called out to her then opened the door. She jumped into the car, fully excitable, jumping all over the back seat, wildly licking me. It was indeed incredible. Where, I wondered, was Sambo? I decided to drive round the bushy environs, about a half mile away from our previous Danyame bungalow, and suddenly from a bushy thicket, Sambo also emerged. I opened the car door, he jumped in and the reunion exercise by his mother was repeated all over again! The jumping and licking by the dogs continued as I drove home. Yolande and the boys looked on incredulously and in excitement. It was an excellent and priceless gift of thanks from the Hohoe couple! Dogs have an uncanny sense of recognition and express their warm welcome in a most excitable manner when they have been separated from their owners for a long time. They both had a habit of running along the road to meet the cars as we drove in; they could recognise them easily. Shortly after Ronnie was born, Yolande's youngest sister, who was a student at Columbia University, arrived at Accra airport to spend her summer vacation with us and also to be his godmother. I drove to Accra to meet her. As Yolande, who had been to visit a friend, returned home with the infant Ronnie in his carrycot on the back seat of her car, she accidentally hit Coocoo, whom she did not see, in the head. She ran from the point of impact straight on to the front verandah where she died. A dreadful experience for Yolande. Her sister, phoning to announce her arrival just at that moment, hearing Yolande's tearful voice and that someone had died, experienced a moment of panic until she understood that it was our dog and not our newborn son, who had unfortunately perished! Sambo died of old age quite a few years later. They were both buried in a part of the garden, along with other pets.

Our growing family enjoyed a happy and comfortable existence in a spacious environment. Yolande and I shared the master bedroom, the adjoining two bedrooms with its bathroom between were shared by Brian and Neil, with Dugald on his own in the other until he was five and Ronald arrived. We had our meals together in the dining room around the elegant stylish round table, except for breakfast, which we had on the back porch. Sunday morning breakfast was often held on the front garden lawn, which also served as the playing field for the boys and their visiting friends. Evening entertainment was limited because of the unreliable television service, with frequent interruptions from the transmission substation in the region. Yolande and I watched TV when it functioned while the boys did their homework. Yolande often played Scrabble with them, usually at the weekends. With my collection of classical music gramophone records, the boys had an early and prolonged exposure to classical music, especially of the opera genre. On Sunday mornings, I played highlights from operas, symphonies and concertos of my favourite composers. Although the older boys had experienced a longer exposure, it was Ronald, the youngest, who caught the bug of the love of classical music, especially operatic music. Although we led a Christian life, we were not regular church attendees. We attended the Ridge International Church infrequently; for special occasions I occasionally attended the E.P. Church, my mother church at Amakom. The christening ceremony services for Brian and Dugald were held at Danyame in our garden and the one for Ronald at Kplomdedie, also in our garden and officiated by Presbyterian pastors.

Our circle of friends widened following our move to Kplomdedie. I had become the gynaecologist to the small, but affluent Lebanese community. Some of the women took a liking to Yolande and so we were frequently invited to their homes for Lebanese and Ghanaian meals.

The Abaka family lived in a close by bungalow at Nhyiaeso. They became close family friends. Charlotte was a Dentist at KAH and Edwin was a Lecturer in Electrical Engineering at KNUST. Charlotte was the sister of Mr P. V. Obeng, the politician. She and Yolande shared much in common in political ideology.

Yolande and I were entertained to dinners and parties both by Ghanaian friends and those of the international community, and of course had to reciprocate. In this field, Yolande held her own. The climax of our entertainment was our annual Christmas party, always held on 23rd December. As one could rely with certainty that in the Harmattan month of December there would be no rain showers, the party was regularly held on our front lawn, with the thatched roofing gazebo as the centre point while the tall trees provided an arboreal ambience. The guests, usually numbering about 50 to 70, were a mix of friends, colleagues and other associates. We did not engage the services of caterers; the snacks and all food items were prepared by Yolande and the domestic assistant. The bar in the gazebo was inexhaustible with a variety of drinks, of which Yolande's Caribbean rum punch was a hot favourite. Fairy lights and Xmas decorations among the branches of the trees, especially assembled for years by a young electrician called Mr Larbi, provided the Yuletide atmosphere. The party usually started at 7pm and went on till the departure of the last guest, usually Austin and Naarkaley Tetteh. It was a party to which our numerous friends and associates looked forward. It was a party we continued to have in our years in the diaspora, whenever it was possible, and also on our return home at Kate Amaville on Agbamo Lane in Accra.

As members of the Kumasi club, we attended social functions such as New Year's Eve parties and cinema shows which they staged. The City Hotel, then in its prime, held popular dinner/dances which were well patronised. We did not miss these events.

In 1975, I attended a luncheon which was to me memorable for more than one reason. It was a luncheon hosted by the Asantehene, Nana Opoku Ware II in his house at the Ridge on Neem Avenue.

The luncheon was held to honour Dr Kweku Bandoh, the Medical Physician, on his elevation from the membership to the Fellowship of the Royal College Of Physicians of London (MRCP to FRCP, London), the first Ashanti to obtain this highly coveted qualification. I had known Kweku, a brilliant student, since our student days at UCGC. I, as well as other leading personalities, especially medical colleagues in Kumasi, was invited to this luncheon. It was on a Saturday afternoon, the day the Wimbledon tennis men's final was being played and broadcast worldwide on the BBC. Arthur Ashe, the first tennis star of African descent, was challenging Jimmy Connors, the favourite in the encounter. I tuned the radio to the BBC and listened to the match broadcast attentively. Arthur Ashe took the first set at six-four, but how long would his lead last? I had to leave for the luncheon at this stage. The luncheon was a well-attended and enjoyable affair, convivial company and tasty Ghanaian cuisine on the menu. During the course of the meal, I was called to take an important telephone message. It was a call from Yolande to inform me that Arthur Ashe had just defeated Jimmy Connors to lift the shield, a most historic event; the rest is history. I passed the news to Dr Harry Poku and other tennis cognoscenti. It was a great social, culinary and tennis Saturday.

Over the years in Kplomdedie, we played hosts to some of our friends from Accra as well as others whom we knew less well. Professor Harold Phillips, then Dean of Korle Bu Medical School, came to Kumasi on a brief official visit and enjoyed a lively lunch session with us. Professor Reverend Gilbert Ansre, my cousin, then a don at Legon, stayed with us on a brief one-night visit. Mr Tommy Thompson, a Legon don and also married to a Trinidadian, on a brief visit to Kumasi also stayed with us. Yolande's school mate in San Fernando, Marilyn Lamptey, married to the Ghanaian Psychiatrist Dr Jordan Lamptey, came with her two children (Derek and Lisa) to spend part of their holidays with us.

The Canadian government played an important role in Technical Education in Ghana. They built and established the famous Accra Technical Training College in Accra and a similar one in Kumasi. These impressive institutions provided excellent technical training in technology – an argument could easily be made and supported that developing economies need this expertise as much as technocrats in order to get ahead There is certainly more need for such institutions now than the numerous universities mushrooming all over the country at present. The Kumasi TTC held an important event at which the guest speaker was the Canadian High Commissioner to Ghana. He was accompanied on this visit by one of his senior assistants, Mr Archie Book. Archie and Lorna Book were friends; Lorna was originally from Trinidad, but we had not met the High Commissioner before. The event was held on a Saturday afternoon at the Kumasi TTC. I attended the function, and I was introduced to the Canadian High Commissioner, Mr Anderson, by Archie Book, whom I invited to have dinner with us at home. Brief though my encounter with Mr Anderson was, I was struck by his dignified personality and extended an invitation to him to join Archie for dinner chez moi that evening. He was non-committal and said he would let me know later. I hoped that this was not a breach of protocol by me! About half an hour later, I was informed that His Excellency would indeed honour my invitation to have dinner with us that evening. I returned home later and informed Yolande of our distinguished guest for dinner that evening, around 8pm. We set about frantically preparing the menu. Suddenly in the middle of all this we found ourselves completely immobilized by a total electrical power failure in our area. This occurrence was not rare at that time, but the timing was frustrating and embarrassing for us. I drove to the electricity faults unit to request the most senior personnel to rectify the problem as soon as possible. The officers were sympathetic and dispatched a team to restore power to us. Alas, the electrical fault turned out to be a major one which could not be quickly and easily rectified. Yolande and I had to improvise as best as we could. In those days, perhaps even now, it was always a good idea to keep some coal pots handy! Fortunately, using her expertise with charcoal fire, Yolande prepared an excellent dinner. Mr Anderson and Archie arrived on time, with our house illuminated only by lanterns and candlelight. As we always used a separate freezer (also a must in Ghana), suitably chilled drinks was not a problem. Dinner was served with the elegance of candlelight. It turned out to be one of the best dinners we had ever hosted. Mr Anderson was a well-read economist and an undoubted intellectual, and we shared a most stimulating and convivial evening which we all enjoyed. The atmosphere was so friendly, it was as if we had known each other for a long time; indeed, a very pleasant evening to remember and cherish.

Pleasant and sociable events were sadly interspersed by morbid ones. In Kumasi, hardly a Saturday passed without a big funeral. It was not my habit to attend them per se, as many did. I attended the funerals of a few people, colleagues and friends such as Dr Blankson-Heymans, Dr Agyemang, Mr Thomas Sekyi, and Mr Frank Mensah Bonsu, almost all of whom have received mention in these memoirs. Mr Bonsu, a distinguished and selfless solicitor, had saved me from the entrapment of a dreadful contract. He died after a short illness when he was still at the peak and prime of his profession. His untimely departure was a great loss not only to Ashanti, but the country as a whole. Dr Agyemang, also an Old Achimotan had joined the KAH as an MO when I headed the OB/GY department. He later went into General Practice. His English wife regularly assisted Yolande in running the RIS Brownies group on Saturday. Indeed she later started up a Cubs group with the help of an expatriate father. They lived in our neighbourhood. He died suddenly at a relatively young age. Yolande and Dr Charlotte Abaka played prominent roles in assisting the almost helpless widow in performing the expected Ashanti funeral rites.

There were three other deaths which touched me deeply and for which I had to travel to attend the funerals. They were the funerals for Mr Cromwell Quist, Dr Damanka and Professor Dziwornu.

Dr Damanka hailed from the Volta Region trained and qualified in Canada. He was married to a young Canadian woman, Carol. I got to know him when he was posted to Kumasi as a doctor in the Ghana Army. He referred a patient with a letter to the gynaecologist on duty at KAH, which as the specialist on call that day, I read. I was so impressed by the referral letter that I sought him out. I appreciate merit whenever I see it. Thus began a short, but firm friendship in Kumasi; he was later transferred to the Military Hospital in Accra. Not very long after his transfer we were stricken with the sad news of his very serious illness; he had liver primary malignancy. I made a special trip to Accra to visit him in hospital. His condition rapidly declined and he died early, leaving behind his wife and two very young children. His Canadian parents-in-law came to visit him in his last days. Dr Akude Gletsu was a fellow gynaecologist whom I had known for a long time (from Achimota School through to UCGC). He was a gynaecologist at the Military Hospital and had been widowed a couple of years earlier. He was a close family friend of the Damankas. He seemed to have orchestrated everything to do with the funeral, and provided great support to Carol in this hour of her need. We were not surprised when in less than a year later, they got married and migrated to Canada.

Peter Dziwornu was a Physicist and head of the Physics department at KNUST. I got to know Peter when he entered UCGC from St Augustine College in 1952 to pursue a degree course in Physical Science. He belonged to the early stream of Ewe students who had an affinity for Physics. After a good honours degree in Physics, he went to Oxford University where he obtained his PhD. There was no doubt about his academic brilliance. He was soon appointed head of the Physics Department at KNUST. He had married Rose Cudjoe with whom he had two daughters. Rose and I had been neighbours at Hohoe (the window from my room opened on to their house, separated only by a wall) and we grew up together as children. Now located together in Kumasi, we were like members of the same family. Peter was in the prime of his life as a highly respected Physics don when he was taken ill and admitted to KAH. The diagnosis of a liver primary malignancy was literally a death sentence. He was transferred to Korle Bu Hospital in Accra. A rapid downward course ended Peter's life. I went to Accra once to visit him in his final days. Austin Tetteh and I travelled by car to Dzelukope to attend his funeral. This narrative cannot end without reference to Rose. Rose was an attractive lady of dark hue. She moved to and settled in Accra after Peter's death. Not very long after relocating to Accra, Rose developed a nasty maxima-facial malignancy which ran a rapid course to bring her life to an early end. She passed away at a relatively young age. I was told that one of her daughters, after undergoing a straightforward gynaecological operation on benign uterine fibroids in a private clinic in Tema, developed post-operative complications which proved fatal. This is a sad family story. The cheerless family tragedy continued in another wing. Felix Cudjoe, Rose's elder brother, went to study in Britain and married an Irish lady with whom he had two children. While resident in Accra, one of the children had a cot death experience, the second child was drowned in a swimming pool. Why should fate visit such cruel events on one family?

The name of Cromwell Quist has cropped up a few times in these memoirs. I had been a close family friend of the Quist family. Cromwell and I travelled on the same plane in 1954, our first flight, from Accra to London. We had each played host to each other in Accra and Kumasi. We were like surrogate brothers. Cromwell was a solicitor/lawyer professionally but achieved fame and was more widely known as a television pundit during the NLC days and in the early days of the Busia regime. As a TV pundit, he was the "Jeremy Paxman" of Ghana TV. Cromwell's English wife adapted herself well to living in Ghana. Cromwell slowly developed some mental symptoms, the cause of which was not detected early. He had a brain tumour which proved to be fatal. Cromwell left us at a relatively young age. I travelled from Kumasi to Accra to attend the funeral. There was a massive crowd of mourners; except in name, it was a State funeral.

At this juncture, I wish to recall the funerals of a couple of my revered colleagues, which I travelled from Kumasi to attend. They were those of Professor Bentsi-Enchill and Dr Kofi Newman. May their souls rest in peace.

As a departmental head, I set up as high an academic standard as I could muster. I kept myself updated with current literature and indulged in teaching junior colleagues, which I truly enjoyed.

General anaesthesia for our surgical cases was administered by trained Nurse/Anaesthetists. They were all competent, but Mr Kissi was outstanding and excelled at a very high level. Messrs Seshie and Amoah also later attained his level of excellence. I always sought out Mr Kissi for my high-risk cases.

A Ghanaian doctor anaesthetist arrived later. In his 30s, he had trained as a doctor anaesthetist in continental Europe. I quickly realized that he was incompetent and had no experience. He could not intubate a patient. I therefore decided never to ask him to handle any of my cases. This way, I incurred his deep dislike even hatred of me. My aim was to protect my patients from any avoidable harm or perhaps even death.

Elections were held in the final days of the NLC government. There were two political parties: the National Alliance of Liberals (NAL) and the Progress Party, headed respectively by Agbeli Gbedemah and Abrefa Busia, vying for power at the time. Being a Busia follower, I voted for the Progress Party during the election. Gbedemah was an Ewe and some people with the tribal mentality assumed that all Ewes voted for NAL. The doctor anaesthetist was apparently very involved in the Progress Party politics and was duly rewarded when his party won the election. He was appointed the Ashanti Regional Commissioner, a high ministerial post. He left the MOH and was established in the Ashanti Regional office after this quantum leap from a humble position. He soon adopted a pompous air of great importance, using a walking stick in mimicry of African political Heads of State! Rather comic in a way.

One morning, the KAH Superintendent, Dr Bondzi-Simpson, Physician Specialist, invited me to his office and handed me a copy of a letter he had received from the Director of Medical Services in Accra. The letter was a complaint against me with a heading which was 'This NAL Doctor Must Go'. The letter had been written by the Ashanti Regional Commissioner and sent to the Director of Medical Services in Accra. The letter then listed a number of charges against me. The charges included some of the following:

- Incompetence as a Gynaecologist.
- Performing a lot of abortions to enrich himself.
- Playing delaying tactics with patients complaining of infertility until they pay me some money.
- I was a poor surgeon and a dreadful sight to watch when I operate.
- I rated high in my post-surgical mortality cases.
- Because of my negligence of duty, a named patient had died in labour.
- I was, he went on to state, only good at teaching during my ward rounds. He ended with 'This NAL doctor should be removed from KAH immediately'.

This was an important letter with extremely serious allegations written by a Minister of State. It could not be dismissed lightly; it called for an appropriate response. My reply had to be as factual as possible in seriatim form, point by point.

In my response, I totally denied performing abortions to enrich myself. It was well known that many doctors in private practice derived great income from performing abortions. This was not the case in the department that I headed, especially as the enforcer of the law there.

I had a great interest in the management of infertility. Doctors with the MOH were not allowed to indulge in private practice. Most doctors toed the line, but a few clandestinely charged some patients. I did not charge my patients, but some grateful patients showed their gratitude by bringing me gifts varying from eggs, yam, alcoholic drinks etc., which I of course accepted. I never charged my patients and thus indeed unwittingly earned the sobriquet of "the doctor who does not like money". I therefore refuted that allegation.

The charge entailing my surgical skill, incompetence and postsurgical mortality had to be factually investigated before any denial or comment. I made a list of all the patients who had had an operation in the previous year by all the three gynaecology specialists (myself, Drs Martey and Valnicek). The list was easily compiled from the theatre operations book. I passed the list on to the theatre block sister, Sister Twum, without disclosing to her the reason. I requested her to retrieve all the files of those patients. I then went through all of them very carefully, both Obstetrics and Gynaecology, and collected the summary details I needed and the surgical outcomes and mortality of the cases done by all three Gynaecologists. It was an illuminating and most revealing exercise. The outcome was that I had done more major operations than any of the other two doctors and had a lower mortality rate. The major cases included Caesarean section, Caesarean hysterectomy, total abdominal hysterectomy, myomectomy, vaginal hysterectomy and Wertheim hysterectomy. Dr Valnicek had done slightly more Wertheim hysterectomies than I had; I was the only one who repaired vesico vaginal fistulae. The Caesarean hysterectomy and most of the Caesarean sections were emergencies and the surgical outcome depended often on the patients' condition on admission. All the same, I had the lowest mortality rate, thus refuting the allegation on incompetence, surgical skill and mortality rate.

A charge alleged that as a result of neglecting a named patient in labour, the patient died. What follows now is the detailed account about what had happened in connection with the named patient.

The patient was a multiparous patient who was admitted one evening at about 7pm in labour. Dr Valnicek was the Specialist on call with his MO. The MO was an Akwapim, whose name I have forgotten (he sadly passed away quite young). The patient had been in the second stage of labour for some time and it was an obvious case of obstructed labour requiring an urgent Caesarean section. The MO was informed, but it took him a long time to respond to the call to go and see the patient. He sat on the case and did not inform Dr Valnicek. The patient ended up with a ruptured uterus with severe surgical shock and internal bleeding. It was only at this stage that he informed Dr Valnicek. The patient's condition at that stage was too poor to undergo surgery and she died. I was informed about the case the following morning as the departmental head. I found the management of the case completely unacceptable and the death preventable. The case merited an official enquiry. I demanded and received written statements from all the midwives involved, the MO and Dr Valnicek. The blame and the offence of neglect rested squarely on the shoulders of the MO. I therefore reported him to the KAH Superintendent for the necessary and appropriate disciplinary action. No one else was found to be negligent of duty or culpable. I had discharged my duty creditably as the departmental head and could go no further. The regional commissioner in his letter alleged that I had killed the patient and went on indeed to usher praises on Dr Valnicek that he was a competent and a dedicated doctor - that bit was true.

In my response, I denied all the allegations as best I could and provided the statistics I had gathered from my exhaustive, demanding and most informative research into our surgical performances over the period of the previous year. The allegations were not worth the paper they were written on. I think they were treated with the contempt they deserved. That was the end of the story. There was a tinge of tribal bigotry in the allegation. Sometimes one can excuse a person who attempts to cover up his professional shortcomings in a pathetic way; it is, however, unacceptable when it is done in a viciously malevolent manner such as this.

An Army Colonel, by name Kutu Acheampong, later staged a military coup d'état and overthrew the Busia government. The Regional Commissioner quickly disappeared. The story was that he travelled by road to Burkina Faso and then continued on to Europe. I have not heard about him ever since "Sic vita est" - Such is life.

Although it is not my aim to write the political and economic history of Ghana in my memoirs, it is germane at this juncture to paint the political and economic landscape in Kumasi as the boys grew up. For this picture, I am indebted to the research and scholarly publication by the highly rated historian/journalist Martin Meredith in his book "The State of Africa", where he succinctly drew the picture of Ghana at this time.

"No other African country demonstrated the decline of Africa as graphically as Ghana. Once one of the most prosperous tropical countries in the world, it had been reduced by 1980 to a paper state. The per capita gross domestic product fell by more than 3% a year in the 70s; output declined in all the major sectors: cocoa, timber, mining and manufacturing. The only sector which flourished was "kalabule" – the black market. The Ghana Cedi traded on the black market at up to 20 times below the official rate. Public Services disintegrated. According to a World Bank estimate, only one third of the bus and truck fleet, and one fifth of the locomotives were serviceable. Between 1975 and 1981, some fourteen thousand trained teachers left government service, many heading abroad. Ghana by 1981 had lost half of all its graduates. The economic situation was worsened by a crippling period of severe drought with its consequent insufficient availability of food crops for daily meals. When the rains did fall, the trunk roads became impassable."

My family was cushioned to a great extent against the severe shortage of items, generally labelled as "essential goods". Because of the sobriquet title of "the doctor who does not like money" which I had earned, grocery shop managers and grateful patients assisted me in obtaining the necessary items of sugar, milk, flour, rice etc. Lome in nearby Togo, became the supermarket shopping centre for the affluent Ghanaian. Yolande made the trip twice with a friend to shop for our annual Christmas party. My brother Bill did it once for us. Lome turned into a rescue city for many Ghanaians in many ways.

A Ghanaian timber merchant friend related this story to me. Domiciled in Kumasi, he wanted to speak by phone, even from Accra, at that time to a customer in Germany. He drove from Kumasi to Accra during the heavy rainy season when the roads were almost impassable, found it impossible to make this very important call, from where he proceeded to Lome before he was able to call his German customer! This demonstrated most tellingly the economic depth into which Ghana had descended.

General Ignatius Acheampong, assisted by Major Agbo and Colonel Selormey, headed the army which staged the coup d'état that removed Busia from power. Their aim was to eradicate the evils of the time. Some years later, the army staged an internal coup, replacing General Acheampong with General Akuffo. This was just a week before elections towards the formation of a civilian government in 1979. Again, quite unexpectedly, a group of young military officers, headed by 32-year-old Flight Lieutenant Jerry Rawlings, seized power. They consisted of a radical group of young officers and they embarked on what they called a house cleaning exercise. Eight senior officers, including three former Heads of State, were executed by firing squad. Accra Makola market was razed to the ground, and impromptu "People's Courts" were set up to deal with scores of army officers and businessmen accused of corruption and malpractices. After the election, Rawlings handed back power to the elected civilian government, headed by Dr Limann. Rawlings seized power again in 1981 from the civilian government by a military coup.

Academic education being an important part of parenting, we aimed at providing the best education available for our boys. The RIS played the role in their younger years and Prempeh College fulfilled the role for Brian, Neil and Dugald for some of their years in secondary school. Although Prempeh College was rated as a good school, it was plagued at that time by the disaster which had befallen the Ghana Educational Service; a mass exodus of teachers to Nigeria (Agege) engulfed all the schools. Prempeh College was not exempt from this. Science and Maths teachers were in very short supply. It was therefore necessary for us to engage Maths teachers to come to our house to supplement teaching the school syllabus. We also converted part of our car garage into a science laboratory where the boys could perform their science experiments. This was the extent and level of our commitment and input as parents. All the boys performed well in their regular school examinations.

Brian, the most senior of the boys, prepared and sat for the WAEC (WEST African Examination Council) O level examination in 1983. He had applied and had been accepted to carry on at Prempeh College for his A levels. Brian passed his O level examination satisfactorily with a high grade. He chose to pursue a science course in his A level course. Several weeks after the publication of the O level results, the WAEC announced their cancellation because of the alleged leakage of the questions before the examination. As a result, Brian had to re-sit the O level examination with his fellow students in the same year. Brian passed the re-sit examination creditably. He embarked on his A level course the following year when Neil was in his final year of the O level course, and preparing to sit for the O level examination. Then came another bombshell – the WAEC O level re-sit examination results were withdrawn. Why? Again, it was alleged that the questions had leaked out before the examination. This was a shock to all concerned. What a saga! Stress was building up on both students and parents as well. There was a dominant air of uncertainty about the educational future of our boys, now in their sensitive and formative years. While Brian was pursuing his A level course, he had to be "pari pasu" ready to re-sit the O level examination for the third time!! This entailed extra work and divided attention. The situation was worsened by the paucity of teachers to undertake the teaching of sixth formers. Brian and Neil sat for the O level examination in 1984. Brian for the third time and Neil for the first time. In due course, the WAEC released the examination results. Brian and Neil passed the examination creditably. Sadly, however, a few weeks after the release of the results, they were again cancelled by the WAEC, as on the two previous occasions, for similar reasons. During the examination week, there had been rumours that access to the examination questions the following day could be gained in the Prempeh College dormitories on the preceding night. Brian and Neil, as day students, were not involved in this scam. The next question was how many times did our boys have to sit for this examination? They were at a critical stage of their education. The educational standard had declined precipitously to a low level. Although Neil had applied to do his A level course at Prempeh College like Brian, when the allocation of schools was released, Neil was assigned to go to Navorongo, a place he did not choose. It was very far north of Kumasi. I had no friends or relatives there. It was now necessary to take some serious steps to further the course of our children's education.

Every so often in one's life journey, there comes a time when a momentous decision has to be taken. Such a time had arrived. Yolande would go to England with Brian and Neil for them to pursue and complete their A level courses; they would then return to Ghana for their university education. Dugald was a bright student, but with the current low standard at Prempeh College, an admission to the Accra GIS (Ghana International School) would be sought; admission there was very competitive. He was granted admission on the proviso that he repeated Form three as he was still young; this would hardly make a significant difference to his future studies. Since Accra GIS was not a boarding school, it was necessary to find a family friend with whom he could stay. Ronald was too young to be left with me alone in Kumasi while I engaged myself in a busy clinical practice – he would therefore join Yolande and his older siblings in England. We did not have enough funds nor foreign currency to carry out our plan. Yolande would need to engage herself in some work in England and generate some income to facilitate their stay there – a tall order, but she did not foresee a problem obtaining gainful employment, especially in London

It was a momentous decision, with the future unknown, wise to take one step at a time. It required careful planning to execute. In finding the right family where Dugald would stay, there was the question of the siting of the family's residence (not far from the GIS). Two such families came under our consideration to approach. The first was Dr and Mrs Doe (aka Agbemebiese). Dr Doe (Kwashivie) and Mrs Doe (nee Ruth Quist) were friends of long standing; I was Kwashivie's best man at their wedding at Keta in 1961. He practised as a civilian Gynaecologist at the Military Hospital. His wife, Afi, demure and friendly, was then head of the Government Secretarial Training College, sited near the Accra Morning Star School which was not far from the Accra GIS. The Does had two daughters (Senam and Setor) who had just completed their A levels in Achimota. The Does lived in their own house, at Osu, a location which would be ideal for Dugald. Even though the Does had been long-standing friends, such a demanding request might not be convenient to fulfil. Yolande was less known to them. We travelled to Accra and paid them a visit at their home. During our conversation, I raised the matter of Dugald's board and lodging with them. To our great delight and joy, they willingly agreed to have him stay with them, acting in loco parentis as it were as I was in Kumasi. They had a spare room which Dugald would have, all to himself. Dugald, then 14 years old, would be taken in as a member of the Doe family. We returned to Kumasi in a spirit of great relief and accomplishment of a mission. The next hurdle was the travel arrangements to England and accommodation problems there for Yolande and the three boys. With limited funds, this constituted a major problem. Sometimes in the course of human events good fortune plays a leadership role.

Mr Frank Amankwa appeared on the scene suddenly to solve our initial accommodation problem in London. Mr Amankwa was a successful timber merchant in Kumasi. Medium in height and with a friendly bearing, he always sported himself in shorts and a short-sleeved shirt in his timber yard near the Kumasi timber rail line. His wife had once been my patient and because of this, he was always kindly disposed to me. On learning about my forthcoming accommodation problem in London, he found a solution. He told me that he had a house there in Walthamstow, north London, which was only occupied during his brief visits to London. Yolande and the boys could stay there initially until they finally secure their own place of abode. It was free of any charge, the only caveat was not to use the telephone for outgoing calls. We accepted this kind and generous offer with much thanks. All that remained now was to plan for a departure date and get the flight tickets. The search for schools would commence when Yolande and I arrived in London.

Our family of six had remained under one roof in Kumasi. The execution of our plans would split the family in three different locations as follows: I alone in Kumasi, Dugald in Accra with the Doe family, and Yolande in London with the other three boys. Since all the schools were on their summer vacation before the start of the new academic year, it was the best time for me to go to London with Yolande to hunt for schools for the boys. Mr and Mrs Nugor assisted in getting a trained lady to be my housekeeper. She would be responsible for cooking all my meals and cleaning the house. She had been trained at a house-keeping institute and seemed ideally suitable for the job.

I took part of my entitled annual leave and flew alone to London; Yolande followed a few days later. Mr Amankwa had given me all the details about the house in Walthamstow, North London. I was to contact a relative who was the caretaker of the house. I did not encounter any difficulties in taking occupation of the house, which had been well kept and maintained. We were assigned one large bedroom. Yolande joined me a few days later from Ghana. The travels from Ghana to London by the family was staggered on purpose. About a fortnight after Yolande's arrival, Neil and Ronald arrived from Ghana. Brian was left behind in Kumasi with Dugald. Brian joined his brothers in London only after my return to Kumasi. This way, the boys were not denied the company of their siblings. Joe and Peggy Appiah visited the boys to ensure they were faring well. Neil invited them and hosted them to a cordon bleu dinner which they enjoyed much to our pride.

Because of the limited time at my disposal, Yolande and I very quickly embarked on hunting for a school for Brian and Neil. We approached Father Wilmington, our parish priest at Perivale Anglican Church where we worshipped, for advice. He referred us to another Anglican minister at Southwark (I have forgotten his name). This minister was responsible for educational affairs. He was warm, friendly and was sympathetic to our educational problem for the boys. He assured us that he would find a suitable school for Brian and Neil. A few days after the interview, we were informed that Twyford Anglican School in Ealing would accept Brian and Neil for their A level courses, starting at the new academic year in September 1984. They did not have to pay any fees. The profound relief and sense of gratitude was beyond description; our prayers had been answered.

One hurdle had been cleared but a second hurdle of finding suitable accommodation remained to be cleared. We inspected a number of flats, but found none of them suitable. Moreover, Yolande was keen on finding a flat in Ealing or its nearby suburbs as the boys would be attending Twyford School. I returned to Ghana with this problem still unsolved.

My brief visit was with a defined purpose of finding a school for Brian and Neil. The aim was achieved. I did not attend any opera performances, but I recall a TV broadcast of a magnificent production of Mozart's "Magic Flute". The Olympic Games were held in Canada and broadcast worldwide. I watched them avidly. A controversial British female athlete committed a disgraceful malfeasance in a track event. She deliberately pushed down a fellow athlete who was then in a potential gold medal winning position in the final lap in the long distance event, not far from the finishing line. Her disgraceful action prevented her fellow competitor from finishing and winning the gold medal. The perpetrator was originally a Caucasian South African who was very controversially and hastily given British citizenship in the previous year when she was regarded as a potential gold medallist in her Olympics event. She ran barefooted. It was the Margaret Thatcher government which colluded in this controversial immigration act, a government well known for its anti-immigration stance towards most Commonwealth countries!

A strange case of serendipity on this London visit is worth narrating.

Yolande has three sisters, namely Gloria, Glenda and Erica. Although Trinidadians by birth, they had all migrated to the USA, became US citizens and lived in New York City. Glenda and Erica were on a European tour in the summer of 1984. I had arrived in London from Ghana and was staying in Walthamstow. My address and telephone number were only known to Yolande, who was still then in Ghana. I received a telephone call one day. The call came from Austria and the caller wanted to speak to one of her close friends in London; it was apparently the wrong number and the caller apologized and said that she thought that she was speaking to a Nigerian friend of her friend. She was speaking from a call box. I accepted her apology and went on to say that I was a Ghanaian and not a Nigerian. The caller responded that she had a Trinidadian sister married to a Ghanaian, who was resident in Kumasi. "I am Ted, your brother-in-law and the one you are talking to." We had met only once before in New York several years earlier. It was a coincidence of more than one in a million in a wrong number call made from a callbox in a faraway country! Quite inexplicable, but true.

Yolande's sojourn to England was not her first overseas journey since our arrival in Ghana in 1965. She had travelled home to Trinidad while expecting Neil, our second son. As already chronicled, Kplomdedie was constructed and built by direct labour. This had been a taxing exercise spread over a period of two years. After moving to Kplomdedie, Yolande felt a need, and justifiably so, to travel to the USA with the three boys to visit her sister Gloria. Yolande flew on Pan American Airlines (PAA) with the boys to New York in 1973. It was financially demanding on my resources. Yolande did some lucrative moonlighting in New York and earned some dollars. She managed a visit to Toronto in Canada with the boys where they were hosted by David and Loise Tay. David Tay was a Ghanaian engineer who had previously lectured at KNUST before migrating to Canada. where he had done his degree courses and met his wife Lois. Yolande returned to Ghana with the boys after six weeks. She had done some useful shopping; included in the purchases was a large Whirlpool refrigerator. The boys certainly enjoyed the trip, their first overseas journey. In 1979, Yolande went on another overseas journey; she flew with Neil to visit Gloria in New York. On her return journey, she passed through London where she bought a VHS video recorder; this was a useful acquisition at the time. It would widen our field of entertainment. Video tapes were prohibitively expensive. An enterprising Lebanese in Kumasi established a video tape library of films which had been taped in the UK and elsewhere. You could borrow tapes on a rental basis. The library enterprise soon spread quickly and the number of such libraries increased.

The summer of 1983 was a fruitful one for me and Yolande, filled with reminiscences. Yolande went on a moonlighting trip again, but to England. On this occasion, the Ghana economy was at its nadir. She was accompanied by Ronald, then eight years old. Adawa, my niece, now married to Richard, lived in the Perivale district of Ealing. Adawa had kindly agreed to give them accommodation at their home. With impeccable nursing qualifications, Yolande had no problems doing day and night agency duty calls. Ronald was enrolled into a neighbourhood school and therefore did not have any interruption in his education. Dick and Pat Kassardjian had relocated to London and were living in an apartment at Queens Gate, Kensington; old friendships were renewed. With her handsome earnings, Yolande was able to stock up a few essential items to take back to Ghana. Meanwhile, I coped very well with the three boys in Kumasi. Yolande sent us a parcel whenever she saw a familiar or reliable person at the airport returning home to Kumasi. Aware of my enchantment with Mozart's Magic Flute opera, she went to Oxford Street's HMV shop and bought me a VHS tape of the opera; it cost her thirty-nine pounds sterling (this would now translate to almost two hundred pounds); it was a gift I treasured highly, and will never forget.

The triennial RCOG Congress was scheduled to be held in Birmingham in the summer and I wished to attend. I was successful in getting sponsorship to travel to attend the congress as usual. I travelled to London and joined Yolande there. It was a very hot summer. We booked to stay in a very good hotel (before the starring system of grading hotels), not cheap, but astonishingly, no air conditioning, not even fans. We had the most uncomfortable time there. We tried to switch, but only the Holiday Inn was airconditioned and the smart North Americans and a few Nigerians had booked up all the rooms! We tried sleeping on the floor, but that did not help; their fire doors rules were not helpful either. Some memories stick in your mind because they are good and precious. This one did because of its nightmarish proportions! I met a couple of old friends and colleagues at the congress. Dr Attit, my old colleague in Leeds, came from Bombay to attend. He had not changed in appearance much; round face resting on a rotund figure. He had become a successful Gynaecologist in private practice and was Chairman of the Sub-regional Committee of the RCOG. We had a pleasant reunion.

Seeds of family friendships sown in Leeds, germinated, grew and blossomed during this summer. We met Mr Redman, Mr Beg and Mr Melville and their respective families in their homes. We responded to an invitation from Theo and Jay Redman to visit them in Leeds. They came to meet us at the train station and welcomed us very warmly and drove us to their new home at Mayo Close, a beautiful semi-detached bungalow with attractive front and back gardens. We received VIP hospitality; Theo and Jay were as delighted to see us as we were to see them. We stayed for two memorable days before departing. We took the opportunity to visit Nigel and Janet and their family (former BC Director in Kumasi).

Next, we travelled from London to Dewsbury to honour an invitation from Jim and Jean Begg to visit them. Jim, my former Senior Registrar in Leeds, was now a Consultant Gynaecologist in Dewsbury. Jim, a true Scot, tall and always smartly dressed; we shared a mutual, liking and respect for each other. Jim and his wife Jean entertained us in a grand style. Jim was knowledgeable on malt whiskies and imparted to me some of this knowledge. Jim was a heavy cigarette smoker and this took an ultimate fatal toll on him barely a couple of years after this memorable visit.

Our Yorkshire visit unfolded another unexpected reunion. We had missed our return train to London on a Sunday morning and whilst looking around in the WH Smith shop, I met a gentleman with a vaguely familiar face. Following an enquiry and mutual self-introductions, he turned out to be Dr George Hesse, a Ghanaian and an Old Achimotan, although not my contemporary. He was an Orthopaedic surgeon who had made Leeds his home, and had indeed attended our wedding in 1965. He successfully persuaded us to postpone our departure for London to the following day in order to spend a day with him at his home, a few miles outside the city. He took us there and we spent the rest of the day catching up on all the news and admiring his enormous record collection, some of which he played for us. I was struck by his collection of gramophone records, easily the largest I have ever seen. We had a most pleasant time with him and returned to London the following day, Monday. We kept in touch with him and several years later we hosted him to dinner at our London home and also in Crewe where I was doing a locum at the time.

The shower of invitations in the summer of 1983 ended with the positive response to an invitation from Mr Melville to visit him in Brighton. Mr Melville had been my Senior Registrar in Leeds and was now a Senior Consultant in Brighton. He was originally from Barbados and of Caucasian decent. He had always been supportive of me. Although I had a crowded programme, I went with Yolande to Brighton and renewed an old friendship. He had arranged for me to do a locum job in his department in 1978, a great help financially at the time. He and his wife were delighted to see us; we dined and wined in style. After a most fulfilling summer visit, I returned home to dire Ghana loaded with the stock of items Yolande had purchased, with Ronald in tow. I recall the image of this young, small boy of eight years, smartly dressed and loaded on his back and front with hand luggage walking on the tarmac to board the plane to Accra. We returned to Kplomdedie in a spirit of great accomplishment. I was glad to see the three boys as Ronald also was to see his siblings. Yolande returned home to Ghana a few weeks later. Thus ended the Agble travels in 1983, which preceded the momentous decision already chronicled above.

BOMSO CLINIC

After the debacle of my rather disappointing foray into private practice a few years earlier, I confidently carried on my career as a MOH Gynaecologist in KAH. I was engrossed in a satisfying and challenging clinical practice. With it being a regional referral centre, I was privileged to see a wide variety of obstetrical and gynaecological conditions, probably denied to some of my contemporaries. We had a comfortable family and social life. Our move to Kplomdedie was a very satisfying one which provided room for both physical and social activities. There is no doubt that the one fly in the ointment was our limited funds which precluded family travel and other luxuries, but we felt that we had little reason to complain overall. We lived comfortably.

One day, Mr John Owusu Addo invited me to meet two other doctors, namely Dr Andani Andan and Dr Kwesi Appiah, Surgeon and Paediatrician respectively in a restaurant. Dr Andan was well known to me and was indeed my medical colleague working as a surgeon at KAH. I had met Dr Appiah only once before socially at the house of a friend whom we were both visiting. He was the Paediatrician Specialist at the KNUST hospital and doubled as the Medical Superintendent there as well. John introduced us all formally and after some small talk, he raised the question of a group practice which he thought might be of interest to all three of us, as specialists in different branches of medical expertise. He believed that as top practitioners in our specialist fields, both the community, as well as ourselves, would benefit from such a merger. As there was no such practice in the country, we would be pacesetters. Our ethnic origins covered the Northern Region (Dr Andan), Ashanti Region (Dr Appiah), the Volta Region and the South (Dr Agble). The idea was attractive. Drs Andan and Appiah had worked together before as MOs earlier at Korle Bu Hospital before they each went abroad to specialize – Dr Appiah in Canada, Dr Andan in England They had both held discussions on a partnership before our meeting. I was now being brought on board.

It is germane to add a few notes here on my other two colleagues.

Dr Andani Anda was a most charming person, a skilled and competent General Surgeon. He was an Old Achimotan and a year my junior, he was famous as an athlete in the long distance running events. In those British colonial days, a northerner such as Andan had to obtain official permission from the powerful District Commissioner in Tamale to travel to the south. Andani was one of the very few northerners in Achimota then. He studied medicine and qualified as a doctor in England and worked at Korle-Bu Hospital on his return. He returned to England for his postgraduate studies and obtained the FRCS (London). He was affable and friendly, almost to a fault.

Dr Appiah, short in height, with heavily-rimmed spectacles, was equally friendly. He was an old boy of Prempeh College. He studied medicine in Newcastle, England, worked at Korle Bu Hospital on his return home and later went to do his post-graduate training in Toronto, Canada, where he qualified as a Paediatrician. He joined the medical staff at KNUST as a Paediatrician and was later appointed the Medical Superintendent.

Our dinner meeting ended with the agreement that the group practice was an attractive proposition worth further discussion. After several meetings, the three of us finally decided to pursue the idea practically. At this stage, we approached Mr Frank Mensah Bonsu, eminent solicitor, to advise us on the formation of a partnership. He willingly offered his professional services pro bono and commended the idea highly. He later produced a draft of an agreement which he left us to study jointly and/ or individually and amend as we saw necessary.

The initial prerequisites were finding suitable premises for the clinic and also the financial resources to begin with. Since we could not find suitable premises, we decided to look for a suitable plot of land on which to build the clinic. Next, architectural drawings of the building were necessary in order to assess the cost of construction; the total cost would also include the cost of equipping the hospital. With the knowledge of the estimated total cost, we could then seek the financial input from a bank. We were lucky in our search for a plot of land. Dr Appiah, through some of his Ashanti contacts, found a large suitable plot of land at Bomso, not far from KNUST. After meeting the chief, the three of us contributed funds and purchased the land. Once again, and not for the last time, the services of Mr John Owusu Addo were in demand. He was entrusted with the task of designing the hospital to our requirements; this would engage his full professional commitment and attention. He visited the KAH theatre area to gain first-hand knowledge of theatre environs. He finally produced his architectural drawings; they served the dual purpose of being very functional and attractive.

The plan was horseshoe shaped single-storeyed structure enclosing a courtyard to be landscaped and covered at the front by a honey-combed wall. The right wing consisted of an OPD (Out Patients Department) waiting area which opened into a corridor; the corridor separated the four consulting rooms from the administrative and pharmacy offices. The left wing consisted of the wards; the wards in turn consisted of male and female open wards, labour and delivery rooms and single private rooms. The wards could accommodate up to 25 patients. Linking the two wings at the back were the theatre complex, the Laboratory and the X-ray units. A corridor separated the laboratory and X-ray units from the theatre complex. The theatre consisted of two operating rooms, a recovery room, a doctors' changing room and a Nurses' room, both provided with personal washrooms. The total design was flawless and further conferred on him the sobriquet, "Le Corbusier", the legendary architect.

The search for funding the project was not going to be easy in the prevailing economic climate. The cost of building the clinic if assigned to a reputable company such as A Laing could be prohibitively high. The building would have to be constructed using the services of a supervising foreman with top grade artisans, and our personal involvement to reduce its cost. With the estimate of the total cost of building and equipping the clinic now available, we decided to approach my friends at GCB (Ghana Commercial Bank) in Accra. We made several trips to Accra to present our case. On one occasion, John had to accompany us to defend his drawings.

Although the initial response from the bank was somewhat lukewarm, our hopes were high, despite the protracted nature of the goings-on. Eventually, a source at the bank hinted to me that we might get a quicker response if we applied to the NIB (the National Investment Bank). Apparently, the chief decision maker at the GCB was not very happy with the involvement of one of my partners, hence the procrastinations. With me as the lead negotiator, we made a formal application to the NIB. The CEO of the NIB was Mr J. S. Addo, an experienced banker who had previously been the Deputy Governor of the Bank of Ghana. An Old Achimotan, he was my former classmate as well. His approach was both professional and reassuring. After the submission of our proposal to the bank, a feasibility study team was sent to Kumasi without any delay for an on-the-spot assessment of the need and profitability of the venture. After the study, the NIB management agreed to advance us the money in stages until the completion of the building. A separate loan would be granted for the purchase of hospital equipment, consisting mainly of surgical instruments, laboratory items and an X-ray machine through PASICO, a trading company in Accra. Mr Addo impressed upon us the wisdom in avoiding a large loan which, he said, would result in our working for the rest of our lives to repay and the interest it would attract. Very useful advice, after which we signed on the dotted line. The NIB requested financial collateral payments from each of us. I approached my friends at the GCB personally and succeeded in obtaining the collaterals for my two partners and a separate one for myself. They did not have to do anything but sign for them. Dr Andan was then working in Obuasi with the Ashanti Gold Mines. Without seeming to claim credit unduly, it can be correctly asserted that without my personal involvement, based on my relationship with the bankers, the outcome would have been different.

In Mr Akyea, we found a young builder with talent. He had been recommended by Yolande who had seen his work performance at Opoku Ware School. The foundation of the building was dug and the task of building Bomso Clinic commenced after a long gestational period. Work advanced stage by stage. Dr Appiah, working at the KNUST Hospital nearby, and I kept supervisory eyes on the progress of the building work as did Mr Owusu Addo. My supervisory role was interrupted in 1976 when I had my attack of hepatitis; it was resumed after my full recovery.

Suddenly, the release of funds from NIB ceased and the building work came to a standstill. This followed the replacement of Mr Addo as the CEO of NIB by someone else. Despite fervent pleas on our behalf by a Deputy CEO, Mr Ofori (later the proprietor of Penta Hotel at Osu Oxford Street), the new CEO never permitted the release of any further funds for the building to advance, strange professional behaviour in banking indeed. This lasted about a year. The release of funds was resumed after his replacement by a new CEO, but in a very limited fashion. It enabled the main building with the consulting rooms and the wards to be completed. There was no further release of money for the completion of the theatre, laboratory and X-ray complex.

In 1978, my annus mirabilis, I travelled to London to be elevated to FRCOG by the RCOG. This visit to England with my travel sponsorship has already been fully chronicled in these memoirs. There was no input from the partnership group. I travelled from London to Leeds to conduct business with Down Brothers, manufacturers of surgical and theatre instruments. Fortunately for us, the separate loan for the purchase of these items, the X-ray machine, and laboratory equipment had been disbursed during the time when Mr Addo was the CEO. The entire amount remained with PASICO, the company in Ghana. I spent two busy and stressful days at Down Brothers in Leeds selecting surgical equipment within our limited budget. Dr Andan had planned to join me in Leeds for this exercise as he planned to be in Britain around this time, but this did not materialize. The X-ray and laboratory items had been handled by me already in London. I felt a great sense of achievement at the end of all this activity on behalf of the Bomso partnership group. The items were all shipped to PASICO in Ghana. They were loaded in a container which was despatched to Bomso Clinic at a much later date. The relics of the container remained in front of Bomso Clinic for many years. We, the joint partners, had to keep a dedicated watchman, Mr Akuffo, an elderly man, at the site 24/7. He was paid from our joint account.

Although most of the main building was ready by early 1981, the theatre complex, X-ray and laboratory units were not. There were no funds available for their completion. The equipment in the container could therefore not be installed. Dr Appiah decided to commence work at the clinic in 1981 after resigning from KNUST. He could well afford to do so, as a Physician – all he needed was a consulting room, prescription forms and some stationery to work and earn a living. As surgeons, we required much more, for a start a functional theatre in which to work; to practise gynaecology, this was even more imperative. Dr Andan had at this time relocated to Accra at the newly opened Police Hospital as the uniformed Medical Director, he seemed quite settled and comfortable, there was no urgency on his part. With no funds available to complete the theatre complex, X-ray and laboratory units, I decided to seek assistance on my own. My approach to Mr Simeon David bore fruit. Simeon David was Naja David's younger brother, a Lebanese, and Director of their Logs and Lumber Company. After listening to my story and my inability to commence work at Bomso Clinic because of a lack of funds to complete the theatre complex, X-ray and laboratory units, Simeon made a personal donation of the required amount to me personally, to set up the theatre, X-ray and laboratory unit so that I could commence work at Bomso Clinic. In addition, my consulting room was given an upgrade of a special finish with exquisite Afromosia wood ceiling and panelling. This was all done gratis. It was to be considered as a gift to me, according to him. I remained forever grateful for this singular act of overwhelming generosity. For a period of about one year when Dr Appiah practised alone at the clinic, he pocketed all his earnings with no payments to the group partnership for the use of the rooms. The partnership on the other hand continued to pay the 24/7 watchman from our joint account. Some years later, very sad to relate, Simeon, still in the flower of his manhood, died in an explosion in Lebanon. It was a loss I felt very deeply for a long time.

Among the items we purchased in Leeds was a large autoclave machine. An expert technician was sent to Kumasi from Leeds to install it. I arranged for a theatre technician in Korle Bu to come to Kumasi to be instructed on its regular maintenance. We also recruited a theatre sister of my choice from KAH. Mrs Caesar, a senior nurse at KAH, was appointed as Matron of the Bomso Clinic. Mr Sotomey, a very senior and highly regarded lawyer/ solicitor accepted our invitation to be the solicitor for the Bomso partnership group after the death of Mr Frank Mensah Bonsu. Mr Boakye, a classmate of Dr Appiah's at Prempeh College, and now the Financial Controller at Mim Timber Company in Brong Ahafo, was appointed the Financial Adviser to the Bomso partnership group on a part-time basis. Other key appointments were Mr Asoku (Radiographer at KAH) as a part-time radiographer; Mr Amoah (an experienced and skilled Nurse/Anaesthetist at KAH) as a part-time Anaesthetist. A Laboratory technician at KNUST Hospital was also recruited on a part-time basis. This completed our list of key personnel. We succeeded in renting a lovely newly completed bungalow house on nearby land very close to the clinic, for Dr Andan, who was still at the Police Hospital in Accra, but expected to join us very soon in Kumasi. Mr Wuaku, one of our well-wishers, was our landlord. We partially furnished the bungalow as we waited for Dr Andan's arrival. The dream Bomso Clinic was ready to take off. With everything now in place, I set my retiring date from the MOH as 31st December 1981. I would commence work at Bomso Clinic on 2nd January 1982, the day after New Year's Day. Rawlings staged his second coup d'état on the 31st December 1981.

I commenced clinical work at Bomso clinic on 2nd January 1982. On that day, I conducted my first delivery; I delivered Mrs Gyamfi of a baby boy. For quite some time, Dr Andan had not made a move to join us in Kumasi, and Dr Appiah and I were getting restive and anxious about his full commitment. We indeed nearly lost him to national politics. Quite unknown to us, he had been approached by Mr Imoru Egala, the king-maker of a major political party, to stand as their candidate for the forth-coming Presidential election. Andani was a royal from Tamale, and the party wanted a Northerner as their candidate. Andani decided to fly from Accra to Tamale and seek advice from his royal and ethnic advisers. This delay would prove too long for Mr Egala. While waiting at the airport to board the plane to Tamale, a radio news announcement came on the air to say that Mr Limann, a fellow Northerner, had been chosen as the candidate to stand for the Presidential election by the party. Andani aborted his trip to Tamale forthwith. A long time later, Andani at last came to join us at Bomso Clinic; the Bomso team was now in full operation. It proved to be a ground-breaking success. A little aside here for the records. Both Dr Appiah's wife and Yolande had met – she was a primary school teacher with no professional interest in the clinic. Yolande on the other hand was keen to see it as a place of excellence, although she had no desire to work there. Early on in the planning stage she raised the question of a kitchen and patients' diet. Since Dr Appiah was the specialist whose medical patients would benefit most from a proper diet in line with their medical care, she sought my permission to mention this to him. He dismissed the idea out of hand and responded that the patients would bring their own food from home! There it ended, but after subsequent events she told me that it was then she lost all interest and hope that Bomso Clinic would be a flagship one as she knew I wanted it to be. Dr Appiah was more interested in a mortuary, Yolande thought that this was because of its money-making propensity. She never approved of this partner and gave me several cogent reasons why she thought joining him was a bad fit. Was she right? And was she once again being prescient?

Dr Appiah handled all paediatric and general medical cases; Dr Andan dealt with all surgical cases; and I attended to all gynaecological and obstetrical cases. Our X-ray facilities enabled me to investigate fully cases of infertility and plan their appropriate management. A high clinical standard was aimed at and set up, we cooperated well together, and we held monthly meetings which I chaired regularly as the most senior professional. We remained united and did not condone or encourage divisive forces, against which Mr Mensah Bonsu had advised us. As the first such practice in the whole country, we attained an enviable status. Almost half our income was generated from my gynaecological and obstetrical section of the practice. As an obstetrician, I often had to work unsociable hours in attending to patients in labour, some of whom ended up in emergency Caesarean section operation. I formulated a scheme whereby the theatre staff and anaesthetist received extra remuneration for working during unsociable hours. They found the scheme attractive. Therein lies the essence of private practice. I suggested at a meeting to my two partners and Financial Advisor that since my unsociable working hours contributed generously to our income this should be reflected in my income. I was over-ruled (two to one) on more than one occasion. As unfair as this clearly was, we were all to draw the same salary, irrespective of input or time! I, however, did not allow this to influence my work ethic in any way nor my relationship with my partners. We worked happily together till certain events unfolded.

I promoted and encouraged intellectual activity. Dr Felix Konotey-Ahulu, the renowned Sickle-cell Physician resident in London, paid a brief visit home to give some lectures at Korle-Bu. I invited him to pay a day's visit to Kumasi to give an update lecture on his speciality (Sickle cell disease) at KAH. Mr Gyamfy assisted in providing transport for the return trip from Accra to Kumasi. Bomso Clinic paid Felix an honorarium fee for the stimulating lecture. In 1983, I went to England for the RCOG

Congress; paid for by sponsors I had succeeded in getting on my soliciting rounds. On my return, I purchased books (Recent Advances in Surgery, and Recent Advances in Paediatrics and Medicine) from our joint funds in London for my colleagues. This way, I reckoned, we could keep abreast of current knowledge in our respective fields. My link with Korle Bu was kept and maintained when I was appointed by the GMA as their inspector in Obstetrics and Gynaecology in 1983, which entailed observing the final year examinations on their behalf to ensure that the expected standard was achieved. We held a Christmas party at the end of the year to which all our well-wishers were invited.

My patients covered a wide socioeconomic range. A little anecdote here is worth narrating. I finished my outpatient clinic consultation early one afternoon, went home for lunch and was returning to the clinic to start a quasi-emergency Caesarean section at 4 pm (before the electricity could go off unexpectedly as it not infrequently did). As I approached the Bomso Clinic junction to turn right, I noticed a convoy of cars, headed by a police car, coming from the opposite direction. The convoy turned onto the Bomso Clinic road before I did. When I arrived at the clinic, I noticed that the cars in the convoy had parked at the clinic car park. It was the Asantehene's (Nana Opoku Ware II) convoy of cars. Hours earlier, I had decided to perform a Caesarean section on his daughter who was my patient. She had apparently gone home to prepare and return for the operation, at the same time informing her father about the surgery. He was attending a function at the time at Effiduase, which he decided to leave to come to see his daughter before the operation. I took Nana to my consulting room and explained to him the indication for the urgent surgery. It was a most engaging meeting and he felt fully reassured. There was no doubt that he was very fond of his daughter and concerned for her wellbeing. I went ahead and delivered his grandchild, which was not without its drama! A few days later, the Queen Mother came to donate a large package of provisions to the hospital nursing staff (it was a time when the country was plagued with scarcity of essential food items). This generous act was very much appreciated by the staff.

The hiatus in my transition from KAH to Bomso Clinic needs to be related. It covered significant developments at KAH and the subsequent history of the institution. My deputy as head of the department of

OB/GY was Dr Martey. He was the natural choice to succeed me. He was a competent gynaecologist who adopted a philosophy similar to mine in addressing our local problems innovatively. A few weeks after my departure, Dr Martey organized a memorable departmental farewell party in my honour at the hospital. It was chaired by Dr Doris Hayfron Benjamin, the Regional Chief Medical Officer. Dr Martey in a moving tribute acknowledged my achievements and contributions to the department.

These memoirs would be incomplete without relating the genesis of the Kumasi Medical School, which started from humble beginnings with many teething problems. It is an exercise similar to the one I had done for the Medical School in Accra, at both of which I was a by-stander with a ring-side view. The Korle Bu Teaching Medical School had been established as our premiere medical school and had set a high standard in teaching undergraduates. Suddenly one day in a speech he was delivering, General Acheampong, Head of State announced that a medical school was to be established at Kumasi KNUST immediately with KAH as the Teaching Hospital. Almost everyone was taken by surprise. There had been a growing feeling for an increase in the number of trained doctors; Korle Bu had been producing about 50 a year.

My informed feeling, shared by others of my ilk, was that there was one of two options to adopt in solving the problem. KBTH could easily double its intake of preclinical students at a little extra cost. It was not easy recruiting preclinical teaching staff. KAH was, in my view, relatively poor in standard as a Teaching Hospital. There were the major departments of General Surgery, General Medicine, OB/GY and Paediatrics. The department of surgery needed to be shored up with subspecialities of Orthopaedics, Urology and Neurosurgery to start with. In like manner, the Department of General Medicine needed considerable upgrading with a number of subspecialities. A percentage of the money could be spent on converting KAH into a reputable teaching hospital. It would also serve the dual purpose of being a centre of excellence for the northern sector of the country. After completing the preclinical courses at Korle-Bu, there would be two options: half of the preclinical graduates would be sent to the newly upgraded KAH for their entire clinical course, at the end of which they would take the final MB, ChB (Ghana) examination. Alternatively, in the second option, all the students would rotate in both KBTH and the upgraded KAH (now KATH) and then take their final MB, ChB examination. With this scheme in operation, if in the future there was a need for more doctors, KNUST could then start its own preclinical course for the increased number of preclinical students. This scheme, I believe, had merit on all fronts.

General Acheampong's announcement constituted a decree which had to be followed forthwith. Professor Laing, the brilliant Pathologist, was appointed as the Foundation Dean of the Medical school. Professor Laing, a Dundee graduate and an excellent scholar, was the first Ghanaian to train and qualify as a Pathologist who also studied and qualified as a lawyer. Charismatic and outgoing, he always enjoyed his bottle of beer. Laing set about the task of recruiting the staff of the Medical School. Dr Sydney Adadevoh and Dr Emmanuel Asiedu, in my department, were appointed lecturers in OB/GY. To my great surprise, Dr Arthur Dadzie, trained and at that time also domiciled in West Germany, was appointed to the Foundation chair in OB/GY. Dr Dadzie had never practised in Ghana nor any tropical country before, a factor, I believed, was obligatory in our speciality. As head of the department, I created a professorial unit to be headed by Dr Arthur Dadzie. This unit with Drs Adadevoh and Asiedu would constitute the teaching unit. In addition, we had the pre-existing other three units headed by Drs Martey, Djan and myself. Dr Arthur Dadzie had been my classmate in Achimota up to O levels in 1949. Although my arrangements with Bomso Clinic were well underway, I had not at this stage officially or otherwise communicated anything about my future plans to the authorities. I was surprised that the Dean at no time approached me to discuss with me any offers or possible role I could play in the planning of the teaching side of the department, or changes which would have to be effected. I had irrefutable clinical, administrative and academic credentials and was then an acknowledged external examiner at KBTH. Sad to relate, but relate it must be. The Foundation Professor was found to be clinically incompetent and deficient in basic OB/GY knowledge (the details of this are embarrassing and not appropriate to narrate here). He was soon fired on technically legal grounds. I have always held Professor

Laing, the Dean, in high esteem, but in his choice of Dr Arthur Dadzie as the Foundation Professor in OB/GY, he exhibited very poor judgement, in my view. There was a field of choice.

After this, the Kumasi Medical School later overcame its considerable early teething problems, not without cost to the pioneering students. The school has now flowered into a major teaching institution and as a serious rival to KBTH as the finest medical school in the country. Dr Martey and Dr Adadevoh later headed the professorial units. They both made great contributions not only to the training of undergraduate students, but also postgraduate students.

After the long interlude on Bomso Clinic and KATH, I now return to the family story. I returned from London to Kumasi in 1984 after successfully procuring schools in London for Brian and Neil. I returned to a dwindled family of three now (Brian, Dugald and me). There were no complaints about the watchman nor the house-keeper. Brian was now prepared and packed to travel to London. I drove him, with Dugald, to Accra from where he boarded his flight to London to join the family there. Dugald remained with me in Kumasi until the reopening of the GIS in September when I drove him to Accra. I stayed with him at the Does for two days to see him properly settled before returning to Kumasi. Dugald appeared to be comfortable in his new environment. Now back in Kumasi, I was now alone in the large empty house. A very strange feeling indeed!

I kept in touch with Dugald regularly by driving to Accra on visits or through Nahim, a nephew of Mr Paul Sagoe, my close friend. Nahim was a young emerging businessman in his 30s, of Lebanese/Ghanaian parentage. He made frequent visits to Accra and always availed himself for any messages or parcels for Dugald. Nahim and his newly married wife hosted me and Dugald to a couple of Saturday lunches when he was in Kumasi during the school holiday period. I looked after Nahim's wife, a Pharmacist, and delivered their first baby, a girl. Nahim and I remained in close touch until my days in the diaspora.

In Dugald's early days at GIS, he was dropped at school by Mrs Doe. They discovered early that Dr Blankson, who lived fairly close-by, had a son who was also a GIS student and who was taken to school daily. She then arranged for Dugald to be taken with Dr Blankson's son. It reduced the burden on her greatly and was a relief to us all. Dr Blankson was a Physician specialist in private practice.

Not very long after Dugald joined the Doe family, they also had a major down-sizing of their family. Kwashivie travelled to Egypt and from there managed to obtain a job as a gynaecologist in Saudi Arabia with their Ministry of Health in Jeddah. Setor had gained admission to KNUST to commence a course in Land Economy. Senam was proceeding to Southampton in England to do a degree course in Biochemistry. I had earlier, at the request of Mrs Doe, succeeded in securing admission for Senam in the KNUST Medical School. I had to cancel her placement. Events were moving fast, and there was an opportunity for mutual family support. Although not entirely necessary, I was in the position to be in loco parentis for Setor in Kumasi.

Brian arrived safely in London and joined the London Agble family. Yolande had got a flat at Park Royal. Brian and Neil were enrolled at Twyford Anglican School in Ealing; they started sixth form classes in Science. The best news from the school's Headmaster, Mr Reeves, was that they were both exempted from paying any school fees, thus one major financial commitment was ruled out for us. I was over the moon when I received the news in Kumasi. Ronald also got enrolled into an Anglican school in Ealing. Yolande enrolled with a Nursing Agency which recruited nurses for various hospitals in London. Through the agency, Yolande obtained jobs to earn enough to pay their flat rental and to live on. She was still looking for a flat with more rooms to accommodate the four of them adequately, and Dugald and myself when we went for a visit. Arrangements for taking a mortgage on a property fell through. One day, Yolande received a call from the Nursing Agency manager. She informed Yolande about a job she was not sure Yolande would find suitable and rewarding, but all the same, Yolande should be aware of this vacancy. It was the post of a warden of a home for retired people who lived in their own apartments in the building. The pay was not particularly rewarding, but there were perks and advantages: centrally sited, good residential area, well served by trains and buses, near enough to both schools for the three boys, best of all an almost new, partially furnished apartment consisting of three bedrooms, bathroom and toilet, Rent free! Yolande was delighted by the place, expressed her interest and was offered the post of warden at

Mayo Court. In her own words, 'it was like a gift from heaven' in answer to her prayers. The job as warden was not very demanding: do a twice daily check by personally calling on them, deal with any problems the residents encountered, assist in making doctors' appointments as needed, basic first aid when required, inspect the hallways and fire exits and doors, and oversee the cleaner who maintained the common areas The best part of the job undoubtedly was the really nice and spacious flat. Comfortable enough for the entire family of six. The schools were conveniently within easy reach. Yolande could judiciously engage herself in some agency nursing as well. She secured a regular agency job at the Hammersmith Hospital oncology unit night shift. She added on other duties if time permitted. Brian and Neil covered for her if she was not around at Mayo Court. The job was tailormade for her and she enjoyed her role as warden and association with the residents. She shared a mutual respect with her manager/boss.

Yolande kept me regularly informed about the positive and cheerful developments. If she heard of anyone going to Kumasi at London Heathrow airport, and willing to take along a small parcel, she would send us one, often with some British journals for me and knickknacks for Dugie. The delicatessen items were highly appreciated in those days of very severe shortages of anything considered luxury in Ghana. Because of my busy clinical work at Bomso Clinic, I was far from lonely. I held an outpatient clinic every day, except on my fixed operating days, once a week. I performed all my elective cases on the fixed day, starting in the morning and finishing about 1.00pm. I followed up with performing hysterosalpingograms (HSG) in the X-ray unit with the Radiographer, Mr Asoku. Because of my interest in the management of infertility, patients were attracted from far and wide to Bomso Clinic. (A Liberian lady travelled all the way from Monrovia to see me.) I, however, discontinued my clinical interest in repairing vesico-vaginal fistulae. Clinical work at Bomso Clinic proved to me to be satisfying and most fulfilling.

At the social and sporting level, I carried on as before. As a member of three tennis clubs, I patronized them all, depending on the day and other factors. My housekeeper was an Ewe girl and knew what my favourite dishes were; she was a very good cook.

With the approach of the end of the academic year in June, I had to make plans to travel with Dugald to London to spend the summer holidays with the rest of the family. Dugald had a successful year at GIS, repeating the third year as was scheduled for him. Yolande asked me to bring along with me some paintings to be given as gifts to Mr Reeves (the Headmaster at Twyford C of E school) and also the Reverend Minister who had placed Brian and Neil at the school. I purchased the oil paintings of Ghanaian scenery by the artist at Opoku Ware. We had acquired some of his work ourselves, and admired them. My trip to London was my annual leave, an entitlement. As a gynaecologist, however, I found it always incumbent upon me to find a specialist locum who would attend to my obstetric patients in my absence, particularly so when they were in labour or developed any complication in pregnancy. This obligation did not apply to my other two partners. Nevertheless, we all remained on the same salary. During my absence, brief though it was, I relied on Drs David Asiedu and Sydney Adadevoh, both gynaecologists at KAH. They were not only colleagues, but friends as well; the locum work would provide some extra income for them too.

Dr David Asiedu, son of a previous Parliament Speaker, hailed from Larteh. He trained in continental Europe as a doctor, returned home to Ghana before going to England to train and qualify as a gynaecologist, with the MRCOG. He came to KAH and was an assistant in my unit in my last year at KAH. With his experience, and friendly and affable, but quiet nature, it was helpful of him to provide cover for me whenever I had to travel outside Kumasi; he was always willing to do so. His wife Larissa is Jamaican, they met in England. Our family friendship was to come into play during our years in the diaspora and later on our final return home.

Dr Sydney Adadevoh came to the Kumasi scene in 1976. He had trained and qualified as a doctor and then as a gynaecologist in West Germany. After a long telephone discussion with Dr Grant, the Deputy Director of Medical Services, Sydney was posted to Kumasi (departmental heads had some clout on postings to their departments) to join my department in KAH. His wife Chloris, of striking beauty and a trained Dentist, was also an Ewe. Sydney worked in my unit for a couple of years. With the establishment of the Medical School, he was one of the first to be appointed a lecturer in OB/GY. As with David Asiedu, the Adadevoh family got on well with my family and became close family friends. I had no hesitation in asking Sydney to provide cover for me at Bomso Clinic when the need arose. Sydney rose in status later to head the department and as Professor he made a great contribution to both undergraduate and postgraduate teaching of OB/GY in Kumasi. Now retired, he is prominent on the international scene in the prevention of carcinoma of the cervix and also Family Planning. Chloris is aware of the fact that I rate her Ewe culinary skill highly, therefore never misses any opportunity to gratify my taste buds however busy she may be. Sydney and Chloris are treasured friends.

I travelled with Dugald to London to join the rest of the Agble family at Mayo Court. The Mayo Court building, a splendid red-brick structure, with its own model car park, was very well located. With its spacious rooms, I realized how lucky Yolande was in obtaining the post of warden there. She did not seem to be unduly stressed doing the extra agency nursing shifts at Hammersmith Hospital. It generated much needed extra income. All three boys also earned some income by doing some part-time work in their free time. Brian and Neil worked at a McDonald's, and young Ronald, aged nine, did early morning newspaper delivery rounds before leaving for school. The work ethic was inculcated in all of them early in life. Even Dugald, on this current short visit, did some manual vacation job.

At the time of our arrival, Twyford School had not yet gone on their summer holidays. It was therefore appropriate for me to go to the school and meet Mr Reeves, the Headmaster, and make a gift presentation. I went to the school in the morning, arriving before the school assembly, carrying along with me the oil paintings I had brought. Mr Reeves received me very warmly in his office, called around some of the teachers and introduced me very graciously to them. He expressed his great satisfaction with Brian and Neil, not only on their academic work, but also on their general deportment and sense of responsibility. This was not only verbal commendations to please their father; he had already appointed Neil as Head Boy and Brian as senior Prefect of the school for the following year. I felt great pleasure and a sense of pride in listening to the report on my two sons in their first year at Twyford School. It was also a tribute to the level of educational discipline and sense of responsibility inculcated in them in Prempeh College in Ghana.

I presented two paintings personally to Mr Reeves and a couple to the school. The Headmaster appeared genuinely pleased with the gifts. After introducing me to some of his staff, he invited me to join him at the school assembly where he seated me on the dais, next to him. At the assembly, Mr Reeves introduced me enthusiastically, after which I made a brief reply and presentation of my gift of paintings to the school. During my conversation with Mr Reeves in his office, he informed me that the Reverend Father in Southwark, who had placed my sons in Twyford C of E school, had died suddenly from a massive heart attack, barely a few months after our interview with him in the preceding year of 1984. I had brought some wooden carvings as a gift for him as well. He had looked very healthy when we met him in 1984 when he did a quite unforgettable favour and act of more than kindness at a very critical juncture in the future of Brian and Neil. It is one of the events on life's journey which we shall never forget, it laid the foundation for their future.

I was in London at the right time for the Wimbledon Tennis Championship when a young 17 year-old blond, blue-eyed German emerged on the tennis scene. Ivan Lendl, a dour looking Czech, once again found the Wimbledon Men's trophy eluded him – he had won every other major championship, but this.

A highlight of this London trip was a surprise birthday party for me. Yolande, with the assistance and collusion of the boys had organized a party to which I was not at all privy. Included among the modest number of guests was Mr Trevor McDonald, a Trinidadian who was a contemporary of Yolande's at their respective Girls' and Boys' secondary schools in San Fernando, Trinidad. He was a prominent news announcer on the TV with both the BBC and ITV, one of the very earliest of colour. He climbed up the ladder and later earned a Knighthood.

At the end of the summer holidays, I returned home to Ghana with Dugald after a refreshing family reunion. I felt a genuine sense of relief, pride and pleasure all rolled into one at the way things had turned out for all our sons, education-wise. After all, we were more or less taking a chance in uncharted waters a year previously. Ronald was doing equally well in school. I returned to Bomso Clinic full of zest. I brought along a couple books on Recent Advances in Surgery and in Medicine and Paediatrics for my colleagues. I also brought a large consignment of disposable syringes and needles which I had obtained in London at no cost to the clinic. Bomso Clinic benefited immensely from my summer sojourn.

Mrs Ruth Doe, with whom Dugald had stayed in his first year in Accra, decided to join her husband in Jeddah, Saudi Arabia. I therefore had to look for new accommodation for him. Yolande and I had a discussion with Kwesi and Jackie Zwennes (Jackie is a fellow Trinidadian) very good friends, with whom, even though they lived in Accra, we still maintained a close friendship, especially our children. They kindly agreed to accept Dugald as Nana, their son, was also a GIS student, making the interminably long and difficult trip twice daily between McCarthy Hill and Accra. Hopefully, an added child would not prove too burdensome for them. Jackie and Kwesi had met in London when they were both law students. They married and returned to Ghana, where they settled in Accra, establishing a law firm of considerable repute. Kwesi was an old Achimotan and my contemporary, his sister Victoria had also been my classmate at the UCGC; the Zwenneses had been family friends for some decades, it was therefore natural to approach them at this time of great need.

I drove up from Kumasi to Accra with Dugald and left him under the care of the Zwennes family. He stayed with them for one academic year after which he had to leave as Nana had transferred from GIS to Achimota boarding school, necessitating Dugald's change of abode. Getting a third abode would not be easy, but providence came to our aid in the persons of Yaw and Gwen Agyarko. Mrs Gwen Agyarko, a British Guianese, met her husband Yaw, in England, where they married and came to Ghana. An Akwapim from Mampong, Yaw was a respectable gentleman, well and quietly spoken, who was a very successful chartered accountant. Always smartly dressed, whether in western suits or native attire, he made a very favourable impression on those who met him. Gwen, was truly a jacklyn of all trades. A nurse by profession who trained first as a teacher, was a florist providing wedding bouquets, as well as funeral corsages and decorations, an excellent cook of both local and international cuisine and hostess, had been Yolande's friend for many years, both sharing a real love for and interest in the brownies and girl guide movements. They lived at the airport residential area in a large, beautifully designed house with well landscaped and manicured gardens at the front and back. We had been guests in their home on a number of occasions before they readily and without hesitation offered to have Dugald stay with them until the completion of his O levels at GIS. He would have a room to himself and be treated as a member of their family. This being the third abode in Accra for a young teenager, a sensitive stage, I felt reassured and a huge sense of relief.

In Kumasi, there was no significant change in my social and sporting life. My friends, such as the Tettehs and the Appiahs (Joe and Peggy), entertained me to the odd dinner. Mr Gyamfi and Mr Paul Sagoe were anxious to see to any of my needs as was my brother Bill. I had now acquired some VHS videos which I watched at my leisure.

I remained in good health except for an episode of high fever. One morning, I suddenly felt feverish and unwell.

I did not allow this to deter me from going to Bomso Clinic for my routine outpatient consultations. With the passing hours, I felt weaker and more feverish, with my temperature peaking at 102 degrees Fahrenheit; anti-malarial medication proved refractory. I aborted my consultation and went straight home to rest and try some alternative medication. I had been very ill, but recovered quite quickly after about two days. Dugald came from Accra to see how I was faring (I don't know how he found out). He arrived when I was starting to recover and was quite relieved. He returned to Accra the following day, alone and lonely; it was touching.

My clinical practice flourished. The obstetric work consisted of antenatal care and the management of labour; the midwives conducted normal deliveries; operative deliveries such as Caesarean sections, instrumental vaginal deliveries (forceps and Ventouse) and breech vaginal deliveries were done by myself. Termination of pregnancy on social grounds, a major source of income for many doctors in private practice in the country, was not part of my practice. A great part of my gynaecological practice was the investigation and management of infertility cases. Tubal and peritoneal factors were the major causes of infertility. Tubal surgery followed by hydrotubation was the accepted management of this at the time. Tubal insufflation with carbon dioxide gas proved beneficial to some patients. Only very few centres worldwide had embarked on IVF (In Vitro Fertilisation) programmes, following in the footsteps of Edwards and Steptoe. I was fully abreast of the literature and practice in the management of tubal and peritoneal factors for infertility. Indeed, during my London sojourn in 1985, I went to Hammersmith Hospital to observe Professor Winston (now Lord Winston), one of the leading authorities on this condition in the operating theatre. I had visited Bourn Hall in 1980 and met Drs Edwards and Steptoe at work. The success rate worldwide in the management of tubal and peritoneal factors was not high. With the limiting pathological factors, such moderate successes I had were greatly satisfying. Patients were attracted from far and wide. I always complemented any ensuing pregnancy following surgery, just after the first trimester with a MacDonald cervical cerclage prophylactically because of the prevailing high incidence of pregnancy termination by D and C. Polycystic Ovarian Syndrome and endochrinological factors were uncommon as a cause of infertility. Myomectomy and total hysterectomy were routinely performed by me. Success in one's vocation, in my view, was more satisfying and worth much more than millions of pounds or dollars.

I went to Accra in 1986 as the Inspector in the final MB ChB examination in OB/GY on behalf of the GMC. During this visit a sad event began to unfold. Dr Andan, my surgical colleague, after a long period of separation from his first wife, got married a second time to a young attractive lady from his hometown of Tamale; she was a journalist. She was resident in Accra and paid frequent visits to her husband in Kumasi. Yolande and I met her and took a mutual liking to her; we had exchanged gifts with her. In 1985 I learnt that she was pregnant but was seriously ill, and jaundiced. I went over immediately to see her at the private clinic where she had been admitted. I was alarmed by her condition; I sent an SOS message to Dr Andan in Kumasi to come to Accra immediately. He responded and came to Accra without delay. A day later, sickle cell crisis took its toll of Andani's young wife. It was a great shock and tragedy from which Andani never fully recovered. I returned to Kumasi, but travelled to Accra at a later date for the funeral. Andani was left with the three young children from his first marriage: David, Alhassan and Mariama.

During this decade, I made numerous trips to Accra for educational, business, or family reasons. The educational trips were usually to fulfil examination commitments in Korle-Bu. The Medical School provided me with accommodation initially at the Ambassador Hotel when it was in its prime, or at the Medical School guest-house. On these visits, I embraced the opportunity to socialise with friends both in the Oby/Gynae group and other disciplines. Most are of blessed memory now and I pay tribute to them.

On my private or family trips, I stayed in hotels or with Mr Ogbarmey-Tetteh of blessed memory. I was always generously hosted. The Accra trips also provided the opportunity to visit my sister, who never failed to entertain me with my favourite dishes.

My return journeys to Kumasi were regularly punctuated at the GIHOC Pharmaceutical factory at Dome, an Accra suburb; my friend Blukoo-Allotey was the Managing Director of the GIHOC factory. My stop-over visits usually lasted about half an hour; whenever there was a need, I purchased a quantity of some of their products for Bomso Clinic.

My long association with the OB/GY department during a historic period compels me now to give my personal impression of the department. The department was headed by the Foundation Professor Bentsi-Enchill, with Kofi Newman and Ata Ampofo as lecturers; Drs KK Korsah and Tara Ghosh were Senior Specialists in the MOH. They were joined later by a younger generation which included Drs Kluffio, Wilson and Duffour. Prof Bentsi-Enchill ran the department with great emphasis, and commendably so, on teaching; he and his team of teachers deserve to be given credit for producing doctors who were well grounded in OB/GY. Many of their products went abroad later to specialize in this speciality with great success and distinction. The great emphasis on teaching, in my view, derailed some attention to simple research and publications in international journals. Ibadan in Nigeria and Kingston in Jamaica blazed the trail in the virgin territory of Tropical Obstetrics and Gynaecology. It is my opinion that this opportunity was sadly neglected and missed; the research and publication culture was not initiated or inculcated. In Dr Tara Ghosh, the department had, in my view, perhaps unarguably the most outstanding gynaecological surgeon in the sub-region. An Indian from Calcutta, he came to Ghana in the early 1960s. I was privileged to be his first MO in Korle-Bu in 1961. He was a highly skilled, innovative and daring surgeon who was avant-garde in gynaecological and obstetrical surgery. He was a confirmed bachelor, married to the OB/GY journals in his pursuit of excellence. Although I made serious efforts to keep abreast of current literature, I always discovered on my visits to his bungalow in Korle Bu that I was far behind. His dedication to duty and hardworking ethos, in my view, merited the grant of Ghanaian citizenship and an appropriate place of abode without any solicitation by him. He finally left Ghana and returned home to Calcutta where he passed away in the 1990s. He deserves to be in the Korle Bu Hall of Fame.

In the course of human history some years turn out to be eventful and prominent; the year 1978 was my 'annus mirabilis'.

The 1986 year would unfold to be the year of a momentous decision.

Our nuclear family had been split under three different roofs in three different locations as chronicled already. Brian and Neil were performing well academically as sixth formers, and preparing to sit for their A level examinations.

Dr Tara Ghosh

They were expected to progress to tertiary education: Brian wanted to pursue a career in medicine like his father; Neil was inclined towards a career in aviation as a pilot; Ronald was performing well in school. Their various talents and gifts needed careful nurturing. Yolande supplemented her income at Mayo Court by doing Agency nursing assignments; her working hours were taxing. Although my earnings from Bomso Clinic were enough for a comfortable life in Kumasi, it was not adequate to meet the necessary educational needs of the boys in England. We reckoned that if I took a two-year sabbatical leave from Bomso Clinic then go to England and do some work, I could save enough money to put into a savings account for their tertiary education. A two-year period with the family was desirable in many ways; it would in a way ameliorate the sacrifice we had embarked upon on behalf of our boys. I had to make a formal request to my partners for my release.

I did not expect my partners to be happy with my request for a sabbatical leave for very obvious reasons. I was responsible for generating a disproportionately high percentage of the income at Bomso Clinic. Although we had steadily paid a large percentage of the loan to NIB, we still had a substantial amount remaining. I would, of course, have to arrange for a locum gynaecologist to cover my sabbatical period. My singular immense contribution to the clinic could not be ignored in any way. I was responsible to a great extent in securing the loan from NIB and solely responsible for securing the collaterals from GCB for my partners. Simeon David, the Lebanese industrialist, responded to my personal appeal to have the theatre complex, laboratory and X-ray units completed and providing the attractive finish to my consulting room. He had done all that because of me, gratis. When the clinic became fully operational, it took Dr Andan more than a year to join us even though we had succeeded in getting a lovely bungalow for him on an adjacent plot. Not to mention Dr Appiah's commencing work at the clinic a full year before I did and pocketing all the proceeds.

In making my request, I emphasized my total commitment to Bomso Clinic and stated that it was not a ruse designed to run away from them. Indeed, I pointed out that we could all take turns in having sabbaticals, if they also wished to do so. One partner was very reluctant in granting my request. We held a final meeting at my home at which our solicitor/lawyer, Mr Simon Sotomey, and Mr Boakye, the Financial Director, were in attendance; it was an interminably long meeting. My partners finally granted me my request for a two-year sabbatical to my great relief. I reassured them all of my total commitment to Bomso Clinic, a fact requiring no repetition. Mr Sotomey, a legal luminary, known for speaking frankly, calling a spade a spade, whispered to me in our Ewe language as we were finishing off our glasses of beer that he was sure that I would stick to the agreement and not let them down; I concurred.

A momentous decision had been taken, I now had to arrange for an obstetrician to do a locum on a long term basis. I also had to start making preparations, domestic and otherwise for my sojourn.

Farewell party in my honour by the OB/GV Department,
KAH. Dr Hayfron Benjamin & Prof Martey

In looking for an obstetrician, I was lucky to learn that a young English lady would be available to do the locum for at least a year to start with. She and her equally young husband, a Gastroenterologist, had just been recruited from Britain to lecture in the Medical School. She had obtained the MRCOG a year before and had hardly any clinical duties at KATH, she could easily fit in her clinical work at Bomso Clinic. The couple lived on the KNUST campus which was conveniently very near to Bomso Clinic. Because of her apparent lack of clinical experience in tropical obstetrics and gynaecology, Dr Martey agreed to be brought on board for clinical advice and assistance if the need arose. Dr Martey had joined the Medical School, and was then the Professor and Head of the Department; he was my biological cousin. I discussed my case managements with the young gynaecologist and felt comfortable leaving my patients in her care. Dr Martey had been very helpful in my choice, after his assessment of her. All three partners engaged watchmen for our respective residences who were put on the Bomso Clinic payroll. Bomso Clinic did not have a vehicle for doing errands. I owned a car, an Opel Rekord (WR 1999). Rather than leaving it idle for two years, I offered this vehicle to Bomso Clinic for their use during my sabbatical years. My partners accepted this offer made in the spirit of furthering the interests of the clinic.

This was the time to inform my friends who had not been privy to my plans. Among these was the Tamakloe couple, Kofi and Martha. They were both lecturers in the Faculty of Architecture at KNUST. They both later attained Professorial status and lived in their own house, which was located almost directly across the road from Bomso Clinic. We shared a mutual family friendship and respect. In 1976, when transportation countrywide was a nightmare, Martha travelled from Kumasi to Peki in the Volta Region to mourn with me at my mother's funeral; a gesture not easily forgotten. We lost touch during our years in the diaspora.

My brother Bill had been privy to all my plans. After gaining the consent of my partners on my sabbatical, Bill and I travelled to Hohoe by car accompanied by Dugald and Lambert, my nephew, then a student at KNUST, studying architecture. We went to inspect the family property in Hohoe. On our return journey, we passed through Peki and Saisi (Agormenya). It was a pleasurable family trip which Dugald enjoyed – he was introduced to the lobsters at the Adome bridge stop-over, of which he became quite fond.

I was programmed to leave for London in July, but some good news precipitated an earlier departure date. Dr Felix Konotey Ahulu, after being briefed by Yolande on my sabbatical plans, succeeded in obtaining a locum consultant job for a period of three months at London's Central Middlesex Hospital. It had been arranged through Dr O'Sullivan, a senior consultant gynaecologist at the hospital; it was fortuitous and very timely. As I would realize later, such appointments for someone not working in the UK system and coming from abroad were indeed rare. Neil came on a surprise visit from London to assist me in packing and preparing to leave Kumasi; it proved to be a useful visit. I left Kumasi, confident that I would be back after two years of sabbatical leave.

THE BRITISH COUNCIL

During my student days in Aberdeen in the 1950s, the British Council (BC) as already narrated in the memoirs played a pivotal role in my extracurricular life. Little did I foresee that the BC would later again play a significant role in my life.

When Yolande and I arrived in Kumasi, we found that the BC had a regional office in Kumasi which was responsible for its activities in the northern half of the country. The office, housed in a two-storey building, was centrally located in Adum. The ground floor housed the library and the upper floor served as administrative offices. The Director, always a very senior British person, had British assistants, whose number varied from one to three at different times. The librarian and his assistant were Ghanaians. As the bibliophile I had always been, the library drew my attention. The books covered several subjects, but it was the medical books which interested me most. They acquired the series of ELBS medical books which I found a great resource. Prominent in my reading were the two major Sunday newspapers to which I had developed an addiction. Because I did not have enough time to complete reading the papers in the library, I sought and was granted special permission by Director after Director to take the two Sunday papers home on weekends (from midday Saturday to 8am Monday) and read leisurely. I believe I was the only recipient of this unique and singular privilege during all our years in Kumasi.

The BC Director, when Yolande and I arrived in Kumasi, was Mr Bruce Smith. Bruce, a true Scot, was a friendly and affable person. My

Aberdeen and Glasgow background quickly catalysed our relationship with his Scottish wife, Anne, and three young daughters – Jane, Fiona and Sheila. Our two families became firm friends. Quite early in our association, Yolande and I had to travel to Takoradi to collect some items we had ordered from Britain at the port; it would entail a four-day stay in Takoradi. Our two sons, Brian and Neil, were aged four and three years. Anne and Bruce without any prompting or solicitation straightaway offered to have our boys stay with them until we returned. We very much appreciated this act of true friendship. We enjoyed numerous evenings together; with different pursuits. Each BC Director served a three-year period in Kumasi.

In 1974, I decided to attend, for the first time, the triennial RCOG Congress due to be held that year in London. Mr Bruce Smith had been transferred to the BC London office. On learning about my forthcoming trip to London, he extended a very warm invitation to me to stay with them during my visit for as long as I wished. To add spice to the invitation, and entice me more, he said that colour TV had come to England and he was sure that I would tremendously enjoy watching on their colour TV the forthcoming Wimbledon Tennis Championship matches and also the FIFA World Cup football matches due to be held in West Germany. They would be broadcast worldwide on TV. This was a wonderful, most generous and friendly gesture. I accepted the offer with great gratitude. The Smiths welcomed me warmly on my arrival to their house, located at Denmark Hill in London. During the course of my stay there, they held a special dinner party in my honour. The invited guests included Professor Sey, then the Vice-Chancellor of the KNUST, who was on a visit to London. The Smiths were highly treasured family friends. Although we remained in mutual touch for several years, we later lost touch with each other.

Another Scot served with the BC in Kumasi in the early 1970s. The couple was Tom and Mary Aitken. Tom, with a toothbrush moustache, spoke with a typical Scottish accent. He served as an Adviser on Education in Kumasi after a similar role in Kenneth Kaunda's Zambia. A friendly and very sociable couple, they often entertained in holding parties in their Nhyiaeso bungalow. Tom organized a Burns party once at which Yolande and I were invited guests. Tom was also very active in the Rotary Club of Kumasi. He was a prominent guest at my 40th birthday party; he was erudite in proposing the toast to my health.

Mr David Howell succeeded Mr Bruce Smith as the Director of the BC in Kumasi. David, a quiet and gentle Englishman and a Cambridge product (Selwyn College), was then a bachelor. A friendship which started slowly grew and blossomed into one close to surrogate siblinghood. He resided in a lovely bungalow with a salubrious surrounding and well-manicured garden. As the Director, he had to entertain visitors from overseas from time to time. He had a cook/steward who served him. He enrolled me and Yolande to join him in the role of host and hostess on these social evenings. In this way, Yolande and I, in a way, became unofficial BC personnel; we enjoyed and cherished this role. When he had completed his three-year tour of duty and had to vacate his bungalow, we had only just moved into our newly built house. We invited him to stay with us at our home in his last remaining days; as he had seen this project from beginning to its conclusion, often having little picnics with Yolande and the boys on the lawn when it was being completed, it was indeed fitting that he should be our first guest.

In 1978, David, now married to Nancy, was the BC Director in Freetown, Sierra Leone. The West African College of Surgeons (WACS) of which I was a Fellow, had planned to hold its biennial Congress in Freetown. On learning about the Congress, David extended an invitation to me and Yolande to come and stay with them during the congress period. The invitation was irresistible. Yolande and I therefore flew to Freetown where we were met by him and chauffeur-driven to their home in the city, quite a distance from the airport. David and Nancy lived in a most elegant and attractive bungalow, befitting an ambassador, with verdant green, beautifully landscaped lawns. They were as always excellent hosts and we had a most enjoyable time with them sightseeing and other pursuits outside of congress hours. This further cemented our friendship. David then served as Director in Singapore and Australia in succession before finally returning to the London base. While in Australia, he was awarded an OBE, well deserved too. We stayed in touch and wherever we were, on arrival in London, our first outing was invariably with them – the West End plays and shows, restaurant trips, dining at our respective homes; they lived in South London. David also hosted us to lunch on a few occasions at the Oxbridge Club. They were regular guests at our London home in Ealing whenever there was an occasion to celebrate. In later years, Nancy's failing health precluded her joining us. Ronald sprang an unforgettable surprise on us on 15th August, 2008. Yolande and I had arrived in London from Accra on 11th August after a stressful period following the fire in our Accra residence. Ronald had succeeded in obtaining tickets for us to attend an opera performance at Glyndebourne, a most exclusive opera venue in Sussex. We were to meet Ronald at a specified time and place at Victoria train station to board a train to Brighton, and a coach from Brighton to Glyndebourne. To our delightful surprise and pleasure, Ronald came along with David! Such a lovely surprise, as we were not even given a hint of it. We had a marvellous evening at the opera, graced with a splendid dinner in the restaurant, Nether Wallop, during the intermission; the selection from the dinner menu had been done several weeks in advance, as is the tradition in order not to delay the performance unduly.

Not long after, Yolande and I left London for New York. News of David's failing health reached us in New York in 2009. Brian, our eldest son, and his family visited him in hospital a couple of times, as did Ronnie and Dugald. It was with deep sadness that Yolande and I received the news of his death from his brother, Keith, by a telephone call. I had never before spoken to Keith. Nancy, after a long illness had predeceased David some years ago. Our three sons in England (Drs Brian, Dugald and Ronald Agble) represented the Agble family at the funeral. David's loss is irreparable.

After the departure of David Howell as the Director of the BC in Kumasi, he was followed in the three-year tours in succession by Mr Nigel Ross, Mr Edmund Marsden and Miss Monica Smith. They all stayed in the same residential bungalow. Our close association with the BC continued undiminished; Yolande and I were frequent guests at British Council events: receptions, dinners, cocktails, lectures etc. Different cultural groups came on tours to give performances at various times. A theatre group which came to perform some plays included Miss Judi Dench. We were both on the sofa and I chatted with her for quite some time. This was a few years before I saw her in the film "The Browning Version" in which she played an excellent role as the wife of the Latin master (John Mills). It is one of my very favourite films of all time. Nigel, young and vivacious, and his wife Janet had a daughter, Karen, and son, Angus, around the same ages as our boys,= (Neil and Angus were great LEGO buddies), and attended the same school. They entertained us frequently and it was at one of their Saturday luncheons that I was introduced to the game of croquet on their lawn. Nigel and Janet were part of the group of six supporters who accompanied Mr Bob Barclay at the ceremony in 1977 when the OBE was conferred on him by Prince Charles. In 1983, Nigel was serving as Director of the BC in Leeds when Yolande and I paid them a visit. In 1999, Yolande and I, then based in Tabuk in Saudi Arabia, went on a cruise which took us to Cyprus. As the saying goes, "it is a small world" (piccolo mondo). Nigel and Janet were as delighted as we were to meet them in Cyprus. Nigel had retired from the BC and they had gone to settle there, in a most attractive house, perched on the top of a hill. They accorded us the warmest of welcomes on the day on which we visited them.

Mr Edmund Marsden followed Mr Ross as the Director in Kumasi. Tall, dynamic and bright, he impressed me as someone who was destined to attain heights, career-wise. Our relationship with the BC remained unchanged. At my request, he succeeded in obtaining for me a BC Travel Fellowship to attend the triennial RCOG Congress in 1980 held in Edinburgh, and also official visits to my alma mater hospitals in Leeds and Aberdeen. I remain to this day greatly indebted to the British Council and especially its branch in Kumasi and all the good and wonderful directors and staff for their magnanimous kindness to me, and by extension, my family.

The last BC Director in Kumasi before our departure on our long sojourn abroad was Miss Smith. Monica Smith, tall and with rounded features was a careerist. She extended to me and Yolande the same courtesies we had received from all her predecessors. A two-volume tome on Gynaecological Oncology had just been published in Britain; it was naturally quite expensive. On learning that I would like to have a copy of the books, she arranged for the BC to acquire the two-volume tome for me. This was at a time when the Ghana economy was in the doldrums and obtaining foreign currency to travel or purchase books was not at all easy. Some years later, in 2008, when I was no longer in clinical practice, I donated the two-volume books with other books to the library of the Ghana College of Physicians and Surgeons.

The BC had played an important role in my life during my student days in Aberdeen. In Kumasi, the Directors one after another, made priceless contributions to me and my family. Friendships which were formed blossomed in later years. It is an association I shall always cherish.

My brother Bill lived with his family at the Kwadaso Agricultural Research Station, where he was the Director of the Crops Research Unit. His wife, Dorma, was the Matron at KAH. They had five children; they were the twin sisters (Jemima and Patricia), Marilyn, and the two boys (Lambert and Kafui). Bill, with an MSc and PhD degrees from USA had specialized in Plant Genetics and Plant Breeding; he was the first Ghanaian Agricultural Scientist. His contributions in agricultural research to the nation was perhaps without equal at the time. The Research Institute at Nyankpala in the Savannah region was his brainchild. He conceived the idea and with generous assistance from the West German government, it came to fruition; his dream was achieved. He forged the post-graduate education and training of many Ghanaian agricultural scientists; his contributions in his field were manifold. It still remains a puzzle to me that the Ghana Academy of Arts and Science has not enrolled him as a Fellow. When we moved from Danyame to Nhyiaeso, Yolande and I regularly hosted Christmas lunch for the joint family while Bill and Dorma did the same on Boxing Day. From 1976 onwards, both Agble families went to Peki for an Easter family reunion; this went on until our years in the diaspora.

Some of my Ghanaian friends and associates were the following: Messrs John Drah, Francis Morny, Jacob Wuaku, Ellis Aryitey, Atiase and Drs Kofi Tagboto and Amengor. Although I was not a regular church attendant, I attended the Ewe Presbyterian Church services at Amakom on a number of occasions. Indeed, the Pastor, Reverend Minister Peer, a Swiss, asked me to read the lesson once; it was a passage from the Old Testament (OT). As all Ewes know, the Ewe translation of the OT is not easy to articulate properly; nevertheless, I think I acquitted myself creditably. A few notes on the gentlemen above are germane.

Mr John Drah, hailing from Peki, had been a store assistant to my father in Hohoe in the 1940s, after which he moved to Accra and later

Kumasi where he was the storekeeper for the trading firm S D Karam, traders in textile goods. He seemed to be doing well. I regarded him as a distant cousin.

Mr Jacob Wuaku, also from Peki, had worked with the hardware and building materials company of Paterson and Zochonis (PZ) for a number of years before setting up his own store of building materials. Jacob, light complexioned with a lip-wide bushy moustache, always dressed in white shirt and shorts, was a hardworking and deeply religious gentleman; he was a successful trader in his field, he was of immense help when we were building Kplomdedie. On one occasion when Yolande and I had to spend a few days in Accra when Papa was ill, he loaned us his brand new red Austin Mini car. We shared a very close association until he passed away; I was abroad at the time.

Mr Francis Morny, from Gbi Klejoe, had been known to our family in Hohoe since the 1930s. His father was a storekeeper with the Swiss Trading firm of UTC (Union Trading Company). Francis attended Mfantsipim Secondary School and obtained the Cambridge School Leaving O Level Certificate in the early 40s; he was probably the first person from the Gbi area to attain that level of education. After a brief period as a junior civil servant in the department of Education, he went to Britain for further studies. He studied Optometry and qualified as an Optician. With our Hohoe background, he was a close associate in Kumasi; he was the closest friend of my brother Bill, who, when he was not at work, could be found in Francis' shop on Harper Road. He was a prominent member of the Amakom EP Church.

I first met Dr Kofi Tagboto in 1961 when I arrived in Kumasi as an MO in Kumasi Central Hospital (now KATH). Kofi had just left government service to commence work in private practice as a GP. On my return to Kumasi in 1965, Dr Tagboto was very well established as a GP and had as a partner my very close friend, Dr Emmanuel Asare. An old Achimotan hailing from Kpando in the Volta Region, and several years my senior, he was probably the first medical doctor from that part of the country. He attained an iconic image in the region as a brilliant scholar in his school days in Achimota. It was as a keen tennis player at the Kumasi Tennis Club that our association crystalized. Dr Amengor also joined him as a partner later.

I had known Dr Ebenezer Amengor, who hails from Peki, for a long time, dating back from our school days in Hohoe EP Senior School where he was two years my senior. After his secondary school education at Accra Academy, he went to West Germany where he trained and qualified as a doctor. On his return home he joined Drs Tagboto and Asare as a partner.

Mr Henry Atiase, also from Peki was a manager at the Guinness Brewery company. His wife Amewu was somewhat related to me. Amewu was the daughter of Ephraim Amu, the legendary musicologist. Her mother was the daughter of Mr Yao. Mr Yao, a cousin to my father, was also one of his closest friends. He was the Manager of the Presbyterian Books Depot, then a prestigious post and the first African to occupy that position. I met the Atiases for the first time in Kumasi. Some years later, when we lived in London, it was a delight to entertain Auntie Christie and Mr Amu to lunch.

Mr Ellis Aryittey, from Ada, was in the business of renting heavy vehicles for constructional work. He was a keen member of the Kumasi Tennis club.

Mr Kwabena Senyah did not fall into the tennis, medical profession, academia, nor the expatriate group of friends and associates. An Ashanti with the belying name of Senya, he did not fall into the Ewe group either. A self-made businessman, he was well built and very dark hued. He was introduced to me by Chris Adomako with whom he had been a student at St Augustine College. A close friendship which proved to be long-standing developed. As he lived in Nhyiaeso, we met frequently. During our years in the diaspora, he fell victim to an illness which greatly reduced his mobility and general health. We always made an effort to see him on our infrequent visits to Kumasi. He remained a true and loyal friend until he moved on.

Chapter 9
PRE-SAUDI LONDON

arrived in London after taking a gigantic step in leaving a flourishing and most satisfying OB/GY practice in Kumasi for a two-year sabbatical to unite with my family, and also for the education of our sons. The accommodation at Mayo Court was ideally sited and comfortable. On my arrival, Brian and Neil were still at Twyford School, preparing for their A levels, while Ronald was attending the Christ Church School in Ealing. Yolande performed her duties as warden at Mayo Court and her nurse Agency duties at Hammersmith Hospital. Dugald was attending the GIS in Accra and staying with the Agyarkos.

I commenced work soon after my arrival as a consultant gynaecologist at Central Middlesex Hospital. The locum was for a three-month period. The department functioned with three consultants and one Senior Registrar at the senior level. I can't recall the number of staff at junior registrar and houseman levels, but I had one junior registrar assigned to me. The outpatient clinic load was relatively light because my registrar was familiar with the case management of the consultant whose locum I was doing, he saw most of the routine cases and only referred a few cases to me. Gynaecology had now been transformed into subspecialities; two decades earlier a gynaecologist dealt with all the cases with which he was confronted. In the current milieu, three major subspecialities had emerged, namely Oncology, Urogynaecology and Gynaecological Endocrinology with Infertility. There were still general gynaecologists who were practising, and I belonged to this genre. Also emerging was the field of laparoscopy. Most gynaecological laparoscopists employed it as an investigative tool rather than in a major operative procedure. I belonged to the former category of gynaecologists. Low midline or paramedian abdominal incisions for laparotomy were gradually being abandoned in favour of the Pfannestiel incision for cosmetic reasons. Great changes had taken place in Obstetrics Ultrasound; originally invented by Ian Donald at Glasgow University, it was now firmly established in patient care and management. The most profound of the changes and advances was the monitoring of patients in labour with electronic cardio tomography (CTG). From its early beginning, it had become routine in the labour ward in Britain and other developed countries. Although I was aware of this technological innovation, I was not familiar with its use and interpretation. Practising in Ghana where it was not in use was a handicap; this lack of familiarity applied to all my contemporaries in Ghana. I quickly realized that I had to remedy this shortcoming if I was to be worth my weight as a consultant obstetrician, at home with the blood and thunder of operative obstetrics. I would need to adjust myself quickly to the demands of modern changes.

On my first day on-call for obstetrics, I went to the labour ward in the morning. It was necessary, I thought, to introduce myself to the medical team, see the layout of the labour ward and also review the cases in labour; a practice which I thought was mandatory. The Registrar on-call with me and midwives were surprised by this apparent intrusion. Very politely, the Registrar remarked that it was not necessary for me to review the cases; he would review them all and report to me any which merited my input or opinion; this was their normal practice; I could therefore go to the coffee-room and await his report; I obliged. And so it was that even on my on-call day I merely had to be available to take phone calls from my Registrar, to be briefed about patients in labour who might require Caesarean sections, which would be done by him after my approval! The onus of responsibility of reading and taking a decision on an abnormal CTG rested with the registrar, and was removed from me. On further reflection, I realized that the system had remained the same since my days at SJH in Leeds. Then I controlled the labour ward when on call, took decisions and phoned the consultant for just a nod of approval; no change had taken place in this respect.

In the first week of my locum, while I was on call, labour had to be terminated by Caesarean section in a case with an abnormal CTG tracing; the baby died after about five minutes (a perinatal death). It was mandatory on my part to write a detailed report on the cause of this perinatal death. With my background of being unfamiliar with abnormal CTGs, it was not an easy or pleasant exercise for me. I quickly set about erasing this deficiency. I arranged to go to one of the busy labour wards in one of the teaching hospitals (I think it was at the UCH) to observe and learn as much as I could about monitoring labour with the CTG; the Senior Registrar was very helpful. I spent a whole day in the unit and felt a bit more confident in that field; I have always maintained that one is never too senior to learn from junior colleagues.

The Senior Registrar at CMH, a budding Oncologist, ran a colposcopy clinic once a week; I attended his clinic to observe and learn from him about colposcopy; he was promoted to consultant status in Oncology at CMH a few years later. During this period, I went to Hammersmith Hospital to observe the gynaecological oncologist operate during his operating sessions; he was a young friendly fellow from Glasgow with a strong Glasgwegian accent. The learning process does not stop.

I completed my three months locum at CMH with great satisfaction, both financially and professionally. Soon after the consultant whose locum I was doing returned to resume his duties, he decided to retire from the hospital service. On his retirement, the hospital board, on the recommendation of the other gynaecology consultants, decided to appoint me as locum consultant for one year until the appointment of a new substantive consultant. The Medical Administration requested me to submit my passport for routine clearance for such a long term appointment. To my great surprise, shock and disappointment, the administration ruled that I could not take the appointment because I did not have a British passport, nor leave to remain. I was told by the Administrative officer that it would constitute a breach of the Home Office regulations if I was given the job. In support of the offer, Mr O'Sullivan, the senior consultant gynaecologist, wrote a letter to the Home Office, stating that I was a very well qualified gynaecologist who the CMH would be honoured to have fill the post until the appointment of a new permanent gynaecologist. I received a telephone call from a senior officer in the Home Office. It was a friendly female voice, probably elderly. After my response to a few questions, I felt that the Home Office was in favour of my appointment. A few days later to my great surprise the CMH registry informed me that the Home Office had written to state that they were not permitted to offer me the consultant post on immigration grounds. It was humbling and devastating news.

I had gone to England in the summer when the sporting events of Wimbledon Tennis championships were on. Young Boris Becker again played brilliant tennis and successfully defended his men's singles title; he proved that the title he had won in the previous year was not by fluke.

The quadrennial football World Championships were staged in Mexico. It was one of the most exciting championships, but from England's point of view, best forgotten; England lost its quarter-final match against Argentina. Maradona of Argentina was the most outstanding and the best footballer on the planet in that generation. Two of the goals he scored in that match against England remained in everyone's memory; the first was the one which received the sobriquet of "the hand of God"; the second was the unstoppable solo onslaught run from mid pitch towards the England goal when he dribbled past almost half the England team of defenders before netting the ball in the England goal; it was a breath-taking and sensational performance by the short and stocky football magician; it confirmed Maradona as an all-time great. The argument about who was the greatest footballer ever still rages and will continue. Is it Pele or Maradona? I cast my vote for Pele. Argentina beat West Germany to lift the World Cup.

I think it was during this summer that the West Indies Cricket team, captained by Gary Sobers, defeated England in the Test series. A renowned BBC Cricket commentator at the time paid a tribute to the West Indian team at the end of the series. When in his tribute, he came to the bowlers, he said that the team had four world-class outstanding bowlers; he mentioned the names of two fast bowlers; next, as a fast bowler, he mentioned Sobers, then followed a pause before he went on to pronounce again the name 'and Sobers'. Sobers was an outstanding spin bowler and also a great medium-fast bowler. He was a legendary batsman, once scoring 365 runs in a first class innings; he was the greatest all-rounder in the game of cricket I had ever seen; he later obtained a knighthood for his achievement in the game.

My musical interests, opera in particular, received some attention; I attended ENO opera performances at the Coliseum; I tried to interest my boys in this pastime but this met with no success. There were some excellent TV opera broadcasts which I enjoyed watching; indeed, I tape recorded all of them. I also attended concerts at the Barbican and the Queen Elizabeth Hall.

Yolande never failed to host and entertain our friends in Ghana who were on visits to London; among these were Ike Ogbarmey-Tetteh and George Swaniker, both of blessed memory. The children of some of Yolande's Caribbean friends also came to stay with us at Mayo Court for some time. Yolande was selfless and hospitable, a commendable exhibition of friendship.

After the three months' locum at CMH and before the debacle of being barred by the Home Office from working on immigration grounds, I did several locum jobs as a registrar or consultant in some London hospitals including St Mary's in Paddington and May Day in Croydon.

The Mayo Court chapter was drawing to a close, and a new chapter began to unfold. Yolande's contract at Mayo Court would end after Christmas 1986; and she did not wish to renew, having other prospects in mind. The warden's position had served an excellent purpose at a very crucial time, but we had to relocate into a residence of our own. Brian and Neil had passed their A levels very successfully; Ronald was shaping up as a brilliant student. One of the reasons for taking the sabbatical was to work and generate some income to finance the tertiary education of Brian and Neil to start with. The Home Office decision barring me from working in Britain was a serious blow to my plans; challenging the decision, though necessary, would prove to be time consuming and in the end likely futile, as most Home Office rules and regulations are often set in cement!. Once again, an important decision had to be taken.

Yolande and I decided to apply for a mortgage to obtain a property. As Yolande had the legal status, she had to play the lead role, by being the first named on the mortgage application. Brian and Neil would take a year out before proceeding to university; I would look out for a job in the Middle East, most preferably in Saudi Arabia for the remaining period of my sabbatical. The search for a house proved surprisingly short. After locating a suitable property, not too far from Mayo Court, and the commencement of negotiations, Neil drew our attention to another house; it was 47 Mary Peter's Drive (47 MPD).on a new housing development We drove down to have a look. The house had been built only a few years earlier and the current occupant was the first; he was an interior decorator and had kept the house in pristine condition, it could be occupied straight away without doing anything to it. We instantly fell in love with the house, contacted the estate agent, paid the necessary fees, saw the mortgage company, completed the necessary paperwork, after which seventy five thousand pounds was handed to the owner's solicitors and we became the new owners of 47 Mary Peters Drive! Amazing how quickly it all happened! We would live there for almost two decades, after which it was rented and then sold. We would always retain and cherish fond memories of our time spent there. The nearest tube station was Sudbury Hill on the Piccadilly Line, and the housing development was sited on a previously huge sporting complex, which now housed the famous David Lloyds Sports Centre, an imposing building. It was in the sporting district with the huge Lloyd Sports Centre nearby; most of the streets and lanes were named after sporting legends such as Roger Bannister and Mary Peters.

The house was a three-storey building. The ground floor consisted of a front garage, a living room, toilet and a kitchen; adjoining the kitchen at the back was a store-room, a split staircase led to the first floor of a large master bedroom and a large living room; the second and third floors consisted of single bedrooms and the main family bathroom. There was a powder room on the ground floor and we put in a shower room adjacent to the storeroom. A small garden was at the front; at the back was a medium-sized garden with a tall hedge providing appealing greenery at the back of the house. A lane at the back of the house separated the Mary Peters buildings from an adjacent forest of trees. Our neighbours at 45 MPD were a couple of old age pensioners, Ed and Ella Kilshaw, very nice and caring neighbours.

A couple of years later we made some substantial conversions to the house. By using the carport for the cars, we incorporated the double garage into the main house, converted it into a sitting-cum-dining room, converted the existing sitting room into the master bedroom and incorporated a small bathroom with it and so then had a four bedroomed house with three bathrooms and lavatories. Mostly Yolande's idea, with Neil's help and cleverly executed by some Eastern European artisans.

While still at Mayo Court, before our move to 47 MPD, it became obvious that I had to seek for greener pastures in Saudi Arabia. A couple of my friends from Ghana had been lucky to have obtained jobs in Saudi Arabia. They included Drs Doe, Teddy Christian (Pathologist), Professors Foley (Physician), and Lade Worsonu (Surgeon) – some of the cream of the Ghana Specialists. The approach was to constantly check the BMJ (British Medical Journal) advertisement section for any available jobs and submit your application. In general, there were three categories of hospitals in Saudi Arabia where vacancies were advertised. First was the MOH hospitals, which catered for the general public, followed by the Armed Forces hospitals, catering for members of the Armed Forces, and the Security Forces hospitals catering for the members of the Security Forces The employees at the Security Forces hospitals were paid the highest salaries, followed by those in the Armed Forces; the MOH employees were paid the lowest salaries. King Fahd Hospital, which catered for Saudi princes and royalty, paid their employees the highest and most enviable salaries for their hospital staff. Recruitment into the MOH was handled by the recruitment branch of the Saudi Arabian Embassy at Cumberland House on Edgware Road, near Marble Arch. Different and various recruiting agencies handled recruitment for Armed Forces and Security Forces hospitals and for the Universities.

There were certain background factors worth noting for a successful application for a gynaecological post. The Saudis, with their religious-cultural ethos and bias, would at all costs, prefer a female gynaecologist to a male; secondly, from my observation, in the Security and Armed Forces hospitals in particular, the Saudis preferred to have doctors of Caucasian stock, all things being equal. It was under this daunting maelstrom that I threw myself. The BMJ came out weekly on Fridays and I responded to the appropriate vacancies week after week. I was invited once for an interview for a consultant post in the MOH; a young Indian gynaecologist, a Registrar, was offered the post. The recruiting agencies could easily tell from your name and CV (curriculum vitae) whether you fitted into the position their clients wanted; the result was that I was not called for any interviews for several weeks; The standard reply to my applications was that the position had already been filled, which of course could not have been the case every time. The repeated rejections over a period of several weeks resulted in inducing a feeling of depression and low self-esteem.

In April 1987 the gloom which had descended on me was lifted. In response to an advertisement in the BMJ, I was invited to attend an interview for a locum consultant job at the Armed Forces Hospital in Khamis Mushait in Saudi Arabia for only a month. After the interview, I was offered the locum job, which I accepted – after all, every journey, however long, begins with the first step. My papers would be processed and a visa obtained before my departure for Saudi Arabia.

I had a fortnight to prepare for my departure to Saudi Arabia, but two disasters were waiting in the wing to strike.

Dr Sydney Adadevoh had travelled to England on a professional assignment. When he finished his mission, he phoned us before returning home. Delightedly, Yolande invited him at very short notice to come over for dinner. It was to be an early dinner because she had to report for work at Hammersmith hospital later that evening. We had planned to have fondue dinner, which was always nice and informal. About half an hour before his expected arrival time, Dr Adadevoh phoned to cancel his dinner appointment – he had received an urgent telephone message from his wife, Chloris, in Kumasi that their eldest son, Nuku, an Engineering student at KNUST had been admitted to hospital in a critical condition; he was requested to return to Ghana as soon as possible .He succeeded in getting a flight and proceeded to Ghana.

Sadly, Sydney missed out on seeing Nuku alive on his arrival; he had already succumbed by the time he arrived in Kumasi.

The dinner with Sydney was cancelled, but I decided to have the fondue with the boys all the same. While I was in the kitchen with Yolande, who was ready to drive off to Hammersmith Hospital, I heard Brian calling out and shouting from the dining room to me, "Daddy, fire, fire". I rushed to the dining room to see the fondue pot with its content of oil aflame; the flame was high, almost reaching the low ceiling which was millimetres away from the rapidly rising flames. I reacted instinctively to grab the extremely hot handle of the fondue pot to remove it from the table, as I did so, I dropped it involuntarily, spilling the boiling hot oil on to the entire back of my right hand! We quickly brought in water from the kitchen to douse the fire; the house was saved from an imminent catastrophe, a rousing fire! The back of my hand sustained very serious second-degree burns. Yolande still had to leave for Hammersmith Hospital for her duties. I went by taxi to Ealing General Hospital where I received initial first-aid treatment consisting of bandaging of my hand. I was referred to the Burns unit in another hospital for definitive management the following day, a Saturday. The extent of the burn, both in area and degree was worse than I had thought. There was excruciating pain.

Yolande drove me to me to the Burns unit at the referral hospital the following day, quite some distance away from our home, where I was seen and treated by the Senior Registrar. Ealing General Hospital had phoned and given them details of my case. The Senior Registrar was friendly and sympathetic. I informed him about my planned departure for the locum job in Saudi Arabia in a fortnight's time; he was cautious in his pronouncement of the prognosis for my undertaking manual clinical work, although function was not grossly impaired. The skin covering the back of my hand was bloated and jet black in colour; the surgeon carefully excised and peeled off the portion of the skin which was dead and non-viable; he then dressed the burnt areas carefully and bandaged the hand. The dressing was to be left in situ until the review of my hand, after a week. This apparently long period before the review, I thought, would very seriously jeopardise my Saudi Arabia appointment. I could only pray that the natural healing process and time, over which the doctor had no control, would be fast. I now fully appreciate why some renowned pianists insure their hands for large sums of money; I wondered for what sum did Messi and Neymar insure their legs? Anyway, after overcoming all the odds and at last obtaining a job in Saudi Arabia, although only for a month, I was determined not to give it up.

I spent the week quietly at home. The healing process entered its most painful phase; I then realized how densely populated the hand is with sensory nerves, probably unlike any part of the body, except perhaps one other. I reported for the review after the stipulated one-week period. Healing was progressing satisfactorily, but there were some raw non-epithelised areas. New dressings were applied and I was provided with an ample supply of new ones to carry on with at home, as was necessary, which Yolande would undertake to do.

I still had to report at the Recruiting Agency office to collect my visa, other documents and ticket for my journey to Saudi Arabia. I cleverly disguised my hand injury and skipped that menacing ordeal with the official. I was now set to fly to Saudi Arabia. The hand injury was healing satisfactorily in the short term, but full epithelisation took several months; the resulting scar is still visible.

Brian and Neil had performed very well in their A level examination and could proceed to their tertiary courses. Our finances at the time and the immigration constraints could not enable commencement of their courses in the 1986/87 academic year; Brian had to compete for admission, therefore I had to postpone their tertiary courses. Entry into medical school in Britain was very competitive. On the other hand, he was eligible to compete for entry into the highly rated medical school in Accra's University of Ghana where I had served as an external examiner and Inspector in OB/GY. I forwarded Brian's application to the medical school in Ghana. Brian was accepted and offered admission starting in the 1987/88 academic year.

After deciding to study Engineering, Neil applied for admission to Leeds University, Queen Mary's in London and on the advice of his Aunty Jackie (Yolande's very close friend, Jackie Zwennes,), London's prestigious Imperial College. Queen Mary's was the first with an offer, Leeds University offered Neil a scholarship to study Engineering Science for a bachelor degree. London's Imperial College also offered him a place to study for a bachelor's degree in Material Science Engineering, with home student status. These were two tantalizing offers from which to make a choice. Pari pasu with my attempt to go to Saudi Arabia, Yolande was also making enquiries about suitable vacancies there for herself, in order to generate income and boost our funds. Signs were beginning to brighten on the horizon. If Yolande and I were both located in Saudi Arabia, and Brian went to Ghana, Neil would need to stay in London to look after and keep an eye on Ronnie, and indeed Dugald when he moved to London for his sixth form. Without hesitation, London's Imperial College received the nod. Although the decline of the offer from Leeds could be done by correspondence, because of the generous nature of the offer, we decided to drive up to Leeds and explain to the Engineering Department the reason for our decline. They appreciated our position, and I think that the fact that we came in person to explain made a good impression. They went on to say that

Neil would be welcome in Leeds in the future if he wished to pursue a postgraduate course.

Our drive to Leeds served a second purpose. I had not seen my mentor, Mr Redman, for almost three years and the Redmans had not met any of our children before; this visit was an excellent opportunity for Theo Redman to meet Theo Agble (senior) and Neil Theo. Theo and Jay Redman received us very warmly; they were delighted to see us and were both very impressed by Neil. I explained to him about my plan to go and work in Saudi Arabia. Now in retirement from the NHS, he had been to Riyadh for brief spells to give lectures in OB/GY. The remuneration, he revealed was lavish; he fully supported my plan to go to Saudi Arabia for a spell. He also very willingly offered be 'in loco parentis' for our boys in England while I was in Saudi Arabia. Neil and I returned to London with a feeling of a successful accomplishment of a mission.

As I approached the end of my first sabbatical year, I was going to embark on my journey to Khamis Mushait in Saudi Arabia. The duration of the locum job did not meet my full desire, but it was an opportunity and perhaps a first step into the unknown future. The following two months were going to prove most critical and decisive in my pursuits on behalf of my family.

My flight from London to Khamis Mushait was a two-leg one on Saudi Airlines; the first leg was London-Jeddah, and the second was Jeddah-Khamis Mushait. After a midday take off from London, we arrived at Jeddah at night. The well illuminated city of Jeddah, viewed from an aircraft, is always a marvellous sight to behold; it looks like a widely spread Christmas tree which stretches endlessly into the distance. The second leg landed me in Khamis Mushait. An awaiting vehicle conveyed me to the military base where the hospital was located. The base consisted of an Air Force base and a Land Forces base; Saudi Arabia had several military bases which were scattered around the Kingdom. There was a Naval base in Jubail.

The hospital was sited in the Cantonment area; the residential accommodation area was close to the hospital complex. The hospital complex was modern, with up-to-date facilities. It catered for members of the Armed Forces, and dependants like wives, children and parents.

There were the major departments of Surgery, Medicine, OB/GY and Paediatrics. The hospital was headed by a senior Saudi soldier.

My residential accommodation was a spacious bungalow with more than one bedroom; it was comfortably furnished with a well-equipped kitchen to meet my needs. I shared the bungalow for a brief period with other locum consultants at different times.

I arrived on a Friday, the Muslim holy day. The head of the OB/GY Department, Dr Rafael, an Egyptian with MRCOG, came to the bungalow on Saturday morning to welcome me. He took me to the hospital and briefed me on the working regulations, duties, etc. There were about three or four other doctors, with whom I would share the duties. There were no junior doctors of registrar and houseman rank; you worked on your own as a doctor; midwives in the wards would call you directly if there was a problem requiring a doctor's attention; there were no intermediaries. The Labour ward Sister carried great responsibility and was held in high esteem.

I quickly realized that all the other doctors were also short-term locum consultants (I can recall two Scandinavians, an Egyptian and an Indian lady). The young Egyptian, with MRCOG, and the Indian had been recruited from England. Dr Rafael was leaving soon at the end of his contract to take up a permanent post in England. There were no Saudi doctors in the hospital; all the doctors were expatriates.

I confronted Dr Rafael at our first meeting with my problem, the recent injury to my right hand. I would not be able to perform any manual clinical activity for at least a week. Although Dr Rafael was not exactly pleased about it, he made the necessary adjustments to the duty roster. I was therefore assigned to outpatient consulting only in my first week. The department obviously needed doctors to fill up the existing vacancies on a longer term basis; I saw this as a great opportunity to put myself on the market. I was therefore anxious to commence full time duties as soon as possible. After an examination and a report on my hand by a surgeon at the request of the authorities, I was given clearance to start full duties schedule; this of course entailed digital pelvic examination and operative procedures. I acquitted myself creditably for the rest of my locum period; the workload was not particularly taxing.

I was introduced to the Saudi Medical Director in my first week of arrival; he gave me a warm broad smile which I thought augured well. However, when he was later informed that I was keen on having a longer contract, he persistently turned a deaf ear and was not interested in making me an offer. The young Egyptian, who had only recently obtained the MRCOG, was being heavily persuaded by the Saudi Medical Director to take a longer contract; he turned down the persuasive offers because he already had a job lined up in Newcastle, England. He told me that he countered their offer by telling the Medical Director that in me, Dr Agble, they had a very good, highly experienced gynaecologist whom they should keep on a longer term basis. The Director would not budge. He continued to give me a broad smile on the few occasions that I ran into him. The female Indian doctor proved to be embarrassingly incompetent, but a longer contract was being offered to her; for some strange reason, she was not interested in staying on. There was obviously an operative factor, not stated, which governed the Director's decision; I know what I thought the problem was, but there was nothing I could do about it.

The multinational nature of the medical and nursing staff provided an opportunity for social intercourse. With the strict sexual segregation, only married couples could admit or entertain females in their homes. There was a large Recreation Centre which provided communal entertainment for all the international staff. The management staff at the centre arranged weekend trips to the surrounding countryside, towns and cities in the region. I discovered to my surprise that the popular image of Saudi Arabia being entirely a desert was untrue. I was amazed on one of our trips to see forested land, almost virgin in character, with monkeys by the roadside. The verdant scenery of the mountainous landscape, stretching for miles, was striking to behold.

I met a friendly group of Scandinavians, Australian and British doctors. There was a female Sierra Leonean Paediatrician consultant; she said her husband was a Ghanaian, a Biochemist, and that she had worked in Korle Bu before. A medical couple hosted an excellent dinner party one weekend for about 20 of us. The Khamis Mushait environment was an appealing one and this further increased my desire to stay on longer.

There was a medical school in the nearby city of Al Khobar where Professor Foley taught Medicine. Following my phone call to him, he drove up to Khamis Mushait the following Thursday accompanied by Dr Doe, gynaecologist, who was on contract there in the hospital. It was a great delight for all three of us to meet in Khamis Mushait, a faraway place from home, the Volta Region of Ghana. After a convivial half day spent with them in Al Khobar, they drove me back to Khamis Mushait.

The end of my locum was fast approaching and I would soon be leaving Khamis Mushait. It seemed that what should have been a very good opportunity to really set myself up with a good position was going to slip by. A consultant gynaecologist from Finland was sharing the bungalow with me in my third week when he was just about to leave and return home to Finland. During our conversation, he asked about my future plans. I told him that although I was keen to stay on longer, the Saudi Medical Director was not interested in making me an offer even though there were vacancies; he expressed disappointment at the Director's attitude because he knew the standard of my professional performance, having worked with me. He told me that with a bit of luck, he might be able to get me a consultant job in Tabuk at the North-West Armed Forces (NWAF) Military Base, where there was a hospital similar to the one in Khamis Mushait. He had worked there as a consultant for a couple of years before and knew the Chief of the Department, a Swede, very well. He was aware of a vacancy there and would speak to the Chief to offer me a contract consultant post in OB/GY. The following day, my Finnish colleague broke the news to me. Dr Joern in Tabuk had agreed to offer me a contract for a consultant position in Tabuk as soon as I was ready to go there. Unbelievable news! Just like that! My despair lifted.

I asked my colleague to have the offer sent to me by fax so that I could proceed with my preparations. A fax message was sent from the NWAF hospital very promptly from Tabuk with an offer of a consultant gynaecologist for at least one year. My prayers had been answered. If I accepted the offer, I would need to go to London for a medical examination and then sign the contract documents. From the nadir and doldrums of depression, my spirit was lifted sky high. I responded immediately by fax to accept the offer and comply by going to London for the medical examination and signing the contract documents.

My gratitude to my Finnish colleague remains immense. He returned home to Finland a few days later. I deeply regret forgetting his name now, even though I kept in touch with him for a number of years after.

Events now proceeded at a fast pace. About a fortnight after I left London for Khamis Mushait, Yolande was offered the post of Nursing Supervisor at the Jubail Naval Base Hospital in Saudi Arabia, a job she had applied for. Neil, Brian and Ronald were left on their own in London. Brian was expected to leave for Ghana to commence his medical course at the University of Ghana. I wasted no time in conveying the good news about Tabuk to Yolande now in Jubail; she was equally delighted with the news. My next move was straightforward: fly back to London, undergo a medical examination, sign the contract documents and fly back to Tabuk.

At this juncture, it is germane to restate an old adage which goes as follows 'never count your chickens before they are hatched'. This adage will prove its truism in the events that followed.

I arranged for my two-leg return flight to London on the same day. I discussed my impending flight with a friendly young consultant Physician in our hospital, an English fellow. He cautioned me on my travel arrangements and advised me to leave Khamis Mushait at least a day before my second leg from Jeddah to London because, he opined, I might need to get a visa endorsement from the British Consulate in Jeddah to proceed on to London. Hitherto, I had travelled to London without an entry visa endorsement; the rules had apparently been changed by Margaret Thatcher. Aware of the change, my English colleague passed on this information to me. I flew to Jeddah a day earlier in order to obtain a visa before my second leg flight; I stayed at the Holiday Inn hotel in Jeddah.

The following morning, I went to the British Consulate to join a long queue of people wanting visas to enter the United Kingdom. Ahead of me in the queue was Dr Teddy Christian, the Pathologist and my old mate in Achimota School; he got his visa without any difficulty or delay. To my immense shock and surprise, I was denied an entry visa and my passport was stamped as such. I was told that my only option was to go to Accra and make a fresh application for a visa; this was a serious setback for me. It would be expensive and time consuming to fly to Accra to obtain a visa; there was no guarantee that the offer of the job in Tabuk would remain valid for an indeterminate period of time. Since I had a valid Saudi Arabian Airlines ticket from Jeddah to London, I decided to take a gamble and utilize it that night. I phoned Yolande in Jubail to tell her about the unexpected and foreboding developments.

I reported at the airport in the evening to check in. A friendly African descent Saudi airline official checked my passport, and handed it back, along with a boarding card; so far, so good, I said to myself. I boarded the flight to London and landed at Heathrow airport between 6 and 7 am. At the immigration desk, after perusing my passport, the immigration officer beckoned me to move aside as he signalled another officer. This other officer informed me very bluntly that I could not enter the country and chastised me for not paying any heed to the ruling in the Jeddah Consulate that I could not fly to the UK. I was taken to another room where all my personal papers were taken out and scrutinized with a fine toothcomb as if I were high up on the Interpol wanted list! A most humiliating experience. Neil, having been briefed by phone by his mother on the developments, was at the airport; he was very visibly upset to see his father being handled in such a manner almost like a criminal. I had to be flown back to Saudi Arabia. So it came to pass that I boarded a flight on Saudi Arabian Airlines from London to Jeddah, landing in the evening. The Saudi immigration officer treated me with courtesy and respect, unlike his counterparts at Heathrow. Yolande has always asserted that the most uncouth immigration officers are to be found at Heathrow. At JFK irrespective of the problem they are more likely to be respectful and not so uncouth. Very often they are former illegal immigrants whose status has been regularised, given a job in which they can feel powerful and overzealous to please their masters. The airline's official who gave me the boarding card to London was seriously reprimanded verbally. The following morning, a senior officer reviewed my case; I had no choice, but to arrange for a flight from Jeddah to Accra; I had to pay for this, of course.

I had set out from Ghana almost exactly a year ago on my two-year sabbatical with no other plan pencilled in for a return after a year. I returned to the Holiday Inn hotel to consider my options and future plans. The Ethiopian Airlines ran a two-leg flight from Jeddah to

Accra via Addis Ababa. I shared my predicament with two Ghanaian colleagues in Jeddah, Drs Doe and Christian. After booking my flight from Jeddah to Accra, I phoned Mr and Mrs Agyarko in Accra to expect me; my son Dugald was staying with them and it was not necessary at that time to disclose the purpose of my trip.

My journey to Accra was uneventful. On board the plane was also the mother of Dr Adiku who was returning home after visiting her son in Jeddah. Dr Adiku, hailing from Peki Tsame, my town, was a consultant Nephrologist at the MOH hospital in Jeddah. I was very warmly welcomed and received by the Agyarkos; Dugald was delighted to see me as indeed I was to see him. I did not initially divulge why I had made this unexpected visit to Accra.

Although I had to go to the British High Commission, I first of all planned to go and see Mr Dennis Beasley, now the CEO at the Tata Brewery (he had been the British consular in his days in Kumasi) to prepare the ground for me at the British Consulate Office before I went there. As an old friend, I assumed that he could be of some assistance in my obtaining a visa. The following morning after my arrival, I went to see Mr Beasley in his office. Dennis, heavily bearded and with his benchmark characteristic charisma, was delighted to see me after several years. I briefed him on the purpose of my visit. Although he was sympathetic, he ruled himself out in assisting me with the British High Commission; he was not in their good books; indeed, he went on to say that any effort on his part would be more likely to ruin my chances of getting a visa. I left his office in despair, but determined to try another line in the pursuit of obtaining the visa.

A few years earlier, my friend Mr Joe Appiah had introduced me to Mr Bruce who was then the Senior Immigration Officer for the Ashanti Region in Kumasi. Mr Bruce was now the Director of the Ghana Immigration Services in Accra. On leaving Mr Beasley's office, I went straightaway to the Ghana Immigration Office to see Mr Bruce. I was told that he was absent from his office; I had to wait for an interminably long time before he eventually arrived at his office, very near the closing time of 5pm. He had apparently spent almost the whole day at the Castle (the seat of government). Mr Bruce, a Ga, was personable and easily approachable. He was clad in mufti, and not in uniform. He recalled our previous meeting in Kumasi several years earlier. I briefed him about my urgent need to obtain the UK visa. I showed him the fax from Tabuk with the offer of a job there and stated that all I required was to go to London to sign a contract. Mr Bruce was sympathetic and appreciated my need. Although he shared a good mutual working relationship with the British Consular Officer, he could not say whether his input would end in success. He promised to phone him the following day to arrange for an interview for me. The following day, Mr Bruce phoned to inform me that after speaking to the most senior officer at the British Consular Office, he had succeeded in arranging for my interview at the British Consular Office. So committed was Mr Bruce to assisting me that he went on to say that despite his heavy schedule, he would personally accompany me to the Consular Office for my interview; this was heartening news, although the granting of a visa was not a foregone conclusion or a certainty, the chances were still precariously poised. By this time, I had briefed my brother on my mission and what was going on. The countdown to the verdict had begun.

On the fateful morning of the following day, I went with my brother Bill to the Ghana Immigration Office to meet Mr Bruce. Bill looked as stressed as I did and felt obliged to accompany me to the British Consular Office. The three of us drove to the British Consular Office. The waiting room was full and I was given my appointment number. I recognized the English lady, Mrs Acquah, who was handing out the appointment numbers as the Headmistress of the Accra GIS who had admitted Dugald, my son, on his transfer from Prempeh College to the GIS in 1984. She had apparently retired from that institution.

My wait was a rather long one, and Mr Bruce had to leave and return to his office, but wished me well. He passed on a piece of information to me which sounded ominous – the senior officer to whom he had spoken had travelled to Lome in Togoland and as a result, I would be interviewed by someone else!

My number came up and I was ushered into a room to meet my interviewer – a heavily built ethnic Indian gentleman. It was not an easy interview by any means. My papers and fax document from Tabuk did not seem to make much discernible impression on him. He told me that it was not easy to reverse the decision which had been taken in the Jeddah Consular Office which I had further complicated by travelling to London. Finally, following my pleading, he decided to grant me a conditional visa. He would grant me a visa to remain in Britain for only five days to permit me to sign the contract which I was being offered. If I breached the five days visa condition and stayed on longer and this was discovered, I would not be permitted to enter the country thereafter forever. He added that by granting me this visa, he was in fact putting his own position on the line; thus my visa to the UK for only five days was granted. I left the office to join Bill who had been waiting anxiously for me. The feeling was not so much of joy, but that of an incalculably heavy burden being lifted from my shoulders; it was an immense relief. I went to Mr Bruce's office to convey to him the good news and also to thank him for his great contribution and immeasurable help and commitment. He told me that my chances of success had been rated at 50/50, an outcome which he could not predict.

A major hurdle had been scaled. I was now in a position to disclose to Mr and Mrs Agyarko an edited and sanitized version of the preceding events and the reason for my visit to Ghana. Dugald, then only seventeen years old, was given a simpler sanitized version.

I still had some obstacles to overcome. I had to ensure that my contract would be ready in London for me to sign on my arrival there so that no time was wasted in appending my signature; quite often, bureaucratic procedures could be time-consuming and I could easily find myself overstaying in London longer than the stipulated five days. I phoned the NWAF hospital in Tabuk to instruct their recruiting office to have all the necessary documents ready before my arrival in London. To my relief, I was told that the agency in London was aware of a delay in my time of arrival there and was waiting with all the papers for me to sign. I then phoned the London office for confirmation that all the documents were ready for my signature. With all these assurances, I was now in a position to book my flight from Accra to London. I booked a Sunday night flight on Ghana Airways, arriving in London on a Monday morning. This way, I would have ample time in working days to complete all the essential business I had to do within five days before departing for Saudi Arabia. I made all the phone calls from the Ghana Telecom offices soon after leaving Mr Bruce's office. The successful booking of my flight was cathartic. All the stress and feeling of low self-esteem of the preceding fortnight were replaced by a feeling of great accomplishment. and relief. As my sister-in-law Glenda would say 'Thank you Lord, thank you Jesus' Amen and Amen.

I had a few days left in Ghana before my flight from Accra to London. I decided to pay a brief visit to Kumasi; I phoned Mr Gyamfi to inform him about my intended brief visit; he was excited and pleased about seeing me in Kumasi. He promised to arrange accommodation for me for a night at my request. I travelled on the State Transport bus to Kumasi; I was well received, warmly welcomed and entertained by Mr Gyamfi; he had booked me into a comfortable guest house in Nhyiaeso. I restricted my telephone calls to only a few friends and Bomso Clinic. I returned to Accra the following day. The remaining few days in Accra were spent in a relaxed and peaceful mode with the Agyarkos and my son Dugald.

An uneventful Ghana Airways flight from Accra landed me at London's Heathrow Airport on an early Monday morning. To my surprise, with irritation and great anger, an officious Immigration official prolonged the perusal of my passport and asked me to move aside for further questioning. In a retort to my assertion that I had a valid visa to enter the country, he told me that my entry was not automatic, and that he had the authority and right to verify it to allow or deny me entry. I was finally allowed to enter. I straightaway went home to 47 MPD and phoned the recruiting agency office to report my arrival and follow any instructions they had for me. I was instructed to go to see a doctor in Harley Street for a physical medical examination and then call at their office to sign the contract documents. I went to the Harley Street address where I saw the GP. He was a friendly, courteous gentleman; he conducted a physical examination on me. After the medical examination, I went to the recruiting agency office.

The contract on offer was that of a consultant gynaecologist at the NWAF hospital in Tabuk, starting in May 1987 for two years. I explained to the official that since I shared a partnership in Kumasi, Ghana to which I was obliged to return, I would prefer a one-year contract. He was surprised at my request and pointed out that there was a long list of gynaecologists who wanted that job if I declined it. Bluntly put, it was a two-year offer, take it or leave it; the decision was obvious. I signed on the dotted line. It appeared that Tabuk was as keen on getting me as I was also keen on going there. The referees I had cited with my formal application included Mr Redman and Professor Sir John Dewhurst (a Past President of the RCOG), both eminent figures in OB/GY. They both held a high opinion on me. I was sure that their written references on me were honest and also flattering. I still had a few days left to burn in London. I collected my ticket for the two-leg flight from London to Tabuk.

Collecting the ticket and boarding the plane at midday on the Friday flight to Jeddah brought to an end a journey of twists and turns and uncertainty, each successfully navigated by providence and destiny. The truism in not counting your chickens until they are hatched cannot be denied.

Chapter 10
DIASPORA YEARS IN TABUK, SAUDI ARABIA

With the weeks of anguish and angst behind me, I boarded the Saudi Arabian Airlines flight at midday on a Friday from London Heathrow to Jeddah. I carried with me one suitcase and a briefcase. After settling down on the plane, my spirit was one of a quiet triumph and a mood of exhilaration. I was embarking on my journey to Tabuk to fulfil my two-year contract with the NWAF hospital in Tabuk. The flight was uneventful. The immigration procedure entailed a thorough check of my suitcase and briefcase to rule out the importation of any prohibited items. Prominent among the list of prohibited items were alcoholic drinks, drugs, the Holy Bible and any insignia pertaining to the Christian religion. The second leg of my flight two hours later from Jeddah to Tabuk lasted one and a half hours; we landed at night in the NW city of Tabuk airport with the magnificent lighting viewed from the plane as it came in to land, characteristic resplendence of Saudi Arabian cities.

On board the flight were a few passengers bound for the NWAF Hospital. We all boarded a bus which had been awaiting our arrival. There was no official on the waiting bus to meet and direct me on where I should go. Luckily, one of the passengers was a Senior Nurse Supervisor for the female wards to whom I had explained my mission; she knew her way around the hospital very well. She sought and arranged a room normally assigned to doctors on call duty at night in one of the medical wards. I was given the room for the night; and there it was that I spent my first night in Tabuk, NWAF hospital. The following morning, I reported at the Administrative Office; I was allocated an apartment in a large block, located about 440 yards away from the hospital; it was a block assigned to senior male staff who were doctors. The apartment consisted of a single bedroom, a living room, a kitchen and a bath/toilet room; the rooms were all suitably furnished. In the kitchen was a small consignment of grocery items to last for a week. I was given my initial briefing and asked to report to my departmental head later.

Less than a decade earlier, Tabuk was reportedly a small village settlement; it turned into a sizable city after the building of a major Armed Forces and Air Force Bases in this NW region; it was to play a very major role some years later in the Iraq War, also named 'Desert Storm'.

The hospital was located over a sprawling area of the Military Base; it was much larger than the one in Khamis Mushait; there was a smaller satellite hospital at the Air Force Base, about eight miles away from the Military Base. Other major structures at the hospital establishment were two large female apartment blocks, each with very tall barbed-wire wall enclosures, a large super-market, recreation centre, tennis courts, basketball court and a bus transport station. The hospital complex itself was an imposing and impressive architectural edifice. There were three floors and a roof with a helicopter landing platform. In the middle of an expansive ground floor were two gigantic elevators which serviced the two floors above; each of the first and second floor area was about half the ground floor area. The ground floor housed the Medical Administration offices, Pharmacy, Laboratory, X-ray, ER (Emergency Room), Out Patient department clinics and the Mosque, as well as indoor gardens. The Programme Office with its Administration, wards, Nephrology Unit, Operating theatres, Antenatal, Post-natal and Labour wards, NICU, and Obstetrics offices were all located on the first floor. A number of wards was located on the second floor. All the floors were kept at a high level of sparkling cleanliness. The hospital was equipped and staffed to provide not only primary and secondary health care for members of the Armed Forces and their dependants, but also health care at tertiary level. The hospital staff was almost entirely expatriate in composition. The top level consisted of consultants in the specialities of Medicine, Surgery, OB/GY, Paediatrics, Laboratory medicine, Public Health and Dentistry: this category of staff, by their contract entitled them to be housed in a bungalow or a town-house with or without their spouse and children. The bungalows and town-houses were fully furnished and equipped with electric cookers, washing machines, refrigerators, dishwashers and convertible heater/

air conditioners. The lower level professionals were accommodated in twinblock apartments; the large force of semiskilled and unskilled workers were accommodated on a campus several miles away from the hospital complex, constituting a township on its own. The houses were constructed of wood and varied in their levels of size, equipment and furnishing. The contracts of the occupants excluded them from bringing with them their wives and/or children. An attractive aspect of the contracts was the free provision of water and electricity; the salaries were paid in full without any deductions of tax or anything else. Telephone was provided in all the apartments; all local calls were free but outside calls, both national and international, had to be paid for. This was the most significant cost for an amenity.

The NWAF hospital had a unique administrative structure. Perched at the top of the pyramidal structure was the Programme Director with his administrative staff on the second floor. The Programme Director was a senior Saudi soldier of military rank of Colonel or Brigadier General; his administrative staff was a mixture of Saudi and expatriate civilians. The medical, nursing and auxiliary services were contracted to a company which carried much weight. The company, always Western, usually a British company or institution, was awarded the contract five-yearly; the bidding was always fierce and competitive. The company, headed locally by the Project Director, was responsible for recruiting all the medical, nursing and auxiliary services staff to run the hospital. The Medical Director and Nursing Director were key personnel in the pyramidal structure; their appointment came directly under the purview of the Project and Programme Directors; the Medical Director was in turn responsible for advising the project Director and Programme Director on the appointment of the Chiefs of the clinical departments; the Chiefs of the departments were responsible for short-listing the applicants for consultant posts. The Chief's recommendations carried much weight; the Chiefs were powerful in their own way. Such was the administrative structure when I stepped into the NWAF hospital complex murals.

The OB/GY Department located on the first floor had, in addition to the wards already mentioned, the following: a conference room, a wing with a few rooms; the wing comprised the Chief's office, the Deputy Chief's office, a single bedroom suite with bath/toilet room, desk for the doctor on-call and a large changing room with lockers for the midwives. The labour ward comprised six single bedrooms for labouring patients, the Sister's office, the station desk, a triage room and a coffee room. Each labour bedroom had a CTG machine and monitor; a corridor led to the adjacent NICU; a corridor from the Labour ward led straight to the operating theatre complex. The theatre complex had four theatres, one of which was always set in readiness for any emergency use, such as an emergency Caesarean section at any time.

On my first day, I went to see Dr Joern, Chief of the Department in his office. A true Swede to the letter, he was tall, blond, blue-eyed, he was a man in his mid-fifties. Familiar as he was with my CV and references, he received me with great courtesy and respect. He gave me a good briefing on the department and supplemented it with a folder on the departmental guidelines, a characteristic feature in all departments; this was a refreshingly new thing to me. There were three other consultants and one Senior Registrar; the consultants were Dr Loftstrand (a Swede), Dr Silvapath and Dr Silva, both Sri Lankans; a Senior Registrar, Dr Shan was also a Sri Lankan; there were no junior doctors at the time. Next, Dr Joern took me to the Medical Director's office to formally introduce me to him. The Medical Director was Dr Anderson, a middle-aged American, a Paediatrician with penetrating eyes; he was knowledgeable and was held in high esteem and awe. I was briefly introduced to him formally and he in turn welcomed me into the medical establishment; the meeting was brief and business-like.

The hospital at this time was in a state of flux; the hospital management contract was changing hands from one company to another; the individual contract of some doctors was up for renewal or termination. In this state of flux there were several locum senior doctors recruited by the new Project Management Company.

The restaurant/cafeteria at lunch time served as a meeting ground of the staff; breakfast and lunch times were the busiest. There was a limited but a good choice in the menu at reasonable prices. There was a strict segregation of the sexes in the restaurant in compliance with the religion and culture. With the multi-nationality of the staff, the seating in the restaurant naturally reflected this: the few Africans tended to sit at the same table as did the Egyptians, the Sri Lankans and those from the Indian subcontinent. At the time I arrived there were four Africans: Dr Paul Dabella (Cardiologist and Chief of Medical Department), from Uganda, Dr Obineche (Nephrologist), a Nigerian and two other Nigerians on short locum jobs. The salary scale of the consultant medical staff depended on the country where the doctor obtained his qualification: the highest were those with the American Board qualification, followed closely by those with the British ones (MRCOG, MRCP, FRCS), next those of Continental Europe, and last at the bottom were those with qualifications from Egypt. The Americans had played a major role in the development and growth of the country and therefore they carried much clout and influence in the country. The Americans set the pace and it was their medical care system which was adopted. Their Quality Assurance policy kept all care givers alert and helped to maintain high standards of care.

I commenced my clinical duties without much delay; I had been engaged as a consultant, but I found that contrary to the practice in Britain, there were no junior doctors of houseman or registrar rank, and I had to function as a houseman, registrar and consultant, all rolled into one. When I was on-call I had to prove my ability and competence to justify my position as consultant. The appointment would only be confirmed after a mandatory three-month probationary period; failure in confirmation would result in termination of my contract. Years, indeed decades, of experience in the tropical Obstetric setting in Kumasi (or Accra) was no guarantee for navigating the probationary period; the management of labour with CTG monitoring and other aspects had undergone such great changes that the ignorance and lack of hands-on knowledge and experience could very easily be exposed and negate confirmation and indeed demand instant termination. Fortunately for me, my exposure to the changing phase while at London's CMH had to a great extent closed the gap sufficiently. I borrowed the appropriate books from the hospital library, and very quickly familiarized myself with foetal monitoring as well as the use of the ultrasound machine in the Labour ward. There was no doubt that if I had gone to Tabuk straight from Ghana, and immersed myself in this new OB/GY environment, my lack of hands-on experience with the current technology would have resulted in an instant termination.

The weekdays of Saturdays to Wednesday began with a morning meeting at 8am prompt of all the departmental doctors, chaired by the Chief, Dr Joern, in the conference room. At this meeting, all the admissions and deliveries of the previous 24 hours were presented by the on call doctor and critically peer-reviewed, taking into account the departmental guidelines; operative procedures had to be justified. All this was of course new to me; in the British, nay Ghana system, there was no such thing as guidelines at that time; each consultant managed any case under his care in a manner as he saw fit without justification to his peers, unless there was a serious outcome or very rarely a mortality. I adjusted myself to the change quickly and indeed found it refreshing. It served as a constant learning process and it enabled others to learn from my own wide experience. There was no morning meeting on Thursday; the on call doctor handed over directly to the on call doctor for the weekend.

At the close of the meeting, we dispersed to our different assignments for the rest of the day. The on call doctor did a round in the labour ward with the midwives, reviewing cases in labour. The other doctors proceeded to do their rounds in the antenatal, postnatal and gynaecology wards. After the ward rounds, the doctors retired to the restaurant for their breakfast. After breakfast, the doctors scheduled for the gynaecology outpatients' clinic proceeded there to attend to the patients who tended to be few in number. After the clinic was the break for lunch, a busy time at the restaurant, the congregation time. The antenatal clinics were held in the afternoon of all the weekdays of Saturday to Wednesday. Any elective operation was done in the afternoon, with prior arrangement with an anaesthetist.

It is now germane to state the nature of our workload. Our patients were the female dependants of the members of the Armed Forces, implying wives, children and occasionally, mothers. Our patients were therefore all young and in the reproductive age group. The strict religious and cultural practice of sexual abstinence until marriage and an absolute ban on extramarital sexual indulgence served to preclude the occurrence of STD (sexually transmitted disease) with its sequelae. The dawn of family planning was only slowly breaking in; high multiparty was the order of the day. The Tabuk civilian population of Saudis and some expatriates were not entitled to receive any medical care at the NWAF hospital. The overall result in terms of clinical practice was that obstetrics alone accounted for more than 90% of our practice. Such gynaecology as there was, was confined to irregular bleeding disorders and infertility of non-tubal aetiology. The resulting virtual absence of the opportunity to perform major gynaecological operations, an exercise I savour, became a bitter pill I had to swallow. My love of major gynaecological surgery, I plead, should not be viewed as sadistic; I regard it as a calling.

The Medical Director, Dr Anderson, championed continuing medical education (CME) very laudably. On every Saturday during the lunch hour from twelve to 2pm, there was a grand round lecture. The lectures rotated among the clinical departments. and were delivered by consultants; sometimes eminent doctors were invited from other hospitals in the Kingdom to give the lecture. Dr Anderson, always seated in the front row, in the left hand corner, was credited with the high standard of the lectures. A delightful, varied, free buffet lunch was served as an added attraction to attend; I tried my best not to miss any of them. Mostly they were stimulating and illuminating.

It was this medical milieu in May 1987 into which I found myself and in which I aimed at holding my own. With time, I acquitted myself creditably in patient management, operative procedures, case review discussions and outpatient consultations. My two-year contract was confirmed after the three months probationary period; there were occasions when appointments were not confirmed and the appointees' contracts terminated.

Yolande was fulfilling her year's contract at the Naval Base hospital in Jubail, in the Damman region, which was a considerable distance away from Tabuk. Yolande decided to pay me a visit; this could only be done if I were housed in married quarters. I submitted an application to Dr Anderson to that effect; he was sympathetic and wasted no time in getting me appropriate accommodation – it was a two-storey townhouse, the superior of the two types of houses available. It was well located and within five minutes' walking distance from the hospital, and very near the tennis courts.

Without delay, I moved into this splendid townhouse: the ground floor consisted of a large living room which led to an adjacent equally large dining room, a second living room (meant for females) and a large kitchen plus storeroom. The upper floor housed a large ensuite master bedroom with an adjoining partially roofed balcony, two large bedrooms and a shared bathroom with toilet. On the ground floor, behind the second living room and the kitchen was a large yard comprising a garden and a cemented area. All the rooms were very well furnished and carpeted, except the kitchen. The wide, tall, almost ceiling-height windows were fitted with elegant curtains. The kitchen was fitted with a cooker, washing machine, dishwasher and a large refrigerator. A dual purpose air-conditioner was provided on both floors, the A/C mode for cooling and the heater mode for heating during the cold season. There were two telephones: one in the master bedroom and the other one in the living room on the ground floor. The house was ideal in almost every respect. The previous occupant had kept and maintained it well and had cultivated a very attractive garden, thus making it easier for me to keep and maintain an attractive arboreal environment.

Yolande made her first two-leg flight visit from Damman to Tabuk (Damman to Riyadh; Riyadh to Tabuk). Each leg was more than an hour in duration. She could only stay for a few days, but it was the first of several such visits. She had the opportunity of meeting the colleagues with whom I associated.

I in turn took a few days off and went to visit her in Jubail. Yolande's hospital had arranged for an apartment for us to stay in – as a senior member of staff she was entitled to have this perk. During this visit, I met a number of Ghanaian doctors who were working in Jubail and Damman; these included Drs Asiedu and Amanianpong, both gynaecologists working in Jubail. On a visit to Damman, I also met Professors Adu Gyamfi, Engman, Lade Wosornu, some of the cream of Korle Bu Hospital.

The Ghanaian diaspora in Saudi Arabia was not confined to the major centres in Jeddah, Damman and Riyadh. In the course of time, I had the opportunity of meeting other Ghanaian doctors in more urban areas.

On my arrival at the relatively remote township of NWAF hospital in Tabuk, I met, to my surprise, two nurses from Ghana working in that hospital; one was a midwife who informed me that there were three Ghanaian gynaecologists working in the civilian MOH hospital. The second was a very senior nurse who was the supervisor of the operating theatres. She was married to an Englishman, and at the time heavily gravid and near term. She indeed gave birth within a fortnight after my arrival. The news of my arrival at the NWAF hospital was conveyed to them, and they wasted no time in coming to welcome me one evening while I was on call. I had not met any of them before: Drs Kumi, Duah and Ahmed Yumunusah, all with the MRCOG, they were consultants in the civilian hospital. It was an entirely unexpected and friendly visit which I highly appreciated. They were all much younger than I was. Dr Duah was a younger brother of Dr Adjei Duah, my former mate in Mfantsipim and UCGC and colleague at KAH. At a much later date, Dr Yumunusah related to me the following story: during his MRCOG viva voce examination, he had faced Mr Redman (my former boss in Leeds) as his examiner. Mr Redman's first question to him after realizing that he was from Ghana was "Do you know Dr Agble?". To which he responded that he did. (Dr Yumunusah had never met me before, but had likely heard about me.) After his response, Dr Yumunusah informed me that Mr Redman spent the next few minutes singing my praises as his former SHO (Registrar); rather flattering. The three doctors paid me several visits. On some visits, they brought along several delicious Ghanaian dishes on which we feasted; we had a wonderful time together while they were in Tabuk. Drs Duah and Kumi returned to England and to Ghana later. I was very saddened to learn later that Dr Duah passed away at a rather young age not long after his return home to Ghana. His older brother, Dr Adjei Duah (my friend and former mate), and another older brother had all predeceased him at young ages. Dr Kumi spent his last evening in Tabuk with me before returning to England.

Being a Military Base, entry into the cantonment was strictly restricted to the residents only. Social activities centred around the recreation centre whose management through the Project organized weekend trips to beaches for those who had an interest in pastimes such as snorkelling, scuba diving and ordinary beachcombing. The centre organized entertainment with film shows and other creative activities. Married couples could entertain guests of both sexes in their houses; permission had to be requested and granted for such parties. Alcoholic drinks were of course not obtainable. Campuses were provided for some major Western companies, notably American ones, which had the attractive privilege of being allowed to show restricted programmes, limited in scope and variety. The Saudis being soccer crazy, there was an ample coverage of the European soccer leagues. The Italian league was the most prominent and entertaining at the time and was as well covered as the English league. A number of Filipinos were good at tennis and constituted a group with whom I regularly played. I acquired and adopted a new life ethos. Which I regarded as all to the good!

My partnership at Bomso Clinic never escaped my thoughts. Following the confirmation of my two-year contract, my awareness was all the greater. I had been granted a two-year sabbatical in 1986 which would end in August 1988, a year earlier than my new contract in Tabuk. I would need to write to my Bomso partners to request for an extension of one year in order to complete my Tabuk contract. Aware of my role at the clinic, I knew that it would be a difficult problem for them. I delayed writing to them for a couple of weeks and finally did so. I explained to them fully the circumstances leading to the two-year contract, pointing out that Tabuk would offer me a two-year contract or none at all. I suggested that on my return they could also take turns at sabbaticals abroad if they wished. Since Bomso Clinic had practically no funds in England for any purchases, I offered to donate a sum of two thousand pounds sterling from my savings into our joint account in Britain, which I considered a reasonable amount. I addressed the letter to our legal adviser, Mr Simon Sotomey. I prayed several times for my colleagues to accept and grant me my request for the extension of my sabbatical for an extra year. After a long and anxious wait, I received a reply directly from my two partners. The letter was very blunt and to the point; my request was refused and I was to return to Bomso Clinic as originally agreed. My failure to do so would mean I would no longer remain a partner. The letter went on to say that I always placed the interest of my family above those of the clinic. It was time, the letter continued, that I placed the interests of Bomso Clinic above my family's interests. The letter was written and signed by the two partners (I had no doubt about the main and principal author). There was notably no input by Mr Sotomey, our Legal Adviser.

I was very disappointed by their refusal to grant me the extension and depressed by the uncompromising tenor of their letter. I had contributed a disproportionately higher level to the establishment of Bomso Clinic; it was my input which had secured the financial loan to build the clinic. In the running of the clinic, I had been unselfishly generating more income than either of my two partners; although we were all on the same salary. Any time I raised the matter of separating the ownership of the fixed assets of the clinic from the running of the clinic, I was always outvoted and the proposal turned down. None of these stated facts seemed to have influenced their decision to deny my request. My generous proposal to donate two thousand pounds sterling to the clinic seemed to have made no positive impression on them.

With my input and commitment to Bomso Clinic, I felt very depressed by the letter. I harboured no intention of leaving Bomso Clinic, nor did I intend to break my contract with NWAF Hospital. I pondered and pondered over the issue. I decided to take my leave from Tabuk near the expiry time of my sabbatical around July/August 1988. I would then spend a month in Kumasi, working at Bomso Clinic after the expiry of my sabbatical leave, thus fulfilling the contract terms. I would have a meeting with my partners and Mr Sotomey and plead with them for the extra year extension. I was leaving no stone unturned.

As planned, I travelled to Ghana with Yolande and Ronald in July 1988 for my working vacation at Bomso Clinic. A friend, a lawyer, whose services Yolande had used before, and her son of Ronald's age, accompanied us on their first visit to Ghana. We stayed at Kplomdedie. Our Kumasi friends were pleased to see us.

I discussed my Bomso Clinic affairs with Mr Joe Appiah, a close family friend and a person held in high regard in the country. He concurred with my decision to plead with my partners for an extension of the contract for one more year. A meeting with my partners was arranged to be held and chaired by Mr Sotomey at his house one evening (I had by then completed working at the clinic for a month and been paid my salary). I invited Mr Joe Appiah to the meeting and he agreed to attend. I told one of my partners, the more pleasant of the two, Dr Andan, that I had also invited Mr Joe Appiah to the meeting. He raised no objection and indeed said Mr Appiah was quite welcome to attend. I did not tell Dr Appiah about it. Accompanied by Mr Appiah, I went to Mr Sotomey's house at about 7pm. Soon after, Dr Andan arrived. We were all warmly received by Mr and Mrs Sotomey and served with choice drinks. The atmosphere was cordial and convivial; we were all well-known to each another over a long period of time. About fifteen minutes later, Dr Appiah arrived and was equally warmly received by our hosts. Dr Appiah gave Mr Joe Appiah a peculiar look and moved to the seat offered by the host. He declined to have the drinks on offer; the rest of us kept on chatting over our drinks as Dr Appiah sat and remained mute. About five minutes after his arrival, he got up and left the living room for outside without saying a word. We all thought that he had left to retrieve something from his car. When he failed to return after about ten minutes, Dr Andan left the living room to check on him. Dr Andan returned to say that Dr Appiah had apparently driven off, without a word to anyone. Mr Sotomey therefore declared that we could not hold the meeting that evening as originally planned and postponed to the following morning at 9am at Bomso Clinic. My flight from Accra to London on my way back to Tabuk had been planned and fixed for two days later.

The aborted meeting and the manner in which it happened was indeed a great blow, it also set me thinking seriously and deeply on what my next move should be in light of the hostility being overtly displayed by one of the partners. I thought it over and over again without discussing it with anyone else. It was obvious to me that a plea for an extension was no longer an option. I should decide whether my family and its future should come before Bomso Clinic. I had done a lot for Bomso Clinic, which had received neither acknowledgement nor recognition. In view of the hateful atmosphere generated by Dr Appiah, the time had come for me to place the interests of my family above those of Bomso Clinic. My mind was now made up for the meeting for the following morning.

I arrived at Bomso Clinic at the appropriate time the following day. The three partners and Mr Sotomey were present at the meeting. Mr Sotomey declared the meeting open. In his review he alluded to my earlier request for an extension of my contract. I stopped him at this juncture and craved his indulgence for me to make a statement. In a short, I made it known that it had been my sincere intention to seek for a year's extension to my sabbatical. Recent events, I went on to state, had caused me to make a different decision. I no longer sought for an extension but now sought to place the interests of my family above those of Bomso Clinic. I had in the past sought in vain for the separation of the ownership of the fixed assets of the clinic from the clinical practice. The legal consequences of my decision would of course follow. My partners and Mr Sotomey were shocked almost into disbelief and appeared visibly disappointed at my decision. The meeting was then declared closed by Mr Sotomey. I asked for the minutes to be sent to me later.

In the course of human affairs, there comes a time for a momentous decision and action; this was one such moment. Its importance and unforeseen consequences would unfold in the ensuing narrative. Later the same day, Yolande, Ronnie and I left Kumasi for Accra and later for London. Earlier, after our arrival in Kumasi, I had heard a comment which was not comforting nor reassuring for my safety if events took a certain turn. Yolande was very eager that we should leave Kumasi as soon as possible, she was never very keen on one of the partners and had a deep mistrust of him.

We returned to London after purging my mind of my commitment to Bomso Clinic; the education of our boys was now the issue to address. They were all very bright and merited the very best education we could afford. Brian, perhaps with a little obligation and loyalty to me, had decided to pursue a career in Medicine. Our finances would preclude a medical school education in Britain. The University of Ghana Medical School was reputable and would be appropriate for him. Although highly competitive, his application to gain a place was successful – his UK 'A' level results were indeed impressive. We commenced making preparations for him to go to Accra. Neil had received a scholarship offer to study Engineering at Leeds University. He had also received scholarship offers to study Engineering at London's Queen Mary's College, Leeds University and the more prestigious Imperial College. This last he only applied to on the advice of his Aunty Jackie (Zwennes) a very close friend of Yolande's whose family was close with ours for decades. Dugald had obtained excellent results from his O level examination and was moving to City of London School, where he had gained admission for his A level course; Ronnie was attending this same school and doing extremely well. The educational blocks were in the process of being laid. Yolande and I were set to go back to Saudi Arabia, but to different cities, Tabuk and Jubail.

I returned to Tabuk in a new spirit – the Bomso Clinic Sword of Damocles was now extinct. The initial building blocks of tertiary education for Brian and Neil had been laid. And the continuing secondary school education for Dugald and Ronnie was on course. Because of his age, 75% of Ronald's fee for education in this public school, a sizable amount, was paid by my employers as part of my contract agreement; this was a tremendous boost to my earnings. Dugald was also a beneficiary of this, but only for one year on account of his age. Several weeks after my arrival in Tabuk, there were certain developments regarding Brian's education. The University of Ghana was closed because of political strike action. An indefinite period of waiting followed and began to make Brian restless and uncertain in London. My absence from London and Ghana did not help in assuaging his fears. His brothers had all in the meantime commenced their respective courses. He received an offer from Bristol University to do a B.Sc. course in Anatomy. As an allied medical science subject, he informed us, there was a good chance of gaining entrance into a medical school after the B.Sc. Course. His restlessness settled and a probable worse development by accepting the offer. Brian therefore enrolled at Bristol University and abandoned the Ghana University offer.

My commitment to Tabuk was now total. Contracts were renewed every two years, but this was not automatic; it depended on the assessment of your performance. No matter how well you performed, one unfavourable incident could negate a contract renewal or indeed end in forthright termination. Nothing could therefore be taken for granted; such was the shadow under which you worked. I received great support and recognition from Dr Joern, the departmental Chief, and Dr Anderson, the Medical Director. About six months after my full confirmation, Dr Joern appointed me as the Deputy Chief of the department, much to the chagrin of another consultant who hankered for the position. In practice, I acted as the Chief whenever the substantive Chief was away. I was also appointed as the department's representative on the Medical Education Committee. This committee, chaired by Dr Anderson, played a significant role in post-graduate and continuing medical education; it was highly regarded. My contributions at the meetings of the committee partly accounted for the high opinion Dr Anderson held about me.

The terms of my contract entitled me to attend one study leave course in the two-year period, fully paid for by my employers. I took full advantage of this opportunity to attend a few courses in Britain and the RCOG triennial Congresses. The study leave courses I attended included one on Ultrasound at Queen Charlotte Hospital in London, conducted by Dr (later Professor) Nikolaides; it proved to be a very useful tuition course in this field. The Royal Free Hospital in London also conducted a course on Laparoscopy, which I attended. Laparoscopy was then emerging to the fore in gynaecological surgery, and I benefited from the exposure at this course. I attended one in Sheffield on Colposcopy; it proved very beneficial in my CME. Another course at Warwick University Hospital on Assisted Reproductive Technology (ART) was mainly didactic, aiming to update the attendants; I found it useful. These courses, to me, were sine qua non for staying on course educationally, as well as updating my knowledge. Surprisingly, not all the consultants took advantage of this great opportunity to broaden their knowledge and keep abreast of current trends. The hospital library with its stock of journals and volumes of standard OB/GY books provided an adequate resource for CME. I had the privilege of being the adviser on the choice of literature on OB/GY and this I exercised wisely. I had my own personal library of books which included the OB/GY regulars such as the yearly Advances in OB/GY and Progress in OB/GY. My interest in OB/GY persuaded me to buy and send copies of Progress in OB/ GY to Korle-Bu and KAH Maternity Units in Accra and Kumasi. Dr Wilson graciously acknowledged and thanked me for the gift.

I was able to attend the triennial RCOG Congresses in 1989 (London), 1992 (Manchester), 1995 (Dublin). These provided a wonderful opportunity to meet old friends and colleagues and make new ones. I attended a FIGO (International Federation of Gynaecologists and Obstetricians) Congress for the first time, which was held in Singapore in 1991. The FIGO Congresses were more international in character; the membership and attendees extended beyond the confines of the old British Commonwealth of nations. I attended the congresses with Yolande, as holidays, they were all memorable. Dugald was on summer break from Imperial with friends in Malaysia at the time and flew over to Singapore to pay us a brief visit. Yolande enjoys travelling and she accompanied me to all the ones I attended. At the FIGO Congress in Montreal, Canada in 1994, which we greatly enjoyed, I met Dr Henry Richter, my Achimota and UCGC classmate; indeed he and his wife were staying in the same hotel as us. We had not met for decades; therein lay the pleasure of congress reunions.

These congresses and courses contributed to making me well informed and a confident practitioner in my trade; I felt that I could hold my own in most circumstances. I took my turn delivering the Grand Round lectures in the hospital. I recall giving more than four of them; the topic was left to the discretion of the speaker.

Grand Round lectures demanded an exercise in scholarship and some research; it should, in my view, rate at a standard which merited publication in a journal of repute.

Very early in my first year, I was requested to deliver my first lecture. The topic I chose was on Symphysiotomy 'The Kumasi Experience'. I think it was very well received. Dr Anderson personally congratulated me on the delivery and wondered if it could be incorporated into our Tabuk repertoire. I pointed out that the medical scenario in Tabuk did not call for Symphysiotomy. My second Grand Round lecture was on Caesarean Section – 'The Tabuk Experience'. A third lecture was on 'Vaginal Breech Delivery – The Tabuk Experience'. Vaginal breech delivery had become very controversial in obstetric practice and, indeed, I was one of a diminishing breed who championed the art of safe vaginal breech delivery. Other Tabuk colleagues and some senior visiting obstetricians did not share my view. Our Tabuk experience registered very favourable data; our Tabuk results were applauded by the audience and appreciated especially by members of the OB/ GY department. The department felt justifiably proud about my advocacy, guidance and delivery. One of my last lectures was on 'Pelvic Malignancies—Our Tabuk Experience'. Well researched, it was a most revealing lecture. Pelvic malignancies were not only a rarity in Tabuk, but in the Kingdom of Saudi Arabia as a whole. My contribution in delivering Grand Round lectures was highly appreciated; the lecture hall was always full. Not every consultant, nor even departmental Chief, embraced the privilege of giving these lectures.

My contracts were renewed at two-year intervals by my departmental Chief or the Medical Director when I served as the substantive Acting Chief of the department. I had my first renewal in 1989.

In 1989, rather suddenly and unexpectedly, Dr Joern resigned his post as Chief of the department. This resulted from an incident which would be inappropriate for me to narrate in full, but only to state that it centred around the clinical management of a patient in labour. Dr Joern had been a good obstetrician and departmental Chief; it had been a pleasure to work with him. To him I owe my recruitment to join the staff of NWAF Hospital.

Following the resignation of Dr Joern, I was appointed the substantive Acting Chief of the department, with an increase in my emoluments. Several months later, the post of the substantive Chief of department was advertised in the British BMJ, and applications for the post were invited. Although I was the substantive Acting Chief, no approach was made to me, but I saw the advertisement for the post in the BMJ purely by chance. Dr Anderson, the Medical Director and my immediate superior, held me in very high regard. In his assessment for my contract renewal, he had given me the very rare and highest score of 28 out of 28 and laudable comments. I approached and sounded him out on my intention to apply for the post advertised. He was very positive and encouraged me to apply for the post. I duly applied for the vacant position of Chief. I was nevertheless aware of the fact that no matter how highly qualified I might be for the position, and how supportive of my application the Medical Director, Dr Anderson, might be, the final nod of approval rested with the Programme Director. He was a young uniformed Saudi medical doctor, then ranking as a major. He was bright and intelligent with a sense of maturity. This officer, Major Dusari, had earlier embarked on specializing in Paediatrics before diverting his interest into medical administration. There were probably other contingent factors at play (in Saudi Arabia, one never knows) but the Saudi Programme Director overruled the professional recommendations of the Medical Director, Dr Anderson (a Caucasian American). I was retained as the substantive Acting Chief for the next two years until 1991. A new company in the nature of the Royal College of Surgeons of Ireland (RCSI), Dublin had won the contract to staff and run the Tabuk NWAF Hospital for the next five years. In their mandate, they appointed Dr Hoyle, FRCOG, as the new Chief of the OB/GY department. I reverted to my previous position as the Deputy Chief, with a drop in my emoluments. Over my 14 year-period in Tabuk, I was the substantive Acting Chief for a total of five years. In retrospect, I was probably fortunate in not obtaining the position of substantive Chief of the department; I most certainly would not have lasted the critical 14 years to see our boys through their entire courses in their tertiary education. Apart from Dr Ben Moore, who signed up as Chief for only one year, and completed it, none of the others lasted the duration of their contract agreements.

The NWAF Hospital had started off as a modest tertiary hospital with minimal facilities. A pioneer American Obstetrician, on a sentimental visit to Tabuk, told me that there were probably fewer than 20 cars when he practised at the NWAF Hospital barely a couple of years before my arrival in Tabuk. Now on this visit, the number of cars was into the thousands. All the basic routine laboratory blood tests done on pregnant women were done by a laboratory in London. The results for some of the patients I looked after were still in their file. This had all changed before my arrival. The hospital laboratory was now a large modern outfit which could perform many blood tests in minutes or seconds and some of the very latest ones, too. The laboratory was headed by a knowledgeable Laboratory Physician. The X-ray department was equally modern and sophisticated and well-equipped. Routine X-ray, ultrasound and electronic body scan services were available. Not long after my arrival, MRI imaging was procured and was in use. The NICU, which adjoined the labour ward, was comparable to any in a London Teaching Hospital. The Nephrology subunit of the medical department had a Renal Dialysis section. There was a compelling desire to transform the hospital into a centre of excellence comparable to those in Riyadh, Jeddah and Damman, the pace-setters in the Kingdom. The hospital expansion programme demanded a commensurate increase in medical and allied staff. Initially there had been a mere sprinkling of Saudi doctors. Dr Khodair (the Deputy Medical Director) was a civilian Saudi doctor who had attempted to obtain the MRCOG in England and had practised briefly as a gynaecologist in the hospital; he was a friendly and pleasant person.

The underlying wisdom of the programme was to seek recognition of the hospital by the appropriate institutions in Britain for the training of doctors for the higher prestigious medical diplomas. With this aim, the door was opened for recruiting junior doctors in all the relevant departments. An application to the RCOG for the recognition of the department for the purpose of training for the MRCOG Part Two Examination had been submitted before my arrival in Tabuk. An Inspector from the College (RCOG), Mr Lamki, indeed arrived in Tabuk for the inspection exercise shortly after I joined. Mr Lamki, an ethnic Omanian, was a Consultant gynaecologist in Belfast, Ireland. Dr Joern, the Chief in OB/ GY was a Swede with a Swedish diploma and not the British MRCOG or FRCOG. Since I was the most senior, with the FRCOG, Dr Joern decided to use me as the heavyweight advocate for the recognition exercise. I found myself in an awkward and difficult position. I should explain why. For recognition as a training centre, the unit should handle a certain minimal number of normal deliveries a year with a commensurate number of abnormal cases a year. There should also be a minimal number of gynaecological cases and operations a year; this would expose the trainees to a full spectrum of cases in the speciality. The delivery rate of three thousand cases a year, in my view, was adequate for the training of two doctors in Obstetrics for an eighteen-month period. With barely a total of four cases of hysterectomy a year, it could in no way be recognized as a training centre in gynaecology; figures should not be falsified for a recognition exercise, this will clearly defeat the laudable purpose of the training requirement.

At the end of the day, a trainee for the MRCOG should have received a full and intensive proper training in the speciality. I expressed my opinion in a very diplomatic way so as not to appear to be sabotaging the recognition exercise. The process dragged on for some months, possibly a couple of years. After the departure of Dr Joern, the key role of seeking a form of recognition fell on my shoulder as the substantive Acting Chief of the department. We eventually got a partial recognition from the RCOG on the condition that the trainee would require another minimum period in a gynaecology hospital where he or she could be exposed to gynaecological cases. We also sought recognition for the Arab Board Diploma. This was the mandatory diploma to practise in several Arab countries. A few years later, we were granted recognition for training for the Arab Board Diploma. I was made a Fellow of the Arab Board later in my tenure in Tabuk. Following the association of the hospital with the RCSI (Dublin), recognition was granted for their Diploma in Obstetrics. The examination for this Diploma in Saudi Arabia was conducted in our NWAF Hospital. The RCSI appointed me one of the examiners on their behalf. I performed this role on two occasions.

Initially, as already noted, there was barely a handful of Saudi doctors in the hospital. These included Dr Badawi (OB/GY resident), Dr Dusari (Paediatrics resident) and Dr Saad (Surgery resident), all uniformed soldiers. Dr Saad went to France to train and qualify as a Plastic Surgeon. He returned to Tabuk and had a rapid climb up the ladder. Short in height and affable in manner, he was a skilled surgeon who combined clinical activities with demanding administrative work. At the time of my final departure, he was the Programme Director. I regarded him highly. Dr Dusari was drafted from being in a Paediatric resident post into the Administration when the RCSI arrived on the scene. Astute and reserved in nature, he scaled the ladder and wielded enormous power when he held the position of Medical Director and later as Programme Director. At the time of my departure, he had attained the rank of a Brigadier in another hospital. Dr Badawi, the OB/GY resident, soon abandoned OB/GY and was catapulted into Administration in Riyadh after a short course in the USA. After the arrival of the RCSI there was a quantum jump in the number of junior doctors in all the departments. The gate was opened to both Saudi and non-Saudi doctors. The Saudi doctors were uniformed and non-uniformed; the non-Saudis were Egyptians, Sudanese and Palestinians. There was a limit on the number of doctors we could accept in our department; this was dictated by the recognition criteria and also the need for hands-on experience. The numbers accepted in Paediatrics and Internal Medicine was more generous, and therefore attracted a lot more junior doctors as residents. Surgery also required hands-on experience and entailed overcoming the 'pons asinorum' (the hurdle) of passing the Part One of the Fellowship Examination in the basic sciences which required rigorous preparation. Surgery, therefore, did not attract local Saudi doctors; the residents at my time there were mainly Sudanese and Egyptians.

With the complement of resident doctors in the OB/GY department, the workload on us, the consultants, eased greatly. We no longer had to sleep in the hospital when on call. We were, however, required to teach the residents and prepare them for the important and necessary examinations. A young Senior Registrar in the person of Dr Ani, a Nigerian, had joined the department. He had only recently obtained the MRCOG and was knowledgeable and hard-working. He was appointed the Medical Educator for the department. As his remit, he was to assist and supervise the resident doctors in preparing for their examinations. I spent endless time emphasizing to the residents that they had passed the stage of being spoon-fed and that they had to read up on the basic sciences, themselves. We arranged for tutorial inputs from the Pathologist and Bacteriologist. We conducted mock examination rehearsals for them at the appropriate times. As the Substantive Acting Chief over critical long-stretched periods, I was deeply involved in these educational activities.

In 1990 the RCSI won the competitive bid to staff and run the hospital. Leading their team was Professor MacGowan. He had been a Professor in Dublin and was a distinguished academic and Surgeon, astute and widely travelled. He did not reside in Tabuk, but visited it often. In Mr Wayne Terry, an American, they had a resident Project Manager. Mr Terry wielded great power and influence; he deliberately made himself not easily accessible to discuss problems. The RCSI brought in their own team of consultants; they replaced Dr Anderson the Medical Director, with one of their own doctors, an Irishman. Very sadly, Dr Anderson, whom I had held in high esteem, had to leave. Therein lay some of the brutal aspects of working in Saudi Arabia.

After the takeover of the Project by the RCSI, some element of chaos descended on the Medical Administration. A senior Irish Surgeon was appointed the Medical Director, with Dr Zain, a civilian Saudi Surgeon, as his Deputy. Dr Zain had been a Senior Registrar in the hospital for two years. The Irishman was sidelined by the Saudi hierarchy, and in frustration, he resigned and left after only a month. Dr Dusari was appointed to replace him.

Professor Ward, a renowned Paediatrician, was brought to head the Paediatrics Department with Dr Woodbridge as his deputy. Dr MacCelligot, an evil Negrophobist, was appointed Chief in the department of Medicine. I did my utmost to avoid any encounter with this fellow. Fortunately, our paths never crossed professionally. Professor MacGowan, distinguished Project Manager, with whom I shared a mutual respect, always sought my opinion on the appointments to senior positions in the OB/GY department. He was in no apparent hurry to appoint the Substantive Chief for the OB/GY Department as he seemed satisfied with my performance in the Acting role. He finally appointed Dr Hoyle, FRCOG as our Chief.

Dr Hoyle came to Tabuk when I was away attending a FIGO Congress in Singapore in 1991. On my return to Tabuk, I met Dr Hoyle for the first time as I walked along the corridor to attend our morning meeting. On seeing me, he greeted me with the words 'Dr Agble, I believe'. I responded in the affirmative. With a warm smile and a welcome handshake, we continued walking to the meeting and introducing ourselves formally. He had apparently heard positive things about me, I was overcome with a slight feeling of embarrassment at the compliments paid. Although Dr Hoyle did not engage in clinical activities, he projected a positive image. He identified himself with our African group in the restaurant during the breakfast and lunch break periods. Rather sadly, his tenure as Chief was short-lived. As a result of some disagreement with the Saudi Medical Administration, his contract was terminated. I genuinely liked him and felt sorry at his departure. The little experienced Saudis were wielding their power. Power corrupts and absolute power corrupts absolutely. And so it was that the mantle of the Substantive Acting Chief again descended on me.

Part of the responsibility of the departmental Chief was assessing and reviewing the performances of the consultants and Senior Registrars, recommending their contract renewals or terminating them. The Chief also had the responsibility of selecting applicants from a list to fill any vacancies at Senior Registrar or Consultant level. The Programme had a bias in favour of female applicants and this factor had to be taken into consideration.

The Sri Lankan group of obstetricians all left voluntarily at the end of their individual contract periods; they were replaced by new appointees. The new group included Dr Usha Kuneru and Dr Bhatacharya as consultants, and Dr Chalasani as Senior Registrar. They were all Indians. Drs Kuneru and Chalasani were female doctors. Dr Kuneru's husband was a Urologist in the Department of Surgery, Dr Chalasani's husband was a Primary Care Physician. Dr Loftstrand retired voluntarily and returned home to Sweden. He was replaced by Dr Husted from Denmark. Dr Husted was the most senior and experienced of the new arrivals; he had a special interest in infertility and was therefore assigned this area in his clinical duties. Other recruits to senior registrar and consultant posts followed in later years. Dr Ani was promoted to a consultant post later. It was my responsibility to make the recommendation for all these appointments and promotions.

It took a considerably long time for the Project to appoint a Chief after the untimely departure of Dr Hoyle. Eventually, Dr Ben Moore came from Hereford in England to fill the vacancy for a year. He had taken a sabbatical from Hereford as a Senior Consultant. I continued my role as Deputy Chief. Dr Moore and I shared a mutual respect for each other; he had a good sense of humour. Dr Moore delegated a lot of administrative assignments to me. After a year I went back to my role of Substantive Acting Chief. Professor MacGowan appeared not to be in a hurry to appoint the next Chief and indeed sounded me out on certain interested applicants.

The circumstances leading to the appointment of the next Chief merit narrating.

When I planned to go on my annual vacation leave to England and Ghana, the Saudi Medical Director made it conditional on my finding a local locum Gynaecologist from the Kingdom. Hitherto, our locums cane from abroad. Through my Ghanaian colleagues in Damman, I succeeded in getting a gynaecologist from Damman University; he was a University Professor, by name Yahyia, a Saudi national. He had apparently trained in Canada and obtained the Canadian Fellowship in OB/GY, a suitable choice for the locum job. He arrived in Tabuk on the morning of my departure day on leave for London; I was due to fly off in the evening. He appeared to be a friendly person and thanked me profusely for offering him the locum job; he

445

agreed to do the locum for the prescribed period. I took him along to introduce him to the Medical Director. After the initial introduction, I was asked to leave; Dr Yahyia promised to see me soon after leaving the Medical Director's office, probably after half an hour. After spending a considerably longer time with the Medical Director and later the Programme Director, he came back to see me at my house; he was in a joyful mood. On my return from leave he returned to Damman. A month after, he returned to Tabuk as the substantive Chief of our department for one year in the first instance; the University had granted him a one-year sabbatical. The job had apparently been offered to him after I introduced him to the Medical Director. I was in no way offended; one could argue that the manner in which it was done was indeed unusual, this behaviour would be unlikely in western countries, like the UK or USA, but manners and cultures differ, and at the end of the day all foreigners working here should consider ourselves as custodians. It is in their interest to be in charge of all their departments, institutions, corporations, etc as soon as they can do so efficiently. He delegated much of the Chief's duties to me to execute. After a year, although he expressed the desire to stay on, the University apparently was unwilling to grant him an extension of his sabbatical.

More seriously, an incident in our hospital marred his ability as Chief. His contract was therefore not extended. Dr Ani, on his recommendation, was appointed the new Acting Chief; I reverted to the position of a Consultant. Professor MacGowan on his next visit to Tabuk sought my opinion on selecting the new Chief from a list of applicants. Our agreed choice was Dr Peter Hill from Canada. A Professor, he had trained and graduated from Liverpool University. He had the British FRCOG and the Canadian Fellowship in OB/GY. Dr Peter Hill arrived in Tabuk to take up the Headship of the OB/ GY Department. He was knowledgeable and had an interest in gynaecological endocrinology. He was a much younger colleague, but we hit it off well together. The politics entailed in holding on to a Chief's position by a non-Saudi were becoming complex to navigate. In my view, although Peter tried his best, the local powers did not allow him to complete his contract period. His departure was unexpected and sudden, having nothing to do with his clinical performance.

When I was the Acting Chief, it also fell within my ambit to select doctors for the junior posts as residents. Saudi doctors were automatically selected. The residents included Sudanese and Palestinians. There were two Saudi residents, namely Dr Abdul Azziz (male) and Dr Kwala (female). The two non-Saudis were Dr Sherry (male Palestinian) and Dr Zaki (male Egyptian). The latter two were hardworking, outstanding and brilliant; the two Saudi resident doctors were also good. Dr Zaki passed the Part One of the MRCOG examination and we succeeded in arranging for him to join Dr Ben Moore's unit in Hereford, England to complete his training in gynaecology for the part two MRCOG examination. Dr Sherry was the first to pass the Part One Arab Board Examination in our department. He went on to Riyadh to complete his training. He later attained a Consultant post in Riyadh quite early. He was destined to be an achiever. I met him once some years later at an international congress.

In addition to our daily morning meetings when we reviewed cases, we also held monthly departmental meetings when perinatal mortality and cases of interest were discussed; the attendees included all the doctors and midwives. The Consultants took turns in chairing the monthly meetings, the aim was to improve on the management of cases; it was not a court to prosecute offenders. It was meant to be educational and instructive.

In the 1990s the hospital embarked on a major exercise of upgrading in various ways, most prominently in the department of Surgery, with laparoscopic surgery at the fore. A team from Dublin came to Tabuk to inaugurate and train a couple of surgeons in the hospital. Dr Zain, Chief of Surgery and now the Medical Director, followed up with a further course in Dublin. On his return, he embarked on laparoscopic surgery on a grand scale; he had acquired dexterous skill and expertise in this field quite speedily. Tabuk soon emerged as the leading centre in the Kingdom in laparoscopic cholecystectomy. Training courses were organized and conducted in our hospital; indeed two Ghanaian surgeons working in the Kingdom attended the courses. The RCSI appointed Drs Zain and Saad, in my view in their courtship exercise, examiners for the Part Two Fellowship Examination held in Dublin and later in Tabuk.

I suspect the financial benefits to the RCSI were not small.

The hospital at the same time embarked on setting up a cardio-thoracic unit which could perform heart transplant surgery. A young South African surgeon, Dr Stefan, was recruited to head and run the unit; funding was not a problem. Dr Stefan, a Caucasian, brought along with him a heart-lung machine technician, a young indigenous South African. An invasive cardiologist physician, an ethnic Indian from Holland, was recruited and brought in. Thus a cardiac centre was established in Tabuk and started functioning. Stefan struck a firm friendship with me and Yolande; he showed us much respect and regard and treated us in a filial way. He was the highest paid doctor in the hospital. After chalking up some great success, he decided to leave for the USA. During his time in Tabuk, he took the examination to practise in the USA and was successful. He left for the USA despite much persuasion by the Saudi authorities to get him to stay. He abandoned cardiac surgery and moved into Family Practice; I was saddened by this change in career – Stefan had a really bright future as a cardiac surgeon. We kept in touch with each other for several years, but finally lost touch.

The wind of upgrading and modernization was blowing and our department was not to be excluded. As already stated, our clinical workload was 90% obstetrics, while the gynaecological part was minimal. I have always been aware of the doctrine which had been inculcated in me by my revered mentor, Sir Dugald Baird. Simply stated, the doctrine dictates that Medicine should be practised by taking into account the milieu of social, economic and indeed I would add the religious and political factors in which one is practising. This way, the management of a case may differ in Accra, London or Tabuk.

On my arrival in Tabuk, the mind-set was that the population growth was to be encouraged at all costs (the Saudi Arabian population was quoted to be 11 million, out of which seven million were Saudi nationals and four million foreigners). Birth control was to be discouraged and not offered to patients; birth control advice could be provided only when requested. Some years later it became acceptable to tell the patient of the availability of the service and the benefits without their requesting it. High multiparty as well as a high number of repeat Caesarean sections prevailed. Tubal ligation was not viewed favourably unless after three repeat Caesarean sections.

Total hysterectomy was frowned upon; it could only be justified as a last resort or for a malignancy. One of my experienced and trusted consultants performed a total hysterectomy on a patient in her late thirties. This followed the investigation of debilitating backache. The gynaecologist counselled the patient and offered a hysterectomy finally as the treatment. The patient accepted the advice, agreed to have the surgery and signed the consent form. Some weeks after the hysterectomy, my colleague was accused of unnecessarily removing her reproductive organ and thereby depriving her of bearing a child in the future. As Acting Chief, I stoutly defended him when I was summoned for my opinion. Despite my strong defence in his support and my equally high marks and written opinion on his assessment for his contract renewal, they refused and his contract was terminated. He had been a pillar of strength in the department. Such indeed were some of the vagaries of working in Saudi Arabia. Indeed, by the Grace of God I went and worked there for 14 long years and survived it!!

The RCSI and the Programme in their pursuit of creating a centre of excellence in Tabuk thought that it would be a good idea to have an IVF (In Vitro Fertilisation) Unit in the hospital. As the Acting Chief at the time, my opinion was sought. I felt that I had to give a candid and professional opinion based on facts and needs, not necessarily on financial resources and funding. I checked on the numbers of infertility cases; the number was small. With the relative absence of tubal and peritoneal factors, our hardcore cases were cases of PCOS (Polycystic Ovarian Syndrome). Some cases responded favourably to therapeutic management, leaving only a small number of refractory cases which would benefit from IVF. The number could be increased if the facilities in our hospital were extended to the Tabuk civilian population. An IVF Unit would require a gynaecologist and an Andrologist or Technician who would need to have a reasonable turnover number of cases a year to keep the unit sufficiently busy in practice. In my view, with these factual constraints, I did not see my way clear to recommend the setting up of an IVF Centre in the hospital. A gynaecologist indeed travelled from Dublin to Tabuk to convince and sell the idea to the Programme big guns; luckily for me, I was only an Acting Chief. I do not know what fate would have befallen me if I had been the substantive Chief. I was certainly not popular with the gynaecologist from Dublin. Indeed, I very likely incurred his wrath! The stakes were high, but I survived my tenure as acting Chief. Heed was paid to my opinion and the notion of an IVF centre in the hospital was discarded for the foreseeable future. The department was fully equipped to practise obstetrics at the highest level. Our statistics on the three thousand deliveries a year were impressive; gynaecological surgery was very limited because of the paucity of cases. In my 14 years in the department, I performed only two vaginal hysterectomies with pelvic floor repair. I was the only gynaecologist to have performed this operation in the department during this period. I repaired two very difficult cases of vesico-vaginal fistulae per the abdomen with the joint assistance of a Urologist. The longstanding fistula had resulted from a vaginal insertion of a powerful corrosive substance; there was a concentrical vaginal stricture which precluded any vaginal approach to the repair. The repair was successful and the patient was very grateful. I reluctantly had to accept the fact that my stay in Tabuk would entail a period of starvation from gynaecological surgery, a practice to which I was partial, if not addicted to.

It is now germane to chronicle two events which in different ways illustrate the environment in which I practised.

While I was consulting in the outpatient clinic in the afternoon with my Egyptian interpreter (a smart and alert lady), my next patient entered the consulting room. She was a plump Saudi girl in her late teens; she was partially veiled and dressed in a burka attire. She was accompanied by her mother of a similar dark-skinned hue and build and similarly attired. She complained of amenorrhea of an unspecified duration, she was a student and unmarried. She fitted into the clinical image of PCOS (Polycystic Ovarian Syndrome). I went through the routine examination. Being rather plump, the abdominal examination was a bit challenging, but on palpation, to my great surprise, I felt the top of a mass suggesting the top of a gravid uterus of about 22 weeks gestation. On auscultation with a Pinard stethoscope, I heard foetal heart sounds. A look of great concern and deep worry from the interpreter spoke volumes. The mother and daughter showed no concern about what was going on; indeed, the daughter's face was one of curiosity and smiles. I told them nothing, except that the daughter would need to have an ultrasound examination. The ultrasonographer was alerted and told not to disclose any findings to the mother and daughter, who were still unaware of the diagnosis of a pregnancy. The ultrasound examination confirmed the pregnancy and the gestational age. Since the girl was not married, it posed an extremely serious social, religious and cultural problem. I informed my Chief who in turn informed the Saudi Medical Director. After about an hour of conferring among the Saudi authorities, the following instruction was passed on to us at the clinic: the girl was to be admitted immediately to the medical inpatient ward (Note MEDICAL and NOT ANTENATAL). A 24-hour military guard was posted outside the door to the single-bed room in the medical ward. No visitor was allowed to visit her; I cannot recall whether her parents were also included in this ban on visitors. After 24 hours in the hospital, she was transferred to a female prison. She remained in prison until she went into labour at term and was admitted to the labour ward. She had a normal delivery of a live baby and was transferred back to prison with her baby. Rumours from the cognoscenti were that her admission with the guard protection and later transfer to prison was designed to protect her from an honour revenge killing by a close member of the family. I do not know what happened to her later. I hope she is alive and safe; her image still rests in my memory.

The second chronicle also involved me when I was the Deputy Chief to Dr Yahyia, the Saudi. One of the consultants was Dr Malas, a Syrian. Dr Malas, MRCOG, had been a Senior Registrar until his recent promotion to consultant status on my recommendation. I was consulting at the outpatients clinic one afternoon when I received an urgent telephone call at about 2pm to come to the operating theatre immediately at the request of Dr Malas. He had encountered a severe life-threatening bleeding during a Caesarean section operation. I left for the theatre quickly, abandoning a patient on the examination couch in response to the urgent call. I changed into operating apparel quickly and entered the theatre to see what was happening. The patient of high parity was undergoing a second Caesarean section on account of a large breech presentation. She had also made a request for tubal ligation. After the extraction of the baby and removal of the placenta, a severe post-partum haemorrhage followed, and it was on account of this that I was summoned for assistance.

On a quick glance at the presenting picture, with the patient not responding to oxytocic drugs, I realized that the patient needed to have a fast total Caesarean hysterectomy performed on her. I was the best equipped to carry this out. I did not hesitate at all in taking over the operation; it had been a bread-and-butter operation in my days of yore in KAH in Kumasi. I scrubbed up very quickly, gowned and took over the operation. After clamping and ligating the right adnexa, I commenced similar procedure on the left side with speed. I suddenly realized that the blood looked dark and cyanosed; I alerted the consultant Anaesthetist to my observation (he was an Eritrean normally based in West Germany). He in turn summoned his departmental Chief, Dr Filibos, an Egyptian (he was an excellent Anaesthetist, probably the best I had ever worked with before). The patient then had a cardiac arrest, but responded favourably to external cardiac massage. I proceeded with the operation as fast as I could. The blood kept oozing all over the operating field, failing to clot, a veritable picture of DIC (Disseminated Intravascular Coagulopathy). Blood was quickly taken from the patient for laboratory tests before the administration of Fibrinogen intramuscularly. The most likely diagnosis of the precipitating cause of the DIC was amniotic fluid embolism; this condition carried with it a high mortality rate, as high as 80%. On realizing the diagnosis, I asked Dr Malas to summon Dr Yahyia (the Saudi Chief) to the theatre immediately. Hitherto, I had not had a maternal death in the Kingdom. The response from Dr Yahyia when he was summoned was that he was at a meeting and therefore could not come. I told Dr Malas that as the consultant in charge of the case, he had to insist on Dr Yahyia's presence in the theatre. I was very aware of the fact that there had been no meeting scheduled for that afternoon; besides, no meeting can override an emergency summon to the operating theatre. Meanwhile we had received the blood fibrinogen level result; it was zero. Dr Yahyia eventually turned up at the theatre, unchanged and ungowned, peeped at the operation going on and left after about five minutes without saying a word! We persevered to control the DIC and eventually closed the abdomen. The patient received a large amount of blood transfusion and coagulants; her condition remained critical and she was transferred to the ICU (Intensive Care Unit). Very sadly, the patient died at about 6pm; our first maternal death since my arrival in Tabuk. We had done everything possible to save her life.

On another separate occasion, I had to scrub up quickly and take over the operation of a Caesarean total hysterectomy at a critical stage from the substantive Chief and expeditiously perform the operation to save the patient's life. Dr Filibos, the ace Anaesthetist, played a major and critical role in the outcome of that case. Plaudits and kudos to this first class anaesthetist. I revere him!

The consequences following any maternal or post-operative death for any non-Saudi in the Kingdom were fearful: your passport was retained and not handed back, thus preventing you from leaving the Kingdom for any purpose whatsoever. The case would undergo an investigation which was always protracted and interminably prolonged. If you were found culpable, your contract would not be renewed and a colossal fine in cash would be imposed. The consequences of any death were therefore not taken lightly. Likewise, some complications following surgery could invite some severe punishment for non-Saudi surgeons. While on contract, consideration of surgical risks and postoperative complications always had to be borne in mind.

It was quickly established that Dr Yahyia was not attending any meeting when he was summoned to the theatre the first time. Bluntly stated, he was dodging any involvement with a serious case for reasons best known to himself. This incident certainly did not favour the extension of his contract as he had wished. He cut a very poor image of himself as the Chief of the department. He did some other deplorable and disgraceful things as Chief which I do not wish to chronicle in these memoirs.

As a result of the post-operative death, I, as well as others involved in the case, was barred from travelling outside the Kingdom until the investigation was concluded. The initial investigation was conducted by a team from the Riyadh Military Hospital, headed by a Senior Naval Officer, a Brigadier; also included was a consultant gynaecologist. To my great surprise, astonishment and indeed anger, I was listed as an accused. I had prepared myself well for the investigation by collecting all the relevant medical literature on amniotic fluid embolism with mortality rates and made several photocopies for my interview. The Naval Officer, a non-medic, was very attentive and appeared to be an intelligent person; he asked me several relevant and intelligent questions. I missed no opportunity in describing Dr Yahyia's negative contribution. The Naval Officer, to his great credit, at the end thanked me for my brave and committed action to save the patient's life, despite the unfavourable outcome of her demise.

After the submission of their report, the trial of the case was listed at the Sharia Court in Medina. Fortunately for me, I was listed as a witness, not as an accused. Dr Malas, the Eritrean anaesthetist, and the scrub nurse were all in attendance; Dr Yahyia, now back at Damman University, was summoned to attend. Fortunately for us non-Saudis, the trial date had been expedited because the project review renewal exercise was going on and any legal affairs had to be completed expeditiously. I made my presentation to the Sharia Court at their request with the support of copies of the medical literature on amniotic fluid embolism; I answered all the questions put to me. The trial lasted a full day. Dr Yahyia was interrogated. The final verdict was that the death was not caused by the doctors; it was unavoidable under the circumstances. Dr Yahyia was severely censured by the court for his refusal to answer his call to the theatre in the first instance. The Sharia court decision was fair; I cannot fault it. I left Medina with my reputation intact and a belief that not only the Western court system in which I was bought up could deliver justice.

Another event needs chronicling in these memoirs.

Dr Joern, a Swede, now and again recruited a Swedish gynaecologist for a short spell as locum. As his Deputy Chief, I thought that a suitable Ghanaian colleague could reap some benefit from my presence in Tabuk. Dr K. K. Korsah, a Senior Consultant in Korle Bu, fitted the role very well. I had admired "KK" since my Achimota school days (he was four years my senior, and a famous athlete/sportsman). A brilliant gynaecologist, he was the first Ghanaian FRCOG to have been invited to examine in the Part Two MRCOG Examination in London by the RCOG. During my first vacation leave in Ghana in 1988, I met KK in Accra and suggested the idea of a locum to him. After an initial reluctance, he agreed to do one in Tabuk in 1989, for a maximum of three-months – from April to June, after which he would go to London to attend the RCOG triennial Congress. His wife would travel from Ghana to meet him in London. I returned to Tabuk with his vintage

CV for approval of his application for a locum position. After an initial non-approval on grounds of age, Dr Anderson, after a discussion with me and my reassurances that he was fit, approved and KK was offered the three-month locum. I felt quite pleased with this outcome. What follows next is a brief summary of events, a synopsis of a sad saga which unfolded.

Dr K.K. Korsah arrived in Tabuk on a Friday evening in April in apparently good health. I was delighted to see him and welcomed him warmly. We chatted about his trip and, more importantly, the work schedule. He would start work on Monday, be on call on Wednesday. We spent a quiet weekend, Sunday was spent sorting out the paperwork and he started work on Monday. I saw him on Tuesday to find out how his first day was, only to hear from him that he had developed an infection on one of his toes which was very painful. Suffice it to say that this quickly turned into a serious condition which necessitated admission into the ICU. As soon as his condition stabilised and he was fit to travel, I contacted Dr Doe to meet him in Jeddah to help with his plane journey and Dr Konotey-Ahulu in London to meet him at Heathrow and take over from there, which they both did. The Saudi authorities were furious with me and it was only the intervention of Dr Andersen which spared me from some serious sanctions. It was a very stressful period for me, and I was thankful when he arrived home in Ghana safely. I actually broke down when I was packing his personal effects in his apartment prior to emplaning from Tabuk, not only the disappointment of the aborted locum position, but to how poorly he became in so short a time. I never again offered anyone to help with a locum job in Tabuk. A very, very harrowing experience.

In June 1989 I went to London to attend the RCOG Congress. Yolande accompanied me to visit KK in the hospital where he had been admitted; he also received a visit from Professor Graham Harley of Belfast University who was also attending the congress. If the worst had resulted from KK's illness, I was in no doubt about the cynical comments which would have been made about me; I never again offered to assist anyone to get a job in Saudi Arabia.

When I first arrived in Tabuk in 1987, there were two Nigerian doctors in the hospital, an Ophthalmologist on a locum assignment and a Nephrologist. The latter was Dr Obineche, a Glasgow University graduate; he left for greener pastures in another Middle East country. Dr Amoah, a young Ghanaian Nephrologist came as a locum for a few months before leaving for a long contract post in Riyadh despite much persuasion to keep him in Tabuk.

The oil boom in Nigeria in the late 1970s and early 1980s began to fade in the late 1980s. This set in motion the diasporic phenomenon of Nigerian doctors seeking jobs in Saudi Arabia. A significant number from Ghana had come earlier. Not long after my arrival in Tabuk a significant number of Nigerian doctors and nurses came to Tabuk; they came mostly from Enugu, Ibadan and Lagos Universities. The doctors included the following: Sam Ohaegbulam (Neurosurgeon), Edwin Okoroma (Paediatric cardiology), Olu (ENT surgeon), Gregg (Ophthalmologist), Ani (gynaecologist), Iphe (anaesthetist), a Dermatologist from Lagos and an Endochrinologist from Ibadan. Dr Alfred Neequaye (Physician) and his English wife Janet Neequaye (Paediatrics) from Ghana came to join the West African contingent; so did Gifty Owusu (dentist); several nurses and midwives swelled up the number. Mr Leslie Nyarko, a Ghanaian Neurology Technician, was recruited for the neurosurgery department. As the most senior West African doctor who had been longest in the hospital, I cultivated the habit of inviting any new West African doctor to my house for dinner within his first fortnight. It was an opportunity to welcome him into his new environment and brief him about life in Tabuk and offer such advice as I deemed necessary in a non-patronising way. This practice seemed to be well appreciated by all the doctors. We almost all sat at the same table in the restaurant during lunch hour; I was the doyen of this group.

All the doctors were consultants and were therefore housed in townhouses or bungalows. All the doctors, except the Neequayes, lived singly unless they had visits from their wives and children. As adults, we lived our lives separately and privately, and cultivated our individual friendships.

Some of my associates merit some mention. The Ghanaian group was small: the Neequayes, Gifty Owusu and Leslie Nyarko. We naturally socialized together rather infrequently. Leslie, a friendly and helpful fellow, was a good cook of Ghanaian dishes. Gifty's husband was an anaesthetist in a hospital in Riyadh. Gifty never missed the opportunity to treat me and Yolande to a great fufu lunch whenever her husband came to visit her in Tabuk. Janet and Alfred surprised and treated me to Ga kenkey meals prepared competently by Janet, Alfie's English wife who made amazing kenkey from scratch. Elizabeth, a Public Health Nurse was another Ghanaian on site in Tabuk. Elizabeth, then widowed, had spent much of her professional life in Nigeria before coming to Tabuk. She bestowed the honour on me to give her away in her next wedding in London to a West Indian fellow.

Dr Sam Ohaegbulam was one of my closest friends in Tabuk. After training and qualifying as a doctor in Cairo, Egypt, he met and married Marcel, an Egyptian. He trained in Britain to obtain the FRCS as a Neurosurgeon. He had been the Vice Chancellor at Enugu University in Nigeria before coming to Tabuk. He was a skilled surgeon and was held in high esteem and highly respected by all in the hospital establishment. His wife and three sons paid periodic visit- to him in Tabuk.

Dr Edwin Okoroma, a Mayo Clinic-trained Paediatric cardiologist, equally held in high esteem, was another Nigerian with whom we shared a warm friendship. His wife and children visited him periodically. Dr Museri and Dr Mrs Museri were a Nigerian couple with whom we were friends. She was a consultant anaesthetist; he was recruited from Riyadh as a consultant cardiac surgeon. They left Tabuk for England and later went to the USA.

The staff in Tabuk was very cosmopolitan in character; my friendships therefore extended beyond the West African region. I can recall a few of these friends. They included Drs Filibos, Mark Hanley, Stefan David and Wanasuriya. Dr Filibos, an Anaesthetist, was my neighbour in the townhouse. We both shared a love for soccer and this further bonded us together. Dr Mark Hanley was a young Caucasian Zimbabwean who had trained and qualified as a doctor in Zimbabwe before specializing as a Pathologist in England. Mark was brilliant, knowledgeable and very well-read; he was a staunch member of my opera group. Articulate and charming in manner, Mark was an excellent raconteur. He regarded himself as a true African (he spoke the Zimbabwean language fluently). He sat with us at lunch time at the West African table. After one year, despite a considerable pressure on him to stay on, he left Tabuk for the USA for a more conducive atmosphere. I have already made reference to Dr Stefan, the young South African cardiac surgeon. Dr Wanasuriya was a Paediatric consultant whose townhouse was directly opposite mine. His polysyllabic name obviously disclosed his Sri Lankan nationality. Middle-aged and of a friendly disposition, he was an academic and a highly respected clinician. We both shared much in common. Dr Wanasuriya and his wife had a daughter, an only child who was bright and well brought up. On completing her A level course successfully in Sri Lanka, she gained admission into the prestigious London School of Economics and Political Science (LSE) for a degree course. Yolande assisted them by advising them on being an overseas student in London. She returned to Sri Lanka after completing her degree course. We enjoyed their company at our parties (as they did) as well at their memorable parties; we shared a warm relationship with them. Dr Wanasuriya returned to Sri Lanka to take up the Chair in Paediatrics at the University of Sri Lanka. There was another Sri Lankan Paediatrician with whom we shared a warm relationship.

He was Dr David, short, bespectacled and with a charisma all his own. He was the Chief of his department when I arrived in Tabuk. He resided in a townhouse with his wife and daughter; she was an employee in the Programme. Dr David was an enthusiastic member of my opera group. He was a Christian and once hosted and organized a brave function on an Easter Sunday in his house. Yolande and I were among those invited, numbering about 15. A service was held with the singing of Easter hymns followed by a most delicious buffet meal, with an assortment of tasty items. In the Saudi Islamic setting where anything pertaining to Christianity was strictly forbidden, this was a brave act by Dr David. Taking a leaf from their book, Yolande and I repeated the Easter Sunday feat at another Easter time. Ronnie, our son, had come to Tabuk on holidays. He led us on his flute in singing Eastertide hymns; we numbered about 12. We ended it with a buffet dinner.

Because of the religious and cultural divide, partying and social intercourse did not cross the expatriate barrier. Despite this, I was hosted on three occasions by Saudis in their homes on the cantonment. Dr Saga, one of our resident doctors, hosted all the consultants in the department to a splendid dinner in his house; we all enjoyed and very much appreciated it.

The second occasion was when a visiting gynaecologist from the RCSI, Dublin came to Tabuk. Dr Yahyia was then Chief of the department. During this very brief visit, Dr Yahyia decided to host a dinner in his honour to which I was invited. Despite his many faults, he deserves credit as a host; we had a most convivial evening.

On the third occasion, I was asked by a Sudanese Physician consultant to accompany him to attend an exclusive function in the house of a very senior Saudi General. It was a very traditional Saudi function with several top military officers in attendance, clad in Saudi attire. There were, of course, no females around. The dishes were tasty, varied and plentiful, and consumed by all using our hands. These constituted the three occasions when I was hosted by Saudis.

In 1991, I attained a non-biological paternal status. The manner of this attainment merits chronicling.

One of the Saudi residents was Dr Kwala, a very strict Muslim, always heavily veiled. She was of Tabuk parentage and was very fluent in English. She had trained and qualified as a doctor in Riyadh and now wished to specialize in OB/GY. I was the Acting Chief of the department when she joined Caesarean section; I engaged her in a chat, as was my habit during surgery. At one point during our dialogue, I enquired about her father. To my surprise and discomfiture, she told me that her father had passed away; I apologized for my probing question and tactfully moved on to something else. After the operation as we both walked down the corridor leading to the labour ward, she made a request of me: since she had no father and she heard me say that I had no daughter, only sons, would I consent to be her father? It was a most unexpected and rather interesting request. I cannot recall my immediate response, but we carried on our walk to the labour ward where we joined the midwives in the coffee room, where we all sat around the oval table. It was one of the few places where people of both sexes could sit together in the same room. Dr Kwala, heavily veiled, sat at the head of the table. She then terminated all conversations and craved permission to speak. She said that as she had no living father, she was requesting me to consent to be her father from now on; if I agree to do so she would forthwith proceed to unveil herself to me in the coffee room. A period of deadly cathedral silence followed. To me the complications were deep and complex; the relationship between the two sexes in the religious-cultural milieu of Saudi Arabia were not straightforward. I needed time to think it over. I therefore mumbled some words in response, neither rejecting nor immediately consenting to her request. She therefore did not unveil herself.

I told her later that in my culture, I would need to discuss her request with my wife before imposing on her the role of a surrogate mother. She understood this solution and agreed with what I told her. At that time, Yolande was based in London. I informed her about our dual parentage status and she agreed that we accede to her request. Yolande was due to travel from London to meet and accompany me to attend a FIGO Congress in Singapore. Yolande brought along with her a gift for Dr Kwala to seal our new relationship. On my return from Singapore, I briefed Drs Chalasani and Usha, both female consultants, about the private and formal presentation of a gift to Dr Kwala and requested their joint presence in my consulting room. Thus I formally became Dr Kwala's father. Dr Kwala later in turn brought presents to me; they included a copy of the Koran. She, however, never unveiled her face to me; I did, however, on two unguarded moments catch a brief glimpse of her face accidentally as she was having a consultation with a patient in her consulting room. She very quickly covered her face. She was very pale in complexion. She never introduced her mother nor any siblings to me. She got engaged to a young man who sought me out and introduced himself to me. A grand wedding was held later which Yolande attended; I do not recall any invitation to me.

The story with another Saudi female doctor was different, but they both shared a similarity in one aspect.

Dr Nadia Hejazi, a Saudi female doctor (of African descent; Saudis come in all different hues and racial origins, very interesting), with a residential home in Jeddah, had trained and qualified as a doctor in Riyadh. She came to Tabuk NWAF Hospital to start a post-graduate specialist course in Paediatrics as a resident. Yolande and I went to the airport in Tabuk to welcome Ronnie, our son, who was arriving from London. Nadia was also at the airport, fully veiled. When she saw me with Yolande (not veiled) she came over and greeted us warmly, addressing me as Dr Agble. I did not know her and had never spoken to her before, but she seemed to know me quite well. I introduced Yolande and Ronnie to her She exchanged phone numbers with Yolande; this way a relationship commenced. Yolande invited her to our house during the brief period she came from London to Tabuk. Yolande returned to London and not long after, Nadia moved from Tabuk to Riyadh to continue with her residency course. Nadia later introduced me and Yolande to her family in Jeddah. Like Dr Kwala, her father had passed away. Her mother and two siblings of a brother and a sister resided in a family apartment in Jeddah. Both siblings were well educated and fluent in English; indeed, her sister Rheem taught English and her brother Khalid worked with the Saudi Arabian Airlines as a flight attendant. We were treated as family members. When Nadia and a female colleague went to do a brief course at the Hammersmith in London, Yolande arranged accommodation for them in a flat. I saw Nadia's face for the first time during a London visit. Without any ceremony, Nadia had attained the status of a surrogate daughter. On a visit to Riyadh, Yolande and I introduced Nadia to our Ghanaian friends there, namely Dr Alex Bruce Tagoe and Mr Herbert Dakwa. Nadia took us on a shopping spree. Nadia's brilliance and ambition propelled her to go to the USA in pursuit of further studies. While she was in the USA, she was introduced to Yolande's sisters in New York, namely Gloria, Glenda and Erica, as well as their mother. Following the introductions, Nadia was accepted into the Garraway family. Yolande and I remained in touch with her even after our years in the diaspora.

Nadia got engaged and a wedding day was fixed for a date in August 2004; she asked me to perform the paternal role of giving her away. Yolande and I were then back in Ghana, and our eldest son, Brian, had chosen to have his wedding in Trinidad in September 2004. Yolande and I travelled to the USA at an earlier date than we had originally planned to fulfil our role at Nadia's wedding. All the Garraway sisters, as well as their mother, were in attendance, Yolande's niece Renee was one of the bridesmaids at the wedding, thus providing full family support. Nadia's mother and sister travelled from Saudi Arabia to be present. Nadia is a pretty young woman and a loving daughter of whom we are proud and whom we all wish well. On a visit to London,

Yolande and Nadia went to Selfridges to do some shopping. An agent for a well known brand of cosmetics approached Yolande and asked whether she would allow him to use 'her daughter' to model some of their products in the store!!! The acquisition of our two Saudi daughters assures a permanent link with Saudi Arabia.

The lifestyle and ethos in Tabuk were different from the London ones. I had to devise my own form of relaxation and entertainment. The English channel of the Saudi Television provided adequate news coverage and in many ways, very satisfactory entertainment programmes. The Saudis love soccer; soccer matches from the Italian and English leagues received full coverage. The Italian league was then the best in Europe. AC Milan with Ruud Gullit, van Basten and Frank Rijkaard were the best performers at the time. The FIFA World Cup matches were also fully televised; my interest in soccer was fully satisfied. I not only watched many matches, but went further to record some of them on video tapes. The English channel often screened programmes of classical music of various composers; it was a great pleasure to watch.

My readers would note that I am a keen opera fan; I had made a collection of all my favourite operas on video tapes (the DVD era had not yet arrived). When I was on leave, I purchased the video tapes of the operas I reckoned I would enjoy. I also met Professor Minford of Liverpool University at a luncheon party in Liverpool. He was an Economics guru who was then a Special Adviser to the British Prime Minister, Margaret Thatcher, and spent a day each week in London. He was an opera buff and had access and also the facility to record many operas on video tapes which were then not available in shops to purchase. Realising my keen interest in opera, Professor Minford made it a habit to tape many operas for me; these were kept in London by Yolande for me to collect from time to time. With my relatively large library of opera tapes, I indulged in watching operas in Tabuk. A number of my colleagues expressed an interest in doing so with me. The result was that a small group of about eight was formed who came to my house regularly on Thursday afternoons at about 4 pm to watch the opera of choice for that week. I made photocopies of the synopsis of the chosen opera and distributed them to the group members on the preceding day for them to familiarize with the story of the opera. We always had a period of intermission during which time I served some refreshments. My favourites were fruit salad with ice cream and several non-alcoholic drinks and snacks. I was forced after a while to agree to a popular request to allow the regular guests to take turns in providing the items for our refreshment – this worked out well to everyone's satisfaction. Some of the regular members were Drs David, Ohaegbulam, Okoroma, Mark Hanley and Mr Barry (a middle-aged friendly Englishman, who taught English to senior Saudi officers). Mr Barry was a keen member who was responsible for printing the photocopies of the synopsis for me to distribute. They were convivial and memorable weekends we all cherished. Some of those attending were introduced to opera for the first time in these sessions and expressed their pleasure and appreciation for the opportunity.to be exposed to this new form of entertainment.

While I pursued my profession as a senior gynaecologist in Tabuk, Yolande was fulfilling her contract at the Naval Base Hospital in Jubail as Nursing Supervisor, and acting for the Nursing Director on occasions, a post she took up in May 1987. Naval Base Hospital was small in comparison to other Armed Forces Hospitals, but it catered for senior naval personnel and their families. She enjoyed working there and was particularly into the Quality Assurance programme which she herself encountered for the first time. There were other Ghanaian medical luminaries in other locations in the Kingdom including Professor Foley, Drs Bruce Tagoe, Teddy Christian and KG Korsah. Their temporary professional loss to Ghana was perhaps compensated for by their contribution to the invisible financial gain in the Ghana economy and perhaps the tertiary education of their wards abroad or in Ghana for the next generation of Ghanaian professionals.

Despite the physical separation, Yolande, and the boys and I kept in touch with each other by phone. All the boys were in educational institutions: Brian at Bristol University, Neil at Imperial College, Dugald and Ronnie at City of London School. After her two-year contract in Jubail, Yolande decided to update herself educationally – she possessed a good academic brain and an unstoppable ambition for excellence in all her pursuits.

The Liverpool University had started an MPH (Masters in Public Health) degree course for qualified medical doctors only. The school decided to open up the admission to carefully selected nurses in 1990 when they admitted the first nurse for the MPH course. At the end of the year she excelled and came at the top of the class, and by her brilliant performance she opened the way for other aspiring nurses. Yolande applied to do the course for the following year and after an interview of a short-listed group, she was one of three selected. The University provided accommodation for those who needed it, so she lived in the postgraduate Mulberry Hall. She combined her role as a mother and that of a student; she stayed in Liverpool during the week and went to London by train to spend the weekends with the boys.

Yolande had joined an elite group of students which included doctors and a couple of non-medics; there was a Caribbean man and a lady from Botswana, the wife of the Botswana Minister of Health. The head of the Teaching staff was Professor Peter Pharoah. Yolande had a great admiration for him as a teacher and as her personal tutor. Yolande pursued the course with great diligence, more so because of the elitist composition of the group. She braved through a difficult, but necessary course in Statistics. They were taken through the rudiments of the then emerging computer technology. She acquired new friends and made a positive impression on her tutors. This was evident on one of my visits to Liverpool, while on leave from Tabuk. I accompanied her (the only student invited) to a Sunday luncheon party hosted by one of the senior tutors; it was at this party that I met Professor Minford, the eminent Economist and an opera buff. At the end of the course, Yolande had to sit for a written examination and also present a dissertation successfully to obtain the Master's degree. The subject matter of her dissertation was 'Risk Factors in Cerebral Palsy'. She passed the written paper and her dissertation received approval. Ronnie, Dugald and I made the memorable journey from London to Liverpool to witness the graduation ceremony. We all felt proud of her achievement. Yolande remained in London to continue to play the role of a mother to the growing adults at 47 MPD. Brian had graduated from Bristol University and commenced an MSc course in Neuro-Anatomy at London's University College. Neil had graduated from Imperial College with a Bachelor degree in Engineering (Material Science) and commenced working. Dugald had entered Imperial College for an MSc degree in Chemical Engineering. Ronnie had gained entrance into Emmanuel College at Cambridge University to study Medicine. Yolande took up an appointment to be the Health Supervisor for a group of schools in the East End of London; this secured a permanent job for her in Britain.

Yolande's ceaseless interest in international affairs and politics propelled her to undertake a PhD course. She enrolled with the University of Washington as an external student. She chose as her subject 'Africa in the 21st Century – Survival or Extinction', The International Policy of African Countries as her research subject. She researched the literature, wrote and submitted her thesis. The thesis was accepted and Yolande was awarded the PhD degree. Yolande updated her address prefix from plain "Mrs" to "Dr Mrs" __ quite an achievement and an inspiration to others.

Yolande's motherly role was extended beyond her biological offsprings. Kwame, son of Mr and Mrs Yempew (formerly of Prempeh College), came from Ghana to stay with our family while in search of an educational avenue in England; his French mother had returned to France from Kumasi. Kwame was treated as a member of the Agble family. Yolande had also met the young Aubrey Bruce Tagoe at Liverpool University. Aubrey was then in his first year of study for a degree in Economics. Aubrey was the nephew of Narkaley Tetteh, a very close family friend. Aubrey was invited to spend his holidays with our family in London, which he did. Yolande had always been generous and friendly to the children of her friends. Selfishness in this respect was not in her dictionary; the parents appreciated this role.

During my years in the diaspora, 47 MPD was our home base when I returned from Saudi Arabia on leave and where our family lived. In Ed and Ella Killshaw, we had friendly and good neighbours at 45 MPD. Ella, petite in build, was reliable and knew about everything going on in the neighbourhood. I tried to take my vacation leave around Christmas time so as to observe the Yuletide with the family and host our yearly party on 23rd December for family and friends. Our invited friends included the following: Drs Felix Konotey Ahulu and his wife Rosemary, the Neequayes, the Seddoh family, Emmanuel and Sandra Anka, Afie Doe, Nana Duah, Cynthia and Peter Grant; we never missed an opportunity to invite Mr David Howell.

We entertained Dr Ajedu Armar and his father, Augustus Armar, to a memorable dinner when Augustus came from Accra to visit his son in London. Dr and Mrs Amroliwala also deserve a notable mention.

Dr Fred Amroliwala was a Registrar in the department of Medicine in SJH at Leeds in 1965 when his friend and mate Dr Attit from Bombay and I were resident doctors in the OB/ GY department. Fred was a Parsee Indian who had trained and qualified as a doctor in Bombay with Dr Attit. On the day Dr Attit and I received our letters that we had passed the MRCOG examination, it was in his house in Leeds that we went to celebrate with champagne and dinner. I returned to Ghana in December 1965. Fred joined the RAF later, but then we lost touch with each other. During the Gulf War when I was in Tabuk (the Military and Air Force Base played a major role in the war), I met a British RAF officer and enquired about Fred. He told me that Fred was one of their high-ranking officers in the RAF. When I returned to London, I made efforts to seek him out and succeeded. We agreed to meet and have a little reunion. I invited him and his wife to dinner at 47 MPD. Fred had risen in rank in the RAF to become the most senior medical doctor, attaining a rank equivalent to a Vice Admiral. It was a great delight to see him after a long time and we enjoyed our sentimental reunion dinner. Yolande and I responded positively to a return invitation to go to spend a day with them at their home at Swindon. Their children had all done well: one of them as a presenter/ news anchor on the BBC-TV.

Dr Ajedu Armar is the son of Dr Augustus Armar, my former senior colleague in Kumasi. On one of my visits to Dr Konotey Ahulu at the Cromwell hospital in the 1990s, he told me that Dr Ajedu was in the adjacent room consulting as a gynaecologist. I had not seen him since his boyhood days in Kumasi in the early 1960s. I went over to his consulting room, introduced myself to him and related to him my close association with his father. Thus commenced a relationship of a surrogate uncle-nephew nature. It was a delight to host father and son to a splendid dinner at 47 MPD when his father came on a short visit to London. Our close relationship extended over several years; I attended Ajedu's OPD clinics as he consulted and also his Operating Theatre sessions to observe the recent developments in laparoscopic surgery, one of his interests. Ajedu had attained a commendable status as a consultant gynaecologist in London's Central Middlesex Hospital, and we felt proud of his achievements.

We have always been a close-knit family. Some of my nieces and nephews lived in London and I kept in touch with them on my visits to London. My visits to London provided the opportunity to attend church services at our parish church in Perivale; Yolande had adopted the Perivale Anglican church since 1983; indeed Ronnie served as an acolyte to Reverend Father John Wilmington when he was young. 1992 was the 10th anniversary of my father's death. With the assistance of the presiding priest, we held a fitting memorial service in Papa's honour at the Perivale Anglican church. The three lessons were read by the eldest grandchild of my mother's three children. I read a tribute. It was a moving memorial service. We followed up with a reception at 47 MPD. Very sadly and disappointingly, the self-styled professional video-recording technician produced a very poor recording after collecting a handsome sum of money.

Yolande and I had so far been lucky and blessed in our accomplishments. My two-yearly contracts were regularly renewed and I was accorded remarkable respect by my peers. Yolande, with MPH and PhD degrees, held the very respectable post of a School Health Supervisor. She had an inclination to politics which she exhibited by writing articles for the West Africa weekly magazine. She collaborated with Dr Felix Konotey Ahulu in forcefully expressing their opinion on Aids in Africa, a topic which generated much controversy at the time, as did the prescription of morphine and opiates in the management of pain in patients with sickle cell disease. Only two of our four boys were in London at this time; Brian had gone to Kingston, Jamaica and Barbados later to study Medicine at UWI (University of West Indies) while Ronnie had gone to Emmanuel College at Cambridge, also to study Medicine. Neil, after graduating with a BSc (Eng.) degree from Imperial College, started working but not as an engineer. Dugald was pursuing an MSc course in Chemical Engineering and following that later with a PhD at Imperial College. With no biological daughters around with its associated parental anxieties concerning their friendships and education, Yolande thought that the time had come for her to leave London and join me in Tabuk. It was deemed necessary to get a suitable job with the NWAF Programme; it was not going to be easy. A suitable vacancy in the Public Health department, headed by Dr Mamoud, an Egyptian, surfaced. They needed a School Health Supervisor and Yolande was eminently qualified for the post, literally tailor-made. She had an extra advantage of not requiring separate accommodation by joining me, in my townhouse. The paperwork was expeditiously carried out and Yolande came to join me in Tabuk as a Programme employee on contract.

Yolande's arrival led to a change in the house and the scale of our entertainment; with a female in the house we could entertain guests of both sexes. Yolande acquired her own circle of female friends, a few of whom joined the opera group. Some afternoon parties were entirely female affairs. Our back porch, with the adjoining well-tended garden, provided an attractive green ambience for both afternoon and evening parties. The Tabuk townhouse was another home from home. With her long experience in School Health, Yolande was innovative in her assignment.

My contract terms permitted our boys to visit me in Tabuk: Ronnie visited us several times; Brian visited once and Dugald visited twice. They played a lot of tennis on their visits. Philip Husted, the teenage son of my Danish colleague, Dr Husted, was a tennis addict who played a lot of tennis with Ronnie; he was always sorry and saddened to see Ronnie return to London. He aspired to play professional tennis in the future.

Yolande and I did not confine ourselves to Tabuk, but did some travelling around in the Kingdom, some for pleasure, and some on business: on a few occasions, we had to go to Jeddah or Riyadh to fulfil some requirements to obtain visas for travel purposes. We stayed in hotels on some of these trips and sometimes we were hosted by some Ghanaian friends on our social trips. Our hosts included: Dr and Mrs Doe, Dr and Mrs Adiku and Dr Kofi Berko, all in Jeddah. Dr Adiku (a Consultant Nephrologist), hailed from Peki Tsame, my hometown in the Volta Region. Their son was attending one of the best schools in Jeddah and was being very well brought up and was receiving lessons on the piano keyboard; he was musically talented. I was indeed very impressed with his performance on the keyboard. I believe he went to Germany later to study Medicine. I predict he will be an achiever; a credit to his parents.

Dr Kofi Berko was a Neurosurgeon with the MOH hospital in Jeddah; he hailed from the Kwahu mountains. He had trained in Germany and was one of the earliest Ghanaian doctors to come to the Kingdom. He obviously enjoyed his popularity as the Neurosurgeon in Jeddah. He hosted me and Yolande in his apartment on a number of occasions. In return, Yolande and I invited him to Tabuk; he came and stayed with us for a few days. Dr Teddy Christian, the eminent Pathologist, was also based in Jeddah; I met him once in his apartment.

Riyadh had also attracted our attention. I had previously visited Riyadh on my own to obtain an entry visa to the UK. On that visit I stayed with Dr Korsi Atubra, a consultant gynaecologist. He had been my MO in Kumasi in the 1960s; he was the best MO I ever had. Even though he was now a Senior consultant, he respectfully still addressed me as Papa; he was a perfect host. In my subsequent visits to Riyadh with Yolande, we stayed in well-appointed hotels. We met Dr Alex Bruce Konuah and Mr Hebert Darkwa, a UNDP official; they were both Old Achimotans. They had both been in the Kingdom for several years. They entertained us to an evening dinner; Nadia was in Riyadh at the time and we took the opportunity to introduce her to our Ghanaian friends; they included Dentist Otoo who also joined us for dinner. When Yolande and I were ready to leave the Kingdom finally and for good, their advice and assistance proved to be very useful and crucial.

Yolande and I were guests of Professor Adu Gyamfi, Anaesthetist, and his wife Mokor (a Primary Care Physician) at Damman University; they had been in the Kingdom for several years. They were excellent hosts; they organized and held a luncheon in our honour. We met other Ghanaians in the diaspora in Damman; these included Professors Lade Wosornu and Larbi.

Yolande and I arranged for a visit to Al Khobar where Professor Foley, the Physician, was based. This city was in a different part of the vast Kingdom with an entirely different topography and vegetation. We flew from Tabuk to Al Khobar. Although we stayed in a hotel, we were basically guests of Professor Foley and his wife. It is a picturesque part of the country with mountains, deep gorges, forested and with monkeys and chimpanzees. It had much to offer in sightseeing and we exploited the opportunity to do so most fully. The Foleys were good hosts. We were introduced to another Ghanaian, a lecturer in medical biochemistry. We invited the Foleys in turn to visit us in Tabuk. They responded to our invitation and came to spend several days with us there. We held an evening dinner in their honour; they met other West African colleagues. We arranged some sightseeing visits for them, but nothing as spectacular to match what was on offer in Al Khobar.

Our final very memorable excursion visit took us to Aramco. Our hosts were Dr Michael Agamasu and his wife Hawa. Aramco was a state within a state. Saudi Arabia was and still is the world's leading oil-producing country. Aramco (Arabian American Oil Company) is the company which produced the oil. It was America's largest single private overseas investment anywhere in the world. None of the restrictions in Saudi Arabia applied to this territory. There was a Christian church in which we attended Easter mass, other places of Christian worship; expatriate women could drive freely; alcohol was openly sold in the supermarket; both sexes mixed freely. The salaries of the doctors were higher than any other in the Kingdom and they had an attractive pension scheme if you worked continuously for ten years or more.

Dr Agamasu was a Ghanaian gynaecologist from Afede near Fodome in the Volta Region. Korle Bu trained, Michael obtained the MRCOG and was working in England when he secured this most desirable job as a consultant gynaecologist with Aramco. Michael and Hawa welcomed us as their revered guests for more than a week. Michael was a jovial, friendly person; he and Hawa showered on us the proverbial Ghanaian hospitality. Their company was never a bore. Their children were being educated at the time in England. After more than a week of being pampered, we returned to Tabuk. Our next meeting with the Agamasus was in Kuala Lumpur, Malaysia in 2006 at a FIGO Congress. They stayed in a modern five-star Ritz Hotel. They entertained us to a splendid dinner at their hotel on their last evening. Michael was still his unassuming self. We hold him and Hawa in high regard and cherish our association. I had returned to Accra after my years in the diaspora. We parted on the understanding that they would contact us in Accra when they came to Accra for Christmas that year as they had planned to do. We failed to hear from them and assumed that they had changed their travel plans. We had not exchanged current addresses.

We were in New York for several months and returned to Accra in April 2010. It was with extreme shock and sadness that I received a call from a colleague to inform me that Michael had passed away in England in the month of June from an illness which ran a swift course. Michael had apparently been ill for some time and suddenly succumbed to a deterioration of the condition in Plymouth, England. Michael had died at a relatively young age. The burial and funeral rites were held at Afede. Dr Klaye drove me in his car with Drs Kofi Dow and Yumunusah also accompanying us to Afede. The Ghanaian Saudi Arabian group was well represented: Professors Lade Wosornu and Adu Gyamfi and their wives were in attendance.

Tabuk and its district had some places of interest. Foremost among them was the beach on the Red Sea which attracted water sports enthusiasts; those interested in snorkelling and diving spent their weekends there. Indeed, some enthusiasts apparently signed contracts to come to work in Tabuk so as to enjoy the beach at the weekends. We were not enthusiasts and so went to the beach only twice. Drowning fatalities sometimes occurred.

The Saudis were aware of the fact that oil resources were a finite source of income. They therefore started a process of diversifying their economy by promoting agriculture and animal husbandry in a major way. Large model agricultural farms with enormous acreages were set up, irrigated, and fertilized for cultivation. They cultivated wheat and other crops on a large commercial scale. In horticulture, a wide variety of flowers was grown and exported. They exported some of them to Holland (Holland was famous for exporting its home-grown flowers). Their dairy farm was also impressive. Although almost all the employees were foreign expatriates on contract, the Saudis were making an economic statement that they could be independent of the oil reserve. The Saudi monarchical political establishment spent much of the oil income consistently on building and laying an infrastructure to the benefit of its civilian population. The health service, education and road network could not be faulted. Our neighbours in Nigeria and indeed many other African countries, including Ghana, could take a page from the Saudis' book on how to use the country's resources to improve living standards for their people.

Yolande and I undertook some sightseeing tours. We took advantage of our geographical location in Saudi Arabia to visit a number of countries in the Middle East like Jordan, Cyprus and Israel.

Jordan is a neighbouring country which shared borders with the northern part of Saudi Arabia. The two countries are linked by a good road as well as the air route. We boarded a very comfortable coach from Tabuk to Amman, the capital of Jordan, for our trip. The drive took us through a picturesque landscape of desert and mountain. We made Amman our base in for the week we spent in Jordan. It was a country of both Biblical and secular history. Historical monuments and Biblical relics were great tourist attractions. A ride on the back of a camel and dipping into the water of the Red Sea (having a high specific gravity) come nostalgically to my mind. We did as much sightseeing as possible before returning to Tabuk.

The visit to Cyprus was much more extensive and fulfilling than the one to Jordan. Cyprus is an island state, a Republic of virtually two countries in the Mediterranean Sea. The two components are the Greek (the larger portion) and Turkish ones. We flew from Tabuk to the Greek Cyprus and stayed in a modern large hotel for about a week. From Cyprus we joined a holiday cruise to Israel and the Holy Land; the cruise liner brought us back to Cyprus.

Cyprus had been a British colony that later gained its independence following a national movement of agitation which was led in the 1950s and 1960s by the Archbishop Makarios of the Greek Orthodox Church. The Turks, backed by their Islamic neighbour, Turkey, broke off and established their own Federal state on the island. Britain still maintains a military base on the Greek side of the island. It was indeed fortuitous that we ran into three friends, all three then resident in the country. They were Nigel and Jane Ross, Fred and Koomi Amroliwala, and Ben Moore. The truism in the adage "Piccolo Mundo" (It's a small world) could not be more apt.

Yolande and I had known Nigel and Janet Ross in Kumasi since the 1970s when Nigel was the British Council Director there. Now retired, Nigel and Janet had settled in Greek Cyprus. They invited us to their home in Paphos; it was a most beautiful house, perched on a hill and reached by a meandering road. The view of the surrounding part of the country was breath-taking as the sun shone. We spent a whole day with them reminiscing about our various experiences; their children, Karen and Angus, all grown up now, like ours are, used to be playmates with Brian and Neil.

Dr Ben Moore, the consultant gynaecologist in Hereford who came to do a spell of one year as our Chief in Tabuk engaged himself on a long term locum in the British Military Hospital. He certainly moved around quite a bit, doing jobs in several places. We caught up with him in Cyprus to our great surprise. He invited us to dinner at the officers' mess in the military base. We learned from him to our great surprise that Dr Fred Amroliwala was also at the Base hospital, working as a physician. Thus we met Fred and renewed our friendship at Akrotiri. Fred and his wife Koomi entertained us to a memorable reunion private dinner at an exclusive restaurant. Unexpected and unplanned meetings with old friends are so uplifting.

We went sightseeing in various parts of the Greek sector; our visit to the Greek/Turkish border, a mere formality, was unspectacular. I was impressed by the widespread use of solar energy. Solar roof panels were installed on a large number of buildings in Nicosia and Paphos. The Cypriots certainly took full advantage of solar technology to exploit the relatively long hours of sunlight. Ghana should also be able to benefit from this technology of clean energy with good government interest.

Next, we joined a cruise liner bound for Israel; it was a great opportunity to fulfil a life-long desire to visit the Holy Land. We sailed to the port city of Haifa; from Haifa we were driven in a coach to Tel Aviv. A significant observation was that on entry into Israel, our passports were not stamped as is customary on entering any other country. This was because we had come from Saudi Arabia and were due to return there; we would be barred from entry into Saudi Arabia if our passports were stamped indicating that we had been to Israel, we very likely would be denied re-entry The Israelis, being aware of this, accommodated visitors from Saudi Arabia. This was one of the foibles of the Middle East political game. We were taken to several tourist centres, including the Wailing Wall and a famous industrial diamond centre where I bought my wife a ring at a discounted price for tourists The climax of our tour was arriving in Jerusalem and the Holy Land. The Christian Biblical names, sites and images conveyed their own vivid sanctity of the events in the Christian Biblical literature. A day was far too brief a period to spend there; it was nevertheless a memory to cherish for a lifetime. We returned to Cyprus on the cruise liner. We finally flew back to Tabuk in a mood of spiritual fulfilment.

All employees in my category were entitled to an annual leave of six weeks. A free return ticket from your point of hire (London in my case) on Saudi Arabia Airlines was also an entitlement. It was beneficial to start a leave on a weekend, taking a Thursday afternoon flight from Tabuk to London via Jeddah. The timing of the leave had to be negotiated with the departmental Chief so that the workforce was not seriously depleted at any one particular time; not every consultant could go on leave at Christmas ; this needed to be taken in rotation and the Chief had the final ruling.

London was always my first port of call and where I received my first welcome from my family. I went to Ghana almost every year during my annual leave in all the 14 years spent in Tabuk. The Ghana destinations were invariably and obviously Accra and Kumasi. My brother Bill and sister Felicia were resident in Accra and this was the occasion to see them; most of my friends resided in Accra or Kumasi. In our earlier diaspora years we stayed with Yaw and Gwen Agyarko at their airport residential house; they were excellent hosts to us, they made us feel as members of their family. In later years, while on our visits to Accra, we stayed at the Sunset Guest House, also located at the airport residential area, on a couple of occasions.

In our earlier years, on our brief visits to Kumasi, we stayed as guests with Nadia and Saleem Hadad in their house at Nhyiaeso, not far from Kplomdedie. We also stayed once with Dr Emmanuel Adinkra. They all hosted us generously. In later years, we stayed in our own house when our visits to Kumasi were longer. On these visits we boarded at Cicero Hotel for a few days as we cleaned up our house before moving in; Cicero Hotel was diagonally just opposite our house.

The visits were occasions to renew friendships, some of longstanding. If circumstances permitted, we did not fail to host a party. On one such occasion in 1993, accompanied this time by Ronnie who was then an undergraduate at Cambridge, we held a memorable Christmas party. Our friends in Accra and Kumasi hosted us to lunches and dinners. These friends included the Hadads, Adus,

Adadevohs and Tettehs in Kumasi; the Accra friends included the Blukoo Alloteys, Adomakohs and Harold Philips. Emmanuel and Joan Asare treated us and Ronnie to an unforgettable Christmas lunch in 1993; two other guests were Mr and Mrs Ofori. Both Joan Asare and Joan Ofori had taught Ronnie at the Kumasi Ridge International School and were pleased to hear of his academic achievements. Friendships are like flowering plants; they need nurturing like watering to sustain them.

I had my moments of sadness and solitude in Tabuk. I was in Tabuk when I received with shock and great sadness the news of the passing away of Harold Ebo Philips. He had travelled from Ghana to London where he had a successful surgical operation. While having an apparently good recovery, he suddenly succumbed several days later to an unrelated natural cause. He had hosted me and Yolande to a splendid dinner in his house in Accra a year before; that was my last time of seeing him. His eldest son, Brian, a medical doctor, had predeceased him at a young age. I had been the best man at his wedding. Gladys was left in great grief which I shared.

The next one was of no less magnitude. I had shared a long period of friendship with Austin Tetteh; it dated back to our student days at the UCGC and attained a near-siblinghood status when we were in Kumasi. I received a message in Tabuk from Yolande in London that Austin had been admitted to Korle Bu Hospital in Accra in a seriously ill condition. When I spoke to his wife, Narkaley, in Accra for the first time, I held the chances of his recovery very high; my next call gave me devastating news: Austin had passed away. I had been denied any chance of seeing Austin before his departure. These were very sad moments for me.

I lost two associates in the Tabuk cantonment. One was a Nigerian Consultant Physician Endocrinologist. He was recruited from Ibadan where he was a Professor. Middle aged, he was friendly with me and Yolande because he had had part of his elementary education in Ghana. Yolande and I had entertained him for lunch and dinner. He attended my opera sessions a few times although he had not turned into an enthusiast. He had been on admission for a few days in the medical ward for what most of us thought was not a serious condition. The shocking news of his sudden death in the ward was conveyed to

475

me at an early stage of a party I was hosting; it was unexpected and was received by all with shock and sadness. The body was conveyed to Nigeria for burial.

The second was the death of Elizabeth, a young English woman. A slim nurse in her 30s, she was a very close friend of two of my friends and had visited me a couple of times with one of our mutual friends. She was a heavy smoker. She died in her room in the female apartment block from a non-natural cause; her death saddened all of the hospital community, especially those of us who knew her well.

Saddam Hussein had set his sights on two ambitious aims: namely his prominence among Arab leaders in the Middle East and dominance in the oil world market. He was counting on the first to come with the shift in the balance of power away from Egypt, which he believed had been too willing to accommodate the USA and Israel. He believed that the second would come with the control of Kuwait, which he had accused of stealing Iraq's oil and ignoring OPEC output ceilings.

In August 1990, Saddam Hussein suddenly invaded Kuwait with his troops and took over the country's oil reserves; Iraqi troops and tanks poured into Kuwait in their numbers. This created a new geo-political conundrum in the Middle East. The Emir of Kuwait and his family fled to neighbouring Saudi Arabia. If the invasion of Kuwait surprised the Saudis, they were more shocked by the inaction of countries they considered as their friends, especially their biggest client on their payment roll, Yasser Arafat of the PLO (Palestinian Liberation Organisation). Arafat came out to support Iraq; so did King Hussein of Jordan. Libya, Tunisia, Sudan and Mauritania reportedly, distanced themselves from Saudi Arabia. Although Saddam Hussein did not disclose any intention of staking claims to Saudi Arabian oilfields, this was a possibility; his new friends would not object to it either.

Saudi Arabia was forced by circumstances to turn to Egypt, an Arab friend, and most importantly the USA, a non-Islamic country, but this was a mandatory military requirement; a beggar has no choice. Colin Powell, the American Chairman of the Joint Chiefs of Staff assigned General Schwarzkopf the role of Commander in Chief for "Desert Storm".

It took another five months before the Desert Storm military attack was launched. President Bush carefully and painstakingly prepared the ground. The United Nations Organisation approved of the attack if Saddam Hussein failed to withdraw all his troops from Kuwait by a deadline in mid-January 1991.

Tabuk, located as it was in the NW of the country, was not far from the potential war zone. The Air and Military Bases constituted legitimate military targets if war broke out. There was a steady build-up of a large American contingent with planes. The Saudis faced another predicament: an American military would lead to an influx of female military personnel who drove cars on the streets in Tabuk; this bred hostility with the Uleama.

Saddam Hussein was known to have used chemical warfare in his war against Iran. He was therefore capable and likely to use it again against Saudi Arabia with missiles. Preparations for war had to take this possibility into consideration. All non-Saudi employees were given the option of voluntarily terminating their contracts and leaving the country. Several countries made provision to assist their nationals in leaving the Kingdom. A few employees availed themselves of the option and left the country. Preparations were made in the hospital to receive casualties from the war zone. Admission for elective surgery was stopped, curtailing admissions to only emergency cases and patients in labour. We were put through rehearsals for combatting the dropping of chemicals of mass destruction; some of us received face masks to wear in case of need (I still keep mine as a memento). An alert sign of chemical warfare would be the dropping down from the skies of dead birds. Personnel in appropriate apparel rehearsed their rescue roles in specially designed tents constructed for the purpose. The atmosphere of uncertainty about dire events and preparation impacted on all of us; it was a time of great anxiety.

The Gulf War (aka Desert Storm) was short and swift, an exercise in military precision. Saddam Hussein failed to respond to the UN ultimatum in January 1991. A large coalition from an impressively long list of countries led by the Americans attacked Hussein's forces in two remarkable phases. The first phase consisted of ceaseless bombardment of the Iraqi Air Force in Iraq, thus completely crippling and rendering the Air Force impotent; this was achieved with modern guided laser precision missiles which the Americans had master-minded. The bombardment lasted several days with many of the flights originating from the Tabuk Air Base. In response, Iraq landed a solitary guided missile in Riyadh; it was a random one. Hussein, however, landed several missiles in Israel; this raised some concern and anxiety in Israel. Israel seriously considered using its nuclear bomb in retaliation, but yielded to American pressure to refrain from doing so.

The second phase was a ground force attack on Iraqi forces in Kuwait. The attack had been expected for some time, but nobody knew exactly when. I was in the middle of a Caesarean section operation one night when it was announced that the land force invasion had commenced. A large armoured force invasion started in the Kuwait quarter. The full Iraqi land force engaged the coalition force in this area in full combat. Unknown to the Iraqi forces, the much larger coalition invasion force in a pincer movement entered Kuwait from a different direction and completely encircled the Iraqi forces from behind, thus cutting off their supply line from behind. The military victory was achieved in days. The much feared and vaunted Iraqi military force was humiliated by General Schwarzkopf. His Deputy was, for obvious political and nationalistic reasons, a Saudi and a member of the Royal family; all the shots were called by the Americans. The coalition forces could have continued their conquest and invaded Iraq, but chose not to do so. President Bush stated that the goal was the liberation of Kuwait and not the conquest of Iraq. He went on to say that the coalition was determined to destroy Hussein's nuclear bomb potential and his chemical war hardware facilities. Hussein responded to the military defeat by setting the Kuwait oilfields on fire; the Americans put out the fires. The allied troops stopped short of Baghdad and Hussein continued to remain in power. He reputedly moved from one secret house to another so that the coalition forces did not succeed in capturing him.

The events of the war were comprehensively reported blow by blow by the African American CNN reporter from the front line. General Schwarzkopf and his troops received a heroes' ticker tape welcome on their return home to the USA. The casualty rate was reported to be low.

The successful end of the war brought us all great relief in Tabuk. I conveyed the news of my safety to my family and friends in Ghana and England; they had all been concerned for me.

This decade also witnessed some major world events which merit mention. The events I recall in these memoirs are not to be regarded as the history of the period. The events include the following: Fall of the Berlin Wall and the unification of East and West Germany into one Germany of the present day. The break-up of the Soviet Union Republics; the release of Nelson Mandela from prison and the collapse of the apartheid regime in South Africa; the death of Princess Diana.

The Berlin Wall had been fearsome and separated the prosperous West Germany from the poor Communist East Germany and Eastern Europe then under the Communist Russia yoke. With the fall of the wall, the whole of Communist Eastern Europe collapsed like a pack of cards followed by the creation of several new states in its wake. The creation of the Soviet Union in 1917 had followed the collapse of the Czarist regime. The death of Communism in the Soviet Union under President Gorbachev eventually ended in the dissolution of the Soviet Union into Russia, Ukraine and Belarus. Yeltsin replaced Gorbachev as President in a dramatic and bullish manner.

In 1990, after 27 years in jail on Robben Island in South Africa as a political prisoner, Nelson Mandela was released and freed. He had been the towering symbol and head of the struggle against apartheid in South Africa. The vivid picture of the smiling Mandela, holding the hand of his wife, Winnie, and walking out with an air of dignity still persists in my mind; the event received worldwide media coverage. In his speech, he urged the native South Africans to keep up the pressure on President de Klerk, who had ordered his release from prison. The apartheid regime came to its end shortly after. Under the new constitution which permitted NSAs (Native South Africans) to vote, Mandela won the Presidential election overwhelmingly. Mandela, in his wisdom, appointed de Klerk as the Vice President. They were both later jointly awarded the Nobel Peace Prize.

Princess Diana, Princess of Wales, ex-wife of Prince Charles, heir to the British throne, the darling of the media all over the world, died tragically in a car accident in Paris. Dodi al Fayed, her Egyptian boyfriend who was in the car with her, and the driver also died in the car. Dodi was the son of Mr Fayed, the billionaire owner of the famous Harrods departmental store. The car was being hotly pursued at very high speed by paparazzi when the fatal crash occurred. Dodi's father for many years insisted that this was a conspiracy to kill the two lovers and that it was not an ordinary accident. I do not subscribe to this view. It is an outlandish opinion. It was an extremely sad event for which we all mourned. I set aside my personal prejudice against her lifestyle and in the most unwise interview she had held with Martin Bashir, a journalist, a couple of years earlier. Her two sons were then young boys in a public school as boarders when she disclosed some details about her family life with her husband, Prince Charles. In my view, the disclosures in the interview were thoughtless and showed little consideration for the potential impact on the young boys in a boarding institution.

Television had transformed the coverage of events, minor or major. History-making events were vividly brought to you as you sat in your living room sipping your tea, coffee or a non-alcoholic drink.

Our four boys were not abandoned and left on their own in London for too long a period by their parents while initially both Yolande and I were in Saudi Arabia. Dr Felix Konotey Ahulu kindly agreed to be in 'loco parentis' for us in London. Yolande's two years in Jubail was followed by her MPH course in Liverpool. The boys pursued their individual courses with diligence. Ronnie being the youngest and most impressionable naturally received the most attention. Ronnie was one of a tiny ethnic minority in the City of London School, an excellent and prestigious school with a very good academic record. It was important for Yolande to attend the PTA (Parents and Teachers Association) meetings; I also attended two such meetings when I was in London at the times the meetings were held. Discussing problems with the teachers imbued the wards with more confidence. Ronnie took part in the school's extracurricular activities; he took delight in being a member of the students' cadet corps, attaining the rank of a sergeant major. He enrolled for and commenced lessons in playing the flute. He was lucky to have a dedicated tutor. He pursued the course with great enthusiasm. He finally attained the eighth grade, which qualified him to play in any orchestra; he joined the City of London School Orchestra. Yolande and I shared the pride in watching and listening as he performed in the school orchestra and in a duet at the school's concert. His interest in playing the flute remains intense and undiminished.

The personal interest of a master in a student can play a significant role in the development and achievement of that student. Such was the case with Ronnie who passed the GCSE examination with distinction. Following the publication of his performance in a small column in an Ealing local paper, Mr Harry Greenway, the local MP (Member of Parliament), phoned to personally congratulate the 'Ealing Boy' who had done so well. Mr Bass, the Headmaster of the school, in conjunction with a vote by the student body and teachers, appointed Ronnie Head Boy when he was in the sixth form (the second Agble Head Boy in a school in London). Ronnie was also awarded the John Carpenter Prize (a prestigious prize named after the Founder of the school), a highly acclaimed prize and an adfinitum award.

Ronnie and his brothers were not bookworms; they also indulged in sporting activities, tennis in particular, much in the footsteps of their father. Brian and Ronnie took to the game more seriously and joined the Ealing Tennis Club; this club also attracted visiting Wimbledon Championship Tennis contestants just before the annual championship matches. Brian, Dugald and Ronnie developed a flair for the game to become very good players. At 18 years, Ronnie won the Ealing club under-twenty championship tournament; he also played regularly at the Queens Tennis Club. A few years later, he captained the Cambridge University Tennis B Team. Brian, a few years later, also was the tennis coach at UWI when he was there as a medical student. Dugald was a gifted tennis player, but devoted less time to this game; he was consumed by his interest in chess. The Agble family, and this includes Neil, has always been absorbed by the game of tennis. If any of my leave from Tabuk coincided with the Wimbledon championship fortnight, Ronnie could always be relied upon to secure me tickets for the centre court or Number 1 court. While a student at Cambridge, Ronnie assisted in manning the scoreboard at Wimbledon.

Although my pastime did not include chess, Dugald embraced the game and represented Imperial College in tournaments during his undergraduate years. He carried this participation to a higher level in his postgraduate years when he was a deputy warden in Bet Hall (a resident hall for post-graduate students). He organized monthly chess tournaments, as a full day event on Sundays, open to all those interested in the game. Full refreshments were served and prizes were awarded to winners at the competition. It gained great popularity and reportedly became the most famous chess tournament in the London area at the time. This revealed an entrepreneurial talent in Dugald, absent in his siblings.

Yolande and I did not participate in any of the students' activities during their undergraduate years, except on one occasion. This was at the May Ball at Cambridge University on an invitation from Ronnie. The Ball, much touted, and which takes place in June, strangely, had a long history. Since I was in Tabuk, I had to time my leave to coincide with the time of the May Ball. Yolande, Dugald and I travelled by train to Cambridge and to Ronnie's flat, changed and dressed up for the dinner and dance event. I had not been on the dance floor for some years and this was a reminiscent occasion for me; it was an occasion to cherish.

When I was forced to take a decision in 1988 on my future with Bomso Clinic, I had placed my family above the clinic; foremost in my mind was the provision of the best education I could provide for the boys. Now, I was beginning to see some light at the end of the previously unknown tunnel. Neil had completed his three-year Engineering degree course at Imperial College and commenced work. Brian, Dugald and Ronnie had all obtained their first degrees from equally high-ranking universities and advanced on to their postgraduate or professional degree courses. It is now germane to annotate these educational pursuits.

Brian graduated with a BSc in Anatomy from Bristol University after three years. His maternal grandmother, aunt Gloria and cousin Renee came over from New York to accompany me and Yolande to witness the graduation ceremony. Brian followed up with a Master's degree course in Human Anatomy at University College in London. This course entailed the writing and presentation of a thesis; Brian thus obtained an MSc degree. With an aim to pursue a career in Medicine, he gained entrance to UWI (University of West Indies). He went to Kingston, Jamaica for the pre-clinical course and completed his clinical course in Barbados. Brian participated in sporting and social activities at both campuses. He came to England for his elective semester.

Dugald gained admission from City of London School to Imperial College of London University to read a four-year MSc degree course in Chemical Engineering. Dugald's Chemistry teacher had described him as one of the best Chemistry students he had ever had (he was a teacher whose teaching career spanned several years). In his third year at Imperial College, he applied to attend a course which was open to all Chemical Engineering students in both East and Western Europe. The venue was Paris and over 3,000 applied for the 30 places. Two hundred of the applicants including Dugald were interviewed in Britain; three places were allocated to Britain. Dugald was one of the three selected from Britain for their allocated number. The 30 students were accommodated in a five-star hotel in Paris. At the end of the course, three of the students who attended the course were asked to make presentations; Dugald was one of the three selected to do so; this was a notable feat. He successfully completed the Master's course and obtained the MSc degree in Chemical Engineering.

Partly in recognition of his academic prowess and talent, we successfully persuaded him to do a PhD degree. The three-year PhD course entailed an original work of research; some of the research required to be conducted at zero gravitational force; he had to go to the European Space Centre in France for this purpose and undergo the exercise and perform the necessary experiments. On realizing that the Chemical Engineering Society into which he enrolled as a member did not have a journal, he decided to remedy this anomaly. He raised funds from appeals sufficiently to launch the Chemical Engineering Journal of Imperial College. The first issue, a copy of which I proudly own, was a glossy premier issue. Despite all this, Dugald always maintained a low profile and declined any opportunity to draw attention to himself; this was Dugald, "sui generis".

Not very long after commencing his postgraduate PhD course, the post of sub-warden of Bet Hall (a hall of residence for postgraduate students) became vacant and applications for the post were invited. Dugald applied and was shortlisted for an interview. Unfortunately, Dugald was away in the USA on holiday on the day scheduled for the interview; the interview was cancelled and postponed to another day on which he was able to attend. He was indeed very fortunate to have been offered the position of sub warden, at which he served for three years, until he completed his PhD course.

In summary, it can be stated that Dugie acquitted himself very well in all respects at Imperial College; our family is justifiably proud of this.

At the City of London School, Ronnie had passed the GCSEs with distinction and in his sixth form Yolande and I went to a meeting at the school; we sat in the school hall with parents whose wards had just gained admission to the school or had wards for whom they wanted admission. The parents had been invited to come and ask questions about the school. Sitting on the dais was an eminent group consisting of some members of the school board, Mr Bass and Ronnie; Mr Bass presided as Chairman at the meeting and answered most of the questions, but depending on the nature of what was being asked, he referred it to Ronnie to be answered, from time to time. Ronnie's performance in answering the questions won admiration from many in the hall. Apart from being awarded the John Carpenter prize, Ronnie was also a member of the school orchestra.

Without any pressure from us at all, Ronnie decided to study Medicine. In the application form one had to list five medical schools of one's choice in a sequential order of preference; gaining admission to only one was all that was required. Some of the medical schools conducted interviews before making an offer for admission. Ronnie made his selection of five with Emmanuel College, Cambridge topping the list. Ronnie was called for an interview at Nottingham (a highly rated medical school) and made an offer of admission; this was a tremendous achievement as he had already been offered admission to (and accepted) Cambridge. One of the teachers at the City of London, a Cambridge graduate, had to eat his words when Ronnie told him that he had applied to go to Cambridge to study Medicine; he told him that he stood no chance of gaining admission to Cambridge. Here it is germane to relate this irony: in 1954, the British Colonial Office applied to place me at Emmanuel College, Cambridge University for my medical degree, but this proved unsuccessful; I was as a result placed in Aberdeen University.

In a spirit of excitement Neil drove Ronnie and their mother from 47 MPD to Cambridge for Ronnie to commence his studies. Ronnie settled down quickly and enjoyed his course there.

The Oxbridge medical course had two phases. The first phase, lasting three years ended with a BA degree; this was followed by the clinical course which ended with the MB, ChB (Bachelor degrees in Medicine and Surgery) degrees. Ronnie completed the first phase with a BA degree. Dugald, Yolande and I attended the graduation ceremony. Neil and Brian were not in England at the time. Commemorative photographs of parents and their begowned son Ronnie were taken on the manicured verdant green quadrangle; these are treasured pictures.

While at Cambridge, Ronnie continued to play tennis seriously as already chronicled. Although he failed in getting the captaincy of the A team, he captained the B team and represented the University in matches. His association with the Wimbledon championship has already been narrated.

Ronnie is a classical music devotee and plays the flute in a Chamber music orchestra. At its annual election the Cambridge Medical Students' Association elected Ronnie, then in his penultimate year, as the President of the Association. In this capacity he had an official office and served as the medical students' representative at Faculty board meetings; this was the acme of his leadership role in his student days. He played this lightly without any airs or graces.

Ronald turned of age in 1996 when he was in his clinical years. We planned and organized his birthday party at the Ritz hotel in London. The guest list included (apart from his three brothers) some of his close friends from Cambridge, Mr David Howell with his wife Nancy, Dr Felix Konotey Ahulu with his wife Rosemary and most importantly Mr Bass and his wife. Mr Bass had retired as the Headmaster from City of London school. He travelled all the way from Grimsby in Yorkshire to come to honour the invitation; it was a great pleasure and honour to see him. Ronnie's aunt Gloria and maternal grandmother came from New York for the occasion. It was held during the Wimbledon Championships fortnight; indeed Ronnie had to rush from a Wimbledon assignment at SW19 to the Ritz at Piccadilly, change quickly from sweaty sporting attire into an appropriate evening attire. An informal drinks reception was followed by a formal, but intimate dinner party. The ambience at the five-star Ritz hotel, drinks and splendid cuisine provided a befitting grandeur to the event. The round of toasts and speeches brought the evening to an end. It was a memorable celebration of Ronnie's birthday and also for all the blessings which had come our way.

During his student days at Imperial College, Neil had the added role as the titular head of the family at 47 MPD. Yolande and I were in Saudi Arabia and Brian was in Bristol. Neil kept me regularly informed by phone and letters about all that was going on. In his role as the Foreign Students' Officer, he had to liaise with other students abroad who were on exchange programmes with Imperial College and vice-versa.

Neil was a Ghanaian and felt proud to be so. During his degree course in Material Science Engineering, he was required to spend a semester in relevant locations for a research programme. He had a choice from two places, namely Namibia and Obuasi Gold Mines in Ghana. Without hesitation Neil chose Oboasi in Ghana as did two other colleagues. Neil had not visited Ghana for at least four years and was full of excitement and told them a lot about Ghana. I had driven Neil and the rest of my family to Obuasi many years before on a visit. On arrival in Accra, Neil and his fellow colleagues were met and driven to Obuasi. They were welcomed by an official on arrival at Obuasi. They were then assigned to their respective accommodations for their semester engagements. The officer in the exercise of his duty unveiled a shock: Neil's Imperial College colleagues were assigned furnished accommodation in management bungalows with the use of the management social club house; Neil was assigned accommodation in the artisans' quarters with poor facilities (in Ghanaian parlance, "Zongo Lane"). Neil's colleagues were Caucasian and Neil is not. The very crude element of discrimination à la apartheid was clear for all to see. Neil complied as there was no alternative choice. Yolande and I happened to be in Kumasi at the time on holidays from Saudi Arabia and saw Neil's accommodation when we went to visit him at Obuasi. We were appalled and decided to protest, but Neil restrained us and said he would handle the discrimination himself. He soon after joined his colleagues in the bungalow accommodation including the managerial facilities. But that this should have happened at all! In Nkrumah's Ghana, during Rawlings' PNDC government! Yolande was incandescent with rage, and wanted to contact President Rawlings at once, she was sure his reaction would have matched hers.

Neil stayed on and carried out his research project and returned to London after the semester. Yolande and I left Kumasi for London after our brief visit. Neil organized and staged a party in our house Kplomdedie (le grand maison) for his colleagues and some senior officers; he asserted his Ghanaian status and pedigree pointedly. One of his colleagues, a female, apparently returned to Obuasi Gold Mines later after graduation to take up a lucrative appointment. Neil's experience on arrival could influence any decision on seeking employment in his home country. His sixth form allocation to Bolgatanga could not be easily forgotten. Our fate in life is often decided by factors and forces beyond our control.

The closing chapter on the boys' education was finally drawing to an end. Brian had qualified as a Medical doctor with an MB, ChB degree (in addition to a BSc and MSc) in Barbados. Ronnie had also done the same in Cambridge with BA, MB, ChB degrees. After obtaining their full medical registrations after their house jobs, their names appeared in the British Medical Register, along with mine, as the three AGBLES in the Medical Register.

One day while Yolande and I were in Tabuk, we received a phone call from Dugald in London; Dugald had obtained a PhD in Chemical Engineering from Imperial College. We were overcome with joy and thanked the Almighty for the blessings He had showered on us. Dugald's PhD was the academic jewel in the crown of his academic achievement. The day for the convocation was fixed and was due fairly soon. Yolande and I attended the graduation ceremonies for Brian and Ronnie at Bristol and Cambridge respectively. We decided and were determined to fly and attend Dugald's day of academic honour and celebrate the occasion in style and with gratitude. Dugald was entitled to two tickets for the convocation ceremony. We booked our two-leg flight with Saudi Arabia Air Lines from Tabuk to London. The Saudi Airline was a dependable one which kept to a strict and regular schedule. We went to the Tabuk airport in a spirit of excitement and anticipation in the late afternoon to board a flight to Jeddah on the first leg. At the appointed time, the plane returning to Jeddah had still not arrived from Jeddah. After an anxious and a very long wait, the Saudi Airlines official announced that the flight to Jeddah was cancelled because there was no plane to undertake the journey; there would be no other flight that day. The next flight would be on the following day.

We consulted the most senior Saudi Airlines officer to find any possible way to make our journey and connect to our flight from Jeddah to London; it was a frustrating exercise. It became quite clear that we would not be able to be in London in time for the convocation to see Dugald fully and distinguishably robed in the academic gown and receiving the PhD certificate. It is one disappointment in my life which I still have not forgotten nor overcome. It was with a great feeling of sadness that I conveyed the news to Dugald by phone. Two of our close friends were in London at the time and were pleased to go to represent us at the convocation ceremony. They were Mrs Jacqui Zwenes and Mr David Howell. Dugald was formally conferred with a PhD degree.

We threw off the London disappointment and planned for a Tabuk event. We invited Dugald to come to Tabuk on a celebration visit. He duly came and stayed on for about a fortnight. We celebrated with two parties in his honour. We invited almost all our Tabuk friends to the first party; it was a buffet dinner with drinks. The second was limited to 10 invited guests (close and senior friends); it was more formal.

Yolande prepared and served a delicious sit down to table meal, which we all enjoyed. We drank non-alcoholic champagne and toasted to Dugald's past and future success; we all felt proud of his achievement. He spent the fortnight in relaxation before returning to London. Although the visit compensated to some degree for our absence from the convocation ceremony, that void can never be filled.

During our fading years in Tabuk, Yolande and I spent a unique Christmas in London. The whole family had been spending Christmas together at 47 MPD. With the boys now scattered in different locations, Dugald suggested and arranged a package Yuletide celebration for me and Yolande at London Ritz hotel in Piccadilly; a four-day package which included Christmas Eve and Boxing Day. We checked in on 23rd December. The room was beautiful and classy; the décor was like from a magazine picture; the bed was wide with a very attractive white bedspread over it. There was a chilled bottle of champagne in an ice-bucket resting on the coffee table to welcome us; the bathroom was in pristine white and chrome, the dressing gowns and towels were made of fluffy 100% white cotton. Breakfast was served to us in our room, wheeled in on an elegant trolley; the breakfast offering was superb. We dined in the restaurant in the evening. The hotel arranged for those who so wished to attend the Christmas Eve service at Buckingham Palace Church, St James Church; it was the church for the Palace household. We were conveyed there in a coach and driven back to the hotel after the service. Dugald and Ronnie came to join us for the Christmas Day dinner at the hotel; it was a unique and memorable Christmas for all four of us.

Every story, every event, has a beginning, a middle and an end; so has my sojourn in Tabuk. I had arrived in Tabuk in 1987 to accomplish a mission of educating my four sons; this aim had now been achieved to an extent beyond our dreams. The time had now arrived for me to depart from Tabuk and return home. The unique Christmas at the Ritz hotel in 1999 was my swansong in my final year in Tabuk.

We had made a home from home in our townhouse residence for more than 14 years. Preparations for our departure had to be planned carefully and carried out.

We had established a comfortable abode in 47 MPD in London which served as a home from home. Although I had acquired an entitlement to stay in Britain, my national home was Ghana; our residential home was in Kumasi. There was, however, no haste in returning to Ghana. I would still have to practise my profession as a gynaecologist for many years to come, but in the private sector. Bomso Clinic was of course completely out of consideration. A medical colleague in General Practice in Kumasi had extended an open invitation to me to join him at any time I was willing to do so; it was a kind, thoughtful and generous offer, but there were some limitations regarding facilities for an OB/GY practice. I was moving on in years as well as my siblings who were resident in Accra; some of my close friends in Kumasi were no longer there. I still had my vacant plot of land at Agbamo Lane at the airport residential area. I had had a long-standing invitation from Dr Kwame Nyaho Tamakloe to practise at his Medical Centre in Accra whenever the time for me was ripe. Bearing all the foregoing points in mind, it was obvious that I would have to relocate from Kumasi to Accra on my return home to Ghana. This decision would naturally have a bearing on our preparations to leave Tabuk finally. Although our relocation to Accra was not in doubt, the matter of our residence was not quickly nor finally decided until our final departure for London. Some years earlier, we had received advice from a long-standing friend, Mr David Amankwa, who was an entrepreneur in the building and construction business. The quotation for the building on our plot of land would exceed our financial resources. My mother had bequeathed me a bungalow at Kokomemle on Abele Road in Accra (the street was reportedly named after her, Agble, with a misspelling for erecting the first building in that area which at the time was undeveloped low virgin grassland). We invited an architect to design an attractive extension to the bungalow for our occupancy. The architect designed an appealing extension, but again, his quotation cost of building was prohibitive; it is always prudent to explore other options.

We received information about an Estate Agent who was putting up very affordable bungalows in a new environment in Accra. On one of our visits to Ghana, we indeed went to view some of them and found them of a reasonable standard. On our return to Tabuk, we made an attempt to pay a deposit into the London bank account of the Estate Agent, but this was unsuccessful as there was a snag with their account. The failure proved later on to have been fortuitous. At this juncture we decided to put our Accra residence on a back burner.

Our return to Ghana would have to be phased into two; in the first phase we would reside in London; whilst in London, I would gainfully do some locum jobs to earn some money; I would at the same time map out phase two in Accra with special reference to our residential accommodation.

Our activities in Tabuk then centred on purchasing items we would need in Ghana, packing and finally shipping them to Ghana. With negligible tax on merchandise in the Kingdom, it was prudent to buy every affordable required item there and ship them to your desired destination. We composed a list of all desired household items; this included a large refrigerator, cold storage, a combined gas and electricity cooker, washing machine, dishwasher and eight air conditioner units. We also purchased a modern 52inch TV set and an elegant chandelier for our living room; we purchased a large garden umbrella. Our friends in Riyadh (Dr Alex Bruce Tagoe and Mr Herbert

Dakwa) assisted us in the purchase of a new Toyota Corolla car in Riyadh.

We had acquired a lot of items in making a home in Tabuk; we sold several household items, but kept some for shipment to Ghana. All our belongings were securely packed by professional packers who also engaged a shipping company to load all of them in a container for delivery in Ghana. They would await our arrival in Ghana for clearance and collection.

Masalama is a departure farewell party held in honour of a departing colleague by his or her associates and co-workers. It varies in degree and extent depending on the esteem in which the honouree is held and also the length of time the honouree had spent in the establishment. Not everyone is accorded a Masalama party; success also depends on how much money has been raised from contributions. In my final days, I was accorded three Masalama parties by three different groups. My fellow colleagues from Nigeria, all doctors, hosted me and Yolande to a dinner party at the most prominent hotel in Tabuk. After a few farewell speeches and a group photograph, I was presented with a marvellous gift: it was a large clock which played a short melody of classical music before announcing the hour; it hangs prominently in my living room in Accra. The second Masalama was a grand and bigger function, organized and staged by the nurses and midwives in the OB/GY Department; it was held at the recreation centre. Anne, a nurse/midwife from Cameroon, was one of the chief organisers of the party. I was encouraged and requested to invite and come along with as many friends and colleagues as I wished. My Nigerian colleagues and my Egyptian Anaesthetist friend, Dr Filibos, were all in attendance. There was a good spread of varied and delicious dishes. The doctors in the department were also there and played their role. One touching tribute followed after another.

It all ended with my speech of thanks in paying tribute to all of them for their generosity in according me the memorable Masalama; it lasted three to four hours. The nurses and interpreters at the Out Patients Department organized and staged their own small, but very touching Masalama party, the third, for me. It was brief and was held after a morning clinic with everyone still in their uniforms. Drinks and pastries were served; the speeches were brief, but moving. It all ended with the presentation of a farewell gift, signatures and brief goodbye wishes. These were emotional occasions. One does not know when, where, how and whether one would meet any or all of them again; it could be tearful.

Thus ended my final days in Tabuk. I collected my two one-way tickets to fly to London, my recruitment point of hire. We travelled to London with a sizable amount of luggage. A great mission truly accomplished.

Chapter 11
AN ADDENDUM BY YOLANDE MARILYNNE AGBLE

INTRODUCTION TO THE ADDENDUM

I decided, after consulting with my husband Ted, that his story was not really complete by ending it in the year 2000. So many things had happened with, to and in our family during the almost 20 years since. Not least of all we now have four grandchildren, the oldest of whom, Noah Kofi, has written a story dedicated to us, his grandparents, when he was nine years old. It appears at the end of this missive. This makes Ted's story an Agble chronicle.

The story of how we met, our marriage and life together from 1965 to 2000 has already been told. The years when Ted worked in Saudi Arabia and the rest of our nuclear family lived in England deserves a mention by me, since many of our friends wondered how we coped with the separation. Strange as it may seem, our union, already several decades old and spent, for many of those years, in Ghana, was quite strong and solid. My happiest times were those travelling to spend 8 or 10 weeks in Tabuk with him. I worked in schools in London which allowed me the long holidays with our sons, especially our youngest, Ronnie, as the others were in tertiary institutions. We had no visa problems visiting the Kingdom and we spent many happy times visiting. I also worked there for two spells, totalling six and a half years. Our marriage grew in strength. A case of absence making the heart grow fonder? Perhaps!

2000: A MILLENNIUM AND A NEW BEGINNING IN ACCRA

We knew that our retirement would be spent in Ghana. After our first abortive attempt to get a house for this purpose, already mentioned by Ted, we decided it would be an idea to develop the plot of land in the Airport Residential Area so generously obtained for us by one of our dearest friends, now of blessed memory, Jake Blukoo Allotey, several decades earlier. Ted's dad, also of blessed memory, had walled the plot and put a small foundation on it to prevent it being grabbed by unauthorised people wanting land to develop. This was a very common practice in Accra in those days and I believe it still happens even today. By some stroke of good luck our land remained untouched and we went about making plans to put our dream house on it. Despite having a really nice place with spacious grounds in Nhyiasu, Kumasi, where our sons were brought up and had very fond memories of, living in Accra was now a serious option. It was not a very easy decision. I fell in love with Kumasi as a place in which I wanted to live the very first visit I made there at the end of 1965 as I really did not like the hot, dry, dusty and arid environment of Accra at all. We knew that our circumstances had changed, with Ted and I being retired, all four sons abroad and likely to stay there since they had jobs/ careers into which they were well settled, so we expected to be travelling back and forth. I also wanted to spend time with my own family, most of whom were settled in New York and because of this my mother spent a lot of time there. I had not lived with my family since I left Trinidad in 1963! It would be more convenient to live where the airport was situated if this was what we intended to do.

Mr Yaw Gyamfi, our old businessman friend from Kumasi, relocated to Accra where he had an office on Aviation Road and as was our custom whenever we visited Ghana, he was always on the list of people we dropped in to see, usually at his office. It was on one of these visits that we met an old boy of Opoku Ware School, where I had worked when we lived in Kumasi. We got around to talking of our plans to return and to build a home in Accra, when he mentioned a friend of his, a young architect just returned from abroad. He gave us his details and we contacted him; he came with us to the plot on

Agbaamo Lane, in the airport Residential Area. We discussed what we wanted and before we left for London he had provided us with a satisfactory set of the building plans. He assured us that he would be responsible for the building as he had just set up his own company, so we gave him the go ahead to start and arranged to make payments through Mr Gyamfi as we wanted him to start immediately.

On our return to London both Ted and I got part time jobs and started preparations to return home to Ghana. The boys were pleased, as they could envision themselves visiting us there. All four of them had a soft spot for Ghana as their ancestral home, even Ronnie who had left it when he was eight. Our third son, Dugald, was the most attached as he had his secondary education at GIS in Accra and had the all-important group of 'class mates', so valued by Ghanaians. We expected to make a few trips to Accra while the building was being constructed, but were sadly disappointed at what we saw on our first visit after it had started. As is usual in Ghana, without strict professional supervision things will fall apart at some point. Luckily for us, this had been detected when it was still possible to rectify the numerous faults.

Later that year 2000 Ted and I attended the FIGO congress in Montreal, Canada. After the Congress we met Sydney Adadevoh and Professor Hugh Wynter of the UWI Medical School where our son Brian had his training. A fine medical school whose products had the distinction of being awarded the very necessary UK recognition by registering with the General Medical Council (GMC) after graduation. The school maintained its links with certain British medical schools and always had UK examiners who could vouch for their standard. We had a great time socially, apart from the accompanying persons trips sightseeing around the beautiful city. We visited our close friends David and Lois Tay who were then settled in a suburb of Toronto. Lois was godmother to our son Dugald and I was godmother to their daughter, Heather. Although they only lived in Kumasi for about three years, we became firm and fast friends.

We decided that the sensible thing to do if we wanted a decent house was to give the project to an established construction firm. Friends in the know recommended MICHELETTI, an Italian company operating in Ghana for several decades and which had a good reputation for quality and reliability. We stayed at the Shangri La Hotel on our next visit, when we made an appointment to see the manager of Micheletti, Mr Nocce, to discuss engaging his company to take over the construction. On the morning of the appointment we expected to meet with an Italian gentleman, instead not only did we meet with him, probably a man in his sixties, but he had an entourage with him of about seven people, including a smartly dressed secretary carrying a portfolio, a quantity surveyor, Mr Humphrey Amegadoe (who turned out to be extremely helpful in the long run), a building supervisor and other assorted professionals from the building trade. It was very impressive, but also quite alarming, knowing that we had a strict budget with which to work. We decided that at the first opportunity we would discuss this with Mr Nocce, and we did. We found him very understanding as he assured us that he would indeed take over the building to completion. Although we did not have nearly as much land as we had in Kumasi, we had decided on having a swimming pool which we could use for exercise, and this was included in the original plan. Considering all the corrections and changes which had to be made we were promised a completion date of sometime in 2002 which we thought reasonable.

Back in London, Ted started work at a hospital in Colchester where he stayed during the week, returning to spend the weekends with us, except when he was on emergency calls. Early in September a first cousin of mine from Trinidad, Lennox Marcelle, a Senior Legal Draughtsman, was passing through London to attend an international legal conference in Rome at which he was representing his government. He decided to spend a few days with us. On the afternoon of September 11th 2001 (GMT) I drove to Shepherds Bush with him where there is a large ethnic market selling a great variety of foodstuff from all over the world, including the Caribbean and Africa. I had promised him a Ghanaian meal and we went there to get some ingredients. As we entered one of the shops, we could hear excited voices coming over the shop radio; we asked the shopkeeper what was happening and she responded very casually that there was some sort of plane crash in America. As the voices on the radio became more frantic, it sounded to us as more than just a plane crash; we stopped to listen and the horror of 9/11 revealed itself to us. What we were hearing was the crashing of the twin towers and as our second son, Neil, worked and lived in Manhattan and one of my two sisters-in-law worked in a building near Wall Street, shopping was abandoned, and I drove home with a pounding heart. Television brought the full extent of the horror to us even more. I proceeded to call New York frantically, but no calls were going through. Ted and I communicated about our concern for the two family members who were likely to be affected by this tragedy. My cousin Lennox and I spent the time glued to the TV sets in our house, not wanting to miss a moment of any news. Later in the evening we had word from one of my sisters whose perseverance in trying to contact us paid off – she knew how worried we would be. Although Neil had to walk through the heavy cloud of dust from the fallen twin towers to get to his apartment from work (they were all sent home early), he was otherwise unhurt. My sister-in-law, because she had to take her mother to a doctor's appointment on Long Island where she and my brother lived, did not go to work that day, which was fortuitous as the exit from the subway which she used for work was blocked off by debris and remained closed for several weeks. My abiding memory to this day of 9/11 is the sight of desperate people jumping to their death rather than die in the inferno which the burning towers had become. I still wish to this day that they had been able to put nets around the places from which they were jumping. But there was so much happening all at once and it was so unexpected. For a long time, the sadness of 9/11 lived with me, and even now every anniversary which I spend in New York, causes me to relive the pathos of that day.

In the meantime, our building was going ahead, we got the best French bathroom fittings from a shop in London and sent them to Accra. Part of the agreement to keep costs within our budget was that we would get most of the hardware abroad and ship them to Accra. The nightmare of clearing goods from the Accra ports need not be narrated here. Most Ghanaians returning home from abroad who read this story would have gone through similar experiences or known someone who had. Suffice it to say that we were still young and energetic enough to get through it relatively unscathed! Ted's mother of blessed memory had built him a small bungalow in Kokomlemle, a suburb of Accra off the Ring Road. It was the first building there in what has already been described in the main memoirs as a quite undeveloped area of Accra. Later, when the city council decided to name the road, it was called after her Abele Road (a corruption of AGBLE, a name with which they were not familiar). We decided to move there from London early in 2002. Ted's brother Bill had been the caretaker of this property for decades, during which time a number of different people had lived in it as tenants, including the late Lawyer Kom. We now took it over, and it proved very useful as a base for going to the ports and checking up on our building. Living in suburban Accra was a different and interesting experience in itself, about which an entire book could be written!

Our swimming pool was built by a young entrepreneur based in Kumasi, but who paid regular visits to Accra to supervise the work. It was a very good pool and all who saw and used it agreed. At last, towards the end of 2002, our house was ready for occupation. Moving into a new house anywhere is tough work, but we were so excited and happy at the thought of our own home as retirees at last that nothing daunted us. At Xmas that year our four sons arrived to spend the holiday with us and we had a big house warming party which we combined with the usual Xmas party we always held on December 23rd when we lived in Kumasi. The house was of ample size with every one of the four bedrooms ensuite. Our master bedroom and bathroom were just what we wanted – large, with separate shower and jaccuzzi and best of all, two separate wash basins and separate toiletry cabinets (very useful for avoiding marital tensions when getting dressed to go out!). We were delighted with all of our house, and so were our sons.

A NEW LIFESTYLE

We started our travels abroad almost at once, as soon as we were settled. In 2003 we attended the FIGO congress in Washington DC. A beautiful city to visit with lots of cultural entertainment, apart from the Scientific sessions. FIGO, THE INTERNATIONAL FEDERATION OF GYNAECOLOGISTS AND OBSTETRICIANS, holds a congress for its members and accompanying persons –wives, children, significant others – triennially. Various countries bid three years in advance for the opportunity to host it, usually in the Americas or Asia. We visited an Ethiopian restaurant and had our first taste of the cuisine of that country. Not bad, and popular with visitors. We observed that there were many Ethiopians in Washington, they were more visible than other groups from the continent, many of the taxis we used were driven by them. After the Congress, we spent a week visiting one of Ted's nieces, Patricia Kuma Doamekpor, and her family in Akron, Ohio. Both she and her husband were on the staff of the University there. We had a lovely time sightseeing and getting to know their kids, the third generation of contemporary Agbles – Dela and Edem. Then on to New York to visit my family – mother and sisters. We always returned from trips to NY (especially) laden with shopping, a great place for buying linen and other household items. We were fortunate in not being jetlag sufferers, and this made our travels truly enjoyable.

Life in Accra was good for us, but the usual problem of securing good quality staff remained a problem. Despite the mushrooming of companies claiming to be able to supply 'trained' staff, this was rarely the case. One ended up having to train them oneself, and while some did not mind being shown what to do, most did not like it. I admit to being 'fussy' and 'particular', but we were not a difficult couple to work with by any means and we were generous to our staff. We did manage, somehow, by chopping and changing staff. There was definitely a lack of interest in housework among many young women in Accra; sometimes the young men were better. One needed to have a watchman, gardener, a pool cleaner, a driver and house person. People who had lived in other developing countries like Ghana told me that it was a very common practice to have one person combine jobs, as an example for a couple like us who needed a driver only occasionally, one could get that same person to do some gardening, or perhaps some cleaning for more pay. In Ghana, drivers are quite happy to sit in their owner's car for several hours running down the battery by having the doors open and the radio on, when not actually sleeping! Decidedly a work-shy group! I liked to do my own cooking, even Ghanaian dishes, some of which I did quite well, but I always appreciated having help in the kitchen with food preparation and other basic chores. But, as I said, we managed.

We have always been very sociable people wherever we have lived – Kumasi, Accra, London, Jubail, Tabuk, New York, wherever. This period in Accra, surrounded by our very many friends, afforded us ample opportunity to entertain and be entertained. I knew nothing, or very little, of opera, before I met Ted in 1964, I was more interested in ballet, which was encouraged at my school. He was definitely an opera buff and took me to a few operas at regional theatres in and around Leeds when we dated. Later, I realised that a few dance hits played by the most popular dance band in Trinidad when I was a young person there, Sel Duncan, were actually arias from well-known operas, very expertly executed by him. When we got engaged, one of my engagement presents from Ted was a trip to Covent Garden to see the late Joan Sutherland perform the lead role in La Sonnambula. It was pure magic, not just the performance, but the entire ambience. His love of the opera rubbed off on me and we bought very good DVD productions from the Met in New York and Covent Garden (now the ROYAL OPERA HOUSE) in London and took them to Ghana. Quite a few of our friends were keen on opera and we soon had a group who came to us on the first Friday of every month when we were around for an opera evening. We usually had this projected on a wall in the garden, with people sitting around the pool or in the gazebo. On the few occasions when it rained, we held it on the front veranda.

I would like to devote a whole paragraph to mention our friends in Accra, a few of whom are of blessed memory now. We valued and still value their friendship wherever we are and the happy times we spent/spend with them. Jake+ and Cynthia Blukoo Allotey, Chris and Vic Adomako, Sammy+ and Charlotte Brew Graves, Barbara Baeta, Sammy and Virginia Ofosu Amah, Henry+ and Morriah + Sekyi, Sydney and Chloris Adadevoh, Pius and Heidi Amegayibor, Theresa Scott, Adalita and Hope Bediako, Janet and Alfie Neequaye, Judith and Aki Sawyerr, Star Annan+(now deceased} Janet Tamaklo, Yaw and Susan Saffu, Reggie Amamoo, Genevieve Nassar, Manu and Akua Herbstein, Joe and Glenda+ Butah, Kwesi+ and Jackie Zwennes+, Charlotte Gardner, Jeanette Hayfron Benjamin, Breid and Joseph Amamoo, Tommy and Setor Klaye, Estelle and Kweku Appiah. Star Annan's favourite opera was TURANDOT by Puccini. When she passed away suddenly, on our next opera evening we showed it in her honour. We still continue this practice whenever we are in Accra, our apartment in Villagio has a nice big wall on which we successfully project our DVDs.

Early in 2003 Ted secured a position as Consultant Oby/Gynae at Nyaho Clinic, now Nyaho Medical Centre. A short walk from our house, it was just perfect. Obstetricians are used to emergencies in their career and so it would be very, very convenient when he had emergency calls late at night. He enjoyed his work there immensely; my husband has always shown enthusiasm for his chosen speciality and even though I lay myself open to the charge of bias, I think he was excellent at what he did. For one thing, he kept up to date with current practice in his field, by attending conferences, lectures, courses, buying and reading current publications etc. Our last attendance at a FIGO Congress was in Rome in 2012 when he was 80! I was not keen to work, despite being very well qualified to make a useful contribution to any public health programme in the country. I loved my garden and took great pride in working in it. I love trees as much as I do plants and shrubs and I had a field day in Kumasi when we were building our house there, it being a perfect place for planting and growing things. I had help occasionally, but made sure that I had all the tools I needed to work on my own. I enjoyed looking after our home too, and writing up my diaries and political articles mainly to papers abroad. Apart from the Legon Observer and Ashanti Pioneer, I have never had any luck having anything published in the Daily Graphic or Ghanaian Times! Very curious! Even when I worked in Saudi Arabia, I had letters and articles published in the papers there! I was kept well occupied anyway. Perhaps my writing was not up to the standard required by these two illustrious Ghanaian dailies.

Later in the year, around September, just before we left for NY to spend a family Xmas, I had a rather strange medical experience. I went from our bedroom to the kitchen which was on the other side of our house to get a cold drink. As I passed our bar returning to our bedroom, I suddenly felt as if my right leg was not attached to my body, it was absent! A total lack of any feeling! I shouted for Ted, but with the bedroom being so far off, the study door closed and the air conditioner on, he could not hear me. Before I could decide what to do next, and just as suddenly as it left, feeling returned to my leg. I could hardly wait to tell Ted of my weird experience. He checked my vital signs, all normal, I felt fine in myself, and we could find no explanation for this strange event. I slept well, woke up with no other signs or symptoms emerging, so we both put it out of our minds.

We left Accra at the end of November for our family Xmas in NY. We both enjoy the hustle and bustle, the beautiful lights and decorations which herald the Xmas season in NY and London. Shopping leisurely for gifts for family and friends, we find it all exciting. One late afternoon we decided to visit one of my sisters, Glenda, in Elmont, Long Island and her daughter Renee offered to take us there. We emerged from the subway and sat in the Burger King which was our agreed meeting place. As she approached, delighted to see us, I suddenly felt that my lips were twisted, that my speech sounded heavy and my right forearm suddenly dropped, like a small log! Neither Ted nor Renee noticed what was happening and it took a while before I was able to draw their attention to it. Ted immediately called his cousin, Jones Adzimah, a cardiologist practising in Brooklyn, who was still at his clinic and advised that I be brought there asap. No further episodes on the drive there, but mega anxiety. When I told him about the previous experience a few months ago in Accra, it confirmed his diagnosis of a TIA (trans ischaemic attack) and he explained about clot forming and that I would have to be on a blood thinner, perhaps indefinitely. He assured me that it was not life threatening if managed properly. He prescribed PLAVIX, which I started taking at once.

We had really great Xmas spent with all the family, visiting with my sisters and brother and their families, attending the midnight New Year's Eve mass to ring in the new year, just perfect. We returned to Ghana early in 2004 and had notification of the WACS biennial conference which was due to take place sometime in February, which we planned to attend (West African College of Surgeons). The venue was the capital of Benin, Cottonu, a place we had never visited before so we were really looking forward to it. As we were responsible for making our own accommodation arrangements, I called up one of the very few hotels from a list given to us. Using my schoolgirl French I made a booking for us for the five-day event.

We left Accra very early on Saturday morning on a mega sized bus hired to take the Accra delegates to the conference and return us the following Friday. The trip was uneventful until we arrived at the Lome border, which was closed as there had been a coup d'etat the day before. Special permission had to be given to allow entry through to Cotonou. This, of course, caused some delay and we arrived there after 4 pm. We were in for quite a few surprises! In the capital many of the roads were unpaved and mopeds seemed to be the main mode of transportation. Hohoe in the Volta Region looked more like a town than this did. The mega bus drove into the sandy driveway of the hotel, which did not at all look appealing from the outside. As I had made the booking and wanted to ensure that they got it right, I left Ted to get our luggage off the bus and proceeded to the check-in desk, where there was a large crowd of men, all milling around, trying to get the attention of the two check-in clerks. As I stood a bit away from the crowd, I suddenly felt my right leg disappear, almost a recurrence of the Accra episode! I spotted a familiar face in the crowd, Professor Achampong, head of Surgery at the Legon Medical School, and asked whether he would help me to a seat, which he very kindly did. I explained to him what had just happened and just then Ted approached with our luggage. He suspected at once what was wrong. With this medical emergency, we were quickly seen by a clerk, checked in and shown to our room. Ted was naturally very anxious to get me settled in bed, but one look at the room and we knew that spending the night there was never an option. The lighting was poor, the very lowest wattage bulb hung from the ceiling, even in the dimness one could see that the room was dingy, the bathroom was shared and I had mental visions of mice (my mega bete noire) scuttling around). By now, although some sensation had returned to my leg unlike the other occasions, I felt a bit unwell. We quickly went downstairs, luggage in tow, to ask for another room. The only spare one he had was a chalet downstairs in the grounds and this was much better, own bathroom, brighter bulbs and a working ceiling fan. I immediately increased my dose of PLAVIX. We knew that we would have to find alternative accommodation come the morning. I spent a rather fitful night, very concerned about my health, but not wanting to worry Ted unduly. We were so relieved when morning broke and we could start getting all the problems sorted out!

At registration, we met a colleague of Ted's who told us of a better hotel and we made our way there. There was a three star Hilton Hotel, but it was fully booked – streetwise delegates who had been to Benin before (Nigerians mainly) had snapped the good rooms up. Anyway, the hotel recommended was much, much better than the one I had booked and they were able to give us one of their 'deluxe' (so called) rooms, but we could definitely sleep there and it was ensuite! There were pay phones which worked for international calls and we called Neil to let him know that we had arrived and the TIA problem. We have four sons but Neil, the second of them, always considers it his duty to keep track of our whereabouts, wherever we are in the world. He immediately started making plans for us to fly to NY by the next day. Only problem was that the borders were all closed, we were totally locked in on all sides. Everything was tried; there was no way out. Neil was quite worried, he called us every day, about three to four times, to check up on how we were. I cannot remember ever feeling so helpless. When I accepted the fact that there would be no quick exit from Benin, I just prayed and left it to God. At the end of the first session on day one, we ran into Sam Ohaegbulam, first class Nigerian neurosurgeon, a very good friend and neighbour from our Tabuk days. We were delighted to see each other and he immediately offered to take us out to dinner that night, which we accepted. Rather surprisingly, for such a rundown looking place, there were a few very good eating places – the French influence no doubt. As we were catching up on news of family, friends, colleagues etc while we were enjoying our dinner, Sam's fork was suspended half way to his mouth when I mentioned that I had experienced my third TIA in six months yesterday! Shocked. He was quite shocked. According to him, in all his many decades of neurological practice he never had a patient with more than one TIA episode which did not convert and that we should see a colleague of his, one Dr Andrews, without delay. The rest of the week was uneventful, we were very much looking forward to our departure on Friday. At the hotel in which we stayed a number of delegates were from the Ashanti Region, and in casually chatting with them we heard that they were returning early Friday morning and passing through Accra. As we really wanted to get to Accra early to get an appointment to see Dr Andrews asap, we asked whether there was room for us to join them and they readily agreed. Great! We informed the Accra group that we were leaving early and were ready at the appointed departure time of 9am. We boarded the Ashanti coach and were driven to the first hotel where we stayed on arrival to collect some of the delegates staying there, when alas disaster struck! The four massive rear wheels fell into a ditch in the driveway and with the sandy terrain, it could not be driven out! The upshot was that we had to leave with our original group which left at 4pm, leaving the Ashanti coach behind as they had to wait for mechanical assistance! What a to-do! One felt almost as if destined to stay in Cotonou forever! As the coup was still ongong, with borders still closed, it took the intervention of the Ghanaian ambassador to get permission to drive the bus to Accra. We arrived at midnight, thankfully safe and intact. I was never happier to see our very comfortable bed and beautifully clean rooms, especially the bathroom. Shower followed by bed and up early next morning to catch Dr Andrews before he became swamped with patients. He agreed to see us at once and as it was my practice to visit Sraha market in James Town to buy fish and local vegetables, we stopped off on Aviation Rd on our way there. After a physical examination, he could find no neuro deficits, but requested a brain scan on Monday at the SNIT Hospital in Osu. Quiet uneventful weekend, up bright and early on Monday to have the scan done, after which the report and film were given to Dr Andrews. Confirmed his diagnosis of TIA of non neurological aetiology and referred me to the cardiologist at Korle Bu Cardiac centre. We were fortunate to be given an appointment for a few days later that same week. I was seen at the Cardio thoracic centre and after a thorough set of tests and examinations, my TIAs were determined to be cardiac in origin. I was diagnosed with Atrial Fibrillation and became a patient of Dr Mawuse Tetteh under whom I received excellent care until we relocated abroad in 2009. I have nothing but the highest praise for the treatment I received under the staff at the Cardio Thoracic unit.

In the June of 2004 Ted and I went to Aberdeen for his medical class 45th reunion. Always a great occasion, his medical class being a small one, they were a very closely-knit group. All his classmates called him Teddy and a jolly time was always had by all. It was a year of many trips abroad. Early in July we travelled to New York and then with all my family to Maryland for the wedding of our adopted Saudi niece, Nadia. Ted had the honour of being the father-giver. We formed the largest group of her supporters, including my mum, whom she regarded as her grandmother. It was a splendid occasion and prepared us for the next wedding on September 18th – that of our eldest son Brian to a young Trinidadian woman, Rhonda Lewis, whom he had been dating for a couple of years. I have been jokingly accused of wanting my son to marry someone from my island, but I plead innocent to the charge of anything apart from giving my approval after we had met her. Apparently, according to my daughter-in-law's mother, her big dream growing up was to have her wedding at the uniquely built upside-down Hilton Hotel in Port of Spain, Trinidad's capital. And a splendid one she did indeed have. About 200 guests, including three of Ted's nieces - daughters of his brother Bill and wife Dorma - Jemima (with her husband Eric), Patricia and Marilyn attended, representing the Agble family, which was really pleasing and appreciated, as they had all travelled long distances to be present.

AN IMPORTANT MILESTONE AND A SIGNIFICANT EVENT

On October 2nd, 2005, Ted and I celebrated our 40th wedding anniversary; it was a great occasion. My mother of blessed memory (who had been present at our wedding in Leeds, bringing everything with her except the kitchen sink, as she was sure that some very necessary items for a successful wedding would not be available in England) came from Trinidad to attend it. As did my youngest sister Erica, who loves Ghana with a passion and would never pass up any opportunity to visit, and my eldest niece Renee, whose own father was Malian and who is very fond of her Uncle Ted and all things African. Our eldest son, Brian, came with his wife Rhonda, as did our other sons Neil, Dugald and Ronnie, who were all still single! Barbara Baeta's catering company Flair provided the setting in our garden and the lovely food. We had excellent weather, so the garden was just perfect. Our youngest son Ronnie, who is a very good flautist and has played in his school orchestra, amateur orchestras in London, and at weddings for his various friends in international settings, treated us to a moving rendition of Mozart's Clarinet Concerto K622 in A MAJOR, which was well received. We were fortunate in having our best man, Dr Peter Mensah, present, and he proposed the main toast. It was a truly splendid celebration with about 50 of us family and good friends thoroughly enjoying this wonderful milestone event.

Just.

MORE INTERESTING TRAVEL – A SLOW TRAIN TO CHINA

Ted has always been very keen on keeping current in his speciality and this entailed attending conferences and congresses internationally. As there were always interesting activities for accompanying persons, and being now retired, I attended all of these with him. Fortunately, we are both keen on travelling, irrespective of the mode – sea, land, air, and we were good travellers. In 2006 we attended the FIGO congress held in Kuala Lumpur, Malaysia. The very first of these FIGO congresses we attended was in Singapore very many years before, when we both worked in Saudi Arabia. At one of big hotels in Kuala Lumpur where we had dinner one night, we ran into one of our very close friends from Accra, the late Kwesi Zwennes, SAG, one of the very top lawyers in the country. He was in Kuala Lumpur on government business as chairman of some Shipping Organisation, a quite unexpected, but delightful meeting, as usual whenever we met. Sydney Adadevoh, a close friend and Professor at the Kumasi Medical School, was also keen on keeping his knowledge current and attended FIGO congresses regularly. We met him, too, in Kuala Lumpur. When we worked in Saudi Arabia, Ted and I spent one Easter in Aramco, the big oilfield complex which was like an American state. There was a Church where we attended Easter Day service and women (NOT the locals) drove around the compound and to the supermarkets in shorts, quite incredible, really. We stayed with a young Ghanaian medical couple, Professor Yaw Gyamfi and his wife Mokwa, nee Blay, whose eldest sister Adwoa was a good friend of ours. They were wonderfully hospitable to us and it was on this visit that we met another young Ghanaian couple working and living in Aramco – Michael and Hawa Agamasu. Michael was an OBY/GYNAE too. They were also at Kuala Lumpur and we had a lovely reunion at one of the city's nicest dining out places. I mention this as it was the last time we saw Michael alive. He passed away a couple years later, rather prematurely. We were very sad at his passing; Ted attended his funeral in the Volta Region.

Since we were in the South East Asia region, we took the opportunity to visit Hong Kong and mainland China after the Congress. In Hong Kong we stayed in one of the most modern hotels we had ever been guests at – the Novotel. Everything was chrome, silver and white. Entirely spic and span. We went to Xwangchou by train, an interesting journey, and spent five days there, visiting different parts of the province. Here we saw one of the most rundown and dilapidated settlements anywhere on our travels. The closest one to it which I had seen was in one of the African townships in Cape Town.

A GRANDCHILD AT LAST! AND A BIG CHANGE OF PLANS

On August 24th, 2007, our first grandchild was born in Kent where his parents, Brian and Rhonda, lived. Brian was a GP in a practice there. A boy, born on a Friday, he was called Noah Kofi, like his father. A delightful little fellow, bright and alert when we first saw him aged four months in December when they came to spend Xmas with the family in New York. It was a true family celebration with four generations – of the Garraway/Marcelle /Agble family together. In this year Ted was also asked to Chair a committee enquiring into maternal mortality in the Oby/Gynae Department at Korle Bu. He considered it a great honour and as was his practice with anything he was asked to do professionally, he did it with a sense of great responsibility. The other colleagues on this committee were Dr Sowaah and Dr Boadi, still practising in Ghana, and the late Dr Nana Ffoulkes Crabbe. They all got on very well together and worked assiduously, eventually producing a useful and comprehensive report. It was during this time when he narrated some of his experiences to one of the secretaries, that she said to him he should write a book; she found the narrative so interesting! And so began the idea for 'My Story'.

We were making many trips overseas, including family visits, and the domestic staffing problem grew worse, particularly with gardeners and pool cleaners who, despite receiving their monthly pay cheques from kind friends who agreed to do us this favour in our absence, had no compunction about neglecting their work and only turning up a few days before they knew we would be back. When the pool became green with algae and some of my prized pot and garden plants perished, Ted and I, knowing that we would continue to travel abroad with our expanding nuclear family, decided that it was time to downsize. About this same time, a few companies started constructing apartments in different residential districts of Accra, mainly to accommodate middle level expatriate staff who were arriving in Ghana to work for the new international companies, including the oil and gas ones. The really well-built apartments were spacious with modern appliances and fittings, and set in attractive landscaped grounds, offering 24-hour security. They were by no means inexpensive. The plan was to rent out our house and get one of these apartments which would require no external upkeep of grounds and garden. This would afford us peace of mind and the freedom to travel whenever we wished. We discussed this with our sons Neil and Dugald. Neil, because he was always at the helm of decisions to be made in our interest – our house in London was his idea, as was the first car I bought there, a second hand AUDI in very good condition rather than the old Ford I originally planned to get; Dugald, because he was then spending a lot of time in Accra as part of his job with an investment company involved in business ventures in quite a number of African countries. Also, he is unarguably the shrewdest and most business minded of our four sons – the others pale beside him in this regard.

Neil, who was quite settled in his job in New York and had become a US citizen, was all for it. Dugald saw the apartment in which we were interested and declared that although it was attractive it was far too expensive, cheaper ones in good areas were available, according to him. He promptly took us to see one of them on his next trip to Accra, which was situated in Cantonments, not far from FLAIR. The first negative for us was the attitude of the proprietor, who occupied one of the apartments himself. He was rude and surly and behaved as if we had gone there to hold him up, rather than to enquire about his apartments with the likelihood of purchasing one! I was already not impressed with the surroundings as compared with the one we first saw, and did not hesitate to walk out from his place as quickly as I could. We saw another one just off the main airport road driving to the Mall. It was not yet occupied, but already plumbing was a problem – the entire ground floor was flooded! None of these apartments was even reasonably priced by any standard used, especially since they were being quoted in US dollars.

A STROKE OF GOOD LUCK?

In the meantime, we contacted an estate agent about renting our house and she had no problem getting a really good tenant for us. He was the local CEO of KOSMOS, one of the oil companies beginning operations in Ghana. He was a very impressive looking man and behaved in a similar manner. After viewing our house, which was to be rented fully furnished, he offered more than the asking rent. According to him, his wife would really love our place and especially the large kitchen with its American appliances that we had purchased in Saudi Arabia. Ted and I knew that the next step would be the sale of our beloved 'KPLOMDEDIE' (Fare Thee Well) in Kumasi. Our youngest son was born there and had been christened in the lovely garden of the house, the older three had their special memories, too – birthday parties, playing football, having their friends from school over for weekends, our lovely dogs Coocoo, Brownie and Sambo, watching us grownups dance on the front porch when we had our parties; even our nieces Jemima, Patricia and Marilyn shared these fond and happy memories. It was the most difficult decision of our life and the boys had very mixed feelings about it. But we needed to move on, and moving on meant disposing of this lovely home in which we had no intention of making our residence ever again. We engaged an estate agent in Kumasi to put it on the market. As he also operated in Accra, we thought that he was well placed to get a good buyer. We made it clear to him that we wanted the buyers to be occupiers, likely people with a young family so that they could experience the happiness which our family had experienced there; we did not want it sold for business purposes. He agreed. This was, of course, reflected in the asking price. As a prospective buyer, he brought to see us a well-dressed woman, possibly in her late forties who hailed from Ashanti. We got along well, chatting about children, schools etc. She told us that she loved the house and was looking forward to moving in with her family. She agreed to the price, did not even ask for a reduction as was the usual Ghanaian custom, and a deal was made. What we got was about half the asking price of the apartment we wanted to buy, and we certainly had no way of raising the rest, but Neil offered to get a loan on his apartment in NY to make up the balance. Bless him for that. The rent from our house, Kate Amaville, would be used to repay him.

Everything was now set in motion for our new lifestyle – a great tenant for our house, a very nice apartment where we would stay when we were in Accra, no worrying about gardeners and pool maintenance workers; life was very good indeed. The one condition which the CEO of KOSMOS requested was that the house be insured. In Ghana, mortgages were almost non-existent at that time and when they were available by a few companies the interest rate was prohibitively high. As an example, interest rates for mortgage loans in the UK and US were 1½ to 2½%, in Accra they were over 20%! As most people built from their own resources, home insurance cover was not mandatory. In retrospect, it should have been made so before it was occupied, even by the owner, possibly by Government statute. State Insurance was by far the biggest insurance company in the country and Ted had always insured our cars with them. It was natural that when we had to insure our house before renting it, we would go to them. We contacted them and they sent two young women from their staff to assess the place; everything was covered, including the pool and the extent of cover was agreed, with all the papers being signed. This was on a Friday, the last one in June and they left with the promise to return with the policy the following Monday at which time payment would be made by cheque and the policy handed over.

We wanted to hand over the house in a perfect condition with everything working well. The electricity supply in Accra had been a mega problem for decades. People lost appliances, there were a few fires in suburban areas attributed to the fluctuation and unstable surges in the power supply. Those of us who could afford it were advised to put every electrical appliance on surge control and we followed this advice to the letter. Although it was on a wired-in surge protector, our double door Samsung refrigerator was still affected – one shelf in the freezer kept thawing. I contacted the Samsung representative in Accra who sent round a technician on the very Monday we expected the State insurance people. He removed the refrigerator to their workshop, promising to return it within two days. We had a smaller refrigerator in our bar which was situated between the dining room and the television room – all this entire area in our house was open plan. I asked him to remove it to the kitchen while the Samsung was repaired, which he did. This small fridge had only an extension lead surge protector which was not very easy to put in place because the Samsung had been wired in, but after a few attempts, he managed to get it in place.

The other area which needed a repair job was our driveway. We contacted the fellow who had made it originally. He had a small company and agreed to get it done quickly as we explained it was going to be handed over for renting at the end of July. Ted and I were booked to leave Accra for London on Sunday August 10th, where we would spend a few weeks before going on to New York to stay, possibly for some months. On Monday the driveway contractor decided he needed some materials which he had to get in Accra. Because of issues with purchasing building materials in the past, Ted decided to accompany him to Kantamanto, an area popular for the availability of building supplies. Shortly after they left, the State Insurance ladies turned up. Ted had made out the cheque, but had taken it with him, in case there was time after purchasing the items to pass the SI office in Accra. As it turned out, the traffic, which was always horrendous, was unusually bad that day, possibly because the next day was Republic Day, a public holiday in Ghana. After waiting for some time, the SI staff left just before 4pm. I apologised and asked them to return the next day, but they informed me that as it was a public holiday they would return on Wednesday July 2nd instead. Ted and the driveway contractor came back after 5pm, complaining about the traffic. We also had a painter, a fellow called Peter, whom we had used in Kumasi and who was quite good, staying with us. We did have a tendency to use workers with whose work we were familiar, as we did not find it easy to get good calibre artisans in Accra, for some reason. As there was no maid using the room allocated for one downstairs, we asked Peter to stay there. Ted and I had started packing our things to travel and also personal items for storage in the Kokomlemle place. As usual for us, we went to bed quite late. Having both worked at jobs which required the ability to wake up from sleep quickly, we are light sleepers. About 3am in the morning we were awakened by Peter's voice shouting outside our bedroom window that there was a fire. We had the presence of mind to grab our dressing gowns and rush to the bedroom door ready to exit through our main front door, which was a sliding one.

AN UNEXPECTED EVENT:
A FIRE – KATE AMAVILLE BURNING!!!

There is a very interesting story about our door keys. We had two key racks – one in the kitchen just at the exit door to the garage, which was convenient for hanging keys when we returned home or take them when we were leaving. But Ted always insisted on putting these keys outside our bedroom door where the other rack was. I always left them in the kitchen. This habit of Ted's probably saved our lives. Houses in Ghana were usually built with strong burglar proofing to keep robbers at bay – this would usually be when no one was at home and ours was no different. But this same burglar proofing could act as a barrier to getting out in case of a fire or some other disaster, as we found out that night! Because fires were a rarity in places like the Airport Residential Area where we lived, no thought was given to constructing collapsible burglar proofing which would be a useful exit route in case doors became impassable. When we left our bedroom, Ted grabbed the front door keys so that we could let ourselves out, but the short hallway to the main door was thick with smoke and Ted started feeling its effect almost immediately. The keys fell from his hand and there was a moment of panic. I reassured him that we would find it as we felt around the floor with thick smoke and flames billowing behind us, moving closer all the time. We found the keys and the first one put in the door was the right one. We made our way to the garden where Peter had had the presence of mind to set some of the garden chairs. There was no 911 or 311 or any emergency number to call, or which worked, but nearly everyone in Ghana had a cell phone – for a developing country with a very poor communication infrastructure, this was very necessary and quite remarkable. The loud blast of breaking glass of the windows in the kitchen and guest room wing from the extreme heat, woke the neighbours. This appeared to be where the fire had started, according to Peter giving an account of how he first became aware of it.

We sat and watched as the flames leapt across the roof; even at that early stage we could tell that it was an electrical fire as it followed a clear path over the ceiling and roof. Some kindly neighbour was able to contact the fire brigade through some means, possibly by driving down to their headquarters, which was only about two and a half miles away, and at that time of morning quicker than placing a call, even if we had a number. A small crowd gathered on the street, Agbaamo Lane. People were wondering if we were in Accra or abroad. After I cannot honestly say how many hours, the fire brigade arrived and proceeded to drench everywhere with lots of water. It did not take them long to put out the fire and I have very little recollection of any interaction with them while they were there. We were very fortunate. Apart from being able to get out before we were overcome by smoke, the damage to the house was almost entirely confined to the roof, which, because it was constructed of concrete tiles was able to restrict the major damage to the guest wing and kitchen only. Most of the damage done to the other part of the house was water damage to our books, papers, photo albums and items in our study from the firemen's water hoses. But back to the morning of the fire. We hardly knew any of our neighbours as we were away so much, but that did not deter them from extending a helping hand to us, offering a place to stay and help in many other ways.

In the immediate aftermath of the fire, one of the first people on the scene was the driver of the Sekyis – Henry and Morriah, both of blessed memory. She had prepared a big breakfast and sent it to us with her driver. I guess news of the fire would travel fast, being such an unusual event in a residential area. Next was Chris Adomako, who lived a few streets away. Ted had been the best man when he and Vic got married and we had maintained a close friendship with them. At the time of the fire, Vic was abroad. Mr K.B. Asante, of blessed memory (Voices from Afar, Daily Graphic), who lived with his wife on the same street, came by to offer their commiserations and whatever help we needed, including accommodation. We were overwhelmed by visits from friends, neighbours, family and those who were just curious! GBC reporters came by, but they were clearly not impressed by the absence of drama, and after being told that the elderly couple sitting talking quietly to their visitors were the people who were in the house at the time of the fire, they left! I am not even sure that it made the news at all. They expected to find loud wailing and weeping and shouting and must have been quite disappointed. Ted's brother Bill turned up later with the quantity surveyor, Humphrey Amegadoe. He took a look at the damage and went away to cost account what he thought would be required to repair it. It was very clear that the damage could have been much worse had the materials which were used in construction been inferior. The tiled roof undoubtedly contained the fire. Later that day, Jake and Cynthia came around and offered us their guest wing to stay for as long as we needed; in fact, they insisted. As they were among our closest friends and lived quite nearby, we accepted their offer. It would facilitate our making the daily trips to the house from early morning to late evening as we knew would be necessary to sort out the place. One thing Ted and I were sure about from the very beginning was that we were not going to cancel our BA flight to New York via London on August 10th. This meant a lot of cleaning up and clearing out in just under six weeks. But we felt quite up to the job, so determined were we.

There were many instances of good fortune. One was that all the security doors were intact, not at all damaged by the fire, so we were able to get one reliable security man along with the painter Peter to keep an eye on the place. We got our cell phones from our bedroom, which was largely intact, removed our suitcases which were partially packed in anticipation of our impending trip, and set off to Jake's and Cynthia's in our faithful Toyota Corolla, bought in Saudi Arabia eight years before. In those days there was a chronic water shortage in Accra; most people had tanks. But it was still a problem which had to be managed carefully to ensure a supply for family and staff who lived in. Guests would be an added concern and we thought of this. But Cynthia always ensured that there were buckets of water in the bath, when the water was not running in the taps, for us to use. And how we needed those baths! I shall never forget the water running off our bodies almost black from the soot which had settled after the fire on everything, indoors and outdoors.

Our long-term plans had to change almost in their entirety. We now had to contemplate the repair of our house, the loss of a great tenant, and lack of a place to stay permanently when we were in Ghana. All our friends rallied round and were impressed by the way we seemed to be managing, without any sense of panic, but Ted and I complement each other in that way. Either one of us could talk the other into not worrying when there was a problem. Best of all, we could listen to each other's views and come up with a solution. The ability to do so stood us in good stead at this period of our lives. Three of our four sons came to visit shortly after the fire. Brian, to give moral support, Neil and Dugie for more practical reasons – they wanted us to set about having the house repaired as quickly as possible. My sisters in NY were of course informed about the fire and the youngest of them, Erica, without being asked, decided to come over to help in whichever way she could. As it turned out her help was invaluable. We asked the estate agent to inform our prospective tenant about what had happened. Another agent had also got a tenant from one of the Scandinavian embassies and he turned up on the second day – a viewing had been arranged for him before the fire, but he was only able to come on that day. He was of course disappointed. Ironically, although many people in Accra were busy selling their prize land, and in some instances homes, to construct what were for Americans and Europeans largely substandard apartments, good bungalows with decent landscaped gardens were still in demand by senior level expatriate staff coming from those countries.

AFTERMATH OF THE FIRE, LIFE GOES ON

Ted and I immediately planned our movements and soon settled into a routine. Every morning we got up pretty early, got dressed and went across to our house. We went about room by room, salvaging and cleaning items which were only damaged by soot. The most painful area to handle was our study which had a lot of water damage, not only from the fire brigade hoses, but also from some torrential rainfall which we experienced a few days after the fire. Although some books and photo albums were destroyed, most were salvageable. The plan was to move all furniture and everything we had been able to save to our place at Kokomlemle which we had still maintained. This was where my sister's help came to be of great value. She sat on the truck moving our belongings from Kate Ama Ville while Ted remained at Kokomlemle with a couple of workers to pack them. Sadly, this was very necessary. The level of dishonesty even among staff you knew and whose services you had used for years, and to whom you had always been generous, was so deep and ingrained that no opportunity to take something which did not belong to them was ever missed. Even with all this overseeing we still lost a few items of furniture, including a large cane bedroom chair which was over 40 years old at the time. This chair was beautifully made, one of two for Ted and me to use in our bedroom, made from a picture in an American homemakers' magazine, by a Czech furniture manager who worked for a company based in Kumasi. But one learns to live with this petty, and sometimes not so petty, stealing over many decades.

The serious business of getting the house repaired had to be broached. There were two companies which were considered. One was owned by a young Ghanaian of mixed race, who was brought up in England, had a good tech background in construction and had decided to come home to Ghana to set up business. He and Dugald had met somewhere in Accra socially, and we were quite impressed by him. I felt that we could trust him, which was very important, with us likely to be absent for most of the repair time. There was also an Italian company associated with the company which had completed the building. In the end it came down to the garden. As previously mentioned, apart from the roof, the guest wing and kitchen, the compound itself was largely unscathed by the fire and I wanted to preserve the garden and the pool. The young, newly arrived builder, who was not yet familiar with the Ghanaian workforce, we felt would be less able to prevent his workmen from ruining the garden and pool. I had visions of the pool being used for mixing cement, washing bodies at the end of the workday, and wrapping, paper and cans strewn all over the garden as I had seen in dozens of building sites around Accra. We felt that a well organised expatriate company would be better equipped to control its workers in this regard and indeed it was the one specific clause in the contract which I emphasised and which was taken seriously and with which I was satisfied on completion.

As I mentioned before, our friends gave not only moral support, but practical as well. Jackie (Z), one of my very oldest friends, and Adalita (B), a more recent one, brought over lunch to us regularly and just helped with cleaning up whenever they came by. My sister Erica stayed at Lavender Lodge, a small hotel within a stone's throw from Jake and Cynthia's place. This was very convenient and Cynthia included her in the evening dining for the period she was in Accra. The kindness and hospitality and care shown to us by Jake and Cynthia could never be sufficiently praised or have our gratitude expressed.

At last the time came when we could see light at the end of the tunnel as far as clearing up the house and leaving Accra with the stress of the events of the past few weeks behind us. We were quite determined not to be deterred by anything at all, and we put all our effort into this goal. Jackie came to see us on the final Saturday and she even drove up to Kokomlemle with our last load for the storeroom; it was around 11pm when we said goodbye to each other and we drove to Jake and Cynthia's. We had a watchman at Kokomlemle, Peter was still staying at Kate Ama Ville. A carpenter, Mr Kingsford, whom we had known for a few years since we came to Accra, a fairly skilled fellow, very willing and whom we quite liked, but over a period realised that he was not very trustworthy (our very elderly Muslim watchman at Kokomlemle observed some disturbing movements by this fellow which he passed on to us) was also around assisting us. He returned to the Agbaamo Lane house with Peter even though he lived way off on the other side of Accra. We got him a cab and asked him to go home. A few odd things had happened during this last trip which had aroused our suspicions. This was likely prescient. As I was putting our things together for travelling, I could not find my carryon bag in which I had all my travelling clothes and toiletries. We assumed that it must have been taken out and put in the storage in error and decided that first thing next morning we would go to retrieve it. When we awoke, we could not find the bunch of keys to open the Kokomlemle property, not in the car, not in our bedroom, not anywhere – and we did look most thoroughly. I had a distinct memory of putting it into the car, likely on the dashboard sill, just before we set off with Peter and Kingsford to drop them at the house, when we insisted that the carpenter should go to his own home and not stay with Peter as they both planned. Nothing to do but have the locks, all six of them, changed. There was another carpenter whose services we had used before, a very experienced fellow called Kwaku, very taciturn in his manner, but a very skilled workman. He was in church and it was several hours before we were able to contact him on his mobile phone. He agreed to come, but the big problem was that almost all the shops in Accra where locks were sold would be closed, it being a Sunday and no country having more churchgoing people than Ghana. Eventually he came and set off with Ted in the car to drive around Accra, looking for shops owned by Muslims which would be open and have locks and other materials needed for changing them. He then had to return to Kokomlemle to change them all by himself as he was unable to contact his apprentice, who had likely gone to church as well! A veritable nightmare.

In Ted's absence I packed the things we were taking along, last minute items would be left in our locked car so that the guest room which had been our home for the past six weeks, could be vacated entirely. At any rate, the car was being left in the garage at Jake and Cynthia's. Ted came in around 7.30pm, the time we should have been checking in for our 11pm flight! He quickly showered and dressed, and we set off for the airport, which was less than two miles away. If we had not been travelling Business Class, we would have missed the flight altogether. But thankfully we got on and the first truly relaxed moments Ted and I had enjoyed in six weeks was sitting back comfortably on the plane and later sipping a glass of champagne. What utter bliss!

EARLY ARRIVAL IN LONDON – ACCRA A DISTANT MEMORY!

All our sons love us, and we have ample proof of this. But Neil has always been the one who has shown the most care and concern and always very solicitous of our welfare. Knowing what we had been through, he booked a 5-star hotel for us in Queens Gate, Kensington, for a week, before we would go to spend time with Dugie and Brian at their respective homes. Check-in time is usually 3pm, but Neil got in touch with the hotel manager and explained our situation, and he promised that we would have an immediate check-in room on arrival. Not only that, a car was waiting for us at the airport, our luggage came out very early and we were driven to this super hotel, and taken to our room which was all white with a lovely bathroom and oh so soft towels and sheets! Although we had showered in Accra only a few hours before, we both showered again and went to bed wrapped in the lovely clean sheets. We slept until late evening, got dressed and walked around Queens Gate, enjoying the sights and sounds of this London neighbourhood. Back to the hotel and dinner, we watched some TV in our room and then to bed, totally zonked out, making up for the hours of sleep deficit we had accumulated since the fire.

Two days later, Ronnie came to take us to Glyndebourne. Although the youngest of our four sons and the one who had the least exposure to the classical music and arias which were our Sunday morning fare when they were growing up in Kumasi, he is the one who has taken to classical music and opera, at his earliest age, almost as if it were a genetic trait. His father used to be able to sit and discuss operas and composers, maestros, performers and all things operatic with him, but now his knowledge far surpasses Ted's. According to him, he had a surprise for us. And indeed, it was - a big one! Waiting on the platform at Victoria Station to get the train to East Sussex where Glyndebourne is located, was David Howell! David Howell (Uncle David to our sons, they have known him since they were quite young; in Ronnie's case, since his birth!) was the Director of the British Council in Kumasi and we became firm friends. Our friendship lasted even when he left Accra and was stationed in Freetown, Sierra Leone, where he invited us to visit. When on retirement he settled in London with his wife Nancy, whenever we were in London, we always went out together, to watch a play in the West End with dinner afterwards usually, or dinner at our house or a lunch at their place in South London. Sadly, Nancy had passed away in 2006. David was also very keen on opera, and Ronnie had invited him to Glyndebourne for an opera evening with dining in one of their splendid dining rooms - the carvery at Nether Wallop. Some attendees go for the elegant picnic in the grounds, but we always preferred the formal dining. For one thing, the weather was always variable - one could never be sure that a shower or two would not turn the beautiful grounds into a soggy affair. We had a very enjoyable evening, with thoughts of Accra and the fire far away in the past. This outing to Glyndebourne arranged by Ronnie with David as our guest, was fortuitous and timely. He passed away the next year, in 2009. We miss him even now when we are in London as we enjoyed each other's company so very much.

After a few weeks in London, we proceeded to New York. Before we left Accra, we had contacted an estate agent, Richard Assenso, to sell our Kokomlemle property, not immediately, but as things can take a long time to get going in Ghana, we thought it a good idea to start then. We could see that being in New York where my mother spent a lot of time visiting her other three daughters and one of her two sons domiciled there, it might be a good idea to have a base there. Ted and I are very independent-minded people who enjoy being on our own, free to go where and when we please. Staying with my sister Gloria was an option, but she lived out in Elmont, Long Island where most people have at least two cars. I hated driving – as soon as I did not need to, I stopped, years before. All the activities in which Ted and I were interested were in Manhattan. Neil had an apartment there, but it was a very expensive place to live, perhaps less so than London, but expensive, nevertheless. For Ted, the main criterion needed for living in New York was the Metropolitan Opera House! Neil had given us a subscription as a Xmas gift the year before, so he was quite amenable to relocating there. New York was always fascinating to me, since I was growing up in Trinidad. As a teenager, all the music, movies, everything American fascinated us, and America largely meant New York. The idea of being around my family, which had not happened for over 50 years was exciting, too. We began the search for somewhere suitable; we traipsed literally all over NY looking at apartments with the right criteria – safe neighbourhood, near to public transport, easy access to Manhattan, reasonably priced! We first rented an apartment in the Forest Hills area of Queens. A small privately owned apartment complex with one- and two-bedroom apartments, mainly occupied by UN and Embassy staff, a very quiet street not far from the subway. This was important, as we intended using the subway and buses for our trips in to Manhattan for the theatre and opera and other activities. It was reasonably safe, too, which was also another important consideration for us. The supervisor, Michael, of Polish descent, was friendly, competent, helpful. This was in marked contrast to the one we had in the more upmarket building on the Jamaica Estates into which we moved in February 2009!

A GENTLE FORAY INTO LIFE IN THE BIG APPLE

America has an abundance of Public Holidays, and that first year we were there for most of them, the most significant being Thanksgiving and Xmas. Both holidays were spent with my reunited family: mother, sisters, brother, nieces, nephews, very enjoyable and lavish in the typical American way. On December 31st we even ventured out in the freezing weather to Times Square to watch the ball drop! We wanted to experience what it was like. It is the sort of activity one does only once when you are elderly. If we were offered a large sum to repeat that experience today, we would emphatically say NO THANKS!! Much better, more comfortable and for us more sensible, to watch it from the comfort of your apartment sofa on your wide screen TV!

Ted and I started to look independently for a more permanent place and our niece Renee put us in touch with an Estate agent, a young Trinidadian woman, Janet Mahabir, whom she had used in getting her own apartment shortly before. We had word from Richard that an offer was in the making for our property at Kokomlemle, which was very welcome news. Apartments in suburban New York were much cheaper than in London, and after looking at a few and checking out the asking prices we realised that buying one was a real option if we sold Kokomlemle. The one which really attracted us was on the Jamaica Estates two streets away from our niece's. After Mr Trump became President, we found out that the house in which he and his family lived when he was a child was three doors down from our apartment building! Our claim to fame, what?

A MEGA RIP OFF IN ACCRA

We returned to Ghana at the end of March and I had the shock of my life. Apart from the horrendous cost to repair our house, the only commendable thing I could point to was that our garden and pool had not been vandalised. The first absurdity was that the water heater for the house was sited in our study! The worst eyesore ever. Our bedroom, which had not been damaged, had had the floor tiles removed and replaced with an obviously cheap and inferior type, black replacing our white porcelain! Our beautiful chrome and white bathroom had been completely altered with black floor tiles, our double washbasin had been replaced by a single one, our jacuzzi replaced by an ordinary tub as had the medicine cabinets and all our lovely French bathroom fittings had been removed and replaced by inferior ones of job lot quality, likely brought in from Spain or Turkey, which are noted for having poor quality sanitary ware which they offload on African and other 'third world' countries. No doubt they produce good quality ones, but we do not see them in our part of the world. The most painful thing was that there was absolutely no damage to that part of the house and therefore no need to do anything except perhaps some cleaning up and painting.

The other three bedrooms, which needed only repainting and decorating, were also vandalised. The very worst thing was that our red tiled roof which we had specifically asked to be rebuilt using concrete tiles, was replaced by some cheap aluminium. We knew that the fire had not been as devastating as it could have been because of the solid tiled roof. It was a nightmare to behold. Most irritating was that despite chasing this Italian builder to various offices in Accra and leaving letters requesting a meeting with him, to this day we have never met him! Only in Ghana could such a travesty happen. We engaged three different firms of lawyers to initiate legal action against him, but there was a clear lack of will on their part to do so. His being a European foreigner, managing a mega construction firm whose services they may well need at some stage, could well have been a factor. Our living abroad made us easy targets. The only justice we had was in getting the Judicial Council to rule in our favour when we took one law firm before them to get a refund of fees which we had paid to them in foreign exchange and which they insisted on keeping although they had not filed any action or even sent a letter on our behalf to the person responsible for the vandalization of our house. I cannot remember any of the members of that Committee except Mr Sam Okudzeto, a very distinguished legal practitioner in Accra, and a lady judge who was the chairman and who kept observing how old we were. I could only conclude that she had never come across people so old who could represent themselves so well! Still, Ghana is fortunate in having a few people who could clearly perceive right from wrong and act on this perception. We could wish that there were more.

The house was rented fairly quickly because some expatriates, especially senior ones, still wanted to live in a house with a garden, rather than some poorly constructed small apartment. Because of the shoddy workmanship and cheap materials used, we almost had another fire!! The new tenants were having breakfast on the back porch when they saw smoke emanating from the kitchen. Fortunately, they were around and had a fire extinguisher handy. It turned out that the builder had used a smaller gauge of electrical wire than he should have for the bigger air-conditioners which had been installed after the repairs! Again, only in Ghana could something like this happen without consequences. That we were not able to seek damages in a court of law is perhaps the greatest injustice I have personally experienced in my lifetime. In New York I have had on a few occasions taken workers to the small claims court, on one occasion a store and another a travel agency, I always had judgment in my favour. This unrecognised injustice which is all too common in Ghana and with which one has to contend very frequently, in all aspects of living there, is one of the reasons we hesitate to live there permanently. Neil paid the builder almost TEN times in repairs, some quite unnecessary, as we had spent to put up the original building! If I am to confess to harbouring ill feelings against anyone in my eight decades of life, it is decidedly against this roguish fellow.

We were in NY for the electioneering campaign of Barack Obama to become President of the United States. I threw myself into it big time. He was a true African American – born of a Kenyan father and an American mother of Irish descent. He was confident, bright, articulate, spoke well and just plainly looked the part. I was over the moon with millions of others when he won the election handsomely. I was glued to the television set for weeks, viewing everything right up to the inauguration. To this day every time I hear the song 'At Last' I could picture this handsome couple, Barack and Michelle Obama, waltzing at their numerous balls, eight I think. To this day our apartments are littered with pictures of the family, the couple, I was so happy for them. My ardour cooled when he supported Hillary Clinton for the Presidency in 2016. He demeaned himself in my view by doing so. How could he? A less deserving candidate there never was. I was one person who rejoiced at Trump's victory, and I have never been able to hate him as so many do, especially those of African descent, to the extent that they will vote for a clearly mentally incapacitated fellow with a running mate, an Indian, who did not realise that she was black, until he selected her. If he does become president as the pariah news outlet CNN is predicting, I fear for America. He definitely would not be president for long and America will be ruled by a woman who has very little to offer but her chameleon qualities. God pity America!

In May of that year, 2009, I celebrated my 70th birthday and we went on a Mediterranean cruise with my mother and my friend Genevieve Nassar. My mother, Ted and I flew to Heathrow from New York, met Genevieve in London and took the train to Southampton to join the Queen Mary. It was a splendid trip, taking in Rome and Barcelona to mention two of the places we visited. Later in the year, Ted and I attended another FIGO congress in Cape Town, the very first time it was held on African soil. We were very excited, going to South Africa, we had always been curious about it, but because of its apartheid system, doubted that we would ever see it. When we worked in Tabuk we made a lasting friendship with a South African midwife, Pauline Sono, and her daughter Larissa, so we always had a wish to visit her country. The Cape Town congress was very well organised, and well patronised, especially by the African delegates. We were very keen to see all the places of interest, so we stayed on for some extra days, visiting Robben Island and Nelson Mandela's prison cubicle, which was the main attraction for us, a vineyard and a winery, went on a day trip Safari and lots of other interesting and unusual pursuits. It was while we were in Cape Town that we heard of the passing away of one of our close friends in Kumasi, Victor Adu, of the Soil Research Institute. He and Ted had been contemporaries in Aberdeen and we became friendly as a couple with his wife, also called Vic, when we lived in Kumasi, just three houses away from us. Vic is the most truly Christian person I know. Her belief and her faith are so strong, they shine through. Apart from my abiding fondness for her as a friend, I truly admire her. We lost another old friend from our Kumasi days too, in 2009 – David Howell, retired British Council Director.

After the South African Congress, Ted and I flew to London to attend the installation of our good friend, and colleague of Ted's, Mr Henry Annan, Senior Consultant Oby/Gynae, as president of the Oby/

Gynae Section of the Royal Society of Medicine, a very high honour indeed.

In November we drove with Neil to Maryland to spend Thanksgiving with a friend of his and his family. Thanksgiving in the US is perhaps a more family-orientated holiday than is Xmas, and families get together for lavish celebrations. We stayed at the 4-star Marriott hotel in the town and drove to Neil's friend's family venue where the celebration was held. It was really grand and we enjoyed it immensely. While in Maryland we were also able to make contact with Ted's nephew, Kafui, a computer programmer who lived with his wife Susie and three kids at the time not too far away, somewhere in Virginia. The roads, especially the highways, in the US are so good that long distances are not a problem if you have a good vehicle, and most people do. He came to visit us at our hotel. We also visited our adopted Saudi niece, Nadia, and her husband David, who lived in a really rural part of the county – deer and other mammals can be seen roaming in the back garden!

We set off on Monday afternoon for New York and Neil mentioned on the way that Brian was unwell! Why on earth had he not told us this before? He then called him from his phone in the car, put it on speaker so that we could all communicate with him. The news was not good, his condition was worse than when Neil had last spoken with him two days before. Rhonda, who was just over five months pregnant with their second child, was advised to have minimal contact with Brian as it seemed to be flu of some sort; his mother-in-law was staying with them and trying to cope. It was the work of a minute for Ted to say he was going to Kent to see the situation himself. Neil called up his travel agent and got Ted a flight leaving JFK at 7.30pm that very evening. As soon as we got home, I helped him to pack and Neil took him to the airport. He was due to arrive next morning after 7am.

At Heathrow, Ted took the train to Paddington, where he was met by our third son, Dugald, and they drove down to Kent. Brian by this time had been taken to the local hospital where Ted and Dugie were met by Rhonda's parents in the waiting area. Brian, being a practising family doctor, had worked extra shifts on occasion at this hospital. Even so, it took a call to a Ghanaian lady consultant, who was not even on duty yet at the hospital, to expedite the process and get him admitted to ICU. He had picked up this infection from one of his patients – apparently there was a particularly virulent strain of flu going around at the time. When Ronnie heard that he had been admitted to the ICU, he, too, came down from London to see how he could help. Brian was in a bad way. His oxygen level was 89 when it should have been 98 to 100. He had to be given oxygen and remained in the ICU for three days. Ted's presence was an immense boost and reassuring to Brian and Rhonda. I never have a problem with young people today who say that they have taken a decision not to have children. Those of us who have them know that it is a lifetime commitment, you never cease being a parent however old or well qualified your children may be, and your natural instinct is to run to their aid whenever there is something wrong. If people think that they do not wish that sort of total lifetime commitment, then they are quite right not to have children. Ted stayed just under two weeks, ensuring that Brian was better and well and truly on his feet before returning to New York.

Xmas that year was spent at one of the best Double Tree Hotels in New York with Neil, two of my sisters, Gloria and Erica, and our mum. Such a treat, getting dressed up to the nines and sitting down to a five-course dinner with all the seasonal trimmings in a beautifully decorated festive ambience, being served by well-trained friendly staff, pure bliss. Then to Neil's apartment on Park Avenue South, also festively decorated, for more Xmas goodies and going home by cab to our nice, cosily warm apartment. That year Ted and I decided to go out on New Year's Eve and we booked a trendy Club in midtown Manhattan, between 47th Street and 49th St at 6th Avenue. Quite a nice way to see in the New Year. We did not know anyone there, but they were all so friendly and we dined and danced into 2010.

ANOTHER GRANDCHILD! IT'S A GIRL!

On February 23rd, Brian and Rhonda presented us with our first granddaughter – Danielle. Rhonda is fortunate with her labours – no long drawn out three stages for her! She is a precipitate labour person! With Noah, at least she had time to get to the hospital. With Danielle, Brian had to do the delivery himself in the kitchen, before the ambulance arrived. The instant pictures of her were of a bouncing, alert little girl, we welcomed this new female to the all-male Agble nuclear family. We met her in the summer when we visited. Neil had got green cards for us pretty quickly and Ted and I were becoming quite used to living in three places. We socialised with some of our Accra friends who also moved around a bit between Accra and London and London and New York, like Alfie and Janet, Aki and Judith, Sammy and Virginia.

Rather interestingly, the only place I had a problem entering was Ghana, this despite being married to a Ghanaian and living in the country since 1965 to 1984, and off and on after then. During the PNDC era there was a move to make life easier and legal for foreign-born wives of Ghanaians, but I do not think it lasted after the government changed. I can only say that my many trips to the Immigration Office, talking to senior officers, amounted to nought. On one occasion when I applied to the Ghana Consulate in New York for a visitors' visa I was treated in such a hostile manner by the female person who interviewed me that I risked it and travelled to Accra without one. I was eventually allowed in after paying a couple of hundred US dollars for a visitor's visa.

Ted's dad had built a property for each of his children on family land in Peki, their hometown in the Volta Region. I had always liked this place with its hills and valleys and almost daily showers which always seemed to happen between 4nad 6 pm, stopping as abruptly as they had started. We both enjoyed spending time there. Papa was buried in the church yard in Peki Tsame, one of the many little villages which make up the town. It was quite a decent house sited on an incline up a hill. His brother Bill had the apartment above us. We moved quite a few pieces of our furniture from Kumasi to Peki, including family pictures and books, of which we had a big collection. Some of them belonged to me before we were married, but which I still treasured. Peki was the perfect, permanent place in which to store them. We made it very comfortable and habitable, and spent at least a few days there whenever we visited Accra. It was an easier place to get some domestic help – although untrained, they were willing and hard working. We made it a point to have the flat thoroughly cleaned on each annual visit and over the years we have repainted and done improvements like putting in a shower room attached to our bedroom so that the main bathroom could be left for visitors; we also converted part of the garage into a room for domestic help and were very pleased with the outcome. Earlier a few friends visited us for a couple of days at a time and this we really enjoyed; the great country ambience, so very different from hot and humid Accra, was a real treat. Occasionally we went to Ho, the regional capital, where there was a very good market, with the freshest vegetable and fruits to be found anywhere in Ghana.

ANOTHER SIGNIFICANT BIRTHDAY, HAPPY 80TH, TED!

As time passed, we were getting used to living in New York and seeing different parts of the vast USA. We visited our South African friend Pauline in Arizona where she lived at the time, and my oldest chum from Trinidad and her husband, Cynthia and Peter Grant in Florida, to which they had partially relocated from London. Like us, they moved between both venues and we visited each other often when we were in London. Some of these trips to other states we made by air, but our favourite mode of travelling through the USA was by AMTRAK train. Both Ted and I enjoy long train journeys and we always travelled first class so that we could take full advantage of the best of rail travel. There are some states which we had no desire to visit. Texas was one of them – for some reason I have always thought of it as a dangerous place with lots of gun toting people! I am sure that I was wrong to hold this view, but nevertheless we have never been there.

In 2011, Ted celebrated his 80th birthday and the family consensus was that it should be celebrated in Accra. We had by now converted the garage at Kokomlemle into a cosy little bedsit which we used, while we gave the bungalow to other members of my family who came to Accra to celebrate this great birthday event with us – my mum who was already in New York, my youngest sister Erica, and a cousin from my mother's side of the family – Anne Alexis Dove, who had never visited any country in Africa and was looking forward to her first venture on to the 'motherland'. She was, I think, shocked at how sophisticated a place she found Accra, especially how well dressed the women were, going to church and social functions. Like many people from the Caribbean, she had fed into the myth of a poor downtrodden Africa, with people not quite living in trees, but not the smart modern houses she saw and visited in Accra!

We held a small celebratory party for a few family members and close friends in the little garden on the compound. Noah made quite an impression – at almost four he was very articulate and could carry on a conversation with any grown up. We were quite proud of him. The main birthday event took place at the African Regency Hotel. Dugald had been school mates with the now MD of the hotel, Chief Addo Kuffour, and this influenced the decision to hold it there. It was a very happy event with family and friends; all our sons were present. Ted was still enjoying good health and even ventured on to the tennis court every so often. We spent the next couple of months in Accra before returning to New York via London, as we almost always invariably did.

In 2012 Ted and I flew from New York to Rome to attend what would be our last FIGO Congress. It was the least impressive of all the Congresses we had ever attended. The venue was the first problem – it was quite a way out of town and involved a convoluted train journey plus a fairly long walk. It is the only Congress from which we have very little to show. Usually there is a decent bag for attendees and something less significant for the accompanying persons. There were some trips like to the Vatican and Colosseum, and other places of interest, and Rome is of course a unique city and we enjoyed our time there. On our way back to New York we spent time in London visiting our sons and grandchildren.

A SPIRITUAL HOME ON FIFTH AVENUE

Ted and I had chosen as our main place of worship St Thomas Church on Fifth Avenue after trying out a few churches around the city and in Queens with my sister Gloria. For me, this was the perfect church as the form of worship was exactly the same as I remembered it from my childhood and young adulthood in Trinidad and later in Leeds, England, where I attended St Michaels in Headingley and where Ted and I got married. The Episcopalian Church in America, which is the closest to the Anglican Church in the form of worship, is not exactly the same. Finding St Thomas was like finding my spiritual home, I could follow the form of the services and needed no prayer book as all the prayers were familiar to me. Although it entailed a journey of about 45 minutes on two trains, getting there every Sunday was not a problem.

What particularly endeared us to the Church was the music. There is a Choir School attached to it and they train about 31 boys to the highest standard of rendering choral music. Apart from the boys, the choir consisted of men, around 20 in number, whose voices, when blended with those of the boys, produced the most excellent musical treat, which we never took for granted. It was a privilege to belong to a church with such a high standard of music. Every year at Easter, when there is special choral music, their rendition of MISERERE DEUS fairly transports one into heavenly realms. Father Meads, the Rector at the time we started worshipping there, and his wife Nancy, were a warm and lovely couple who looked after their flock very well, and we were very fond of Father John Andrews, an English priest who was once Rector of the Church.

St Thomas also had several ministries for lay people, among them the Soup Kitchen, which I joined shortly after becoming a member of the Church. This had started several decades earlier when boys from the Choir School decided that they wanted to perform some regular act of kindness to the homeless people whom they encountered on the streets on their way from school to the Church. The soup kitchen meets every Saturday morning and different groups of us do various things – making the soup (Winter and Fall) or fruit cup (Spring and Summer), sandwiches and cookies, placing the food, napkins, and cutlery into bags . The more able bodied among us walked around with carts handing out these food bags to the homeless around certain areas of Manhattan. A few of our customers actually come to the reception area of the Church to collect them. Occasionally we added toiletries to the bags. The Soup kitchen is proud to say that since it started this work not a single Saturday had ever been missed, irrespective of the weather conditions. This is important as several hundred bags are given out every Saturday and the recipients depend on them. The Church has a strong pastoral section which looks after its seniors, both socially and spiritually. There are lunches, teas, dinners throughout the year, and despite being a large Church with a few hundred parishioners, it is still friendly and caring. Seniors in particular will be contacted if they have not been seen at Church services.

The present Rector, Rev. Canon Cael F. Turner, and his wife Alison, who is also a minister of religion, are both English and have been in charge since 2014. They have been very innovative by introducing new activities to the church life like a pub quiz, Ascot tea party, Italian and French nights when there would be a focus on that country's music and food. There is also more focus on families with children, and Mother Alison Turner heads this Ministry.

SPREADING OUR WINGS AROUND THE BIG APPLE

Through a Soup kitchen associate, Rose, now of blessed memory, Ted and I joined the Wagner Society of New York. This is a group of like-minded opera lovers with a special affinity for Richard Wagner, the great German composer. I find him a bit heavy and only enjoy some of his less dark music, unlike Ronnie and Ted who are avid fans. Our membership of this society put us in touch with other groups of New Yorkers. Lectures and talks by top international singers, conductors and cultural attaches are held regularly and we very much enjoy the annual cruise around the Hudson in the summer, during which our group boards a luxury boat and have a leisurely cruise with lunch and all the trimmings, and as our special guests some of the singers and musicians appearing at the MET in Wagner's operas at the time. A memorable trip was one we made by coach as a group from New York to the Princeton campus for the day to see one of Wagner's very well-known works, The Flying Dutchman, after which we had lunch, tea, good convivial company, and not to mention a great opera performance.

Through another acquaintance at Church, we joined the Church Club of New York – an umbrella organisation of Episcopalian Churches in New York. Another very interesting Club with diverse members, all with one thing in common – committed Christians interested in the Church and increasing their knowledge of its teachings, as well as meeting like-minded people. We also participated in some very interesting activities, like volunteering to help at a large food kitchen on Martin Luther King's Day at which over 1000 people were served a three-course meal. Most of these clients were not homeless, just down on their luck, perfectly well dressed and in some cases well educated.

We learnt that it was very easy to slip from being independent and self-sufficient to a state of helplessness and dependence. Ted actually helped at this food pantry and found it quite interesting. These places are never short of volunteers. The Church Club also hosts a black-tie dinner annually either at the Harvard or Yale club in midtown Manhattan. Both venues were splendid places for hosting these events and we enjoy them immensely.

Settling down in New York was very easy for us – with all these various activities and interesting friendly people we felt quite at home, and when people asked whether we liked living in New York the answer was always a resounding 'YES'. All places have their good points and their negative ones. Ted and I found the freedom and independence to go about by public transport, which was more reliable than not, just great. No drivers to turn up if they wished or late if they did not feel like it. Our neighbourhood on the Jamaica Estates (nothing to do with the Caribbean Island) was quite safe and in the early years we would return by our local train, the 'F' which terminated locally, after midnight when we went to the opera or Carnegie Hall or Broadway to see a play, or just a night out in Manhattan, and walk home quite safely, under very bright street lighting. Not that we were complacent about our safety because apart from criminals, there were a fair number of mentally disturbed people around who could turn violent with no provocation. But we never encountered any problems on the seven-minute walk from the subway station to our apartment, thank God.

New York, despite being such a large city with a population of over 10 million, and very cosmopolitan, was by no means an unfriendly city. To the contrary. We cannot count the times when complete strangers, usually of Caucasian descent, would stop to offer to help us get out of or into a car or public transport, or to carry a bag or something. We could never complain about unkindness or hostile behaviour; the same is true of London. Of course one meets rude individuals everywhere, then our response is to deal with such situations appropriately. I confess to being someone who complains when I feel that I have been treated unfairly, but by the same token I am very quick to commend good behaviour or /and positive interaction to the highest authority and have it recognised. This works very well for me. Ted is more prone to ignore it. I always complete surveys which ask for my feedback on service, product or anything at all. Ted, not so much!

HAPPY DAYS WITH MUM AND A SAD FAREWELL

2013 started out well. One of the best things for me about being in New York was the reunion with my family – my mother, three sisters and the older of my two brothers. My mother loved Ted to bits, he got along very well with her and also my sisters. They admired his quiet, gentlemanly demeanour and my mother actually said to me some time ago that if ever there was a problem in our marriage, she would blame it on me!! This reunion allowed us to do things together, like going on a Caribbean cruise with a group from my sister Gloria's church, various picnics and outings in the summer, lunches and dinners together. Mummy was a big part of the reason why I was able to persuade Ted to relocate to the 'big apple'. Mummy always stayed with Gloria, who had a fairly roomy house in the very leafy and pretty suburb of Elmont on Long Island – she travelled by herself between Trinidad and New York annually. Check-in clerks at airports anywhere she travelled always asked if the age shown on her passport was correct – apart from being a stylish, well-dressed lady, she was really smart and conducted all her banking and other business by herself, well into her 90s, very independent indeed, and I think she passed on this trait to all her daughters. She usually spent the months between June and February in New York and the other months in Trinidad. This year she had no sooner arrived than she was wanting to return home. Gloria also complained that she was completely off her food and not her usual active self. She was 97 and although we should have expected some slowing down, we were so used to having her as centrepiece that it was indeed worrying.

I called a family meeting at which we were all present, except our youngest brother Ronnie who lived in Trinidad with his wife Rita and two children, David and Daniece, and with whom Mummy stayed when she was there. The meeting was really to try to get her to remain in NY and I used the argument that since all of her daughters were in New York, two of whom were nurses, and all willing and happy to look after her, it was more in her interest to stay here rather than to return to Trinidad where our sister-in-law Rita, who worked full time, would have to manage on her own. She agreed with some reluctance. Neil, who loved his grandmother and was on site, brought her different flavours of a food supplement – ENSURE – which she seemed to enjoy.

Xmas that year was a bit of a sombre affair, with Mummy not her usual self. And she apparently started saying to certain family members that she wanted to go home – not to me or my sister Gloria, but to others and even to my brother Ronnie in Trinidad, with the result that he and Glenda decided to arrange for her return. He sent his son David to New York to accompany her, and that was the first we knew that she was returning to Trinidad early the next morning, January 17th, 2014. This caused a rift in the family, but as the eldest child I had to rise above this and accept that if going home was what she wanted we should all agree to it. After all, she was fully compos mentis.

Our sister Glenda accompanied David on the Caribbean Airline flight which departed JFK very early next morning and which took her home to her beloved Trinidad. Gloria and I followed a few days later. Although her mind was clear as a bell, it was very evident that she was going downhill. A recent X-ray had shown an advanced stage of stomach cancer. She knew that her life was coming to a close. Mummy remained as stoic as ever, uncomplaining, refusing morphine as she claimed the pain was not severe. Rita's brother, Philip, who was a general practitioner, checked up on her regularly. I realised that there was very little I could do. Mummy was being very well looked after by Glenda and Gloria, with help from Rita, Ronnie and David and that I would have to make arrangements to return shortly with Ted. On Thursday 30th January I received a call from my youngest sister Erica to say that Mummy had passed away peacefully in her bed at home, as she wished, at 4.13am.

We left on a Caribbean Airline flight to Trinidad on Saturday 1st February. The custom for burial in our Caribbean culture is as shortly after one's demise as is practically possible, and Mummy had requested that she wished to remain no longer than three days after she passed on. Mummy's burial service was held at St Pauls Anglican Church where our family had worshipped for decades and at which she and our brother and his wife and family were prominent members. As her oldest child, I was asked to read the eulogy. She was interred in the same grave as her mother, our beloved grandmother Ada Charles, at the Paradise cemetery near to the church. May they both rest in peace.

There are so many occasions on which I want to know or check up on something and I think of asking Mummy only to remember that she was no longer around to ask. She was a font of knowledge of family and community affairs and had such a sharp sense of remembering incidents, places, people. I am so very glad that we spent these last years with her! Neil did not attend her burial; he explained to us that he could not bear to, he is very emotional about such things and he did so love his grandmother! All our boys did. Gloria held a Memorial service for Mummy at her church, St Stephens in Jamaica. As she was a regular congregant there, going to services with Gloria on a very regular basis, she was very well known and the service was very well attended. Ted told me that Mummy showed him several exercises which she did on a daily basis and which he himself does up to the present!!

NEW EXPERIENCES, NEW FRIENDS

On our return to New York there was an invitation for us in the mail from a leading company, Castle Connolly Medical Ltd, a prestigious health care research company and information company which help consumers select the best doctor in all categories, around the country. Apparently, the company uses rigorous methods in carrying out their research for Best Doctors. Not quite sure how these assessments are done, but we have been assured that it is a quite detailed process. The award ceremony to which we had been invited was being held at the Waldorf Astoria, one of the city's most famous hotels. Ted and I decided to attend. Despite it being a real wintry evening and not knowing anyone who was attending, we set off for the Waldorf! It was well worth the trip into Manhattan, very well attended, super ambience, great food and company. We were seated at a table with an Oby/ Gynae award recipient and his family, which was great as he and Ted could talk shop. He was very interested when he heard that Ted was from Ghana as it was a country he dearly wanted to visit and possibly do a stint of volunteer work. Ted offered to make some enquiries on our next trip to Ghana, and the evening ended on a happy positive note. In May we received a phone call from one of his sons telling us that his father had passed on after a short illness, which was later diagnosed as an immune suppressant strain. Ted and I arranged to go to Silver Springs where the funeral was to be held. A man in his prime cut down by an illness of such short duration! We were very saddened by his demise. There was a large gathering at the funeral and his colleagues spoke of his dedication and high standard of work ethics. Very moving. A man in his fifties, with whom we had sat at a happy proud event, being laid to rest three months later! It was brought home to us all over again how tenuous our hold on life is and why we should live our life to the fullest every single day.

In June that year we travelled to London on our way to Aberdeen to attend Ted's medical class 55th reunion. It was actually held in Edinburgh and Deji Femipierce, Ted's Nigerian class mate and very good friend, attended it with one of his sons. It was his last one as he passed away three years later. We also travelled to Accra before returning to New York in October.

Myself and Richard Williams, father of Venus and
Serena Williams at the 2013 USA Open.

Ted and I had enjoyed relatively good health in New York, but in February 2015 there was a change. Ted is and always has been a committed soccer fan, especially the European leagues, but not exclusively, and he kept up with this wherever in the world he happens to be and TV viewing would allow. In our apartment complex we were not allowed to have washing machines or driers, but these were available in a laundry room in the basement of our building, for a charge of course! Ted always volunteered to do the laundry as he used the time to catch up with his reading while the machines were running. He would usually be gone about two hours. This particular morning he was back in our apartment after half an hour – he had returned to watch an important soccer match. I was in the kitchen trying to decide what to do with a punnet of green apples given to me by my sister Gloria. I decided to stew and freeze them to be kept for a crumble at some stage. I needed to get some cinnamon which was in a cabinet too high for me to reach and so I called out to Ted for help. There was no response. I went to the kitchen door to repeat my request when I realised that he seemed to be trying to remove his shoes unsuccessfully. When there was still no response, I rushed over to him and realised he was not coherent. I immediately called 911 and after taking the details needed to locate us, the operator assured me that an ambulance was on its way.

In the meantime, I placed him flat, turned his head to the side and performed other first aid measures to prevent an obstructed airway. In a few minutes the EMTs were there. I gave them a brief account of what had just happened and his medical history: no diabetes, controlled hypertension, nothing else of significance. They checked his BP and it was well within normal; he had to be taken to hospital to be diagnosed and treated. Which hospital was now the question? We were about equidistant between the Jamaica Hospital and Long Island Jewish. The senior of the EMTs decided that Long Island Jewish it should be and there we went. It was indeed a fortuitous decision from what I learnt about the other hospital later on. Suffice it to say that Ted had the best care available and on time, which made the big difference to the ultimate outcome – no neurological deficits on discharge five days later! A truly great outcome. In the first hour of his admission he was seen by two teams of doctors – cardiac and neurology – to determine just where the focus of the stroke was. The most impressive of all was the way in which they made me part of the decision making of Ted's care and how thoroughly every action was explained to me. We have nothing but the highest praise for the Long Island Jewish Hospital and the care Ted received. We consider ourselves extremely fortunate to be resident in their catchment area.

As a subscriber to the AMERICAN PROSPECT, a liberal political quarterly magazine, I was invited to attend their 25th anniversary early in May 2015. This was to be held in the trendy HYATT hotel in downtown Washington DC, not far from the White House. Ted and I decided to attend, combining it with a few days' holiday visiting Nadia and David in Glenn Close, Maryland. It was an impressive affair and the Guest Speaker was Elizabeth Warren. She gave a powerful address, and I thought at the time if the Democrats were so keen on having a female president how did they miss this eloquent, brilliant woman and were so obviously hell bent, even then, on Hillary Clinton?

A MEGA MILESTONE, A MEGA CELEBRATION

On October 2nd of that same year, Ted and I celebrated our 50th wedding anniversary. No big decision of where to have the party – Accra, of course, where most of our friends and family would be. We went to Ghana that August to prepare for our big day. Shortly after we arrived we were invited to a function at the British Council in Accra at which a large number of well-known people in academia were present. As with most similar events in Accra, drinks and hors d'oeuvres were served. This was unusual only in the way the service was being carried out. Elderly guests were served first, encouraged not to join the queue and were treated with such care and regard that I was truly impressed. The food served was also better than what one usually gets at this type of function. I asked one of the servers for the phone number of the proprietress and was rather surprised to learn that she was present! I asked to see her and we got along really well from the very first. I introduced her to Ted and we made a decision to engage her as the caterer for the celebratory 50th wedding anniversary event which we would be hosting on October 1st at the VILLAGIO compound where we lived.

It was one of the most fortuitous meetings we ever had with someone from a service aspect, and we have remained firm friends to the present. Maud is an exceptional Ghanaian business person. She keeps to time, is reliable, efficient, kind, thoughtful, innovative and helped us to organise a very successful 50th anniversary party that I really do not know how we would have managed had we not met her at the British Council that evening. She did not rip us off either! As sometimes happens to deserving people, her business has grown exponentially. And we thank God for that. She truly deserves it. We had permission to use the rooftop of one of the very tall buildings in the VILLAGIO compound, which gave a beautiful view of the city. Maud organised the decoration of the area, beautifully done with lights, plants, flowers. About 60 of our close friends and family were present.

By this time Dugie and Evelyn were engaged. We were delighted that our third son Dugald had at last found the love of his life. A bright and beautiful young woman who was born in the Brong Ahafo Region of Ghana, but had migrated with her parents to the UK at the age of three. She was a medic, doing very well for herself as doctor in charge of a community hospital in Watford. She had the right combination of Ghanaian respect for family values and London sophistication. We were really looking forward to having her join our family. Brian and Rhonda were present, as were Neil and a close friend at the time, and Ronnie with long-time partner Cat, a very pretty, well-mannered and good-natured girl who could give William's Kate a run for her money. A very happy occasion, with all our sons and their partners present, as well as my sisters Gloria and Erica, and my very close friend Pauline from South Africa. On Saturday the 2nd, the actual anniversary date, our sons hosted an equally large party at the African Regency Hotel, just across the road from our VILLAGIO compound. This was the night for speeches, toasts, and photos galore! Maud saved us from a really awful incident. My sister Gloria, who had decided to visit Ghana for the first time on this auspicious occasion, made the anniversary cake. No one makes a better Caribbean rum, black cake than she does – even though she is my sister I can say this in all honesty. Knowing that we were likely to have a large number of guests, she made two 15" diameter cakes, 3 ½ inches thick. A newly arrived from London Ghanaian woman, supposedly a top of the range cake decorator, was recommended and we engaged her services. Her charge was quite high, but we agreed to it – this was after all a special once in a lifetime event. To our shock and my sister Gloria's considerable annoyance, only one cake was decorated – she clearly kept the other, and we found this out only on the 2nd of October, the night of the hotel event. She of course denied keeping the cake and we had to use the single layer which she had tried to make larger with a thick frosting. But it was clear to see when it was cut that there was only one layer!

Whenever I am asked about life in Ghana, I carefully explain to people that your chances of being killed or maimed by a trigger-happy policeman, or a gang member, or a mentally deranged person are almost nil. But being cheated or ripped off or having your personal items disappear are quite high, and usually from people around you, too. Because of Maud's intervention, though, the cake situation was saved. Ted's closest and oldest friend, Jake, with whom we had stayed after our fire, although not in very good health, attended with Cynthia and was one of the speech makers, along with Chris, another friend of many decades. Ronnie also reunited with Kwesi, a friend of his since they were six years old and who now lived in the USA. His parents, who had been our friends decades ago in Kumasi, were guests and as Kwesi was around, we invited him too. It was another great night and we could truly say that we enjoyed our 50th wedding anniversary, perhaps more so than our actual wedding day!! The hotel gave us a free night's stay as an anniversary gift, which we took up several weeks later when we were leaving Accra for NY via London. Our sons had combined resources to give us a trip to Salzburg during the annual festival in July/August as an anniversary gift. We spent about two weeks there, visited Vienna twice using the train, went to the opera twice and dined one evening at a very good restaurant recommended by Frank Reinauer, head of the soup kitchen ministry at St. Thomas and a friend of ours who travels extensively himself. Great anniversary year altogether!

A FUNERAL AND A WEDDING, AND
TWO SERIOUS FAMILY ILLNESSES

2016 turned out to be a very eventful year – we had a funeral, a wedding, two serious family illnesses and a 50th birthday at the end of the year, in December. In early March we had a call from Accra informing us that our very close friend, Jake Blukoo Allotey, who with his wife Cynthia had so very kindly and generously invited us to stay with them after the fire in our home, had passed away after a short illness. There was no question that Ted and I would have to attend the funeral, Neil immediately made travel arrangements for us to fly to Accra. Our sons all knew how dear their Uncle Jake was to our family and that we would go to Accra to give moral support to Aunty Cynthia and the family. Some days later Neil contracted what had started as a cold. As he is not married nor does he have a live-in partner, when he is ill we consider it our duty to keep an eye on him and although he often would not tell us when he was unwell because he thinks we worry and fuss too much, it was a jolly good thing that he did so this time. He started feeling unwell on Monday; we took some chicken soup to him on Tuesday, and he said he was feeling better. When he had to return from work on Wednesday we began to be concerned and advised him to see his doctor. He did and she told him it was only a cold – bed rest and lots of fluid, was her advice.

He became progressively worse and with a fever when we saw him on Friday, by which time we thought we should accompany him to the local hospital a few streets away. He was seen by a succession of Physicians' assistants who observed him and after a few hours with no improvement that we could discern, discharged him! I must confess that I have always had my concerns about this group of health care professionals, I could not understand what their training equipped them to do which well-trained RNs could not. My scepticism was very well justified when Neil, early next morning, took himself to the Lennox Hill hospital and was admitted at once in critical condition! I had just arrived at Church for my Soup Kitchen stint when I had the call about his admission, I left at once for the Lennox Hill hospital and stayed the entire day; Ted joined me later.

Neil was admitted to the ICU and had several fluid input lines, his breathing was laboured and rapid, with a very low Oxygen level, and the doctors let us know of their concern as they were unable for some time to make a diagnosis, but were trying everything. This was Easter weekend, too. It was then decided that only Ted would go to Accra for Jake's funeral, I would stay to be with Neil. Ted flew off by BA on Easter Monday night to get to Accra on time for the funeral on Thursday. For a couple of days it was touch and go with Neil, but by Wednesday he began to show signs of improvement. I spent every day at the hospital, not going home until late at night as I stayed in his apartment at 21st Street and Park Avenue. He had wonderful support from his numerous friends, bless them. He was an ICU patient for a week, the medical and nursing staff were truly wonderful! We were really happy that he recovered in time to be a groom's man at his brother Dugie's wedding in May.

We were in London for the 2016 UK referendum on whether the UK should remain part of the European Union or leave it. As registered voters, Ted and I, along with all our family members, voted to remain. We could see very clearly why it would be good for the country to stay in the EU and did not at all share the optimism of those who felt that leaving was the thing to do. Well, the rest, as they say, is history.

My sisters Gloria and Erica, both of whom love Dugie as a son, decided that they would definitely attend his wedding, as did my niece Rolanda, the youngest daughter of the older of my two brothers and her fiancé, Keiron, to represent her parents. The date was set for May 28th and we planned to get to London on May 24th, having to arrange for the decorating of the groom's cake, made by you know who! We stayed at the Kensington Hilton until the Monday after the wedding when a flat in Earl's Court would be ready for us. The day after we arrived, we went all the way to north-east London to get to the cake decorators, Gloria chose the design she wanted and the collection date and time were arranged. On Friday night there was a bride and groom party to which we and a number of our friends were invited. It was held in a darkish basement room at the Gore Hotel in a smart part of South Kensington. The next day, Saturday, was the BIG ONE; the wedding would have two parts – the cultural, Ghanaian one which was first and the second traditional 'Christian' one, both booked to take place in a popular event place in London, the Hurlingham Club, with beautiful spacious grounds, perfect for pictures on a good day!

All the main participants, like the bridegroom and their various attendants, as well as parents and close relatives, would have to change attire – from Ghanaian to western. In my haste to get to the venue on time, I forgot my hat, specially bought at John Lewis for the occasion. Ronnie very kindly retrieved it for me from the hotel. A very strange thing happened at the hotel on that very day. We had been having some problems with the safe and we of course needed to secure our passports, credit cards, cash and my jewellery. We reported this and were assured that it would be sorted out. On our return we found that all our cash was gone! It was the first and only time in all our decades of hotel stays that we had money stolen from a safe. You would have thought that it would have been easy to find the culprit, but not so. With most hotels relying on the influx of migrants from Eastern Europe to boost up their work staff, hotel guests are finding that more of these incidents are occurring, even in reputable hotels like the HILTON.

It was a perfectly beautiful May day for the wedding, not a cloud in the sky, everything went to plan and the just over 200 guests of 39 different nationalities, a perfect reflection of the couple's varied friendships over the years. Both Dugie and Evelyn had had their tertiary education at London universities – Dugie at Imperial College up to PhD level and Evelyn at St Mary's Medical School, both popular places of higher education with overseas students. We sat at a table with Janet and Alfie Neequaye, Jemima and Eric Ayree, representing Ted's brother Bill, Felix Konotey-Ahulu, Cynthia and Peter Grant. Tunde and Alan Kwabwe represented Tunde's parents, Kwesi and Jackie Zwennes. It was a beautiful wedding and guests were particularly impressed by the cultural part, when Evelyn had to sit on my lap to signify that I was welcoming her to our family. We were all dressed in our very colourful traditional Ghanaian attire for this part of the ceremony. Dugie and Evelyn had a short honeymoon in Spain somewhere and a longer one later in the year when both their work schedules allowed it.

Back to NY where we continued our life of Church activities, opera-going, Wagner Society events, Church Club events and a summer which you expected would be mainly sunny and warm. Tracy Gamrat,

Maud and Jeff's daughter, was studying at a college in South Dakota and extended an invitation to us for her graduation. Although it seemed very far away on the map and we had never been anywhere near there before, we decided to go. We really felt that we should support the family as a show of appreciation for the way Maud had handled our 50th anniversary and had looked after Ted on his trip to Accra when he attended Jake's funeral. We set off from JFK then changed to a small plane at O'Hare airport then on to South Dakota. The college town was a quaint place, more like an English town, quite easy to get around and we enjoyed the few days we spent there. Tracy had done well in her studies and planned to go on to obtain a Master's degree. Maud and Angel were very pleased to see us, Tracy, whom we were meeting for the first time, was very warm and welcoming.

Back in New York, I had to see a Vascular surgeon recommended by my Primary care physician, Dr Akwasi Achampong of Elmont Medical Centre, for an ulcer on my right leg which came up as if by magic – no prior injury, bruise or anything one would associate with a lesion serious enough to need the intervention of a vascular surgeon! A debridement was done, scans were taken which revealed incipient arthritis of my knees, but very little else of significance. Compression stockings were prescribed. I also became the patient of a Nigerian cardiologist in an area a few miles from where we lived, still in the Queens Borough. His office walls were decorated with award certificates for best doctor, his office was nearly always filled with patients, he was very pleasant and respectful to Ted and me. But I am not sure that he took my complaints of weakness, lassitude and a general lack of wellbeing very seriously or that there was anything he could do about it. I had numerous tests done. Atrial fibrillation had been diagnosed years ago which is why I had been prescribed a blood thinner and an EKG had revealed some mitral valve malfunction, but with a well-functioning pumping mechanism, no further treatment was suggested or tried. In so far as our routine continued – travelling among New York, London and Accra – I decided to adopt a 'c'est la vie' attitude.

Back to London in early December for another big family event which was going to take place before Xmas – our eldest son Brian would celebrate his 50th birthday on the 16th. His wife Rhonda had arranged a family celebration at the Ritz of London, where they really know how to host such events! Meant to be a surprise for Brian, it all went very, very well. We stayed on for Xmas, but this was marred by our granddaughter Danielle's illness. She fell ill suddenly, a few days after the wonderful celebration for her father's birthday, with what appeared to be a stomach bug, but became so serious that she had to be admitted to the local hospital where paediatricians were preparing to have her transferred to Great Ormond Street, the specialist children's hospital in London, as they were concerned about her kidney function. We were very, very worried and considered postponing our return to NY on the 28th December. Fortunately, her condition started to improve while we were arranging to do so. But it could have been very much worse; prayer is powerful indeed.

MAJOR DECISIONS - SURPRISING INTERVENTIONS

2017 continued to be a year of uncertain health for me, especially the reduced mobility due to painful knees as a result of incipient arthritis. But as I have always been aware of the limitations of the medical profession in curing all our disabilities and making us better, my visits to them were infrequent. I did go to see some 'doctors' in a pain clinic on 6th Avenue who charged huge fees, but whose treatment was largely ineffective. Quite correctly, most insurance companies refuse to pay for the dubious cures they claimed to offer. After spending a few thousand of my own dollars on this rip-off treatment I stopped after I noticed a swelling on my left knee, which was the one last treated. The medical staff were mainly foreign and had no compunction at all of living the American dream by taking advantage of vulnerable people in pain. One used to be protected from this sort of irregular medical intervention in England, but news of ways to make money easily spread quickly across the Atlantic and soon enough in London a similar group sprung up, more open in their practice, but by the same token more dangerous as they openly advertised their services in the Evening Standard, a very popular free newspaper available to thousands of people in and around London. They proved to be just as ineffective at relieving arthritic pain. Sometime in May my youngest sister Erica, who is a very well qualified health professional herself, recommended a new cardiologist she had seen for an unrelated matter. She was impressed by his knowledge and his manner. He listened to his patients and was not averse to other forms of treatment than the usual ones recommended by the most mega money makers of all – the drug companies!

With a little persuasion from my sister I made an appointment to see Dr Marc Nolan. Found him very pleasant and down to earth. He said that he would request a report from my previous cardiologist and gave me another appointment. By the date of the next visit, when he still had not received the report from the cardiologist Dr Ola Akinboboye, he decided to do his own examination and investigations. His diagnosis, which was not new, was that I suffered from atrial fibrillation, an abnormality of the heart beating mechanism, which had been detected several years ago. He believed that it was due to the mitral valve malfunction which could be repaired and he felt that I would benefit from a repair, despite my age as I had no other significant underlying diseases and had never smoked. He could refer me to a cardiac surgeon if I decided to have this done. Ted was surprised at how quickly I decided that I was interested in having the surgery. After all, this was cardiac surgery when I had only ever had spinal surgery in 1999 in Saudi Arabia during the time we worked and lived there. I surprised myself too, as I have a dreadful fear of anaesthesia, not the surgery itself. I was very fortunate that when I had my spinal surgery in Tabuk, SA, we had an excellent Egyptian anaesthetist who was a neighbour and a great soccer buddy of Ted's. It was such an unexpectedly pleasant experience, I woke up almost immediately after 4 ½ hours of surgery, with no ill effects from the anaesthesia, such as a sore throat, malaise, sickness or tiredness. The surgery, too, was a huge success, so my previous experience had indeed been a great one, which was probably why I was so ready to consider having this one. I was referred to a cardiac surgeon that same day at Lennox Hill Hospital and was called up on Monday, given an appointment for Thursday. When I met the surgeon, Dr Nirav Patel, I instinctively felt that I would be in good hands, he, too, was also very reassuring. He was also a product of my alma mater, Liverpool University in England, which made a bond. We had already booked our summer trip to London; he was going away in August. I could either have the surgery performed the next week Thursday or on our return from our trip. I made another quick decision to have it on the next Thursday, to Ted's utter surprise. My reasoning was that if I were going to have the surgery, better sooner than later. It all happened very quickly after that. Ted and I moved into Neil's apartment on Monday as he was abroad on a business trip. We went to Lennox Hill hospital on Tuesday morning, had the admission procedures completed and settled in. I had a few visitors on that day: two of my sisters, Frank our Soup Kitchen supervisor, and my Rector, Father Turner, who prayed with me, using one of my favourite comfort prayers – Animus Christi. Others called and I received several beautiful floral arrangements. I felt quite relaxed, slept well. On Wednesday morning, my pre-op day, I was taken to the pre-op theatre where I had a procedure done to check the patency of my arteries, all okay. Dugald flew in from London; although he is not a medical doctor he wanted to be around and also to give moral support to his dad. He did have a few very relevant and pertinent questions for the surgeon and the anaesthetist and was reassured that everything should be alright. Medication to ensure a restful pre-op night was given, effectively, and Thursday dawned, with me still in a tranquil mood. Ted and Dugie were there bright and early, the anaesthetist (the most important player as far as I was concerned) came to give me a pep talk. Then I was wheeled into the area for patients and staff only. My next recollection was being back in a bed in an isolated room. Apparently, all went well with the surgery. In an operation like the one I just had done to repair a heart valve, you are put on a heart lung machine for the duration of the procedure – in my case four and a half hours. The machine takes over the function of the two main organs. My previous experience of anaesthesia for an operation of similar length was an extremely pleasant and uneventful one. As far as post op complications went, this was equally good.

I had a fairly uneventful hospital stay of six days. My sister Gloria, a retired RN of considerable experience, insisted that I stay with her to recuperate, and we happily accepted knowing that best care with her was guaranteed. On my very first day and while the home care nurse was visiting, I had a slight temperature rise and a discharge from the drainage removal site. I was readmitted to the sister hospital of Lennox Hill, the Long Island Jewish, where despite my protestations and the easily accessible records of the tests done less than 24 hours earlier when I had been discharged, they were nearly all repeated. A huge bill to be paid for by my insurers. This is one of the big flaws in the US health care system, and which makes it so costly. When I saw what the bill was, I dearly wished that I could discuss it with my insurers at the time, FIDELIS CARE. But rather surprisingly, they were not at all interested. Amazing! It makes one wonder who the real beneficiaries are of this money driven health care system.

In September, Evelyn called to say that she was expecting, and a few weeks later while I was at the doctors' she called from her obstetrician's to say that a scan had revealed TWINS!!!!, due in March 2018. Excitement galore at the thought of welcoming two more grandchildren into the Agble clan. After two follow up visits to the Cardiology Clinic at Lennox Hill Hospital, Dr Patel declared that I was fit to travel and we left for London early in December. We had discussed with all our sons the possibility of the joint purchase of a flat in central London as a permanent place for us to stay when we are in London. Dugie took up the offer and we got a flat ideally placed just off Marble Arch on the Edgware Road. Close enough to both our Church and our GP's. Only problem is that it was a basement and the elevator stopped on the first floor! Although there was 24-hour concierge service and the security men were always happy to help us down with our shopping, the idea of a basement flat did not sit comfortably with us, and we gave it up after a few months. We had a wonderful Xmas, our London Church, St James' in Paddington is such a warm and welcoming place. With a much smaller congregation than St Thomas's, I have the same feeling of spiritual fulfilment when we attend services there. Our wonderful Rector, Father Paul Thomas (an Uxbridge graduate) and his two assistants Father Martin and Father Michael (very young) provide for the needs of the growing congregation. We have seen it grow from just a few congregants when we started going there in 2008 to the present. Young people and elderly ones who have been worshipping at St James for several decades. The Church has a strong musical tradition and young musicians use it as a place to hold concerts, at least twice weekly some cellist, flautist, soprano or baritone will perform mostly at lunch time, but occasionally in the evenings. Having these places of worship is a blessing for us, especially at times like Xmas.

After a lovely midnight mass and a lie in, the entire family had Xmas Day lunch at a great little restaurant which served traditional Xmas fare. We saw in the new year, 2018, in London.

First big event in 2018 was the arrival of our two, brand new grandbabies on March 9th, the day before their father's birthday on March 10th. A boy, Joshua Senam, was first, followed by his sister, Sarai Dzifa. A true case of two for the price of one! Both Dugie and Evelyn decided that they did not want to know the sex of the twins until they were born, so it was a surprise to all the family. How clever they were, having one of each – they could decide that their family was complete now. To say that we were delighted would be to understate how we felt. More so because we were in London and could be a part of it all.

Shortly after, another ulcer appeared on my left leg, again seemingly out of nowhere! All the usual tests were negative, but this one grew bigger with a vengeance, and oh so very painful. It had to be dressed thrice weekly at our GP surgery Westbourne Green, by the tissue viability nurses, a group specialising in wound/ulcer care. Despite this, I was eventually referred to a vascular surgeon by my GP, Dr Olukanwa. A Harley Street surgeon, Dr Constanz Kyriakides, was highly recommended by our daughter-in-law, Evelyn. He was a very good looking, middle aged fellow of Greek descent, and we got along very well. He later told me that when he first saw the ulcer, despite the fact that there was no history of diabetes, he feared it would be of a long-term duration! I became a devout follower of St Anthony during this period. I cannot remember having such unrelenting pain, it was nerve damage pain, which is really the worst one could have. A big problem for me was my sensitivity to many medications, especially painkillers. The smallest dose of some kept me awake and alert, while others sent me almost comatosed. Eventually, Mr Kyriakides suggested treatment with maggots. I had heard about this vaguely some time ago during my training, as one heard about leeches – I imagine that they acted in a similar fashion. I agreed to it.

There was only one factory in the world where they were produced and this was in Wales. Nevertheless, despite its proximity to London, it was quite expensive. In using it, timing had to be right. Basically, this was a bag of carefully selected maggots' eggs which would be placed on the ulcer and would feed on the decaying flesh! Horrible sounding, but I was ready to try anything which might work. The first lot was applied and I had to try desperately to take my mind off the fact that there were little organisms eating away at my flesh. It was painful, too. Suffice it to say that this worked; the second batch of eggs was inert. By mid-June it was well healed, much to the very pleasant surprise of my surgeon. We returned to New York at the end of July, in the middle of a really nice summer, already preparing for our next trip before Xmas. We had decided that spending Xmas with the family was a priority. With our declining years it was important to spend more time with the family, especially our grandchildren. Noah and Danielle were at the age when we could converse with them sensibly and Joshua and Sarai were changing so fast and such a pleasure to be around that we did not wish to miss out. Xmas that year was spent at Brian and Rhonda's home in Kent, which had ample room to accommodate the family, a really enjoyable affair, with Josh and Sarai less than a year old, crawling around and into everything, and so very, very cute!

ANOTHER VERY SAD LOSS

Lent and Easter in 2018 were celebrated in London and while we were there, on March 19th, we had a call from Dugie, passing on some shocking and very sad news – Kwesi Zwennes, one of our closest couple friends, had passed away suddenly that morning. It was so unreal! We prepared at once to leave for Accra. We had seen Kwesi and Jackie the year before in October when they were in London. We had very happy memories of an evening out at the Dorchester for dinner, a great get together. We have always been aware of how important it is for us to make much of each other whenever we can, and Kwesi's passing brought it home. We took comfort in the enjoyment of that last evening together. We arrived in Accra on the evening of the 7th April with a return booking for the 17th. Jackie and Tunde were very pleased to see us. Kwesi was buried on April 12th; a very sad affair, we were still struggling to accept that we would not see him again on this earth, his loss was so sudden and unexpected. RIP, Kwesi, we shall miss you every time we see Jackie. We spent Xmas in London at Brian and Rhonda's, including Neil and Ray, then set off for Ghana on the 27th December, staying there until March 8th 2019. Ted had a an appointment for his green card renewal in New York on March 15th 2019, but the Americans could be so helpful and civilised with such matters that part of the process was carried out at their Consulate in Accra to facilitate him in case he was late getting back. When we left Accra on the evening of March 8th, we flew into London just in time to celebrate Josh and Sarai's first birthday on the 9th which was an entirely family affair. We were driven straight from Heathrow to a rather posh restaurant in central London for a breakfast celebration. Very enjoyable to see how they had grown from a few months back, Sarai walking around very confidently, while Joshua seemed content to crawl, at a very fast rate, behind her! On to New York and to the Immigration Office where within half an hour Ted was given a temporary green card, the substantive one would be sent to him in a few months. In the meantime, this one was valid for travel, including international travel. No waiting around for hours, very quick, straightforward and efficient. These are the practices which one would like to see Ghanaians emulate – less obstruction and hostility and more willingness to help and accommodate at the official level.

THE BIG 80 – JOINING THE RANKS OF THE OCTOGENS!!

I turned 80 in May 2019 and it was a great event, celebrated in New York at one of the trendy Park Avenue South restaurants – Union Square Cafe All the boys were in attendance with their wives/partners and our two youngest grandchildren, my siblings, one of my nephews and about a dozen of our good friends in NY. Nadia and David came down from Glenn Close in Maryland for the entire weekend and what a lovely surprise that was! They took us to dinner and to the theatre in the heart of Broadway and it was like old times. Rhonda, Noah and Danielle were the only family members missing. Noah had a very important exam to sit for entry to Tonbridge School, one of the top schools in Kent for Boys and where the competition is very keen. Rhonda thought it best not to risk travelling, cutting it so fine, the exam being on the Tuesday after the party on Sunday. I fully understood how she felt being that sort of Mum myself and when the results came that he had topped the pass list in Maths and Science, we were so overjoyed and felt that missing my 80th was well worth it! It was after this that we had a conversation with all our sons about spending more time in Ghana with a view to eventually settling down there. Hard to think about missing all these pleasurable activities in New York and miss them we shall. Later in May we spent five days in Washington DC to attend Tracy's Graduation from George Washington University. We stayed at a Hampton Inn just opposite to the hotel in which Maud, Jeff and Angel stayed and it was a really great ceremony, Tracy earned a distinction in one of her subjects and we played the role of proud in loco 'grandparentis' very well.

Ted's medical class at Aberdeen University in Scotland, celebrated their 60th anniversary in June. As their numbers had diminished from their last gathering at the 55th in 2014, it was held at a small family-owned hotel on the outskirts of Edinburgh city – the Dunstan Houses. It rained non-stop from our arrival on Wednesday 12th June and only tapered off three days later as we were about to depart! This is not so unusual for Edinburgh, an otherwise lovely city. There were two events planned – a drinks reception on Wednesday and the formal dinner on Thursday. Both were held at the Dunstan Houses. Ted's class is very special and they are always very comfortable in each other's company. Being only 60 in number when they started, it was easy to become very friendly towards each other over the six-year course. They tend to have a reunion every five years, and we have attended every one since the inception of this practice at their 25th anniversary in 1984.

Yolande & I with classmate Morris Graham in the Garden of John Reid at 45th Class reunion held on the Channel Islands.

Christine, Yolande, Ronnie and I at formal dinner for the 35th reunion in Aberdeen.

*Myself with Ronnie and Jamaican Class mate Betsy
Davis and her guest at the 35th Class reunion.*

*Yolande, Ronnie and Class mate Christian Robb at the Craths
Castle ground during the 35th Class Anniversary.*

*Yolande, Ronnie and I at the Craths Castle ground
during the 35th Class Anniversary.*

*My Medical class '59 (with spouses) at an informal lunch which took place
at a trendy restaurant in Edinburgh, prior to their 60th reunion in 2019.*

My Medical class at 60th reunion in 2019

My Medical class with our spouses at 60th reunion in 2019

Early in July, Ted and I went to Wales as part of the Church Club of New York to participate in a retreat/pilgrimage organised by US Friends of Gladstone. Gladstone was an 18th century UK Prime Minister who served four terms, was very well known for his prolific writings, his Christian beliefs and his philanthropy. He had somehow acquired admirers and followers of his teachings in America, hence the Friends Society. He built a famous library and it had been converted into a place of study with a small number of rooms for lodging; people came from all over to do short courses on myriad subjects and disciplines. We spent a very happy, peaceful and interesting week there, each morning started off with a service in the little chapel just around the corner from our room, which made it very convenient for us. Different people, both lay and ordained, conducted the simple service, each with a different theme, after which was a typical British breakfast with all the trimmings, and trips sightseeing various famous churches, talks / lectures on interesting topics, three course dinner, evenings free at one's leisure. We visited the famous Chester Cathedral and attended a lunch time organ recital there. The last but one day was free to do whatever we wanted and we chose to visit Liverpool city, home of my old Alma Mater, Liverpool University. We went by train with Susan, director of the Church Club of New York, and her partner, Rick. We actually visited the Beatles Museum on a beautiful mild summer day when queues were forming to get in! Somewhat daunting for seniors with canes! But it was well worth it as it brought back vivid memories of my youthful days. Ted and I found this retreat/ pilgrimage most rewarding and spiritually uplifting. We have nothing but praise for and gratitude to the people in our group, mostly seniors like us, with a few sexagenarians and one young woman perhaps in her late 30s or early 40s. Ted and I were by now using canes and everyone was so solicitous of our welfare! It was very touching. So very glad that we were able to make this trip!

In mid-September we journeyed by air to Pittsburgh to attend the wedding of Ted's grand-nephew, his brother Bill's grandson. As the oldest member of the Agble family resident in the US, Ted had to attend and indeed we wanted to; we very much looked forward to meeting Patricia and the family – we had last seen them as teenagers several years ago. Another new place to visit, too. Both of

Patricia's children had studied medicine and Frederick Edem was an internist at a Philadelphia Hospital where he met and fell in love with a colleague, Jessie Meyer, herself from a very distinguished family. We looked forward to welcoming her to the Agble clan. It was a very grand wedding, the bride and groom both had large families who were generous in their support. It was a delight for us to meet all the nieces and nephews and their children, some of whom were in tertiary education already! How time flies! We later had the pleasure of having Edem and Jesse and Jackie Dela and Patricia at our apartment in Accra for dinner January 2nd, 2020. The young couple seemed to be enjoying their short stay in Ghana very much.

We spent a week in London from December 22nd, where we attended Xmas Eve Mass at our St James Church, spent Xmas with all our family, except Neil and Ray who were in Ghana, at Brian and Rhonda's in Kent, a lovely supper with Father Thomas and his family and a few other parishioners at the Vicarage on the 26th to celebrate St Stephen's Day, and off to Accra on Saturday the 28th.

LAND OF THE FREE AND THE BRAVE

As I get to the end of my addendum, I feel that it is pertinent that I should give an overview of the three countries in which I have lived over the period. I have already mentioned my fascination with America since my earliest years. Living there for some time was a natural progression, though not consciously planned. And I do enjoy living in New York, with all its activities, despite our diminishing mobility. That America consists of some very brave individuals cannot be in doubt. Every day one hears of acts of bravery, both at home and abroad, committed by Americans which are truly remarkable. I would say from my observations that they are instinctively brave. 'Land of the free' is where I have misgivings. What do they mean when they say that America is the 'land of the free'? Many immigrants, especially those from developing countries, would claim that they were in the US because of that freedom. I have my doubts whether political freedom is what they have in mind. Freedom to make money by any means is more the reason. Ripping off is prevalent among immigrant businesses, in Queens they have captured the car service business and they can and do increase their charges with impunity. Fast food is also another popular business venture and although there are health rules in place to ensure that eating places are kept to a high standard of food hygiene, not many observe them. Some of the other freedoms with which I have an issue is the one where you are bombarded with unsolicited mail. Every day I have to deal with at least 12-15 on average, not counting magazines. Living the American dream is another phrase with which I have a problem. Making money at whatever cost and living above one's means, especially in the immigrant communities, is a more apt description!

I have always been a donor to certain causes and have done this in England for decades, the same charities, modest amounts, consistently, without any problems. Here it is a different kettle of fish – give to one charity and your personal details are passed on to others (I am told, but I have no proof of this) or worse, every month one can get two or three begging letters from the same charity, no once or twice a year donating for them. When I think of the wanton waste of paper I could cry. But then as one quickly finds out, everything is about money. Robert Kuttner, a contributor to the American Prospect, describes it as 'predatory capitalism'. The American Prospect is one of the few magazines for which I have a subscription. It is also one of the few whose writers and contributors dare to describe capitalism as seen in the US in less than glowing terms.

Freedom, unfortunately, does not extend to consumer rights. I have a vivid memory of an American whom I admired from thousands of miles away in Trinidad as a teenager growing up – Ralph Nader. He was a champion of the rights of the average American consumer; I often wonder what became of him. Consumer rights are not a big issue anymore, and corporations are free to treat their customers unfairly with impunity. TIME WARNER CABLE changed its name to SPECTRUM and raised prices for their seasonal services by 300%, with hardly a whimper from most of their customers. Their latest thing is 'going paperless', ironically. While one section is allowed to send unsolicited mail every day, customers of some of the multimedia companies like VERIZON are forced into using 'apps' for nearly every single interaction like paying bills, and other mundane interactions. There is an 'app' for everything and they are not user-friendly. But they are what VERIZON wants, saves them money and as a matter of course, customers who would prefer to get their bills in the traditional way, including the elderly, are not given a choice. Of course, the Better Business Bureau can be very effective as I found out on the few occasions on which I have had to use them, but corporate bullying is the order of the day. Healthcare is a huge problem. The best healthcare probably in the world is available here, but many people are as far away from receiving it as if they lived in poor areas of the world. Money is wasted on other aspects of living; healthcare is not considered a priority. When people here talk of the NHS, the British healthcare system, it is usually scoffed at and mildly derided. There is no denying that the NHS has deteriorated significantly in the last four decades, ever since the late British Prime Minister Margaret Thatcher, in her love of and admiration for all things American, thought that the health service could be run successfully as a business. She got rid of Matrons, very well trained and experienced nurses, the very backbone of the system which kept delivering best care, and substituted them with graduates in Social Science and other unrelated subjects to be at the helm of managing the service. It was only a matter of time before it all collapsed and we were indeed lucky that this has not been completely. Radical changes in practice, like nurses having to spend more time on computers and less time on quality patient care, using ordinary water to clean the hospital wards and other areas with heavy use by patients, rather than with tried and tested cleaning agents because of some spurious research which claimed that the outcome was the same. Cross infection and hospital acquired infection began to rear their ugly heads.

Without a doubt, Ted and I have benefited from the healthcare in America, which partly depends on where you live. Our catchment area has some outstanding hospitals like the Long Island Jewish and we are indeed grateful for this. We do see the flaws in the system and now some politicians, described in derisory terms like 'left wing', 'liberal' and worse, are not afraid or embarrassed to advocate a fairer and more equitable healthcare for all. The insurance system of providing healthcare encourages bad practice. Not in every case, but I would definitely say on the whole. And in a society where having lots of money is so very important, providing best care will not always be top priority. The ugliest face of capitalism is to be seen here. On the other hand, no other country has as many philanthropists and the arts and sciences benefit greatly from their philanthropy.

THE RIGHT TO BEAR ARMS

In the mid-60s when American Foundations like the Ford and others were actively involved in trying to help some African developing countries improve their healthcare, especially maternal health care, birth control was top of their priorities, Ted was selected to go on a tour of hospitals not only in America, but Mexico and Venezuela as well. To my utter surprise he returned to Ghana from one of these trips with a gun, which he had bought from a shop In New York! He had decided to do this on the advice of a senior police officer in Kumasi, as a means of protection in case we ever had a problem with armed burglars. Although this was not a common occurrence in Ghana by any yardstick, a recent coup was thought to make the likelihood of this possible. The interesting thing about this was that he did not have a clue as to how to use it, I never wanted to see it and it was kept in a cupboard in his wardrobe; he was the only person who ever went there. It was never used and he passed it on to a colleague years later, who also never used it! It was a white elephant. Most people in Ghana would never have seen a gun up close, let alone owned one. In America guns are commonplace and policemen are all armed and not afraid or reluctant to use their armour, sometimes recklessly. They seem incapable of shooting to disarm and almost always shoot to kill. Homicides are commonplace among ordinary civilians too, not only by guns, but knives and any other weapon which could be used. The figures are astronomical. I recall a few years ago when in a London suburb two terrorists had killed a young soldier. The British police were soon on the scene and the assailant was disarmed with one shot. In the US no less than forty shots would have been fired by several officers. I hope and pray that the UK continues its policy of not routinely arming their police officers. Not infrequently, ordinary passers-by get caught in crossfire and are killed or maimed. I have become almost addicted to a television programme – Investigation Discovery – it tells the stories of real crime including murder, enacted, with accounts by real family members. The determination and tenacity which the law officers display in solving these crimes, sometimes after several decades, have caused them to rise in my esteem and I do have great respect for them. Every so often, about a few times yearly, some mentally disturbed person, or someone with a grudge against his co-workers, goes on a shoot up and several people are killed. Even schools are not protected from this madness. In fact, schools have been in the news over the past decade for being the sites of some of the worst and most heartrending shootings. One would think that churches, God's places of worship, would be exempt from gun violence, but one would be mistaken. Several places of worship – Christian churches, Jewish synagogues, Muslim mosques – have all been wantonly attacked by gun wielding maniacs. Nowhere is sacred! Attempts to control this have not been popular with some of the population, even normal sounding ordinary citizens who are quick to point out that their right to bear arms is enshrined in the 2nd Amendment of the constitution. To say to those who hold this view that this amendment was perhaps necessary in the days of frontier America, when the wild, wild west was very real, is a huge waste of time. Although there is a big hue and cry every time a mass shooting occurs, it is difficult to see how the government and citizens of the 'world's greatest democracy' could ever end this too frequent carnage of innocent people. The very powerful National Gun Rifle Association has one of the most influential lobbies in the government. Another anti-democratic practice in my opinion is that of the role of 'lobbyists' who comprise individuals and groups representing special interests, based in Washington DC, at the heart of government. Their main function is to influence law makers with whichever cause they are espousing, not always for the good of the ordinary American. It is believed to be a very financially lucrative practice. But there is hardly any sense of outrage at how powerful they are. In my opinion emerging democracies in poorer areas of the world should think twice or even thrice before they decide to adopt the American system of democracy, which does not even work well for Americans themselves. And if they are unable to make it work to the benefit of their citizens, then how much less for poorer democracies?

They stand a better chance with Parliamentary democracy I think, from what I have observed.

It is a shock to the system when one encounters lawyers advertising their services, like retail shops do their goods, on the TV screens. Doctors, perhaps, have a code of conduct imposed by their regulating bodies, which discourage this sort of practice. They do not advertise in such open ways, but lawyers have no such compunction. Some may think that it diminishes the profession to sell it like merchandise, but it is perfectly respectable and acceptable in the great USA! Doctors have found a way of making up for this, however, and being aware of the big rip off by the major pharmaceutical companies, many have formed themselves into companies touting alternative medicine as the answer to almost all the ailments present in the populace. The FDA is the regulating body which has the last word and gives final approval for any drug put out on the market. The clever doctors who produce and advertise their homeopathic medicines advertise via pamphlets and booklets, very convincingly put together, and in very, very fine print, almost as if it were an afterthought, it is stated that their product has not been approved by the FDA!!! One thing all the products have in common is that they are usually in liquid form or as large capsules.

THE MEDIA AND FAKE NEWS

Although not a popular person in many countries, mainly because of the bad press he gets at home for being such an unorthodox President by many standards, one thing Donald Trump has said which has resonated with very many is his concept of fake news. Many people globally are suspicious of the media. Even the BBC, known internationally for its accuracy and fair reporting, is viewed with suspicion in many quarters nowadays. I have always been sceptical and select my news sources carefully, but I saw first hand how the media in the USA strives to influence the average population. This was during the 2014/15 presidential campaign. Fair and unbiased reporting was never even a consideration from the way most of the media behaved. CNN was the worst culprit and I have never watched it since. The Republican candidates, who admittedly were a pretty unimpressive bunch, never had a chance. The media almost to a man wanted Hillary Clinton to win and certainly did their best to see that this happened. Poor Bernie Sanders, whom I admit to supporting, and who had a powerful message which drew thousands to his rallies, especially young people, also did not have a chance. Despite polls which showed that he was the only candidate who repeatedly trounced Trump, the powers that be in the Democratic party had other plans. I was happy to see that two of the women mainly responsible for this fiasco were sacked from the party, rather ignominiously, but too late, too late, was the cry.

The media were shocked and disappointed by Trump's victory. For a start, he definitely did not fit their idea of a US president. Being rather unorthodox in his manner and utterances, not from the Washington political crowd, prone to making ridiculous statements, even though they were sometimes true, and worst of all made no bones of his contempt for the media, all contributed to a recipe for a total disconnect and war on their part. It was never going to end until they got rid of him, not by the ballot box and not by guns, but using their ever-flexible constitution. Whatever his faults and his failings, I am not sure that I agreed with the way he has been vilified by the media. It could never be a good practice to so weaken your president as to make the rest of the world realise the contempt in which he is held at home. It has weakened America in the eyes of the world. The fact is that not all of his policies were wrong or different from what other heads of states were doing. And yes, I am daring to say this fully aware that large numbers of my friends and family will totally disagree with me.

ENGLAND, THE UK ET AL

I have already mentioned my affinity with the UK, having gone there on a British passport in 1963, successfully completing my studies and having had only good, positive experiences while I was there. Like meeting Ted, getting engaged and married to him and fully enjoying the country about which so much of my education had been the focus, visiting all those ancient places which had only been in my imagination when I had read about them. While most of my class mates were heading to Canada, or less so to the US, I believe that I was actually the only one who had this yearning to go to England. When Ted and I left shortly after our marriage in October 1965 for Ghana, it was 18 years before I visited it again in 1983. This time I lived in London, not Leeds as previously, and it was a totally different London from the one in which I had arrived in 1963; I could barely recognise it! It was a trial run to see whether I could live there as it became increasingly clear that if our sons were to have a decent education, a change from Ghana would be imperative. Ted has already mentioned the numerous problems and terrible experiences they had been through with their education.

From 1984 when three of our four sons and I relocated there, I have wholly or partially lived in England, London to be more specific. It was a good move, only good things happened to all our nuclear family. In fact, it is no exaggeration to say that all our sons fared much better educationally and professionally than they would have done in Ghana. They were treated fairly and according to their ability, no leg up or affirmative action. Ted had leave to remain as the spouse of a UK citizen and he voted more times in England than he ever did in Ghana! We were not a burden on the NHS at all, not having any serious ailments while we were there, but we have benefited immensely from the perks which one gets in a developed country that is not insanely capitalist. Free travel for the over 60s on public transport is one which we appreciate the most as this could be a huge financial burden if one wishes to move around. Free medication on the NHS, in fact free treatment in almost all cases. Not as quickly as in the USA for those fortunate enough to have health insurance and depending on where they lived. It is this relatively long waiting time to be seen and treated which attracts so much scepticism from Americans.

Apart from a creeping tendency towards American-style violence, but with knives rather than guns, the UK is still a pretty quiet place to live, a very good standard of education is still maintained on the whole, and racist tendencies are not so blatant as in the US. There is decidedly more integration at all levels, and there are very few totally segregated neighbourhoods. Children of all colours and races can be seen playing together, leaving the same school. They speak the same language, literally. In the US one can easily distinguish an African American accent as distinct from that of a Caucasian one. This is because there is so little fraternisation between the groups. For one brief period a couple of decades ago, African Americans were encouraged to have their own language, even to the point of being educated in it – Eubonics. Thank God reason stepped in before another nail in the coffin of African American demise was hammered in.

Ted and I are very happy that our grandchildren are being brought up in the UK. We are delighted with their progress in school and their good manners. We consider ourselves fortunate to have an alternative home there, despite BREXIT, for which we did not vote, and all the other upheavals which we should expect as a result, we are fairly confident, to use one of their favourite sayings 'it will be alright on the night'!

GHANA – THE REAL CONUNDRUM

Writing a few words on Ghana is not really easy for me, as there is so much I want to say. From our earliest meeting Ted had narrated a story to me about someone who was bitterly complaining to God that He, the Almighty, had given Ghana so much by way of natural resources, climate, land site, etc, why had He so favoured the place? God smiled knowingly and replied, 'Do not worry, you just wait and you would see the people I am going to put there!' Ted was never very clear from where this little pearl of wisdom originated, but how very, very true and prescient! Never had a less deserving people been given more. It is my view that despite words of praise and admiration in abundance from some western governments, there is not the improvement in the standard of living, malls and designer shops notwithstanding, which one expects and which should be a natural progression over the decades and despite all the big noise about western democracy being in place. In my 50-plus years' association with Ghana, little has changed, little of significance, that is to say. There are more modern cars, more private schools, more houses (not sure that they are better – in the get rich quick haste, quality has been a mega casualty), more people travelling abroad, all superficial signs of prosperity. But the electricity supply is worse than ever; water, admittedly is not so bad, although many would disagree with this view; certain roads, even in the city, are impassable because of terrible potholes; despite being an oil producing country, petrol and petroleum products prices are sky high; health care is haphazard – if you are rich enough you can attend one of the many new hospitals springing up all over Accra where decent standards of medicine and care are available, or you could travel to South Africa or the UK or even the USA! Ghana is an openly capitalist society and very proud of it. Apart from Nkrumah's governments I could think of only one which did not seek to emulate America and everything American – that of Rawlings' PNDC.

I have always held the firm belief that poor countries should not be bastions of capitalism, and socialism has never been a bad word in my dictionary. The seed of this belief was very likely planted by my father, who told me in a reply to a question from me about communism when I was about eight, in very simplistic terms, that it was about a country's wealth being shared equally, not a small number of people being sickeningly wealthy while others starved. The result of this disparity can be clearly observed in Ghana. As an example, people like us who have worked very hard for the modest means we own are perceived to be 'wealthy', we are fair game for all, including the government, for big time rip off. If you can be identified you are made to pay taxes to make up for those whom they miss, deliberately or otherwise.

We had a discussion with our sons that it was probably time for Ted and me to spend more time in Ghana. I admit that although it was with some misgivings because of all the negative experiences we have had, I promised myself that I would have an open mind.

Ted is the youngest of three siblings, all of whom are still around – his brother Bill, 94 and sister Felicia, 90, both of whom he dearly loves. He is also fond of hot weather. Not that he ever complains of the cold in NY or London, as we do dress up warmly in winter and are fortunate to live in what I consider an overheated building, without any individual apartment heat regulating system. I would admit that although I have grave misgivings because of the previous bad experiences, I promised myself to approach this with an open mind. Despite the willingness on my part to have an open mind about this very important decision, here are some of the encounters we have met during the few short weeks in which we have been back here:

We arrived on the evening of December 28th met by Stanley and a driver from Lavender Lodge, where we would spend that first night as is our practice. Next morning, Stanley came to take us to the VODAFONE outlet at the Mall to get our internet up and running. He is very good at having all the necessary information at hand to enable us to renew the contract. We paid for a certain amount of data, more than ample over the period of a month, to be renewed monthly, were given a receipt, were told that we could start using it later that day. To date after several visits to their head office, their shop in the mall, telephone calls lasting several hours with reassurances being given by several of their staff at all levels, we still have no VODAFONE service as I write, February 13th 2020! The person with whom I most wanted to speak, the CEO or her secretary, seems to exist in an ivory tower, not to be disturbed by ordinary mortals. I was not even allowed to contact her secretary. This is what being CEO of a large corporation in Ghana is like. I do not give up easily, but when I realised that this interaction, or lack of it, with VODAFONE was ruining my health, I decided to leave it alone. But is it fair? Is it right? It shows total contempt for the customer, without whose patronage your company would not exist, but which is so common here and which frightens and frustrates me. There is no redress to be sought either. Fortunately, Stanley who is a computer tech at BUSY Internet, brought his own gadget BUSY MI FI for me to use and so I was able to get some internet access. There is no consumer affairs regulating body to which one could complain.

The next encounter has a better ending because of the CEO and the persistence of our son, Neil. Our 350 ML car which was being used by Neil on his arrival in Ghana, had an accident. I had warned him in an email of how careful and alert he needed to be when dealing with personal drivers and all grades of local helpers – his response to me was that I was 'sooo dramatic'! I was not unhappy to see that his own experience caused him to rethink that view. He left the driver with the car key while he was upstairs in his hotel room. The driver took the car on a frolic of his own – without permission, of course, as is their practice – and had an accident. The Insurance company was contacted and arranged for the car to be repaired. When the car was returned, the new battery bought in January 2019 and used for seven weeks and which worked perfectly during the first few days before the accident, was flat! Neil knew that something was wrong, suspected that the battery had been stolen and replaced with a dud one. The headlamps had been replaced with home used ones which quickly blew out the first time they were used. Neil was determined that we should not be saddled with car repair problems. He was fortunate enough to be able to speak to Vanguard CEO in Accra from NY, EST and GMT, notwithstanding. He had a profuse apology, a promise to call us, and that all repairs would be sorted out completely and thoroughly. And he kept his word to the letter. Mr Frederick Saka of VANGUARD is indeed an unusual CEO for a large Ghanaian company. Apologising, rectifying wrongs and keeping to his word. More like him and Ghana could be going places.

Problem 3. We shipped most of our books, DVDs, CDs from New York using a shipping company, Modern Shipping Ltd based in New York/New Jersey with a Ghanaian manager/proprietor, Joe Adjei. He was recommended to me by a very reliable, well brought up Ghanaian friend. Her uncle had used him on a few occasions to send personal effects to Ghana and had found him satisfactory. It was important to have this endorsement as any Ghanaian or person associated with Ghana would know. Not that it would mean that one could sit back and think that all would be well, but at least there is some link. We duly engaged the services of this shipping company, paid for it and awaited the arrival of our 11 boxes in Accra. The company offered door-to-door service, which was an added attraction. Of all the many nightmare situations one could endure in Ghana, clearing items from the port of Tema ranks with the worst. With the very unreliable VODAFONE service, we were not sure if the landline would be working, so we gave the name of a trusted reliable friend whose line of business entailed a working phone. The clearing agent duly contacted her when the items arrived, but instead of 11 boxes, there were 10. They claimed to have found the 11th box and delivered it. When the boxes were opened, one was not ours. It contained 16 backpacks, a brand-new suitcase in a box, several cartons of crayon – perhaps the assignee had a school or was thinking of starting one. At any rate, the box did not contain the items we had shipped – books, Great Courses and opera DVDs, CDs and other of our personal items. When the clearing agent was informed of this, his response was that he would come to our apartment next day to collect the wrong box and would give me the address and phone number of the person as she/ he might have ours in error!!! I knew that this was not a person I should be talking to about finding our missing box. My friend in New York told me that Joe Adjei was in Accra and gave me his number; several attempts to reach him and the clearing agent over four days were unsuccessful. Of course, my local small claims court in Queens NY is a way through which I could seek redress successfully as the company is registered in the US. He had better make sure that his immigration status is okay!

About six Xmases ago, which we had decided to spend in Ghana, a whole box containing Xmas gifts for all our family who were spending it here with us, plus a top grade carry on of great sentimental value, not to mention all the Xmas food and drink, went missing! The box was put on the plane at Heathrow according to BA records, and it was placed on the carousel in Accra. Clearly it was stolen blatantly from the Airport. This is perhaps the one improvement to which I can attest – the new airport built by the last government. The waywardness and the pilfering which were the hallmark of the last one, have now been put under some control, it seems. For this small thing, we thank God.

Problem 4. We have had five different drivers in almost as many weeks. All dismissed for one dishonest practice or another, despite being well paid by Ghanaian standards. One of these was an unemployed fellow with three kids. I did not actually fire him, but I think his conscience was at play – yes some of them do have consciences, hard as it is to believe. He advised himself and did not turn up for work after that. There were only three of us in the car – he, Ted and I. Since the money had gone missing in the car from my bag, it had to be one of us.

The Police in Ghana get a bad press, although I think that this is less so now. They used to be paid appallingly low wages, had very little by way of amenities, unlike their counterparts in the armed forces, and as a result suffered from low self-esteem. The first Rawlings government was very aware of this and started to improve the lot of the Police. Ted and I rely on their intervention whenever we have a problem with the various miscreants with whom we have to deal. They always make time for us, however busy they might be, acting as mediators, and most are very good at it. Since we arrived a few weeks ago, Ted had called up a fellow whose services he had used a few years ago to sort out our BANG and OLUFSEN multi CD player, a very good machine sound wise and very attractive – slim, non-intrusive. We swear by it. As it was not working properly, he decided to contact him. He is always difficult to reach – not answering his phone, out of town, excuses. Eventually he said he would send his brother who worked with him to have a look. His brother came and after a few minutes said he needed to take the machine away We had not met the so-called brother before and so I was apprehensive, but Ted thought it was alright especially since he gave an assurance to call next day with feedback. Not surprisingly, there was no call for several days and attempts to reach either of them were fruitless. They only answered when it was a number which they did not recognise. We got a message when our computer adviser called him, that there was a malfunctioning part which he could not get in Ghana. We asked that it should be removed and given to us so that we could get it abroad. More assurances that it would be brought, but no sign of it. We got our driver to ask for directions to his shop so that we could retrieve it ourselves, all to no avail. Nothing for it but to make a report to our local CID at the Airport police. Eventually his brother brought them and placed them on the living room floor, not on its stand from where he removed it. When asked about the screws to replace the centre on its stand he claimed that he gave them to Ted! After the intervention of Sergeant Thompson, he said he would bring them. The upshot was that the CID officer turned up on Monday morning with both men in tow, supervised them while they fixed the machine with the screws on the stand. Were it not for him we would not have retrieved our music centre. For people like us the police are a great resource in dealing with petty criminals who abound in Ghana.

A few decades ago, Ghana had a president called Busia who is best remembered for his execution of the Aliens Compliance Act. He was an Oxford graduate sociologist who decided that it would be a good idea to get rid of all the foreigners in Ghana, even those from the neighbouring countries who were born here, mostly people who were petty traders in small towns and villages. In doing so, especially the inhumane manner in which it was carried out, with indecent haste, he caused hardships to his fellow Ghanaians. Ghanaians are notoriously bad at business and people relied very much on foreigners; small traders were mostly Mamyalatahs in towns and villages and Lebanese and Syrians in the big towns. This last group make good immigrants, they are hardworking, innovative, integrate easily, they quickly learn to speak the local language of whichever place they have settled, they employ and train Ghanaians. Ghana is fortunate in still having some of them around doing business. There is one Ghanaian shop which I patronise fairly often. They sell greeting cards and other novelty gifts, a useful little shop. On a couple of occasions when I have been to the shop on a Sunday, there is one man, usually on his cell phone, showing no interest at all in welcoming customers. He always claims that the cash register is not working and will give you the wrong price in a heartbeat. I caught him out two Sundays ago, a mark-up of fifty percent! I forced him to give me the correct price by looking it up, and also to give me a proper receipt from a book as he claimed that the register was still not working. The owners of this shop were very likely in church, leaving this typical Ghanaian worker in charge of it. This is one of the reasons why their businesses invariably collapse. They have not caught on that businesses cannot be run by remote control, one has to be on site, Sunday church service notwithstanding. Another good example of Ghanaian businesses are those at Opera Square. All the items in their shop are covered in dust. When you purchase anything, you have to ask for it to be dusted off. It never occurs to the owners or their staff to clean the dust off their goods every day in the periods when they are not otherwise engaged in sales.

To run an enterprise successfully in Ghana you virtually have to be present at all times; the Lebanese and Syrians know this. Although they employ Ghanaian assistants in their shops, they are ALWAYS present. It is no exaggeration to say that Ghanaians can easily ruin the most successful venture if left to their own devices. There is an inbuilt lack of attention to detail in most, with very few exceptions. Is there any hope? And can they change sufficiently and in large enough numbers to make a difference to their country of so much promise? It is a question most intelligent Ghanaians ask and have no answer to. When I think of what the Israelis would have done with this land mass had God given it to them!!

Is Ghana to remain a mediocre country despite its many talented citizens, never reaching its full potential? Will it remain a country with boastful people who talk a lot and yet achieve so little? Will it be the same in fifty years? I see a glimmer of hope in the return of some very determined born and brought up abroad Ghanaians who want to return home. They bring with them not only their skills, but their attitude and ethics to work. We must be careful not to drive them away.

If I could speak Ga, I would hold a series of meetings and invite all the vendors at Slaha (Salazar) market, who are mainly women, make sure that they registered to vote and advise them to vote only for the candidate who gives them a written promise to build them a decent market within a year. After all, the Chinese are constructing hospitals to isolate and treat COVID-19 patients in two weeks. (There is another country from which Ghana could learn some useful lessons.) The plight of these poor women, many of whom have lost their livelihood because of the shocking state of the partially demolished market, is enough to drive one to tears. Does the MP for the area ever go there, or any of the very many female MPs who make so much noise about women's rights? Is going to the polls to vote every four years just aping the western countries, but in reality, an exercise in futility? Democracy needs to be seen working, improving people's lives, not a talking shop to determine whose English is better and to impress foreign observers.

Chapter 12
CORONAVIRUS

The End Of Civilization As We Know It? A Plague Of Biblical Proportions? A Wake Up Call?

Sometime in early February Ted and I became aware of a strange virus coming out of China, but we did not think too much of it. It was our third son, Dugald, on a trip to Ghana who told us that we needed to be very careful as it was a very serious new virus that was spreading quickly with a fairly high mortality rate. Dugald is not a medical doctor, his PhD is in Chemical Engineering. At one stage during his sixth form he did consider a career in medicine, following in his father's footsteps. City of London Boys School had a programme for its sixth formers where they were paired for a few weeks with professionals of their career choice. Dugald was unfortunate in the specialities assigned to him – Geriatrics and Orthopaedics. That experience put paid to any desire he had to become a doctor. He had always excelled in Chemistry, even from his days at GIS in Accra, and went on to study Chemical Engineering at Imperial College; right up to PhD level. He has always maintained an interest in Medicine, however, and he was able to discuss with us quite comprehensively his concerns about this new virus. It was after this that we began to take an interest in what was going on globally.

We closely followed the international news daily, several sources – BBC, SKY NEWS, AL JAZEERA, SABC to mention a few. I hardly ever watched CNN, having become quite disillusioned with most of its news anchors years ago in the US. I also went to various other sources on my iPad – especially the global newspapers. In fact, it would be no exaggeration to say that it obsessed me. I was impressed with the way the Chinese were handling this problem which WHO quickly declared a pandemic. It all happened so fast. Italy was overrun by the virus and the number of Italians who succumbed to it rose exponentially. Italy, especially the north, which was the epicentre of the virus, is known for its well-equipped and competent healthcare system, but this quickly showed signs of strain. France followed, then Spain. While all this was unfolding before us, the UK government under the premiership of Boris Johnson, 'sleepwalked' into a looming disaster. If some of us were shocked and disappointed when he won a landslide election last December it was because we doubted his ability to cope competently with this position. He might be good for BREXIT, but what about the rest? There are many descriptions of Mr Johnson – jovial, ebullient, optimistic, racist (at least, anti-African – news reports are replete with disparaging and contemptuous comments he has made over the years about Africans and people of African descent), charming, glib, tricky, chameleon-like, clever by half, none of which I consider essential traits in any Prime Minister, least of all a British one to whom many, in and outside of Britain, will look to for some sort of leadership in times like this.

Apparently, when he did take time off from his obsessive BREXIT mindset to think about how to handle the pandemic, which was rapidly engulfing most of the world, it was to adopt a principle of 'herd immunity' whereby the virus is allowed to run wild among the populace – most people will come into contact with it, catch it and develop some immunity. Of course, some people would die, but never mind, the price of their deaths would be well worth it. He and his cabinet claimed that it was the scientific advice which they had received from the group of scientists charged with the task of advising the government. This has all been denied and the truth might only be revealed when there is some form of inquiry into the whole comedy of errors, which has been the hallmark of the UK government's response to this very sad tragedy.

The worst thing about the situation in the UK is that there are no strong, reliable members in Mr Johnson's cabinet. This was brought home sharply not so long ago when he became ill with COVID-19. At first the country, indeed the world, was told that he was just isolating because of mild symptoms, but after the period of isolation some of his colleagues who had fallen ill around the same time as him, bounced back to work and he did not, it became a little disturbing. Next thing we knew, he was admitted to hospital, then to intensive care. Those of us with any medical knowledge felt that it was not a good sign – ICU is a place for very ill patients. It was only after he was discharged that we realised how seriously ill he was, by his own admission. He was generous with his praise for the NHS and the nurses (neither of whom was British) and the doctors, both called Nicholas, after whom he named his newly born son, for literally saving his life. Apparently, he had a very close brush with death. Ill winds do not blow, and we can only hope that this experience will influence the prime minister, who has been very critical of the NHS in the past, will continue to see it in a very positive light and that there will be no further rumours, or otherwise, of it being sold to America, that it should be strengthened and supported to the highest degree, to the flagship status which it deserves.

Back to Mr Johnson's cabinet. News reports have it that most, if not all of them, are people who backed BREXIT to the hilt, some to the same extent or more than he himself. The result is the very many 'ninos' (apologies to Achimotans) around him. The one left in charge in his absence, but with very limited authority, was Dominic Raab. Some reports described him as having the look of a 'rabbit caught in the headlights' during his tenure. But undoubtedly the worst of this bunch is Matt Hancock, the Health minister. Every day I torture myself watching the daily updates on COVID-19 and see him tying himself in knots, trying to defend the indefensible. Most of those who stood with him performed similarly, but he undoubtedly was the worst.

At last the day came when it was clear that the herd immunity thing was not going to work as the advisers thought it would and some drastic action needed to be taken like in Germany, Italy, France, Spain, Holland, Australia, New Zealand, in fact practically everywhere else in the world. It was likely kicking and screaming, as Mr Johnson prized the 'freedom' of the British people and was loathe to start taking this 'freedom' away. China has been derided, amidst grudging admiration, for the fact that it was its authoritarianism which had allowed it to handle the spread of the virus so successfully. Many people, though, given a choice, might choose life over his brand of freedom. Therein was born the UK lockdown. Too late, too late shall be the cry. Indeed. Then came the PPE saga. To this day, when I see countries like Ghana producing their own PPE and masks, I am at a total loss as to why this became such a huge problem for the UK, but a mega problem it was and a survey by the BMA showed that more than half of GPs had to purchase their own PPE or accept donations. Yet day after day we were told by cabinet ministers as they stood on the lectern that there was enough PPE in the system, that there was a problem with delivery, and up to now, as I write this, the problem has not been sorted out. This is a government very long on words and very short on action, all very glib and disingenuous, not a good idea to believe anything they say, to take all pronouncements with several teaspoons of salt! Numbers are massaged to score a point, shamelessly. In all the decades I have been following British politics, never have I seen such an inept, incompetent bunch in charge, on either side of the aisle. The country is likely to have the dubious distinction of having the highest mortality rate in Europe and the second in the world after its special relationship cousin, the USA. Scotland, meanwhile, should be thankful for and proud of its level headed and smart First Minister, Nichola Sturgeon.

Are there signs of any acknowledgment of errors in judgment at the outset of this pandemic on the part of the UK government so that it could move on to a better handling of the situation? Not really; except that Mr Johnson has now participated in a global fundraising to develop a vaccine, headed by the EU. This is after unwisely deciding to ignore an offer early in February, when the virus was just getting started, from the EU to participate in a plan to obtain PPE and other gear which would be needed to manage treatment and containment. According to some of his ministers there was a mix up over the email sent by the EU: it went to the wrong address!!! Of course, this was shortly after their victorious exit from the EU and their newfound independence. Germany and some other European countries, which had acted smartly at the outset, managed the COVID-19 crisis far better, had a much lower mortality rate and it would hardly be surprising if their economic recovery was quicker. Global admiration for Angela Merkel's Germany is widespread.

The USA, with its more than 362 million population, and the high volume of international travel by its citizens, was just a disaster waiting to happen. They had a very strong economy, the strongest in the world, credit for which has to be given to the much-vilified president, Donald Trump. Their first cases were on the west coast of the country, in the state of Washington and quickly grew. Although it definitely was not taken as seriously as it should have been, seeing what was happening in Europe, this is a country with 50 states, all of which are pretty autonomous and as politics governs everything in America, this included managing the virus. The president, a larger than life person, prone to saying whatever comes into his head and not at all a favourite of the media, especially in the USA and the UK, very likely made things worse as his concern for the economy was quite clear when it collapsed almost before his very eyes. All the indices on which capitalism relies to show continued growth and prosperity went into freefall – jobs, stock markets, the price of oil – and the death rates rose, especially in New York State and its city, exponentially. Everything seemed to happen at once. Dire predictions abounded, and at one stage for a few days the price of oil was negative, i.e. buyers were PAID to take it away. The country was thrown literally into a state of panic with conflicting practice, advice and treatment the order of the day. Even in a non-election year politics would have played a part, more so now, when come November Americans will vote in presidential and other important elections. Of course, in line with most of the rest of the world, lockdown had to be one of the methods to which America eventually resorted, culminating in unprecedented joblessness, federal borrowing of alarming amounts of greenbacks. In short, the great USA almost brought to its knees, economically.

In the midst of all this the New York governor, Andrew Cuomo, stood out and became flavour of the month, with his pragmatic policies and his willingness to do whatever was needed to save his state. His daily updates on the state of COVID-19 were broadcast on some of the international networks. There were serious calls for him to replace the so far missing in action Joe Biden as the presumptive Democratic candidate. The Democratic establishment, for the second time, will miss an opportunity to have a dynamic, caring president, a people's president, and they fluffed it by rejecting Bernie Sanders. Their money-driven healthcare system is probably one of the reasons why so many lives were lost and continue to be lost, especially among ethnic minorities Seventy thousand as I write. To President Trump's credit, after cutting off America's contribution to WHO for being too friendly to China, whom he has blamed for the turmoil in which the world, and mainly the USA, finds itself, he actually phoned up some

African countries to find out how they were doing – notably South Africa and Nigeria. Not sure if Ghana was included in this specially favoured group. Each day the picture in America becomes more confused and uncertain. The election of Joe Biden will be unlikely to do anything to solve America's problems, especially the economic ones, 'nice guy' though he may be.

In South America fortunes are mixed, small case numbers rising, death rates not yet overwhelming, but potentially so, according to the 'experts'. Brazil stands out, described by political media pundits as having a very right-wing president, who for a long time refused to see the seriousness of COVID-19. The country seems to be suffering the same fate as parts of Europe, with substantially more cases and deaths than any of its South American neighbours. Venezuela, pariah of the USA where a recent attempted coup, allegedly foreign-sponsored, was foiled, seems to be holding out, at least not yet facing the oblivion which its critics are forecasting. Costa Rica, with its forward looking government on green issues, seems to be managing the COVID-19 admirably. This is another area of the world for which dire predictions are made by our know-it-all media pundits. The Caribbean islands seem to be handling the pandemic by themselves, being very quick to refuse docking privileges to cruise ships which very early on were identified as a source of rapid spread of COVID-19 among their passengers. They do have the advantage of being small islands where, with reasonably decent healthcare systems, epidemics and pandemics can easily be controlled. I remember growing up as a young child in Trinidad and Tobago how easily malaria was eradicated, not by drugs, but a simple public health practice – specially trained workers paying regular visits, especially to villages and rural areas, frequent spraying of homes and compounds, ensuring that water kept in drums and other vessels were not left uncovered. Not so easy in great land masses if the government does not have the resources.

The Asian giants outside of China – Japan, South Korea, Singapore – appear to be handling their COVID-19 situation with confidence, caution and a measure of success. They have all very wisely adopted policies and practices to suit their individual populations and have largely avoided the calamitous results seen in Europe, the UK and the USA. Even India, Bangladesh, Pakistan and Sri Lanka are coping, somehow. The one thing all these countries have in common is the confidence and the ability to use their own resources to adapt the management of the Virus to suit the peculiar circumstances of their respective populations.

And now for our dear Africa. What is to become of us? With our dreadful living conditions, poor sanitation, lack of water, deplorable housing, perennial hunger, widespread endemic disease, fragile and often non-existent healthcare systems (2000 ventilators on the entire continent), surely a recipe for annihilation by such a pandemic as COVID-19? And indeed, early predictions were that this would happen in a fairly short space of time. It was the AIDS pandemic all over again, when certain major countries would actually stake an interest in whichever parts of the continent they wanted after the decimation. Rather surprisingly, this has not happened, yet. And I cross all my fingers, as well as my toes, not to mention saying fervent prayers to the Almighty if He has anything to do with it, that this will not happen. Very true that we do not have the health resources to cope with the kind of outbreak we are witnessing in the world's major economies. The north of Italy where COVID-19 is taking its highest toll is the richest, most successful part of that country. Ventilators, considered key at the outset of the outbreak to recovery for severely ill patients, were woefully short in most African countries – even Nigeria, the continent's economic giant, had only 169, Ghana 200. South Africa, with its more developed healthcare system, had many more, but still not enough to cope with a massive outbreak of COVID-19 cases. (Thinking on the use of ventilators has altered, less intrusive methods of delivering high volumes of oxygen to patients have been used successfully when it was realised that there was a 50% to 60% mortality rate with its use.) On the whole, African countries have behaved with an admirable sense of responsibility. Realising the rather precarious state of their healthcare systems and all the other negatives afore mentioned, they acted swiftly, taking proactive measures to avoid calamity. Ghana has adopted a really mature strategy which would make its founding father, Kwame Nkrumah of blessed memory, proud. He always wanted an Africa which was proud, confident and independent, working with other countries, especially on the continent, using innovative methods. Begging was definitely not his thing!

Ghana's scientists have proved themselves to be on the ball since the pandemic reared its head, and to my very pleasant surprise the Ghanaian population has shown itself to be mature and compliant. We bought face masks for our driver and home help when the initial lockdown was partially lifted, as wearing them outdoors was a condition, only to discover that they had bought locally made ones themselves, at a reasonable price, they told us. Most of Ghana's big supermarkets like Koala, Maxmart, Palace, pharmacies (all of which were left open under the essential services category) etc have good, preventive practices in place: sanitizers, gloves, spraying of carts and baskets after use and since the partial lifting of the first lockdown, no entry without masks, big signs proclaiming this everywhere. People are voluntarily distancing in shops and as there has been no stampede or panic buying in Accra, it has been relatively easy to venture out for weekly shopping even at age 80 plus! Even in the public markets there are plastic drums/ buckets with taps (designed by a Ghanaian woman during a cholera outbreak decades ago) and liquid soap for washing hands; what is impressive is that people are using them. Even the tro tro drivers, notorious for cramming their vehicles to the hilt, are taking fewer passengers, encouraged no doubt by the presence of traffic wardens and police posted at the stations. Ghana has been mentioned favourably as a country using innovative practices to handle COVID-19 in both the NYT and TIME magazine. Using drones to collect virus samples, from remote areas in Ashanti region, testing and tracing of contacts, and even working on the development of a vaccine. Those at the Kwame Nkrumah University of Science and Technology, as well as the Noguchi Institute, Ghana's oldest such institute, set up in Nkrumah's time, are at the forefront of these innovations. Ghana had closed all its borders early on, and those who managed to slip through via the Togolese borders whose airport was still open, were tracked and quarantined. Nigeria has continued to have fewer cases than Ghana, but then they are probably doing less testing. On the other hand, Nigeria has a really commendable track record on the EBOLA epidemic, managing the small number of cases they had so that there was no spread. Senegal, along with South Africa, has been quite forward with its testing and tracing. WHO, too, has sounded the alarm, stating that there could be as many as three million cases and 300,000 deaths in Africa if nothing is done. The comforting news is that things *are* being done, all over Africa, limited resources notwithstanding. The mega question for well-wishers, detractors, the international media, Africans living on the continent, those in the diaspora, et al: will Africa escape the fate of the UK, USA and some European countries? Having survived the devastation of AIDS, could they make it through this much more easily spread COVID-19? With the mother and master countries in disarray themselves, and largely unable to help or advise, is there any hope for Africa? A recent question and answer programme on the BBC – FOCUS ON AFRICA – hosted by Zeinab Badawi, which discussed Africa and the COVID-19, consensus was a resounding YES. To which, from my observations in Ghana and following what is going on globally on the pandemic, almost obsessively, I concur! Knowing over the years how attached to the Western way of running their country most past elected governments in Ghana have been, except perhaps Rawlings' PNDC (I clearly remember one newly elected past president of Ghana, being interviewed by the BBC in London, boasting about how eager he was to get Ghana on to the globalization bandwagon!), I was pleasantly surprised and encouraged when the current President during his original lockdown address stated that it was not going to be 'a one size fits all' exercise, obviously recognising the country's special circumstances of its population.

Large numbers of Ghanaians earn their living through working outside – home helps, drivers, gardeners, shop assistants, nannies, bus and taxi drivers, tro tro drivers, artisans, computer techs etc. Very few, if any, African governments would find it affordable to find safety net cash for these different groups, all of whom are keen to get back to work to earn their livelihood. Supermarkets were never closed, there was never any panic buying, no shortages of any essential goods and the shopkeepers behaved responsibly, to their great credit. Another thing, the 'fragile health systems' have so far held up. The hand of GOD? We simply do not know, great respect for science and scientists, et al notwithstanding. With this new virus, I am in agreement with all who take the view that we should use whatever works – the list includes presidents, governors, professors, medics and myriad others. What does not kill, usually cures, a very appropriate Caribbean saying in these COVID-19 times. This virus is a very new phenomenon, so far mutating into several strains. There is already evidence that the strain in the USA was a weaker one than that ravaging parts of Europe. So clearly what works for some groups may not work for others. The FDA, which regulates drug use in the USA, has banned the use of chloroquine there, claiming that there have been reports of heart failure with its use. Yet it has been used successfully in Australia and some British scientists are trialling it with four other drugs. Of course, chloroquine is off-patent and this will not go unnoticed in the USA where money and medicine are great bedfellows. Madagascar has proclaimed the use of a herbal liquid which was traditionally used in the treatment of malaria, but is now being used for COVID-19, supposedly to prevent spread of the virus and perhaps even cure the disease, but of course it has not been officially put through the usual scientific protocols. Overwhelming anecdotal evidence is enough in a serious pandemic as COVID-19, in my opinion. If ever a simple cure is found for COVID-19, big pharma will lose out big time. On the other hand, there are trillions to be made with a vaccine that works. I was startled recently when Matt Hancock, the UK health secretary, cautioned that there may never be a vaccine! True, it is all trial and error at this stage.

When during the US election campaign in 2016 presidential candidate Donald Trump coined the phrase 'fake news' to describe some of the very negative reports about him, we had no idea that it would enter the English lexicon of well-used phrases, but it has. Relations between Mr Trump and most of the media have always been fractious, especially when they tried so very hard to help Hillary Clinton win, by covering up all her serious shortcomings. They were devastated when she lost, they really did not expect him to win, and they have never forgiven him for it. They influenced the global media to disparage the president, and he made it very easy for them by being himself – an unorthodox American businessman from a self-made background, saying whatever came to his mind and not caring too much about his image with the media. It never failed to surprise me that whenever I said we lived in New York, how most people would ask in some form or another, 'how can you live there with Trump as president'? Well this coronavirus has given them a field day! The president's strong suit is the economy and it soared under his watch so far, until the coronavirus when it all dissolved almost before one's eyes. In a wantonly capitalist country like America the news was dire, and the media, both local and international, knew just whom to blame and whom to mock. The COVID-19 was not the only enemy facing Mr. Trump! Two examples stand out for me. On one of the daily briefings he advocated the use of chloroquine, which he had heard was working for some communities abroad. He was torn to shreds by the media for saying this, among other things accused of trying to undermine the saintly Dr Fauci (those of us who remember him from the days of the AIDS pandemic may be forgiven for not sharing this view of the doctor). Two days later Andrew Cuomo mentioned that he had heard that chloroquine was working in the treatment of COVID-19 and advocated its use in his state, and not a single media voice raised an objection! More recently he made what I thought were musings about the use of Solar power and disinfectants to be used in fighting COVID-19. I watched the update live and thereafter a couple more times of the video. I never heard him say that it should be injected into humans, and I took it as just mulling over loudly what the latest new thing was. I was really shocked when there were claims that hundreds of people rang up asking what the dosage for Lysol and Dettol was when taking it as a cure, to the extent that the makers of both disinfectants had to issue a warning that they should not be ingested by any means!!! If this were true and not fake news, then there are more dim-witted people in the US than one would have thought! But never mind, the media including SKY NEWS and the BBC America service went to town on it, ad nauseam. To the extent that a British female journalist interviewing one woman, obviously expecting to hear that she would no longer support Trump because of his handling of the COVID-19, and that he advocated the use of disinfectants, like me she did not think that he was advocating its use by ingestion from what he had said.

The British reporter could barely hide her disgust. Most of them ask leading questions and they appear to seek out interviewees who are known Trump bashers. When they occasionally get a reply that is clearly not going to indulge in president bashing it ruins their day. In the meantime, Boris Johnson and his cabinet seem to be getting a pass for their equally poor handling of the COVID-19 situation, with less reason since they are dealing with a population less than one fifth the size of the US and a proportionately higher death rate, most of which many claim could have been avoided had he acted sooner. Trump has very good reason to accuse most of the media of bias – there is hardly an impartial one in their midst. They showed great support for the women who accused Harvey Weinstein of sexual misconduct, even though some of them were in relationships with him. They showed similar support for those who accused Bill Cosby of similar behaviour. Both men have received long prison sentences. Then Tara Reade comes along with a fairly credible account of sexual misbehaviour by Joe Biden, the fellow the media is actively supporting to be the next US president, and just like the chameleon changes its colour, so does the media. Suddenly this woman is not telling the truth, there are flaws and inconsistencies in her account, according to them. Knowing the media, she is going to be hounded and vilified big time, and especially by the sister women supporting Mr Biden. And they wonder why so many people around the world mistrust them!

The Media and Africa during the COVID-19 pandemic.

As mentioned before, it was taken as a foregone conclusion at the outset of COVID-19 that Africa with all its myriad shortcomings and negatives would be wiped out. When it did not happen you could see the shock and often disappointment on the faces of various journalists, male and female, that this was not happening, especially when they saw the awful situation in the developed European economies. Instead of visiting the continent to see why this was so, they do what they are best at – surmising, guessing, theorising. Nothing the news outlet love more than some calamitous occurrence that they could pontificate about. Since the pandemic, I have taken to watching and reading reports from most of the English-speaking parts of the world and it has indeed been an eye opener. I would recommend to those who can, to watch SABC, the main South African news network. Al Jazeera started out being impartial, but there are a few of their anchors who tend to cover Africa less objectively. They were among the first to predict a wipe-out of the continent. Unless you want to be fed a constant menu of Trump bashing and substantial fake news, CNN is to be avoided.

BBC world service is probably still the best for Africa with two relatively fair programmes on Africa – FOCUS ON AFRICA and BUSINESS AFRICA, of significance, is that these programmes are presented by Africans. This is very important because some other ethnic groups tend to adopt a superior tone and attitude when reporting on the continent. When we are in New York, Ted and I have a New York Times subscription, and I have one for TIME magazine, so we were quite pleasantly surprised to read in both those publications positive comments on Ghana's handling of the COVID-19. Both the USA and the UK are battling with reports of a high mortality rate among ethnic minorities, especially those of African descent. Both are claiming socio-economic reasons as the cause. One would have thought that Africa, being the home of people of African descent, would be the place to look for any causal link. Or can it be concluded that living in either country for this group of people during COVID-19 is very, very bad for your health? Americans of African descent have managed to establish that they wish to be described as African Americans in the same way that there are Asian Americans and not yellow Americans. Not so the British, and this is partly to do with how little influence they have there, especially economic. When we lived in England several decades ago and shortly after the influx of Asians mainly from Idi Amin's Uganda into the UK, the British media tended to regard people of various shades of brown/black, as black. The East African Asians, used to their exalted status in East Africa, were not having any of it – they have a particular aversion to the colour black as a skin colour, their Dalits are indeed usually the darkest hued among them, in their notorious caste system, and this is very important to them.

With the economic power and business acumen which they brought to their new country, they lost no time in establishing that they wished to be referred to as Asians, and so it was. People of African descent, never quick to pick up on these things, and having very little clout as a group in British society, continued to allow themselves to be described as 'Black' irrespective of their skin hue! It was as if they were unaware of all the negative connotations the word 'black' carries, whether written with a capital 'B' or a common one. And we do have an identifiable origin, even those of us who have other origins, too. Subcontinental people know that 'black' is a bad, negative word.

So did white apartheid era South Africans. I, for one, as a matter of principle, always run a line through (often with a red pen) the section which asks for race with the heading BLACK and the various categories of black when completing forms in the UK. I write 'of African descent'. There is a more unwise and very sad reason for this on the part of people of African descent, especially those from the Caribbean. It is high time that their BAME become AAME or OADAME.

These are interesting times, worrying times, sad times. Many believe that we have to look forward to a 'new normal', that our way of life will never be the same again. If this means that the grossly unfair trading and other practices by one 'superior', powerful, 'clever' group against another, causing them to live in abject poverty in perpetuity without the basic amenities for a decent life, would take a pause; if it means that militarily powerful nations would stop invading weaker ones; if it means that people would stop and think seriously about saving the earth for future generations; if corporate greed would take a backseat in the most rabidly capitalist countries; if more justice and equity would prevail in all countries for their citizens irrespective of race or colour; the list could go on; then COVID-19 would be like an ill wind, which blows no one any good. In other words, ill winds do not blow. Amen and Amen!

Chapter 13
2020 AN EPOCH
MAKING YEAR

And It Is Only five Months Gone!

In the afternoon of Monday, the 25th May, what should have been a relatively minor incident, set in motion a series of quite incredible scenes almost worldwide. An African American man, George Floyd, 46, allegedly used a fake 20 dollar note to purchase cigarettes in a small café in Minneapolis, a city in the North-western state of Minnesota. The shop owner called the police and pointed out the man, sitting in his car. Reports (videos support this account) state that the man was completely compliant with all the arresting officers asked him to do, even addressing them as 'sir'. In what must be the most regrettable instant of his life, the arresting officer, now ex, put the man on the pavement in the prone position, placed his knee on the man's neck, and proceeded to keep it there for eight minutes, 46 seconds. Two of his colleagues joined him by sitting on George Floyd's back, so he was totally deprived of oxygen. He cried out that he could not breathe and begged the officers to get off his neck, he invoked the help of his deceased mother, but the brutish police officer and his equally savage accomplices ignored his pleas. Horrified passers-by added to the man's pleas, one even daring to attempt to help, but the brute pulled his gun on him and so he retreated. A clever, God bless her, 17 year old who was part of the group standing around had the presence of mind to film it on her phone. Eventually, Mr Floyd, having had all the oxygen pushed out of his system, gave up the ghost and died. Large numbers of American police officers are inveterate liars, especially those with the propensity to murder helpless citizens. Immediately came the usual lies – Mr Floyd was resisting arrest, he was being violent and had to be restrained. There were too many people as witnesses for this lie to stand, and the video of Mr Floyd's murder went viral. As a commentator remarked, 'Steve Jobs', who made it possible for videotaping on phones, has done more for the justice of ordinary citizens than any politician, and he was right. Almost immediately, lockdown policies flew through the window and thousands, indeed hundreds of thousands, in America and beyond rose up in fury over this wanton act of murder which played out on their phones anytime the video was shown.

The brutal murders of unarmed African American men and boys was not a new phenomenon. We lived in New York when Errol Garner was similarly murdered. This, too, caused horror by right minded citizens; there were protests, too and street marches. Errol Garner's mother, a strong woman supported by the Rev. Al Sharpton, demanded justice for her son. The killer cop, arrogant and unrepentant, sure that as usual he would get away with murder, denied any wrongdoing – American cops have a licence to kill, like 007 of James Bond fame. They are covered by some law known as 'qualified immunity', which is meant to protect government and state officials from lawsuits when on official business. Although Errol Garner's mother won a lawsuit of unlawful killing and had a monetary award, I am not sure if her son's killer served jail time. I seem to remember that he was sacked, amid huge protest by his fellow officers and bosses. Talk about a group of people completely amoral, with no sense of right and wrong and no respect or regard for human life, especially when it is one of African descent.

What has been striking about these protests is the way in which they transcended age, race, nationality, status, so many variables. BLACK LIVES MATTER, a movement started some years ago to address the very issue of police and white supremacist (another group with a licence to kill people of African descent and other minorities) wanton murders. When one considers that as a man (or person of colour) you could leave your house in the morning and not return as expected, having been murdered by some sadistic cop for the slightest infringement just because of your skin hue, it is frightening indeed. The BLM movement shot into the spotlight and gained the sort of recognition as a well organised movement well able to bring people together for peaceful protests on a large scale which it has always wanted. When it comes to protest, I am all for peaceful ones. Violence is only justified as a response to immediate violence. As for looting and burning, I saw nothing wrong with the comment 'when the looting starts, it is time for the shooting to start', honestly. My heart goes out to those people who have had their (usually small) businesses looted, vandalised and burnt. In my view, mayors, governors etc, should not sit by helplessly while this goes on. I deplore these actions as much as I do those of the brutish killer cops. Anyway, the mega protests, which went on for several days, were largely peaceful, despite provocation by some aggressive and bullying police officers, and quite a few protesters were caused injury by some of them. One suspects that the protesters, knowing how difficult it is to hold police officers accountable for their criminal actions, wanted to make sure that the killer cops would be charged for their crime this time round. The Minneapolis authorities were quite swift in their sacking of all four officers, but it took a couple of days before the main perpetrator was charged with third degree murder and third-degree manslaughter. Almost a week later his three accomplices were charged with aiding and abetting, and his charges were elevated to second degree murder and second degree manslaughter. Bail was set at quite a high amount as the rogue cop, Derek Chauvin, who had had at least 18 complaints filed against him in the past for various serious offences against citizens, was seen as a flight risk. There would be no shortage of far right, racist extremists to help him in this, including some of his brother cops.

As everything in the US is highly politicized, this being an election year, this aspect of the tragedy was going to be HUGE. Nothing Trump said or did would be right and some people, as well as most of the media, local and international, were going to help the Democratic, largely MIA Joe Biden win the Presidency mainly by denigrating Trump and blowing up negatively every utterance he made. Worldwide marches were held. In Australia, people expressed support for the Aboriginal people who suffer a milder form of abuse, occasionally murder, at the hands of their police. Indians protested against the hypocrisy of their upper castes and movie stars who expressed their horror at George Floyd's murder while their immigrant and lower castes are treated despicably across the board. All the big European countries, still in partial lockdown most of them, had large crowds of protesters marching – catching COVID 19 did not appear to be a deterrent.

Unsurprisingly, the next big protest was bound to happen in the UK. Although the British police are not quite as vicious or murderous as their US counterparts, their hands are not exactly clean. The fact that they are not armed is likely a factor. The only time I would ever consider joining a protest is if there was ever talk of arming them. I fear that there would be some in their midst who would be just as murderous as their American cousins, and the victims would very likely be people of African descent. Their systemic racism was acknowledged quite openly in the Macpherson Report when it held an enquiry, nearly three decades ago, into the death of Stephen Lawrence, an 18 year old British student of Afro Caribbean descent. He was a bright, well brought up young man from a stable family, who was planning to attend university to study architecture and his only crime was being at a bus stop when some murderous thugs stabbed him to death for no other reason than his dark-skinned hue. It was definitely a racist killing. Our youngest son, Ronald, was one year younger than Stephen Lawrence and I became very fearful for his safety, even though we lived in an area which was quite safe and relatively well mixed racially. I cried every time Mrs Lawrence appeared on television to talk about her son, I truly felt her pain.

The Metropolitan police, who were really racist at that time, stopping and searching every young (and some older ones, too) African descent male with impunity, had no real interest in finding Stephen Lawrence's killer, despite clear evidence. It was many years later that one of them was brought to justice and received merely a slap on the wrist sentence. Those were the days of Margaret Thatcher, who never hid her contempt for her citizens of African descent – they were poor and had no money to contribute to her party, mostly in low paid jobs, unlike some other immigrant groups. The insidious and not so insidious racism started then. With another successful favoured ethnic group eager to join their ranks, she and her party could boast that they were not racist, but African descent kids, even those whose parents were middle range workers, and some of professional parents, just could not reach their full potential, the odds were so firmly stacked against them. I was shocked a few weeks ago when I watched an interview of a young British African student say that teachers often gave them low grade forecasts, which they often exceeded, but this greatly affected the offers they had from the better universities. I could not believe what I was hearing. Thirty years ago, I was writing about this in London! It was unbelievable that this was still the case. When Ronnie went to Cambridge, in his medical year there were five British African students. I have to admit that there is a lack of enthusiasm on the part of many Afro Caribbean parents to spend money on educating their children – they are quite content to leave that to the State system which consistently and persistently fails our children. All circumstances being equal, subcontinental Asians have a much better record of making sacrifices for their children's education. Ronnie was extremely lucky. When he went to City of London School, he was one of four pupils of African descent among the 600-plus boys. The headmaster at the time was one Mr Bass and our son, despite being one of such a tiny minority, was made to feel very welcome there. He was a day student – I have never believed in boarding schools, being quite confident that I was far more equipped to bring up our sons rather than people we hardly knew. This way any concerns, fears, problems (and there were bound to be some) which they encountered could be addressed at once. I would give this advice to any young parents educating their children in the UK.

Mr Bass, as with so many of the teachers at City of London School, was a wonderful man, with not a racist bone in his body and he set the tone for the rest of the staff. Ronnie went on to be head boy there, and not only did he do well academically, but he also turned out to be a well-rounded, confident person with no hang ups. This has stood him in good stead to this day. Brian and Neil had a similar experience at Twyford High School in Ealing when they went there for sixth form. These good and positive experiences notwithstanding, I am well aware that many British African parents face mega problems with their children's education. It is this lack of good quality education, which treats ALL pupils equally, with teachers being trained to stop discriminating and denigrating their pupils of African descent, making them feel unwanted, devalued and performing well below their real ability. Other brown and dark hued pupils do not share the same fate. When I worked in schools in London it was not lost on me that even at ages three and four, children of African descent were the ones often put out of their classes for being 'disruptive'. This continued through the years and caused many of them to become disenchanted with the system and eventually to drop out of it altogether. I have no doubt that this is at the core of the gang and knife culture so prevalent among British African youth. Many parents feel helpless to challenge the system. Some native (white) British teachers could behave quite haughtily and dismissive when complaints are made to them. Parents are likely to become frustrated and resentful by this attitude and the trouble starts from there. Terms like 'hostile', 'aggressive', 'loud', 'disruptive' get bandied around, often quite unjustly, and the children suffer. British African parents need a level of confidence and indeed a strategy to handle racist teachers. Another good policy is to form informal groups of parents at the same school, and it may well be that they are concerned about the same issues. There is strength in numbers.

And so, BLACK LIVES MATTER appears in the UK. News of proposed marches by protesters surfaced on the Friday before and the Health Secretary, Matt Hancock, asked people to remember that there was partial lockdown still in place, as well as social distancing because of COVID-19, and while the numbers were going down, he strongly advised people not to join mass protests. He did say that he, too, was shocked at the death of George Floyd and understood people wanting to show how they felt. All this was said in a moderate, conciliatory, understanding tone. I have not been one of Mr Hancock's admirers in the past, but his manner caused me to soften my attitude towards him. Then the Home Secretary appeared on the scene, with her best Thatcherish tone and manner, demanding that people should not join protest marches, that it was against the law and that the police will be authorised to ensure that the law was obeyed. Her manner was decidedly hostile. I was more than happy to see that people cocked a snoop at her orders. Ms Patel is one of the most hostile members of Boris Johnson's cabinet. I am not at all surprised that a very senior civil servant from her department has taken the government to court, claiming that he was bullied by her and that her manner was not conducive to working peacefully. She exudes pomposity, a lady with problems, clearly. Her inflammatory remarks when there were scuffles with the police do not augur well for future protests, peaceful intentions notwithstanding. Perhaps she should change portfolios with Mr Hancock!

The crowds protesting were huge and there was a great sense of relief that it was all so peaceful, unlike those in the US, until late evening when a few scuffles with the police ensued. I was quite disappointed by this. The Metropolitan police had behaved with remarkable restraint and civility, and every effort should have been made by all those protesting to reciprocate, even if there might have been a couple of cops determined to show their muscle. Violence should never be a part of any peaceful protest, especially when so much is at stake – it undermines the serious message and the point which the movement hopes to make. When a couple of journalists asked different participants since they were wearing masks, but not practising social distancing, about COVID-19, their response was that racism was a more serious pandemic! All the pent-up grievances to do with racism from the police stop and search, to tasering, even giving out fines during the lockdown (the Met police was apparently still applying their bias), came to the fore, like a burst abscess! Senior voices of reason, those who believe in 'to thine own self be true' urged the police to listen to what the protesters had to say; the Prime Minister grudgingly admitted that while there were some injustices in society, Britain was not a racist country as such. Unsurprisingly, there was very much sympathy for the views expressed by the protesters from Sir Keir Starmer (dear God, why did Jeremy Corbyn not resign sooner, say like three years ago?), the new Labour leader, a man who exudes quiet competence and reason, totally unlike his mendacious, blustering opponent. It is clear that very many disparate groups have problems or very bad feelings about some aspects of life in Britain and this was a clear opportunity to reveal them, and one which they were not going to miss.

The statue of Colston, the notorious slave owner whose statue occupies place of pride in the main square in front of Bristol University, and which apparently has been a sore point with very many of the city's citizens for a very long time, was brought down by a group of protesters in the twinkling of an eye, and Sadiq Khan, London's mayor, immediately set up a committee to look into which statues around the city might be good for the chop – men who had done bad things along the way to becoming famous. Some native British people, usually young ones, did not seem to mind these changes, some thought them long overdue in the 21st century. Some were totally against it. I saw an elderly man interviewed on TV, becoming almost apoplectic at the thought of removing Baden Powell's statue. The belief was that he had Nazi sympathies, liked Hitler and reviewed Mein Kampf favourably. And so, all around the country, conversations are taking place to remove 'offensive' artefacts, much to the horror of a great many people. One protester in London had dared to scrawl on the plinth of Churchill's statue in Trafalgar Square 'was a racist'! I am ambivalent about these happenings, we cannot and should not want to rewrite history. This is the home of native British people, a free country, and if they wish to revere the statues of their people who did terrible things, I honestly think that they should be allowed to do so.

Immigrants and their descendants living in the UK could be likened to 'chickens coming home to roost'. Most British people have a live and let live attitude to life, many do not really like 'foreigners' at all, especially those of a quite different hue, even though they spend hours in the sun trying to become brown (but NOT too dark brown). Many can tolerate light brown and then there is that very wonderful dish – curry – which for a number of years has replaced fish and chips, and roast beef and Yorkshire pudding as the most popular food in Britain. When I first arrived in Britain in 1965 most landladies would complain bitterly about the smell of onions and garlic being cooked by their overseas tenants. What a turnaround! British society has always been layered, not unlike Indian society with its very many castes, often associated with skin hue. This is a perfect home from home. Younger people are changing, having grown up with people of different colours and cultures most of them seem to be more accepting, which is why there are so many mixed-race people seen in Britain.

The experience of the Asian immigrant is quite different. I smile to myself when I think that some of the racist charges against Churchill have to do with his treatment of Indians in India in colonial times, his total opposition to Indian independence and his opinion of Gandhi, the Indian saint. He would be rolling in his grave if he could see how firm a hold the descendants of the very people so disdained by him now occupy in so many commanding positions in his beloved England. In fact, the country could not do without their economic input. The biggest steel company in the UK is Indian-owned, not to mention myriad smaller ones. Margaret Thatcher was very prescient in recognising their worth. They are well represented in every scientific department, the law, medicine, journalism, the media, the Police and in government. Boris Johnson has seven Asians in his cabinet! To quote Zahra, a young woman of South-East Asian descent, interviewed by the Metro recently: 'I could never speak for the specific pain of 'Black' people. The levels of racism and discrimination that 'Black' people face is on a different level to other people of colour'. She goes on to admit that she has faced some racist abuse and been held back by structures which endlessly favour 'white' people. My experience is that when many Asians speak of abuse or racism it is usually when they were young and some child or young person in a playground or on the street called them 'paki' or said 'paki, go home!'. Asian Muslims may have slightly different experiences because of religion, rather than by race. Her American counterpart, a lawyer originally from Guiana, whose older brother was killed in police custody in 2008, and a recent past president of the South-east Asian association of lawyers adds, in supporting the Black Lives Matter protests: 'I recognise the relative privilege of my own brown skin – regularly sheltered within the model minority construct and armed with a law degree, I am no longer afraid of my past repeating itself, my brown skin hue has allowed me to do something that Black skin cannot –!!' I wish the many brown hued African Americans and Latinos living in Queens could read his rather simplistic view of skin hue! But it was constructive and illuminating to hear these pearls of truth emanating from Asian immigrants, both in the USA and the UK. This is why dismantling racism in Britain, and righting the myriad injustices, will not be an easy project.

Instead of worrying about inconsequential matters like statues and artefacts, let us get the important things right, like making sure that the education system in this country stops failing our children. Investing in our own children's education, even if it means making sacrifices. Educate ourselves, participate in the voting franchise, we do not all have to belong to the same party, diversify a bit. Get to know our representatives, council people, form groups among ourselves or with others of like minds to ensure we get the benefits in the society to which we are entitled as lawful citizens. Above all, when we have children pass on our great African/ Caribbean values to them. Talk to them, find out how they feel about what is going on around them. When I worked in schools and had interviews with parents, I always advised them to talk with their children, not while driving them home in the car as important concerns could be missed when doing so, but when you get home or at supper time, or even at bed time. Take complaints seriously and act on them. Your children's future and possibly their life depends on your interaction with them.

The USA is a totally different kettle of fish. After decimating most of the native Americans and appropriating their land, they went to Africa, or bought African slaves from their British cousins, took them to a land so very far away that they were never ever going to see their homeland again. They were freed from the slavery, but could not return to their motherland. This meant that they had to put roots down in this strange place to which they were brought. They have every right to believe that they have a stake in it, to receive the same treatment as the other people who were there at the same time. It is wrong from every angle that this land of the free treats those whom they welcomed at Liberty Island (and begged that they be given their poor and their destitute) far better, allowing them to ascend to every height of existence in America, while the ones whom they brought here against their will remain at the bottom of the pile. African Americans and their descendants have a right to all that the great USA has to offer. By now they should have to stop fighting for even the air which they breathe. They, too, have to use their franchise sensibly and intelligently to get the sort of people in place who would make their life better. In my view they fluffed it again this time round when they rejected Bernie Sanders. Joe Biden, nice fellow as he may be, will not do it for them, it will be more of the same, only with a smiling face. It should be of concern that recent immigrants occupy positions in high places – nearly every group of them is better off by any measure used – education, health, the judicial services, government, social housing, you name it.

To my African American cousins, I say let George Floyd's death be a catalyst for real change, not only an end to police brutality and murder, not only from white supremacists who think that you should not walk on their streets or even breathe the God-given air, but by taking education seriously, using all the avenues open to you as the generations of your citizenship entitles you. We share your pain every time some sadistic cop shoots or murders in any form, one of you, and we are rooting for you that this time, there will be meaningful change. You have the inalienable right to all the good things America has to offer, you have been there long enough, and you helped to build it, big time. The time is long past when the slave owner and his descendants should get his knee off your neck and back, and allow you to breathe and live free.

Chapter 14
A STRANGER PLANET
BY NOAH AGBLE

It was the day before school when I was taken through a cyclone to a strange planet, a very strange planet...

I was clueless, confused and scared. I didn't know what to do before it became even stranger.

Aliens were swarming around me, with a loud voice inside me screaming. I felt an unsettling shiver running down my spine. Murmurs seeped from the mouths of these creatures. I backed away...

These things gave me the creeps I desperately wanted to go home. I couldn't stand another moment on this planet, this very strange planet. An uncomfortable feeling crept sinisterly upon me, I felt as if I was shaking, shaking, shaking very hard. I wondered if this experience could get any worse.

The planet just got colder and colder, and moving anxiously I rummaged through my pockets hoping to find some gloves.

NOTHING.

All seemed hopeless, I was surrounded by aliens, I was freezing and couldn't think of how I could get out of this planet.

A dark blue light swallowed the planet looming over us and I had a funny feeling that I was the only one feeling terrified.

I kept hoping and believing that I would find my way out soon, but with every breath I felt otherwise. The aliens were still swarming around me and still whispering among themselves. Night was slowly rising (you couldn't tell very well because it was a dark planet). I cautiously ran to lie down on the rock planet.

Hopeless, I lay, and I couldn't think of much else, but to escape from this place I thought of home and how my family must be missing me so. I tried to get it all out of my head.

Suddenly an angry man emerged from some shadows, shadows that I had noticed before. He came closer, screaming at me.

I felt like just giving up as I felt I had 0% hope of leaving the planet. It was a terrible feeling, just terrible especially with this man staring at me.

The man yanked me up onto my feet and every time I attempted to get out of his grip it got even tighter. I shook and shook until I eventually released myself from his grip. I ran. I ran and ran and ran and ran until I could run no more. I crouched down exhausted behind a rock knowing that the man and maybe the aliens would come looking for me.

I kept moving to try to get away from these creatures or whatever they were...

Stay tuned for more from the Stanger Planet.

*THIS IS A SPECIAL DEDICATION TO MY
GRANNY & GRANDPA FROM GHANA,*

APPENDIX 1

RETIREMENT OF DR T. K. AGBLE

Head of Department of Obstetrics and Gynaecology, Konfo Anokye Hospital, Kumasi.

APPRECIATION BY DR J. C. MARTEY, JANUARY, 1982

INTRODUCTION

'SI MONUMENTUM REQUIRIS, CIRCUMSPICE'.

-If you would see his monument, look around.

(Ref. Sir Christopher Wren 1632 – 1723, St. Paul's Cathedral in London, UK)

WHAT has Dr Agble done for us?

Apart from numerous patients treated – Best Achievement – Best Department: Parable: 'The Tree and the Branches' **Secret of success:**

Application of Brilliant Brain.

'The strategy of Indirect Approach'

'Masterly Inactivity'

(Ref. Human Relations in War and Life, British House of Lords and Obstetric Practice – Management of Labour!)

WHO is he? The life and Times of Dr Theodore Komla Agble (Ted, T.K).

BORN: Hohoe Volta Region July 21, 1931 – Celebrated 88th birthday last year.

Father: Mr Erastus K.Agble of Peki, Volta Region – Nonogenarian

Mother: Kate Ama Agble nee Apo, hailed from Saisi – Agomanya Krobo in the Eastern Region, from well known Apo and Nartey families – related to Martey family. In fact, Dr Agble and Dr Martey are second cousins.

EDUCATION

Elementary School: Evangelical Presbyterian school Hohoe up to Standard 5 in 1945.

Secondary School: Achimota School 1946 – 1949. Note

Record – First to be admitted from Standard 5 straight to form 2 – Second year at Achimota.

Played for school Soccer Team.

School Certificate Examination 1949 – Grade I with 6 As. London Matriculation – First Division – one of 12 in the Gold Coast.

Pre-University Course: Mfantsipim Secondary School, Cape Coast, April – June 1950. Dr Agble and Dr Martey first met at Mfantsipim over 31 years ago.

University College of the Gold Coast, Achimota (now University of Ghana Legon) 1950 – 1954 Graduated B.SC (London) – June 1954 (Zoology, Botany & Chemistry).

Medical School: Left Ghana for Great Britain 1954. Attended Aberdeen University in Scotland 1954 – 1959. Qualified as Doctor with MBCHB June 1959.

Housemanship: Scotland and England 1959 – 1960 (Medicine, Surgery and Obstetrics in Aberdeen and Warrington). Came under influence of Sir Dugald Baird – Renowned British Obstetrician and Gynaecologist and Emeritus Professor Aberdeen University.

Medical Officer: Had to return to Ghana when Osagyefo Dr Kwame Nkrumah (our first President) wanted Doctors for the Congo Crisis in 1960. Arrived home from UK November 1960. Disembarkation leave of only five days. (c/f Nowadays several months self-imposed leave in Age of Revolution of Rights versus Duties).

First Post: Winneba Hospital 1960 for one month only

Second post: Korle Bu Maternity Accra 1960-1961

Third Post: Komfo Anokye Hospital, Kumasi 1961 – 1982 i.e. 21 years ago.

Postgraduate Training: Returned to Great Britain to Specialise in Obstetrics & Gynaecology 1962 – 1965

Glasgow – Southern General Hospital

Leeds – St. James Hospital – came under influence of Mr Redman and Mr Agar among other reputable gynaecologists

Passed MRCOG (Membership of the Royal College of Obstetricians and Gynaecologists, London, U.K.) July 1965

Marriage: While working in England at Leeds St. James Hospital, Dr Agble met a lovely and lively West Indian nurse from Trinidad with Maiden name Yolande Garraway'. It was, indeed, a romantic encounter. He dated her, courted and married her in October 1965.

Returned: to Ghana December, 1965.

Senior Medical Officer & Specialist: Posted to Komfo Anokye Hospital again December, 1965. Head of Department of Obst/Gynae 1969 – 1981. Succeeded Dr A.A. Armar as Departmental head of Oby Gynae.

FRCOG (Fellow of the Royal College of Obstetricians & Gynaecology) 1978

Family Life: Dr Agble's better half, Yolande, has been a wonderful and well matched partner, has been of tremendous help to him during all of their 16 years' plus of life in Ghana. Their marriage has been blessed with four children, all male.

Hobbies: Lawn Tennis, Soccer all international leagues, Opera, Classical music, especially Beethoven, Mozart and Wagner

Smoking masculine Pipes, Whisky Connoisseur from Scottish influence. Voracious Reader of Good Books and British Newspapers, Collection of Top-class Classical Music Records and other musical genres.

CONCLUSION

"Lives of great men all remind us
We can make our lives sublime,
And, dope ting, leave behind us
Footprints on the sands of time."
"Let us, then, be up and doing,
With a heart for any fate;
Still achieving, still pursuing,
Learn to LABOUR and to wait".

(From 'A Psalm of Life' by Henry Wadsworth LONGFELLOW, 18071882, USA Poet and Professor of Modern Languages at Harvard University.)

Dr Agble has laboured splendidly for Ghana, Komfo Anokye Hospital our Department of Obstetrics & Gynaecology and his numerous patients day and night. In spite of his eventful prolonged labour of twenty-one years (21yrs), he has not been blowing his own trumpet so loudly as to jar on our ears and nerves. It is, therefore, sweet and fitting to THANK him, praise him and honour him. Congratulations! 'Aye Koo'!

He has now handed us the proverbial baton from the Obstetric 'Tree and Branches'. It is our bounded duty to nurse the whole tree so well that it will continue to produce more golden fruits among the best in Africa.

We hope he will remember us in his 'paradise' at BOMSO CLINIC. We trust that he is only lengthening the 'Umbilical Cord' between him and us and that he will not sever the connections completely.

We wish Dr & Mrs Agble and their partners GOOD LUCK, GOOD HEALTH AND HAPPINESS in their new venture in private practice.

MAY GOD BLESS THEM ALL.

APPENDIX 2

UNIVERSITY OF GHANA MEDICAL SCHOOL

Phone: 65401

My Ref. No. MS-03275?

Your Ref. No.

P. O. Box 4236
Accra

14th August, 19 80

Dear Ted,

I wish to express my personal gratitude for your continued interest in the welfare of Obstetrics and Gynaecology in this country. Your regular discussions, encouragement, provision of books are a big help to the Department.

I feel sorry that my last letter to you never arrived. I hope that this will reach you safely to express my gratitude.

We were able to visit K.K. in London Hospital on two occasions. He seems to be really in very good spirits and had improved very considerably. We hope he will recover fully and return to continue to help the Department especially the Post Graduate Programme.

Once more I am grateful for your help and hope that you will continue to do so for the benefit of Obstetrics/Gynaecology and mothers in Ghana.

Thanks very much.

Yours Sincerely,

DR. J.B. WILSON
HEAD OF DEPARTMENT

DR. TED AGBLE,
47 Mary Peters Drive,
Greenford Middlesex, UB6
OSS Consultant Gynaecologist,
King Abdul Azziz Military Hospital,
TABUK, SAUDI ARABIA. M.1965

608

APPENDIX 3

الشركة العربية العامة للخدمات الطبية المحدودة

GENERAL ARABIAN MEDICAL & ALLIED SERVICES LIMITED

مشروع إدارة وتشغيل مستشفيات القوات المسلحة بالمنطقة الشمالية الغربية
MANAGEMENT & OPERATION PROJECT FOR ARMED FORCES HOSPITALS. TABUK

P O Box 100
TABUK - KINGDOM OF SAUDI ARABIA
TEL   968 (04) 423-3988
FAX   968 (04) 423-2795 GAMA SVC LTD
TLX   881043 WKRTBK SJ

ص.ب : ١٠٠
تبوك : المملكة العربية السعودية
هاتف : ٩٦٨(٠٤)٤٢٣-٣٩٨٨
فاكس : ٩٦٨(٠٤)٤٢٣-٢٧٩٥ جاما إس.في.سي المحدودة
تلكس : ٨٨١٠٤٣ وكرتبك إس.جي

27 June 1990

TO WHOM IT MAY CONCERN

It is my pleasure to respond to the request of Dr Theodore K. Agble, Consultant Obstetrician and Gynaecologist, to write for him a testimonial relating to his professional activities at the Hospital.

Dr Agble came to this Hospital in June 1987 following a prestigious career in a large regional hospital in Kumasi, Ghana. Initially his assignment was that of Consultant and in this role he demonstrated medical knowledge of exceptional magnitude and sound judgement marked by commendably seasoned maturity. The quality and high standards of his professional activities have been exceptional and commendable. In addition, he has always shown himself to be a willing participant in supporting all Medical Staff activities, both professional and social, both in his department and outside his department.

In view of the above observations plus Dr Agble's mature and gentlemanly manner he was considered to be the natural successor to the Chief of the Department of Ob/Gyn when that post became vacant and he has served ably as Acting Chief since December 1989. It should be pointed out that policy in this Hospital is such that one must serve in an Acting capacity for a number of months before being named Chief of the Department.

609

Dr Agble adds a highly valuable dimension of dignity and wisdom to our Medical Staff and therefore it would be much preferred that he continue his fine work and many contributions here; however, should be elect to pursue his career further in other locations, we sincerely wish him well in all his future endeavours.

Sincerely,

H.W. Anderson, MD, DTMH, MScCHDC, FAAP
Chief of Professional Services

APPENDIX 4

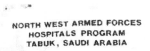

NORTH WEST ARMED FORCES
HOSPITALS PROGRAM
TABUK, SAUDI ARABIA

برسامج مستشفيات القوات المسلحة
بالمنطقة الشمالية الغربية /تبوك
المملكة العربية السعودية

26 January 2000

To Whom It May Concern

Dr Theodore K. Agble

This hospital is a tertiary care military hospital delivering approximately five thousand women per annum in the department of Obstetrics and Gynaecology. Many of these patients are previously unseen, and a very significant number can be classified as of extreme risk. The extremely active out-patient service reviewed over 42,000 patients in 1999. The department offers a full spectrum of specialist care, tertiary care obstetrics, a tertiary intensive care neo-natal unit, and full gynaecological facilities: some minimally invasive surgery is offered, and the infertility program is particularly active.

'Ted' has made a most particularly valuable contribution to this department. Since his appointment as Consultant Obstetrician/ Gynaecologist in June 1987 he has been a true statesman of the department, reflected in his wealth of clinical experience, his vast surgical and technical knowledge and capacities, and his constant availability as a fortunate resource to all his colleagues.

In addition to a comprehensive clinical practice Dr Agble has taught widely, has presented departmental rounds frequently, hospital wide grand-rounds on many occasions and audited widely a number of clinical issues of his particular interest. He has made contributions on a wide range of hospital administrative levels, has steered a number of issues of local cultural and clinical relevance, and for substantial periods of time has acted as Chairman of this demanding department.

It is difficult indeed fully to compose a description of the attributes of a senior colleague whose personal clinical lifetime experience is vast, whose professional conduct is ever beyond reproach, and whose universally dignified professionalism is a constant feature of his interpersonal courtesy.

2/............ Dr Theodore K. Agble

Dr Agble is a highly respected colleague of immense resource, from whose personal and professional support each member of this department has truly and generously benefited. He would add grace and dignity to any professional environment of his choice, and it is my privilege to offer this letter of unhesitant recommendation on his behalf.

Yours sincerely,

Dr Peter Hill
M.D.,F.S.O.G.O.,F.R.C.S.C.,F.R.C.O.G
Chief of Obstetrics and Gynaecology
Professor, Royal College of Surgeons of Canada
Hon. Professor in Obstetrics and Gynaecology, Royal College of Surgeons in Ireland.

APPENDIX 5

S E A S O N ' S   G R E E T I N G S

9th December 2002

Dear

Please forgive our long silence since we left London, but sometime in the not too distant future we promise that you will read all about the last seven months here, in a book! To those of you who know Ghana already we can only say that it is not the Ghana you knew and that does not imply improvement. They now have all become pseudo Americans, imbibing all the worst traits of that nation, and none of its good characteristics like hard work, good customer care, cleanliness and efficiency, Driving is hazardous, Ghana has now overtaken Nigeria in the road accidents table- 2nd highest in the world!

We have now completed our house which is quite nice and spacious, if we say so ourselves and Ted does 2 days weekly at a private hospital three minutes walk away from our house, which is really nice. Socially, life is great and we are invited out quite a bit, we are starting to repay hospitality by having a Xmas cocktail and house warming for 45 on December 23rd. DV, the boys would all have arrived safely and we are looking forward to having them and their friends/partners for a couple weeks. The completion of this building would have laid flat lesser mortals, but Ted and I have an inner and outer strength which is truly a gift worth having!

Despite all the problems we are glad to be back- being with old friends and relatives makes it worthwhile. The heat, which I really hate and is probably the only thing I really miss about London (lack of heat/cold weather, grey skies and rain) is back with a vengeance, although we have been having some heavy downpours which are very welcome indeed.

We are now hooked up to the internet at home, and what a pleasure it is not to have to drive round to internet cafes to access our mail. We lost all our friends addresses when we did not use our mail service for 5 weeks and as I had none of the address books with addresses in, we have been

Printed in Great Britain
by Amazon

17093014R00350